Index

LUCE
and His Empire

W. A. SWANBERG

CHARLES SCRIBNER'S SONS · NEW YORK

For Jessica

Printed in the United States of America
Library of Congress Catalog Card Number 73–162778
SBN 684–12592–7 (cloth)

Contents

v

List of Illustrations and Credits

xi

I

1. THE SPRING IN ROMANTIC CHUNGKING

When Henry Robinson Luce looked down on the muddy Yangtze on October 6, 1945, he had reason to feel exultation in the consummation of one of the great dreams of his life. China had won. Almost a half billion people—about a fifth of all humanity—were saved for Christianity and democracy. The dimensions of what had happened in the eight weeks since the Hiroshima bomb were so vast that not even Luce could see all the way to the edges, but that part of the panorama which was visible was inspiring even if there were a few villainous faces lurking in the background.

But his political jubilation was clouded by distress at a momentous decision of his wife Clare, the beautiful and astonishing Congresswoman from Connecticut.

Their marriage had been beset by difficulties perhaps inevitable between two brilliant, driving, power-seeking people who were often in intellectual competition with each other. The difficulty this time was a religious one. Clare had been in spiritual torment since the death in an automobile accident of her nineteen-year-old daughter Ann. An indifferent Baptist, she had decided to become a Catholic and was taking instruction from Monsignor Fulton J. Sheen "in order to rid myself," as she would explain in McCall's magazine, "of my burden of sin." A woman of such combined beauty, wit and finesse at disparagement naturally had enemies inclined to discount the sincerity of her conversion, undertaken by one of the most famous of priests. Luce had given her every sympathy and support in her bereavement. But he was, after all, the son of missionaries and one of America's leading Presbyterian laymen. For all his ecumenism and enjoyment of friendship with Catholic dignitaries including Cardinal Spellman, he was not *married* to Spellman.

Now he was riding first-class in the plane of Major General Robert B.

1

McClure of the American China Command. Strangely, since despite his ties with China he had not a drop of Chinese blood, his eyes had a subtle slant that rendered his lean face striking if not quite handsome and made him seem doubly at home over the rippling Szechwan landscape. It is safe to say that he chain-smoked and talked a blue streak, as he almost always did. From his notes it is evident that, characteristically, he pumped McClure for information, eying the general closely as a possible Time cover subject to go with a six-page story on this unparalleled Asian drama.

"McClure thinks Generalissimo made a mistake in ousting Lung Yun as Governor of Yunnan," Luce noted in his diary. "Looks to me like Generalissimo did an important job very neatly."

"Generalissimo" meant Chiang Kai-shek, who was and would remain in a sense the most important man in Luce's life—his pride, joy, worry and disaster. Never for a moment did he forget his own enormous power in shaping American public and official opinion. There was a joke around Time that he was about to call a five-power conference to divvy up the postwar world—the United States, England, Russia, China and Time Inc. Although the various company editors and executives, some of whom had known him for years, differed sharply about his character and motivation, there was partial agreement that he felt close to God—perhaps even a little chummy—and that the two were collaborating, in Luce's view, on the solution of world problems. He had used his power and would continue to use it for the Christian Chiang, the America-oriented Chiang, the Communist-hating Chiang.

Despite some reservations, Luce venerated Chiang as the savior of China. He was impatient with American ignorance of China, American disillusionment with China and cynicism over the diversion of its mercifully intended dollars into official Chinese pockets—with American GI's who called their own government "Uncle Chump from Over the Hump" and gave Chiang Kai-shek the revolting nickname of "Chancre Jack." It is not impossible that General McClure's offhand remarks about the Lung Yun incident, questioning Chiang's judgment, were a factor in keeping his likeness, in four colors, off Time's cover.

The jumbled buildings and winding alleys of Chungking came into view—the malodorous provincial town that had become China's wartime capital and had swollen to a million people who now, with the war's ending, were scattering again. The American soldier's disenchantment with Chungking and all it stood for had been expressed in ripe verse by General Joseph Warren Stilwell:

> I welcomed the spring in romantic Chungking.
> I walked in her beautiful bowers.
> In the light of the moon, in the sunshine at noon,
> I savored the fragrance of flowers.
> (Not to speak of the slush, or the muck and the mush
> That covers the streets and the alleys.

2

Or the reek of the swill as it seeps down the hill—
Or the odor of pig in the valleys.)

The plane descended between cliffs—an experience that could be unnerving to travelers less seasoned than Luce—and touched down at the riverside airfield. It was in honor of the publisher rather than General McClure that a deputation of important people waited.

"Met at airport," Luce noted faithfully, "by General Shang representing the Generalissimo; K. C. Wu, who is to take charge of my arrangements here; General [George E.] Stratemeyer and [Walter S.] Robertson [Counsellor of the U.S. Embassy, in charge now that Ambassador Hurley was in the United States], and Commander Reynolds of the embassy."

He was *not* met by his former protégé, Theodore H. White, until recently Time's valued Chungking correspondent. White, who loved China almost as extravagantly as Luce, had, as Luce interpreted it, broken under the strain of seeing great world events through a Szechwan fog. He had come to regard the Gimo as a power-mad dictator, a reactionary surrounded by bandits, a burden that China's suffering millions could no longer support. His dispatches to New York had said this, but they had not appeared in Time that way. They had been revised in the Time-Life Building by the foreign news staff under Whittaker Chambers, a former Communist agent who had become the most zealous of anti-Communists and who, like Luce, would not permit a bad press for the anti-Communist Chiang. White had seen the import of his dispatches altered. Items unflattering to Chiang were removed. Criticism of Chiang became praise of Chiang. White had protested by mail and by cable against what he described as "making Time a Chiang house organ." The New York alterations continued. White hung a sign on his office door: "Any similarity between this correspondent's dispatches and what appears in Time is purely coincidental." Luce, who was fond of White and valued him as a reporter, would yield to no one in his understanding of China, where he had been born and reared.

It was his magazine, after all. He could print what he wanted. He was at the center of newswires from the whole world, informed in the round, privy to events unknown by White. Time policy could hardly be made in the boondocks by a twenty-five-year-old reporter. Luce had held his temper and tried to soothe the young man by giving him a byline on several dispatches and printing his picture.

But White had continued in a rebellion that had its counterpart among correspondents in Europe and among a group in the home office. That was the year of the Great Schism at Time—a tug-of-war between those who were suspicious of or hostile to the Russians (who were still America's allies) and those who were sympathetic with them or, if suspicious, anxious to give them honest treatment and the benefit of the doubt in the belief that every effort must be made for postwar amity rather than postwar war.

3

Thus, Luce and the staff at Time were among the first to raise in such inter-necine struggle the question that would become the great issue of the twenti-eth century—indeed of all the centuries, since human survival would depend on it.

The Presbyterian Luce being violently opposed to godless Communism, the outcome of the argument at Time Inc. was never in doubt. White had been recalled three weeks before Luce arrived in China and eventually would be cashiered. To "repair the damage" Luce had cabled his tall, Tory "star writer" Charles J. V. Murphy in Guam and dispatched him to Chungking.

For fifteen years Luce had roamed the world, communed with the great, watched and weighed the news, his mind absorbing facts which his aston-ishing memory preserved in mental microfilm. The intense effort he had ex-pended in self-education would have exhausted a lesser man. Now, at forty-seven, he was at his peak, not entirely without justification in feeling that he was the best-informed man on earth. He knew of the corruption around Chiang. But he felt Chiang himself to be unblemished, the leader who op-posed the Reds in the world's most populous nation. Peace and time should heal China, as they would America—which was not without its own scoun-drels—and ultimately the complaining Theodore Whites would realize their folly.

Now Luce, who had traveled a week, was just in from Calcutta and Kun-ming and should have been bone-weary, swung smartly into the kind of eat-drink-and-talk program of fact-gathering that had always stimulated rather than tired him.

He was whisked in an embassy limousine up the hill to town and given a suite in the handsome home of Lieutenant General Albert C. Wedemeyer, Stilwell's successor as the top American officer in China. Wedemeyer, absent in the field, had been idealized in a Time cover story of June 4 as "born to sol-diering," "tireless," "brilliant." Two hours after landing, Luce was having cocktails at the American embassy as the stag-dinner guest of Counsellor Robertson, a banker-turned diplomat whose good manners did not conceal his consciousness of old Virginia ancestry. Manners were unimportant to Luce because they took extra time and got in the way of fact-finding, and his own were negligible. He was worried about the impression of Chiang harbored by many GI's, who would carry it back home and spread it among the voters.

"Stratemeyer says majority of G.I.'s will go home sympathetic to the Chi-nese," he noted in his diary; "Robertson says no. I am sure that the G.I. reac-tion to China is a problem."

2. THE ODOR OF PIG IN THE VALLEYS

Next morning, Sunday, he attended the Protestant church service (". . . a very poor sermon by the Army chaplain"). He lunched with the current Time

Chungking staff—Murphy, Annalee Jacoby and Marjorie Severyns—talking incessantly, asking for information and barely giving them time to reply. But this was after he had expressed sympathetic concern for Mrs. Jacoby, whose husband, Melville, a Time correspondent, had been killed in an airplane crash in Australia. ("Talk with Annalee was most painful," he recorded.) He rushed away from the trio, jumped into a waiting Cadillac and was driven twelve miles into the country to join the mighty. He had tea in the ornate mansion of sixty-four-year-old Dr. Kung Hsiang-hsi—always Anglicized in Time as Dr. H. H. "Daddy" Kung—the Shansi-born Yale graduate who had married the eldest of the powerful Soong sisters, amassed a fortune as Standard Oil agent in China and had served his brother-in-law Chiang and his ruling Kuomintang party in many important posts, including that of premier. Luce had met him often in New York. The amiable, triple-chinned and politely predatory Kung had nevertheless spent most of the war in grubby Chungking while his family preferred the luxuries of Hong Kong and America. He was proud of a family tree that made Walter Robertson's six generations look stumpy, for he was deemed a direct descendant of Confucius in the seventy-fifth generation.

"Dr. Kung recalled my telling him," Luce noted, "on July 3 in New York that the war with Japan was already militarily finished; he complimented me on my prognostication of a probable end to the war in the very near future."

Next came the ultimate honor, dinner with Chiang himself. He had abandoned his magnificent home across the Yangtze and was living near Kung in a smaller villa surrounded by blooms and famous for its tiled bathrooms trimmed with chrome. Bathrooms were almost unknown in Chungking, much less tile and chrome, and it was said that coolies who had heard of the wonderful conveniences in this one would almost have forfeited the good will of their ancestors if only they could have seen it and tried the various levers.

Luce had performed enormous services for Chiang and his Kuomintang dictatorship and could perform more. He had been the moving spirit in founding United China Relief in New York, which had funneled American millions to China and had also become a powerful American political lobby backing Chiang. His magazines had made the Chiang couple not only famous but heroic in the United States, whose government had poured billions into the Kuomintang coffers and, it was devoutly hoped, would keep on pouring. At the same time he had helped render Chiang's most dangerous enemy, Mao Tse-tung, infamous. He would permit only gentle criticism of Kuomintang abuses in his publications, always stressing the positive. The departure of Theodore White, recently so bitter toward Chiang, was the latest sign of his partiality. White had become a terrible threat. The Kuomintang people had been holding their breaths about him, so anxious were they about their image in America, and even though much of his criticism had not got into Time magazine, his departure had caused celebrations in Chungking. The New Re-

public and other liberal American publications had taken to sniping at Chiang, and even if their influence was negligible in comparison with the mighty Time, Life and Fortune, it was a disturbing trend.

Luce had arranged for his powerful magazines to become propaganda vehicles for the Nationalist government of Chiang. He had once assured his managing editor of Time, T. S. Matthews, that he would never permit any political use of his publications "unless I thought the Republic was in danger." He had no doubt that the greatest possible danger to America and the whole democratic world would be the takeover of China by the Communists. He had used and would continue to use every ounce of his power to prevent this. Only Chiang, he reasoned, could bring democratic unity to this disordered land. ". . . [W]e should realize," he had written in a "strictly confidential" New York policy memorandum, "that China's top priority is the need for Unity. Remember the priority that Lincoln gave to the Union." He added, "The most difficult problem in Sino-American publicity concerns the Soong family. They are . . . the head and front of a pro-American policy. It ill befits us therefore, to go sour on them."

Time Inc. had not gone sour. The man on whom Luce had conferred the unique prestige of appearing most often on Time's cover was not an American. He was Chiang, recently pictured there for the sixth time, gravely impressive in uniform, along with a triumphant four-page story ("At 57, Chiang Kai-shek stood at one of the pinnacles of his own and his nation's history"). Madame Chiang had decorated the cover three times—twice with her husband, once alone. Madame and the Gimo had been given enthusiastic attention on the cover and inside pages of Life. That thick magazine for businessmen, Fortune, had been admiring too. Some of Chiang's subordinates had also been treated warmly, and the Chinese people had been represented as devoted to Chiang and to America—the kind of perspective most likely to keep American aid coming.

There had also been agreeable personal visits and exchanges of gifts between Luce and Chiang. Chiang's interest in him seemed totally expedient. But if it came to that, Luce himself was imbued with a Calvinist expediency governing his effort to shape the postwar world with his own hands. If he could make use of Chiang on the side of God and democracy and meanwhile get a few journalistic scoops—hallelujah!

"I found Generalissimo and Madame," he wrote, "having tea with the High Command of China Theatre—Generals Stratemeyer, Ho [Ho Ying-chin, Chiang's chief of staff], McClure. After a few minutes I was taken away to a guest cottage. Returned for dinner alone with Generalissimo and Madame and K. C. Wu."

The plump, American-educated K. C. Wu, wartime mayor of Chungking, was a favorite of Chiang's. Madame, Chiang's consort, was Mei-ling, the Wellesley-educated youngest of the Soong sisters, brilliant, haughty and still beautiful at forty-nine. With Luce's help she had coaxed so many millions for

6

China out of the United States that she was said to be worth ten divisions to
the Gimo. She was the "baby" of a family too fantastic for fiction. Her father,
Charlie Soong, had gone to America at nine, found a wealthy sponsor, studied
for the clergy at Vanderbilt University, and had returned to China as a Methodist missionary briefly before he flouted the biblical warning about the camel
and the needle's eye and made his fortune as a merchant. Since Luce's father
had been a Presbyterian missionary in China, and both his sisters were
Wellesley graduates, he and Madame were linked by strands of sentiment and
Protestantism; she had been his guest in New York, he previously had been
her guest in Chungking, and each had great respect for the other's sphere of
power. Besides, he spoke virtually no Chinese, and Chiang spoke no English.
It would be up to Madame and Wu, a Grinnell College graduate, to interpret
for them. The tall, distinguished American, always a little humble when he
felt himself in the presence of true greatness, faced the smaller but very erect
Chinese who claimed the governance of a population three times that of the
United States, whose shaven head shone, whose face was immobile except for
the quick Mongol eyes, and whose speech was punctuated by the occasional
clicking of poorly fitted false teeth.

"After dinner had wonderful conversation with the Generalissimo," Luce
told his diary, "mainly of a philosophical nature. For the first time I learned
what the concept of 'freedom' meant in Chinese thought. The Generalissimo,
discussing the Chinese character for freedom, said it connoted 1) movement
and 2) naturalness. The character suggested a fish in the water—moving
freely and naturally. . . . After the Generalissimo retired the Madame and I
talked for an hour or so. Her main point: the Government now has a terrible
responsibility not to disappoint the hopes of the people."

The Gimo's lecture on freedom had no visible connection with his rule in
China. Under him, the Chinese had been unable to move freely and naturally,
like fish. Luce, always aware of moral issues, knew that he faced one in
Chiang—one that affected more human lives than any in history.

It was not only Chiang's unrealized promises of reform, the democracy un-
fulfilled, the sale of army commissions, the routine appropriation by officers of
wages intended for their starving men, the theft of American supplies until recently brought at peril over the Hump and their immediate appearance on
the Chinese black market. It was also the decay and rapacity around the
Gimo himself, the luxury of his family and favorites in the midst of the misery
of millions, the atrocities committed by his secret police, the injustices for
which Chiang, though always said to be personally honest, could not escape
blame.

Luce knew something of this. It did not pain him as much as it should have
pained a good Presbyterian. He overlooked it in view of Chiang's Christian
anti-Communism, and perhaps put more faith than was justified in Madame's
high-sounding pronouncement.

W. A. Swanberg

3. SANTA CLAUS PRIMUS

Any doubt of Luce's position in Chiang's regard would have been dispelled next day when he appeared at the dinner honoring the Communist leader Mao Tse-tung. While Roosevelt, Churchill and Stalin had all recognized the Gimo's group as China's ruling government during the war, and Chiang and Madame had sat with Roosevelt and Churchill at the Cairo Conference, the Chinese people had never had an opportunity to vote him into office. He had won whatever legitimacy he possessed by force of arms. During the war he had made an uneasy accommodation with Mao, who controlled his own fiefdom to the north, on the theory that they should fight the Japanese instead of each other. American war material sent with such difficulty, however, had gone to Chiang as the recognized leader. Chiang had had an exasperating tendency to let the Americans fight the Japanese while he hoarded his supplies and men for his postwar effort to destroy the Communists. Now the Americans, still recognizing Chiang, hoped to solve the problem by encouraging a coalition government that would join China in peace as it reoccupied the areas taken by the Japanese and accepted the surrender of Japanese armies which were as yet waiting for someone to appear to whom they could surrender. The U.S. ambassador, General Patrick Jay Hurley, the Oklahoma eccentric who liked to regale heads of state with Choctaw war whoops, had coaxed Mao to come to Chungking with Chou En-lai and begin parleys with the Kuomintang.

Luce was the only non-Chinese among the three hundred dinner guests. He was placed at the speakers' table next to General Chang Chih-chung, who presided in behalf of Chiang and who sat next to Mao himself. Although he never permitted any slackening in his detestation of Communism, Luce also never lost his reporter's interest in newsworthy personalities. He essayed a conversation with Mao, who spoke a little English, telling him they had several mutual friends. "He was surprised to see me there," Luce observed in his diary, "and gazed at me with an intense but not unfriendly curiosity. His remarks: polite grunts."

General Chang addressed the group about China's great need for peace and said that the negotiations with the Communists had achieved about 70 percent agreement.

"Then it came Mao's turn to step to the mike," the diary went on. "His face is heavier and more peasant-like than that of most national officers. His sloppy blue-denim garment contrasted sharply with his host's snappy beribboned uniform. He started slowly, with a slight clearing of the throat between nearly every phrase, but he built up gradually to a full-throated shout at the end. He said about what Chang had said plus: that the 30% of the problem which remained to be settled 'will be settled by discussion *and by no other*

8

means' (great applause) and that China must find 'unity under Chiang Kai-shek.' "

This was a declaration that Luce himself could applaud. Unfortunately, similar sentiments had been uttered before by both sides in this savage struggle, always ending in more throat-cutting.

Next day saw the arrival from Shanghai of Wesley L. Bailey, a Time representative who had spent three years as Luce's personal assistant in New York. Bailey was at once impressed into service as secretary and general expediter of the Boss's activities, a duty he described as "like riding a tornado." Luce made it a rule while on tour to discuss problems with all the most important people from the top down, and could be irascible about staff work that was less than perfect. Bailey had become his New York assistant after successfully promoting United China Relief, and had also been an effective aide in the campaigns that had twice elected Mrs. Luce to Congress. Luce had rewarded him with kindnesses that included the gift of seventy valuable shares of Time stock. Bailey admired Luce, was acquainted with much of the Chiang hierarchy through his work with UCR, and was as willing as the Boss to work overtime. ". . . [A]s usual we are off in a cloud of dust," he wrote his wife in New York.

Luce dined with China's number two man, the impassive, Harvard-trained, wealthy banker T. V. Soong, the hard-driving brother of the Soong sisters, who was premier in his brother-in-law Chiang's nepotic government. Soong had appeared on Time's cover the previous December 18 along with a flattering sketch of his career. Only recently he had met with Stalin in Moscow and hammered out the Sino-Soviet treaty that had humiliated Mao and his Communists by ignoring them as a factor in China. Neither he nor Luce trusted Stalin despite the treaty. "He [Soong] had seven or eight of his cabinet there," Luce recorded. "T. V. was in a very relaxed mood and the conversation rarely got more serious than a discussion of the food—we had a much admired fish from the Yangtze; also deer's tendons, etc. . . . The serious talk was about Russia. What a terrible nuisance Russia is; if it weren't for her we could have surcease from the politics of crisis."

He dined again with Chiang: "The Generalissimo had most of the cabinet to dinner and laid on a fancy version of my favorite but very bourgeois dish: jow-tzes. After dinner Mao Tse-tung came to spend the night as the Generalissimo's house-guest!"

He chatted with the number two Communist, the charming Chou En-lai: "We had a nice talk—and completely frank from the moment we sat down. He said we [the Lucepress] hadn't been very nice to them recently. I said that was too bad because we had a world-wide battle on our hands with world-wide left-wing propaganda—and it was just as nasty as a skunk."

He called on Chen Li-fu, co-leader of the right-wing "C-C Clique" which was said to have a sinister political dominance over Chiang. "I found him a man of great charm who had thought deeply about human affairs. He gave a

brilliant brief exposition of Confucian ethics centering around 'love' in the aspect of filial piety. As a basis for family and solid cohesion he thought there was something to be said for love in the aspect of father and son in contrast to the Western emphasis on love in the aspect of boy-meets-girl."

Love was something China could use in any aspect. Luce discussed China's outlook with many others, including the minister of finance, the minister of education and the president of the National University of Peking. He met with groups representing various specialties and endeavors—a committee of United China Relief officials, a gathering of Chinese newspapermen, a committee of UNRRA executives, and a deputation of alumni from Yenching University in Peking. Luce's father had helped found Yenching a quarter-century earlier, and these graduates had come to honor both father and son.

On October 11 he took off in an army plane provided by General Stratemeyer, with Murphy and Bailey in his party. He wanted to see as much of postwar China as he could, visit with generals and officials, find out if possible how the nation's crisis would be resolved, and help Murphy write a story about it. They would enter areas still controlled by Japanese troops whose surrender so far was purely theoretical—areas possibly dangerous for Americans—but Luce was not in the least intimidated. Their first stop was Chengtu, where the jeep transporting them from airport to town broke down immediately.

"Presently," Luce wrote, "a truckload of G.I.'s come by and they take . . . [us] aboard. This isn't so pleasant. I sit on the floor of the truck. . . . As my tail is being beaten by the bumps and my eyes watch the retreating Szechwan landscape, I listen to the chatter of the sergeants. Sitting about me [*sic*] is one of those typical Americans who speaks slowly and deliberately repeating guide-book facts with what appears to be deadly accuracy. Most of the facts he recites are unflattering to China . . . Up ahead there is the loud-mouthed wisecracker. . . . We pass a battalion of Chinese soldiers carrying guns. The loud-mouth yells out 'The war's over; so now you're going to fight.' . . . As we enter the town the scholarly fellow explains about Chengtu. . . . There are two whore houses, he says, one for 200 and one for 700 (China dollars or something). The $700 one is pretty good and even the $200 [one] isn't bad—they are or were government inspected. . . ."

In Chengtu Luce and his party dined with the Chiang-appointed governor and inspected the Kuomintang-controlled West China University. In the next three days they touched down at Sian, Taiyuan ("Grubby town," Bailey wrote in his diary. "Lunch in Jap-controlled railroad hotel.") and Tsinan before alighting in Peking on October 15. Here Luce took a suite at the expensive Hotel de Pekin and enjoyed the luxury of a bath. He was driven to Yenching University and greeted there by the president, his and his late father's old friend Dr. John Leighton Stuart, and visited the Luce Pavilion on the campus provided by Luce money. Bailey, impressed by the ceremonious greeting given Luce by officials everywhere (greetings rendered all the more

ardent because of his friendship with the Chiang couple), wrote his wife, "I don't think any foreign visitor . . . has been so welcome since Marco Polo as HRL and his party have been."

Accompanied by an interpreter, Luce stopped at a jade shop, where he instructed the proprietor to bring a few dozen fine pieces to his hotel where he would make a choice. Meanwhile Murphy, a tall, handsome Harvardman for nine years a writer for the Lucepress, had noticed four bottles of Gordon's gin on a shelf in a shop near the hotel. It was the first time he had seen this cheering label in the Orient. He bought all four bottles, along with some vermouth, returned to the Hotel de Pekin suite and made martinis.

The dealer arrived with the jade, each piece beautifully wrapped in silk, and Luce began bargaining with him through his interpreter. He had an astonishing strain of innocence for so experienced a man. He was certain that the Chinese, grateful for America's aid during the war, would not take advantage of an American—particularly one friendly with Chiang. If this was a principle not recognized by the dealer, Luce was unaware of it. As he would demonstrate on other occasions in buying pearls for his wife or Swiss watches as gifts for his friends, this brilliant exponent of hard-sell in mass advertising was the soul of ingenuousness when face to face with a salesman. Now and then he dropped in at Murphy's room to sip at a martini and speak enthusiastically of the jade.

Whether it was in celebration of China's deliverance or in sorrow at his wife's current difficulties, the temperate Luce took aboard more liquor than usual. He was feeling gay when he, Murphy and Bailey left to be the dinner guests of Hsiung Pin, the Chiang-appointed mayor of Peking, at the Chinese Bankers' Association. Many high officials of the municipal government were present. Each of them insisted on drinking *kan peis*—bottoms-up toasts in rice wine—to the American publisher hailed by the Peiping Chronicle as "a sympathetic friend of China" who in Chungking "was entertained by Generalissimo and Madame Chiang at dinner." The loyal Yaleman Luce was overjoyed to discover that one of the city officials was Y. L. Tong, class of '13— "A classmate of Ambassadors Bullitt and Harriman," he noted, being wrong about Bullitt, who was '12.

Tong and Luce had further *kan peis* in behalf of Yale, Bullitt and Harriman. A pretty Chinese girl in charge of cultural affairs for the city topped it off with a whole salvo of toasts honoring the American friend of Chiang and China. Luce got up and spoke a few words of acknowledgment in diction less chiseled than usual. He ended by singing several bars of "Boola Boola" in his rather nasal voice, a song perhaps meaningless to the mayor and most of the guests but surely bringing a glow of nostalgia to Y. L. Tong.

"He got just a wee bit tight," Bailey wrote, ". . . and he and I took a rickshaw ride under the stars to cool *him* off . . ."

Next day, Luce bought rugs and Chinese silks for his wife. He saw Bailey admiring two lovely blue-and-white vases and said, "Take them—a gift from

11

me." Meanwhile he was watching General Stratemeyer's planes perform a gigantic feat in transporting what would become a total of 200,000 of Chiang's troops to take over East China from the Japanese, and the landing of American troops to help them. He bombarded his editorial director in New York, John Shaw Billings, with cables about what was going on: "The reoccupation of China by the Chinese with American aid is something I believe unique in history. . . ." "The city of Peking is in good shape. . . . The city is bouncing back rapidly to normal, peaceful life. . . . A new energetic municipal government seems well established under Mayor Hsiung Pin. . . . Law and order prevails throughout the city . . ." He was, it could be seen, thoroughly approving of Chiang's leadership.

He spoke at a banquet of the Chinese-American Institute of Cultural Relations held in his honor. He was interviewed by the press. He dined at the French embassy. On October 18 he moved on to Tientsin, where he found many factories closed for want of raw materials. "The notorious inefficiency of our State Department," he cabled Billings with typical scorn for the Truman administration, "is once again exhibited by the fact that the American consul has not yet arrived in this great commercial center . . ." But he was cheered by the presence of 25,000 American Marines in Tientsin: "The desire of local Chinese officials to show their appreciation of Americans and to have Tientsin make a good impression on them cannot be exaggerated."

His next stop was Tsingtao, on the Shantung peninsula, where he luxuriated in nostalgia, an emotion rare in one so obsessed with today-and-tomorrow. Tsingtao was hardly more than 100 miles from his birthplace. As a boy he had come here with his family to loaf and swim in the summer. Now, gazing at the beach, he yielded to a familiar Luce mental-visual defect, one so chronic particularly in his view of China that it had alarmed Theodore White and some of Time's more realistic editors. He saw it the way it ought to be rather than as it was. He seemed unaware that years of war and neglect had left the beach overgrown and the cottages shabby.

"Isn't it beautiful?" he said. "I shall take a Sabbatical and bring Clare to live here for a year."

Murphy, who could be blunt, saw it as it was. "It looks like Far Rockaway," he said, realizing his tactlessness when he saw the instant frown on Luce's face.

Tsingtao, another monument to the Western exploitation that had weakened and humiliated China, had been seized by German troops in 1898 and expanded into a German city. Luce took a suite at the Edgewater Hotel with a magnificent view of the Yellow Sea and—after the usual reception given him by the mayor—went for a swim with Bailey and Murphy and told them of boyhood experiences here almost forty years earlier. When he heard church bells ringing, he noted, "I recognized the tone at once; they were the deep, rich clanging voice of the old German church."

Dedicated as he was to a world mission for which he felt himself uniquely

equipped, gripped by an American patriotism that was religious in its origin and intensity, he was moved alike by the bells, by the defeat of Japan and by the glorious sight of American warships in the harbor so that he fell back reverently on the Psalms: "The earth is the Lord's, and the fullness thereof. . . ."

And he was seized by an impossible idea. He wanted Bailey to organize— immediately or thereabouts—facilities for the printing of Time and Life in China. When Luce had an idea, it was not politic to throw cold water on it. Bailey pointed out, with all the tact at his command, that the country was still in chaos, fighting continued in many localities and that even if adequate printing and paper supplies could be found somewhere (which he privately thought impossible), there could be no distribution over the shattered high-ways and railroads for many months. He suggested Tokyo. The magazines could at any rate be published there, though distribution in China would still be limited virtually to seaport areas.

"He was vastly impatient with this kind of talk," Bailey later recalled. "It seemed to be a dream of his, to publish quickly in China. It was one of the few times I ever saw him utterly unreasonable."

Of course he wanted *his* magazines to be first to publish in *his* China. All his life he had made his dreams come true by dint of hard work and intelligent planning. He was in entire sympathy with the aggressive American pride in accomplishment exemplified in the Air Force motto: "We do the difficult immediately; the impossible takes a little longer," and he was apt to suspect indolence when he was told that something could not be done. But good cheer returned as he dined with the Chinese governor, lunched with the American general in command, then went out by gig to dine with Captain Noble of the U.S. cruiser *Alaska* and saw a flat-top and other elements of the fleet anchored nearby. "Incredible military power is represented by the Stars and Stripes," he wrote with that patriotic ardor that often edged into jingoism. "And the autumn so rare and bright makes the heart joyful."

Then on to Nanking October 22, where he pursued another fast schedule ("Visited Jap hospital, barracks, arsenal") that included lunch with the mayor at the ugly tomb of Sun Yat-sen on nearby Purple Mountain. When he reached Shanghai at 3:00 P.M. October 24, he should have collapsed in exhaustion in his penthouse suite at the Cathay Hotel. Not at all. Four hours later, Bailey having handled the arrangements, Luce gave a convivial Chinese dinner for the eight Time-Life people then in Shanghai.

"He acted as host and master of ceremonies, and asked a thousand questions," Bailey recalled. "Perhaps there was a shade of the return-of-MacArthur air about him, but mainly he wanted to know from all of us what we had observed in China and what was likely to happen next."

In his remaining time in Shanghai he gave detailed instructions to his news representatives, discussed with Murphy the approach to be taken in his series on China, addressed a YMCA group, gave a press conference, dined with

13

Chiang's Mayor Chien Ta-chun, lunched with Chiang's General Tang En-po (who presented him and his aides with swords taken from the Japanese), gave a dinner for the wealthy American "old China hand" C. V. Starr, gave a tea for Chinese newspapermen, addressed the China Foundation and wound up by giving a lavish dinner at the Cathay for the American commanders in Shanghai, Admiral Thomas Kinkaid and General Stratemeyer and their staffs. On October 29, wearing a gray double-breasted suit and gray fedora, he boarded a plane at Shanghai's airport and headed for America.

In his twenty-three days in China he had been conferred attentions such as he had never received at home. From Chungking to Peking to Nanking to Shanghai he had been exposed to the most alluring of Oriental blandishments. Naturally he would have liked to think that all this homage was given without guile to Henry Luce the man. But as a hard-headed tycoon he must have known that in some part it was given to Henry Luce the powerful publisher who had influenced American public opinion and American policy in favor of Chiang and could, if so inclined, continue to do so.

Luce did not forget the changing Time-Life staff in Shanghai. At Christmas—a time when Americans could be lonely in the Chinese metropolis—he cabled Bailey: "You are hereby given temporary rank of Santa Claus Primus to provide for yourself and all [in Shanghai] a big extra bundle of Christmas cheer chargeable to the Old China Boy. . . . Merry Christmas."

Bailey spent $200 of the Old China Boy's money to buy gifts for the eight staff people then in Shanghai.

II

1. INTOXICATED WITH GOD

Henry Robinson Luce was born April 3, 1898, in Tengchow, China, under circumstances that had a part in providing him with a dazzling spectrum of talents and failings. Both his parents were descended from Englishmen who landed in New England long before the Revolution. Both were distinguished in their character and abilities. His missionary father, Henry Winters Luce, was a man so physically and mentally energetic that few could keep up with him. Within him there was a struggle of extremes—a sweetness of spirit combined with a temper as fiery as his red hair, fundamentalism and modernism, humility and determination, quiet persuasiveness and a bluntness of speech that sometimes offended his churchly elders.

Born in Scranton, Pennsylvania, in 1868, son of a wholesale grocer of modest means, Luce was active in Presbyterian church work as were his parents, but he intended to be a lawyer. It was not until shortly before his graduation from Yale in 1892 that he was stirred by an irresistible call to the ministry. His parents, surprised at his shift in aim and his subsequent enrollment at the Union Theological Seminary in New York, were something more than surprised at his next decision.

"God willing," he wrote in his diary, ". . . I purpose to go to the foreign field and witness for Him as best I may in the uttermost parts of the earth." He chose China as his field.

The missionary movement had then reached a pitch of ardor that would be chastened by later experience. The assumption of the transcendence of Christianity and the American culture, and the conviction that representatives of other cultures would be grateful for our role in their improvement rather than resentful at our interference, had become a national article of faith championed by four successive Presidents. The tide of religious fervor whipped up

15

by the Moody-Sankey style of evangelism had washed every corner of the nation. Women's missionary societies burgeoned, Sunday school children gave pennies and nickels to save the heathen, and returned missionaries were heard with veneration. The Student Volunteers for Foreign Missions were establishing organizations in scores of colleges. Luce's good friend and classmate, Horace Tracy Pitkin of Philadelphia, was the leader of the movement at Yale.

There was a world-saving urgency in the appeals for more young missionaries. The Reverend Adoniram J. Gordon of Boston told missionary candidates that they must become intoxicated with God: "God wants that kind of men today, men inebriated with the Holy Ghost; men that may be counted insane sometimes because of the tremendous earnestness of their fire and zeal." Others, such as the veteran missionary Hudson Taylor, stressed the need of haste with the gospel. "A million a month in China are dying without God!" he said—a reminder that those million every month were doomed to eternal hellfire because our missionaries had not arrived soon enough to save them.

The piety of Horace Pitkin—one of those vulgarly called Jesus' Little Lambs by the more worldly collegians—was formidable. Luce was editor of the Yale Courant, with Pitkin an associate editor. Wine was served at the more important Courant dinners and at other Yale functions. As Luce put it, "Not a few earnest men felt that it was sufficient to go, and manifest their position by having their glasses turned down and thus unfilled; but Pitkin could not look on it in this light and so stayed away altogether." Sherwood Eddy, a close friend of both of them, noted of Pitkin, "On the question of dancing, cards, the theatre and similar amusements, he took a stronger stand than any man in the college."

Pitkin, who hoped to become a missionary in China, contributed a humorous piece to the Courant about a Chinese emperor who roared, "Off with his head!" when anyone annoyed him. By a ghastly irony, Pitkin himself was fated to be decapitated in China eight years later. When Luce, Pitkin and Eddy went on to the theological seminary in New York, they were inseparable friends. "Once each day," Luce wrote, "and often several times a day, we met to pray over the things pertaining to our 'great purpose' . . ." He believed that he had been divinely selected. He was deeply responsive to his religion, intensely loyal to it, ready to work endlessly for it, dedicated, unshakable—qualities that his oldest son would apply to secular life with startling results.

Many of the influences that affected him would also affect the son. These two would form a bridge over which several nineteenth-century attitudes and doctrines including Manifest Destiny came thumping into the twentieth—doctrines and attitudes which in turn would affect important men and institutions, among them Dwight Eisenhower, Chiang Kai-shek, Wendell Willkie, the Kremlin, the American embassy in Rome, and indeed the domestic and world policies of the United States.

Finishing at Union, the elder Luce joined the Student Volunteer movement for a year as a traveling representative, cramping his length into upper berths as he traversed the country to speak at colleges and campaign for more missionaries. His kindly eloquence astonished Edward H. Hume, who as a Yale freshman looked forward to becoming a physician and had an active antipathy toward missionary work until Luce visited his alma mater. "He got hold of me one day and took me for a walk," Hume said. "We stood on a hill and looked toward the horizon. 'Let this be a hill of vision to you,' he said. 'Let your view include the whole world. Where else, except as a medical missionary, could you possibly find so unlimited a place of opportunity and service?' That night I went back to my room and signed the Student Volunteer card." Hume would later rise to become head of Yale-in-China.

Luce's father went on to Princeton, where he received his Bachelor of Divinity degree in 1896, then returned to his travels for the movement. On a visit home he met tall, dark-eyed Elizabeth Middleton Root, who had come to Scranton as a YWCA worker among factory girls. Daughter of a lawyer of Utica, New York, Miss Root was a young lady of great tact and charm who was already slightly handicapped by deteriorating hearing caused by childhood typhoid. She was less rigid and doctrinaire than the rather intense young man who asked, with all the formality of the day, for her hand in marriage. Both were courageous, knowing that eleven missionaries had been murdered in China in 1895. They were married on June 1, 1897, and they sailed for the Orient in September. Fittingly, however, their first son had already been conceived in the United States of America which he would always uphold and exhort and reproach and defend and glorify.

The son was an unseen presence when they stopped to sightsee in Japan, where the father showed a trace of the inflexibility that would appear in the child. He could not bring himself to admire the beauty of the heathen Buddhist temples, whereas his bride glowed.

"You haven't said so, but don't you think they are beautiful?" she asked. "Oh, do say they are!"

"Yes," he replied, "I think they are beautiful—and very, very sad."

At Shanghai the travelers transferred to a coastal vessel for the voyage to Chefoo, on the Shantung peninsula. A rough two-day trip in a *shen-dzi*—a conveyance on poles slung between mules—took them the last fifty miles to Tengchow. Here they became a part of the East Shantung Presbyterian Mission, and here Henry Robinson Luce was born in a house without gas, electricity or plumbing.

A few dozen Western people and a few score of Chinese students inhabited the compound which, with its high stone wall, was a fortress against a dangerous outside world. Government was uncertain, law enforcement minimal, and violence was almost as common as the hunger that often caused it. Bubonic plague, smallpox, typhus and cholera were so prevalent that strangers were

17

not admitted and when missionaries returned from their evangelizing labors they were quarantined in a house outside the gate.

2. ENLIGHTENING THE HEATHEN

The Chinese, despite appalling ignorance and poverty, were the conscious heirs of a culture long antedating the Age of Pericles, much less the discovery of America. Certainly no great nation had ever been so systematically invaded, exploited, partitioned, oppressed, threatened, robbed, insulted and humiliated as theirs. The kindly motives of the missionaries who poured into the country in increasing numbers after 1890 were largely vitiated by their lack of tact and understanding.

The Chinese discovered that the various Western religions which set out to "show them the way" were in disagreement and competition with each other even though they worshiped the same god. The Presbyterians felt that they could save Chinese souls better than the misguided Catholics, and the Congregationalists were happy if they could snatch converts from the Baptists. The confusion was compounded by the fact that the different Western religions had five different Chinese names for what was presumably the same Western god, in addition to disagreements over his description, age, pronouncements, jurisdiction and mode of operation. Hence Voltaire's story of the Chinese who, after listening to a theological disputation among a Catholic, a Protestant, a Quaker, a Jansenist, a Jew and a Moslem, finally clapped each of them into separate cells as insane.

Voltaire could see more humor in it than the Chinese. They did not enjoy having strangers arrive and pronounce them absurd in their deepest beliefs, especially since the foreign guests, while temporarily more affluent, were millennia later in achieving civilization. Their conviction that they were God's ambassadors was not humbling. China was overladen with missionaries whose good intentions never could make amends for their complacency.

While all Western missionaries were guilty in this respect, the Americans usually were more so because of the young, aggressive vigor of their nation and the tendency of American missionaries to mix patriotism with their religion. They had "no squeamish doubts about the superiority of American life," which they attributed to their brand of Christianity and government. They were not only drunk with God but with country too. Yet their lot was not easy because their first experience with Chinese mass destitution aroused their immediate sympathies and their desire to help. It seemed evident to most of them that China needed American democracy and American know-how as well as American religion. The very humaneness of the missionaries thus led them to pile disparagements of China's government on top of their reflections on Chinese religion.

Although it was known in America that the Chinese were difficult to convert, what was less known was the overwhelming preponderance of those

who resisted conversion, the determination with which they resisted it and the sense of outrage they felt. They resented being looked on as benighted heathen, resented the American ban on Chinese immigration, resented their whole treatment as an inferior race. One of the most xenophobic of peoples, they regarded the invaders as barbarians. They were offended by missionaries who condemned "infidel" Confucianism, belittled Chinese politics and institutions and even insisted that Confucius was expiating his sins in hell.

The number of converts was minuscule, never exceeding more than a fraction of one percent of the population even after more than a century of proselytizing. No one was sure how many of these converts were opportunistic "rice Christians." With these few exceptions, the Chinese hated the missionaries with a passion, used every stratagem they could to thwart them and occasionally murdered them.

Not until years later would the American churches themselves become aware that the effort in China was stronger in zeal than in judgment. It would take an exhaustive Protestant laymen's inquiry to discover that mismanagement was common in mission work, that it was impossible to "speak of the total impression with the high enthusiasm we should like to offer," and that while some missionaries exhibited real devotion and power, "the greater number seem to us of limited outlook and capacity." Their report also made an astonishing concession—that Christianity was only one of many great religions and could no longer claim the exclusive approval of God.

Similar thoughts would come to Pearl Buck, daughter of a missionary in China, who had spent many years there. She would admit disillusionment with the mediocrity of the Christianizing campaign and its ultimate failure. ". . . I feel that Christian missionaries are basically good," she would write. "Certainly I never knew of any who were thieves or rascals. I did know one or two who had illegitimate children—lonely men without their wives—but they were immediately dismissed. Yet, while missionary standards were high for moral conduct, missionaries themselves were not usually people who understood the Chinese or made much effort to understand the people whose souls they wanted to save—this with some notable exceptions, among them my own mother and father. In general, missionaries lacked the education for a country where the culture was as old as that of China."

Henry and Elizabeth Luce joined in this enterprise with intentions wholly benign. Unlike some of the earlier missionaries, they were well educated and of exceptional intelligence and ability, and if they had little previous instruction about their new land, they would make it their business to learn and appreciate Chinese history and culture. They were superior people except for the Christian prejudice without which they never would have gone to China. Henry Luce indeed was specially imbued with that mischief-making politico-theological doctrine of the time, being an ardent patriot convinced that God had given America His particular blessing and had entrusted the nation to spread not only Christianity but democracy.

19

When he had mastered enough of the Chinese language for simple conversation, he joined the faculty of the mission-founded Tengchow College, an institution of less than actual collegiate rating where young Chinese were prepared for the Christian ministry. Although he had had only one elementary course in physics at Yale, he became the physics instructor simply because one was needed. Vigorous and enthusiastic, he had the gift of communicating with the young. But he suffered some discomfiture and possibly even damaged his own career because of his bullheaded opposition to the standpat older missionaries who were interested only in saving souls. He saw the need for curricular improvement and a better all-around education for the mission's young Chinese charges, and he was blunt in saying so. As even his sympathetic biographer put it, "The elder statesmen within the Mission struggled to exercise Christian patience in showing this brash young colleague the error of his ways."

But if mission work was grueling, it had its compensations. Missionaries were a privileged class. Chinese servants removed all need for menial work, and leisure was provided by school vacations. The Luces spent the summer of 1898 at the seacoast town of Petaiho, where Luce was overjoyed to meet his Yale classmate, Rev. Horace Tracy Pitkin, who now also had a wife and son and was a Congregational missionary at Paotingfu.

3. GOD AND OLD GLORY

The Luces had become part of a holy crusade which had fallen into tyrannical practices. The Protestant missionary movement, which began in China in the 1830's, had by degrees arranged for special privileges backed by the power of the United States. The belief that God had participated directly in America's founding had encouraged an aggressive collaboration with the Almighty and had maintained a conviction of essential goodness as Manifest Destiny ordained the appropriation of the West, then Hawaii and the Philippines. President McKinley, a Methodist, explained that it would have been shameful to neglect the Filipinos:

> . . . [T]here was nothing left for us to do but to take [the islands], and to educate the Filipinos, and uplift and Christianize them, and by God's grace do the very best we could by them, as our fellowmen for whom Christ also died.

Mr. Dooley saw it in a different light:

> We're a gr-reat civilizein' agent, Hinnissy, an' as Father Kelly says, "So's th' steam roller." An' bein' a quiet man, I'd rather be behind thin in fr-ront when the shtreet has to be improved.

Expansionists such as Theodore Roosevelt and Captain Alfred Thayer Mahan saw in the widening network of missionaries a useful instrument in ex-

20

tending American power and commerce. One witticism had it that American missionaries and the Standard Oil Company had the same motto, "Let there be light," and that one group sought the souls of 400 million Chinese while the other went for their pocketbooks. The writer Margherita Hamm returned from the Orient and pointed out that notice of the missionaries' possessions created a demand for them among the people. "From this point of view," she wrote, "every missionary is a salesman for the manufactures of Christendom!" In a phonograph record made by William Howard Taft, he praised foreign missions on one side and urged a bigger army and navy on the other. The most orotund coupler of God and Old Glory was Senator Beveridge, who echoed Kipling's "White Man's Burden" and would himself be echoed decades later by the journalist Henry Luce:

> God . . . has made us the master organizers of the world to establish systems where chaos reigns. . . . He has made us adepts in government that we may administer government among savage and senile peoples. Were it not for such a force as this the world would relapse into barbarism and night . . . He has marked the American people as His chosen nation to finally lead in the regeneration of the world.

Sections of the Chinese melon had been seized by the English, French, Portuguese, Russians, Japanese and Germans. China, with the largest population of any nation, had sunk to the peculiar status of a colony not of one country but many. America, arriving late, had taken no territory but had demanded every advantage exacted by the other nations. China had been forced by treaty to admit American missionaries and businessmen, grant them extraterritoriality, guarantee their safety, and to pay indemnity for offenses against them. The missionary organizations, determined to spread God's word despite the people's hostility, had pressed hard for these imperialist concessions. American businessmen in China generally dissociated themselves from the missionaries in the hope that they could thereby escape the hatred felt for them.

The corrupt Empress Dowager was helpless to prevent these humiliations, or to prevent foreigners from taking over more and more of the port facilities, banks, railroads, mines and other enterprises. In the international race for booty, China had become infested with plump foreign merchants and promoters whose clubs excluded the Chinese. But the most intolerable affront was the attack of the missionaries on their sacred beliefs. As Nathaniel Peffer observed:

> . . . [T]here was fundamentally something unhealthy and incongruous in the whole missionary idea. If the endeavor had been confined to primitive savages something could have been said for it. But to go out to a race of high culture and long tradition, with philosophical, ethical, and religious systems antedating Christianity, and to go avowedly to save its people from damnation as dwellers in heathen darkness—in that there was something not only spiritually limited but almost grotesque.

21

Not a year had passed without sporadic outbreaks against the foreign religionists. The Chinese were fertile in their invention of ingenious torture and protracted execution. Missionaries of various sects had met death in many forms, ranging from dismemberment to crucifixion. All this paled before the violence that occurred when the secret organization of the Boxers, dedicated to the extermination of the "foreign devils," launched their great bloodletting in the spring of 1900.

One Boxer manifesto began: "The Catholic and Protestant religions being insolent to the gods and extinguishing sanctity, rendering no obedience to Buddha, and enraging Heaven and Earth, the rain-clouds no longer visit us; but eight million Spirit Soldiers will descend from Heaven and sweep the Empire clean of all foreigners."

The New York Times of June 12 listed the Luces as among those in danger as Boxers streamed into Shantung. A week later, its headline over a story about the many Caucasian nationals in peril was, "CHINA IS AT WAR WITH THE WORLD!" By the end of June the whole Presbyterian colony at Tengchow was forced to flee for their lives—a process made difficult for the Luces because their second child, Emmavail, was only three weeks old and Henry was still a baby of two.

With an amah helping them, they escaped on July 1 on a boat operated by friendly Chinese. Ultimately they were taken, along with other refugees, in a larger vessel across the bay to Seoul, Korea, where they spent the summer with sympathetic American missionaries while American and other troops dealt with the Boxers. They learned that Pitkin was among those killed, decapitated with a heavy sword. His wife and son would have suffered the same fate had they not been vacationing in America.

"What days these are for China!" Luce wrote. "Days of suspense, days of suffering and persecution, days of blood and death! But in it all the missionaries have not lost their quiet and calm, standing firm in their determination to pour out their lives for China."

Missionaries in China, as elsewhere, tended to be determined, undoubting men. There seemed no feeling among them that it might be better to pour out their lives in their own imperfect homeland. With few exceptions they returned in their hundreds to their posts when peace had been restored. Altogether some 136 Protestant and 44 Catholic missionaries and 53 children of missionaries had been killed, in addition to about 30,000 Chinese converts to Christianity, who were regarded as traitors. Life was cheap in China, anger ran high and the savagery of the killings was shocking, many of the victims being decapitated, burned to death or mutilated with slow torture.

Incidents in Peking after the troops had driven off the Boxers and rescued the foreigners there illustrated the strangely inverted attitude of some of the clergymen. Angered by the Boxer atrocities, some American missionaries appropriated Chinese mansions and palaces whose owners had fled, looted them and sold their silver and furnishings. The practice was justified on the ground

that Christians, including Chinese converts, deserved to be indemnified for their losses. Yet this seemed a high-handed method of seeking indemnity, as did the fact that a part of the profits was used for such things as speculation in rice and the purchase of land for a "summer residence for missionaries."

News of this, as well as churchly demands that the McKinley administration exact summary vengeance, took aback readers in America, one of them being Mark Twain. "Sometimes," Twain wrote in the North American Review, "an ordained minister sets out to be blasphemous. When this happens, the layman is out of the running; he stands no chance." To missionary replies that they had only followed local custom, Twain rejoined that the Commandment should be revised to read, "Thou shalt not steal—except when it is the custom of the country." The missionary defense that they had taken in indemnity only a little more than the value of the mission property destroyed, Twain likened to the girl who, when reproached for having an illegitimate child, said, "But it is such a little one."

In America, a small minority of critics drew from these events the reflection that we had no right to impose our religion on the Chinese and that if we did so it should be at the missionaries' own risk. But the American people as a whole entirely missed the lesson of the rebellion. They still regarded the Chinese masses with sentimental affection, feeling that the Boxers were a group apart, a band of fanatics who should of course be brought to retribution.

Punishment was ruthless. Boxer leaders were publicly beheaded. Poverty-stricken China was compelled to pay an indemnity of $333 million to the various injured nations and to extend greater concessions to Western business interests as well as to permit the stationing of a foreign garrison in Peking.

The killings and the destruction of church and business property resulted in hundreds of individual claims for indemnity on the part of businessmen, missionaries or their families. The Horace Pitkin estate, for example, filed a claim against China for $100,000. Herbert Hoover, who would later be a Waldorf Towers neighbor and friend of the Henry Luce who was now only two years old, asked $52,707 to reimburse him for the three-year engineering job in Chihli Province which he had been forced to give up because of the turmoil. The claims commission, learning that he had soon found another job almost as good, allowed him only $10,759.

By late fall the Luces and their colleagues were back at Tengchow and the school and mission were functioning again. Rev. Henry Luce, an ecumenist ahead of his time, was now winning the disapproval of some of his elders by urging educational consolidation with other Protestant groups in Shantung. ". . . It is both uneconomical and a denial of our unity in Christ," he said, "that the Presbyterians are attempting to carry on their own little college, with insufficient staff and funds, while at the same time several other American and British missions are also trying to establish and maintain colleges with equally inadequate resources."

In 1902 his exhortations were heeded when a collaboration with English

Baptists, something unprecedented, was agreed on. In 1904, soon after the birth of their second daughter, Elisabeth, the Luces moved to the new arts college at Weihsien, 125 miles to the southwest. Here Luce was made head of the physics department—a tribute to his independent study of the subject. And here young Henry, easily the handsomest boy of the mission, began to exercise his intellect.

Obviously gifted, he received more than ordinary encouragement from his parents. At age three he had attended the Chinese Christian church as well as the Sunday service in English. At five he "delivered his own sermons—to the neighbors' children, or anyone else who would listen," his sister recalled, and his proud mother wrote them down for his father. The other children stared when the sandy-haired young Harry, as he was called, declaimed: "He has established the earth and he founded it upon the seas. For the tower of Babel, it was a wicked thing that man should do, and Jehovah smashed it. . . ."

Not unaware of his keenness, he might have been an insufferable little peacock but for his great seriousness and his intention to do good in the world. It was the mother who was the disciplinarian and who turned him over her knee when he needed punishment. The father, for all his stubbornness and occasional temper, was the lenient parent. He had an axiom from the Greeks, "character means destiny," which the son would adopt as his own, and he would urge, "Use your native Lucepower" to encourage effort and determination. He was patriotic, a believer in America, an extravagant admirer of Theodore Roosevelt. There was in this family perhaps even more of the strong love of country commonly felt by missionaries far from home. And they had gone through the Boxer Rebellion, an experience blending the religious and patriotic as nothing else could. The Luces would never forget their escape from Tengchow. And they would remember and retell the story of the arrival of American troops in Peking, coming gloriously to the rescue as the hard-riding cavalry was wont to do in melodramas. The advance of the flag to the great Oriental capital was at once an act of God, a merciful deliverance from barbarism run amuck, and an event inspiring deep national pride, the proof and vindication of America as a world power.

All this was absorbed by the young, intelligent, patriotic and religious Harry Luce. Years later, some of his colleagues would swear that if one looked sharply he could see Old Glory rippling in each of Luce's blue eyes.

"I have the globe ready to teach the history of George Washington," he told his mother at age six; ". . . the boys like to hear about Isaiah . . . but Paul is the easiest of all Bible men . . ."

III

1. LAND OF THE FREE

Early in 1906 the excitement in the Luce family was almost unbearable as, after vast preparations, they sailed for San Francisco. Rev. Henry Luce was on a money-raising mission for Weihsien that would take more than a year. For young Harry it was his first glimpse of the great republic he had heard so much about, the country that was *his* country even though he had never set foot on it before.

He was, for such a bright boy, astonishingly literal. To him, the nation was in actual fact the land of the free and the home of the brave, just as the anthem said. He marveled at the wonders of America, where even the poor seemed rich by Chinese standards and were blessed with the vote, and where Theodore Roosevelt sat in the White House, put there by those millions of voters in a democratic way unknown in China.

The most important stop the Luces made was at a turreted brownstone palace encircled by a spiked iron fence—the home of Mrs. Cyrus Hall McCormick at 675 Rush Street in Chicago. Mrs. McCormick, the enormously rich widow of the founder of the International Harvester Company, was as devout a Presbyterian as her hard-shelled husband had been, a generous contributor to the church and its missions. She and her late husband had been the largest donors in the construction of the huge Fourth Presbyterian Church nearby, which therefore became known colloquially as The Church of the Holy Harvester, or sometimes as The Church of the Divine Reaper. She so liked Rev. Henry Luce that she asked him to bring his wife and children from their hotel. Petite, regal, surrounded by crystal and footmen, she was drawn to the missionary family who had made such sacrifices for the faith and whose very clothing showed signs of Chinese design and needlework. Perhaps a further reason for her appreciation of them was the fact that she, like Mrs. Luce, was

25

deaf—she used a jeweled serpentine ear trumpet—and that the Luces had all acquired the habit of speaking distinctly. She took an immediate liking to the handsome, articulate, grave-faced, eight-year-old Harry Luce.

The palace contained such wonders as a hydraulic elevator and, on the ceiling of the main hall, an intricate painted design which had as its central figure a glorified version of the McCormick reaper. At Mrs. McCormick's insistence, the Luces called on her several times during their fifteen-month stay in America. She would remain their friend and benefactor as long as she lived, donating generously to the mission, contributing to the children's education and corresponding with Mrs. Luce. She was so fond of their boy and so fearful that life in China might impair his schooling and opportunity that she offered to adopt him and educate him in America. In later life he never forgot his terror at this proposal, having taken a strange notion that she wanted to "buy" him from his parents. The Luces prayed for guidance. They decided that they must keep their son, but they could not refuse Mrs. McCormick's offer to pay for a new house for them at Weihsien.

Harry's tonsils were removed while the family was in America. He emerged from the anesthetic before the surgery was finished—a painful experience to which the parents ascribed the stutter which tormented him for years afterward. In June, Rev. Henry Luce received an honorary Master of Arts degree at Yale in recognition of religious writings he had done in China, solidifying the family attachment to his alma mater. They visited Mrs. Luce's relatives, the Roots, in Utica, where Harry showed an aspect of the naïveté he would never really outgrow. Attending church there, and seeing a stained-glass window bearing the quotation, "I am the Vine and Ye are the Roots," he remarked that he had not known of his direct relationship to Christ.

Meanwhile Rev. Luce solicited contributions from his Yale classmates—now men in their mid-thirties, even the "unsuccessful" ones prosperous enough to make a missionary feel poverty-stricken—and other wealthy men. "Trudged through the rain all day," he noted on one occasion. "Tried to see ten men, seven of them refused to see me." But his persistence—his "native Lucepower"—brought results and by the time the family was back in China in April 1907, the little college's prospects were at any rate improved.

Harry read avidly in the family library—from H. G. Henty to Dickens to Gibbon. The Luces were richer in books than in modern conveniences. One of the vivid memories of the daughters is the huge annual order the family mailed to the Montgomery Ward company in Chicago. Both mother and father worked over the order list, which included everything from stationery to canned goods, clothing and gifts. Since it took almost a year after the order was sent for the shipment to arrive, a special difficulty was to estimate how much the children's feet would grow in specifying the size of shoes. "When the shipment finally came," Emmavail recalls, "it was a holiday for all of us. We were allowed to skip school for the day while we helped father and mother open box after box and check each item off against the order list."

Family life was warmly simple, the children gathering to sing as Mrs. Luce played the piano, or joining with other missionary families in sociables or outings. The excitement of 1908, however, was the building of the new eight-room house provided by Mrs. McCormick—a dwelling they hoped would end the makeshift accommodations they had endured, having lived in thirty houses or parts of houses including an abandoned temple to Kwan Yin, during their eleven years in China. It was mentioned in a charming letter written by Harry to his favorite magazine, St. Nicholas:

> My dear St. Nicholas,
>
> I am a boy born in China. I live in the country near Weihsien (Way Shen) city, in an enclosed compound or big yard about two blocks large. There are eight dwelling houses, a boys' and girls' school, a college, a big church and two hospitals.
>
> A new house is being built (the house we are to live in) by Chinese carpenters and masons.
>
> It will take about eight months to build it. What a long time! The Chinese have no saw-mills, but every log has to be cut and sawed by hand.
>
> I think you are fine.
>
> Your true friend and reader,
> Henry R. Luce

By now his sisters were being tutored by a formidable widow, Frau Netz, whose kindness of heart was hidden behind the sternest Prussian discipline. His equability vanished whenever she was called on to aid him in his school work. They struck sparks immediately. His willfulness toward Frau Netz decided his parents on taking him out of the mission school and sending him away to a private school where he would escape the heavily feminine influence at home, submit to a prescribed discipline and get better training for Yale, where he would of course eventually matriculate. At ten he was sent to the British boarding school at Chefoo, on the Shantung north coast.

2. IT WAS ALL GOD

Although he later said of Chefoo School, "I hated it and I loved it," it was the dislike that seemed to linger. On top of the displacement of his adoring parents by despotic masters who enforced regulations with canings, the young patriot was a member of a minority. The masters were all Britons, as were four-fifths of the hundred-odd students. His stuttering, about which he was painfully sensitive, could not have failed to provoke occasional taunts, nor could his aggressive Americanism. His imperfect sense of humor deprived him of the saving capacity to understand a joke and enjoy it rather than resent it. His ambassadorially serious estimate of himself and his country, which was discernible at a considerable distance, doubtless made him the butt of jokes he otherwise would have escaped. He later recalled that a British master in-

27

sisted that Ohio was pronounced "O-hee-o." He recalled that the "British code—flogging and fagging and toadying—violated every American instinct." He recalled having a fight with "a British bastard who had insulted my country."

One classmate remembered him as a "quiet, solemn, aloof boy," and went on to describe a part of the training at Chefoo: "He received the British discipline intended to train empire-builders and administrators and learned the code."

The empire building stuck, but so did many other things, for he had a capacity for concentration allied with his endless intellectual curiosity as well as that phenomenal memory. Homesick, he sent home a torrent of letters, mostly well phrased, mostly serious. He attended sermons and hung on words that most boys shut out in protective daydreams. "The best sermon I ever heard," he wrote at age eleven, ". . . on the redemption and what the death of Christ means . . ." And he could exhibit a formidable familiarity with God, as when he wrote home:

> I am *going* to get into the fourth form. I do not care if I die for it. I must get inside. I must. I will. And God has, is, and will help me. Just take my 100% in Algebra. It was all God. I prayed he would guide my hand from all careless mistakes and again in the middle of the exam.

Probably no other Chefoo scholar wanted so desperately not merely to succeed but to excel, or sought God's help not only before the examination but in the middle, seizing a minute or two from his equations to renew the prayer that God might have forgotten in the press of business.

At home on vacation he joined other mission boys in "war games" in the fields and showed a historical bent in his re-creation of battles such as Waterloo with toy soldiers in the house. "He was always nice to us," Emmavail recalled, "but he warned us not to knock his soldiers over." The birth of a second son, Sheldon Luce, in 1909 expanded the family to six, but housework and child care were largely taken over by the half-dozen Chinese servants. The Luces and other missionary families acquired summer cottages on the beach at Iltus Huk, Tsingtao. Harry, growing tall and muscular, swam there with his friends but was always more the scholar than the athlete.

Back at school, determined to overcome his handicap, he deliberately courted the horror that most stammerers avoid—public speaking. "We have just founded a debating society . . . tonight we debate 'Should Mary Queen of Scots have been beheaded?' " The "quiet, aloof boy" could talk like one of Mr. Edison's phonographs when he had a properly appreciative audience. His best friend was Harold Burt, whom he knew from Weihsien, the son of a British missionary there. Another classmate was Thornton Wilder, whose father was American consul general at Shanghai and with whom he would have a sporadic friendship that ended curiously: "I had a long talk with Thornton Wilder on Darwinism. He says that it is quite the thing in the U.S. He says that until he came here he thought everybody accepted it!"

Anger gripped him on Independence Day, 1912: "To my utter contempt of American citizens here in Chefoo, the 4th of July passed without note to sound the glories of our day. Has patriotism fallen to this degraded state? Is there no spark left to show our ancient glory?"

His national loyalty would always be a blend of Roosevelt, Beveridge and Dink Stover. At Chefoo School he did what would always come naturally to him, wringing from it every drop of learning it could offer. He raced against time as he would always race against time. He studied the Bible, worked at French, Latin and Greek, reveled in history, pored over the Yale bulletin, followed current events, watched politics both in China and America, cherished photographs of Roosevelt his father sent him, and indulged a promising creative urge. "I am still—I suppose foolishly—desperately keen on poesy," he wrote, still only thirteen, "and am in the midst of writing a long epic . . . on the missionary's sacrifices and rewards . . . and an essay on capital punishment." Before he had finished the epic, a new enterprise claimed him:

> Now a surprise . . . a school paper has been urged. . . . I am Editor-in-Chief (an elephantine title!). . . . The plan is to [make] 30 copies to be sold at 10¢ (weekly paper), ten pages: Poetry (classical and jocular), Editor's Arena, Short Story, News Columns (anecdotes like your "Campus Note Book"), Criticism on Works, Burlesque . . .

He already had executive ideas about the journalism that would ultimately claim him. Perhaps even more prophetic words came in an earlier letter, a remark tossed off with seeming carelessness except that this young man was never careless: "I would like to be Alexander if I were not Socrates." He wanted to be both conqueror and philosopher, and during the next half-century he would have some success at both.

At fourteen, in the fall of 1912, Harry said good-bye to family and friends, boarded a steamship at Shanghai and was off, alone, for England. He had won a scholarship at Hotchkiss School in Connecticut, but first he would spend a year in a school at St. Albans, north of London, whose headmaster had had success in curing stammerers. At Singapore his admiration for the botanical gardens gave way to his social conscience: ". . . I will not rave over a city where Botany is apparently first and Humanity second. Time in this city could be sold for a flower an hour while in the city of Life time is valued by the dollars per minute."

Ceylon, Suez, the Mediterranean—he recorded keen impressions in daily letters home, valuing his minutes like dollars. At Naples he first set eyes on Europe, a continent he would later crisscross with his pathways, and was simultaneously transported by a beauty which "scorns description by such as I," and indignant at its slums: ". . . with all its beauty, its churches, its ecclesiastical finery, there is a terrible poverty and hence a hotbed of socialism—no wonder!"

Reaching England and the St. Albans school in October, he used it as a

base for bicycle tours to castles, cathedrals and "the grassy remains of the old Roman walls, telling in a way that words fail to show: the *fact* of Ancient History." He read English newspapers and magazines. He called on his good friend Harold Burt, now back in London to prepare for Oxford. He explored the city, visited Parliament: ". . . I have attended a debate in the House of Lords, the greatest debate of the year . . ." But alas, there seemed to be little improvement in his speech. He was itching to see Europe and in February 1913 he got parental permission to visit the continent. For a week he investigated Paris, then went on to Switzerland and Rome: "Spent my 15th birthday [April 3, 1913] in the Forum . . . I have carried away with me some parts of Rome that can never be taken from me."

As he returned to finish the school year at St. Albans, his indefatigable family at Weihsien planned a European reunion and tour that was a continuing demonstration of the venturesome way they regarded the world as their oyster.

When Rev. Henry Luce again visited America that spring to raise more money for the college, the rest of the family—Mrs. Luce, Emmavail, Elisabeth and four-year-old Sheldon—accompanied him. The latter four continued on to Europe and took a pension at Lausanne. When Harry's school year was finished, he and young Burt joined them at Lausanne for hiking and mountain-climbing around Lake Geneva. (The mountain-climbing would foster in him a poetic idea about the distant Matterhorn.) Next, Mr. Luce rejoined the entourage, intent on broadening his religious education. Taking Emmavail with him because her German was excellent, he visited the "Martin Luther country"—Eisleben, Erfurt, Leipzig and Wittenberg—thence to Wernigerode, where they met Mrs. Luce, Elisabeth and Sheldon, Harry having meanwhile traveled down the Rhine with Burt, who returned to London. At Wernigerode, the two girls were put in a boarding school operated by the sister of Frau Netz, where they would spend a year. The high-stepping Rev. Henry Luce, not even breathing hard, joined Harry in Hamburg, where they embarked for New York. Mrs. Luce stayed on for a time with young Sheldon, visiting galleries and museums in Berlin and Leipzig before she and her youngest son in turn sailed for New York. These were people who got around.

IV

1. AMERICA!

Hotchkiss School's row of handsome brick buildings with white cupolas surmounted a wooded hill near sleepy Lakeville, Connecticut, which overlooked a lake with a mountain beyond—a scene suggestive of a Japanese print. The school was purposely inaccessible in order to keep parents and other distractions away from the 250 boy scholars. The pompous headmaster, Dr. Huber Gray Buehler, known as The King, always wore a cutaway, and beginning students were told by upperclassmen that he went to bed that way. Tuition fees were high, the masters demanding, and the stiff collars required at daily chapel sawed 250 necks. Though the school professed to be nondenominational, it was heavily Presbyterian. The more active boys complained that on Sundays they were permitted only to breathe, and that quietly.

Hotchkiss catered to sons of the affluent who were expected to go on to college, most of them heading for Yale. Rosenberg's and other tailors from New Haven and New York sent representatives there to take orders for expensive tweeds, and the boy who did not wear Frank Brothers cordovans and carry his own matched cowhide luggage was out of it.

Into this uppish milieu came Henry Luce, wearing scuffed shoes and a suit oddly tailored by a Chinese who had studied the general drift of American styles in an old magazine illustration. He stammered badly at times. He arrived at the Lower Mid (sophomore) year so that he was a stranger among classmates who had known each other a year. He was ignorant of American slang—a grave handicap—and could remain blank-faced at jokes that made others split their sides. He was promptly nicknamed Chink, which he loathed. Being a scholarship boy—that is, an object of charity—he cleaned classrooms and occasionally waited on table.

These multiple humiliations he managed to endure. If he knew that he

31

would never win his H at football, or hold a group spellbound as he spun out a joke, he also knew that he had talents of his own. Few of his classmates could match him scholastically or creatively, and not one of those well-turned-out boys from luxurious homes had his background of world travel, self-reliance and independent thought.

Still, he could not be blamed if, in some of his conversations with God, he requested improvement in things worldly so that he could meet the Rosenberg-and-Frank Brothers boys on closer terms.

He was immediately an honor student. He quickly became a leader in St. Luke's, the religious organization, and won a place on the Hotchkiss Literary Monthly. "Next Saturday," he wrote his parents, "I deliver an oration, competing for the Forum Literary Team of five. It will be, so to speak, a very crucial point in my life here at Hotchkiss."

Every effort he made was crucial. An oration was especially so, with the nightmare possibility of breaking down in stammering. He did not break down, having discovered that words flowed more freely in a prepared speech, and he made the Forum. But in recitation or conversation he would get stuck and would suffer. In his room he studied a book of instructions for stammerers. Courage and will were evident in his lonely battle. Meanwhile his two sisters left Germany hurriedly before the Kaiser's ultimatum. It seemed that if the globe-girdling Luces were not escaping Boxers on one side of the world, they were dodging Uhlans on the other.

Luce was not on close terms with his noisy classmate Briton Hadden, who came from a prosperous banking family in Brooklyn, had a passion for horseplay and baseball, and would ultimately join him in the strangest of partnerships. He became friendly with another classmate, Culbreth Sudler of Chicago—himself an outstanding student with literary gifts. Sudler was impressed by Luce's habit of listening carefully to a chapel sermon, evaluating the speaker "and never questioning his competence to pass judgment on him." Sudler and Luce would hike to the lake on Sundays before chapel, Luce talking in the explosive way of the stammerer. "Harry's tie would be askew," Sudler recalled, "his jacket with a button missing . . . and his eyes would still be remembering the passage from Milton we had to memorize for the next day's English class. . . . For him the purpose of those walks was to sort out the contents of his mind. Was Alexander Hamilton or Thomas Jefferson ultimately right for the American people?"

Luce and Hadden measured each other in a singular relationship that always contained more of rivalry and respect than friendship, and would continue on that basis for fifteen years. Both won staff positions on the bi-weekly Record, the school news publication. In their senior year Hadden won the coveted post of editor-in-chief, but Luce stayed at least even in the competition, remaining as a Record assistant editor and becoming editor-in-chief of the Lit. If Luce had a wide margin in scholarship, Hadden's bluff good humor surrounded him with friends. Luce excelled in the Greek class they attended

together, and yet it was Hadden who would find a use for Greek that would enrich them both. Hadden, who could write good prose, could not match Luce's flights into verse. Since Hadden's ability at baseball did not equal his love for the game, and neither boy gained the athletic prowess obligatory for "top men," they viewed each other a trifle warily from the subsidiary level of editorial and intellectual excellence. Each was going to Yale, and at some point along the way each recognized the other as a foeman worthy of his steel.

". . . [U]nless we race we rot," Luce wrote his parents as he sprinted. There was a no-nonsense toughness in him, a practicality, a belief in brain over heart that would later cause him to be thought hard, and which made him pen one line remarkably hard-boiled for any youngster, much less one of such churchly rearing: "Not for one sentimental cause shed one small tear . . ." He would throughout his life reject sentiment for what he saw as pragmatism. Not that this placed any limits on his schoolboy ambition. That was high and sure, perhaps because of confidence in his own brain and its freedom from softness. He could lampoon in verse the average man's limited aspiration, his passive content to climb a "little hill"—a poem ending:

> Thus, thus, he spake,—the man earth-born
> Who feared to gaze on Matterhorn.

It was Matterhorn or nothing for Luce. Though he had not yet decided on a career, and his admiration for Milton and Wordsworth tempted him to take up poetry in earnest, he wrote his father that he was not "aiming at anything paltry" and would depend on God to help him choose. But here was one young poet not defeated by a column of figures or a practical problem. Along with the numbers, he possessed the logic and acumen needed in business. On the one hand he could pen a sentimental vignette, innocently celebrating his own travels, West and East:

> Oh, lights of Venice shining
>   A-through the mist to me;
> Oh, golden sun reclining
>   A-down a silver sea;
> Oh, paper lanterns darting
>   In Niko-in-the-hills;
> Oh, love-light at departing,
>   —Our world with glory fills.

On the other, he could travel to New York City, dicker with printers for the Lit, watch the October Scribner's magazine come off the presses, and call on the great Dr. Lyman Abbott, editor of The Outlook (and a friend of Theodore Roosevelt's!), to ask his advice on running the Lit ("I had expected five minutes with the distinguished gentleman. I got a good half hour").

On the one hand he could glorify adventure in China with lines that had a good gallop even if overlong (eleven stanzas) and rough in spots:

Oh, give me a Shantung shen-dzi,
And the life of a muleteer!
Oh, give me a load
And a mountain road,
The way of a pioneer!

Farewell to the ships at anchor,
And the junks from old Shanghai.
I'll see them again
In the month of ten,
When the snow is lying high. . . .

On the other, he could conceive an unprecedented money-making scheme for the Lit—a special automobile advertising section at $12 a page which brought in revenue from Pierce Arrow, Dodge and other leading makers.

He made his class football team despite his athletic ineptitude, sang in the glee club although he was nearly tone deaf, made the debating team as if he had never wrestled with a consonant, wrote a play contrasting Cromwell and Milton, worked for the $10 Virgil prize, intentionally embarrassed the frock-coated King in Bible class by asking, "Why should we have to ask an all-protecting God not to lead us into temptation?," and during the Christmas vacation went to New York largely to hear three sermons in a row, one of them by the sonorous John Henry Jowett at the Fifth Avenue Presbyterian Church, who preached about the cherubim in Isaiah I, never dreaming that the gist of his message would cross the Pacific and be carried at last to the Luce parents in Weihsien by a junk from old Shanghai and a Shantung *shen-dzi*.

In the Record, Hadden found fault with Luce's Cromwell-Milton play but praised his *"shen-dzi"* stanzas as "by far the best poem that has appeared in the Lit this year." Doubtless both hoped for more than routine recognition at graduation time when the senior class voted for its "best." Alas, it was the athletes who took the honors. Luce was irked enough to enliven his last issue with a blast at the shin-guard mentality and a frank tribute to Editor Hadden of the Record, not to mention Editor Luce of the Lit.

"After we graduated," Sudler recalled, "to my complete surprise, Harry sent me a note with a check for $40 or so as my share of the profits of the Lit." Luce took his own profits to Springfield, Massachusetts, where he had a summer office job at eight dollars a week with the local daily Republican. He economized drastically in the hope of bettering his financial position at Yale. It happened that cantaloupe was plentiful and cheap in the Springfield area that summer. So many of his meals consisted of cantaloupe and ice cream that he could never thereafter recover his enthusiasm for either. But to his delight, he was occasionally allowed to fill in as a reporter.

"The reporting work becomes more and more fascinating," he wrote his parents in his 457th letter since he first went to Chefoo (his letters were later edited and numbered by his sister Elisabeth). ". . . As a matter of fact, I be-

lieve that I can be of greatest service in journalistic work and can by that way come nearest to the heart of the world."

2. SMOKE AMONG THE ELMS

When Luce entered Yale in 1916 he was eighteen years old and for the first time participating regularly in a society which, in its thought and talk, approached that of mainstream America. He had skipped entirely an ordinary American boyhood. His fiery Americanism was that of his parents out of the previous century. In matriculating at Yale he was consummating a family dream and was also beginning a more studied battle for mastery with Briton Hadden. The kid rivalry now escalated into a more mature combat which would reverberate along High and College streets for four whole years, trailing smoke among the elms. The accounts of a few of the surviving witnesses of the class of 1920—Culbreth Sudler, John M. Hincks and Perry Prentice—attest to the severity of the struggle. Even the narratives of Yalemen of slightly earlier or later vintage—Archibald MacLeish, William Benton, Allen Grover and E. V. Hale—touch on it. An interesting aspect was the fact that both Luce and Hadden were heavily armed with abilities but, with the exception of their enormous drive and common gift for journalism, they were as different as if they had come from opposite sides of the world, which they had.

Since Rev. Henry Luce's day, Yale had subdued its stress on religion and the classics. It had become a four-year exercise in which fellowship still outranked scholarship but a more practical accommodation had been made toward mundane success. While any college modestly hoped that its graduates would be self-supporting, Yale trained its men assiduously for business, political and social supremacy. If it was true that the Battle of Waterloo was won on the playing fields of Eton, Yale wanted to make it equally certain that the battles of Wall Street, Fifth Avenue and Washington, and all their smaller counterparts throughout the country, would be won in the ivied realm between Grove and Chapel streets. As Henry Seidel Canby, a graduate who taught English there and had Luce and Hadden as students, observed:

There was no fiercer competition in the business world than the [Yale] undergraduate competition for social awards. Beside its strenuosities the pursuit of marks or even of scholarship glowed dimly. . . . [C]ollege life . . . inculcated ideals that were viable in America as it was then, and these ideals were adaptations of general idealism (even of Christianity) to the needs of an industrialized, get-rich-quick country. It educated specifically for the harsh competitions of capitalism, for the successful and often unscrupulous pursuit by the individual of power for himself, for class superiority, and for a success measured by the secure possession of the fruits of prosperity. I do not see how a better education could have been contrived for a youth that wanted the wealth, the position, the

individual power that was being worshiped just then in America—and wanted to get them quickly, easily, and with no public dishonesty.

Yale's gospel of success held out rewards to the faithful and withheld them from the dissidents. A Yaleman's orthodoxy was almost as visible as a Heidelberger's dueling scar. The trickle of Yalemen into Wall Street was becoming a stream. The system permitted endless individuality so long as it did not conflict with the college concepts of loyalty, religion, patriotism, success and elitism. But if Yale was conformist, WASPish, dilettante and materialistic, it enveloped its purposes in rousing good fellowship and the glamour of elderly traditions, handsome buildings, ardent young men, mandolins, noseguards and secret societies. It took itself and its values seriously. When Yalemen sang "Bright College Years," they came down with a roar on the last line—"For God, for Country, and for Yale"—and especially on the last word, never seeing any anticlimax in this emphasis.

"This first Sunday at Yale," Luce wrote his parents a trifle rebelliously, ". . . there was a Freshman meeting at Dwight Hall . . . rather sickened me . . . One thing is certain, that . . . an over-dose of this fervid Xnity stuff, has completely alienated my friend Brit Hadden from its holy halls."

But he was in perfect conformity with Yale's emphasis on the earning and accumulation of power. Power was the reward for competitive achievement, and so it was in life. Power of one kind or another was what made the world go round and kept it in order. The most thrilling example of it in his own background was the arrival of Old Glory in Peking with the American soldiers who helped put down the Boxers—righteousness armed with might and suppressing evil. The fight for power and the use of power that would mark and ultimately disfigure his life took their justification from the Bible and the flag. The Bible and the flag represented the power of God and country. Those paternal axioms about "native Lucepower" and "character means destiny" reflected the aggressive missionary whose own power depended on the Bible and the flag. The son had been unusually preoccupied with power since boyhood. His mention at twelve that "I would like to be Alexander if I were not Socrates," suggesting the struggle in him between conquest and contemplation, had been followed in other letters by mention of his more muscular interest: "Worthy men to place in power," "God's gentleness is power in restraint," "the power of the British lion," and "America's leadership of the world."

Luce and Hadden plunged immediately into the battle for a place on the Yale Daily News, a grueling six-month ordeal called "heeling" for several dozen young men of whom only four could win minor posts. Membership on the News staff, though an enormous honor in itself, was part of a complex system of awards leading as time went on to the greatest honor of all, membership in one of the three senior societies, Skull and Bones, Scroll and Key, and Wolf's Head. Many freshmen who would have denied having read *Stover*

at Yale had nevertheless learned something about the "society system" from that book, wherein the knowledgeable sophomore Le Baron explained it to the freshman Dink Stover on the first day at school:

"You'll hear a good deal of talk inside the college, and out of it, too, about the system. It has its faults. But it's the best system there is, and it makes Yale what it is today. It makes fellows get out and work; it gives them ambitions, stops loafing and going to seed. . . ."

"I know nothing at all about it," said Stover, perplexed.

"The seniors have 15 in each [society]; they give out their elections end of junior year, end of May. That's what we're all working for."

"Already?" said Stover involuntarily.

"There are fellows in your class," said Le Baron, "who've been working all summer, so as to get ahead of the competition for the News or the Lit, or to make the leader of the glee club—fellows, of course, who know."

"But that's three years off."

"Yes, it's three years off," said Le Baron quietly.

Luce's utterly serious cast of mind combined with what one friend described as "a kind of terrifying egotism" deprived him of the popularity that inundated Hadden. Hadden's jovial shout at Luce, striding across the campus with responsibility etched on his face—"Look out, Harry, you'll drop the college"—underlined one difference between them.

"This heeling business is awful. . . ." Luce wrote his parents. "[It] not only uses up all your energy, it robs you of the mood or frame of mind to do anything like studying or reading or writing letters."

He had assured them that he would do his best to make the News, and that ultimately he would make Phi Beta Kappa. His one-word cable to them in China in March 1917 showed the extent to which they were engrossed in his lonely New Haven competition. It said simply, "Successful." The Luces, having been coached in advance by mail, understood with delight that he had won one of the coveted News posts. But Hadden was top man among the winners.

3. A PIECE OF THE RHINE

Luce fought his customary handicaps in scaling the New Haven Matterhorn. The prized collegiate quality of sophistication eluded him. Some thought him arrogant. His lack of poise, camaraderie and humor would classify him later as a square, and his lack of money would classify him any time as poor. He walked on thin soles in a class that included Morehead Patterson, son of the American Machine & Foundry mogul, Harry Davison, son of a Morgan partner, and scions of the du Pont, Hanes, Heffelfinger and other fortunes. Since his father had been able to send him only $500 toward his initial expenses, he could not with real feeling sing that hearty Yale ballad:

O, father and mother pay all the bills,
And I have all of the fun.

With few exceptions he avoided girls. He eschewed Rosenberg's. He got free meals by organizing an eating group. He did what Yalemen and all young men dislike doing. He economized.

Theodore Roosevelt was in paroxysms over President Wilson's pacific "emasculation" of America's righteousness and manhood, with Luce in agreement about the nation's duty to stop the Kaiser. America's entry into the war in April electrified him, although he felt it so late as to lose all moral authority and appear motivated by mere self-preservation. When summer came, with his family still on the far side of the world, he worked at a farm near Scranton owned by old family friends, the Linens. Back at Yale in the fall he earned money by taking orders for ROTC uniforms, including his own. He, Hadden and the rest fell in at 6:45 for campus calisthenics, working up a dripping sweat which they carried noisomely into classes before they could shower at noon. Everybody was singing "K-K-K-Katy" and "We Don't Want the Bacon, All We Want Is a Piece of the Rhine," and Luce badly wanted to go overseas.

Along with his classmates Hadden, Sudler, Walter Millis and Thornton Wilder he was elected to the determinedly literary Elizabethan Club. He was pledged to Alpha Delta Phi, while Hadden joined the somewhat more prestigious Delta Kappa Epsilon. He read his Bible regularly, gave occasional short sermons at the Yale Hope Mission, and was known by some as a "Christer" just as his father in his day had been one of "Jesus' Little Lambs." But the great question was—for the moment even eclipsing the war—who would win that most cherished of sophomore awards, the chairmanship of the Oldest College Daily?

It was between Luce and Hadden. In their subsidiary positions on the paper they had battled each other with outward amiability. Luce roomed with Sudler that year in Durfee Hall, but Sudler seldom saw him because Luce spent every spare minute grinding at the News. On the day of the balloting, the voting among incoming board members was known to be very close. One of the members, Perry Prentice, who voted for Luce, declares to this day that it would have been a tie but for the fact that another of the members believed that Luce preferred that Hadden should have the top position—a preposterous notion.

"Briton Hadden is chairman of the News . . ." Luce wrote his parents bravely although his competitive heart was surely breaking. "I am managing editor, and am to write a share of the editorials . . . Happily, I have the greatest admiration and affection for Brit which, in some measure at least, is reciprocated."

If his diction was stuffy, he did have a generous appreciation of talent wherever he found it. Hadden, who was not scheduled to take charge until the junior year, got the office abruptly when the incumbent chairman joined

the Army, and Luce rose with him. The college seethed with a fervor of enlistment that reduced enrollment by 40 percent and also threw heavier News responsibility on Luce—welcome in more ways than one, for the paper made a substantial profit from advertising that was distributed to the staff. The younger professors joined the colors. Yale became virtually a military school. "We give three weeks to Aristotle," Luce observed, "—Aristotle who founded twelve sciences!" Intercollegiate athletics were suspended and cultural courses suffered. It was said that Professor Edward Bliss Reed, formerly an academic tyrant, lectured his class in this wise:

> Now take this down. It is important for the examination. We come now to Edmund Spenser, spelled with an s. Be careful about that. He wrote the *Faerie Queene*, spelled F-a-e-r-i-e Q-u-e-e-n-e. Got that? It will be necessary. Now we come to Christopher Marlowe.

Hadden and Luce made the News a propagandist thorn in the Kaiser's side. "I have written 40% of the editorials and Hadden 30%," Luce wrote home. ". . . I can confidently say that we have played a major part in changing the spirit of Yale. There is now no college in the country more thoroughly and intensely patriotic—and *intelligently!*" He argued in a letter to the News against holding the Junior Prom as usual while men were dying in Flanders. Hadden responded with an editorial *favoring* the Prom, but at the patriotic price of a Liberty Bond. The yeas had it, but Luce did not attend. With Hadden's roommate and closest friend, John M. Hincks, he took the train to New York and bought standing-room tickets for *Aida* at the Metropolitan Opera.

Hadden's compulsion to keep the paper lively sometimes led him to use unorthodox techniques. At one time when news was slow, he wrote and published a fake letter signed "Divinity Student," complaining of the noise and uproar at Berkeley Hall. He then addressed an angry reply from an equally mythical student resident of Berkeley, signed "Old Hatchet Face," who was in turn answered in anger. Soon the whole college was engrossed in the imaginary quarrel. Luce meanwhile tried soberly to shape campus opinion on larger issues. He sent the News home to China and to the family benefactor, Mrs. McCormick, in Chicago, as he had done with his Hotchkiss efforts. Despite the fierce pressure on his time, his energy and concentration were such that he still contributed regularly to the Lit, which was also sent to China and Chicago.

Luce and Hadden were among the many Yalemen who were overjoyed to become full-time soldiers in the summer of 1918 when their unit was sent to Camp Jackson, near Columbia, South Carolina.

"Of course in the eyes of the Eternal," Luce wrote his family, "the days of preparation and the days on the field of battle are one. I pride myself most on my small share in pushing Yale to a more intensive war-training life . . . The one greatest thing to do now is to fight, with all the life one has, so that the continuity of history 'toward the truth and the right of things,' shall be main-

tained." He described the French officers who gave instruction in the 75-mm. gun as "worthy of the greatest artillery nation on earth." His habit of dissecting moral issues removed him from the "regular fellow" category, as did his refusal to tell racy stories. But by now perhaps the innocuous song the artillerymen sang to the tune of "My Bonnie" did not offend him:

> Saltpeter they put in my coffee;
> Saltpeter they put in my tea;
> Saltpeter they put in my oatmeal;
> Oh, bring back my manhood to me.

Army life loosened him a trifle. He, Hadden, Hincks and the rest of the Yale contingent celebrated with cigars when they were commissioned second lieutenants. As Luce later recalled it, it was at Camp Jackson that he and Hadden first discussed the idea of collaborating in the founding of a newsmagazine—a recollection Hincks is inclined to doubt.

Alas, six weeks after they were transferred to Camp Zachary Taylor near Louisville, the war ended and with it their dreams of battle command. It was a crushing blow to Luce. (More than two decades later, when an even greater war began, his second wife noticed that he still felt bereaved at his failure to see combat duty on the Western Front. "He had missed his war," said Mrs. Luce.) "I have absolutely lost all military ambitions," he now admitted dolefully, since military ambition was useless without a war.

In January 1919 the warriors were back at Yale, where Luce and Hadden returned to the News just in time to record the death of Theodore Roosevelt. The event evoked a front-page story and an editorial probably written by the admiring Luce (". . . a spirit unique among men . . . [like] that which imbued Napoleon. He possessed courage which never flinched . . ."). The college years—normally the years when the devil is abroad sowing doubt—left his arrangement with the Almighty unchanged. When Culbreth Sudler's Presbyterian beliefs were shaken by courses in science, Luce told him calmly, "Fundamentalism isn't all there is to religion, you know."

Luce the incessant questioner seems seldom to have questioned the dogma of his fathers. The oddly shy-but-aggressive Christer, the Chinaboy so lacking in finesse, was at a disadvantage socially with that master of the quip and horselaugh, Hadden. Luce competed with him nevertheless in every area where they touched, and was the better man in some of them. But it would be difficult to measure the lifelong effect on Luce, the competitor who so badly wanted to be first in everything, to be pitted for seven years in prep school and college against a rival he could never match in magnetism and popularity.

Together they took Henry Seidel Canby's advanced writing course, English 40, an exceptional class including Stephen Vincent Benét, Thornton Wilder and Walter Millis. The class was often visited by recent alumni, among them Archibald MacLeish, John Farrar and Philip Barry. Again there was competition with brilliance. The precocious Benét had already published his third

volume of poetry, and MacLeish and Farrar were writing verse of considerable polish. In such company, perhaps Luce decided that he could not lead in every field and had better concentrate on those more promising to him. Thereafter, his budding poetic gift seems to have drawn less of his attention.

With the April 1, 1919, issue of the News, Hadden and Luce's names went on the masthead as Chairman and Managing Editor, making official the duties they had already exercised. They continued and enlarged a News tradition of covering the more important national and international events. This was a time of world concern over the fate of Russia that drew Luce's deepest attention. In his boyhood, Czarist Russia had been under permanent suspicion among American missionaries because of its "imperialist designs" on China. Now the shaky Bolshevist government was threatened by several foreign armies and also that of the counterrevolutionary Admiral Kolchak. What was to be done about Russia—and indeed whether Communism should be permitted to exist—was an engrossing question in America. The earliest News story in the Hadden-Luce regime concerning it told of the return to Paris of William C. Bullitt (Yale '12)—a man later to be oddly linked with Luce—with a report to President Wilson "so favorable to the Bolshevist Government," as the News put it, "that it is dangerous to make it public."

It was dangerous to be favorable in any way to the Soviets during this period of anti-Communist turbulence. The News told in a later story of the national concern about the menace of Bolshevist propaganda spread by "insidious soap-box orators, who appeal to the uneducated masses," and of the plan sponsored by patriotic Americans to counter it with college-trained speakers who would expose their falsities. The News splashed the story of the unsuccessful plot, laid to Communists, to send bombs by mail to John D. Rockefeller, Jr., J. P. Morgan and others. These ominous doings were forgotten in what must have been the greatest day in Luce's life to that moment, Thursday, May 15, 1919.

On that day he was elected (along with Walter Millis and fourteen others) to Phi Beta Kappa, a laurel Hadden would never achieve. And he was one of the fifteen tapped for Skull and Bones—a great honor and well deserved, even if the order of selection placed him behind Hadden. Bones, founded in 1832, had on its "secret" roster so many of the wealthy and influential who were sworn to help other Bones men that cynics said a membership properly implemented meant lifetime social and financial assurance. As Le Baron said to Stover, "I'm frankly aristocratic in my point of view, and what I say others think. . . . You may think the world begins outside of college. It doesn't. It begins right here. You want to make the friends that will help you along, here and outside."

This aristocratic-elitist philosophy was one to which Luce would subscribe all his life. But he was appealingly modest about PBK, later admitting that this came about through hard work rather than brilliance, that he was indeed a greasy grind but was so fearful of gaining that reputation that he did much

of his studying in the dormitory bathroom. And he wrote his parents, with a generosity not easy for one so competitive: "Brit Hadden, if ever a class had *one* big man, is the big man of our class . . . my rival since early Hotchkiss days . . ."

That fall, the Bolshevist question stirred even more excitement, with Kolchak suffering reverses in Russia, Attorney General Palmer's men raiding suspected Communist meetings in the United States and radicals being deported. Certainly the politically minded Hadden was interested in these events. Luce was doubly absorbed, politically and religiously, detesting the Bolsheviks on the score of Marxism and atheism. The News, continuing to follow Soviet developments, also ran a long article of opinion headed, "Kolchak is Hope of Russia," specially prepared by Max Solomon, instructor in Russian at Yale, and doubtless solicited by the editors. Luce, who would seldom admit that any subject was beyond his ken, had been further emboldened by his travels to regard international relations as a specialty. He was the leading anti-Bolshevist and pro-Kolchak debater when the Yale Union argued the question of intervention in Russia. As the News reported it:

> [Luce] told how this radical group of Communists, despotically controlling a large part of Russia, was opposed by various groups of conservatives. In Kolchak, he said, the conserving influences of Russia converged . . . Kolchak, in order to win, must have assistance.
>
> Luce then turned to the general question of international relations, drawing the conclusion that if we do not intervene soon Bolshevism will undermine the civilization of the world. He concluded by stating that this menace must be fought and overcome on the frontier of civilization.

Millis opposed him on the ground that Kolchak represented a minority, and David Ingalls argued that Bolshevism would die out eventually if let alone. But the Luce call for intervention won the audience vote by 45 to 18. It was the first well-publicized anti-Communist appeal by the young man who would become the Great American Anti-Communist. The basic Christian-moral-patriotic convictions that would drive him all his life were already well developed at Yale. And his concept of a morally superior America, destined to lead the world, was the stuff from which he composed a speech in his bid for the DeForest Prize.

At Woolsey Hall on April 26, 1920, a few weeks before his graduation, he won the prize with an oration about America bristling with mention of "power," "strength," "greatness," "honor and glory," "force" and "moral challenge." He described the nation as a powerhouse without purpose, a moralist *manqué* which had failed to rise to its duties as world leader and international policeman:

> . . . When we say "America" today we connote power. We hold the purse strings of the world. . . . We sell in the markets of every nation. . . . America is power in industry. . . . The glory of our strength flatters us. . . . America is

power, and it sits astride the globe. But is our greatness after all great merely for the sake of greatness? Are we big to no purpose?

There was the rub, he said. America did not believe in her world mission. For three years she had ignored the moral challenge of the war in Europe and had finally fought out of self-preservation rather than honor. She had lost much of her early spirit of adventure and democracy, and Luce urged on his own generation a rebirth of the national pride and spirit:

> But when we say "America" twenty years from now may it be that that great name will signify throughout the world at least two things: First, that American interests shall be respected, American citizens entitled to trade and to live in every corner of the globe, American business ideals recognized wherever the trader goes; second, that America may be counted upon to do her share in every international difficulty, that she will be the great friend of the lame, the halt and the blind among nations, the comrade of all nations that struggle to rise to higher planes of social and political organization, and withal the implacable and *immediate* foe of whatever nation shall offer to disturb the peace of the world. If this shall be, then the America of this century shall have glory and honor to take into that City of God far outshining the glory and honor which the kings do bring. . . . For if America will be a defender of good faith throughout the world, hers will be an adventure more brilliant than Eldorado. . . .

The facetious Hadden would have bellowed, "Look out, Harry, you'll drop the world." But the DeForest Oration given at twenty-two, almost line by line would be Luce's theme for the rest of his life, forty-seven years and three wars after Woolsey Hall.

V

1. THE MOST WONDERFUL GIRL

Luce's $1500 share in the profits of the News, plus a $1000 commencement gift from his fairy godmother in Chicago, Mrs. McCormick, made him richer and freer than he ever had been in his life. He had decided on a year of graduate study at Oxford with two classmates, his fellow Bonesman Morehead Patterson and his fellow Phi Beta Kappa member William Whitney, a Rhodes Scholar.

But first he rode to Chicago with Patterson in the private railroad car of the latter's father, Rufus Lenoir Patterson, an inventive genius who had made a fortune devising tobacco-processing machinery for James B. Duke and had done even better on his own. The Patterson car, like the palace of Mrs. McCormick, was one of those exhibits of American luxury likely to arouse envy in a young man of the modest Luce circumstances. As he later admitted, one of his dreams was to own a chauffeur-driven automobile. In Chicago he attended the Republican National Convention, his fascination with politics being part of his solicitude for an America he felt was laggard in its destined world leadership. He saw the nomination of Harding, of whom his opinion was low. He paid his shouted devoirs to Mrs. McCormick, who promised him a job at International Harvester when he returned from Oxford. Riding East again in the same Patterson opulence, he joined two other classmates, John Hincks and Walter Millis, and boarded the *Olympia* third class with them in July. Hincks, son of a Bridgeport investment banker, had been twice captain of the swimming team and was Bones. Millis, son of a well-traveled Army engineering officer, could be forgiven his Wolf's Head affiliation since he was Phi Beta Kappa, Elizabethan Club, a fencer, class secretary and managing editor of the Lit in his senior year.

Luce had written his old friend Harold Burt, recently graduated from Ox-

ford, and had told his two Yale friends how tall and powerful Burt was. He had not seen Burt for seven years. Hincks and Millis were amused at Luce's astonishment when they reached London, met Burt and discovered that he had stopped growing in the interim and was now undersized. Burt invited them to a dress party. Luce, always too absorbed in thought to mind his apparel, had lost the vest to his tuxedo. At a store in the Strand he asked for a black vest. The clerk, dumfounded, said he had vests only in white or pink. Luce in turn was astonished until he recalled that in England a vest was an undershirt, and solved the situation by asking for a black waistcoat.

After visiting Stratford-on-Avon, the three Yalemen donned their old Army fatigues and hiked for several days through Devon and Cornwall, then went by train to Wales and made a pilgrimage to the tomb of Elihu Yale. Luce was in good spirits. Perhaps a part of the reason was his escape, after seven years, from the overpowering personality and endowments of Briton Hadden. Continuing into the Lake District, they climbed the 3100-foot Helvellyn, England's nearest approximation to Matterhorn, before going on to Edinburgh and back to London, where they separated. Hincks, who thoroughly enjoyed the tour and would remain a good friend of Luce's as well as Hadden's, could not recall that Luce made any mention of a plan to start a news publication, and indeed there are signs that his ultimate aim at that time was politics.

Luce, for whom this jaunt was a mere warm-up, crossed to Paris and there by chance encountered another classmate, Hugh Auchincloss of Providence, son of a mining entrepreneur. They boarded the Orient Express for Constantinople. Apparently it was on this journey that the eternally curious Luce began his custom of stopping at American embassies for information and advice. "Excellent lunch at American Embassy," he wrote from Constantinople, ". . . and exceedingly intelligent aides." They stopped at others, including the legation in Bucharest. They spent hours in the Parliament in Budapest, which Luce found "the most beautiful interior I have ever seen."

As his colleagues would notice in later years, there was something about a tour—any tour—that exhilarated him far beyond mere interest. He always returned beaming, or sometimes bursting with indignation, but invariably stuttering in his eagerness to impart new knowledge which often turned out to be more opinion than knowledge. Now he wrote exuberantly, "Somehow I feel as if I know 500% more about Europe, its problems and its national passions, than I ever knew before . . . a full account would fill volumes!"

At Christ Church ("Well, here we are at Oxford and Christ Church is grand!"), where he specialized in history, he and Patterson had spacious rooms and a servant to wait on them. Luce, unable to match Patterson's pink-coat-and-foxhunt opulence, was satisfied with tennis for recreation. He relished the fact that he could be addressed at "Ch. Ch. Oxon Eng," and that any post office in Europe would identify it. He immediately learned the history of the various colleges, faithfully observed traditions and planned for the future, writing his parents:

45

My desire is to go into public life and whatever I do in the next ten years is preparatory to that . . . publishing? . . . business? . . . financial independence so I can go into politics without being entirely dependent upon the boss for my bread and butter.

Public life. Politics. These were his objectives, and journalism only one possible way to attain independence for a political career. It is hard to resist the thought that Luce already had his eye on the White House. Fascinated as he was by power, he wanted to attain power himself and use it in pushing America into her rightful place of world power. America as a world power with a world mission was on his mind to a degree uncommon for a Senator, much less a man recently out of Yale. "Through it all," he wrote after his latest look at Europe, "one realizes that the magnificence is now of America. May it prove to be a moral and spiritual magnificence!"

Love, however, complicated his life for the first time. With William Whitney he journeyed to Rome for the Christmas holidays and there met Thornton Wilder, studying at the American Academy. "Thornton Wilder," he wrote, ". . . watches over us. He illumines art and reads to me his plays which show a very great dramatic adroitness and subtlety of characterization."

Wilder did more than that. He took them to a New Year's Eve party at the Academy. Among the guests were the students at Miss Risser's School in Rome, a finishing school for American girls of wealth. Luce spent the entire evening with one of them, Lila Ross Hotz of Chicago, a graduate of Miss Spence's in New York. One friend described her: "Tall, dark, with very white skin and dark brown curls spilling away from her temples and neck, she was one of those dazzling ethereal people who hardly seem to be on the ground at all." She came from a family of wealth and social position, she was a Presbyterian and her brother had gone to Yale. An annual visitor to Europe since childhood, she knew the museums, cathedrals, palazzos and spas far better than Luce. She liked music and poetry and dashed off occasional verses herself. A blithe spirit, she was fluent in Italian and French, possessor of the natural warmth and charm Luce lacked. She later recalled that he was "a bit of an intellectual show-off at the time, and he talked a blue streak." He spoke of books he liked, said his favorite poet was Francis Thompson and startled her by asking suddenly, "Are you popular?"

One of the many surprising things about Luce, appearing as he did so impervious to tenderness, was the violence with which love smote him. Two days later, Perry Prentice—another member of this remarkably well-traveled class of 1920—was standing outside the Pitti Palace in Florence when someone touched his shoulder.

"It was Harry," Prentice recalled, "on his way back to Oxford. He said he had just met the most wonderful girl in the world and he was going to marry her."

To his parents Luce described it as "a perfectly delightful sojourn," with-

out specifying its chief delight. He kept letters speeding from Ch. Ch. to Rome. Their reversed initials—HRL and LRH—seemed proof of the intervention of destiny. He raised a mustache, bought a cane. During the March vacation he met Lila again in Paris, where she stayed with an aunt, but then he returned stoically to the business of learning. He went on alone to Prague and Berlin, seeing important people and asking questions: "Prague—entertained by legation, German industrial baron, called on Foreign Minister Beneš, chatted with young Masaryk. . . . Berlin—inspected schools, trade unions, Bolshevik club headquarters, a factory and one of the biggest German newspapers . . ."

He seemed consciously preparing himself for greatness. He turned twenty-three on April 3—a reminder of inexorable time, so valuable in building a career, so sinful to fritter away. He frittered it away with every appearance of enjoyment during the gala May Week festivities at Oxford, when Miss Hotz was his guest at a dizzying round of parties, polo matches, dances and punting excursions on the Isis, and among the many personages present were John Masefield and his rather whiskery wife. All too rarely did the too serious, too ambitious young man permit himself such warmth and relaxation. "Ah, but there's no style to these English women," he wrote his parents, not saying that he saw style only in one girl, an American.

In June the halcyon English interlude was over. Luce sailed for New York, his money nearly gone.

2. STUDYING PIANO

Dr. Luce, whose strong opinions had caused arguments in Shantung, had meanwhile resigned his post to become vice president and second in command to Dr. John Leighton Stuart, president of the newly organized Christian Yenching University in Peking. He was as determined as ever to Christianize and democratize China. Alas, Yenching needed money urgently. Who was an experienced fund-raiser? Dr. Luce, of course.

The family now lived in New York while he resumed the old Pullman-car routine and pursued donors all over the country. When Harry arrived from England, Emmavail and Elisabeth were on vacation from Wellesley College and Sheldon was still in grade school. It was seldom that the six wandering Luces got together, and (if the father was home) perhaps this was one of those times—a great occasion to a family so devoted.

But soon Harry was drawn to Chicago by the presence there of Lila Hotz, the promise of a job at International Harvester being a contributing consideration. If he had visions of a Harvester job grand enough to enable him to marry an heiress, the vision faded. The 1921 depression was severe. Alexander Legge, the vice president of the company, was candid with the serious young applicant. Yes, he could have a job, since Mrs. McCormick had promised him

47

one, but it would mean that another employee, probably a married man, would have to be fired to make room for him. Luce recoiled at the thought of bringing hardship to someone else. "Of course I don't want you to fire anyone," he said. Looking around, he landed a job as legman for Ben Hecht, whose column "One Thousand and One Afternoons" was a feature in the Daily News.

To have one's first experience in metropolitan journalism under Ben Hecht must be likened to learning the banking business from an embezzler or studying piano in a bagnio. Hecht, a gifted romancer, never let facts interfere with a good story. He wrote daily about odd Chicago characters—an astrologer, a midwife, a snake charmer, a punch-drunk boxer. It was up to Luce to find such characters and supply a few basic details. Hecht would flesh them out with colorful flights of imagination presented as truth. Hecht himself, as improbable as any of his characters, had left his first wife and run off with another woman and as a result was dodging attorneys as well as bill collectors hounding him for the $20,000 he owed various people. He was forever darting out the Daily News back door to escape such annoyances. Chicago was then the journalistic battleground of the Hearst, McCormick (no relation to the Harvester McCormicks) and Lawson newspapers, a rivalry in which probity often suffered, and Hecht was only the most outrageous trifler with it.

One could make out a case for the proposition that Hecht's cynicism had a baneful effect on the young, innately truthful but malleable Luce, that it was the root cause of his later eccentricity with fact in his publications, and that if he had had his first training instead under someone like the solid Walter Lippmann he would never have taken such liberties.

A better argument would be that neither Hecht nor Lippmann would have made the slightest difference in the ultimate career of this determined young man who was already bursting with the philosophy and the message that would make him view the news less as news than as a vehicle.

". . . [M]y salary is about 10¢ a day over carfare," Luce wrote home, not saying that much of his carfare was spent on trips to call on Lila Ross Hotz.

Until he found permanent quarters, he stayed at the spacious near North Side home of his Yale roommate, Culbreth Sudler. He admitted to Sudler that he intended to propose to Miss Hotz. "When he finally came in about 2:00 A.M.," Sudler recalled, "he looked very striking in his black tuxedo with a white vest spanned by a gold chain with the Lit triangle which he always wore. He was immaculate except for a bow tie slightly out of place and an incongruous bright red gloss on his lips."

Clearly he had not met total rebuff. He was less successful at his job, writing home in September: "I have been fired—this department was instructed to cut off five men and as I was the last to come I must be the first to go . . . may be for the best as I wasn't getting very far around here . . ."

Thirty-seven years later, on his television show, Hecht said Luce was not fired for economy but because Hecht complained to the editor that "this fel-

48

low is much too naïve. Nothing he writes makes any sense. I haven't been able to get a paragraph out of it."

While it is interesting that he remembered Luce's naïveté, one can scarcely place any more credence in Hecht after thirty-seven years than could be placed in one of his 1921 daily columns. In any case, the worlds of Ben Hecht and Henry Luce glanced off and separated after this brief collision, the better for them both. But at the moment, Luce's need for money was urgent because of his determination to marry Lila Hotz and the equally firm disapproval of her banker stepfather, Frederick Haskell, of a jobless and penniless suitor.

Here a piece of luck intervened. The brilliant Walter Millis was then working for the Baltimore News. He was doing so well that the News wanted two more young men of his caliber and was willing to pay $40 a week for each. He reacted in the Yale tradition, writing Luce in Chicago and Hadden in New York.

Hadden meanwhile had worked for a year for the prestige-laden Ralph Pulitzer-Herbert Bayard Swope New York World. Although he was still a low-ranking reporter, he was a veritable Floyd Gibbons or Webb Miller in seasoning compared with Luce. The fact that he was willing to jump the World in favor of the third-rate, tank-town, Munsey-owned News, and at the same salary as Luce, indicated his eagerness to join Luce and plan their newsmagazine project. He was aching to get started. A few months earlier, when he and John Hincks had gone to Houston to usher at the wedding of their classmate and Bonesmate Peavey Heffelfinger, Hadden had jumped off the train at every stop to buy a local paper and had talked incessantly of starting a publication based on newspaper accounts. "I think during that trip Brit got newspapers in at least twenty different cities," Hincks recalled. He felt that Hadden was the prime mover in the venture, and the evidence seems to support him. Luce had not shown quite such journalistic enthusiasm, had made his try at Harvester and had mentioned "publishing" as one possible avenue to his career in politics.

"If we are ever going to start that paper," Hadden now wrote Luce, "this looks like our chance."

Luce said good-bye to Lila Hotz, left for New York, conferred with Hadden and then rode with him to Baltimore. Soon they were working on the News, an afternoon paper, and rooming together on Charles Street. If Luce's editorial dreams had somewhat faded, they quickly revived. These two high-powered young men became totally preoccupied with their idea. When their salaried work was finished in midafternoon, they returned to their apartment and began unpaid labors that often lasted far into the night and generated thick cigarette smoke. They became known among their Baltimore colleagues as "the Yale locks." Millis sometimes joined them, though he lacked their afflatus. It is not impossible that working long hours with two such aggressive and intense companions was not Millis's idea of pleasure.

In Baltimore, Luce was seized by one of those spasms of hero-worship

which would affect and sometimes impair his judgment throughout his life. During an interview with Archbishop Michael J. Curley, he was so impressed by the prelate and perhaps also by the power he wielded that he returned for further discussion and quite fell under the archbishop's spell. For a time, as he wrote Lila perhaps only partly in jest, he considered embracing Catholicism, entering the priesthood and ultimately becoming a cardinal.

While some friends came to regard this hero-worshiping trait as evidence of an open mind, as indeed it was, it also marked a mind so eager for ideas as ideas, for the new and stimulating, as to resemble a hungry terrier that will snap at anything. His incessant curiosity would prove endlessly valuable to the journalist Luce. Yet his lack of discrimination would occasionally mislead the politician Luce, the philosopher Luce or the world-saver Luce. *Snap* would go the mental teeth on a new morsel, sometimes swallowing it whole, sometimes ruminating a while, finding it flavorless and spitting it out. Those who worked for Luce, and those seeking to understand him, would have to be careful about that *snap*.

The handling of stories in the News gave Luce and Hadden a daily fare of discussion and criticism. How differently would they treat news in their magazine? How could news be more quickly told for busy readers? How could it be better organized? How could it be made more visually attractive? How could they maintain readers' interest in a weekly whose news would necessarily be far in arrears of daily papers with international wire-service facilities?

They studied the newsmagazines they would have to buck, headed so decisively by the Literary Digest that they hardly had to consider the others. The Digest seemed to settle any doubts that "old news" was readily marketable. It was a national institution, circulation 1,200,000, fat with advertising, seen on every respectable fumed-oak table and assigned to high school and college students for its coverage of current events. Its "news service" was very nearly scot-free. It consisted of subscriptions to the more important American newspapers and a few published elsewhere in the world. The Digest frankly stole its news from these papers, usually quoting them directly. The victims seldom complained because the magazine gave them full credit and because by the time it used their property it was several days old—waste material by daily journalistic standards. In that sense the Digest ran the most profitable news junk shop in the world. But it performed a useful service, an advance over the breathless patchwork and discontinuity of the dailies and bringing vital issues into more leisurely focus. It gave two or more sides to contentious issues by quoting newspapers holding opposing opinions—important to a public that wished to be informed, but often done with tiresome verbosity.

Luce and Hadden thought they could do better with Facts, the working title of their creation. "Work progresses," Luce wrote his family with the curtness of a busy man. "First sample issue of Facts nearing completion."

On a free Sunday they hurried to New York with their dummy. Unknown as they were, they made full use of the few avenues of influence open to

them—relationship, friendship and Yale loyalty, which included Bones, their fraternities, the Elizabethan Club, the prestige of the Yale Daily News and the fact that Hadden had been top man of the class of '20 and Luce not far behind him. They showed the dummy to their former writing instructor, Henry Seidel Canby, now editor of the New York Evening Post literary supplement. Canby was warmly encouraging. He agreed that there was need for a better newsmagazine, and emphasized the importance of developing a clear and concise prose˙ for it. The advertising man Bruce Barton, on the other hand, told Luce the idea was impossible and they would lose every nickel they put into it. A friend of Luce's father, Samuel Everitt, treasurer of Doubleday, Page & Company and experienced in the publishing of books and magazines, tilted the balance the other way with his optimism.

Luce and Hadden returned to Baltimore, where they were cautious enough to make a deal with the editor of the News to give them what amounted to a seven-weeks' leave without pay and the option to resume their jobs if they reported back by April 1.

"I am confident," Hadden wrote his mother, "that in the seven weeks prior to April 1 we shall be able to determine whether or not the paper Facts is going to be brought into existence. We propose to devote our time in New York to working out our ideas and having them criticized by able journalists of the Swope type."

On February 8, 1922, Luce and Hadden left for New York.

3. THE STATUTE OF EQUALITY

Had wealth been their primary aim, the more logical place for them to go would have been into an established business or into Wall Street, where the money was—not into journalism, the riskiest of all enterprises. Wall Street was full of Yalemen. Had Luce and Hadden, with their impressive records, hurled the same formidable energies into finance as they did into journalism, the odds would have been heavily in favor of much quicker and greater pecuniary success. Instead, they were plunging into a venture which many conservative friends viewed as folly. Even Luce's parents seemed to have little confidence in it. Luce, if not his partner, would soon display a remarkable acumen that would have carried him far in virtually any business venture. Luce, far more than Hadden, had known lifelong impecuniousness that might logically have driven him into the sure thing rather than the gamble. And he had to demonstrate reasonable financial soundness before HRL could marry LRH, to whom he was writing daily.

One must infer that Hadden, always the journalist, had rekindled Luce's enthusiasm. But these two very shrewd young men did not truly love each other. Their seven-year rivalry still simmered. They had high respect for each other's abilities, but they were not cronies (Luce never had a crony—Hadden

had more than he could use) and there were actually elements of discord between them. They must have known that these frictions would increase as they worked closely together on a plane of vague "equality" that could never be quite equal, and as they decided matters of business and policy on which they would not always agree. Each knew that the other was determined and cocksure. They seemed on a collision course.

A further consideration on Luce's part was that he was subtly second man in the picture. Hadden had not only won the Yale sweepstakes but had the enormous advantage of a full year with one of the nation's greatest papers. Hadden had saved a little cash, whereas Luce barely had cigarette money. Would not the noisy extrovert Hadden run roughshod over the proud Luce? Was not Luce indeed the crazier of the pair to enter into such a preposterous arrangement?

If all these things were true, nevertheless in their collaboration perhaps they paid each other the greatest compliment possible between two men short of warmest affection. They implicitly agreed that the factors drawing them together were more urgent than the factors alienating them. They needed each other. Each loved journalism in his own way. They knew that in their differences they complemented each other.

On the World, Hadden had absorbed some of the enthusiasm that had trickled down from the great Joseph Pulitzer. He had worked obscurely among inheritors of that tradition, big men themselves—Frank Cobb, Walter Lippmann, Rollin Kirby, Heywood Broun. More than that, journalism excited him passionately. For him, no joy could surpass that of polishing his own—or someone else's—copy into lines that crackled. The evidence suggests that Luce, on the other hand, viewed journalism as a stimulating road to influence and power. He had those ideas about government, religion and international relations which he wished to promote. He had written at eighteen, "I believe that I can be of greatest service in journalistic work and can by that way come nearest to the heart of the world." "Service" and "coming near the heart of the world" could perhaps be translated as gaining and exerting power. The urge to power was a driving force, the greatest in his life. A great news organ was an avenue to power and to public office.

So the two young madmen were perhaps not really mad. They devised a plan to assure observance of their Statute of Equality and to keep out of each other's domain. Once they got started, they would alternate in running the business and editorial sides, each to his own. And after all, they were both Bones, sworn to eternal friendship.

4. THE MANIFESTO

Hadden thriftily moved in with his family in Brooklyn Heights. Luce, as frugal, became a non-paying guest at his family's apartment at 514 West

122nd Street near Columbia University. They rented office space in a decaying building at 141 East 17th Street for $55 a month, supplied by Hadden. Luce wrote to Culbreth Sudler in Chicago to urge that he leave his job with his father's lithographing firm to become head (and only member) of the promotion and advertising sales staff of Facts. Sudler arrived in New York and room was found for him in the Luce ménage.

"If I had only $1,000 I would put it all in . . ." Luce wrote his traveling father. "Right now I wish I hadn't put it into Oxford, although fundamentally I suppose the Oxford year is indirectly invested in the paper."

They consulted Melville Stone, the recently retired head of the Associated Press, as to the propriety of lifting news from daily papers. Stone assured them that news was public property after a day or two of aging. None of them was satisfied with the title Facts, and Luce later said it was he who hit on the title Time as he rode home on the subway in exhaustion late one night. Alas, the evidence trips him in a mendacity. A magazine named Time, edited by Edmund Yates, had been published in England from 1879 to 1890, with a distinctive logotype identical in its hand-lettered design with that taken by its American descendant, and in fact Hadden had a bound volume of his own, still to be found in the company archives in 1970. The trio slaved over a prospectus that buttered the upper-crust educators and financiers from whom they would solicit prestige and capital. It warned them that they risked being unenlightened because until then "NO PUBLICATION HAS ADAPTED ITSELF TO THE TIME WHICH BUSY MEN ARE ABLE TO SPEND ON SIMPLY KEEPING INFORMED." Time would inform them swiftly because of its condensation and systematic organization of the news.

Luce and Hadden were so anxious that prospects not dismiss Time as "another Literary Digest" that they used four paragraphs to emphasize the difference. And under the heading, "EDITORIAL BIAS," they promised fair news treatment *without* objectivity—an opening that would become endlessly useful:

> There will be no editorial page in Time.
> No article will be written to prove any special case.
> But the editors recognize that complete neutrality on public questions and important news is probably as undesirable as it is impossible, and are therefore ready to acknowledge certain prejudices which may in varying measure predetermine their opinions on the news.
> A catalogue of these prejudices would include such phrases as:
> 1. A belief that the world is round and an admiration of the statesman's "view of the world."
> 2. A general distrust of the present tendency toward increasing interference by government.
> 3. A prejudice against the rising cost of government.
> 4. Faith in the things which money cannot buy.
> 5. A respect for the old, particularly in manners.

6. An interest in the new, particularly in ideas.

But this magazine is not founded to promulgate prejudices, liberal or conservative. "To keep men well-informed"—that, first and last, is the only axe this magazine has to grind.

These prejudices about the shape of the world, cost of government and the desirability of courtesy did not represent any reckless defiance of existing orthodoxy. As Laura Z. Hobson would later point out, it was rather like coming out firmly against muddy streets and in favor of blueberry pie. But the admission of prejudice opened wide a gate through which Hadden would drive odd contraband and through which Luce would ultimately send endless truckloads.

The prospectus was as cheeky as its authors, twenty-three going on twenty-four, who served notice that they would not always be satisfied to report the news but felt qualified to interpret it to some degree. They took it to many famous personages, including Nicholas Murray Butler, the recently paralyzed Franklin Delano Roosevelt, Herbert Bayard Swope, Bernard Baruch, John Grier Hibben and, to be sure, President James R. Angell of Yale, succeeding in getting endorsements from them. Luce, Hadden and Sudler felt they could float their magazine on $100,000 in capital, thinking it should be simple to get ten of their richer Yale classmates to put up $10,000 each. There was the question of stock. They consulted John Wesley Hanes (Yale '15), a Wall Street banker, who wounded them by saying they were mad to think of competing with the Literary Digest but made amends by adding that if they were going ahead anyway they should keep stock control.

"How the hell can we do that if we haven't any money?" Hadden demanded. Hanes outlined a simple plan whereby they could reserve 80 percent of the common stock for themselves as entrepreneurs—a plan that ultimately would mean millions to them.

Less easy was the task of finding ten classmates willing to invest $10,000. They could not even find one. The 1920 men either did not have it, could not coax their fathers to part with it or simply could not help scoffing at the folly of bucking the Digest. A modest penetration was made with Henry P. Davison, Jr. ('20, Bones), now working for J. P. Morgan & Company, where his father was a senior partner. Young Davison, though skeptical, subscribed $4000 and also introduced the promoters to Dwight Morrow, another Morgan partner, who congratulated them on their enterprise and signed up for $1000.

But the going was slow. By midsummer they had raised only $35,000. The gloom at times was thick at 141 East 17th. Prospects eyed them suspiciously and showed them the door without really getting the Time message—an experience that gave Luce a keener understanding of the fund-raising trials of his father. Most infuriating was the you-can't-beat-the-Digest argument. In August the literary-inclined Sudler left to take a salaried job with Doubleday,

Page, thus losing a fortune which he would later recoup in his own advertising business, but never losing his admiration for Luce and Hadden. Luck turned through a steer given by Wells Root (class of 1922, chairman of the News in his own time, now with the New York World). Root introduced them to *his* classmate, William Hale Harkness, related to the multimillionaire Rockefeller partner Edward S. Harkness. Young Harkness not only pledged $5000 but suggested that his mother in New York might be receptive. Luce and Hadden gave Mrs. William L. Harkness the ultimate in persuasion. She was very deaf, and the story has it that she heard little of what they said. She read the prospectus, liked their looks and said, "That will do, boys. You may put me down for $20,000."

It happened that Mrs. Harkness's daughter Louise was married to David S. Ingalls, a classmate and Bonesmate of Luce and Hadden—the same Ingalls who had opposed Luce in the debate about Russia. Ingalls, now at Harvard Law School, was so unfeeling as to say they had a nerve to think of competing with the Digest. His wife, however, signed up for $5000.

By October they had squeezed every dollar out of every available prospect and still had only $86,000. They decided to proceed with publication and try to raise more as they went along. Luce could not afford the $60 annual Yale Club membership fee, so he habitually signed in under Hadden's name at the new Vanderbilt Avenue establishment. So far, the partner-rivals were getting along, observing the Statute of Equality. When they met the kindly but expensive public relations counsel, Edward L. Bernays, at the Yale Club, and asked him to publicize their venture as well as invest in it, it was Luce who did most of the talking while Hadden listened and put in only an occasional word.

"Luce was so intense that he stuttered and spluttered and yet he made a strong case for Time," Bernays recalled. It was not strong enough, for he declined their offer of $125 a week for his services, saying he would not take their money, nor did he care to invest, being unconvinced that they could compete with the Digest. Thus did Bernays (who later kindly handled their first public announcement of Time as a favor) thrust away a fortune, which he would amass anyway by his own efforts.

The headstrong pair hired Manfred Gottfried (Yale '22, Elizabethan Club, from Chicago and having the unequaled advantage of knowing Lila Hotz and her family) as a writer at $25 a week, Luce again doing the talking. They hired Roy E. Larsen of Boston as circulation manager, Hadden this time handling the details. Larsen's dash and personality were so impressive that he not only overcame an unfortunate choice of colleges (Harvard '21, business manager of the Harvard Advocate) but joined up at $40 a week as against the $30 Luce and Hadden were paying themselves as editor-publishers. They rented larger office space at 9 East 40th Street and gathered a few more full- and part-time staff members including the part-time Stephen Vincent Benét (Yale

'19, the Lit) and the part-time Archibald MacLeish (Hotchkiss '11, Yale '15, Bones, Phi Beta Kappa and Lit). They put together two complete typewritten dummies of the week's news by way of practice. The first issue of Time, after more than a year of preparation, was dated March 3, 1923.

VI

1. A LITERARY CHAIN GANG

The purpose of Time, said the New York Herald Tribune in a two-paragraph notice hidden on page 7, "is to summarize the week's news in the shortest possible space." Volume I, Number 1, sold only 9000 instead of the expected 25,000 copies, part of the loss blamable to college-girl workers hired by Larsen who ineptly sent some subscribers several copies and others none. It compressed the world's events into twenty-eight pages, minus six pages of advertisements sold at give-away rates. Although this was a time of big news—the American quarrel over Prohibition, the French occupation of the Ruhr, the German protests, the turmoils of the League, the famine in Russia—Time's account of it all could easily be read in a half-hour.

It was of course not for people who really wanted to be informed. It was for people willing to spend a half-hour to avoid being entirely uninformed. The editors so well redeemed their promise of brevity that Time seemed the capsulized abridgment of a condensation. Yet, considering the youth of its founders and the hectic conditions of its production, it was a surprising achievement. The news was fired in bursts of short sentences. Later tricky economies would include the elimination of the definite article and the use of "and" as a connective wherever possible, the frequent use of the ampersand also giving the reader a sensation of solicitude for his valuable time and lending the message something of the urgency of a telegram. Solemnity was avoided. The news was given a jaunty personal point of view. Readers felt instinctively that Time was the work of collegiate young men who were a little amused and a trifle superior but engaging fellows for all that. (That same week's issue of the Literary Digest was Volume 76, Number 9—eighty-eight pages thick, with thirty-nine pages of advertising, many in color, such as

Goodyear tires, Heinz and Cadillac, but its newswriting seemed the work of elderly gentlemen.)

"Congratulations on most interesting publication afloat . . ." Lila Hotz wired Luce from Chicago.

Few readers would have guessed that Time was digested entirely from the dozens of newspapers it subscribed to, gaining its greatest free lunch from the opulent tables of the New York Times and New York World. Education Editor MacLeish, for example, was working in Boston as a lawyer and teacher. Weekly he received in the mail from Time a batch of newsclippings bearing on the subject of education. He rewrote them in condensed form and mailed his finished work back to New York—hardly a picture of frantic deadlines. MacLeish, who was married and had a family, was glad to add an easy $10 weekly from Time to his income.

"Dear Lassie," Luce wrote Lila in Chicago, "it's a quiet Sunday afternoon, a little Spring in the air, and the wheels seem to be grinding slowly & smoothly in the production of Vol. I No. 2 of Time. Not until tomorrow can we have any indication of how No. 1 was received." He and the rest were exhausted by a succession of twelve- to sixteen-hour working days. Anguish over the poor sale of the first issue was healed by improvement in the next. April saw an upsurge, May a decline again. Nevertheless, in July they moved to larger if dingier quarters in a malt-redolent building at 236 East 39th Street once occupied by Hupfel's brewery. Time was a literary chain gang. The partner-rivals enjoyed this slavery to their own creation, took for granted the same enjoyment in others and were surprised when an office helper named Nancy Ford quit not because of dissatisfaction but in sheer exhaustion.

All of them exerted every wile in promoting the magazine. Friends were not only urged to buy it but to tell other friends about it and to urge them to urge *their* friends to spend a dime for Time. Lila created demand by asking for Time at Chicago newsstands and showing incredulity and annoyance when told by dealers that they had never heard of such a magazine. When Time got its first small Colgate advertisement with a coupon, Lila and her brother coaxed a dozen friends to send in the coupon in order to impress Colgate with Time's potency as an advertising medium. Even her stepfather relented and agreed that the magazine might succeed.

Luce planned to marry her in December. Their letters had passed each other on the Twentieth Century Limited and on dozens of ocean liners. Hers, in her travels with her parents, had borne postmarks ranging from Chicago to Canterbury, Grenoble, Lausanne, Rothenburg, Bad Gastein and Florence. His had invariably been postmarked New York. Once on reaching Paris from Switzerland she had found five of his letters waiting for her. His affectionate salutations for her included "Angel," "Carissima" and "Darlingest," while among hers were "Enrico," "Belovedissimo" and, not at all in jest, "Cher prince du journalisme." She clearly saw greatness in him and said so, but she also said that he worked entirely too hard. "Dearest," she protested in a letter

from Brides-les-Bains, "do you HAVE to stay at your office till 2 a.m. and then get there at the crack of dawn the following morning?"

She and Luce had met when she passed through New York, he being deep in publishing problems as he always would be. In Paris in the fall of 1923, with her mother's help, she selected her trousseau and before leaving for America she wrote Luce from her hotel on the Rue de la Paix in a charming vein of sentiment:

> Alone in a taxi this aft., I made my first verbal farewell to Paris, driving up the Champs Élysées and back across the Concorde and down Rivoli, across Vendôme and now here. Paris looked so appealing in her dress of pink and gold of the evening, and she reproached me sadly for being so anxious and glad to leave her. I was quite emotionized . . .

On December 22, 1923, Luce and Lila were married at Chicago's huge Church of the Holy Harvester on Rush Street, the church of Luce's late fairy godmother. (Time that week had only fifteen columns of advertisements including a full page for the Yale Review that was surely given away.) Luce stayed at the Sudler home while there. The ushers were all classmates and most of them Bones—among them Hadden, Sudler, John Hincks and William Whitney—and Morehead Patterson was best man. The bride and groom, after a honeymoon at the Homestead in Virginia, were at home on Fifth Avenue and 97th Street in New York.

Although men of large ego, vigor and ambition usually make poor husbands, the marriage got off well. Lila's mother, averse to seeing the young couple skimp on Luce's paltry salary, sent increments that doubled their income. Instead of a two-room apartment unattended, the Luces had a four-room apartment and a day maid.

2. SHAMBLING, SNARLING AND SIMPERING

After a summer slump, Time had picked up somewhat but was still selling only about 20,000 copies weekly by the end of 1923. It had lost $39,454. Yet the partners audaciously raised their own salaries to $40 a week and issued an optimistic report to the stockholders, saying, ". . . Time has grown from an idea to an established institution . . . accepted by an increasing number of people as part of their weekly reading."

From the beginning there was no one in the shop with a tiresome sense of responsibility toward the news as something untouchable, something to be passed along to the reader unchanged in its fundamentals. On the contrary, the whole Time idea was change of approach and change of style, which quickly led to change of substance. Hadden's editorial ingenuity was devoted to the slicing, trimming, flavoring, coloring and packaging of the news to make it more interesting and more salable than it was in real life. Seizing and

running off with an old Pulitzer maxim that people in the news should be more than mere names, he began draping them with jazz-age versions of the Homeric epithets he had learned in Greek. People in Time became gray-thatched, gentle-spirited or beetle-browed, and as Hadden grew bolder they became pot-bellied, tough-talking, snaggle-toothed, sour-visaged or bag-jowled. Remembering the dislike of his writing instructor at Yale, Professor John Berdan, for quiet verbs, Hadden seldom let people merely say something. They barked, snapped, gushed, muttered, growled, blathered, grunted, cooed or shrieked. Nor were they permitted to walk. They dashed, shuffled, ambled, pussyfooted, sashayed, lumbered or lurched.

Various combinations of these adjectives and verbs could be used to give an attractive or unlovely coloration and supply the reader with extra drama or amusement. A *trim-figured, keen-brained* politician who *strode* in and *unfolded* his policies had no complaint against Time. But a *flabby-chinned, gimlet-eyed* candidate who *shambled* and *snarled* was apt to lose votes, while a *temperament-ridden, firmly-corseted* prima donna who *minced* and *simpered* would have to be in good voice to retrieve her fame.

Other Time novelties were the reversing of subject and predicate, the use of alliteration and an insistence on middle names—a trick that seemed to give a new dimension to people often in the news and which delighted Hadden when, for example, he could unmask the man long known simply as James A. Farley as James Aloysius Farley. More and more, Time accounts took on the technique of fictional narrative. The reader was given a little story with snappy title, beginning, middle and end, sometimes complete with a bit of mystery or suspense which was resolved neatly in the last line. This required imaginative interpolation, since Time's news sources, the daily papers, failed to supply all the items necessary for the scenario. A touch here, a dash there —how it brightened dull fact! None of this tended to imbue the staff with regard for the sanctity of news.

The external mannerisms of Timestyle would gradually increase to and even over the verge of grotesquerie that would offend British and other ears. One English journalist called the dropping of the definite article "a parsimony such as used to be thought of as natural only to the natives of Bengal." St. John Ervine referred to it as a style in which "adjectives are used as verbs, and nouns are telescoped to such an extent that a sentence looks like a railway accident." London's Cassandra would call it "as vile a piece of mangling as ever stripped the heart out of prose." Marshall McLuhan would suggest that "nobody could tell the truth in Time style." And even Westbrook Pegler would complain, diagnosing it as "a nervous disease of the typewriter." Time's collegiate tone was enhanced by the hiring in 1924 of two of Hadden's cousins, Niven Busch and one-armed John Martin, both Princeton men and admirers of Hadden. The former brewery sheltered imaginative young men racking their brains for new twists and effects. Cracking the whip over them was Hadden, who would groan and hurl his thesaurus against the wall when

offended by a losing effort but would shout with glee over a winner. Luce, running the business office and having time only to write Religion and fill in on other departments, was less the originator than the collaborator.

Probably these two never suspected that a growing threat to their harmony was George F. Babbitt of Zenith. Sinclair Lewis's acid etching of the go-getting businessman who blocked all enlightenment had provoked a nationwide controversy. In Hadden it aroused not only amusement but anger that commercialism should be so vulgarly triumphant and that struggling young Time was at the mercy of these Babbitts for its advertising. He liked to point out such types on the street, growling "Babbitt" under his breath.

Luce disagreed sharply. He thought Lewis's portrait a malicious caricature, a libel on the men of business who were builders of the nation's greatness.

While no one could seriously identify the keen Luce with the stupid Babbitt, Luce's shining faith in business and his admiration for successful businessmen were traits of similarity Hadden could not miss. Obviously Luce became aware that in Hadden's mind he was not free from Babbittry. Whether Hadden went so far as to point out that George F. Babbitt was also a Republican, a Presbyterian and a super-patriot who named his own son Theodore Roosevelt Babbitt is not known.

Hadden had nothing against money. His goal was to make a million by the time he was thirty and he was enjoying every minute along the way. Business details bored him. When he did undertake them he was not impressive, a fact that faced Luce with unpleasant alternatives: If he insisted on citing the Statute and taking his turn as editor while Time was in delicate infancy, Hadden's fiscal errors might slaughter the babe. Hadden's misgivings were the reverse —that Luce might introduce a malign editorial flavor. When Hadden decided that he needed a vacation in Europe, part of it to be spent with his fellow bachelor Larsen, Luce protested this simultaneous desertion of two of Time's three most important people. He was overruled by his breezy partner, who rather upstaged him at times. Hadden even made Manfred Gottfried managing editor in his absence, telling him, "See that Luce doesn't meddle." Amused members of the staff fashioned a fake Time cover adorned with Luce's sober face and captioned, "He doesn't meddle."

Luce *did* meddle. Probably he was more than ever determined to do so when Hadden cabled from Paris for an additional $1500—Time's lifeblood— to pay for gay parties held aboard ship and continued on land. There had been discussion of a move to a more central point because the railroads were getting Time to Western readers a day or even two days late. Hadden, the *bon vivant*, had opposed any move to the provinces. When he returned in May 1925 after six weeks in Europe, he discovered that Luce had made firm commitments to move to Cleveland.

Hadden blew up. He and Luce retired to the Yale Club to quarrel in a private corner—evidently a policy with them, for neither Gottfried, Hadden's secretary, Mary Fraser, nor the red-headed office boy, Joseph Kastner, ever

heard them in open wrangling at the office. Luce's calculations showed that in addition to the improvement in shipping they would save about $20,000 a year in rent, salaries and printing costs. He had won what seemed legitimate revenge.

They could not afford to move their lesser personnel to Cleveland. Hadden kindly raised Kastner's salary the last week so that he could use this as a bargaining point in seeking another job. The employees were notified that they were fired as of August 16 and would be rehired in Cleveland if they appeared there on the 19th. The Penton Building on Lakeside Avenue would be Time's address for the next two years. One of those who made the move was young Laird S. Goldsborough (Yale '24, the Daily News, the Lit, Elizabethan Club). Goldsborough, son of a Purdue University engineering professor, used a cane as a result of a childhood leg accident. A clever, fluent writer, quite deaf and something of a loner, he had a strange career ahead of him on Time.

The Luces took a house in suburban Cleveland Heights with their infant son Henry III, born in New York April 28. They now owned a Chrysler sedan driven exclusively by Lila since Luce, so devoid of mechanical skill that the operation of the dial telephone was a terrible hurdle, could not learn to drive safely. "He kept bumping into things," his wife recalled. He had not approved of speakeasy-infested New York. Middle-sized Cleveland, where people seemed more friendly and entertained at home instead of at night clubs, suited him better, and Cleveland Heights, with its winding streets and substantial houses, was the essence of middle-class respectability.

Hadden loathed Cleveland, where the New York World and Times arrived ten hours late and where the cafés and night clubs did not match his favorite Manhattan spots. Almost every week he would board an east-bound New York Central train, sleeping en route so that he would have more wakeful hours in New York, and would return to Cleveland with revulsion. Only when forced by circumstances would he hand editorial responsibility to Luce. "Harry's a business genius," he told a friend by way of explanation. "And I mean genius."

Winsor French of Cleveland, who joined the staff there, remarked on how complementary the two were: "Brit was one of the few editorial geniuses I have ever encountered. . . . Luce was the business man, hard as nails, cold as ice and inclined toward arrogance. They seldom saw eye to eye, but as a team they couldn't be beaten." Yet Myron Weiss, a Harvardman who also joined Time in Cleveland, found Luce an innately kindly man. "Harry had a habit of focusing on his objective and brushing aside incidentals," Weiss said—a trait that could be unnerving to the man who sensed that either he or what he said was incidental. Gottfried, like Weiss an equable, even-tempered man, worked for Luce for years in positions of high importance. "Harry was easier to get along with than Brit," he recalled, without suggesting that either was the soul of agreeability or concord.

That Christmas it seemed possible that none of them would have to put up

with each other much longer. Time's bank balance sagged to $1976.16. Survival depended on the success of Larsen's drive for Christmas-gift subscriptions, which turned out to be triumphant and saved the day. Despite a loss of $23,829 for the year, the worst crisis was over, for the circulation had risen to 107,000 and more than $100,000 had come in from advertising.

3. FRAUD AND INSULT

A bit of madness was helpful in appreciating Hadden, as shown by French's portrait of him: "His neckties were always askew, his trousers incredibly baggy . . . He either ate voraciously or not at all, thought nothing of putting in 24-hour days when the pressure was intense and consequently saw no reason why anyone else, male or female, shouldn't and couldn't do the same. Hadden also had a quick, violent temper and his wild roaring, drifting down nine floors into the street, caused people . . . to come to an abrupt halt and wonder if someone wasn't being murdered. . . . Yet, for all his eccentricities, I don't think there was a single member of his staff who didn't love him. [One day French checked the absent Hadden's desk calendar to see if he had a luncheon date open two days hence.] I saw the only appointment that day was one with me. It was for 12 noon and read 'Oust French.'

"The day and the moment arrived, the buzzer buzzed and I walked into the office and was offered a chair. It wouldn't be necessary, I told him. What I had to say would take only a second. I was quitting.

"Hadden's roars could have been heard for blocks. But he took me to a two-hour lunch of Martinis, during which he talked about nothing except baseball and possible candidates for my former job. . . . [I]t was impossible to get mad at him. The man had the kind of charm that could bring birds from the trees. . . ."

Luce seemed unaware of these birds. French noted that "both Luce and Hadden were men of very strong opinions" and went on: "Socially they were poles apart . . . The Luces, raising a family, lived quietly on the Heights, entertained simply and were enormously in demand by, shall we say, the more conventionally minded groups."

Luce and Hadden stirred up a 220-member meeting of the Cleveland Chamber of Commerce with a quiz on news events covered in Time, offering a year's subscription to members correctly answering twenty out of twenty-five questions, among them, "At whom did Gridley fire, when he was ready?" and "In what state did Sinclair Lewis locate his imaginary village of Gopher Prairie?" Hadden, his news presentation vindicated by rising circulation, heightened his strategic use of fraud and insult. Never forgetting the sensation he had created at Yale with Divinity Student and Old Hatchet Face, he enlivened the Letters department in Time by drawing readers into fierce quarrels. He touched them off with outrageous screeds he composed himself and in-

63

serted in the name of mythical subscribers. One of these was George Schleiger of Chillicothe, who brought interstate rivalry to a boil with a letter in purest Hadden style:

> What's West Virginia but Ohio's coal bin? Just a dirty disheveled stretch of mine dumps, scraggly mountains, filled with a bunch of ignorants that only know enough to swing picks and drink moonshine. That's *one* reason you can't spend anything but Sunday on Sunday in West Virginia. Everybody is drunk or sleeping it off down there on Sunday.
>
> What President did West Virginia ever produce—what big man has West Virginia got? Senator So-and-So, I suppose, and Senator Whozis. I never heard of them. They can't stack up against Fess and Willis [the Ohio Senators].

Genuine West Virginia readers rose to the bait with attacks on Schleiger and the whole state of Ohio, which were answered by counterblasts from across the river. The Clarksburg, West Virginia, Daily Telegram bitterly protested the smears on the state. The Chillicothe paper deprecated Time's role in the dispute and announced suspiciously, "so far as we have been able to learn, there is no such person in this community as George Schleiger." Another Hadden invention was Mary Elizabeth Robinn, who traveled so much that her address frequently changed. She wrote letters to Time over a period of four years, usually in biting criticism of the Prince of Wales, whose popularity assured heated ripostes. Still another was Morris (Al) Epstein of Brooklyn, whose execrable grammar and strong opinions on controversial subjects drew scornful replies for many months.

The use of disrespect, this side of libel, was cultivated. The Washington Eagle, a paper for Negroes, said that Time's description of Mrs. Mary McLeod Bethune would rankle "if, in the same issue, Mrs. Bainbridge Colby, Mrs. Edward Harriman, and Anne Nichols were not handled in the same flippant yet offhand manner." The magazine drew fire from upstate New York papers when it gratuitously described the home county of a politician:

> This county in the Finger Lakes district is the stamping ground of the famed progeny of two sisters (Jukes) and two Dutch backwoodsmen. Sixty per cent of this hereditary strain are idiots, imbeciles, harlots, murderers, thieves, perverts, felons, loons, sots, paupers, maniacs, etc.

The Auburn Citizen retorted that the county was the birthplace of John D. Rockefeller, George Pullman and Millard Fillmore. Hadden hurled barbs at Babbitts in Cincinnati. An editorialist in that city's Enquirer denounced the "diseased imagination" and "scurrilous slanders" of the Time writer who not only spoke without deference of William Cooper Procter and James Gamble, the city's soap multimillionaires, but added, "Cincinnati has drooped, malnourished, industrially. It has become draggled and dirty." A funmaking offshoot of the Freemasons, the Mystic Grotto of Veiled Prophets of the Enchanted Realm, was offended by Time's lampoon of its "pseudo-Islamic nomenclature" and a description of its convention:

The Grotto technique of smile-spreading is to select a large city annually, have it hung with bunting . . . and for a solid summer week herd thousands of Prophets from all over the U.S. and Canada to the city and tell them to "have fun." . . . They slipped ice down pretty girls' backs and ogled them. . . . They bestrode taxi radiators, waved whisky bottles, assisted traffic cops, spit out of hotel windows. . . . They ran around in bathing suits, danced in hotel lobbies, stuck people with pins, shocked them with batteries.

These violations of journalistic canons entertained and provoked comment. Hadden knew how to irritate and incense to the right degree. He was the spokesman of the flask-on-hip Twenties, the creator of a style tailored to the era. Hotchkiss and Yale were watching. "Two Alumni Gaining Fame in Journalism," headlined the Hotchkiss Record. A newspaper in remote Hot Springs, South Dakota, commented, "It is surprising to see how the taste for 'Time' is spreading." The Hollywood Film Daily noted, "Our passing show: Adolphe Menjou carrying a copy of 'Time.' "

The magazine was catching on with young people. High schools began using it for the study of current events. It was actually cutting in a trifle on the Literary Digest, which nervously souped up its writing style. In mid-1926 a survey of magazines favored by college students showed the Saturday Evening Post in the lead, followed by the American Magazine, Good Housekeeping and the Digest. Time, unheard of three years earlier, had climbed to fourteenth place ahead of such old favorites as the New Republic, the Nation and the Outlook.

Soon the Daily at the University of Minnesota would say editorially: "The heyday of H. L. Mencken has passed. . . . Sophistication no longer lies in that direction. Another literary idol has arisen to take the [American] Mercury's place. . . . It is of course 'Time.' Its style is becoming the mode of college journalism."

As Hadden said with a twinkle, "They're beginning to take this thing seriously." By sheer cleverness and effrontery, Time was on the way to success.

VII

1. THE ALL-AMERICAN BOY

In June 1926 Yale unaccountably went out of its way to wound Briton Hadden, the great man of '20 who had "done most for Yale." It awarded an honorary Master of Arts degree to Luce—the youngest ever to be so recognized —for "distinguished accomplishments in a novel and worthy field of journalism." Hadden who, a trifle more than Luce, had created this "novel and worthy" departure, was passed over, unmentioned even as Luce's partner. The incident caused a stir among the grads of '20. Those who knew them well, such as John Hincks, felt that Hadden's lack of dignity and his reputation for wildness had done him in. Luce in some ways was the perfect Yale graduate—loyal to a fault, punctilious in meeting class and society obligations, a conservative family man, the distinguished undergraduate who had become a successful alumnus.

If Yale's treatment of Hadden was surprising, Luce's own response when he was informed of the honor was as much so. He did not tell Hadden, who learned of it through other sources and was terribly hurt.

In 1927, on the strength of doubled advertising revenue and Time's first rise out of red ink ($8541 profit in 1926) Luce and Hadden persuaded the directors to raise their salaries to $10,000. In June, Luce and his wife sailed for a vacation in Europe. In Paris they visited the MacLeishes—MacLeish had long since quit Time and the law and settled with his family in a cold-water flat on the Boulevard Saint Michel to write poetry. The relationship between these two Bonesmates was unusual, Luce having given up poetry for more promising endeavors but admiring the poet loyal to verse. MacLeish, whose *The Pot of Earth* had been disparaged by Time's nameless but confident critic, regarded Luce with friendliness and interest and also with the judiciousness of

66

the more experienced elder, the friend of Hemingway, Fitzgerald and many others.

"Harry was still careless about dress," he recalled. "He was quite naïve, the all-American boy out to lick the world with his slingshot. He said everything twice, probably a relic of his stammering, and he said, 'How are you–how are you?' "

Luce was no gallant, his manners often unintentionally crude. They all dined at the Tour d'Argent with another ex-Timer in Paris soon to be famous, Stephen Vincent Benét. The Luces went on to Corsica, Luce having perhaps an empathic as well as a historical interest in Napoleon. Lila remembers, "My greatest thrill of the entire trip was the day we arrived at a tiny hotel . . . in Corsica and found a two-year-old copy of Time in the vestibule."

In Rome, the city of their unforgettable meeting, they celebrated that event and Luce endeavored to arrange an interview with Mussolini. Always the student of politics and government, he had an intense interest in the dictator strongly tinctured with admiration. But Time and Luce were unknown in Italy. Several days of solicitation of Fascist functionaries proved unsuccessful. The couple went on to London for a leisurely stay before returning to Cleveland.

At the Time office there, as Laird Goldsborough later recalled, an intrigue had been brewing. Doubtless because of the coolness between Luce and Hadden and the undesirability of a rift in the Time command, John Martin and a few others had urged Hadden to buy Luce out. Hadden, loathing the business details which Luce handled so ably, decided against the idea. But he acted decisively in another direction. After praising Cleveland in the Chamber of Commerce magazine as a place free from "the booster style of city salesmanship that makes one blench as he reads the Babbitt books," and adding "Time is here to stay," he had committed Time to move back to New York. Babbitt was indeed much on his mind.

Probably there was a quarrel about this. There had been cruelty on both sides and it is unlikely that the partners were ever again really friends after the incident of the honorary degree. It turned out that Hadden was right, that Time needed the stimulation and the news sources of the metropolis, especially since Luce was able to work out an advantageous plan whereby printing and distribution would be done in Chicago.

Real riches still eluded them—Time would clear a puny $3861 in 1927—but this was partly due to increased salaries, moving costs and heavy promotion expenses. Luce had no doubts. He and his wife took a fairly grand town house with Italian fountains in a backyard garden in Manhattan's Turtle Bay section at 234 East 49th Street, and rented a country house at Roxbury, Connecticut, seventy-five miles from the city. They wanted to buy a large country place with a view, and they would look around Roxbury for it. Luce was, as he later admitted, consciously aiming to attain the status of what Time called

a tycoon. Tycoons owned country estates. Sometimes his thinking could be astonishingly direct and simple.

Meanwhile, what had become of the globe-trotting Luce family?

Rev. Henry Luce had retired from Yenching University and returned from Peking for ulcer surgery, then settled down again with his wife in an apartment on Morningside Heights to take courses (at fifty-nine) at Columbia and Union Theological Seminary. "By the time I 'get off the earth,' " he said, "I'll begin to know something about it." Sheldon was now a student at Hotchkiss. The beautiful Emmavail Luce, a Wellesley graduate, had recently returned from five years in China, where she had been a YWCA worker, and had married Leslie R. Severinghaus, who had taught at the Rockefeller Foundation in Peking. The equally charming Elisabeth, who had often reviewed books for Time after her graduation from Wellesley, had married a young lawyer from Texas, Maurice T. Moore, who was a junior member of the eminent New York firm of Cravath, de Gersdorff, Swaine & Wood. "Harry asked if our 'important' firm would represent his 'unimportant' company," Moore recalls, "and of course we were glad to."

In New York, Time took small offices at 25 West 45th Street. Luce, so dynamic that he had energy to burn and was uncomfortable unless he burned it, could walk to work in fifteen minutes. On those occasions when he took over as editor, he was more permissive than Hadden, more sparing with the pencil but shrewd in his demands. Vagueness or a wandering story line never escaped him. He would pelt the writer with questions, some of them naïve but always bearing on points important to the average reader. And since Time-style had become second nature to the small writing staff, the magazine still seemed to be written by one impudent man.

Luce had become so fascinated by business that the handling of ledgers was not irksome. His contact with such Time directors as Harry Davison, William H. Harkness and John Hanes had opened up the wonders of Wall Street to him, and Time's gradual acquisition of full-page advertisements from such companies as Prudential insurance, Fisher automobile bodies and Chrysler cars was proof of the greatest bull market in history. In one issue of Time, the "People" department contained paragraphs about seventeen individuals in the news, twelve of whom were tycoons such as J. P. Morgan, Charles Schwab, Julius Rosenwald, Walter Gifford and the same Fisher body brothers. Ted Cook, the newspaper satirist, included in his series of "interesting hobbies" that of a mythical citizen:

> He buys old copies of Time magazine and looks for the word "tycoon." Every time he finds it he pastes a gold star in his scrap book, which now has 4,356 pages which look like the Milky Way.

Turning thirty in 1928, Luce was young enough to think Hoover stuffy, disapprove in principle of Prohibition and vote for Al Smith, although Time cautiously presented the two candidates without partiality. It was his last Demo-

cratic vote for thirty-six years. At home, he liked to perch his second son, Peter Paul, born May 18 of that year, on his shoulder at breakfast as he read the papers with such avidity that he seemed unaware of either breakfast or son.

Suddenly Time was catching fire. Its circulation was soaring, its advertising opulent. Smart people were talking about it. Businessmen found that its concision saved them time and innocently believed its claim to be "Curt, Clear, Complete." It was fashionable. People liked to be seen with it. At long last it was repaying the enormous labors of Luce and Hadden and the long forbearance of its stockholders.

And at last, newspapers long aware that Time was pilfering from them news it cost them and their wire services millions to gather, was reprocessing it and then reselling it *a week later* at fifteen cents a copy instead of the original newspaper price of two cents and was inaugurating a radio news program over thirty-three stations that would cover the whole nation, thereby reusing the stolen news twice—well, newspapers that had let it pass during Time's years of struggle were incensed now that the thievery was so obviously profitable. Editor & Publisher, journalism's trade paper, began a concerted campaign against Time:

> Time puts this stuff on the air with credit to itself alone. The average person, listening to this flow of news at his fireside, might very well gain the impression that behind the little magazine Time lies a huge news-gathering organization, reporters scattered over the civilized world busily observing human action and dashing madly to telegraph offices to file the news to Time. . . . [W]e consulted the editor of the magazine, Henry R. Luce. We put the question: "Where do these news items which appear in your magazine and in your radio service come from?" He promptly replied, "We pick them up out of the newspapers." We asked how the magazine, in these circumstances, could accept responsibility for the accuracy or justice of the statements it blindly publishes about people and institutions, and Mr. Luce answered that his writers use their judgment, sometimes seek to confirm statements and in rare instances even get a news item on their own initiative . . . Mr. Luce sought to justify news lifting by saying that his writers contributed when they rewrote news from an "interpretative" angle. . . . [I]t must be said that Literary Digest is infinitely more fair than is Time in the matter of giving credit. But both are grafting on news organizations which pay their way and are truly responsible to their readers for statements of news.

Having bearded Luce, Editor & Publisher next went after Hadden, and reported:

> The publisher of Time undertakes to justify the parasitical scissors, paste pot and rewrite job, even asserting that it is a "contribution" to the newspapers of the United States, the theory being that it makes those who read Time and hear its "news casting" on the radio more "news-conscious." Now isn't that perfectly splendid of Time? . . . Mr. Hadden says, with some show of indignation, that anyway he had permission, before he went into the Time enterprise, from Mr. Melville E. Stone to do what he is doing . . .

Editor & Publisher kept up the assault for a month, joined by a few protesting newspapers, but got nowhere. Time's practice was perfectly legal although hardly admirable. As E & P said, it was irresponsible. But the irresponsibility E & P referred to was its evasion of the newsgathering function. There was no complaint about the odd things that happened to other people's news when it appeared in Time. Luce's explanation that Time gave "interpretative" reporting indicated a Lucean attitude toward news which was not yet understood in its full proportions and was obscured by the argument over mere ownership of the news. This "interpretative" reporting would ultimately become the most questionable practice of all.

2. DABBLING IN FASCISM

Luce's long and semi-secret liaison with Fascism resulted largely from domestic political discontent. It appears that for a time he hoped to advance his own political career under the aegis of some version or modification of authoritarianism. His ferocious patriotism did not mean that he was wedded to the Constitution and his reverence for the founding fathers did not preclude the thought that their techniques might be outmoded. America, which should lead the world, was lagging. In a 1928 magazine article he described the Constitution as obsolete and called for "a new form of government." He was dissatisfied with the nation's performance under Coolidge, would be equally so under Hoover and (for different reasons) would reach the farthest frontiers of outrage under Roosevelt. A businessman to the core, he rather expected the government to inspire and exact the people's discipline and loyalty just as he exacted these qualities from the staff at Time Inc.

In his search for better government he naturally studied the models on exhibit elsewhere in the world, principally Communism and Fascism. Communism repelled him so strongly on each of several grounds that any one of them would have been enough to make him condemn it out of hand. The sum total of his detestation, which would come to dominate his life, included these factors:

Communism's contempt for religion struck at beliefs he held sacred.

In China, its spread seemed like that of a disease, attacking the missionary and "colonial" establishment that had his total loyalty.

The Marxian dogma that "business is theft" described him and the entrepreneurs he revered as thieves.

Russian Communism had destroyed the Romanovs, liquidated the aristocracy and the capitalists and substituted the vulgar commissar. Luce believed in the need for an aristocracy.

Communism in Russia seemed on the verge of failure, inefficient, unable even to feed all its own people.

Communism there was totalitarian and ruthless, though these qualities

alone would not have offended him unduly if exercised in what he believed a good cause, as will be seen.

Fascism, on the other hand, was a new idea. New ideas of any kind, but especially in government, fascinated him. His speeches and reports for a decade would contain hints and outright suggestions that some features of Fascism might be useful in America. The negative aspect of Fascism—its undying enmity to Communism—won his instant approval, for he took the pragmatic attitude that "The enemy of my enemy is my friend." But there were characteristics that attracted him even had no such thing as Communism existed:

The hero-worshiper in him responded to the Fascist superman who could inspire the allegiance and cooperation of the masses. The Nietzschean *Übermensch* stirred in him the nationalistic fervor of his Yale days and all his days. The Fascist submergence of the masses into the mystic unity of the nation created a seeming discipline and loyalty which, he felt, got excellent results in Italy—a national discipline and loyalty that was badly needed in America.

Fascism, however, abhorred the dead-level proletarianism of Communism, maintained an aristocracy and rewarded leaders of business and industry. Fascism was dynamic, militaristic, aggressive, imperialist—all of them qualities Luce admired.

While Fascism might quarrel with religion, it had not suppressed it and Mussolini would soon come to terms with it.

Although Fascism, like Communism, was totalitarian and ruthless, Luce persuaded himself that Mussolini had risen to power with a minimum of violence and compiled a record that atoned for his peccadilloes. A corollary of Luce's apotheosis of the hero was his dislike and mistrust of the inefficient and unpredictable masses. He detested pacifism with the combined detestation of the militant Calvinist and the practical man who regarded all life as competition.

Perhaps his beginnings in China—his identification with an elite American politico-religious establishment ministering to an ignorant and disfranchised populace—underlay his contempt for the masses. The half-dozen Chinese servants at his command during his boyhood could hardly have failed to nurture the mandarin image. His rudeness to servants was almost lifelong. The cheapness of life in China—the poverty, oppression and woe so inevitably the lot of the people—had to be accepted by missionaries and their families as normal. In order to function efficiently, missionaries felt they had to steel themselves against excessive sympathy, had to inhibit the very emotions of tenderness and compassion which the outsider would assume to be the basis of missionary work. Moreover, since the Chinese multitude were riddled by disease and vermin and had an outlaw element, they were dangerous. The high walls of the mission compound had not only divided the elite socially from the masses but had been necessary for safety. The masses had supported the Boxer Rebellion and sent Horace Pitkin's head rolling into the gutter— things Luce was not likely to forget.

Now a new factor in China abetted his revulsion toward Communism. Sun Yat-sen's successor, the rising young warlord Chiang Kai-shek, had allied himself with the Russian Communists—a policy resulting in anti-foreignism that drove 5000 Protestant missionaries out of China and raised the specter of Communist rule from Canton to Leningrad, from the Pacific to the Baltic.

Thus, a high-powered combination of religion, family heritage, personal philosophy, historical study, political intuition and prejudice gave enormous thrust to his anti-Communist pro-Fascism. He passionately denied the axiom that there are no "indispensable men," saying that on the contrary Great Men (which he capitalized in writing) *were* indispensable and that American politics, though not American business, suffered a shortage of them. This was, he said in an early speech, the era of the tycoon, whom he went to some lengths to define:

> He is almost inevitably a rich man, though not necessarily worth more than a million. . . . Secondly, a tycoon is a man of outstanding importance in some industry. . . . Now, of course, we see that it is not a seat in Congress but on the directorate of the greatest corporations which our countrymen regard as the greater post of honor and responsibility.

As if still stinging from Hadden's barbs, he criticized Sinclair Lewis for misrepresenting the American tycoon. "Mr. Lewis," he said, "knows practically nothing at all about business with a capital B." The businessman was no Babbitt or Dodsworth but the creator of a new "aristocratic principle" that should have wider recognition:

> Business is what we [in America] believe in more than any other agency of society. . . . [B]usiness will never be run on a democratic basis. . . . [B]usiness must be aristocratic. There must be a top and, if possible, the best men must get there.

He pointed to the success of Mussolini in revitalizing the aristocratic principle in Italy, "a state reborn by virtue of Fascist symbols, Fascist rank and hence Fascist enterprise."

Luce admired strong regimes in which the "best people" ruled for the good of all, as he believed the Tories generally did in England. He deplored multiparty systems such as those in France and the Weimar Republic where the "best people" were unable to govern except in coalitions with the "worst people." Communism, in his view, was the deliberate elimination of the best to permit government by the worst. In Mussolini he saw such greatness and in Fascism such dramatic political innovations that he could not contain his excitement. He made his first of many public speeches to a group of businessmen in Rochester in March 1928. It was again proof of his courage and ambition that he would fight his lingering stammer and work to develop an adroitness that might advance his political hopes. He said in part:

> America needs at this moment a moral leader, a national moral leader. The outstanding national moral leader in the world today is Mussolini. And I say

this, heartily disagreeing with nearly all of his moral principles. Fact remains, he has pulled his country up by the pants; he has made Italy stand up, he has substituted self-respect for vanity, patriotism for greed, ambition for boredom. He has made the nation stand up, stand up. That is what a great moral leader does.

He was more complacent than such a student of free institutions should have been about Mussolini's methods—his destruction of liberty, organized brutalities, murder or imprisonment of political opponents, control of the press, and his black-shirt-and-fist-shaking fustian. Luce seemed absent-mindedly to forget that what made Italy "stand up" was tyranny visited on the masses. The element that appeared lacking in his contemplation of ideal government was any real warmth or concern for the great majority of humanity. The poor were simply the most inefficient members of society.

3. A GLACIER WITH FORGET-ME-NOTS

Lila spent the summer of 1928 with young Henry at the Roxbury country place while Luce was so preoccupied with a new magazine project that he stayed at the town house and came out weekends. "Weekends" were Tuesday and Wednesday, the quieter period immediately after Time went to press. Far from resting from his labors, he expected company and spirited talk and he would play tennis with anyone who came along.

His tennis was unexceptional but—like his politics, business methods, religion and philosophy—dedicated to the idea of winning. At least one opponent was fascinated by the way Luce would rush to the net with racket upraised for the kill, his face as ferocious as an executioner's. When his holiday was over, Lila would drive him madly to the New Milford station to catch the 6:42 to New York. From Roxbury she wrote him charmingly breathless letters reporting on their sons' activities, commenting on Luce's absent-mindedness—"Don't forget to get your suit pressed!"—his excessive devotion to work and his regimen of self-improvement. He was reading Count Keyserling's effort to combine the values of Eastern and Western thought—a study that inspired Lila to an interesting description of his varying moods:

> Why do people resent his [Keyserling's] way of writing so? I think he's a very picturesque mountain in the literary landscape. I wonder what kind of a mountain you would turn into with a literary background. . . . Decidedly with a glacier near the top, and with forget-me-nots growing around your feet.

He would reply with a quick rundown of his efforts on Time, which he called "the great cosmic weekly almanac," and mention meetings in town with the Moores and others. He could end gracefully after mailing letters for Lila to her mother in Europe: "But I shall special delivery myself up there [to Roxbury] Monday—because it is a nice place and all. —Always Your Lover." Or he could address her as "Carissima," begin with, "If this day could have

been worse it was. And busy—Hadden off for three weeks," then give her the news and follow with an indulgent-but-serious lecture on what he regarded as her negligence in financial matters:

> I *do* think there is something more than sheer drudgery in household accounts. The creation of an estate or even an estatelette is a sort of work of art (which is *not* to say, no not ever to say, that all millionaires are artists). In it all is tied up a good deal of "getting the most out of life" etc etc etc. Now, as a member of the Board of Directors of Luce Inc, I think you, the management, get an extraordinarily [*sic*] lot out of our meager pickings. You put on as good an act as many people with twice the wherewithal. My only objection is that your [*sic*] a little too inspirational about it and not sufficiently Teuton-methodical. It's sort of hare vs. turtle—and I'm always afraid that in such races the turtle may win. Of course we're in a queer position. In a way it's silly to worry over a penny when, we hope, the penny won't count much anyway. I guess I'm just a little superstitious about it—"If you *don't* look out for the pennies, the dollars *won't*"—although I certainly *don't* have faith in the original saw that if you *do* look out for the pennies the dollars *will* etc.
>
> Anyway, I believe it's much easier to have fun with money than without, and I certainly want us both to have the biggest kind of fun in many a year to come. Selah, Preacher.
>
> Incidently [*sic*], apropos your (somewhat belated!) worries as to next year's rent, I figure on salary of about $20,000—and furthermore, 1930 & 31 (the life of the lease) should see some even further increases in income. Well, they say that Love & Money are the two great magazine themes. This issue has love all mixed in with the cash as maybe you can see.
>
> Your— Harry

But for all his talk about wanting the biggest kind of fun, he never took time for it. He was too wound up, too ambitious, too preoccupied with the future to enjoy the warm delights of life as they occurred. She wrote him: "I am terribly anticipating . . . seeing you take a weekend off." She tried to slow him down:

> Chicagoans go in for kidnapping . . . I am going to kidnap you and take you to some leafy solitude (poetically speaking) to laugh; against your will and better judgment, to laugh. Or lie and listen to the sweet silences that one forgets about when living in big cities.

Not for Luce the sweet silences or lazy laughter. At thirty, an age when thoughtful men are apt to appraise their progress, he might have been well satisfied but for the scope of his ambitions. The grubby struggle for survival was over. He was making money so fast that he would soon be a millionaire—a term still impressive in the Twenties. But money was only part of the goal. He sought influence, power. His pronouncement at fifteen that he was "not aiming at anything paltry" was if anything more determined at thirty. Some felt confirmed in the suspicion that he yearned for the Presidency not only because he took the trouble to correct an erroneous impression that his birth in

China disqualified him but because there seemed White House hunger in his enormous fascination with politics and the moves he made to improve himself and become better known. He was working on a new magazine—his own, not Hadden's. *Never* Hadden's, for it was about business.

"Hard to realize," Lila wrote him from Roxbury, "that while me and my playmates idle away the hours in this pleasant place, men labor in the heat of a city, and that the best of them [Luce] is creating a masterpiece every week [Time] . . . Harder to believe that the same fertile brain is giving birth to a new magazine, wonderful in its way, another brain stroke."

Interestingly, he planned to call it Power. It would concern itself with the assumption of power by America's new royalty—businessmen and industrialists—and the engines of power they commanded. Time had been plugging them as the stock market soared. John D. Rockefeller, Andrew Mellon, Bernard Baruch, Captain Robert Dollar, Amadio Giannini, Vincent Astor, Harry Sinclair, George Eastman and other corporate giants had appeared on Time's cover in 1928. But Time's department about Business was a small one that could not begin to suggest the struggle, excitement, romance, wealth and power which Luce saw in the business world and the men who controlled it. He wanted to capture it all in the most luxuriously beautiful magazine ever produced.

Hadden was opposed. It was not his idea. It did not seem either interesting or likely to succeed. It would be, after all, a journalistic hosanna to men who had to some extent the characteristics of George F. Babbitt. Hadden did not block the allotment of a modest sum for experimental work toward such a magazine, but his attitude was one of disdain and he disparaged the project to Time's directors.

The great problem of Luce's life was Hadden. The most alienated of Bonesmen, they were lashed together in triumph as they had been in struggle. So long as Hadden was there, Luce's missionary use of Time was limited to issues on which they agreed. Two such kingly men could not forever stand the pinch of the same small throne. Just as Time had been chiefly Hadden's creation, Power was all Luce's—his way of asserting his own creativity and enforcing the Statute of Equality. Power was also a Luce vehicle for separating himself from Hadden within the organization. And it seems likely that Luce held in reserve the idea that if Power was successful and relations with his partner became unbearable, the two could sever their corporate connection, each taking one magazine.

4. A THOUSAND DAGGERS FLASHING

Time had shown admiring interest in Mussolini since 1923, when it spoke of his "remarkable self-control, rare judgment and efficient application of his ideas." Its reporting had grown more "interpretative" with success. Here was

an area in which Hadden and Luce agreed substantially. If Hadden's bias was less extreme than Luce's, the partners were alike in their inclination to embellish the news for greater drama and circulation. Another factor was the quick brilliance of Laird Goldsborough. Goldy, as he was called, had been rewarded with the supervision of Time's foreign news (known in the shop as FN, as the National Affairs department was called NA), which like everything else was rewritten from the papers. Goldsborough not only shared Luce's biases but employed such clever writing and skillful embroidery in this hard-to-check field that he turned an ordinarily soporific department into a thing with the color of a gossip column.

Time interpreted Mussolini as daring, brilliant, wise and courageous. The birth of a child to Donna Mussolini was reported in congratulatory vein. Il Duce's forty-first birthday was celebrated by his first of many appearances on Time's cover along with a benign account of his early struggles, his war service ("His great personal courage won him general praise") and his political wisdom ("Bolshevism taught him his great lesson"). Time's interpretation of Stalin's obscure background stressed his "ominous past" which was "kept shrouded in perpetual mystery by his iron censorship . . ." The regime was likened to hard metal by Time's invariable explanation for several years, when the names of Stalin and Molotov were used, that they meant "steel" and "hammer."

Whereas Mussolini was described in one account as "rubicund, jovial, beaming," the best Time could do for Stalin was, "His facial features suggest cruelty—a hard mask of oriental ruthlessness." Unlike the impeccably uniformed Italian dictator, he was "always shabbily dressed." The romantic Duce kept a lion cub named Italia Bella which "crouched, speed-stunned, in Signor Mussolini's lap as the Dictator stepped upon the throttle of his racing car and sped toward Rome." The lion loved him as did the people, said Time's second cover story on him: "To date Il Duce has suffered barely a scratch or two from the claws of Italia Bella. Like her namesake, 'Fair Italy,' she appears to adore him." Stalin, on the contrary, "was never a dreamer or a romantic hero. He is a cold-blooded man of deeds, uneducated in manner . . ." He did not enjoy Mussolini's popularity and was "never overwhelmed with public adulation."

There seemed a disposition to overlook Italian brutalities and difficulties while stressing those in Russia. There, Time said, the revolution had meant "the substitution of one privileged class for another" with the result that "the workers are the aristocracy." This did them no good since "the population as a whole remains illiterate and characteristically apathetic." Orphans of the war "abound[ed] like alley cats" and became "skilled pickpockets and moral degenerates" who made civilized observers shudder "half with pity, half with revulsion." Even non-orphans were so blighted by Bolshevist education that "100,000 vicious ragamuffins roam the streets [of Moscow] today." Time was

amused by the "scientific Communist planning" that made bread cost forty cents a loaf and butter two dollars a pound.

Time's pejoratives and approbatives could infiltrate sentences in subtle and atmospheric ways. A large crowd in Russia, for example, was a *mob*, whereas in Italy it was a *throng*. Russia was *chill, drab, bleak*, Italy *warm, gay, genial*. What was *relentlessness* or *ruthlessness* in the Kremlin became *firmness* or *resolution* south of the Alps. Time often referred companionably to Mussolini as "Premier Benito" and pictured him as truly Italian in his warmth and sociability. His Russian counterpart was usually alluded to by his rather ominous name, "Josef Vissarionovitch Stalin," or sometimes by his true surname of Djugashvili along with mention of his adoption of an alias—a practice common among revolutionaries but associated with criminals in America. Time told of the "black secrecy" within the "thick, awesome walls of the Kremlin." Far from being either black or secretive, Mussolini was forever talking, and on one occasion when he felt himself affronted, Time said, "his eyes flashed like a thousand daggers in the sunlight, his voice sounded like the bellow of a bull."

The running battle between the two dictators was won hands down week after week by Mussolini, whose "logic, reason and curt common sense" had inspired the nation: "Today the ceaseless unremittent work-fervor of Mussolini is triumphantly infused into Italians. From monarch to hod-carrier the nation is at work." The leader who had jerked Italy up by the pants had even yanked the breeches of the king, who "begins [work] at 8:30 each morning," and had more politely won cooperation from Queen Elena who, in addition to welfare work and gardening, was now sewing "garments for the poor." Alas, Stalin if anything had let Russia's pants down. Management was lacking, planning went awry and "50 'kulaks' (rich peasants) were executed" for failing to cooperate with the government program. Stalin could not elicit the cheers that greeted Mussolini when he spoke: "Across the Chamber floated 'Bravo!' in a shrill treble from a woman in the gallery. Instantly *bravos* and *vivas* were engaged in mortal combat for supremacy."

"Throughout the Soviet Union," Time said, "it is a grim jest that neither the Voice of God nor that of the People can be heard above the silence of Comrade Josef Stalin." Every now and then Time translated in capitals the huge sign the dictatorship had erected near Red Square: "RELIGION IS THE OPIUM OF THE PEOPLE." The sinister force of atheism in Russia was a constant Time refrain. Mussolini, however, for all his quarrels with the Pope, had never tried to stifle what Time called "the spiritual veneration of Italians for their quite literally 'beloved Papa' (the Pope)," and he ultimately came to amicable terms with the Holy See.

Time's rewriting of newspaper accounts brought out touches unseen by the newspaper correspondents themselves, for example, in its atmospheric description of the departure of Trotsky from joyless Moscow. The crowd seeing

him off was not only "sullen and docile" but "shuffling and shivering." It was "surrounded by agents of the Secret Police" and Trotsky was "wan and pallid" and "as threadbare as his cloak" as he got into a "drab railway car." Things were not so adjectivally sullen, docile, shuffling, shivering, wan, pallid, drab and threadbare in Italy. The custom of Il Duce's bully boys of forcing castor oil down opponents' throats was interpreted as humorous and at any rate better than bullets, which Time suggested he used with commendable restraint: "Although the Fascisti cannot be absolved from using armed force against the civil population, Mussolini's coup d'état of October, 1922, was largely effected by the potency of his castor oil . . ."

Time consistently permitted Mussolini to "announce," "order" or merely to "say," whereas Stalin either "growled" or "rasped" on those rare occasions when he spoke at all. The Dracula element in Stalin was most ably limned by Time's Laird Goldsborough, although Goldy had not yet been in Russia. One one-paragraph tour de force about him contained the descriptives, *egotistical, ruthless, inflexible, like tempered metal, cold, inscrutable, never interviewed,* and ended *scarcely recognized in his infrequent rides about Moscow in a closely guarded limousine.*

The fact that many of these descriptions turned out to be true or even flattering to Stalin scarcely justified the good press given Mussolini. Since Time's denunciation of Bolshevism was so often counterbalanced with admiration for the Italian brand of enslavement, the inference could be drawn that enslavement *per se* was not automatically evil—indeed that enslavement effected by the right people, employing capitalism and opposing Communism, could be glamorous, benevolent and chivalrous. Time, the defender of a "free and honest press," often lampooned the Soviet line parroted by Pravda and Izvestia ("At long intervals the Dictator simply releases a statement with instructions that it shall appear verbatim"). Once it even criticized Mussolini's muzzling of the press, at the same time evoking his heroic image:

> Exact dynamic utterance is expected from the lips of Signor Mussolini. His capacity for being clear amounts to genius. He likes to be clear. Yet he can use weasel words. . . . Last week *Il Duce* explained to U.S. newsgatherers why he had suppressed the liberty of Italian newsorgans. Weasel words fell from his lips . . .

Time's coverage of Italy and Russia since the beginning had comprised many thousands of weasel words. The young fellows from Yale really had not changed their early attitude toward news as something plastic and susceptible of improvement. Divinity Student, Old Hatchet Face and George Schleiger of Chillicothe were amusing and never did any measurable harm, but the Yalemen were in the big leagues now. Mussolini and Stalin were real people, important to Americans, who deserved to know the ungimmicked truth about them.

5. THE DEATH OF HADDEN

The gentleness and warmth with which religion invests some communicants were absent in the dour, intense Luce, perhaps because he felt he had a calling, that God had special work for him to do. The doctrine of the calling, which Calvin had stressed, encouraged the idea that God had appointed an occupation for everyone and that virtue led to success. Thus there was no conflict between the superman theory and Luce's Presbyterianism, which was so militant and aggressive that one could imagine him shouting his prayers at a God who might otherwise be inattentive and waste his time. The importance he placed on time did not encourage ease or fraternization. Yet when told something that interested him he would respond with purest attention. As one friend put it, "Harry seemed in love with ideas rather than people."

Ideas were avenues to power. At social gatherings he could walk away in midsentence from someone boring him to seek out someone who could give him facts and ideas. He was skillful at framing questions that would elicit them. He could ignore the woman at his right at the table if she proved devoid of facts and ideas and turn an aggressive scrutiny on the woman at his left because she seemed to have a fact or an idea. Food and drink were not only inconsequential but in a sense invisible and nonexistent to him. He positively had no knowledge of whether he was eating filet mignon or finnan haddie so long as he was devouring a fact or an idea, and he was a disappointment to the hostess who expected to be complimented on the dinner which he had eaten without being aware of it.

In October 1928 Time moved to more spacious quarters at 205 East 42nd Street—an event Hadden marked with an appropriate quantity of bootleg gin and an office party. In December he came down with influenza. He was moved from his East End Avenue bachelor apartment to the home of his mother and stepfather in Brooklyn—then, when he developed septicemia, to Brooklyn Hospital. Unlike Luce, he was fussy about food. Disliking the hospital fare, he had his meals sent in from a Schrafft's restaurant, always including a huge bunch of grapes. He was constantly on the telephone with his friends, who included such Broadway performers as Libby Holman.

Toward the end of January he grew weaker and it appeared doubtful that he would live. On the twenty-sixth his apartment mate and old friend (Yale '19), William Carr, who was a lawyer, visited him, took out paper and wrote, "I, Briton Hadden, declare this to be my last will and testament." Hadden spoke so faintly that Carr had to strain to hear him. He owned 3,361 shares of Time stock, worth well over a million dollars (he had fulfilled his dream of becoming a millionaire by thirty) and representing the balance of control of the corporation.

Luce wanted those shares. There had been difficulties enough with them in Hadden's hands—a divided authority and friction. If Hadden left them to

79

someone else, the division would be perpetuated and Luce's authority might be further impaired. With his strong sense of responsibility and proprietorship, it would have been surprising if, during a visit at the hospital, he did not urge Hadden to sell him at least a controlling block of his shares. It is said that Luce did so. If so, here in the odor of antiseptics they played out the mournful climax of the drama of rivalry that started at Hotchkiss School, continued through Yale and then through seven years of struggle and eventual triumph with Time—Hadden always a shade ahead, now losing the race because of streptococci in his bloodstream. One only knows that Luce did not get the shares. In Hadden's interview with Carr he directed that they go to his half-brother and executor, Crowell Hadden III, whom he instructed to "hold my stock in Time Inc., and not sell the same until after the expiration of 49 years after my death." When it was finished he was too weak to sign his name. He scrawled an "X" at the bottom, his nurse, Lucy Wolinski, being called in to sign as a witness.

Hadden's will proved his faith in the magazine he had created. It did not seem to suggest his faith in Harry Luce. If its provisions were observed to the letter, Luce would have been deprived of the power he sought until he was eighty years old.

Antibiotics developed since then probably would have saved Hadden's life. At that time only blood transfusions kept him going, many of them donated by office associates deeply attached to him. Luce himself had his blood tested, though it seems unremembered whether he had the right type. Hadden lingered for another month and died on February 26, 1929, just eight days past his thirty-first birthday.

"I don't know what I'll do without Brit," Luce said to Manfred Gottfried.

In the light of his thorough command of both the editorial and business sides of the corporation, it is possible that the remark was rhetorical, or that he referred to the shares rather than to Hadden. Yet there were times when his self-belief sagged a trifle, and this may have been one of them. He was deep in the preliminaries of an expensive new magazine that forcibly removed him from Time's editorship. He named John Martin managing editor of Time. He began negotiations with the Hadden estate.

As executor it turned out that Crowell Hadden was empowered to consider the interests of all members of his family and was not bound to hold the shares for forty-nine years. Seven months after Briton Hadden's death, the estate sold 625 shares to Luce (at $360 a share, worth $225,000), 550 to Roy Larsen and smaller blocks to other members of a syndicate Luce organized. It was more than enough to give Luce the unquestioned financial sovereignty he wanted and needed.

VIII

1. THE TYCOON AS HERO

An important effect of Hadden's death was its liberation of Luce the ideologist-missionary-propagandist. The derider of Babbitt would scarcely have agreed to the glorification of business and businessmen which Luce now indulged.

Time's Man of the Year in January 1929, while Hadden lay dying, was Walter P. Chrysler ("The doings of Walter P. Chrysler, already prodigious, now become fabulous"). Chrysler was pretty fabulous even if he was a Time advertiser and a friend and business colleague of one of Time's most influential board members, William V. Griffin, even if Time made an exception to its otherwise inviolable rule that middle names must be given. Chrysler, who despised his middle name, Percy, had promised that there would be no more advertisements if it was divulged. Time had capitulated to that extent. Chrysler was lauded for his introduction during the year of Plymouth and DeSoto cars, his purchase of Dodge Brothers for $160 million and his sixty-eight-story Chrysler Building now rising on 42nd Street just west of Time's office. He took solid rank among the business supermen who, Luce felt, were thrusting America into a golden age of power as well as prosperity.

Up, up went stocks. Luce's celebration of the tycoon soared to a record sixteen Time covers in 1929. Among the better known were J. P. Morgan ("The foremost financier on this round earth"), Myron Taylor ("The door of his office is lettered simply 'Mr. Taylor' "), David Sarnoff ("You cannot fool him about mousetraps"), Alvan Macaulay ("Cool, self-possessed, quiet, sure of his facts and figures") and Walter Teagle ("Standard Oil of New Jersey . . . has never passed a dividend").

That fall, at the very time the stock market reeled drunkenly into the collapse that would bring years of disaster and would question the exaltation of

the tycoon, Time's covers featured five heroes of business in succession, with never an athlete or litterateur to break the chain: William Wrigley, Jr., Harry Guggenheim, Ivar Kreuger, Samuel Insull and Thomas W. Lamont, the latter described as "this right hand of John Pierpont Morgan . . ."

The last issue before the crash carried a three-page announcement of Luce's new magazine Fortune (the title Power had finally been given up and the new name selected by Lila Luce from a group of other possibilities) at the staggering price of a dollar a copy or ten dollars a year. Fortune, it said, proclaimed the "generally accepted commonplace that America's great achievement has been Business."

As Eric Hodgins later described it, "Almost on the eve of Fortune's publication, the whole economy of the United States clapped a hand over its heart, uttered a piercing scream, and slipped on the largest banana peel since Adam Smith wrote *The Wealth of Nations.*"

Luce, like more expert observers, thought the market reverse a temporary setback. Fortune went full speed ahead. Indeed, as market victims still leaped from windows, Time saluted several tycoons as heroes who had stopped the skid in securities. It was the financial resources of the House of Morgan, Time said, that effected the rescue. Its visible agent was Broker Richard F. Whitney. Whitney's entrance into the Exchange seemed to Time to have something of the reckless valor of Horatius taking his post on the bridge:

> . . . Whitney strode through the mob of desperate traders, made swiftly for Post No. 2 where . . . the stock of the United States Steel Corp., most pivotal of all U.S. stocks, is traded in. . . . Having broken down through 200, it was now at 190. If it should sink further, Panic, with its most awful leer, might surely take command. Loudly, confidently at Post No. 2, Broker Whitney made known that he offered $205 per share for 25,000 shares of Steel . . . [Prices rallied.] . . . the man who bid 205 for 25,000 shares of Steel had made himself a hero of a financially historic moment.

Time's next issue gave its cover to Lamont, the Morgan partner who had sent Whitney on his historic mission, "the man who steered the ship of U.S. prosperity through the storm, who at length felt the helm respond"—interesting reading a year or two later. As the ship of prosperity crashed sickeningly onto the rocks, Luce topped off his recognition of men of business by making Owen D. Young of General Electric his Man of the Year, because, "Never a moralist, he has said: 'In no other profession [besides business] . . . is the need for wide information, broad sympathies and directed imagination so great.'"

2. HALL OF FAME

The founder of a magazine about business would be expected to gather a staff with degrees in economics, experience in business and acquaintance with

important people in business. Luce *forbade* expertise. He had organized his staff around a small group of enthusiastic amateurs like Russell Davenport (Yale '23, Bones, Elizabethan Club), the craggy-faced poet who had worked briefly for Time. Davenport had recently married the once-divorced, darkly beautiful Marcia, daughter of the soprano Alma Gluck. Mme. Gluck, also divorced, had married the violinist Efrem Zimbalist. The Zimbalists, 49th Street neighbors of the Luces, became their good friends, and since Lila was a music lover and Luce himself not actively opposed, there were frequent gatherings of musical people. According to one observer, "That was about the only time Harry had a relatively normal social life."

For Fortune, Luce wanted young people who had not worked elsewhere long enough to form habit-patterns and could observe phenomena with excitement instead of the old-timer's boredom. The amateur quality of the Time staff, with its imaginative and fancy-woven outlook on events, had proved out in profits, however dubious its standing as journalism. Fortune's first managing editor was Parker Lloyd-Smith, a witty Princetonian who had spent a year at Oxford and then worked briefly for the Albany Evening News. With him were such people as the brilliant Dwight Macdonald (Yale '27) and Margaret Bourke-White, a Cleveland girl who had created a specialty of photographing industrial scenes. The most seasoned amateur was Archibald MacLeish, back from Paris, now the father of three and in need of a stake to enable him to finish his narrative poem *Conquistador*. He was surprised when Luce asked him to write for his new magazine of business.

"I'm flattered," he said, "but I know absolutely nothing about business."

"That's why I want you," Luce replied.

MacLeish put himself in Luce's hands. He admitted that he needed money to finish his poem and that he would be of little use to Fortune unless he *could* finish it. Luce was generosity itself.

"Well, then," he said, "you can work for Fortune as much of the time as you need to pay your bills and take the rest of the time off for poetry."

It was on this unusual basis that MacLeish joined the staff. He never forgot Luce's magnanimity, which indeed made possible the publication of the Pulitzer Prize-winning *Conquistador* in 1932. He was paid handsomely even when he gave half of his time or less to Fortune, and Luce got a bargain for such talents. As MacLeish observed, Luce's naïveté was not a weakness but a strength: "He really thought there was nothing he could not do, so he often did it." Pretty soon MacLeish would be doing a piece about the Elgin watch factory "so imaginative," as he described it, "that the Elgin executives hardly recognized it."

A picture of Luce's dream of industrial paternalism appeared in his own Fortune article on Pittsburgh. It was "a gentle city," he wrote of this roughneck place, where "the brass-knuckled steel barons" had been replaced by men typified by the Mellons, kindly men all of them. Luce was insistent about

their gentleness: "Neither A. W. nor R. B. [Mellon] likes rough-and-tumble. The same is true of their associates . . . mild men . . ." Still another Mellon, James, was "a delightful and subtly humorous gentleman." Luce emphasized "the gentleness of spirit which is inescapable in modern Pittsburgh," paying tribute to the Mellons as a family to whom their city "has been motive, duty, devotion, and satisfaction," and saying that they were motivated by a "principle that makes the Mellon fortune racial in scope, with a feeling for the nation's destiny playing through it." Pittsburgh's windows were washed weekly by contented family servants, he wrote, and the workers were happy and prosperous—97,000 schoolchildren gave a dime each to the University of Pittsburgh, a millworker gave it $5000 and a Magyar woman gave it "the price of a month's meat." Luce's admiration for "the Mellon Raj," as he called it, was plain and his faith in a society so humanely controlled seemed complete. He seemed not to have visited the slums. The article angered the leftish Dwight Macdonald, who later volunteered one of the sayings of the gentle R. B. Mellon which Luce's research had failed to find: "You couldn't run a coal mine without machine-guns."

At this same time Luce came to the attention of Vanity Fair's beautiful fair-haired assistant editor Clare Boothe Brokaw. Assigned to interview him for that magazine's "Hall of Fame," she was unable to see him—too busy. Vanity Fair ran his picture anyway, and Mrs. Brokaw wrote the caption:

> We nominate for the Hall of Fame:
> Henry Luce. Originator of the news-magazine idea; because at the age of 32 he is the successful editor and publisher of "Time" and "Fortune" magazines; because he was born in China; because he was a humble newspaper reporter on the Chicago Daily News; and lastly because he claims that he has no other interest outside of his work, and that his work fills his waking hours.

Mrs. Brokaw, who was twenty-seven and divorced, would in five years confront Luce with a moral dilemma when he fell in love with her. Now his fascination with industry was whetted by a trip to South Bend, where he carried Miss Bourke-White's cameras for her and was moved to nostalgia by the huge Singer sewing machine factory.

"All through my childhood," he told her, "even in tiny villages in the interior of China, I saw that big S for Singer."

At the Studebaker Corporation he was impressed by the efficiency of the assembly line. He talked with the young Paul G. Hoffman, Studebaker's vice president, and with the president, Albert Erskine. (Fortune's later story brought anguish to Erskine, an Alabamian, for its photograph of Erskine was overshadowed by one of a sweating Negro Studebaker worker.)

Luce, whose talents at promotion equaled his command of other phases of business, had made sure that Fortune's first issue (February 1930) was splendidly publicized. With its 184 antique-paper pages plus covers, its weight of more than two pounds, its 30,000 subscribers and scores of advertisements for

luxuries ranging from Pierce Arrow automobiles to Chris-Craft yachts, it hardly seemed a harbinger of national privation and despair. The lavishness of its typography, art and color reproduction were of a piece with its dedication to tycoons and their works, among them Swift & Company, David Sarnoff and his Radio Corporation of America, and the Rothschilds. Its sketch of the multimillionaire Arthur Curtiss James ("Portrait of a Gentleman Funded Proprietor—This Civilization's Best Example") stressed the corporate abilities that had brought him yachts and palaces in New York and Newport. It even had a 10,000-word article on banking by Luce himself which he could not possibly have had time to write and yet did.

The Daily Worker assailed Fortune for "romantically attempting to disguise the rapacity and swinishness of American 'Big Business' . . ." The Nation thought it too eager to "heap encomiums" on tycoons. The San Diego Union loosed a blast:

> It has remained for Fortune . . . to reduce American aristocracy to its final absurdity . . . Plutocracy's pride in the dollar is pitilessly exposed by the elaboration of concealment, and the pose that invective could not shake has been rendered ridiculous and self-conscious by adulation.

There was perhaps an unintended "let them eat cake" impression in bringing out this salute to luxury when national hardship was beginning. Less socially sensitive papers were more in agreement with the Omaha News, which called Luce "the miracle editor." Fortune got off to a good if not immediately profitable start, while Time's profits were enormous. By 1931, with the nation sinking deeper into depression and many corporations showing losses, Time's directors looked with benevolence on Luce. Time stock, which had reached its then high of $360 after the death of Hadden, was about to hit $1000 and to be split 20 to 1.

"Miracle editor" was a proper appellation for a man who could make his stockholders plump in the Thirties. Fortune was a thing of pride but it was Time that washed in a golden tide. It had become an admired part of the American scene. The smart red-bordered magazine which identified itself with God, the flag and business, was virtually unseen in ghettos or tanktowns, its habitat being in libraries, high schools and colleges, church studies, and living rooms with bridge lamps and the new wall-to-wall carpeting. It was read and enjoyed, as Time's own advertising research staff discovered, by people in the upper levels of both income and education. Bankers, sales managers, clergymen and professors not only enjoyed its lively pages but often indulged a quiet yearning that some day they might "make" the cover, or anyway win mention inside. Most regular readers were accustomed to Timestyle and unaware of hidden propaganda. They unconsciously appreciated editorial stands which simplified their own opinion-making, unlike the skidding Literary Digest, whose presentation of various aspects of issues took more time, was confusing and forced readers to make their own judgments. Only a few, such as

the left-leaning editor of the Beverly Hills Script, felt that they were being imposed upon:

> The fellows who got up Time had a peach of an idea. . . . As far as we are concerned, however, the grand idea is beginning to flop, for the reason that the narrator has now turned critic and is editorializing on his news as he goes along. For instance, any items about Russia are narrated with deep contempt; certain public characters are sneered at, and others made ridiculous. The nifty purpose of giving us world news has deteriorated into an apparently young editor's opinion of that news. Ye Ed has returned to The Literary Digest where he reads both sides of important questions and thus is permitted to form his own judgments.

Confucius likened the truth to a virgin who, once violated, can never be the same again. In the Time office the hapless girl received such bruising weekly attentions as to forfeit all respect on the part of her manhandlers. She received further mistreatment in 1931 when the new March of Time radio series began under the sponsorship of Roy Larsen. Larsen's only previous news experience was what he had absorbed at Time. John Shaw Billings, a South Carolina-born, Harvard-trained Time editor who had risen swiftly to high responsibility, noted in his diary:

> Drove down to the Luces on 49th Street for dinner. Other guests were Tom Palmer and his wife, Bill Whitney and wife, Marcia Davenport, Washington Dodge and others. Halfway through the dinner we all dashed out and drove up to Columbia Broadcasting studio on Madison Avenue to watch the March of Time from a glass-fronted cubicle. . . . I was amazed at the number of performers—20 or 25. Then back to the Luces for ice cream and coffee. . . . Luce confided to me he thought the March of Time was a costly bust . . .

Luce changed his mind. The program used Time's already transmogrified news as a basis for dramatizations of the week's more colorful events. Speaking their pieces from scripts one further remove from reality were actors who mimicked persons in the news. Most of the actors could handle at least two voices. William Adams spoke as both President Roosevelt and President von Hindenburg, using German-accented English for the latter. Ted De Corsia enacted both Herbert Hoover and Mussolini, Westbrook Van Voorhis "did" Hitler and Marion Hopkinson enacted Mrs. Roosevelt, Frances Perkins and Princess Marina. A twenty-one-piece orchestra led by Howard Barlow furnished a musical introduction for each episode. Sound effects were imaginative, a decapitation being suggested by the quick slicing of a cantaloupe which then fell into a box of sawdust.

The news-by-cantaloupe extremes of the March of Time would hardly have been attained but for the liberties with the news taken for so long by Time itself as to become custom. The reverse seemed as likely—that Time writers, after becoming indoctrinated with the buskined broadcast of MOT, would abate a shade more their regard for fact. Newspapers at the time—some

whose own concern for responsible reporting was not always above question
—were fearful and critical of radio as a dangerous competitor both in news
dissemination and advertising revenue. There seemed a whiff of self-interest
in the Rutland, Vermont, Herald's condemnation of the exaggeration and lu-
ridity and its reminder of Time's own consistent sarcasm toward such sensational newspapers as the New York Graphic. Still, its editorial, "The Journalism of Fiction," had a point:

> . . . [T]his "March of Time" is as yellow and sensational as any act of any
> newspaper so sarcastically jeered at by "Time" itself. Most of the dialogue is
> purely imaginary as are the accompanying sounds, created for a dramatic back-
> ground. Listeners who recall "Time's" attempt to reproduce the freezing to
> death of little children in a school bus caught in a blizzard in Ohio . . . will still
> shudder at the dreadful and purely imaginary hokum uttered by the actors who
> sought to represent the victims.

Occasionally Luce now called in Edward L. Bernays to advise him on publicity. Bernays, who was a nephew of Freud and had studied his uncle's work,
felt that Luce had a drive for power and a simultaneous drive for good, that
he rationalized the two but had guilt feelings as compensation.

"I always felt as if Harry were flexing his muscles," he recalled.

3. NEVER KILLED AN INDIAN

Around the continent, editors had varying opinions of Time but were seldom indifferent. The St. Louis Post-Dispatch said with tongue in cheek:

> U.S. news-lingo seems set for a big change, due to spreading influence of nosy
> . . . vibrant newsmagazine Time. . . . Old flowing periods of classic writers
> Addison & Steele out of date in fast-moving peppy civilization, which craves
> something snippy, snappy, terse.

The Ottawa Evening Journal, its tongue in place, called Time "bright,
readable, acute," but complained that in a recent Time story about Canada,
"It would be hard to crowd more of ignorance and misinformation into any
equal number of words."

The Fairmont, Minnesota, Sentinel complained about Time's errors in a
story about Minnesota, adding, "Snobs hereabouts who think they are of the
intelligentsia are fond of stalking about with a copy of Time sticking out of
the coat pocket."

The Baltimore Afro-American was indignant because Time's article about
the jazz leader Louis Armstrong called him "a bullet-headed, satchelmouthed
black rascal." But the Afro-American was so much less offended by this than
it was pleased by Time's praise for Armstrong's artistry that it went on to re-
print the whole Time story.

W. A. Swanberg

The Saturday Review, noting that different magazines had human characteristics, commented:

> Time is a bright college boy, immensely and rapidly read, with a tongue in his cheek and his mouth open, while he pounds the news inside out in the attempt to make it exciting.

Marlen Pew, editor of Editor & Publisher, long exasperated by Time's habit of appropriating news from the papers and remodeling it, told of being stabbed in the back by his own legionaries:

> At a recent meeting of the American Society of Newspaper Editors somebody wanted to know why it is that newspapermen will not write fresh and realistic stuff like that written for the magazine Time. It seemed to be the opinion of a number of editors in attendance that conventional and formula press writing has become quite deadly. This week I noticed the following paragraph in Time, taken from a story of a Maryland lynching:
>
> > "A stooped and toothless crone of 71 shuffled along a country road near Kingston, Md., one morning last week. Mrs. Mary Denston was on her way to see her daughter. Suddenly, from behind, black hands were laid upon her. Cackling and kicking feebly she was dragged by a young Negro buck to a clump of bushes. There, amid a flurry of leaves dancing rustily in the autumn sunshine, she was raped."
>
> Well, that's a piece of openwork news knitting, fairly typical of Time, but how many newspaper desks would pass it? . . . The "stooped and toothless crone" stuff might be libelous. The word "rape" is taboo. . . . No nice newspaper editor would dream of dressing up such horror with flurrying leaves dancing rustily in the autumn sunshine. . . . It is the sort of thing that makes Time jingle, but don't tell me daily editors really want it.

Slangy Variety, however, which had imitated Time's insolence, published a report suggesting that Pew and his nice newspaper editors might be a little old-fashioned:

> "Time," the weekly news mag, is now in second place in volume of advertising carried by an American periodical, the "Satevepost" being of course, the leader. "Time" nosed out the "Literary Digest" last month by 22 pages of advertising.

A mere want ad in the conservative New York Herald Tribune seemed to verify the thought that Pew's advice was not holding up well and that other publishers sought the same kind of jingle. It read:

> Former "Time" Magazine writer wanted by Metropolitan publisher . . .

"The trouble with me," Luce told a Brooklyn Eagle reporter who asked about his hobbies, "is that I work nearly all the time. . . . My principal hobby is conversing with somebody who knows something. . . . I'm sorry that I've never done anything exciting," he went on, as if he had not seen more travel and excitement than many members of the Foreign Legion. "Never killed an

Indian or rescued anybody from drowning—wasn't wrecked in the *Titanic* or anything."

The Eagle man noted Luce's restlessness and dynamism. Everybody who encountered him felt his enormous energy and noticed his nervous pacing and his chain-smoking, and the tension that made him repeat phrases as if the words were under pressure, shot out of a gun. He worked, as he said, nearly all the time. Laura Z. Hobson—she had married Luce's classmate Thayer Hobson (News, Bones)—noticed that the Luce evening schedule became tighter.

"Earlier," she said, "you could call Lila and Harry at eleven and have a good chance of getting them to come to dinner that night."

Luce's evenings tended to become black- or white-tie continuations of his days, extensions of his business and his ambitions. His hobby of "conversing with somebody who knows something" meant that an increasing number of experts and specialists were invited to the Luce gatherings—people with whom the conversational preliminaries could be skipped in order to get at their facts and ideas.

"Harry could never really relax," Mrs. Hobson recalled. "He couldn't just lean back, let everything go and enjoy himself."

One feels that on the Luce mountain, the forget-me-nots Lila had admired were receding and the glacier advancing. Luce was under tremendous tension, wound up like a spring, driven incessantly. In his efficiency, drive and imperial ego, he resembled the manic type fairly common in business who works at a furious pace, expects the same from underlings and can achieve such wonders of creativity or production as to become a captain of industry, but occasionally has to be hospitalized for his own good. Luce, evidently a hypomanic, had these qualities without paying the full price of the manic. His personality was so strongly knit that it could operate at almost frightening velocity without flying apart. Grandiose as were his dreams of power, he was able to control them while he used his combination of brains, energy and aggressiveness to achieve them. He valued able men so long as they could adjust themselves to his fast pace and inordinate demands. Those who could, found him outrageous at times but often stimulating, a tonic, and generous in his loyalty as well as his rewards. He could even countenance inefficiency if enough talent came with it, as with Russell Davenport. Davenport was eccentric, easily bored, undisciplined, never an organization man, but so brilliant and so chock-full of facts and ideas that the impatient Luce kept him on.

4. BOLSHEVIKS VS. GOD

Hadden's death, in addition to liberating Luce's worship of business, opened the way for a heavier offensive against Soviet Russia. The machine-gun bursts of a few paragraphs or a column continued as Luce brought up the

artillery and air force. Time thereafter employed the occasional big bomb of a page or even two. The decision of Christian groups to join in prayer for the preservation of religion in the Soviet Union despite official hostility toward it was the newspeg on which Time hung a two-and-a-half-page cannonade, mostly representing a culling of published insult.

The article, titled "All Against Russia," opened with Pope Pius's denunciation of the "horrible, sacrilegious iniquities" going on there and his appeal for a world crusade against the Soviet Union. It quoted the animadversions of clergymen, statesmen and editors in America and capitalist Europe against the "Bolshevik campaign against God." It was replete with such phrases as "[Bolshevik] infamies," "nameless and disgusting Bolshevik atrocities," "the most unworthy and perhaps the most criminal [government] in the world," and "[Bolsheviks are] unattractive animals which, like boa-constrictors and alligators, accept food, only to show their gratitude by swallowing their keepers."

Luce also began a propagandist effort to isolate Russia economically. Time slapped at the publicist Ivy Lee, "peripatetic representative extraordinary of U.S. Business," for his Moscow visits in search of American contracts. United States corporations had done $108 millions' worth of business with the Reds in 1929. This tainted money was leading American business into a trap. Industrialists were warned that it would be to their long-run interest to join the churchly struggle against the common enemy:

> Prayers must be numerous and fervent indeed to stop Stalin, "The Man of Steel," but he can be stopped the moment Business unites with the Church in an economic boycott of the Soviet Union. For Stalin's whole program is based on importing Ford tractors and U.S. technicians, exporting grain and raw materials. Nowhere, last week, was the economic weapon drawn, nor was any plan afoot to draw it.
>
> In Belgium one of that little country's largest match factories went bankrupt last week, because the Soviet Government Match Works is now dumping matches in the Belgian market . . . When colossal Red Russia begins to dump automobiles in the U.S., Britain, France and Italy, the Church may count on Business for help in the Crusade—perhaps too late.

Three months later Time's cover went to new polemic lengths, showing a darkened room hung with a huge picture of a Mongoloid Stalin, under which were four whiskery conspirators plotting palpable evil. The bombs which were not literally shown were suggested with wonderful impact by the desperate and furtive attitudes of the conspirators. The cover caption read, "Stalin & Friends," under which was the line, *His business friends include Ford, International Harvester, General Electric, Radio Corp., du Pont, Standard Oil, Ivy Lee.* The cover story showed Luce's courage in righteousness. While it did not openly attack these and other American firms which did business with Russia (and some of which were Time advertisers), it listed them as Stalin's friends and implied a lack of patriotism.

90

This was in any case a refreshing departure from the usual magazine truck-ling to advertisers. Luce had the temerity to be especially severe with Henry Ford, a man before whom publishers ordinarily genuflected:

> In return for an order for $30,000,000 worth of Ford products, the company is understood to have made available all its patents, blueprints and designs to Soviet technicians for one year.
>
> Mr. Ford knows perfectly well that these patents and designs will be ruthlessly pirated—indeed pirated tractors copied minutely even to the pirated name *Ford* are already made in the Soviet Union—but $30,000,000 is $30,000,000. . . . Business, transcending all frontiers, stifling fear, mocking statesmen who refuse to "recognize" the Soviet Union, casting even patent rights into the discard, now assists the triumph of the very thing which western businessmen most hate—the Communist Ideal.

Time again broached the idea of "an *international* Capitalist boycott of the Soviet State." It agreed that a crackdown on the Communists and a suppression of trade with Russia "would mean a staggering loss to Business—cancellation of Soviet contracts by the tens of millions. However, not all Congressmen are businessmen. Some think that to stamp out U.S. Communism now would be a national boon, cheap at any price." Time bitterly opposed an idea that had some backing—United States recognition of Soviet Russia.

"All Against Russia" and "Stalin & Friends" heralded Luce's intensified cold war, which was to last out his life with only a three-year pause dictated by expediency. His able ally was Foreign Editor Laird Goldsborough, whose copy was always lively, gossipy and, as his colleague Dwight Macdonald put it, filled with every virtue "except such dull ones as accuracy and honesty." Goldsborough, now the highest-paid writer in the shop, drove a Rolls-Royce, lived on Fifth Avenue and went to Europe every year for local color. Critics said he got his Russian news from White Russian émigrés in Paris. His gift for drama was so valued that his peculiar irresponsibility toward news events as yet vexed only the staff's liberals. He would limp into the office on his cane, seize a pencil and write steadily by hand, seldom pausing for thought, turning out accounts as readable as they were unreliable.

Luce's increasing concern about Russia caused him to send Goldsborough there in 1931 to lay the groundwork for a triple-length, five-chapter article which filled about half of the March 1932 Fortune. While some Soviet advances were listed in the finished article, the predominating air of revulsion stressed Russian irreligion, terrors, inequities and failures. The masses were pitilessly ridiculed. The delegates to the Soviet Congress were described as men who "know more about the backside of a camel, polar bear, or cow, than they do about government." The chapter on "The Eternal Peasant" began, "Gross, sensual and greedy, the eternal Russian peasant is no more ashamed of, or inconvenienced by, these qualities than a bear." There was a studied effort to equate Russians with animals, to emphasize their high rate of illiter-

acy, to suggest an accompanying stupidity, and to depict them as drunken, dirty and dissolute people inhabiting a land infested with flies, rats, bedbugs and snakes. A party functionary was described as "a six-foot gorilla," the orphaned children as "human rats" and "rat-children," and there was mention of how peasants would drive to market "with their calves and wives." Under the czars the peasant was a "work-beast," whereas, Fortune said, Stalin now seated "this whip-sore but astonished and delighted bear upon a tractor." It referred to "the baboon-like mating of aboriginal males and females in parts of the Soviet Union so remote that they have not yet even been explored." Russian drunkenness and immorality were suggested by emphasis on the flow of vodka, the ease of divorce, the free abortion clinics and the alleged commonness of illegitimacy. After visiting town, Russian peasants would ride home, "snoring, dead drunk, brought safely home by their wives." A huge colored drawing of a bedbug, showing top and side views, further questioned Russian fastidiousness. And at the end of the article was Luce's long, alphabetical list of American firms doing business with the Soviet Union and which (it was suggested without being stated) ought to know better.

IX

1. OFF TO CHINA

In Haverford, Pennsylvania, Leslie Severinghaus got a surprise telephone call from his brother-in-law Luce in New York, who said he was planning a trip around the world. "I can't think of anyone I'd rather have with me than you," he said. The conversation, a typical Luce time-saver, took less than three minutes. Severinghaus, who was head of the English department at Haverford School, left Philadelphia on May 2, 1932, met Luce in Chicago and rode on with him to Seattle.

Here, awaiting the sailing of the *Empress of Canada* from Victoria, Luce investigated Time's local part-time representative and found him, as he put it, "a sap." Such stringers in the bigger cities handled circulation matters and were expected also to cooperate on occasional local newsbreaks.

"The fact is we *do* muff news from the *U.S.A.*," Luce wrote in a letter to Larsen and Martin. "I *never* leave N.Y. that I don't hear a great story which Time should have had." He urged (that is, ordered) that Time get "30 *right* editorial contacts in 30 key cities," adding, "So far as money is concerned, we *ought* to spend it." He noted, ". . . we haven't given much of a damn about news not appearing East of the Hudson. . . . There's a huge opportunity here—an opportunity to *really* be the national paper. If I and John [Martin] and Billings and all the rest of the staff don't get out to the Mississippi Valley & West more, we ought to be shot."

Having thus punctured complacency back at the new offices in the Chrysler Building—something he did ably and regularly—he apologized for his criticism. With Severinghaus he visited the University of Washington, saw a baseball game with the University of Idaho, looked over the Greek-letter district and was photographed with five pretty coeds. When they sailed on May 7, they found two congenial shipmates: Dr. John Leighton Stuart, missionary

93

colleague of Luce's father and still president of Yenching University in Peking, and the naturalist Roy Chapman Andrews, already famous for a half-dozen expeditions into the remoter parts of China and Central Asia.

"Harry was relaxed, obviously confident of the future," Severinghaus observed. But the word "relaxed" as applied to Luce was purely comparative. He wrote advice on foreign affairs to Laird Goldsborough. He sent orders to Time's financial specialist to buy common stocks. He paced the deck. He discussed China and Asia with Andrews and Dr. Stuart. Although he was run-down from his efforts since Hadden's death and was supposed to be taking a rest, he was congenitally, helplessly restless.

In fact, far from being on a vacation tour, he was on one of the more important missions of his life. He intended to appraise politics, government and society as well as he could in the world's two largest nations, China and the Soviet Union. Out of his own investigations he would write reports for the guidance of his staff back home. Rest indeed! He had already read considerably about Russia. Now he took copious notes as he read J. A. B. Scherer's *Romance of Japan*, H. B. Restarick's *Sun Yat-sen* and shorter material on Sun's posthumous brother-in-law, Chiang Kai-shek, and the Soong family.

From the start, the story of the Soongs had so excited Luce, the Protestant and the politician, that it would engross him all his life. Charlie Soong, returning from America to China as a Methodist missionary to his own people, then making his fortune as a merchant, had sponsored an even greater miracle in four of the children he had fathered. All four were now associated politically or familially with Sun's successor in the effort to unify China, the emerging man of power, Chiang Kai-shek. Time's attitude toward Chiang had of course reflected Luce's. While Chiang was a heathen and collaborating with the Soviet Union, Time had treated him coldly as just another warlord. But in 1927, a pivotal year in his life, he had broken with the Russians, slaughtered thousands of Communists, dismissed his concubines and married the Methodist Mei-ling Soong. Time had melted, granting its supreme recognition, Chiang's picture on the cover. The news emerged that he was studying the Bible and that Christian missionaries were welcomed in his home. In 1931 he was baptized a Methodist, voicing concern about the growth of Marxist thought in China. Time had honored him again. Only the previous October Chiang and his wife had been pictured together on the cover along with a sympathetic story about the double threat to him posed by the Communists and the Japanese. Luce now intended to investigate the Soongs at close range.

The genial, strapping Severinghaus, experiencing his longest exposure to his high-powered brother-in-law, found him agreeable. "Dr. Stuart, Harry and I are just about the last ones to leave the dining salon after every meal," Severinghaus wrote in the meticulous diary he kept of his ten-week journey with Luce. "We get involved in discussions [about China] that seem to have no stopping points."

In Japan there was strenuous but observant Luce sightseeing—Tokyo, the Yoshiwara red-light district, Nikko, the Meiji Memorial Shrine, the Gold Pavilion, Kyoto, Osaka. After crossing the lovely Inland Sea, they reached Shanghai May 29. It was Luce's first visit to China in twenty years, one that filled him with recollections of his departure from this same teeming port as a stammering fourteen-year-old schoolboy bound for England. He went to work at once. After talking with newspapermen, business leaders and bankers, he had an audience with the thirty-eight-year-old T. V. Soong, who paid him the compliment of flying in from Nanking to talk with him at the Soong Shanghai mansion. He had a touch of malarial fever and, as Luce put it in his notes, "He refused to see anyone—except the Editor of Time and Fortune, to both of which he subscribes." The tall banker-politician—Chiang's finance minister—was keenly conscious of public relations. Soong was welcoming an important ally, one he perhaps hoped was not immune to flattery.

Luce noted that Soong's children were attended by an amah "dressed just like the amah I used to have 30 years ago." "Soong started off with compliments for Time and Fortune," he recorded. One result of this interview would be an adulatory Fortune article about Soong, his family and Chiang and their combined "campaign to excise [the] cancerous growth" of the "insidious Communists."

As part of his constant program of self-education, Luce was interested in everything from agriculture to night life. With American friends they drove through alleyways of prostitution and visited cabarets. At one of them, La Dow's, there was a good orchestra and twenty-five pretty Russian girls who would dance with unattached males for a small fee. "I didn't dance," Severinghaus wrote, "but Harry did, several times—a stunning Russian girl, 26, in black evening gown. I went back to the hotel at 2:00 A.M. . . . Harry was still talking to the young lady when I left." "Harry's much sought after by prominent Chinese and Westerners," he added next day, "and I usually have my hands full keeping travel arrangements up to date."

In a creaking Loening amphibian of China Airways, Luce and Severinghaus flew to Nanking, where they called on Pearl Buck, visited Ginling Christian College and drove out to the tomb of Sun Yat-sen—the sight recalling to Severinghaus, an excellent baritone, "It's hard to believe that I sang the solo part at Sun's funeral in Peking in 1925!" They flew farther up the Yangtze to Hankow, where Luce met with bankers, Standard Oil men and churchmen, not to mention dancing girls.

They set out for Peking: "The train never exceeded 25 miles per hour; by nightfall we were deep in the mountains, the worst of the bandit country, but nothing exciting happened. Filthy dining car . . ." And next day: "All day we loafed across the plains of Honan in stifling heat—104 in our compartment . . ." A fellow passenger was a cultivated Chinese Communist who had spent time in Moscow and who spoke English. Inevitably he and Luce em-

barked on an intense but courteous discussion of Communist ideology in which neither gave ground. "I was ignored while this discussion went on," Severinghaus recalled with amusement.

Their arrival in Peking was a thrill to Severinghaus, who had lived there for five years and had many friendships to renew. Luce was now so preoccupied and so accustomed to servants that any hotel room he occupied (always the best, as in the Peking Hotel) became a shambles of underwear, shirts and neckties. Among other things he conferred with the United States Minister, visited the Forbidden City and the Temple of Heaven, went mountain-climbing near Montikuo with his brother-in-law, and dined with a group including the philosopher and classical scholar Dr. Hu Shih, educated at Cornell and Columbia. "Harry, as usual, kept plying questions to these knowledgeable persons about the progress of the republic and international relationships," Severinghaus wrote. "He is always the center of active conversation, and I am continually astounded at his grasp of facts in so many fields."

Luce's prime interest in Peking was Yenching University, which his father had done so much to finance and where Dr. Stuart now made him an honored guest. The thirty-four-year-old editor of Time was well embarked on what was to be the supreme but futile effort of his life—to finish the Christianization of China through such institutions as Yenching, drive out Communism and place the Christian Chiang Kai-shek in charge. This was a dream that glowed like the Grail. It represented the consummation of the work his father and mother had begun when they sailed for China in 1897. It represented also the nineteenth-century dream of that tough, practical Christian, Admiral Mahan, who had been similarly concerned with the state of China's soul and its effect on America's power, trade and well-being:

> [Mahan] warned that one day China might well acquire power commensurate with her mass and would then demand her share of the world's goods. While there was still time, therefore, it was essential to instil Christian values so that "time shall have been secured for them [the Chinese] to absorb the ideals which in ourselves are the result of centuries of Christian increment." Otherwise the world might one day be faced with a dangerous, materialistic, and hugely powerful country unrestrained by either God or the Constitution.

2. SCENES OF BOYHOOD

Next, on what was becoming a test of brain and endurance, was the most nostalgic place of all, Shantung province, where Luce had spent his boyhood. He seemed intent on swallowing as much of China as he could hold. Though they had only an hour's stopover at Tientsin, he insisted on renting a car and rushing through the city. "The curiosity appetite of Harry is insatiable," his brother-in-law remarked.

At Tsinan, the big provincial capital, it was not enough to see U.S. Consul

Meinhardt and to call on Han Fu-chu, Chiang's governor of Shantung. (Luce relayed word to Goldsborough that Governor Han was a "rising star" who should be watched.) On the same hectic day they toured Cheloo Christian University, the leper colony, the hospital, the museum and, of all places, a flour mill that Luce could not bear to pass without inspection. A quick bath and change and they arrived breathlessly to dine with the Meinhardts, where the Luce-inspired discussion was cut short at 8:30 so they could hurry back to their hotel, pack and catch the 9:40 for Taian. ("Harry wastes no time!") Arriving late at Taian, they went to sleep at their hotel at 1:30 A.M., then rose at 4:45 to visit the Methodist mission before making a morning ascent of the famous Sacred Mountain. Luce's father had climbed its thousands of steps on foot years earlier. In view of their loss of sleep, Luce and Severinghaus succumbed to sloth and hired eight bearers, the diarist writing:

> Walking some of the time and carried by our bearers at other times, we went up and up the endless steps, passing through the Nan T'ien Men at 9:30 and arriving at the top at 10 o'clock. For an hour we rested, looking over the countryside from our elevation of more than 5000 feet. . . . The trip down was exciting. We rode all the way, suspended in our chairs between the shoulders of our two bearers. From time to time, while maintaining a perfect stride, bearers would be shifted by simply tossing the chair skyward while two dropped out and two others slipped under the shoulder straps. Looking down the steep expanses of endless steps while descending at a trot was somewhat disconcerting, but the bearers never missed a step.
>
> About halfway down, we encountered an international commission, led by Lord Lytton, enjoying the same experience. We stopped for a chat. Mr. Stimson, U.S. Secretary of State [Yale '88, Bones, on Time's cover in 1929] was a member of the party.

Reaching the bottom, they called on the storied "Christian General," Feng Yu-hsiang who, after his conversion to Methodism, had originated the novel practice of baptizing thousands of his troops with a fire hose. Feng, once a powerful warlord, more recently a high official under the Methodist Chiang, had retired to an abandoned Buddhist temple near the Sacred Mountain to write poetry. He gave them fifteen minutes, although he had turned away the Lytton Commission. "No interpreter," Luce wrote in a letter to Larsen, "so Leslie Severinghaus was for the first time thrown completely upon his knowledge of Chinese to carry us through"—doubtless an emergency service the practical Luce had counted on in the first place.

Next stop, Weihsien, where they arrived hungry and tired at 10:00 P.M. The stationmaster warned them of bandits between the station and the town, so they slept, still hungry, on wooden benches. At 6:00 next morning, June 19, they got a ride in a cart to the old compound:

> Harry was like a ten-year-old, recognizing all the turns in the road, pointing out mission buildings, showing me where he had played as a boy. . . . By 7 o'clock

we were inside the compound—and Harry could not talk fast enough. Our cart pulled up before Mr. Reeder's house, the old LUCE homestead, and with a tremendous thrill I realized that I was entering the legendary land of Frau Netz, Emmavail, Beth, and Sheldon.

They were welcomed by many old friends of Luce's parents, as well as by Grace Rowley, his old Latin teacher at the mission school. Luce, much moved by sentiment, showed his brother-in-law the bedrooms, the study porch, the donkey stall—even the chicken coop. They went walking, "scrambling over walls and into the cemetery where he had played so many games with his friends of yore." In bed that night, "long we lay in discussion of how missionary life has changed under changing world conditions."

At Tengchow, Luce's birthplace and the scene of the former college where Rev. Henry Luce had begun his service, Severinghaus wrote:

> I felt as if I were treading on holy ground. There were the old college buildings, the renovated Buddhist temples where the first missionaries lived, Calvin Mateer's workshop where he translated the Bible, and the old Luce house, where Beth and Vail were born, and where the three of them played as children. . . . Out toward the blue sea lay the hill with its temple, and all around me were the gardens where the Luce children had grown up—and even as at Wei Hsien, I felt what the early life of a missionary family must have been like.

Then to Chefoo, where Luce had both loved and hated his British schoolmasters:

> Harry's pleasure was boundless as he took me through the old buildings, showed me where he had slept, studied, and where his name was inscribed on the Prelim Oxford examination Honors Roll in 1910.

They met the present headmaster, dined with the faculty, then visited the Chefoo mission, where Luce was surrounded by interested people:

> . . . Harry became the answer box for countless questions. For more than an hour Harry talked on present political conditions to the delight and close attention of the people. Time's future success will certainly be in large part assignable to this man's leadership and insatiable absorptive ability. It is fantastic to watch in operation!

Then on to Tsingtao, where they stayed at the luxurious Grand Hotel on the Bund, rented a Graham-Paige car for sightseeing, but also bought bathing suits and actually relaxed when they were not visiting the Presbyterian mission, climbing 3500-foot Lao Ting or nearby Lao Shan, inspecting the old German fortifications, or dancing at the Pavilion. They drove to Iltus Huk, "and again I reveled in Luce history as Harry pointed out the old summer house and other landmarks." Luce was in euphoria, writing, "it has been an absolute knock-out fine trip," and adding:

> You've never seen an ocean, you've never seen a beach until you've seen the Strand and Iltus Huk. And it's got hills and mountains and woods and forests—

everything! Such a satisfaction to know that all these years I haven't been harboring a false illusion of the charms of first-love.

He also read the newspapers, including the stock quotations, commenting, "I learn that Steel on Wednesday was 24. Good Lord! Isn't that damned depression over yet?"

On June 30 they took a coastal steamer to Dairen (which city was quarantined for cholera) and saw the sights hurriedly at Port Arthur before catching their train for Harbin. Manchuria had become Manchukuo, and Japanese soldiers were on the train. When they reached Harbin, Luce was as curious as ever:

> At that late hour of 10:30 Harry and I went to the Harbin Yacht Club. Very fashionably dressed crowd. . . . There was a good Salome dancer. From there we moved on to the Fantasie Cabaret. Many Japanese military men there with Geishas. Not many whites. The Russian girls had very little dancing to do. . . . Harry danced three times; I none. To bed at 1:30 A.M.

3. INTO ENEMY COUNTRY

Luce's introduction to Russia in 1932 was almost as malign as Napoleon's in 1812. During their five weeks in China, he and Severinghaus had occasionally endured horrendous food, dirty accommodations and evil smells, but that had been transitory, always lightened by the certainty that at the next stop they would be in luxury. There had been freedom of movement, constant change, anticipation, nostalgia, the pleasure of meeting old friends. On the Trans-Siberian Railway, however, they would be trapped for six days and six nights— 144 hours of imprisonment, no change, no friends, no abalone and pigeon eggs, no cabarets. For Luce especially, with his genuine need to work off tensions, the durance was vile. Both men felt the effects of eight grueling weeks away from home. Both came down with miserable head colds. Their physical and mental conditioning for this Russian ordeal was inauspicious.

Ironically, it was July 4, Independence Day, when the two men changed from the Chinese Eastern to the Trans-Siberian at Manchuli and were in enemy country. Euphoria was over. Since 1928 Russia had been regarded as safe enough so that cautious Thomas Cook & Son would handle arrangements for travelers, but the long Manchuli-Moscow trek was nothing like the Paris-Venice spin on the Orient Express. The Trans-Siberian had a wood-burning locomotive and an all-woman crew. It made about twenty-five miles per hour, with frequent stops to fuel at wood piles along the way. At Manchuli, Soviet customs men were "remarkably decent" but the amenities dwindled as they rolled westward.

Since there were only fourteen first-class passengers on the deluxe train, and Luce had an almost maidenly concern for his privacy, he and Severing-

haus took separate double compartments. In the small hours of the first night, however, a stop was made at Chita, a crowd of passengers came aboard, there was a banging at Luce's door and after a flood of exotic language he discovered that a Siberian gentleman was to share his room. Although the room was large and the beds screened from each other, he wrote bitterly in the report he kept of the journey:

> [The Russians] have an atrocious body-odor. It is not merely a pungent sort of barnyard odor. It is a decayed odor. It is everywhere the same. The nearest one could come to a definition was: the odor of rotten eggs in a damp cellar.

Severinghaus did not find the odor necessarily linked with any one nationality. He had drawn a young Greek mechanical engineer as his berthmate, but he noted, "My companion smelled so strongly that I got up at 4:30 A.M. and stayed out of the compartment the rest of the night." By morning the train that had been half empty was packed. First-class accommodations meant little, for peasants were herded into the Wagon-Lits. Some were barefooted, all bearded, and all seemed to be sweating in the increasing warmth. "By noon," Luce wrote, "the entire train stank." Severinghaus conferred with him and found him ready to take a calculated risk:

> Harry won't double up with me. He hopes to be given the compartment alone after Irkutsk. Therefore I am deserting my man and doubling up with Mr. Weber, a delightful German of 50. I don't care to ride all the way to Moscow with these people. If one could talk with them, learn something from them, it would be different, but all we can do is smile and smell!

Luce's risk became even more than calculated next day when his male companion got off:

> Well, well! Harry has drawn a new sleeping companion, a Russian woman, and I'm glad I moved in with Mr. Weber. Otherwise I should have had as bedroom mate a 25-year-old mother and her 5-year-old son. She is above average height, and wears a flaring red-silk dress. I'm better off where I am. Harry is welcome to enjoy her company and to share the bathroom with that little tot who goes wee in the washbasin.

Luce, always uneasy with strangers, ignored his roommates entirely. He wrote, "It [the car] continued to stink with that identical stink . . ." He lost the ephedrine that had given him some relief from his cold. Though they passed a train loaded with traitorous Ford tractors, poverty was evident at every stop, the diarist noting:

> Platform crowded with the most dreadful people imaginable. Mongols in all their filth, bearded Russian peasants, Jews from southeastern Europe. Men sleeping on the wet dirt platform, frequently women holding year-old babies in bundles of rags . . . Barefooted women sticking their toes in the mud puddles between the ties of the tracks; fur-lined hats, bandanna scarves, felt boots . . . no shoes at all, flies, dirt, dull expressions, and so on.

The dozen-odd English-speaking passengers clung together, but a few days out of Manchuli "Everybody on the train is getting somewhat on everybody else's nerves." Luce argued heatedly with Frau Ullstein, a German woman who had the nerve to criticize American capitalism. He joined a foursome to play auction bridge to pass the time, darting out at station stops to look around. The food, poor from the start, got worse, and the food on sale in station buffets was worse yet.

At Omsk they glimpsed an English-language Moscow paper with historic news: Franklin Delano Roosevelt was the Democratic nominee for President of the United States.

Alighting at Moscow at long last on July 10, they were met by a chauffeur-driven Lincoln supplied by Intourist and a pretty Russian guide, Miss Vasilieva, who spoke excellent English. Despite Luce's protestations that he had been promised rooms at the Metropol Hotel (where Rasputin had held his orgies), they were taken to the older National, where the plumbing was balky and "the main feature of the hotel is its slow service."

During their five days in Moscow, Miss Vasilieva escorted them on tours which avoided Soviet failures and stressed the triumphs. Luce conferred with American engineers and many news correspondents as well as editors of Izvestia and the Moscow Daily News, but evidently felt it impossible or useless to follow his usual custom of interviewing government officials. Every spare minute was filled with such things as a close inspection of St. Basil's, the Museum of the Revolution, a view of Lenin's tomb that showed him "looking as fresh as though he had died last week," a brisk walk completely around the Kremlin exterior, and a performance of a light opera based on a Gogol comedy, of which Severinghaus wrote, "The production was most excellent, but the air was so foul from body odors that we left after the first two acts."

They escaped Moscow on the fifteenth. Meanwhile, according to plan, Lila Luce, the two boys and old Mrs. Luce had arrived capitalistically in Paris with a maid, a chauffeur and the huge Luce Chrysler. Lila's voice was in shreds from her shouted efforts to make her mother-in-law hear. Leaving Mrs. Luce and Peter Paul in Paris with the maid, Lila and the seven-year-old Henry were driven to Vienna.

Luce had left his train at Warsaw. While Severinghaus rode on to meet the group in Paris, Luce went by train to Vienna and was met there by his wife and older son. He had brought mandarin coats and other gifts for them all, and was terribly glad to see them. They were driven back to Paris, where Severinghaus took over the Chrysler and drove old Mrs. Luce and young Henry through England while Luce, Lila and Peter Paul sailed for New York.

4. THE LUCE REPORTS

As guidance for his editors, Luce composed a joyful 1200-word report on China and a merciless 3000 words on the Soviet Union, the latter dubbed by

wiseacres in New York the Olfactory Lesson. Filled with shrewd comment, they also showed his tendency to simplify complex phenomena and his journalist's awareness of readers' confusions. Chiang was a name in the news which Luce as propagandist wanted to grow bigger. But to Americans, China had such a bewildering array of Chings, Changs, Chiangs and Chongs that a nickname was needed to permit the instant identification that Luce wanted. He observed that some of the Chinese believed Chiang Kai-shek to be the reincarnation of a great sea-beast. Even though the iguana hardly filled the specifications, he suggested, "I think we could nickname Chiang 'Iguana.' " °
As for Russia:

> First of all, I was amazed to find that Russia is, as advertised, 100% proletarian in appearance. . . . Of course there are no well-dressed people—but what astounded me was that there are no *neatly* dressed people. ["People on the streets are neatly dressed but obviously poor," Severinghaus had noted in Moscow.] They are all sloppy and boorish. Even in Siberia and the Urals, the peasants are sloppy; they are not neat and picturesque like the peasants you see next door in Poland, Czechoslovakia and Austria. And you don't see any "good manners" anywhere. If there were such things as peas in Russia (which I doubt) you are sure that everyone would eat them with their knives—except that they would be in such a hurry to bolt them down that they would probably lap them out of the dish with their tongues, dog-fashion.
>
> Thus it becomes apparent that your correspondent took a violent dislike to U.S.S.R. I think it is a thoroughly disgusting place.

He saw the Russians as an inferior polyglot of races sandwiched between the cultivated Chinese and the cultivated West, lacking in Christianity and civilization:

> . . . one reason why Russia is definitely neither Oriental nor Occidental is that it has never developed an indigenous civilization. It has contained whirlpools of Central Asiatic nomads but out of these nomads it never developed that delicately balanced equilibrium of law and custom and *style* which we call civilization. What little civilization it got, it got from the West. In so far as Russia is civilized, it is Occidental. . . . There is a Western civilization and there is an Eastern. But there is no Russian and Russia is neither.

He seemed unduly severe toward the land of Turgenev and Tolstoi. In setting for his editors the new line to be taken on Russia, he wrote:

> The most important specific fact which Fortune's story omitted was that the Russians, one and all, stink. . . . I really think that article was a great performance. . . . But I do think that it omitted the stink and the sourness of Russia— so these notes have been written on the assumption that you are all familiar with Fortune's article and will use these notes simply as slight correctives of the focus.

° The problem of Chiang's nickname was solved by calling him the Generalissimo, or Gimo.

Luce's last paragraphs suggested that the Russian-Polish border was more than an imaginary line:

> We came from Moscow to the border in the same kind of swank but stinky and dirty Russian Wagon-Lits. Looking out the window, the countryside seemed very drab—only half the land was cultivated and the rest was scraggly bushes laden with dust. We got off the train and spent a busy hour in the customs trying to get something to eat. Then we went out the other side of the station, and again mounted a train, which soon pulled out. It was a beautiful sunny day. The windows were wide and opened. For a few minutes I seemed dazed. Where was the dust that should have come pouring in the windows? It just wasn't. We arranged ourselves and looked about. It seemed to be the most beautiful railroad car in the world. Clean, glistening, all-steel, immaculate. A waiter came running up, bowed. Would we have some ice cream and cake? A few minutes later I sat, content, looking out the window. My God! Where were we? In England? In France? Look at the velvety fields, all neat in their patterns of green and gold. The perfectly cylindrical haystacks. The cows! More cows! Milk from contented cows! And people—girls waving at us gaily. And two buxom hausfraus positively stylish in black dresses trimmed with white lace, each under a parasol. And still the fields and a great abundance of dustless air. Paradise! . . . Never in all my tens of thousands of miles of travel has a border seemed to signify so much.

There seemed a lack of compassion for people, for the millions of Slavs who had thrown off the oppression of the czars only to find themselves under a new oppression. The Time approbatives, which had been used up on China, had been replaced here by the pejoratives: *sloppy, boorish, dirty, unpleasant, atrocious, rotten.* An Intourist representative was *nauseatingly cheerful.* The word *odor* as applied to the body appeared four times, and variants of *stink* seven times. Time-Fortune editors were cautioned not to forget the Russian *stink.* (Luce himself talked of it all his life, with various changes in the definition of the Russian smell, among them that it was like sour and decayed dishrags.) In the Timestyle use of pejorative wisecracks, the Soviet leaders were described as having *a passion for inequality,* and the economic situation was *the best-managed famine in history.*

His unanimity of loathing had its amusing side in its revelation of long prejudice exacerbated by weariness, discomfort and irritation. This, one would say, would disappear when the annoyance faded and Luce recovered his balance. But it never did disappear. The loathing was fixed and would be lifelong.

Luce never visited Russia again, although he would skirt its edges. His twelve-day stay in 1932, closing his mind with a sharp final click, was historic. His loathing became the foundation of policy of America's most powerful opinion-maker for the thirty-five years he had yet to live and to propagate opinion.

X

1. THE GOSPEL OF SUCCESS

Luce's impulses still swung toward moderacy often enough so that he could not be ideologically pigeonholed. He took a strong, if academic, interest in Negroes and was as opposed to lynching as Coolidge had been to sin. Time ran a sympathetic cover story on the Socialist Norman Thomas. While it was true that Thomas possessed qualifications inclined to mitigate Luce's suspicions of any doubter of the profit system—he was an Ivy Leaguer, an ordained Presbyterian clergyman, an anti-Communist, an intellectual aristocrat and a perfect gentleman at the head of a party fated to run last and therefore no threat—occasionally Luce could show resistance to the royalists he admired. The Matson Line exerted pressure but failed to keep Fortune from referring to its proud but pitchy liner *Malolo* by her nickname among travelers, "Maloler the Roller." This integrity was said to have cost Luce a possible $50,000 in advertising, but he was believed to be aware that it made his editors stand up and cheer him.

Fortune won "muckraking" fame with no apparent advertising loss with its exposure of the munitions industry, "Arms and the Men." It whacked hard at European arms magnates and mentioned those in America as an afterthought, the du Ponts (one of whom was a Luce classmate) being given an innocuous paragraph. While Time's line hardened, the lordly but liberal Ralph McAllister Ingersoll, recently imported from the New Yorker to head up Fortune, was able to open that magazine to diverse points of view. MacLeish wrote one article criticizing President Hoover and another in praise of Franklin Roosevelt without complaint from Luce, who was so susceptible to ideas simply as ideas that occasionally even a liberal slant could be urged on him if promoted with ingenuity.

Luce's remarkable accommodation of religion, business and politics was a

104

factor that kept him from easy classification. The core of the logic of his whole career, it gave him the extra advantage of heavenly cooperation.

He heartily subscribed to Calvinism's wonderful secularity, its teaching that "the man of God should be a braver warrior, a more enlightened ruler, a more skillful and industrious artisan, and a more successful tradesman because of the divine favor and appointment." Hence, the man of God should be a successful man, whatever his undertakings. Luce made free enterprise and worldly success into a religious creed. The good man was a successful man. In his belief in the Protestant ethic of hard work, success and goodness, he subscribed to the spirit if not the language of Billy Sunday: "Jesus could go some; Jesus Christ could go like a six-cylinder engine . . ." His advertising-tycoon friend Bruce Barton had already written *The Man Nobody Knows*, illustrating the pragmatic effectiveness of religion, in which he said that Jesus "picked up 12 men from the bottom ranks of business and forged them into an organization that conquered the world." Rev. Emmet Fox urged, "Conduct the affairs of your soul in a businesslike way." Rev. Norman Vincent Peale exhorted, "Learn to pray correctly, scientifically. Employ tested and proven methods," and promised that one who followed these rules could attain fabulous capacities: "There is enough power in *you* to blow the city of New York to rubble."

If the good man was a success, it followed that the unsuccessful were not good. The failure was a failure because he ignored the infallible law of hard work and success. The strength with which Luce held these convictions heightened his elitist admiration for the powerful and successful and reduced the common people, the masses, to relative inconsequentiality. Now and then throughout his life he came upon a book which overcame him with what seemed universal truth. In 1932 he encountered José Ortega y Gasset's *Revolt of the Masses*, which so affected him that he quoted it in speeches and conversations for years. Ortega pictured the traditional educated national leader as a man of morality, "which is always an essence, a sentiment of submission to something, a consciousness of service and obligation"—a definition that perhaps fitted Luce's conception of his own role. Ortega's book was a somber warning of the decline of such qualified leaders and the emergence to power of a rabble such as Luce felt he had seen in Russia:

> *The characteristic of the hour is that the commonplace mind, knowing itself to be commonplace, has the assurance to proclaim the rights of the commonplace and to impose them wherever it will. . . . The mass crushes beneath it everything that is different, everything that is excellent, individual, qualified and select. . . . Here we have the formidable fact of our times, described without any concealment of the brutality of its features.*

To similar basic beliefs, Luce added the astonishing selection of businessmen as those specially qualified by American life to lead and to assume the role of the "moral and intellectual elite." In his Chicago speech two years be-

fore he read Ortega he had urged an aristocracy of business, had chided the "best young men" for failing to assume leadership and had derided the notion that aristocracy was an un-American concept. Fortune indeed was a magazine dedicated to business aristocracy. He saw America drifting into a political apathy in which the "best people" refused to exert their power, with the danger that the "worst people" would move in. He voted for Hoover in 1932—"business" meaning Republicanism—and yet was willing to give the victorious Roosevelt (hardly a representative of the rabble) a chance to solve the nation's problems. His friendship with MacLeish was closer than most, and MacLeish knew Roosevelt. Luce gladly accepted MacLeish's suggestion that they visit Roosevelt not long after he was inaugurated.

Luce, in one of his fits of thrift, got a double room at the Carlton Hotel instead of private rooms as they awaited the call of Miss Le Hand to say that the President would see them. Waiting for someone was anguish for him. "I was afraid Harry would go crazy," MacLeish recalled, "waiting and pacing the floor." When Roosevelt did see them he was at his magnetic best, smiling, friendly, brilliant in conversation, exercising all the confident attractions of a personality richly endowed with charm.

"My God!" Luce said as they left the White House. "What a man!"

It was the instant reaction of the hero-worshiper, this one fated to be short-lived. Meanwhile the Luces moved to a splendid apartment at 4 East 72nd Street, across Fifth Avenue from Central Park. To their staff of servants were added two uniformed footmen, at a time when some Americans actually starved. Luce was so insulated from the other half that it took him some time to realize that the depression not only reduced business profits but afflicted many non-readers of Time and Fortune with real privation. He was less inclined to view this as a human tragedy than as a political and economic fact that had to be faced. His own vast success in the face of the slump was an argument in itself. As one of his colleagues put it, "Harry had no patience with the poor slob who couldn't make it."

This seemed implicit in a speech he made before the Chamber of Commerce in his father's hometown, Scranton. (On the back of the program was a motto Hadden would have loved: "If your town is worth boosting, boost it and boost it right. IT PAYS!") Luce argued that conservatives would be wise to embrace two principles that they were accustomed to reject out of hand: "The first is that a livelihood must be guaranteed to every man. . . . The second . . . is that there must be a dwelling for every man, woman and child and that it must conform to some minimum standard of decency."

For Luce these were progressive and humanitarian proposals even if the New Deal had already proclaimed them. He followed them with a third principle, that the "superior man" must be enabled to rise. And his disdain for the great mass of the non-superior, those who had to be guaranteed employment and homes, was outspoken: "Our first two principles concerned themselves with everyman—with the vulgar, the moronic, the unpleasant specimens of

humanity and those who are as poor in spirit as in purse, but whom for some reason beyond our comprehending, Jesus blessed."

2. *THE MILITANT GODLESS*

Time showed its disgruntlement at the American recognition of the U.S.S.R., which had long since been recognized by other major powers including Italy and Germany. It meant that Luce's effort to isolate the Soviets had lost both in the economic and political spheres. Time observed that recognition was not a case of yielding to Soviet pressure but that President Roosevelt had "taken the initiative," repeating the following week (for the third time) that "it was not Russia but the U.S. which took the initiative in proposing recognition." Although the move was inevitable, supported by businessmen and virtually all factions except for the American Legion, Time hatched pejoratives. It described Maxim Litvinov as the "shrewd, sly Foreign Commissar of the U.S.S.R." who arrived in America "baring his canine teeth in a merry grin" over the coup. Under the heading "Opium for the People," Time described Litvinov as "Jewish but an Atheist," described Soviet tactics in discouraging religion, and said that Litvinov's guarantee that the Russians would not try to overthrow the United States government could not be taken seriously:

> Just as President Roosevelt and Comrade Litvinoff were fraternizing last week . . . the Soviet War Council at Moscow, with blazing indiscretion, issued Order No. 173.
>
> Abrupt and militant, it knocked into a Red soldier's turnip-shaped helmet the soothing assertions by Soviet publicists in recent weeks that Russia's leaders have abandoned the objective of her late, great Dictator Nikolai Lenin: to foment "the World Revolution of the Proletariat" by every practicable means including, when advisable, intervention by the Red Army.
>
> Order No. 173 is specific. It instructs every Red Army commander "to train each Red Soldier to be devoted in heart and in soul to the World Revolution of the Proletariat."

Time disclosed how the Soviet would evade its agreement not to attempt the overthrow:

> . . . M. Litvinoff promised that "it will be the fixed policy of the *Government*" of Russia (he could not promise for the *Party* headed by Josef Stalin) to "refrain" in the most scrupulous manner from any interference in U.S. affairs . . .

Although Roosevelt's designee as the first American ambassador to Soviet Russia was a Yale graduate ('12), William C. Bullitt, Time showed him as atypical:

> When smug Philadelphia friends called him a "Bolshevik" and when his first wife divorced him in 1923, Bill Bullitt married the widow of John Reed, the U.S.

107

Communist . . . The new Mrs. Bullitt, an out-and-out Red, appeared in Philadelphia in Russian costumes complete with high boots. . . . In Episcopal Church House, Philadelphia, last week Archdeacon the Rev. James F. Bullitt, uncle of the new Ambassador, flared: "The United States has disgraced itself by establishing relations with a country which is beyond the pale—a pariah among nations!"

The Soviet effort to export Communism to the United States proved to be small in scale but was as unacceptable as the American effort to export Christianity to China with the aid of gunboats. Luce probably never forgave Roosevelt for recognizing Russia, nor did he feel kindly toward American capitalists anxious to do business with the Antichrist. He had clearly lost a battle, but the war went on.

In 1933 Laird Goldsborough endeared himself to Luce with a double coup. He managed an interview with the newly emergent Hitler, then moved on to Rome and talked with Mussolini as part of a study of Italy that filled the entire July 1934 issue of Fortune.

Luce's long interest in Italian Fascism culminated naturally in his decision to devote a whole thick issue to it. In importance it deserved this extensive treatment along with a balance in view which unhappily it did not get. Although Fortune's preamble stoutly asserted a bias against Fascism, the overwhelming tone of the thirteen chapters was one of admiration for its objectives, its discipline, its success, and for the charisma and achievements of its founder. The grandeur and glory surrounding the "amazing" and "brilliant" Duce and his Blackshirt lieutenants was in contrast with Fortune's earlier treatment of Stalin and the Communist hierarchy. What had been "implacable purpose" in Russia was "patriotic dedication" in Italy. There was no mention of rats and bedbugs, no suggestion that recognition of Italy, or trade with Italy, was objectionable. And unlike the barbarous Russian peasants and workers, Fortune found the Italians a once noble race reclaimed to their ancient greatness by the discipline of Fascism:

> Other nations falter or reel hysterically in search of unity. Italy is calm and united under the emblem of common strength and effort which is Fascism. . . . With uplifted hearts and Augustan pride the wops are unwopping themselves.

Mussolini not only made the trains run on time. He made them run faster. He built sleek new ocean liners, drained marshes, eradicated slums, created a vast new air force and radiated such *élan* that the Italians were "fired by the excitement of his purpose . . ." Mussolini's success was so contagious that "Fascism has all but conquered half of Europe and part of Asia . . ." The secret police and Fascist terror were soft-pedaled, although Fortune agreed in careful language that there was a question of loss of freedom which might puzzle and dismay Americans:

> We know that the Italian people have no choice but to support the State and we thereupon think that by this fact the Italian people are enjoined from the

full expression of life, liberty, and the pursuit of happiness, and that they *ought* to resent it even if they don't. This is a confusion, and we can only get over it if we anesthetize for a moment our ingrained idea that democracy is the only right and just conception of government.

Fortune's anesthetic dulled this democratic confusion enough so that the average reader was left with admiration for so enlightened a dictator whose achievements rescued a decaying nation and lifted its once despairing people to pride and purpose. It urged the American to recognize in Fascism "certain ancient virtues of the race, whether or not they happen to be momentarily fashionable in his own country. Among these are Discipline, Duty, Courage, Glory, Sacrifice."

As Luce told the Scrantonians, "The moral force of Fascism, appearing in totally different forms in different nations, may be the inspiration for the next general march of mankind." Anyone who heard Luce's speeches, read his Fortune piece on Pittsburgh, Time's foreign news and Fortune's articles on Russia and on Italy could scarcely mistake the direction of his political thinking.

3. NOT REALLY MATURE

Occasionally Luce would take Martin, Billings and other top editors to lunch at the Cloud Club, high in the Chrysler Building's chromium spire, where he would go over the previous issue with them. "He had a talent for distributing praise and blame," Billings noted, "especially blame. He was often after me because he found National Affairs dull and undramatic. Once I wrote something about the sailing of the *Ile de France*, and Luce said afterward he never once heard the ship's great whistle blow. He was a great one for stirring up ideas and whopping writers out of their routine."

Indeed he sprouted ideas, many of them brilliant. He called in an aide and described what he wanted at the Chicago Century of Progress Exposition: "Just a simple building with a huge representation of Time at one end and Fortune at the other. Inside, comfortable chairs for all those tired people with sore feet—and plenty of Times and Fortunes for them to read while they rest." It was a hit.

Although the company's 1932 profits ($650,000 after taxes) had represented a slight decrease from the previous year, Time Inc. was in solid shape in a parlous time. Most employers were cutting salaries and laying off people not provably essential. Luce pointed out in a memorandum that it would be the "logical thing" to cut all salaries 10 to 20 percent and argued that his decision to hold the line amounted to a salary rise. In return he expected a better magazine because "you and I know that Time can be improved."

Luce told his wife they were lucky in having a rising income at this time of

general decline. Lila, the most agreeable of people, approved of the income but not of his immersion in work at the expense of family life. His preoccupation could blot out what was going on around him. At the office, he would ring for his new secretary, Miss Corinne Thrasher, because he could find no matches to light his cigarette although several matchbooks were under his nose. She finally solved the problem by rearranging his desk so that one drawer was filled with matches. He hated to take time for a haircut. He disliked putting money in his wallet, with the result that when he pulled out his handkerchief, loose currency and change often fell to the floor. Or he forgot money entirely and sponged on his colleagues. He kept losing rubbers, gloves, hats and coats in taxis and restaurants. He forgot that people were waiting to see him. Once, young C. D. Jackson, the charming Princetonian who would rise high in the Time empire, waited to consult him. Miss Thrasher finally reminded Luce that Jackson had been waiting forty-five minutes.

"Any man who'll wait that long," Luce snapped, "is no damned good."

One day Miss Thrasher received a call from Mrs. Luce, who had just had word from a worried valet. "Would you see," she asked, "if Mr. Luce is wearing one brown shoe and one black?"

He was, and a shoe was sent over from the apartment.

The repeal of Prohibition caused a long debate between Luce and his father, who now taught at the Kennedy School of Missions in Hartford but often visited New York with his wife. Dr. Luce, who could talk endlessly and even fatiguingly about his beloved China, had three bugbears: Catholicism, the Japanese and liquor. Liquor, he said, was evil and his son should refuse to advertise it. But Luce was heartily sick of the evasions and illegalities of the Volstead era, and enjoyed a dram himself. Also, he had the stockholders to worry about and it went against the grain to turn away perfectly good money. As soon as the law allowed, Time and Fortune bloomed with advertisements in color that pained Rev. Henry Luce—Golden Wedding, Canadian Club, John Jameson, Dixie Belle.

The debates about it continued by mail when the father was out of town. After all his ailments and travels, Dr. Luce still enjoyed visiting Europe in the summer for religious gatherings or simply for sightseeing and calling on acquaintances of the cloth. Getting off the ship on his return, he would be so far from exhaustion as to hail a taxi and head for the Time offices, call on Foreign News Editor Goldsborough and tell him what he had learned abroad. Like many clergymen, he liked the optimism-dripping Reader's Digest, owned by a pair of solid Presbyterians, DeWitt Wallace and his wife. "In its field," Rev. Luce said, "the Digest helps as much as Time does in its field."

Indeed the Digest was emerging contemporaneously with Time as a propagandist magazine gaining great influence and profit in the face of general business invalidism. Any student of American attitudes from this time on who did not take into account these publications would be ignoring two powerful forces in shaping public opinion. Although Time was more skillfully written

and appealed to a more sophisticated audience, and the Reader's Digest was a purveyor of mass culture along with its rightward slant, the two were complementary and had more similarities than differences. Both were owned and actively controlled by religious people of evangelical inclination. (Both Wallace and his wife were the children of Presbyterian ministers.) Both magazines were marred by factual errors, exaggerations and inventions which did not trouble the proprietors because they were interested in successful journalism and politico-moral messages rather than mere information. Both were not above deception, Time in purporting to be a newsmagazine, RD in claiming to be a digest of other magazines when in fact it quietly "planted" pieces of its own manufacture in other publications in order to go through the rigmarole of buying them back and "digesting" them.

Since they catered to the intellectual laziness of people seeking quick and easy wisdom rather than informed discussion, the two magazines were simplistic. Each stressed in its own way an insular concept of patriotism coupled with hostility toward the New Deal, hatred of Communism and some flirtation with Fascism. Together the two magazines influenced an enormous audience, the Digest corralling readers in the lower spectrum of intellectual vigor. As John Bainbridge observed in a later study of the Digest, its editors had a "perfect understanding of the herd mind." Harold Laski in his own appraisal of the Digest decided that its "pemmicanized" summaries were for the "tired business man who has almost forgotten how to read."

Turning to Luce, Laski described him as "a phenomenon of importance" whose importance was baneful: ". . . he has never become really mature; there is a sophomoric streak in him which makes him identify notoriety with success, power with greatness . . . He is shrewd, in the sense that a speculator on the Stock Exchange is shrewd. He has the American notion that, at some point, the by-product of bigness is grandeur. . . . Behind the façade it [Time] erects of hard brilliance in reporting . . . the real emphasis is always a reactionary emphasis. Most Big Business men always emerge in heroic proportions. . . . No opportunity is missed of attacking Russia. . . . Time makes it possible for [average Americans] to talk . . . it puts into phrases that they like the thoughts they are seeking to shape. It makes the news more vivid by colouring its contents as the readers would wish to see it coloured. And the readers are grateful for the labels of identification which enable them to know just who are their friends. They like the brief glimpse they get, as through a half-shut door, of science and art, of the latest radio gadget, and the real inside story of the Communists in China."

With Lila doing the looking, the Luces at last found their "estatelette"— five hundred acres with a splendid view near Gladstone, New Jersey, forty miles west of the Chrysler Building. Its fine Revolutionary house, remodeled, with twelve rooms and five baths, would shelter them until they could build the stone mansion they planned, though Luce was fated never to occupy it. He was happy about the herd of eighty Holsteins and Jerseys, cared for by

hired men, which fulfilled his dream of a working farm. It was an excellent place for the two boys and for Lila, who delighted in sunshine, flowers and all the rural beauties. They kept the 72nd Street apartment for city use.

Before her marriage, Lila's trips to Europe had been as periodic as springtime. Since then, what with the several miscarriages she had suffered and Luce's preoccupation with business, he had taken her only on the post-honeymoon tour of 1927—the quick return from Vienna after his 1932 global journey hardly counted. In 1934 he made amends by taking Lila and Henry to England to buy antique furniture for the proposed house and to "look around."

This time Luce did most of the looking around while Lila did the antique-buying. Among those he called on was undersized Lord Beaverbrook, the former William Maxwell Aitken, son of a Canadian Presbyterian preacher who fought his way to wealth by age thirty and now owned the money-making London Daily Express. Cynical, exhibitionistic, a woman-chaser, often a journalistic charlatan, a Presbyterian matchless in backsliding, Beaverbrook might have been expected to repel the American. On the contrary he fascinated Luce, who cultivated the friendship at every later opportunity throughout Beaverbrook's life. It was an instance of a trait that would intrigue Luce-watchers: his occasional tendency to strike up friendships with flouters of approved bourgeois morality. Some of his colleagues theorized that for one thing Luce had an ingenuous respect for titles, and for another that his inordinate concern with power fired his interest in those who had won power even by methods not of the manse. He was studying in the flesh the acquisition and use of power.

"Of course my papers are primarily for propaganda," Beaverbrook told him—a remark not inclined to make Luce repent his own course. There was at any rate a winning frankness about the grinning little man whose wife towered above him. The frankness was present also in his theology. A firm predestinarian, he believed that he was damned and "acted on the belief," praising God but enjoying his own exemption from righteousness. Luce found him a "really able, bright and lively fellow."

His 3000-word report of his observations in England, written for the instruction of his editors, was chatty but not without insights. He found the English popular press (as distinguished from its serious papers) "sheer unadulterated DRIVEL." Its lower and middle classes he thought inferior intellectually to America's, whereas "England's Upper Class beats ours hollow." He felt that England was slipping, living on her capital, and saw the increase in homosexuality as one symptom of decay. The Fascist leader Sir Oswald Mosley impressed him as "an able man, intelligent and a good speaker," but "Fascism is more un-English than it is un-anything else. I would back the U.S. to go a variety of Fascist long before England." He seemed to think that Fascism might be useful with a little tinkering. Although his report concerned England alone, it seemed odd that he made only an offhand one-sentence mention

of Hitler's infamous blood purge, which occurred while he was in London. He regretted that its monopolization of British newspaper space interfered with his scrutiny of England: "Unfortunately, at the end of the week, the Hitler assassinations broke the calm and so for the rest of my stay the press was reflecting not England but Germany"—a remark which, coming from a newsman, seemed like blaming a murder next door for interrupting one's knitting.

Presumably the press also reflected England's reaction to this world-shaking news, but he did not go into this. He did attend a dinner given by Victor Cazalet, a friend from Oxford days now a Member of Parliament, and there met the Prince of Wales who, he was delighted to discover, read both Time and Fortune.

XI

1. MEET ME AT THE COMMODORE

On the morning of December 7, 1934, Archibald MacLeish was at work in his office on the forty-second floor of the Chrysler Building when Luce telephoned to ask if he could see him. "I'll come down," MacLeish said.

There was a long silence. "Harry sometimes had telephone silences," MacLeish said later, "as if it were a remainder of his stammer." Then Luce said, "No, don't come to my office. Meet me at the Commodore. I'll be in the ballroom off the mezzanine."

The hotel was, and is, a scant block away. When MacLeish reached the semi-dark ballroom, redolent of stale cigar smoke, Luce was already seated in a corner. There was a stunned expression on his face. He told MacLeish that he had fallen in love with a divorcée.

There were few who knew Luce on his own terms—none who shared his private world. Not even MacLeish did, but his possession of all the mystic college-club-and-key qualifications to which Luce was so loyal, and his qualities of intelligence, candor and understanding, brought him closer than most. This still held although his disillusionment with Luce had begun. If the poet with the active social conscience felt that the Miracle Editor was being corrupted by success, he could not forget his generosity. Nor was he unaware that the secretive Luce paid him the greatest possible compliment by choosing him as his confidant in this shattering crisis in his life.

"Harry was shaken, overwhelmed, infatuated," MacLeish recalled. Smoking nervously, he told how he had met Mrs. Clare Boothe Brokaw the night before at the Waldorf-Astoria Hotel's Starlight Roof. It was not their first meeting but still only about their third, spread over many months. He had told her he meant to marry her. She had laughed, but of course he was serious, always serious. MacLeish listened sympathetically.

114

At thirty-one Mrs. Brokaw had already made a blonde trajectory across the social and literary firmament. Born in New York City on April 10, 1903, she had overcome childhood insecurity and a patchwork education by dint of her singular combination of brains, beauty and a third quality that was often a subject of dispute, her friends describing it as determination and her enemies as effrontery. Her late father, William F. Boothe, a Baptist and a professional violinist, was a poor provider. He traveled erratically to meet orchestral engagements and once raised enough capital to invest in a profitable soft-drink bottling plant. His daughter, whose childhood was spent in brief stays in Racine, Des Moines, Memphis and other towns, was fond of him but later disposed of his business ability in this venture with one of her witticisms: "He sold it to buy a piano factory just as the talking machine was perfected."

Her mother, a former chorus girl and a beauty, very ambitious, was abandoned by her husband when Clare was ten. Through friends of the theater, she landed Clare as a child actress, her most important engagement being with Ernest Truex in *The Dummy*. Her impulsive mother, on the strength of small stock winnings made on a tip given by an admirer, then took her to Paris for an intended year of "culture" that lasted only a few months because of the outbreak of war. On their return Clare had attended the Episcopal private school of St. Mary's in Garden City, Long Island, where she was lonely and was named "most conceited" in the classbook; then a happier interlude at the progressive Castle School in Tarrytown, where she did well scholastically and became a good swimmer. But she had been cautioned at Castle about her "egotism, lack of sympathy, or 'coldness.'" With characteristic determination she had written in her diary, "I promised myself to try to improve," and added, apparently as part of her improvement, "I am to have a very serious *affaire de coeur.*"

Her formal schooling ended when she was sixteen. Money worries were over, however, when her mother married a physician, Albert E. Austin of Greenwich, Connecticut. The doctor took his new family to Europe in 1922, and on the return trip Clare met and impressed that doughty suffragette grande dame, Mrs. O. H. P. Belmont. She became Mrs. Belmont's secretary, a job that carried her into society as well as feminist politics, a movement that would engage her lifelong attention. Three months after joining forces with Mrs. Belmont she met the forty-three-year-old bachelor George Tuttle Brokaw, millionaire heir to a clothing fortune. Although she had reservations about Brokaw, her mother and stepfather thought it an excellent match and she married him when she was twenty. After a honeymoon in Europe they divided their time between the old-fashioned Brokaw town house on Fifth Avenue and 79th Street, and Newport. Their only child, Ann Clare, was born in 1924. The marriage lasted six years—Brokaw drank heavily—and after Clare's Reno divorce, granted in 1929 on the ground of mental cruelty and giving her a trust fund of $425,000 plus $2500 a month, she took a chro-

mium-and-glass penthouse apartment on Beekman Place overlooking the East River.

Having suffered boredom in the stuffed-shirt social crowd, she sought membership in groups in which wealth did not exclude thought. She was still only twenty-seven, and with her remarkable qualifications this objective was attained with ease even if these same qualifications did not always endear her to women less brilliantly endowed. According to a later profile of her, "Her friends are familiar with her habit, at a dinner party . . . of gazing speculatively around the table and silently deciding who is worth talking to." At one dinner party she talked to that waxy-mustached connoisseur of beauty, Condé Nast, publisher of the snooty fashion magazines Vogue and Vanity Fair. She wanted a job with one of those magazines. "Drop into my office," Nast said. She did so at a time when both Nast and his top editor, Edna Woolman Chase, were away. She announced herself as a new member of the staff and got away with it. When Nast and Mrs. Chase returned, the story goes, each thought the other had hired her. She wrote captions at $35 a week. "Her status was vague," Mrs. Chase recalled, "but after a bit she began to prove herself," and added, "Clare had a good mind, although in those days she tended to be a little grand." One of her young colleagues on the magazine was Marya Mannes, as beautiful and intelligent but less inclined to grandeur. Of the two of them Mrs. Chase reported eloquently, "They did not like each other."

Mrs. Brokaw's 1930 "Hall of Fame" mention of Luce in Vanity Fair has been noted. Always a hard worker, she rose in the hierarchy and dealt with such writers as George Jean Nathan, Walter Lippmann and Robert Sherwood. Arthur Krock admired her abilities and her loyalty to friends, which underlay an exterior coolness which made him call her "La Belle Dame Sans Merci." But, reported a woman writer, "Weekly staff luncheons were held at which Mrs. Brokaw always managed to appear to be presiding. The fact that there were also present people who outranked her never disturbed this appearance." The sixty-one-year-old multimillionaire Bernard Baruch, it was said, badly wanted to marry her but was politely rejected. Her salary was $10,000 when she resigned in 1933 to become a freelance writer, using an approach (according to her censorious female profilist) different from that of most ink-stained wretches:

> She would have her secretary telephone an editor and ask him to come to cocktails . . . [H]e would feel rather pleased at being asked to one of Mrs. Brokaw's parties, which generally included only the more celebrated political, literary, and social personages. When he arrived at the apartment on the appointed day, he would find himself the only guest, and Mrs. Brokaw, after giving him a cocktail, would inform him that she had a little time on her hands and thought it might be fun to dash off some articles for his magazine.

Luce had first met her at a dinner given by the Thayer Hobsons, then again a few months later at the Countess Rose Waldeck's. His impatience was al-

ways visible when a conversation did not proceed along lines agreeable to him, and she thought him interesting but rude, especially when he kept glancing at his watch. Although considerable time elapsed between their meetings, something seemed to build up. The crisis came at the huge party at the Waldorf given by that priestess of glitter, Elsa Maxwell, to honor Cole Porter (Yale '13). Luce, walking across the room with two glasses of champagne, did not reach his wife because he encountered Mrs. Brokaw alone at a table. "Is that champagne for me?" she inquired. The lights dimmed, so he sat with her. They had champagne and talk while Ethel Merman sang "I Get a Kick Out of You," with Porter at the piano. Some time later he asked her to go with him down to the lobby because he had something important to say. In the after-midnight cavernousness of the lobby, he told her without dramatics that she was essential to his happiness.

2. A MAN BESIDE HIMSELF

Luce's total exposure to Mrs. Brokaw in three or four social meetings could hardly have been more than fifteen or twenty hours, a good deal of it in group talk. Their tête-à-tête total was much less. He was convulsing his own life, his wife and family and business, over a woman he did not really know. He had no doubts. Lila, terribly distressed, fled for a time to her widowed mother in Chicago, then took the boys to Bermuda in the spring while Luce remained at the 72nd Street apartment. The Luce family in a body disapproved of his decision. For once he was an object of familial censure rather than the clan hero. Indeed he was not without remorse, for he was and would remain deeply attached to Lila, to whom he wrote humbly:

Darlingest— (Because that word meant you and only you for so many years, let me keep it for you only —They were years, too, which in the short arc of life were, and will always be, so important to us both). . . . Someday I shall try to put in writing what I have tried to tell you these weeks—my love and, weak though the word, my deep, my very deep appreciation for all that you have been willing to go through. . . .

On her birthday he telegraphed her in Bermuda, "IF I WERE KING I WOULD GIVE YOU THE MOON FOR THIMBLE RING," and followed it with a letter in which he continued to summon his long-disused poetic idiom:

A good many years ago I undertook the responsibility of being, in a way, the gardener of your heart's estate. That responsibility, I can tell you, weighs very heavily on me now. If it seems unthinkable to you that I could "walk out" on so important an undertaking, it is also true that I cannot construct any "defense" or "justification" for an action that is so unkind. But even though I quit on the job that was so especially mine, I hope you will believe that I am deeply concerned—that I certainly can never be happy unless your garden has flowers in it.

Although she had deferred to his wishes as a great and busy man, their differences in temperament and their divergent interests had become more evident. Her love for music, art and horticulture found little echo in him, and she, with her warm interest in people in all walks of life, was not in tune with his insistent need to know more and more of the great and famous. Many of the scores of Time and Fortune editors who knew her as a charming hostess at Luce's shop-talk gatherings and one who had always remembered their anniversaries and commiserated with them in their sorrows were partial to her. As for Luce, he had become so accustomed to his corporate powers of absolute monarchy that he found legal interference with his wishes maddening. During the inevitable delays he was a man beside himself with impatience, seeing lawyers, writing letters, occasionally dashing off after Mrs. Brokaw. When she went to Miami to visit her mother, he appeared there for a two-day round of sightseeing and soul-searching. When she visited friends in Havana, he left New York again to join her there. She was of course quite wealthy in her own right. Her fertility in wit and ideas was so well known, and Luce's infatuation so evident, that some of the editors feared that she might invade their preserves. Luce at the time was considering the publication of a new magazine devoted largely to pictures, an idea that fascinated her and one which she had vainly pressed on Nast before she left his employ. In the Chrysler Building there seemed some concern that the boss might not only wind up with a new wife but with a new editor-in-charge-of-everything.

Returning to New York, she was soon off to Europe with her daughter Ann, now fourteen. One of Luce's newer executives, the suave Daniel Longwell, who had come over from the Doubleday book publishing firm, was then in Europe in behalf of the March of Time. Luce sent him on to Salzburg to carry his representations to Mrs. Brokaw, vacationing there and looking stunning in Tyrolean garb. Taking her on a scenic drive, he also gave her a message of his own. He advised her not to get involved in the magazines. The best thing she could do when she married Luce, he said, was to stay home and have lots of babies, at which she burst into tears and told him she could not have any more children.

Luce himself went to Europe in June to confer with her in carefully chaperoned meetings. Lila, her own life so rudely upset, likewise sailed for Europe to visit the friendly people and places, and for a time the three principals in the triangle were in Paris simultaneously. Luckily Time Inc. had a solid organization of able men. Editors accustomed to Luce's normal fifty- to sixty-hour work week saw him irregularly for almost a year. Billings, now managing editor of Time, noted, "I'd go weeks at a time during this domestic interlude without seeing him or hearing from him. At times I'd find him listless or blue as if he were sick . . . At other times he would be bright and driving and on his toes."

His parents were shocked. Coming after his acceptance of liquor advertisements, his break with his wife and his infatuation with a divorcée of no pro-

nounced religious affiliation whose chief associations seemed to be with fashion and the theater, appeared to the elder Luces to be signs that he was abandoning the strait and narrow and embracing the world. Luce's father had recently retired, and in the spring of 1935, aged sixty-seven, left for a long-planned trip around the world with extended visits in China. It took him away from the scene as a critic and preoccupied old Mrs. Luce, who stayed much of the time with the Severinghauses in Haverford. Lila, finally convinced that Luce's attachment to Mrs. Brokaw was no passing fancy, went to Reno and divorced him in October. The event went unmentioned in Time—a dispensation not granted others whose divorces made news.

3. ABIDE WITH ME

The marriage of Henry Luce and Clare Boothe Brokaw was set for November 23, 1935. On November 21, Clare's first play, *Abide With Me*, opened at the Ritz Theater with Earle Larimore and Cecilia Loftus in the cast. There were those at Time and Fortune who thought that this near conjunction of dates might not have been accidental and that the producers hoped to get good publicity in Time's drama page. Luce and Clare of course were at the opening. The play, about a young woman married to a sadistic inebriate much older than she, was unanimously panned by the newspaper critics. Richard Watts of the Tribune wrote, "One almost forgave *Abide With Me* its faults when its lovely playwright, who must have been crouched in the wings for a sprinter's start as the final curtain mercifully descended, heard a cry of 'author,' which was not audible in my vicinity, and arrived onstage to accept the audience's applause. . . ."

The normally unflappable Billings wrote in his diary, "What to do about reviewing *Abide With Me?* Can we say it's rotten? We wrote several drafts to get the proper degree of innocuousness. . . . Drafts were written and rushed up to him [Luce], only to be sent back for changes. Luce wanted to eat his cake and have it too—say the play was rotten and yet good. The final version of what he wanted printed didn't get back to me until 8:30 the night we went to press."

Luce had put himself into the love-and-honor dilemma of William Randolph Hearst, which Hearst had solved by throwing honor overboard and giving journalistic hosannas to every picture in which his friend Marion Davies appeared. All of the 620 persons in Luce's employ were watching for *his* solution. Although he came off less badly than Hearst, it cannot be said that Time's review of *Abide With Me* was honest or objective. Luce demanded rewrite after rewrite in his effort to achieve an appraisal that would sound favorable without actually being so. The final draft as published in the December 2 Time was a two-hundred-word lesson in semantic straddling. It concealed the judgment that the play contained "much tedious psychiatry"

119

amid such phrases as "Manhattan's most gilded opening of the week," praised the "excellent cast" and declared that the play "gratified those spectators who like melodrama."

The play, heavily papered, closed in a month. Meanwhile Luce and Mrs. Brokaw were married without attendants at the First Congregational Church at Old Greenwich, Connecticut, and left for a ten-week honeymoon in Cuba. They made an exceedingly handsome couple. If they were attracted to each other by congenialities such as their uncommon industry and ambition, there were also conflicts that would bruise two such imperial egos. Each loved to talk, to command an audience. But here Clare far outshone the jerky and inarticulate Luce with a smooth delivery that often glittered with wit and epigram. This would be a difficulty, as would be her possession of her own career, her own circle of friends. A problem of a different kind was the new Mrs. Luce's connection with the magazines. On her enthusiastic urging, Luce had decided to go ahead with the new picture magazine Life and had given her some encouragement that she might have a high editorial post. After the pair returned from their honeymoon, took a fifteen-room apartment at River House on East 52nd Street and a country house in Stamford, they were invited to dine with Ingersoll and Longwell at Voisin's expensive restaurant on 65th Street. By now Ingersoll had risen to general manager of Time Inc. and Longwell was engaged in planning Life. Luce gave considerable autonomy to editors he respected. He felt, he told his bride, that Ingersoll and Longwell must be ready to offer her an important job.

True, the talk turned on Life as the four returned to River House, but the denouement was unexpected. As Clare later recalled it, the fast-talking Ingersoll, after complimenting Luce on his handling of Time, warned that the new magazine would require as much dedication:

"Harry, you have got to make up your mind whether you are going to go on being a great editor or whether you are going to be on a perpetual honeymoon. When you edited Time you stayed in the office until ten and eleven o'clock every night. Now you catch the 5:10 back to the country. . . . Clare, if she really loves you, won't get in the way of the success of this magazine. And what I have to say to her is that you cannot publish a great magazine with one hand tied behind your back."

Luce for once was wordless. Stunned and hurt, Clare said to Ingersoll, "Harry Luce can publish a better magazine with one hand tied behind his back than you can publish with both of yours free." She burst into tears and fled. From time to time thereafter Luce would, with a winning and unusual humility, ask for some concessions toward his wife in his own magazines. Almost invariably, though not always, the opposition of his editors turned him back.

XII

1. UNTIL REELED THE MIND

Luce's prime function as an editorialist, missionary or propagandist was illustrated by his refusal to establish a newsgathering organization of his own when economy was no longer a factor. Time still lifted its news from the papers. Its scattering of local stringers was little used. Some of its editors, embarrassed by its reputation as a rewrite sheet and the low estate this gave it among the working press, urged the founding of a network of correspondents. Luce rejected the idea, writing:

"Time *is* a rewrite sheet. Time does get most of its news and information from the newspapers. . . . It takes *brains and work* to master all the facts dug up by the world's 10,000 journalists and put them together in a little magazine."

Actually, Time still represented less a mastery of facts than an entertaining interpretation and embellishment of them along with intriguing gossip and speculation. But it was making so much money (a corporate record of $2,249,823 profit in 1935) that its readers clearly were not buying news. They were buying Time's own scenario, which was manufactured in the Chrysler Building more than on the world's newsfronts. A costly staff of correspondents was not only irrelevant, but could be embarrassing.

Time's important people were now so well paid that they occupied vast apartments, drank vintage wines, kept servants and sometimes mistresses. John Billings ($27,000 plus stock profits) rode to work in a limousine driven by a liveried chauffeur. Laird Goldsborough ($26,000 *plus*) drove his own Rolls-Royce. Ralph Ingersoll ($30,000 *plus*) spent $5000 of it on a fashionable psychoanalyst. Roy Larsen's heavy stock holdings made his $125,000 investment profit dwarf his $35,000 salary. Billings, Ingersoll, MacLeish, T. S. Matthews, Martin, Hodgins, Larsen, Davenport and others were listed in the Social Reg-

121

ister. Many belonged to expensive private clubs. It seems that as yet only a few were beginning to feel unhappy about the propagandist or circulation-oriented bedizening of the news. The shaky defense could be made that Time had professed to be non-objective in the beginning, or that somehow news-magazines were not to be judged by the same standards as newspapers, but probably the majority simply grew accustomed to Time's gradually increasing license and thought no more of it. A few of the more sensitive would later write novels about their inner moral struggles over being a part of this tinkering with the news. At least one, Matthews, would wait for many years until after his retirement, when he would disclose his discoveries of improbities at Time.

A part of Time's success was due to its clever exploitation of sex and scandal while ridiculing the tabloid papers which front-paged such stories. Goldsborough's infallible nose for gossip had sniffed the Edward VIII–Wallis Warfield Simpson romance well before other journalists. He sensationalized it week after week with talk of "suburban snuggeries" and rumors that the king was no longer sleeping at Buckingham Palace, so that the British ambassador in Washington lodged a quiet complaint while Time-readers ate it up. Time's coverage of the court battle between the actress Mary Astor and her former husband, Dr. Franklyn Thorpe, over custody of their small daughter, started out with lofty contempt for newspapers which fed on such cases ("circulation managers of the tabloid press howled with delight") as it joined them in appreciation of the actress's racy diary about her friendship with George S. Kaufman. "Browsing through Miss Astor's diary," Time said, "the doctor's lawyers said they found that she had experienced a 'thrilling ecstasy' in the company of George S. Kaufman (*Merrily We Roll Along, Once in a Lifetime*). 'He fits me perfectly,' stated Miss Astor, recalling 'many exquisite moments . . . twenty—count them, diary, twenty . . . I don't see how he does it . . . He is perfect.' " As the columnist George Frazier would later put it, "Time's sanctimoniousness was infinitely more offensive than Miss Astor's honest passion."

Although Time's big guns had now been out of college for a decade and a half, Timestyle remained unregenerately collegiate. It had been refined under Luce to its ultimate in inverted sentence structure, trick words, inventions and epithets. Visitors from England could scarcely understand the magazine. Growing bolder with success, its irreverence had become more than a little insulting and cruel. It was hard to quarrel with success. Matthews, a rising editor (Princeton and Oxford, son of an Episcopal bishop and a Procter & Gamble soap heiress) worked diligently at Time although he would soon come into a lather of Procter money. Tall, handsome, a poet and a prose stylist, he "went along" despite some reservations. He would later call Time a "strutting little venture" whose style was too often "snook-cockery," a "ludicrous, exhibitionistic but arresting dialect of journalese." He was bothered by Time's overworked coinages (*radiorator, cinemansion*) and by its cunning euphe-

misms which conveyed shock without danger of libel, such as *great and good friend* for mistress or for homosexual intimate. Matthews, who had previously worked for the New Republic, observed, "The contrast felt between the New Republic and Time was a contrast between scholarly, distinguished men and smart, ignorant boys. The New Republic didn't exist primarily to call attention to itself; it had the nobler motive (or so it seemed to me) of trying to recall Americans to their better senses."

Edmund Wilson, as a reader and critic, wrote that "Time's picture of the world gives us sometimes simply the effect of schoolboy mentalities in a position to avail themselves of a gigantic research equipment; but it is almost always tinged with a peculiar kind of jeering rancor." Although Laski, Matthews and Wilson mentioned other characteristics of Time, they agreed on one, its immaturity of outlook. Laski had sensed a "sophomoric streak" in Luce, Matthews found Time to reflect the attitudes of "smart, ignorant boys" and Wilson commented on "schoolboy mentalities." Harold Ross, agreeing about the immaturity and the rancor, now gathered his troops for a larger offensive. Ross, the eccentric editor of the New Yorker, had long been incensed by Time's liberties with the language, factuality and its invective. His choler rose when Fortune published an article about the New Yorker which was not entirely worshipful and which embarrassed Ross in his own shop by listing his alleged salary ($40,000) and those of his staff. The article had been written by Ingersoll, who took some long guesses about his former employer and was not always accurate. Ross regarded this as a betrayal of the confidential nature of Ingersoll's one-time position as managing editor under him. The famous New Yorker parody of Time by Wolcott Gibbs was the result.

This had been arranged through Ingersoll, who was told it would be a profile of Luce. Since Gibbs was known as a parodist, St. Clair McKelway, Ross's managing editor, was sent to interview Luce who, having been reassured by Ingersoll, was not averse to being publicized in the journal of the fashionable and wealthy. He talked freely to McKelway. The New Yorker got further information confidentially from "more than a dozen" Timeemployees who, hearing of the projected appraisal, were eager to contribute. When the New Yorker sent advance proofs of the six-page Gibbs piece to Ingersoll in the Chrysler Building, Ingersoll exploded. His upset was perhaps caused less by his own unglamorous portrayal as a hypochondriac surrounded by unguents and doctors than by the realization that he had been taken in.

"Hearst tactics!" Ingersoll shouted over the telephone to McKelway.

On the contrary, such satire could hardly have emerged from the heavy-handed Hearst mill. It was couched in a judicious exaggeration of Timestyle. There were lines readers would repeat joyfully for months, one of them suggesting that the magazine's upside-down diction had gone too far: "Backward ran sentences until reeled the mind." Luce read it with the anguish of a man suspicious of humor and dreadfully concerned about his own image. Speaking of the new Life magazine, it read:

Behind this latest, most incomprehensible Timenterprise looms, as usual, ambitious, gimlet-eyed, Baby Tycoon Henry Robinson Luce. . . . Headman Luce was born in Tengchowfu, China. . . . Under brows too beetling for a baby, young Luce grew up inside the compound, played with his two sisters, lisped first Chinese. . . .

Although in 1935 Fortune made a net profit of $500,000, vaguely dissatisfied was Editor Luce . . . he has been handicapped by the fact that his writers are often hostile to Big Business, insert sneers, slithering insults. In an article on Bernard Baruch, the banker was described as calling President Hoover "old cheese-face." Protested Tycoon Baruch that he had said no such thing. Shotup of this was that Luce, embarrassed, printed a retraction. . . .

In 1935 gross revenue of Time-Fortune was $8,621,170. . . . Time's books . . . show total assets of $6,755,451. . . . These figures, conventionally allowing $1 for name, prestige of Time, come far from reflecting actual prosperity of Luce, his enterprises. Sitting pretty are the boys.

Transmogrified by this success are the offices, personnel of Time-Fortune. . . . In New York, total [employees], 566. In Chicago, mailing, editorial, mechanical employees, 216. Grand total Timemployees on God's earth, 782. Average weekly recompense for informing fellowman, $45.67802. . . .

Accused by many of Fascist leanings, of soaring journalistic ambition, much & conflicting is the evidence on Luce political faith, future plans. . . . Close friend for years of Thomas Lamont, Henry P. Davison, the late Dwight Morrow, it has been hinted that an official connection with the House of Morgan in the future is not impossible. Vehemently denies this Luce, denies any personal political ambition . . .

Most persistent, most fantastic rumor, however, declares that Yaleman Luce already has a wistful eye on the White House. . . . Certainly to be taken with seriousness is Luce at 38, his fellowman already informed up to his ears, the shadow of his enterprises long across the land, his future plans impossible to imagine, staggering to contemplate. Where it will all end, knows God!

Although the Timestyle Gibbs burlesqued was Hadden's invention, Luce had institutionalized it and heightened its malice. Like many purveyors of ridicule, he was shocked and wounded when his own methods were used against him. Actually, Gibbs was not personally vengeful in his satire, and if Timestyle was pilloried, Luce himself emerged very little hurt, if only he knew. A man of urbanity might have shrugged it off with the realization that the New Yorker readership was small and select, heavy in the metropolitan area where Time's was light, and that there was no harm in the article anyway. But Luce seems to have worried about his standing in that very New York upper crust. Possibly he sensed also in the piece a trace of the Babbitt characterization that had so upset him in Hadden's time. He and Ingersoll demanded a meeting with Ross. Ross, who was attending a dinner party that night, suggested the following evening. The urgency of the matter was too great for the two Timemen, so Ross agreed that he and McKelway would meet them that night at 11:30 at his penthouse at 22 East 36th Street.

They argued until 3:00 A.M. Ross, an ulcer victim who did not drink,

brought out liquor. Luce nursed one or two slow drinks while Ingersoll and McKelway made greater inroads on the supply and nearly came to blows. "There's not a single kind word about me in the whole profile," Luce complained.

"That's what you get for being a baby tycoon," Ross replied.

Luce said with utmost seriousness that contrary to the impression given in the piece, he *did* have a sense of humor. He found the going hard. When he said, "There isn't a single constructive thing in the whole piece," Ross replied, "We didn't set out to do a constructive piece. We simply tried to do a *fair* piece." And when Luce said the article was all wrong about Time's salaries and profits, Ross's reply was uncomforting.

"Perhaps," he said. "Perhaps it is—but that, after all, is part of the parody of Time."

In a letter to Luce after the meeting, Ross read him an instructive lecture. Among the points he covered seriatim was that about Luce's Presidential ambitions, which the piece had noted that Luce denied:

> It was regarded as exactly the kind of thing Time is doing constantly; denying the weird, and, as we called it, "fantastic" rumor after starting it, thereby getting the full news value out of it. Moreover, Time enterprises are always speculating on people's ambitions.

Ross quoted Gibbs's own summation of Time's sins:

> "I think Time has gratuitously invaded the privacy of a great many people; I think it draws conclusions unwarranted by the facts, distorts quotes, reprints rumors it knows have little foundation, uses a selective editing in getting together a story from the newspapers that throws it altogether out of focus, and that Time's style is an offense to the ear."

On his own, Ross pointed out that Time was widely considered anti-Semitic, was "generally regarded as being mean as Hell and frequently scurrilous," and observed:

> I was astonished to realize the other night that you are apparently unconscious of the notorious reputation Time and Fortune have for crassness in description, for cruelty and scandal mongering and insult. I say, frankly, but really in a not unfriendly spirit, that you are in a hell of a position to ask anything.

2. HAILE SELASSIE ON BROADWAY

When the liner *Morro Castle* burned off the New Jersey coast at a cost of 134 lives, Managing Editor Billings gave the story to Goldsborough because, as he put it, "Goldsborough was always traveling to Europe and strutting his knowledge of ships [so] I thought he could write this marine disaster in fine style. I was horrified when his copy reached my desk and I discovered that he

thought the whole tragedy was funny and had written the story as high comedy. His attitude evidently was that no self-respecting traveler would be caught dead on that ship."

Billings had the piece hurriedly rewritten without a word to Goldsborough, who disliked having his copy changed.

The incident illustrated the strange humor of "Goldy," in whom Luce placed his trust for covering foreign news. He was one of the old-Timers who had been with the organization virtually from the beginning—a group including Larsen, Gottfried, Martin and Myron Weiss—a group for whom Luce had a special loyalty and whom he called the "Old Bolsheviks." In addition to getting the highest salary of any writer, he was virtually untouchable in his province. The copy of other writers might be butchered, but his escaped the blue pencil because of his seniority, his authority in foreign affairs, colorful writing and his favor with Luce. He still rewrote his racy copy mostly from the columns of the New York Times and New York Herald Tribune, supplying his own slant.

Since his interview with Mussolini, Goldsborough had been more than ever enthusiastic about him. When he defied the League of Nations in 1935–36 and invaded Ethiopia in what he described as a "civilizing mission," Time applauded this spreading of civilization by Il Duce's bombers and mustard gas. It expressed amusement at the efforts of the crumbling League to apply sanctions to Italy and likened the Italian spirit to that of America during the Revolution in its account of the Fascist Grand Council's declaration of "enthusiasm in Il Duce, who realizes the supreme right of the nation to win security in Africa," adding:

> This motion was adopted at massive Palazzo Venezia last week in a tumultuous closing of ranks around the Dictator by Italians who were saying in their own way, "We hold these truths to be self-evident. . . ." With Mussolini stood Grand Councilmen whose names the world knows: Marconi, Volpi, Balbo, Grandi and others. . . .

Time raised a lump in the throat in describing how "tall, fair Vittorio Mussolini, 18, and chunky, dark Bruno Mussolini, 17," petitioned their father for fighting service, and that "Il Duce received his sons with a visible effort to master his feelings as a father, grunted a wordless assent . . ."

Time ridiculed the "savage and illiterate" Ethiopian "blackamoors." It emphasized the "fleas, flies and filth" of the country, which it called the "hellhole of creation," was amused by its women ("fashionably tallowed with Ethiopian grease") and its cowardly soldiers ("At the first sound of an Italian bombing plane Ethiopian officers dive for the nearest Red Cross shelter"). Emperor Haile Selassie was satirized under Time's nickname of "Little Charlie" as an absurd monarch "squealing for protection." His son-in-law was described as "terrified and bug-eyed" and "mounted on a prancing ass." His people, rather than speaking, "jabbered and shrieked." In consecutive para-

graphs they were termed "screaming savages" and "mud-wallowing savages" who castrated their prisoners. When the emperor was satirized as Time's Man of the Year, readers were told of the general "blind sympathy for uncivilized Ethiopia" and the mistaken belief that its people were "Noble Savages." Time went on:

> . . . Haile Selassie reached Broadway as a character in the new *George White's Scandals*. Cries he: "Boys, our country am menaced! What is we gwine do?" From then until the curtain falls amid applause which almost stops the show, His Majesty and guardsmen execute a hilarious tap dance (see cut).

The cut was a publicity photograph showing a black actor, clad in the emperor's familiar white helmet and dark cape, jigging as other blacks looked on.

When Ethiopian resistance at last collapsed, Goldsborough celebrated the posturing Blackshirt dictator in a cover story (Mussolini's fifth appearance on Time's cover, a record so far) and hailed him:

> A scant 14 years ago, the Kingdom of Italy was as confused, irresolute and radical-ridden as are France and Spain today. The years have dignified Benito Mussolini, and he has dignified and tempered the Italian people. As empires crumble other empires rise, and buoyant empire-builders invariably have clear consciences. Italians are not ashamed but proud and happy about Ethiopia. . . . Today ebullient Italians of the mass cheerfully boast from one end of Italy to the other that they are "the world's greatest people."

3. HITLER IN THE JAM CLOSET

At this time of one of history's great turning points, when the lights of liberty were going out and the forces of brutality and oppression were rising, Time was guilty of throwing its considerable weight in favor of Mussolini and Hitler. It consistently belittled the men and the nations opposing the two dictators.

In fairness to Luce, during part of this time he was upset over his divorce and remarriage. He was preoccupied with plans for the new magazine Life, a Presidential campaign, and difficulties with the assertive John Martin, Hadden's cousin, a stockholder and not a man who could easily be told off. To be sure, all this would remove an ordinary man from watchfulness, but not the extraordinary Luce, who could pack at least twenty hours of efficiency into a ten-hour workday. Even a love-stricken Luce did not fail to read Time. He was always consulted about the cover subject and the Man of the Year.

He was back on the job early in February 1936, in the midst of the Ethiopian war, and there was no diminution of Goldy's fun. Luce was, however, mildly displeased by the Mussolini cover story, as shown by Billings's diary.

His entry for July 16 told of a Cloud Club luncheon discussion among Luce, Billings, a Chinese general visiting the United States, Fang Chen-wu,

and a young Chinese graduate student from Columbia University as his interpreter. Since General Fang opposed Luce's admired Chiang, he was not accorded an entirely sympathetic hearing. The time-saving Luce used the intervals when his questions were being interpreted to the general to talk business
with Billings.

"We had a private dining room," Billings wrote. "Fang, about 55, wore a
plain U.S. suit and had handlebar mustaches. . . . Luce would ask long provocative questions. . . . Luce suggested that the Chinese could not beat the
Japanese, and this got Fang very excited. It was cruel talk, and there is something awful about seeing a foreigner deeply stirred in an unintelligible language. During a long spell of interrogation, Luce turned and whispered to
me, 'You're getting to be a picture editor,' referring to last week's issue [of
Time]. 'But I can't give you 100% on the cover story.' That was Goldy's long
ramble about Mussolini."

This offhand remark seems to have been all Luce said—nothing like the
anger and even fury he could exhibit when stirred. The evidence shows that
he was in political agreement with Goldsborough and it also suggests that his
concern was that excessive Fascist partisanship might alienate liberal readers.
In his now complete identification with big business and his growing hatred of
Roosevelt, it seems improbable that he ruled out Fascism as a possible road to
the political power for which he longed. There were not a few in the stricken
Thirties who felt that democracy had failed—Luce himself saw it as on the
decline—and that America's choice lay between Communism and Fascism.
Given such options, his choice would be obvious.

He was of course aware of Goldsborough's Fascist line, which had continued for years. Foreign and domestic politics fascinated Luce. He watched
these departments in Time closely. Goldsborough was a friend, an "Old Bolshevik," one whose thinking Luce understood. He was fully responsible for
Goldy's writings not only in the sense of a publisher's legal responsibility but
in the specific moral sense of having exact knowledge of what he was printing.
He wanted it that way.

While Hitler's more visible brutality and murders cost him the open admiration Time bestowed on Mussolini, he was cleverly handled by Goldsborough in a manner implying guarded approval. His abilities were stressed
("Some orations are of definite greatness, and the speech of Adolf Hitler to
the German Reichstag last week was in that class"). His inevitability and the
underlying righteousness of his cause were pointed out ("The Treaty of Ver-
sailles all but wrote into its text the eventual arrival of Adolf Hitler upon the
world scene"). His barbarities were soft-pedaled, Time's story on the Blood
Purge being so restrained in tone as to suggest that Hitler had been forced
against his will to clean out the homosexuals and some few others in his ranks.
His violations of solemn treaties were viewed with complacency ("Even to intelligent Germans it began to seem that the Hitler regime might be useful in
getting Germany's necessary international dirty work done"). He was often

presented as foxy and somehow amusing ("It has always been Herr Hitler's technique . . . to employ both the heavy Teuton bludgeon and the sweet Teuton sugar-cookie"). Time took a sentimental view of the Nazi reoccupation of the Rhineland, mentioning the "ecstasy" of the Germans and particularly of the "apple-cheeked wenches" who were delighted at this soldierly company, quite as if it were a joyous festival instead of a grave step toward war. And when Hitler coolly announced another treaty breach in the secret Nazi organization of an air force equal to England's, Time described it with great good humor as "Hitler's exit from the jam closet, sticky-faced," and said, "Germany has been naughty but is not to be spanked."

But Hitler was a touchy subject; many Americans were revolted by him, and Time could lose circulation by giving him open praise. The most effective encouragement and support Goldsborough gave the Nazis was by ridiculing the people and nations arrayed against them. He found the sinking of the League and the frustration of men desperately working for peace as funny as he had found the burning of the *Morro Castle*. Time had rather thrown up its hands about the League when Russia was permitted to join it and it was accused by Hitler of being "the platform for world Bolshevism."

Hating radicals, Goldsborough aimed most of his shots (second always to Russia) at floundering France, which had a government of the left. "The tone of the French press," he wrote when that country was trying to block the Hitlerian onrush, "was that of an aging coquette whose friends are about to leave her." Although he respected Tory England, he let John Bull have it when he seemed in solidarity with France against the dictators. He described the "toothy Anthony Eden" as "that self-righteous Briton" when Eden sought to stop the shipment of Italian poison gas through the Suez Canal. And when Winston Churchill, in an election speech, warned against Hitler, saying, "we cannot afford to see Nazidom in its present phase of cruelty and intolerance paramount in Europe," Time dismissed it as the "verbal postures" of electioneering and added, "Perhaps it was the intuition of Adolf Hitler to let this windy provocation pass . . ."

Hitler, whose prime strategy was to divide France and England, seemed to have an ally in the American "newsmagazine." Both also sneered at the League, Time dropping occasional witticisms such as, "the salty admirals who are the king's [George V] cronies over late Scotch nightcaps have never considered the League worth a brave man's belch." And both sought to isolate Russia.

Goldsborough disliked Jews, which perhaps diluted his sensitivity to the Nazi "Aryan" atrocities. In Léon Blum he had a man on whom he could confer multiple scorn since Blum was a radical, a Jew, an admirer of Roosevelt and a politician trying to implement the Franco-Russian treaty aimed at checking Hitler. Goldsborough invariably called him "Jew Blum" in his accounts. When Blum finally managed to get the treaty ratified, Goldsborough got him on Time's cover (a ridiculous picture showing him bandaged and in

bed) and heaped abuse on him in his three-page story. Blum's savage beating at the hands of Royalist thugs was believed suspect: ". . . [E]nemies of Léon Blum charged he was not really hurt but is dramatically 'exploiting a few scratches' . . ." The story began:

> So to contrive that Bolshevist Russia and Republican France should some time be linked in close mutual accord has become a ruling passion with the wealthy No. 1 Socialist of France, that exquisitely cultivated Jew and famed rabble-rouser, M. Léon Blum. From rostrums as varied as the curbstone of a Paris slum and the tribune of the Chamber, long-nosed, stringy-haired M. Blum has clarioned, "Socialism is my religion!" . . . His Socialist spirit is fired with religious fanaticism; he hates Nazis as they can only be hated by one who is a Socialist, a Frenchman and a Jew.

The story spoke of Russian treachery and the likelihood that such a pact would mean the downfall of the capitalistic system in France and elsewhere. It misquoted the writings and statements of Blum, a respected scholar, to make him out an imbecile and invest his Jewishness with ridicule:

> "As far as I am concerned I am a French Jew and I can conscientiously say that I am a good Frenchman. . . . I was brought up as a Frenchman. . . . I attended French schools, my friends were French. . . . I speak French perfectly and without a trace of foreign accent; even my facial features are free of particularly conspicuous racial traits. . . . Yet, though I feel myself to be genuinely French, I do, at the same time, feel that I am a Jew. . . . I have always known that a Jew can be nothing but a Jew."
>
> This emphatic Jewishness makes the No. 1 French Socialist thoroughly at home in Moscow, where it is Stalin's boast that Communism is equally hospitable to Jews, Gentiles, Moslems, Buddhists and persons of all colors.

Blum's success with the treaty drew this comment in Time:

> To a great many Frenchmen the person and program of Léon Blum are so "abominable" that they can think of no other in France equally abominable. Nevertheless the "popular Front" . . . last week finally steam-rollered through the Chamber of Deputies the Franco-Soviet Pact by a triumphant majority of 353-to-164. Among his bandages Jew Léon Blum chuckled . . .

Meanwhile the cinematic March of Time, still headed by Roy Larsen (who had also had an audience with Mussolini) ran into criticism. "People of all shades of opinion," wrote George Dangerfield, "swore that it was going fascist." The New Republic likened it to the Fascist-inclined Hearst Metrotone News. Even the conservative New York Herald Tribune protested its accent on militarism, its "good long cheer for Father Coughlin," its "ecstatic report" on the speed with which America could mobilize for war and its glorification of the French Fascist military organization, the Croix de Feu. Dangerfield described MOT as "almost completely irresponsible." MOT, which was not making a profit, was impressed enough by the protest to tone down.

Luce and His Empire

Time's domestic political news (National Affairs) was written by a succession of editors with Luce always looking over their shoulders. The impression Roosevelt had made on him during their White House meeting began to crumble after the recognition of Russia. Before recognition, Time praised Roosevelt's "careful and cautious start," treated Braintruster Raymond Moley with respect, commented on the industry and honesty of Interior Secretary Harold Ickes and was downright admiring of the abilities of Madam Secretary of Labor Frances Perkins. After recognition the bloom was off the peach and Luce's disenchantment was augmented by his businessman's disapproval of New Deal spending and curbs on business.

A cover story on Eleanor Roosevelt mentioned her prominent teeth, the divorces among her children, and raised the question of whether she was a "publicity-glutton," a "front-page solo character" or a "genuine, warm-hearted woman . . ." It seemed to favor the former idea in its handling of Mrs. Roosevelt's activities and her magazine writings, adding about her daughter, Mrs. Curtis Dall, that she "remains available for advertising since her broadcasting contract with Best & Co. expired." Postmaster General Farley was said to be "adroitly staffing the Government with deserving Democrats—and nobody else," a man who, in a holier-than-Hoover administration, "stands out as the one who makes no pretense of being other than an old-fashioned political sinner," but that the "potentialities of scandal" had not yet been realized. The cutting edge was sharper when Time got around to Undersecretary of Agriculture Rexford Tugwell:

> . . . Dr. Tugwell [was] having his white doeskin shoes cleaned and whitened. His necktie, shirt and socks always conform to a careful color scheme, and in passing a mirror he is apt, perhaps unconsciously, to give himself a glance. . . . Besides being a connoisseur of dress, he is also an amateur of wines.

Time was perfecting its use of such personality touches which could be politically helpful or hurtful. It described Tugwell as a radical who really meant "to redistribute wealth by drastically cutting down private profits," that "in the Tugwellian eyes the New Deal was a grindstone to rub 'rugged individualism' down to a social if not a socialistic polish," and said, "President Roosevelt holds Dr. Tugwell dear . . ." One of Tugwell's radical acts listed by Time reads interestingly now:

> He drafted a Pure Food & Drug bill to enforce honesty in advertising, a bill so drastic that it made not only intrenched patent medicine makers shake in their boots but frightened even honest advertisers.

The Man of the Year cover story ridiculed General Hugh Johnson, head of the National Recovery Administration—a Rooseveltian business control which Luce disliked—and suggested that he was gallivanting with his pretty secretary:

> General Johnson gets $6,000 a year. His secretary, nurse, guardian and constant companion at Washington, in airplanes, on trains, at banquets, Frances ("Rob-

131

bie") Robinson, gets $5,780. When that news got out last month, Man of the Year Johnson hotly announced: "I think that was one below the belt. She knows more about this organization than anyone else. I am sure that nobody here ever thought she was a mere stenographer or secretary. She has been my personal assistant straight through." Not on the payroll is Mrs. Hugh Johnson of the Consumers Board.

Time wickedly illustrated the account with a photograph showing Miss Robinson touching the general's shoulder as she leaned close to him and appeared about to kiss his cheek, although closer examination made it plain that she was only whispering New Deal information into his ear. Under the picture was the caption, "Secretary-of-the-Year/She works for $5,780," while under the picture of Mrs. Johnson nearby was the line, "She works for nothing." The general and Miss Robinson were so interesting that Time returned to them eight months later:

> Ably and conscientiously has "Robbie" . . . "implemented" General Johnson. Last year when some critics carped at his giving his "stenographer" a $6,800 [sic] job, the General justly retorted: "I think that was one below the belt." No mere stenographer was she. The little 100-lb., 5-ft. high "Robbie" is a self-made woman. Washington thinks she is a Jewess, but she has deliberately veiled her early life in mystery. . . . During the code-making days she worked with him [Johnson] often as much as 20 hours at a stretch. She reviewed parades with him. She got herself photographed with him. She attended banquets with him. She went to business conferences at the White House with him. And, above all, she traveled with him—over 40,000 miles to date, mostly by air. She went to the Pacific Coast with him last July, joined his fishing parties, left San Francisco agog with gossip. . . .

The pragmatic Luce had to bow to public opinion when the mid-term elections proved the President's enormous popularity. Roosevelt became Time's Man of the Year and was accorded some cautiously restrained compliments. By 1936 Luce burned to help put a Republican in the White House to replace the man Time said "has so bitterly aroused the enmity of a whole class . . . Regardless of party and regardless of region, today, with few exceptions, members of the so-called Upper Class frankly hate Franklin Roosevelt." He went to Topeka to talk with Alfred M. Landon and returned deeply impressed. Time began a careful Landon build-up, putting him on the cover and applying confidence-inspiring touches including what was known to the staff as the Breakfast Technique, behind which lay the theory that a man's goodness or badness could be illuminated by his morning mood and provender. With Landon, the mood was one of all-American cheer, the food enough to make readers salivate:

> At 7:20 he was down to a breakfast of orange juice, fruit, scrambled eggs and kidneys, toast and coffee . . . husky, broad-shouldered Governor Landon . . . a wide smile crinkling his plain, friendly face. "Top o' the mornin' to you

all." . . . the Governor went for a brisk seven-mile canter. . . . Kansas had again balanced its budget . . by enterprise, hard work, fair dealing and stiff bargaining—he made a fortune . . . honest, cracker-barrel voice . . . able Governor of Kansas . . .

But Landon's poor prospects and inept campaign disillusioned Luce, who had no wish to back a loser. In the last weeks of the campaign he gave up on Landon. Time actually reported the bungling work of his staff, the half-empty halls he addressed and the booing he received in Los Angeles and elsewhere. After the Roosevelt landslide Time admitted it was a "masterpiece" of politics. Luce, who so hated to lose, could do nothing but determine to help name a 1940 Republican candidate who could win.

4. THE HEATING PROBLEM

The new Mrs. Luce told her husband it was time that he junked the battered hats and mousy suits that made him look like an unemployed bond salesman. She directed him to a good tailor—the expensive James Bell—and a haberdasher. Thereafter, although he was personally indifferent to clothing, his tall frame was so handsomely accoutered that he was soon listed among the country's ten best-dressed men. It was said that when he complained of a $7000 bill for lingerie, she replied simply, "Well, are we wealthy or aren't we?" It was fashionable then for New York moguls to own Southern plantations, as Clare's friend Bernard Baruch did. One of the Luce extravagances was to buy one—Mepkin, a 7200-acre spread once owned by the Revolutionary patriot Henry Laurens, on the Cooper River forty miles north of Charleston, South Carolina, for $150,000. As publisher of the money-losing Architectural Forum,° and having a vested interest in good design, Luce brought down the architect Edward Durell Stone to look over the terrain and plan a group of houses to replace the old mansion already on the property.

Meanwhile the French château in New Jersey which was barely begun when Luce's marriage broke up was completed under Lila's supervision and named Lu Shan (roughly, Mountain Road). Luce, always genuinely fond of his first wife, had given her the château with its accompanying farm and stock and a $500,000 trust fund. Lila, on her part, had arranged for young Henry and Peter Paul to visit occasionally with their father, his second wife and her daughter Ann Brokaw, the five of them having gone on a yachting trip off Cape Cod the previous summer.

After a stay at their rented country home in Stamford, the Luces paid $185,000 for a twenty-one-room red-brick-and-marble Georgian house near

---

° Luce, interested in architecture, had bought the trade publication Architectural Forum in 1932. Although it was a small enterprise and never profitable, he clung to it for more than thirty years.

Greenwich, complete with tennis court and swimming pool. They called it simply The House and had that name engraved on their notepaper. It was completely redone by decorators, including one room for Luce's Chinese mementoes, to which Clare added by buying Chinese lacquer pieces including a $4500 chest, some picked up by an interior decorator sent to San Francisco for the purpose. There was usually a servant problem both at The House and Mepkin. Luce blamed this on the laziness caused by New Deal handouts, as Billings noted in his diary, but others were inclined to blame Luce himself. He was often as abrupt with servants as he was with waiters and cab drivers —and, if it came to that, with his editors. His intense voice and instantaneous impatience made the more timid housemaids fear him. The cool-eyed Clare herself had an expert command of sarcasm which cut in a different way from the Luce rasp. The turnover in servants was considerable. Much of the time of one of Clare's secretaries (she always had two and sometimes three and had so many irons in the fire that she kept them very busy) was taken up with the maintenance of the staff. Because of this turnover and because there were long intervals when the Luces did not visit The House, the servants sometimes failed to recognize their master and mistress. Allen Grover (Yale '22, Alpha Delta Phi), a Time and Fortune editor rapidly on the rise, visited there once with his wife and was surprised to have the butler address him deferentially as "Mr. Luce."

Luce, who had always wanted a daughter, established an affectionate relationship with the budding Ann Brokaw unusual for so hard-shelled a man. Never relaxed, always formal in speech, totally undemonstrative, never a chucker-under-the-chin, he was yet fond of Ann and very kind to her, a feeling the girl cherished and reciprocated. While Clare's relationship with the two boys was different—they already had a full-time mother and part-time father—they helped to fulfill her yearning for sons and she got on excellently with them.

With both Luce and Clare, however, children had to be fitted into the many other demands on their time and attention. Their "home life" was a riot of non-domesticity, moves from one dwelling to another, leave-takings for trips, preparations for speeches, departures for the theater or opera, a round of social gatherings which they planned carefully, inviting people of special interest and importance. And Clare, denied a job on Life, still stinging over *Abide With Me* and no more ready than Luce to accept defeat, was working on another play. She suddenly sat bolt upright one evening and said, "Harry, I think I'll write a play about women with no men in it." Luce said, "Why not?" She was fertile in startling ideas. This one was said to have germinated at a large dinner party when the women withdrew to leave the men to their cigars, promptly shed their charm and became spiteful. She did part of her research in the powder room of a night club, listening to women talk for a half-hour while the waiting Luce seethed and snapped, "What, for God's sake, were you doing?" when she emerged.

After spending a weekend with him at White Sulphur Springs, Clare stayed on when he returned to New York and wrote steadily for three days. She brought back with her the first draft of *The Women*, which she then carefully reworked. Produced by Max Gordon, the play opened at the Ethel Barrymore Theater on December 26, 1939. It had no men and forty-four women in the cast, forty-three of them bitchy and the forty-fourth wholesome but stupid. Although the critics were not unanimously impressed—Brooks Atkinson of the Times called it "Clare Boothe's kettle of venom"—it was a striking novelty and a phenomenal hit that ran for 657 performances. It would go on the road all over America, would be produced in twenty-five foreign countries and would be sold to the films. It would make the producer a million and Clare herself some $200,000.

Time's five-hundred-word review was glowing. Luce sent for the notice composed in the Drama department, did not like it and revised it himself to read in part:

> *The Women* is calculated to give the Men two of the most shockingly inform-
> ative hours of their lives and is so clever that few women would willingly miss it.
> . . . All of the play has sharp theatrical impact . . . Clare Boothe's *The Women*
> was received by first audiences with grateful mirth. Clever of line and deft of
> pace, *The Women* is packed with cracks which will doubtless be batted back
> and forth across Manhattan dinner tables the rest of the season. . . .

He also gave *The Women* a three-page celebration in Life, with two pages of scenes from the play in expensive full color. This success proved her a true professional and may have created some problems with her husband in its establishment of a career and milieu of her own. Again this beautiful and clever woman seemed to attract enmity as often as friendship. Margaret C. Harriman, who analyzed her not altogether sympathetically in a later New Yorker profile, noted that she had been blessed by the gods with beauty, wealth, talent and success, and finally with "unpopularity, the distrust of her fellow men and women." Without coming right out and saying so, Mrs. Harriman suggested that the distrust was caused by a partiality for the limelight not visibly counterbalanced by great human compassion. Her genuine lifelong interest in feminism was perhaps unfairly attributed to interest in herself as the nearest and most glamorous representative of that movement. Another biographer, Fay Henle, taking note of Clare's complaints that she was commonly regarded as "shrewd, cynical, hard and calculating, an opportunist, a careful engineer of her own destiny who puts self-advancement before all else," observed: "There is evidence of the justice of much of this cataloguing. There is evidence, too—plenty of it—of Clare's charity and thoughtfulness."

Her acts of charity (such as personally taking cod-liver oil to the Mepkin Negroes for their children) were seldom as visible or as dramatic as her self-advancement. Even her more adulatory biographer, Alden Hatch, stressed the surprise quality in the love match between "two such sophisticated [*sic*],

egocentric, and *spoiled* people as Clare Brokaw and Harry Luce." Women observers, seldom seeing in Clare Boothe Luce a creature of benevolences, could perhaps be accused of jealousy of her abilities or of anger over her treason in writing a play, as one of them described it, that "tied up her own sex crisply in cellophane and delivered it to the ashcan." They might let her be a Lady Mary Wortley Montagu but they would be hanged if they would let her get away with being a Clara Barton too. Even the tart Mrs. Harriman agreed that she was a frequent victim of vitriol, that she attracted criticism and gossip, much of it false. It was said, for example, that she dyed her hair, was a confirmed night-clubber and that she did not write her own plays, all untrue. Her beauty was genuine, she and Luce seldom visited the night spots, her writing was original and her capacity for hard work and concentration rivaled her husband's.

But naturally her less-than-angelic characteristics were publicized as she rose rapidly to become a woman in the public eye. Like her husband, she had vast ego and ambition, and was guilty at times of lapses in taste or judgment. Perhaps the male French architect touched on a deficiency when he said of her, "It is a beautiful façade, well constructed but without central heating." Indeed both Luces had a heating problem that would become a factor in their careers since both were politically ambitious. They were alike in their interest in outstanding people, wealthy people, great people, and in a failure of rapport with or sympathy for "the people."

XIII

1. THE REDS AND THE WHITES

When Time referred to Manuel Azaña, President of Republican Spain, as
"frog-faced" and "obese and blotchy" in the same paragraph, and to his
Labor Minister as "the ex-jailbird," the more knowing workers in the Chrysler Building offices understood. Spain's Popular Front government was getting the business from Goldsborough. It was a coalition of Socialists, Communists and centrists and although it had been elected overwhelmingly in 1936
and was the legally constituted government of Spain, it was well left of center
and Luce did not like it any more than Goldsborough did. Azaña was joining
"Jew Blum" as a Popular Front target of Time.

Both in France and Spain the Popular Front governments were final bul-
warks against Fascism. In Spain the republic represented the dream of peasants and workers crushed for centuries under blackest feudal oppression and
poverty at the hands of the grandees and the church. Spain still lived in the
dark ages. A republican government working for reform and the amelioration
of the lot of its people was long, long overdue. Now the Fascist armies were
tearing it down.

Time's Foreign News editor soon gave over calling the forces of Generalissimo Francisco Franco "rebels," which suggested that they were attacking
the constitutional government of Spain (as indeed they were). And he stopped
referring to the soldiers of the republic as "Government" or "Loyalist" forces,
though that was exactly what they were. He called the Government forces
"Reds" and christened Franco's armies the "Whites," a triumph of propagandist nomenclature. Before many weeks of battle had passed, Time readers
could easily make the error of believing Franco's troops to be those representing the legally elected government. A simultaneous device was the depiction
of Government leaders as unappetizing, absurd and cowardly at the head of a

blood-lusting rabble practicing "violent Left terrorism." The more than ordinarily distinguished President Azaña, who was called "frog-faced" in both the July 20th and August 24th issues, was quoted as saying, "The only person whose views are always correct is Azaña!" Time depicted a "corpulent" Azaña sneaking cravenly out of Madrid as soon as bombs began falling there, telling the soldiers he left behind that his only purpose was "to inspect our glorious Government forces in the field." Similarly, Premier Largo Caballero was described as "fleeing" dangerous Madrid twenty-four hours after he had announced, "Under no circumstances will I abandon Madrid alive! If the insurgents break through, I will shoot myself!" Reaching safe Valencia, said Time, he telephoned Madrid's defenders, "Courage! Our victory is certain. . . . You must give up your lives before yielding another inch of ground!"

Franco, on the contrary, seemed a man of great dignity, being described as "soft-spoken, studious," "serious, close-lipped," a man of "soldierly simplicity," at times "humorous and carefree."

Early in the war, one scornful Goldsborough sentence gave the theme: "The Spanish Government, a regime of Socialists, Communists and rattle-brained Liberals had emptied the jails of cutthroats to defend itself and swell what could be called 'forces of law and order.' " He rang the changes on their disorderliness and desperation: ". . . The Government forces . . . were by last week in great part not Army detachments at all but civilian Socialists, Anarchists and Communists, male and female, for whose benefit the President had opened the arsenals of Spain and handed out some 500,000 rifles, pistols and small arms." He mentioned the inferior social status of Madrid's cowardly defenders: ". . . the Government's militia [was] largely composed of ill-trained, ill-disciplined shoemakers, cab-drivers and waiters who were only prevented from scattering in despair by their officers standing behind them with cocked firearms."

The arrival of Italian and German troops and planes to aid Franco was reported matter-of-factly, leaving readers to decide whether Hitler and Mussolini were good company for the generalissimo. In adjoining photographs of the opposing Spanish leaders, one caption read, "White Franco: *Laughing, he advanced*," and the other, "Red Caballero: *Orating, he fled*." The story read in part:

> Meanwhile, smiling Generalissimo Franco was exhibiting his other distinctive characteristics: caution, thoroughness, quick decision, forehandedness . . . [A]long with attending to military details he was also ready with his own White police force and his own skeleton force of civil servants ready to install them in the Government buildings which his artillery was "dusting" with light shells. Franco police were trimly attired and wore the hard, tri-cornered hats which to Spaniards are the normal symbol of law & order. The Generalissimo's program was Back to Normalcy for Spain.

Normalcy would mean the death of democracy and its hopes and a return

to feudal oppression. One of the many who had watched Time's coverage of Spain with rising choler was MacLeish. He wrote Goldsborough, sending a copy to Luce, complaining about the constant reference to "Reds" and about—

> the presentation of the Spanish civil war as though it were some sort of spontaneous cockfight between Whites and Reds . . . [I]t is my feeling that entirely objective journalism would have presented the facts in such a way as to indicate that the fascists, backed by landowners and church were the aggressors against a popular government lawfully elected. . . . I feel that Time has never presented the war in Spain for what it was—an inexcusable and unjustifiable act of aggression by reactionary forces against a popular government.

Oddly, he did not mention Goldsborough's adjectival virtuosity and the fact that even if an official's acts are reported fairly, he is apt to lose reader respect if he is obese, blotchy and frog-faced. Goldsborough's reply was an 1100-word memorandum accusing the Spanish government of starting the war, affirming that its partisans were indeed Communists and that Franco's backers were "men of property, men of God and men of the sword":

> In so describing them, I presume that I condemn them in 1937 to particularly nether depths [evidently a Goldsborough sarcasm directed at MacLeish's low opinion of those elements in Spain], but what position do you suppose these [sic] sort of men (irrespective of nationality) occupy in the minds of 700,000 readers of Time? Time is obliged to bear in mind the set of values with which we have every reason to believe that our readers are equipped. They do not, I am convinced, recoil at the sight of a United States Marine, a clergyman or a prosperous householder, and they are of a quite contrary opinion as to Communists, Anarchists and even "Republicans" so-called of a stamp who resort to political gangsterism . . .

He seemed to be saying that whatever his own feelings, he had to write expediently to keep from affronting Time's prosperous, Franco-oriented readers. This was a Jesuitical argument from the adjectivist whose Fascist cheerleading had been evident for years. Goldsborough's point of view and judgment were now so patently compromised that his retention as Foreign News editor seemed impossible to some Time and Fortune men who had watched his performance with anguish.

From the clues available it appears that Luce—always bearing Russia and China in mind—was still convinced that the world was moving toward a division between Communism and Fascism. He was honestly, though not openly, picking Fascism, the cause which (so far) favored the aristocracy with which he identified himself and which he saw as vital for the preservation of civilized values. In another connection, Luce wrote MacLeish about the same subject—interesting because it seems his only written pronouncement on the Spanish civil war:

> The Revolution, started by the Rebels, is *per se* an awful thing. So was the Russian Revolution. (From a *per se* point of view Mussolini, with at most one murder to his credit [sic], was the least objectionable of all.)

But are you not absolutely closed-minded to the possibility that the purposes of this revolution maybe [*sic*] valid? . . .

And now suppose that one is neither pro-Fascist nor pro-Communist, but stalwartly and closed-mindedly pro-Freedom and Democracy—does Spain provide the issue for such a one? I think not— Last year, Spain was perhaps Democratic rather than Communist. But there is certainly strong evidence that Spain has now only two significant camps—the Fascists and the Communists (or Left-dominated Popular Front).

Ultimately the world may be divided between these two camps but I do not think it is yet, and I think that anyone who thinks that Communism is to be trusted as an ally of Liberty is, quite simply, a mistaken theoretician and a hopeless politician! I know you will be glad to be called the latter but I trust you would be insulted by the former.

This reasoning was not without Jesuitism either, as long as Time continued to puff the Fascists. Luce was much closer ideologically to Goldsborough than to MacLeish. But some of his most talented men—among them, in addition to the poet, were Gottfried, Ingersoll, Allen Grover and Eric Hodgins, the latter now managing editor of Fortune—were critical of his political line. The brilliant young leftist Dwight Macdonald had just quit in anger over it. Although Luce was expert at placating dissidents with well-phrased memos, it would take more than memos to quiet the anti-Hitlerites. Placation was part of Luce's motive in permitting at this time a four-part series in Fortune, "Background for War," written by MacLeish and others, appraising from a mature and liberal point of view the seething political forces in Europe. "Harry turned up his nose at it," Hodgins recalled, "but he published it." Even if it was sandwiched between articles devoted to tycoons, and Fortune's circulation was one-eighth of Time's, it mollified the office liberals for a time.

One might have thought that even Goldsborough was impressed by the tempest, for as spring arrived in 1937 the adjectives in FN were suddenly modified and human tragedies were not treated as entertaining. When German airmen allied with Franco mercilessly bombed undefended Guernica, Time's foreign news so far departed from custom as to quote a priestly witness who called it what it was, "one of the terrible crimes of the age." Alas, it did not mean reform. It was simply that Goldy was in London for the coronation of George VI and a stand-in had taken over Foreign News.

The anti-Communist MacLeish, an idealistic New Dealer, thought Fascism itself to be one of the crimes of the age. Discussing it thirty years later, he still liked Luce but felt something lacking in him. "Why Harry kept this man who seemed to me to be pro-Hitler and pro-Mussolini," he said, "was beyond me." In 1938 he resigned, writing Luce a letter congratulating him on his achievements but mentioning his growing insensitivity to "the people":

And then there's you. I don't know you very well these days. I probably never will know you very well again. I think you're all right. I don't think the kind of people you are going mostly to see from now on will be able to shake your ap-

prenticeship in loyal journalism. They'll try to. But then you know they'll try to and are therefore forearmed. I wish some things had gone differently with you —though I'd find it hard to say just which. Maybe what I mean is that I wish you hadn't been so successful. Because it's very hard to be as successful as you have been and still keep your belief in the desperate necessity for fundamental change. I think what you have done is amazing and I give you all credit and all honor for it. It would have been very easy for you to forget everything you had believed true when you were twenty. . . . But I don't know—you were meant to be a progressive—a pusher-over—a pryer-up. You were meant to make common cause with the people—all the people. You would have been very happy I think if you could have felt that the New Deal was your affair. Because it was your affair. You would have been very happy inside yourself as one of the leaders in a democratic revolution in this country . . . Maybe I'm wrong. It's presumptuous to guess about another man's happiness but I think you would have been. I think you hate being rich. I think you hate being a pal of the people who want you to be their pal. I think you would have liked to write *The People, Yes*.

2. THE PEOPLE, NO

Despite all the tumult, the evidence suggests that few of Time's top men realized the extent to which Luce had moved ever further away from dealing in news as news and had become the world's most powerful unacknowledged political propagandist. The situation was not unlike that of workmen in a boiler factory so schooled to noise as to become unaware of it. Time was founded in 1923 on noisy excess and invention. Goldsborough's own special excesses and inventions had continued unbroken since 1925, and the NA anti-Rooseveltism had gradually accumulated decibels since 1933. Although the clamor had become deafening in the Chrysler Building, some heard only a slight buzz and very few were feeling the pain in their eardrums which outsiders would have felt.

Even MacLeish, whose ears were hurting, did not hear everything. He did not grasp the fact that Luce had abandoned news journalism insofar as he expediently could and had molded and altered journalism to fit his own prime function as missionary. It was not until later, when MacLeish entered government service, that he became aware of the extent and hurtfulness of Time's news manipulation. "When you're on the receiving end," he said, "you feel it."

And surely MacLeish misread the cloistered mind and heart of his fellow Bonesman when he said Luce was meant to "make common cause with the people." Perhaps instead he was expressing his disappointment in discovering that this was not so. And when he said, "I think you hate being a pal of the people who want you to be their pal," meaning the wealthy and powerful, perhaps he meant he *hoped* so. Luce was studiously cultivating them.

His theory of journalism was both iconoclastic and apocalyptic. "Time," he

wrote in a news-policy memo to the executives, "must have in its make-up individuals of strong personality. . . . But it will never be enough that they should believe in themselves; they must believe in Time. Time is the most powerful publication in America. . . . It has achieved this position by the devotion of a few able men and women to the cause of Time." The cause of Time, he explained, was to apply the morally correct "fundamental attitudes to the reporting of the news." That is, Time must interpret and slant the news, blending it with opinion and editorializing so that the reader got not mere news but a proper understanding of what it really signified and what his own attitude toward it should be. The ministerial seriousness of this injunction, its air of being graven on tablets, impressed virtually all Timen. He was investing them with the responsibility of educating the public in Right Thinking just as his father had saved the heathen. The fact that this Right Thinking referred to Luce's own thinking attested to the same missionary certainty his father had felt, and placed him vis-à-vis the American reader in the same position as Rev. Henry Luce vis-à-vis the Chinese peasant. The likelihood is that the son at this point was as sincere as his father had been.

Some Timen said it helped to have a man at the top who was honest even when he was wrong. Some argued that the New York Times was liberal and the Herald Tribune Republican and that Time was entitled to its own point of view as they were. The fact was that these newspapers—and almost all American papers of importance—carried relatively factual and unbiased news reports, many of them taken straight from the highly objective wire services. They *labeled* their editorials. None dared to sweep away the distinction between fact and comment as Luce did, or to use Time's adjectival slander or puffery. None of them borrowed most of their news, then rewrote every word of it, as Time did, to conform to the "line." There was no publication in the world of such size and influence which was regarded by the innocent as a purveyor of news and yet which succeeded in being an instrument of propaganda.

Indeed, Luce was reversing the whole trend of American journalism, which had been so crudely partisan in the eighteenth and much of the nineteenth century and had at last risen to an almost universal professional ethic requiring the separation of news and opinion. He demanded their blending. As Marshall McLuhan would soon discover, the three Luce magazines assumed "god-like heights of observation" in promoting "carefully engineered political action." Luce would later defend his policy by pointing out the impossibility of true objectivity: "Show me a man who thinks he's objective and I'll show you a man who's deceiving himself." This of course was no argument at all. Perfect honesty was as difficult to come by, and yet the world would be a total jungle if all effort toward honesty were dropped. A trait that would become more and more noticeable was the celerity with which he could rationalize whatever he deeply wanted to do.

Several times he had come close to publicly preaching the need for propa-

ganda in journalism in order to inform and direct the masses. A few years earlier he had urged the newspaper press to stop its slavish division of editorial and news pages and to put on page one "intelligent criticism, representation and evaluation of the men who hold offices of public trust." Now, with the world hurtling toward war, he was making more speeches, practicing them diligently before a mirror to perfect his enunciation and gestures. In Williamstown, Massachusetts, he told a highbrow audience that "all men are *not* equal—except in the sight of an all-merciful God," and that the press must teach, "must assist the people to govern themselves." The press at the time was heavily anti-Roosevelt. In another speech before an advertising men's convention at White Sulphur Springs, he placed his hope in the American press "for turning back the darkness which walks upon us." But he assailed "the-press-that-gives-the-people-what-they-want," on the score that the public did not know what was good for it. (In passing, he castigated the "sensationalism" of cheap newspapers—this not long after Time's delighted prurience in such cases as those involving King Edward and Mary Astor.) He dropped the astounding suggestion that it might be well if advertisers assumed "some burden of ethical and cultural responsibility" as to what should appear in the newspapers. Luce did not seem to realize the implications of this proposal, which could have meant the ouster of the free-speaking editor and his replacement by business interests with their own axes to grind. Evidently he trusted businessmen more than he trusted editors or the public, for he went on in a vein foreign to *The People, Yes:*

> . . . [C]an the public save itself? Can the masses save themselves from the barbarous dominion of the mass-mind? If you have a complete, unqualified, irrational faith in the common man in the new revolutionary world, then you will believe in giving the public what it wants . . . in education, in law, in goods and chattels, in art, in morals, and in all these things at once in the press. It was an advertising man, Bruce Barton, who made me read Ortega y Gasset's thesis on the mass-mind. It begins by making you face the great new physical reality in society—crowds. Not merely Hitler's crowds, or Mussolini's, or Stalin's or Hirohito's, but the crowds on American beaches, the crowds in the movies—the even vaster crowds you advertisers yearn for—mass circulation. These crowds, he says, will destroy civilization.

Luce seemed sincerely determined to save civilization even if a little authoritarianism was necessary. He feared all crowds, but the crowd he feared most of all was Stalin's. Like some of the British, French and American conservatives, he so feared Communism that he had found encouragement in the rise of the anti-Communist dictators. His belief in the survival of democracy as a third international force seemed feeble in view of his write-off of it in Spain and his American pessimism. He had indulged the Duce and Führer all the way to the Rhineland, Ethiopia and Guernica. Very soon, like the British and French gentry, he would have to decide whether Hitler really was an amusing boy caught leaving the jam closet with a sticky face.

3. MAKE MORE MONEY

The disastrous success of Life made magazine history. For many months, the more copies it sold the more money it lost. Unlike Time and Fortune, it was not an original idea, for there had been talk in many quarters on both sides of the Atlantic of exploiting in a magazine the new advances in film and cameras. Luce was merely one of the first to seize the idea (with his wife's strong urging), promote it and invest huge sums of money and talent in it. Under the seasoned Billings as managing editor, and with the fertile Longwell supplying many of the picture-story inspirations, Life first hit the stands November 19, 1936, and quickly sold out its entire press run of 466,000.

Because its advertising rates were mistakenly low, based on a calculated sale of 250,000 copies weekly, and because of the high cost of heavy coated paper required for good picture reproduction, the small predicted loss ran into a frightening $50,000 weekly. It would come to a staggering $6 million before Life began to pay it back many times over.

Luce's confidence was impressive. Although he could have cut his losses by holding down the print order, he preferred to let the sale rise to more than a million so that he could establish a backlog of readership that would justify a quicker rise in advertising rates. He was deeply involved in Life, worked furiously at it, but never attained the mastery of the picture medium that was at his fingertips with Time and Fortune. He was more interested in words than pictures. He tended to distrust the technique of splashing dramatic pictures, and if he had his way about a convention or international conference he would be likely to pack a page with fifty small faces.

Life's beginning had also involved a personality clash between Luce and John Martin, who had first been in charge of preliminary work on the picture magazine. Martin, who had lost an arm in a boyhood hunting accident, was a gritty man who became an expert sportsman and golfer despite his handicap and wore his empty sleeve with pride. One friendly staff member sent him a single cufflink as a Christmas present. A two-fisted drinker when in the mood, it was said of him that he "could edit a magazine lying down, and sometimes did." He was never an admirer of Luce, whom he regarded as stuffy, and it had amused him to slip many shocking double entendres into Time which the innocent Luce missed entirely. At one Life "idea luncheon" he had shouted down a whole succession of Luce ideas as "buckeye," meaning corny. While Luce had managed to hold the fierce temper he had inherited from his father and doubled, this was treatment that he could not countenance. He solved the problem by returning Martin to his former post as managing editor of Time and moving Time's managing editor, Billings, to that same position on Life. Billings, whose picture experience was limited to Time's comparatively modest use of them, nevertheless proved a perfect choice.

144

"Luce was in and out of editing most of the time," Billings recalled. "Sometimes he was a help. Sometimes he was a pain in the neck—especially when he could not make up his mind what he really wanted in the magazine. It took him a long time to learn that you cannot put the front page of the New York Times all into pictures."

He could usually be dissuaded from mistaken picture-story notions. But each time a suggestion of his was voted down he would gain inner points which would finally add up to insistence on some idea in which he would not allow his men to outvote him. This happened once with a picture-text story about a Chinese Methodist missionary that was execrated by all but Luce as excruciatingly dull. Thereafter, any such feature insisted on by Luce despite the groans of his men was called a "Chinese Methodist missionary story."

Some felt that his connections with God and his conviction that private enterprise was a divine institution enabled him to slip through the censors sensational material which less righteous publishers would have lacked the nerve to use. Life was seldom downright vulgar, but especially at the beginning, when quick public interest was paramount, its formula, as Bernard De Voto said, was "equal parts of the decapitated Chinaman, the flogged Negro, the surgically explored peritoneum, and the rapidly slipping chemise."

Luce's daring with Life, when its losses had him in an actual financial pinch, was considerable. There was an impression that his ability to explain his operations to his own and God's satisfaction was a large ingredient in his self-confidence. In a speech in Cleveland in which he attacked the Rooseveltian planned-economy legislation as an invasion of freedom, the wealthy Luce told 650 wealthy Ohio bankers not to forget that they as taxpayers were paying the bill. "Have no embarrassment about making too much," he urged. "Every dollar you make is a patriotic contribution to the national debt. . . . Make money, be proud of it; make more money, be prouder of it."

4. WORKERS IN THE LUCE VINEYARD

Time's first office boy, Joseph Kastner, had been so impressed by his first two employers that when he decided to go to college, it had to be Yale. When Luce made a speech at Yale, Kastner approached him and identified himself. Luce remembered him and said, "Stop in and see me when you graduate," which Kastner did in 1930. Luce was kind, though terribly busy with Fortune, and Kastner went to work for that magazine. Two years later when he was fired by the capricious Ingersoll, Luce heard of it and without mentioning it to Ingersoll he kept Kastner on in another job. Switched to Life in 1936, he began to have more contact with Luce.

"How much are you getting now, Joe?" Luce asked him. Kastner said his salary was $100 a week, wondering silently whether Luce would raise it perhaps to $115. Or $125?

"Well, I guess we can pay you that much," Luce said, leaving it at $100 but seeming to confer an honor in doing so.

He was in and out of the Life offices in shirtsleeves, pondering pictures and ideas. His rudeness Kastner believed to be part of his idea of efficiency, eliminating all time-wasting amenities. Like Joseph Pulitzer and his World, Luce assumed that the bodies and souls of all his editors belonged to Time Inc. He became famous for his staff luncheons, some of them small, taking in only top executives, larger ones including men of the second echelon. It was his method of improving his men, getting corporate use out of them during an otherwise wasted lunch period. The nervous strain was intense. Even if the agenda was known in advance, Luce could put unpredictable questions to which one's answers could raise or sink one in the Boss's regard. Since he frowned on drinking at lunch, before the zero hour some of the victims would zip over to a 43rd Street establishment where assorted nerve medicines were served. At the lunch, Luce would pick a man and fire questions at him, expecting quick wisdom. But what began as a Socratic dialog would often develop into a Luce monolog as he became interested in his own thoughts, which he tended to do more and more. Although at times his monologs could be direct and effective, more often they wandered into stream-of-consciousness excursions without destination, dreadfully boring but better than being on the witness stand.

The worst trial of all was to get a call that Luce wanted to see you, subject unknown. He expected immediate answers to difficult questions. His intensity was compelling. He demanded complete attention. His chilly blue eyes under the thatchy brows bored relentlessly as he inquired about a picture spread or a title and gave it the moment of an international crisis. One felt that if he could not answer intelligently and fast, the whole Chrysler Building might topple into 42nd Street under the stress of Luce's desperation.

This meeting with Luce, known by Timen as the Terror, the Rack or the Last Judgment, became a part of his machinery of efficiency and would be described by various executives down through the years. The brilliant Eric Hodgins, as managing editor of Fortune, found that when he made up his schedule of projected articles for the magazine, he had to defend every item on the list against the cold-eyed prosecutor Luce as if each one were a swindle on the company, and that Luce's sarcasm was devastating if the defense lagged for an instant. Time editors discovered that in discussing the "slant" taken on any news story, Luce could take alternately one side and the other of a question and argue as fiercely on both, seeming to play cat and mouse with his victim and reducing him to confusion unless he were ready and nimble. An executive calling on him to settle policy problems would rehearse his pitch point by point, 1-2-3, getting it letter-perfect so that not a moment would be wasted and above all being sure of his facts. There were no preliminaries, no good morning, just an immediate plunge into the problem. Luce went for the facts as a tiger goes for the throat, and God help the man who

was wrong or uncertain of his facts. The Boss could become an ogre with a tongue that lashed powerful executives before whom dozens of *other* men quailed. This fostered a general feeling of anxiety that drifted down into the ranks and which was believed intentionally inculcated by Luce to keep everybody hopping. There was a high incidence of nervous indigestion in the first and second echelons, but Luce himself never suffered the stomach troubles that had plagued his father.

"No matter how many years you worked for him," Kastner recalled after working thirty-seven years for him, "a summons from Harry would make your palms sweat."

One Timemployee set apart was Luce's younger brother Sheldon. As a boy he scarcely knew his big brother except in family narratives. He was only four when Luce left China and had seen little of him until Sheldon himself left China in 1924 to enter Hotchkiss. From then on he visited Luce and Lila on vacations and when he finished Yale in 1933 he joined Time Inc. as an advertising salesman. In two years he was shifted to the Business department and later became business manager of Architectural Forum. His close relationship to the Boss implied no exemptions, for he often found himself working far into the evening. A tall, jocular man, he would at times (*never* during business hours) pull Luce's leg, asking straight-faced questions which Luce would answer at earnest length until he discovered that he was being kidded. Possibly this delayed Sheldon's advancement somewhat, for Luce was apt to consider a person frivolous who could jest about serious things.

Sheldon felt that his brother had no outside friends on the terms of intimacy usually associated with friendship, though there were three or four men he called his friends, such as Larsen, Billings and Hodgins. Morehead Patterson was the only Yale classmate in whom he kept up any pretense of continuing interest. It seemed to Sheldon that Luce's real friends—the only ones with whom he could relax on a basis of perfect confidence and equality—were his sister Beth and her husband Maurice Moore. The affable Moore, a director of Time Inc., was the man above all others on whom Luce depended for sound legal and corporate advice. Mrs. Moore, who had her older brother's intelligence plus the warmth and friendliness he lacked, was so important to him that he had a private telephone wire between his office and her Park Avenue apartment.

Aside from his maximum use of time, Sheldon thought his brother's greatest ability was his phenomenal memory: "You could give Harry a budget and come back three months later, and if something was changed in that budget, he'd know. There was no glossing over errors."

In the mid-Thirties word got around that Luce preferred to ride alone in an elevator built to accommodate twenty persons—an arrogance not then fully understood. The starter would usher him into an empty car and send it up. Once, Dorothy Hoover, of Life's picture department, unaware of the new ruling, slipped into the car with him. He had just returned from somewhere, so

she said, "Mr. Luce, did you have a nice trip?" Staring stonily at his shoes, he said, "No," and that was the end of the conversation.

Laura Z. Hobson, the dashing Jewish wife of Luce's classmate-Bonesmate Thayer Hobson, had a special place in the thoughts of Henry and Clare Luce because it was at the Hobsons' that they had first met. Beautiful, warm in personality, ambitious, a skilled writer, she won a promotion-writing job at Time in 1935 because of an advertising coup she had scored for B. Altman's department store. Luce recoiled, however, when she let him know she was getting $7000 at Altman's.

"No woman gets that kind of money here," he said.

This woman did because she held her ground—got exactly that same salary on a year's trial basis. During that year she was divorced, and Luce went through the same ordeal. At its end he said, with a frosty twinkle, "Your year's trial is over. I either have to fire you or give you a $3000 raise and a bonus. Which would you prefer?"

Late one afternoon weeks later, he called her in and handed her a sheet of copy. "Here's an ad to introduce the March of Time to Time readers. What do you think of it?"

She read it quickly. "I think it's pompous and dull."

"O.K. I wrote it. Think you can do it better?"

The deadline was next morning. She called off a dinner party that evening, worked furiously almost all night and handed Luce her work in the morning. He looked it over, gave her a complimentary nod, and sent it through.

On that level—the level of stimulating, recognizing and rewarding good work—Mrs. Hobson thought Luce superb. (True, she had the benefit, as did Marcia Davenport and a few others, of womanly beauty combined with intelligence, which could make him almost humanly male in admiration.) On another plane she disagreed with him strenuously. A New Dealer and an admirer of Roosevelt, she could understand a normal Republican opposition but she thought his opposition abnormal. He would go white with rage at mention of FDR. She felt that he was against labor, lacking in sympathy for the underdog. And Time was in its "Jew Blum" phase, favoring Franco, complacent about Hitler and Mussolini. Much as she admired Luce the businessman, Mrs. Hobson thought he was in inner conflict and she made a joke about it which was perhaps truer and less funny than she thought at the time.

"The trouble with Harry is that he's torn between wanting to be a Chinese missionary like his parents and a Chinese warlord like Chiang Kai-shek."

For several years the betting on who would eventually succeed Luce as editor-in-chief was on John R. Hersey, who possessed an unlikely number of qualifications appealing to Luce. Born in Tientsin in 1914, son of a YMCA worker, he came to America at ten and went to Hotchkiss and Yale—surely a good beginning. He was a fine scholar, athlete, vice chairman of the Daily News, an Elizabethan Clubber, a Bonesman. After Yale, he spent a year at Cambridge. Hardly anything more could be asked except that he be hand-

some, charming and possess the social acceptability required for the top job, all of which he was.

In the Thirties, any Yaleman who distinguished himself in writing could have a Time job for the asking. In 1935, while still a junior, Hersey called on Luce in New York and was offered a job on graduation. Time was a young man's company, Luce said, its top men only thirty-five or so. "When we get to be forty," he went on, "we'll turn it over to the thirty-five-year-olds."

In 1937, after his year at Cambridge, Hersey went to work as a Time junior writer. He was not hired directly by Luce and in fact it was a couple of years before Luce was aware he was there. Then he took Hersey and a group of other young Time writers to lunch. By now he was a shade over forty. He told his guests it was a young man's company. "When we get to be forty-five," he said, "we'll give it to the forty-year-olds."

Time seemed to be marching on, or up. Luce was now entering upon his period of loneliness and power. Although some blamed his loneliness on his new wife, who had her own career, it seems to have been largely self-imposed, the end product of his own use of his time. His divorce and his excessive busy-ness had cut him off from his two sons except for infrequent holiday meetings, and his growing sense of infallibility along with his uninterruptibility reduced the number of invitations he received from important people he prized. He came more and more to extend luncheon, dinner or social invitations to younger staff members who seemed especially interesting. One was Hersey. (Another was young Joseph Thorndike, whose brilliant work on Life made up for a Harvard background and the fact that he had never lived in China.) Luce's habit was to drop most favorites after probing their minds. He did not drop Hersey, who ranked high among those bright young men who were sharpening their knives in the struggle for advancement at Time, but who would drop out himself because he did not like the knifing and refused to meet another qualification not yet in question. This was the matter of utter, automatic loyalty as Luce defined it.

Luce even took Hersey to the opera a couple of times. He was able to suppress his powerful ego at such times and treat a fledgling writer with great kindness. Hersey noticed that he had a strong sense of generalization. He liked to fit people and issues into categories which were convenient but not really true, being oversimplified. Journalistically and in propaganda this was successful, relieving readers of the tiresome discrimination necessary for better understanding. He was impressed by the "best people" socially. At the opera during the intermission he pointed out some of them for his young companion: *There's an Astor, there's a Rockefeller, there's a Vanderbilt.*

Roy Alexander, like Briton Hadden, formed a link between the Pulitzer dynasty and Luce. He was hired at the ripe age of forty because Time had scads of young men fresh from New Haven and Princeton and needed an experienced newsman for a change. He came from the St. Louis Post-Dispatch, where in fourteen years he had worked up to assistant city editor and

had only occasionally seen the proprietor, big Joseph Pulitzer, Jr. Born in Omaha, a Catholic graduate of the Jesuit St. Louis University, he broke Time's Ivy League tradition and yet was slated for rapid advancement—the exception who proved the rule.

Alexander, being only a year younger than the Boss, was not told, "When we get to be forty-five, we'll turn the company over to the forty-year-olds." A classicist himself and interested in religion, he enjoyed the way Luce would be off like a shot if one brought up the subject of free will or original sin, quoting John Knox, Thomas Aquinas, St. Augustine and others. Most of all he was impressed by Luce's day-by-day involvement with the news and with his men. If he desired, he could have put John Billings or Eric Hodgins in editorial charge of the company and luxuriated in Antibes or Hawaii, visiting New York occasionally to pick up some money and jack up the staff. Or he could do as old Hearst did—live in a castle and run the show by teletype, or as Pulitzer in St. Louis was doing, so different from his famous father.

Pulitzer ran the respected, liberal Post-Dispatch through his editor, the autocratic O. K. Bovard. Pulitzer was there, all right, but Bovard was always between him and the staff. Luce was both Pulitzer and Bovard and then some, knowing his men personally, studying the news, discussing it with them in ferocious encounters, strong in his own views but occasionally accepting a contrary one if convincingly presented. Although Alexander would disagree with some of Luce's judgments, his overriding feeling was one of admiration. Alexander was one of several men (two others being Sidney James and Otto Fuerbringer) to leave the Post-Dispatch for Time. The liberals who stayed on at the P-D at one-third the salary, and who regarded Luce as the archangel of reaction and news perversion, looked on these "deserters" much as a mother would look on a daughter who went to the big city, poor but honest, and suddenly emerged in mink from a Cadillac in front of the Stork Club.

Still a different sort was Winthrop Sargeant, an artist caught up in the great, whirring Time machine, fitting in first as a small cog, divorced from responsibility and yet having a part in the production of an attractive product conveying the right message. A skilled musician, unemployed for a time during the depression, he had written music criticism for New York newspapers before joining Time at a big salary jump. He began to feel that sense of luxury which the Time organization radiated along with its immanent anxiety—the fear of losing it. Writing at first only on music, he found that his copy was entirely rewritten to the Time formula. Soon he was writing about art "and then nearly everything else." It was rewritten, regardless. As he put it: "My writing was sent on to editors who rewrote it completely, turned it into sausage meat, so to speak, and then stuffed it into the magazine."

Sargeant became reconciled to having his copy turned into sausage meat. "I did not really care what happened to my copy at Time," he wrote—an abdication of news responsibility which the Time machine not only encouraged

but required. Indeed he admired the ingenuity of the sausage grinder. It ground like this:

Time had a weekly editorial conference at which its specialized writer-editors would present ideas for news stories to the managing editor, who was of course in closest contact with Luce. Ideas that were accepted were handed to the large and capable corps of researchers—mostly girls from Wellesley, Vassar or Smith. After a girl gathered the facts on a topic and completed necessary interviews, she would give all this information to the writer involved. From it he would extract the more important and/or interesting items and write his story. He gave it to his department editor, who would rewrite and cut it before handing it on to the managing editor himself, who would usually make fewer changes in giving it finished form. It was then returned to the researcher, who would check every word for accuracy before the copy went to the printer.

As Sargeant observed, "the responsibilities of the writer are minimal." Truth was up to the researcher, and final polish to the editors. This was what Luce called "group journalism." In bouncing back and forth from researcher to writer to editor to managing editor, strange things could happen. While the researcher had to be sure of her facts, she had no power over adjectives, quips, classical allusions, omissions or emphases, and Time's stress on cleverness was so often at the expense of accuracy that its reputation for truth among trained newspapermen would invariably be as low as its reputation for entertainment was high. A stream of collegians who came to Time to receive their first instruction in journalism were perhaps not fully aware of this system's foxy habit of downgrading dull fact and upgrading color, entertainment or message.

But there were others at Time less complaisant than Sargeant, including his friend James Agee, the gifted Harvardman. His copy went through the meat grinder like everyone else's, and although he disliked his work he was improvident and needed the paycheck. He kept a bottle of whisky at his right hand and Benzedrine tablets at his left. He was, as Sargeant said, killing himself, and he ultimately died young.

More eccentric than Agee was Alexander King, whose employment by Life proved that the devil could enter heaven. A book illustrator, playwright, charming liar and occasional user of morphine, King wore only pink neckties. He had worked for Vanity Fair, had known Clare Boothe Brokaw before she married Luce, and claimed that he helped her polish her plays. He later said he was hired on the strength of a letter he wrote Luce demonstrating the kind of zany inventiveness a picture magazine needed. For one thing, Father's Day was coming and he suggested a photo-feature on Whistler's Father, a distinguished but neglected man. Outstanding in impudence and dislike for sham, he saw almost no sham in Luce although he did in many well-paid Luce underlings. His description of Luce on their first meeting in the editor-in-chief's huge office was sharply drawn:

He was a sparse-haired, pale, timber-wolf kind of man, quick in his movements, and very decisive in his speech, as frequently happens with men who are afraid they might fall into a stammer. He had shaggy reddish eyebrows and cold, pale-gray eyes [pale blue, really] that hardly ever participated in his rare smiles.

I felt at once that there was a great deal of dangerous integrity in the man. I mean, the sort of integrity I generally associate with the head of the Women's Christian Temperance Union. An almost unbribable pig-headedness. It was also instantly obvious that he didn't have a shred of humor to cover any part of his almost frenzied intensity.

Hired, King gave a dozen cheap cameras to chimpanzees in a zoo, with which a few of them accidentally took pictures of spectators looking at them through the bars. These were published under the title, "This is what you look like to the monkey in the zoo." Among his many other ideas was a life-size picture of a twenty-one-inch dwarf who just fitted into Life's double-page twenty-two-inch dimension. But he disliked the kind of sanctimonious commercialism he found in the "Ivy League clothes dummies" running the Lucepress. "Nearly everybody was scared stiff of his job," he wrote. He disapproved of Time's eternal propaganda and its tricks such as its habit of following the name of Leon Trotsky with the parenthetical "(né Bronstein)":

> . . . It seemed to me that the editors of Time liked to . . . expose him as just a cheap little Jew who, in the manner of his breed, had, for devious, shady reasons, decided to change his monicker.

He commented on the central evangelical theme:

> Everybody in his right mind knows that Communism is a hell of a way of life. . . . So?
>
> So I'd like to make it plain at once that that still doesn't make unhampered, catch-as-catch-can capitalism into a snow-white maiden. . . . Life, Time and Fortune . . . do unremittingly sponsor the notion that to lack faith in capitalism is tantamount to spitting at the holy source of divine wisdom itself, because man can never hope to aspire to any nobler spiritual plateau than the expectation of six per cent interest on invested capital.

An unfailing party-enlivener, King was a guest of the Luces at Greenwich and at Mepkin, but he tired of his job and quit after only three years. There was general relief, for he was not the type the company liked to encourage. He did not have the faith.

XIV

1. THE MEEK PEOPLE

In 1938 Europe came to such a boil that Luce had to examine it even though his own affairs were cooking in New York. In May, Time absorbed the 250,000 remaining subscriptions of the Literary Digest, which in fifteen years it had beaten into submission. That same month, Time Inc. moved from its six-year home in the Chrysler Building to the top seven floors of the brand-new thirty-six-story Time-Life Building on 49th Street, a part of the massive Rockefeller Center complex. Billings, on vacation in South Carolina, had been implored to hurry back to Life so that Luce could leave. "Luce took me up to see his office on the roof," he told his diary, "—a magnificent double-story affair fit for old Duce or Luce." It would become known as the Penthouse.

Luce took Billings to lunch at the expensive Louis XIV restaurant across the street and sailed with his wife that afternoon on the splendid *Queen Mary*—which could be seen at its pier from the Time-Life offices. Only six weeks earlier the Nazis had marched into Austria, consummating the *Anschluss* which caused the Rome-Berlin Axis to reach unbroken from Baltic to Mediterranean. Luce had recently given a speech predicting world war in which America would be involved, but he did not really believe this. It had been given to an all-Yale group at Montclair, New Jersey, men whose complacency he felt constrained to disturb, saying:

> . . . [W]e Americans are entirely too cheerful. . . . In my time, Yale was turned into a military training camp. I think the chances are at least fifty-fifty that Yale will again be turned into a military training camp within ten years. . . . [R]ight now the gentlemen of England are trying to make up their minds whether they will let Germany grab Austria and Czechoslovakia. . . . War in Europe, war in Asia—and we stay out?

153

And he returned to his theme—indeed his obsession—of Ortega y Gasset, warning that the mass mind was a threat not only in Europe but in America where, he felt, political ideals had withered under the New Deal:

> One of the most brilliant works of our time is certainly Ortega y Gasset's thesis on the triumph of the mass-mind. The mass-mind shows itself in dictatorships. The mass-mind shows itself also in unrestrained and rudderless democracies.

Elaborate plans had been made by the Time organization for him to meet important and knowledgeable people abroad—always his goal no matter where he was. If he resembled a drama lover from Grand Rapids visiting New York to see ten plays in ten nights, it was the only way it could be done. His curiosity and his passion for first-hand observation were unmatched by any of his peers. The European trips of Adolph Ochs, Roy Howard, Hearst and Colonel Robert McCormick were vacation jaunts by comparison.

In London the Luces visited Ambassador Joseph Patrick Kennedy, whose hospitality could hardly have been impaired by the flattering cover story Time gave him when he was Securities and Exchange Commissioner ("an ideal policeman for the securities business"). Kennedy, perhaps not without White House ambitions and thoughts of Lucepress friendship, arranged an invitation for the Luces to a ball given by the Duchess of Sutherland, where they met the Duke and Duchess of Windsor, in whom Luce had a journalistic as well as a social interest. He conferred with Brendan Bracken, Harold Nicolson, Lord Beaverbrook and others. Cassandra, the London Daily News columnist, in noting Luce's visit, recognized both his political power and literary sins:

> They talk of him as a future Presidential candidate. Our elder statesmen and Potent Peers of the Realm curried his company. He was feted, dined, wined, complimented and plastered with praise. . . . Mr. Luce presents the news [in Time] in a way which he describes as being "curt, clear, complete." . . . And that style is as vile a piece of mangling as has ever stripped the heart out of prose.

The London Bystander also mentioned him as a Presidential possibility, adding, "Henry Luce is also a chain-smoker, heart-breakingly punctual, exceedingly idle about his clothes, and unable to forget, when dealing with waiters, that way back in China his father . . . had half-a-dozen 'boys' at his beck and call."

Going on by air to Berlin, the Luces were the guests of a wealthy German businessman at a gathering attended also by an American businessman from Stamford, Connecticut. After dinner, Luce brought up the subject of National Socialism. As he described it in the 6000-word report he made of his trip:

> Herr——[his host] is not even yet a member of the party, but he is a tremendous enthusiast for Germany if not for National Socialism and it was with an al-

154

most pathetic eagerness that he besought [the American from Stamford] to take the floor and explain to us outsiders the merits of Hitler's Germany. This Mr. [————] was glad to do. . . . He said that if he could take a year off to do nothing except study the ways and destiny of man in the twentieth century, the place he would come to, of all the countries in the world, is Germany. Whether or not you like it, Germany is the place where you are most likely to learn most about what you are going to get in the U.S. and elsewhere in the world, he says. . . . The great and first impression I got . . . is that National Socialism is a socialism which works mightily for the masses however distasteful it may be to them personally in many ways.

This patronizing of "the masses" was perhaps unconscious: ". . . in Germany there is no 'soak-the-rich' ideology," he wrote. ". . . The extraordinary thing about Hitler, at least for the moment, is that he has suspended the class war . . ."

The Luces had tea with the Hitler-truckling British ambassador in Berlin, Sir Nevile Henderson. They were driven south in a Cadillac by a relative of their Berlin host and lunched at Bayreuth:

. . . [I]t was there I first saw the paper edited by Streicher and entirely devoted to attacking Jews . . . there has been no exaggeration as to the important role which anti-Semitism has played in the Third Reich or as to the intensity of this brand of hatred. Our friend [the driver] . . . was anything but a "natural" Nazi, but even he accepted anti-Semitism as, at least, a necessary evil in the rebuilding of Germany under the Third Reich.

He listed points, some on the credit side, some on the debit, of this German brand of dictatorship. Fifteen busy theaters in Munich caused him to report, "Any idea that the Nazis have put the kibosh on culture is ridiculous." He thought the Nazis and the New Deal alike in their use of vast sums of money for self-advertising building programs. Luce in several speeches had made sarcastic mention of demagogic New Deal gestures toward "the people" in America. To him, the term seemed to mean a combination of the politically exploited and the *lumpen* that he, along with Ortega y Gasset, feared. He made repeated ironical use of it in mentioning the popularity of the motorbike in Germany:

. . . [T]he German people are on wheels by the millions—the People. Yes, the People. Oh, make no mistake, the People, the meek People who have inherited the earth. We read of Germany as if it were the private domain of Hitler with just enough people to serve him for an audience occasionally, and with an Army to parade around and amuse him. But the *visual* impression of Germany is of a People's land. I never saw Hitler. I saw many soldiers casually here and there but I saw no Army. I saw only The People and The People and The People. I do not know what they are but they did not seem to be slaves. Their chains are not visible.

They took the route Hitler had used in the *Anschluss*, attended the opera

in Vienna and dined with the American consul general, a man named Wiley: "Wiley is married to a charming Polish Jew and is 100% anti-Nazi but he too, I think, agrees that National Socialism is thoroughly misunderstood in the U.S."

At this very time the Nazis were increasing their pressure on the Czech Sudetenland. In Prague, Luce talked with President Eduard Beneš (whom he had last seen in 1921 while on tour from Oxford) and was affected when Beneš swore the Czechs would defend their land, saying, "Ask anybody—anybody you meet in the streets—and he will tell you he will fight." Luce observed, "We saw tens of thousands of good stolid Bohemians going about their business . . . men—*and* women—who would fight and die for country and for liberty. It was a thrill—I confess it—to touch, however briefly—such a people." He added, ". . . I know no such men of courage in America. We in America have totally forgotten what it is like to . . . [be] with men who will fight . . ." But this was Luce the militant, the admirer of courage as a virtue in itself, not Luce the internationalist making any decision of his own as to the merits of the Sudeten question. He made none. "The first German plane which arrives over Prague is, I am sure, a dead plane," he wrote. But after he had gone on to Karlsbad, talked with the Sudeten German leader there and heard his story about the "subjection" by the Czechs of the Germans within their boundaries, he seemed to swing toward the Germans:

> It may well be true that there was no "Sudeten question" until Hitler came along. But on the other hand the real moral of all this is that Europe is not divided into countries but into valleys, and every valley has its history and its local demons and its fairies. . . . Without this deep emotional attachment to *place*, you cannot have civilization, and yet, of course, this very attachment to place breeds conflicts between places. We must not be contemptuous of Europe because it has this Spirit-of-Place, this attachment to soil—what Hitler calls Brot and Boten [*sic*]. We need much more of it in America . . . We must recognize that this is necessary to civilization . . .

In Paris the Luces were the dinner guests of the American ambassador, that odd number, William C. Bullitt, now congenial to them since his former infatuation with the Soviet had swung to the opposite extreme. Charming and an intriguer, Bullitt, if later rumor could be believed, was then pulling strings for a European accord against Stalin that would take strange shape at Munich. His guests, in addition to Cabinet ministers, included André Maurois, Louis Bromfield and M. Bailby, owner of Le Jour, the Paris paper that was said to have received huge secret payments from Mussolini for supporting a French pro-Fascist policy. The air was charged with machinations, into which it is not impossible that Luce may have been initiated by Bullitt, a man who knew the power of the press. Luce wrote, "To the vast glee of Bullitt and Novelist Bromfield and others assembled, I asked M. Bailby to explain to me the morals of the French press and whether its reputation for corruption was jus-

tified." He commented favorably on Pierre Laval and felt that Fortune had been too kind to Léon Blum and the Popular Front—feelings certainly shared by Bullitt:

> . . . Communism is a much bigger thing in Europe than it is in America. There were *millions* of actual official Communist votes in Germany before Hitler. In France there is a very large block of actual Communist votes seating 72 Communist Congressmen and there are whole suburbs around Paris which are Communistic—not merely in the alarmist American sense of the word, but as an actual party organization.

Although he announced no specific conclusions, the tone of Luce's comments suggested agreement with Bullitt that Europe might be approaching a Fascist-Communist showdown in which American interests lay with the Fascists, and a strange air of coolness over the prospect. The Hitler career of international blackmail was on the record, and although Nazi indecencies against humanity were not yet perpetrated daily on fashionable streets in broad daylight, they were known to the world. Luce seemed to walk through this evil without a twitch. He listened placidly to the wealthy Berlin businessman-apologist and the wealthy American businessman-apologist for Hitler, and became in his report a near-apologist himself, suggesting that Nazism was "misunderstood" in America and that better comprehension would place the Nazis in a better light.

2. THE FOUR CHEEKS AT MUNICH

The Luces arrived in New York on the *Queen Mary* June 20, having had Ambassador Kennedy as a companion. Luce took Clare home and hurried to the office as inevitably as a racing addict would have gone to the track. "He sat on my picture table swinging his legs," Billings wrote, "and talking about the bigwigs he'd met. Joe Kennedy, Edward of Windsor—he'll probably entertain the Windsors when they come to the U.S."

Clare's new play *Kiss the Boys Goodbye*, a social satire which she was said to have written in a month, opened in New York September 28. Time's drama critic was now the solid Louis Kronenberger, who remarked that he could Kiss the Boss Goodbye if he did not like the Boss's wife's new play. But his review was bravely lukewarm, daring to say that by comparison with the leading character, some others were "dramatically flat." It got by the Boss without change and he never seemed to hold it against Kronenberger. But he did make handsome amends to his spouse when her play received rousing praise in the following week's Life, which called it "high comedy" and saluted her for smashing the jinx that usually follows a hit by producing another hit. Life's four pages and twenty-four pictures with glowing captions made priceless publicity, the envy of other playwrights less favorably connected.

When Kronenberger later was a guest at Luce parties, he observed, Clare "tended to shake my hand while scanning some far horizon, and to murmur goodbye as though seeing the last of a rather incompetent footman. Once, however, she did remark with a strong hissing sound, 'I'm ssssso glad that we sssso often sssee eye-to-eye about the theatre.' "

On September 30, Luce's prediction that the Czechs would fight was undercut by the turning of "all four cheeks" by Chamberlain and the signing of the four-power Munich pact from which Czechoslovakia, as well as Russia and the League, was excluded. Chamberlain and Daladier, in placating Hitler by awarding him most of the Sudetenland and later informing the Czechs that they must submit, were delaying World War II only by a scant year and for a heavy price—Czech border fortifications that would have stopped the Nazis in a two-front war, plus thirty-five Czech divisions.

Time praised the pact, saying it was easy for those not threatened to criticize: "Really scathing attacks on Neville Chamberlain were made almost entirely from extremely safe distances of several thousand miles . . ." It followed a sly Time propaganda custom by attributing criticism of Munich to people it downgraded, notably "certain Manhattan news broadcasters" of whom it named only "Johannes Steel, a German agent on mysterious missions in Brazil until the Nazis came into power." The following week Chamberlain was Time's honored cover subject. It noted that "energetic, square-jawed" Premier Daladier got a 535–75 Chamber vote of confidence on the Munich question, "nearly all the dissenters being Communists." In the Commons, Winston Churchill drew scowls when he warned, "We have sustained a total, unmitigated defeat . . ."

Time's foreign news had now grown obnoxious to many middle-roaders. Kronenberger remarked on Goldsborough's "pro-fascist, reputedly anti-Semitic" line and how his "week-after-week treatment of the European situation was getting to be as inevitable a topic as Goldsborough's presence in the office was becoming an embarrassment." At the time of Munich, Luce seemed in substantial agreement with his FN chief. He still did not believe war was coming, his journalistic-missionary efforts were devoted to isolating the Russians, and the Axis still seemed a God-given weapon aimed straight at Bolshevism. But within his organization the group protesting this view grew more restive, among them Ralph Ingersoll. As general manager of Time, Ingersoll was also embarrassed by a sag in circulation he blamed in part on Goldsborough. A few weeks after Munich he wrote Luce:

If ever the returns were in on the failure of a major department, the returns are in on Time's Foreign News. . . . Goldsborough has almost consistently been sly, unfair and uninformed. But in the face of the greater charge of being unfeeling, this is almost beside the point. People do not buy hundreds of thousands of copies of the writings of a tired, tired Jesuit. . . . My prescription is that he be given a year's leave of absence. . . . Goldy's gossipy mind was amusing in the

158

20's, it is not amusing now . . . And utterly inconsistent with that basic premise
of Prospectus No. 1, "We believe in the existence of Good and Evil."

This criticism of Goldsborough was also to some extent criticism of Luce
himself, who was beginning to fume at Ingersoll's tough officiousness. But he
knew that even conservatives such as Mrs. Helen Reid of the Herald Tribune
were taken aback by Time's irresponsibility in foreign news. Ingersoll's mention of "Good and Evil," of course referred to Time's original prospectus, so
carefully drawn by Luce and Hadden. Goldsborough was raising a problem of
morale on the staff, and circulation figures were holy symbols. Luce's final
agreement with Ingersoll about the FN editor was on the ground of style
rather than of judicious treatment of the news.

In November Luce took over the editing of Time for a week, in so doing
reading Goldy's copy hot from the pencil. On December 8 he sent a memo
"To all Time Writers and Editors" giving Goldsborough generous praise after
its opening paragraph: "With the best wishes of all of us, and no doubt a little
of our best envy, Laird Goldsborough begins this week his long-overdue sabbatical year." Robert Neville and other younger men thereafter wrote FN. At
the same time Luce made another gesture toward his rule of "handing the
company over" to younger men by retiring Myron Weiss, who had reached
the advanced age of forty-four. Weiss recalls that Luce was very kind, "hated
to do it" and paid a handsome severance sum.

The Luces went to Mepkin for the holidays with the two Luce boys, Ann
Brokaw and a number of guests including the Allen Grovers and the Daniel
Longwells, Mrs. Longwell being the former Mary Fraser, one of the few
women to attain editorial status at Time. The main house was still unfinished
but five guest houses designed by Stone had risen, each air-conditioned, indi-
rectly lighted and having glass walls facing the river. Neighbors were critical
of such functional glitter in a country of pillared verandas and moss-dripping
liveoaks. "Why should I build an old mansion on the Cooper River?" Clare
asked with some justice. "I have no roots there. This is none of my tradition,
and it would be false to ape the old ways."

The common enjoyment she and her husband took in addressing an audience occasionally brought darkness to the Lucean brow, since she could inter-
polate entertaining remarks on her subject while he was articulating his own.
Sometimes, at the long dinner table, the Luces seemed to compete for their
guests' attention, Luce seizing listeners at his end while Clare gathered those
at the other. The serious Luce at times seemed unaware that she could say extravagant things simply for effect which less literal listeners were expected to
discount, and in any case he hewed to the husband-is-master doctrine. On one
occasion when they disagreed about something, it was said, Luce leaned forward and asked icily, "You are sure that you are right, aren't you? Absolutely
sure?" "Yes," Clare replied, "I am absolutely sure." "Well then, if you are
that sure . . . then are you willing to bet one million dollars?" Although the

angry Mrs. Luce did not accept the challenge, it seemed entirely serious and some of the astonished guests realized it was not beyond the couple's resources. The Mepkin duck shooting, too, could create strain, for she was the better marksman and he loathed being beaten at anything by anybody.

Luce posed for Jo Davidson, who was making a bust of him. Meanwhile, in the Time-Life Building, Ingersoll was making a momentous decision. Time's Man of the Year—a selection Luce took with great seriousness—had already been chosen. Newsworthiness rather than righteousness being the criterion, he was of course Hitler. Time had an excellent color picture of him in uniform which, however, did not show his fanaticism and made him appear rather like a banker in khaki.

"I did not see how Time could put this dignified picture of him on the cover without conveying some kind of tacit endorsement," Ingersoll later explained, without adding that Time's dignified textual treatment of him had often given a similar impression.

After much agency search he found a lithograph by an Austrian who had fled the Nazi terror, Rudolph C. von Ripper. It showed a small, diabolical Hitler playing a huge organ which actuated a monstrous wheel from which hung the bodies of his victims. It became the Time cover for January 2, 1939, with the caption: "MAN OF 1938: From the unholy organist, a hymn of hate." With it was a text piece abandoning the attitudes of the three-weeks'-departed Goldsborough, a few passages reading:

> . . . Herr Hitler reaped on that day at Munich the harvest of an audacious, defiant, ruthless foreign policy he had pursued for five and a half years. . . . Hitler became in 1938 the greatest threatening force that the democratic, freedom-loving world faces today. . . . Small, neighboring States . . . feared to offend him. . . . The Fascintern, with Hitler in the driver's seat, with Mussolini, Franco and the Japanese military cabal riding behind, emerged in 1938 as an international revolutionary movement. . . . The Fascist battle against freedom is often carried forward under the false slogan of "Down with Communism!" . . . Civil rights and liberties have disappeared. Opposition to the Nazi regime has become tantamount to suicide or worse. . . . Germany's 700,000 Jews have been tortured physically, robbed of homes and properties . . . Now they are being held for "ransom," a gangster trick through the ages. . . . Out of Germany has come a steady, ever-swelling stream of refugees, Jews and Gentiles, Catholics as well as Protestants, who could stand Nazism no longer. . . .

Had not Time for so long applauded the Fascist dictators, these things would not so badly have needed saying. Luce himself had approved the text after criticizing it for being too anti-Fascist and adding a paragraph listing Hitler's achievements within the Reich, but it seems possible that such sentiments as "The Fascist battle against freedom is often carried forward under the false slogan of 'Down with Communism!' " may have been slipped in during his absence. A breakthrough of near-honesty had been made. It must have puzzled the more pliant readers who had for so long been led by this same

160

magazine to think well of the dictators. As for Time's own liberals, it was said that a large group of them paraded across 48th Street to the Three G's, a favorite saloon, and hung one on.

3. THE GENTLEMAN FROM INDIANA

Ingersoll was a radical who at times spoke obliquely. In a later explanation of the crisis he described himself as a journalist with a social conscience whereas (and here his tongue seems to have been far in cheek), "Harry . . . believed that a journalist should be amoral—with no responsibility except to be accurate [sic] and able to hold the attention of his audience." Ingersoll, already planning to start a newspaper of his own, no longer looked on Luce as his lifelong employer. When Luce returned, to gaze at the Man of the Year issue with distended eyes, Ingersoll described the subsequent interview:

> It was in Harry's room on top of the Time-Life Building, and we were quite alone . . . Harry became visibly emotional, flushing and getting that cold set look he gets when he is very angry. We sat looking at each other for about a minute and then he said simply, "Spilt milk; let's not discuss it."

Luce's official objection was that the cover should not be a deliberate instrument of propaganda. Apparently he forgot his deliberately propagandist cover of June 9, 1930—the portrait of Stalin surrounded by Red conspirators. At the same time he took another blow from the left in the appearance of High Time, published by the "Communist Party Members at Time Inc.," which was secretly distributed around the office and instantly became the talk of New York. Among its many complaints it listed fourteen recent firings and blamed Luce:

> Psychologically, Time Inc. is a one man organization . . . [A]ll his [Luce's] sub-executives are terrified of him, and this terror seeps down through the whole organization. Mr. Luce is fond of ripping apart an entire magazine on the deadline and making it over again. On occasion he does the same to his staff.

"Join the Communist Party!" High Time urged as a way to fight for job security. Its longest feature was headed, "Goldie—The End of Time's Minister of Propaganda," an attack on the distortions of the sabbaticalized FN head. As the New Republic saw it, the article "offers a convincing explanation of Time's curious editorial interpretations of what has been happening in Soviet Russia, in Spain, in Germany, in Italy and in France." High Time also dispensed gossip about upper-echelon personnel. Luce, who would as soon open a brothel as harbor a nest of Reds, was in a passion. Billings wrote in his diary:

> At 5:15 an emergency meeting in Luce's office . . . Gottfried, Davenport, Jackson, Prentice, Paine, Hodgins and Bruce Bromley [a lawyer with Maurice T. Moore's firm] . . . Luce proposed that we try to find out who in our company

was responsible for High Time and fire them out of hand. This precipitated a hot debate. Gottfried, Davenport and Paine warned vigorously against a purge, a manhunt which would get the company bad publicity. . . . The meeting was strongly against Luce's proposal of a frontal attack. . . .

Now Walter Winchell gossiped that Luce had hired detectives to hunt down the Communists of High Time. The New Republic chuckled, "Our detectives tell us that Mr. Luce is going to be very embarrassed when he discovers that those contributors out on the firing line include some people 'way up' on his own staff." Luce, after some thought, sent out an admonitory office memo:

> Most of you have seen the sheet "High Time" put out by the "Communist Party Members at Time Inc." I think that just as a gossip sheet it's a pretty amusing job of writing. I also think that the authors of it were disloyal to the organization and to all their fellow workers. . . . A publication by "The Communist Party at Time Inc." is just as offensive as one would be by a "Nazi Bund in Time Inc." . . . It has been a cardinal principle with us that editors, writers and researchers have a right to spout to one another their views . . . We have had people of all shades of political thought on our staff and I maintain the right of every one of them to speak to every other member of the staff with as much intellectual freedom—and carefreeness—as he would in his own family. . . . *Free speech in confidence* is essential to group journalism. It would be intolerable if our editors had to feel that they could not open their mouths without having some half-uttered thought plucked out and used to stab them publicly in the back. . . .
>
> I think you will agree with me that one of the things *not* to do is to start a Red hunt. . . .
>
> We cannot get along on any basis except that of free expression toward one another in private and assurance that such confidence will not be violated. If anyone feels that he cannot make that confidence mutual on his part, he ought to resign. Certainly if the management discovers any employee making public gossip of matters that are properly confidential between members of the staff, he will be fired.
>
> —Henry R. Luce.

Time's clandestine Communists came back at him in their second issue, saying, "He called it 'gossip.' When you want to suppress free speech, it sounds better to call it 'gossip.' " There was an attack on the use of Life in 1938 as a "Republican Party organ," and on John Martin for steady denigration of the New Deal in Time's NA department: "He does his work by innuendo, by tricky leads, by making New Dealers sinister or foolish and anti-New Dealers dignified and cool-headed." As for Luce, High Time said he had had political ambitions since 1932, had no chance until Life became so powerful, and now seemed to have settled for the role of king-maker rather than king. Perhaps most embarrassing was the charge that Time had suppressed news that would antagonize large advertisers—that it had treated the Akron strikes in a manner hostile to labor and favorable to the tire manufacturers.

Luce and His Empire

Troubled over his own "revolt of the masses," Luce wrote an interminable memo which he never sent out, much of it in rebuttal of the theories of Ingersoll. Just who was Time aimed at? Ingersoll had argued that each department should be handled with enough depth to please experts. Not at all, said Luce. Time was meant to be read cover-to-cover by all readers, not patchily by specialists:

And that means that if you are going to ask one man to read Time from cover-to-cover, you have got to work like hell to edit Time *for one man.* . . . Now, theoretically, the lower the mental content, the wider your audience will be. But that is only theoretically or generally speaking—it is not true in specific cases. The mental content of Life always was about 1000% higher than any other picture magazine and is 2000% higher today—and look at the comparative results. But if you are going to hold 700,000 circulation [on Time], must you edit for the last and dumbest of the 700,000? No—or if that is so, the Board of Directors of Time Inc. will flatly authorize you *not* to edit for same. Time is going to be a damned intelligent paper—let the circulation chips fall where they may. . . .

Time is edited for the Gentleman of Indiana and for Madame the Lady of Indiana. . . . Time is going to write for the Gentleman of Indiana, writing to him as man to man, in straightforward decent language, no punches pulled, but no dirty below-the-belt cracks either at God, the Constitution or his fellow gentlemen of Indiana. . . .

That meant perpetuation of the meat grinder, the writing of every story to maintain editorial "unity" and satisfy cover-to-cover readers with all text at a similar level of understanding. The editor-in-chief also loosed a bolt at Ingersoll:

Someone else around here, call him Mr. "X," is worrying about Time's intellectual or interpretative level. Well, now, what I would like to do is to change places with Mr. "X." Dear Mr. "X," if you will guarantee that Time's newsstand circulation will move steadily forward, I will gladly be responsible for Time's intellectual level. . . . I fancy I could be a pretty hot intellectual myself if I ever had the chance to be. I, too, could probe the European situation to its very gizzard. . . . So, Mr. "X," . . . I'll take on the job of being [Time's] intellectual mentor and elevator. . . .

I do not conceive of myself as having to be the continual Moral Schoolmaster of this place. But I think I cannot escape being the custodian or depository of "Time's conscience." Possibly therefore an informal, unwritten custom should be established—namely that any senior editor or senior executive of any Time Inc. publication who is troubled about any tendency involving editorial conscience should understand that he can and should come to me about it at any time. Practically, and recognizing that we are all frail mortals, it is a question of mutual confidence and respect. If fundamentally any senior does not have sufficient confidence and respect for my ethical attitudes, he should, I think, put me on notice to that effect . . .

163

In April 1939, Ingersoll, who had questioned Luce's ethical attitudes, left Time to start work on the liberal-leftist newspaper PM, where he would prove himself as obdurate in his prejudices as Luce was in his.

4. THE REPUBLIC IN DANGER

Other changes at Time enunciated the banishment of Ingersoll and the renewed hegemony of the Boss. Under Gottfried as managing editor were two associates, Frank Norris and T. S. Matthews. Luce made it plain that he was not only his own publisher but also the top editor, responsible for "general character, tone, direction, ambition and ideals."

None of his three headmen had newspaper experience. Matthews was as close to being politically obtuse as such an otherwise cultivated man could be. A literary perfectionist, he had done much to rid the "culture" departments of the Timestyle excesses which the New Yorker had lampooned. According to Winthrop Sargeant, who had worked under him, Matthews had been "empire building"—that is, aiming for more power and gathering a group of loyal followers with whom he could move in when opportunity came, as it had now. Like most of his colleagues he was nominally a liberal. Astonishingly, despite his ten years at Time, his sympathy for the Spanish Loyalists, his acquaintance with Goldsborough and presumably with his work, he was unaware of the extent to which Time was a propaganda magazine. He had an intermittent sense of journalistic responsibility. In his new eminence he decided that he must get better acquainted with Luce. As he put it:

> I could no longer say that I didn't take Time seriously. I now thought it a barbarous magazine that might, at least in part, be civilized. It had possibilities that hadn't been apparent to me before. I liked my job and wanted to go on with it. But not under any and all circumstances, not under any kind of management.°

He invited Luce to dine with him and four colleagues, Norris, Charles Christian Wertenbaker, John Osborne and Robert Fitzgerald. Luce accepted but insisted that the five instead be *his* guests at his new apartment in the Waldorf Towers on Park Avenue, just two blocks east of Rockefeller Center.

The Luce apartment had the coldness of the habitation of a rich couple pursuing power. Luce, who never knew what he was eating, was hardly more conscious of his surroundings. A couple of the callers had never seen him, much less spoken to him. The dinner gave them an opportunity to see what he was like, and also provided Matthews with two unscheduled meetings with Mrs. Luce. Hunting for a bathroom as the evening wore on, he walked down a corridor, opened a door and discovered Clare before her mirror, preparing

° Quoted from *Name and Address*, by T. S. Matthews (Simon & Schuster, N.Y. 1960).

for bed. Closing the door and retreating, he turned a corner, spied another door, opened it and now was eying Clare from the other side.

"Young man!" she said severely.

But the unexpected view of Clare was less important than a clear view of Luce's aims. "Luce," Matthews recalled, "could hold the floor and hold it." He was ingratiating and convincing in his exposition of his news policies. It grew so late that the conference was continued a week later at the Luce apartment, then again at the Players Club, where Matthews engaged a private room. As he described it:

> When Luce arrived for this meeting he handed us each a copy of a memo he had written. As we read it, we saw that he had anticipated all these final questions and had written his answers. Furthermore he had lifted the argument to a general discussion of journalism, its purposes and possibilities, and ended with a statement of his own journalistic faith. He had cut the ground out from under us. We looked at each other and shook our heads. There was nothing left to say.

Few other press lords would have submitted to questioning by five subordinates, a couple of them far enough down the ladder so that he had never met them. Luce more than once had sent word to Miss Thrasher that he was too busy to see his father, waiting outside. Yet he had given these five a total of ten or twelve hours divided among three evenings. He had gone over the ground so thoroughly in his own mind and was so sure of his ground that he dispersed the doubts of five keen men who had good reason for doubts so soon after Munich and the Goldy crisis. The "soul meetings" with Luce would become a company legend and would form the theme of a novel years later by Wertenbaker.

Matthews's account of the talks names the cast, sets the scene, then leaves out much of the action and dialog. He did, however, name one of the questions he asked Luce. It was in fact the crucial one—the right question in the wrong tense: "Under what circumstances would you consider using Time as a political instrument?" And he gave Luce's answer to that one question:

"If I thought the Republic was in danger."

No one seems to have asked, "Is it in danger?" Indeed Luce performed a forensic feat in winning over the five editors who were, to one degree or another, not sure that they wholly approved of his conduct of the magazine. He could scarcely have done so had he not been morally certain of his own ground, backed by the angels of the Lord. The greatest question that had arisen among the five was the same one that had troubled MacLeish and a few others—the question of bias in the presentation of the news. He had disposed of that masterfully in his conversation and in his memo to them, disavowing any intention to make Time objective and asserting that objectivity was impossible even if desirable:

> Even within our company there is occasionally some confusion on this score. For example, there is a persistent urge to say that Time is "unbiased," and to

claim for it complete "objectivity." That, of course, is nonsense. The original owners-editors-promoters of Time made no such fantastic claim. . . . You will find an acknowledgment of bias in the first circular. . . .

They were bowled over not only by his skill in debate but by the force of his convictions. They believed in him. They believed in him enough so that they did not put questions that would have occurred to really hard-bitten doubters under aggressive leadership. True, the original circular seventeen years earlier had conceded the impossibility of "complete neutrality on public questions" and said that Time would exercise the benevolent prejudices common to enlightened minds such as the belief that the world was round. Only a few thousand people had read it then and had long since forgotten about it. It had been flashed before the readers again on Time's tenth anniversary. Were such warnings supposed to suffice in perpetuity? Would it not be fair to make this point clear in every issue? Should not every reader be informed that he was not reading news but news modified and rewritten to include opinion and suggestion? Did not the subtitle, The Weekly Newsmagazine, assure the reader that he was getting news? Was there not a question of honest labeling of merchandise here? And did not the bias go considerably further than agreement that the world was round? These were logical questions that did not get asked, or, if asked, were turned aside by Luce's impregnable moral assurance.

They were questions that would continue to trouble some of the more thoughtful Timen—questions which in their existence in an unknown number of editorial minds would remain hidden like a skeleton in the closet at Time Inc. for many years, with great excitement arising when someone occasionally was brave enough to open the door.

Aside from Time's skilled adjectival shaping of the news and the people in it, there were at least three levels of communication of its propaganda. There was the relatively rare honest opinion given openly along with an honest news story. There were the opinions cleverly hidden behind the facts of a news story which itself was still essentially true. And there was the twisting of the news itself by exaggeration, selection or suppression. This last could be achieved in many ways—in the case of a public official, for example, by stressing the emptiest or most questionable passages in his speeches and ignoring the constructive and inspiring passages. Time often used this technique on President Roosevelt, not forgetting details like frequent mention of his use of a cigarette holder, which was regarded as a vote-loser in the virile hinterland. The gimmicks available to shrewd denigrators were limited only by the fertility of their imaginations. One of them, reflecting Luce's fairly continuous effort to depict Roosevelt as a potential dictator, appeared in Life, where careful search of picture files turned up Hitler, Mussolini, Stalin and the President all in similar poses of shaking hands, pointing, petting animals and pinning medals. The headline was "Speaking of Dictators," and readers who wrote to complain were assured it was only a joke. Another was Time's cover

story on the American Communist leader Earl Browder whose color photograph, backed by Communist posters, had a clever guilt-by-association line under it: "COMRADE EARL BROWDER / For Stalin, for Roosevelt . . ."

Time's treatment of Roosevelt grew more acid as his second term wore on without real economic recovery and there was some evidence of public disillusionment. It was unequaled in its ability to make a man look incompetent or suspect in the framework of a few compliments that gave an impression of fairness. A cover story on James Roosevelt said the son had grown rich selling "the Roosevelt brand of insurance" to clients whom Time pointedly refrained from suggesting might expect political favors in return. With great good nature Time portrayed the President as a man who liked a drink even better than the next fellow and that "often at banquets the flower vases before his plate conceal as many as four Old-Fashioneds, which he downs before one can say 'Jack Garner.'"

Although Luce was still susceptible to occasional liberal ideas, his growing hatred of Roosevelt tended to steer him from anything even faintly New Dealish. Time Inc. was full of well-paid liberals in the position of being forced to write propaganda that pained them. Their wrestlings with conscience would be documented in works of fiction as well as fact. In the novel *The Big Wheel* by the former Time staffer John Brooks, one such writer bemoans his dilemma:

> "I know I shouldn't go on writing things I don't believe. I know I ought to quit. . . . And by God I intend to, in another year at the outside. But how can I? I tell you, I need ten thousand a year to keep the apartment! Besides, where could I go from here? This is the top, Dick! The top! This is what men spend their time working up to. The only place you can go from here is down."

XV

1. JACK BENNY AND WINSTON CHURCHILL

When Hitler invaded Czechoslovakia, Time said it was the "signal for a belated Stop Hitler drive," as if its own recognition of the dictator's true stripe had been early. Luce said no more about Nazism being "misunderstood." He urged that America, instead of standing in isolation, summon the world to peace "with all the power and energy we can command." He met with the nation's two most honored public men, reporting on it predictably enough so that Billings wrote in his diary: "Editors' and Publishers' meeting at which Luce reported thus: He had lunch with President Roosevelt privately, and soon after, breakfast with ex-President Hoover, privately. Roosevelt was dull and uninspired and had nothing to say. Hoover was exciting and thoughtful and said plenty. So what!"

Late in June the Luces sailed for Europe, "only for a rest." But at Aix-les-Bains Luce received an irresistible invitation from America's ambassador to Poland, Anthony Biddle, to visit that country, which was then arming against Nazi threats. In view of England's alliance with Poland, he flew with Clare to London to prepare himself with a breathless round of interviews with British leaders. They also attended the London opening of Clare's The Women, which had had trouble passing the censor, and met George Bernard Shaw, whose Socialism Luce abhorred. Shaw, unacquainted with American journalism—or was it a Shavian barb?—later sent Clare a postcard ending infuriatingly for Luce, "Kindest regards to you and Mr. Boothe." En route to Poland the Luces stopped briefly at the Ritz in Paris, where he wrote his first wife:

> Dear Lila: Three days in London of the most strenuous interviewing caused me to miss yesterday's boat with the letter I had intended to write. Flew over here today and in half an hour we are off to Poland.

Luce and His Empire

> As you know, I had intended to come over this time only for a rest. . . . But
> in view of the terrific goings on in all parts of Europe, it seemed foolish not to
> avail myself of various unusual opportunities to look around—and so I'm doing
> two weeks of journalisticing. . . . I hope to see you before the summer's end.

In Warsaw, where the Luces were among the guests at a ball given by Ambassador Biddle, he was persuaded that Poland would hold off the Nazis because of its "tradition of military patriotism." Hurrying on to Bucharest,
where he dined with Foreign Minister Gabriel Gafencu, he became optimistic
about the resistance Rumania would offer. "Today there are no braver opponents of Nazi Germany than the governments of the not-so-democratic Republic of Poland and the quite democratic Kingdom of Rumania," he wrote in
the 3500-word report he prepared for his editors back home. (Both countries
would quickly crumble.) Surely Clare was the instigator of their visit, as they
returned through France, with Gertrude Stein and Alice B. Toklas, who recorded it curtly and clearly but incompletely:

> . . . We received a visit from Clare Boothe Luce and her husband. They had
> been to Poland and both were convinced that there would be war. . . . She was
> embroidering in petit point a map of the United States. She was convinced her
> husband would become President.

The world reports of Henry Luce, which would ultimately run into the
hundreds of thousands of words, were already becoming a tradition in the
Time-Life Building. One could never fault his conviction that the way to
learn about world crises was to go to the scene and ask those involved. He
did, however, expect to arrive at solutions rather quickly. The Luce curiosity
still had in it something of the Yale undergraduate pelting his professors with
questions. There was in it also something of the pollster, jotting down quick
answers and going on to the next individual. In his short report on his activities in London, his comment on his talk with Lord Beaverbrook was,
". . . my God, what a man, in his huge London Palace-Prison, in his terrifying and fantastically expensive discomfort—Power, Power, Power . . ."
Whether the English took Clare and her petit-point map as an omen of the
Presidency, they took Luce seriously as a man of influence and molder of
opinion. He was deferred to by "statesmen and potent peers" even more than
the year before. England, haunted by the peril of a war for which she was not
prepared, needed the American friendship which Luce could influence. His
report listed twenty-one persons (not counting Shaw) he had interviewed during his short stay, including Winston Churchill, Lady Astor, Anthony Eden
("infinitely nice"), Viscount Willingden, Lady Sybil Colefax ("most delightful") and Lord Camrose. He added as if in afterthought:

> Oh, of course, the most enjoyable evening of all my political travels! Dinner à
> quatre with the [Lord Robert] Vansittarts . . . in a fashionable restaurant . . .
> and then we returned to their home for a night-cap, inspected the Vansittart an-
> cestors . . .

If the Luce reports let the editors back home know he was getting up in the world, they also let them know that he was the most energetic reporter in the establishment and that they had better put similar effort into their work. But his office reputation as a prophet was poor. "Luce came back from Europe at noon," Billings wrote August 14. "He dropped into my office for 20 minutes and talked world affairs . . . He thinks the Poles will fight for their sovereignty. We laughed to ourselves and kissed the Poles goodbye . . ."

His hunch that war would not come in 1939 was also mishandled by events. A week after his return came Stalin's answer to Munich, the Nazi-Soviet pact. To go with this appalling news was a Jack Benny cover, a million copies already printed in color for the September 4 Time. "Oh, God," Luce protested, "how I hate the idea of Jack Benny this week." The comedian was scrapped and the man hurriedly substituted was Churchill, with whom Luce had so recently talked—a Churchill who was still only a lowly M.P. Next in this parade of world-shaking events came the Nazi invasion of Poland on September 1. Europe was at war, and perversely had consummated it too late to get it into the September 4 Time.

Hitler's accommodation with Stalin at long last destroyed Luce's sympathy for him. "Luce went through the special issue war dummy [of Life] with disastrous results," Billings wrote. "He felt we didn't blame Hitler enough for starting the war, that we were too hard on Britain. . . . I called in Kay [Hubert Kay, an editor] and told him . . . Said he: 'When is Harry going to declare war on Germany?' "

2. THE REX LETTER

"I've met the man who ought to be the next President of the United States," Russell Davenport told his wife after his first encounter with Wendell Willkie. Davenport, now managing editor of Fortune, was bowled over by the charming, rumpled Hoosier who headed Commonwealth & Southern Corporation. When Willkie spent a weekend at the Davenport summer place in Westport, where the lion cub Davenport had given his wife was tethered to a tree, the Luces were interested guests.

The Roosevelt years which had seen Luce attain wealth and power had seen him largely frustrated in touching the Washington springs of power because he was a Republican, an outsider. He was also sensitive about a liberal establishment, with the President at its head and front, which did not take him seriously as an intellectual. He was well along with his collection of honorary degrees and yearned for membership in the Yale Corporation. His protesting, "I fancy I could be a pretty hot intellectual myself" came from the heart. He was said to have told Clare that he could think of no one mentally his superior—a claim that took her aback and made her mention first Einstein

and then John Kieran. Luce rejected them both, saying Einstein was a specialist and Kieran "a freak." It seems likely that Luce ached to be king-maker for a Republican administration that would bring him into the center of power rather than the periphery. He had cheered Willkie's losing fight against TVA. Time had just used one of its subtler pejoratives on Roosevelt's TVA boss David Lilienthal who, it said, had come "out of the White House with his lips twisted in a grin of satisfaction" over the TVA victory. Since Horatio Alger, twisted lips had meant sure villainy and a "grin of satisfaction" suggested the triumph of turpitude.

While Luce investigated President-making, his wife was setting a course for a seat in Congress. She sailed for Italy in February with her friend Margaret Case, a Vogue editor. Miss Case's ultimate mission was to study Paris fashions, Mrs. Luce's to study the quiet confrontation of French and German armies at the Maginot Line which had continued virtually bullet-free for six months and was called in America the Phony War. She planned a book about it which should help her political ambitions. Before going on to France she attended an audience with Pope Pius XII and chatted with Count Galeazzo Ciano, Mussolini's son-in-law and foreign minister, at a Roman dinner party. Quite on her own—she was smashingly independent—she had adopted her husband's moral and political loathing for Communism, though she was not pious.

In Paris she resembled her husband in seeming less critical of Laval's property-conscious rightism than of the Popular Front, the "French New Deal" with its inclusion of Communists. Her mind was keen and tough. What was the French strategy? What did they expect to gain by the Phony War? Did they still hope the Germans might turn on the Russians? Did they believe that Germany would ultimately collapse economically because of the blockade? But what if Germany itself became Communist, a true ally of Russia? She was dubious of the Maginot mind and the French tablecloth generals.

Time had recently opened a small Paris bureau to watch the war. With the aid of its staff and her own acquaintance with Ambassador Bullitt and others, she arranged interviews with public figures and even wangled a visit to the Maginot Line near Metz, where the bored *poilus* were so impressed by her beauty that they brought her roses. She had been accredited as a Life correspondent. She could be as blunt as her husband in asking questions of strangers. She caught a tartar in Mme. Charles Pomaret, wife of the Minister of Labor, when she said: "Madame Pomaret, we Americans who are friends of France feel that American public opinion, which is largely isolationist, is partly so because we don't quite know what France's war aims are."

Her hostess whirled on her fiercely, put down her champagne and spoke of Uncle Shylock in the last war and of Americans who meddled in French affairs. Minister Pomaret, hearing the denunciation, came in. His wife said, "This is Mlle. Boothe. She has been asking me the usual stupid question:

What are France's war aims? America wants to know them!" Pomaret nodded and said, "I am sorry, Miss Boothe, you must go." He opened the door and ushered her out of the ministry.

Undismayed, she cabled Luce urging him to come, adding in the lingo of the dramatist, "The curtain is about to go up on the greatest show the world has ever seen." Luce sailed on the *Rex* April 13, a few days after the Nazi occupation of Denmark and attack on Norway.

It was as if the *Rex* was Luce's Mount Sinai, though of course it was only that he now had time to record revelations long growing on him. The cable he had received, the drama of a Europe licked by flames, the action-lover's consciousness that he would soon be there watching the fire, all seem to have inspired the romantic and the prophet in him. He set down his thoughts in an apocalyptic letter to Roy Larsen. He wanted to impart his message, as he put it, "*before* becoming environmentally involved in Armageddon or whatever it is." The *Rex* letter, as kingly in tone as the vessel's name, contained a distillation of his beliefs as they bore on America and the world of April 1940. First he philosophized about his power, the power of propaganda:

. . . [O]ur great job [at Time Inc.] from now on is not to create power but to use it. . . . The thought has been inextricably bound up in all our work for a decade. Furthermore the use of power and the creation of it are not separate things—they are inevitably bound up together. But I think you and I share a kind of reluctance to use power—one of the deepest first instincts in the American tradition is perhaps the distrust of power. It would perhaps rather create power, take satisfaction in the creation—and let its use be free, "democratic," uncontrolled.

To see Time Inc. in perspective is to realize its tremendous potential power. . . . I don't particularly like it . . . but there it is.

Perhaps he did not intend this last to be taken literally. He next took up the business of using that power, with a President to be elected, a world war to be settled, and a vital American need, as he saw it, to spread itself ideologically:

. . . [T]here is another [reflection] of more immediate application to the shape of things present & to come. The wild waves and the gentle waves have been telling me that the domestic problem of the United States and the foreign problem of the United States are today *one and the same thing*. . . . The problem of preserving, expanding, and developing a way of life which is characterized by ideals of freedom, of the integrity and moral responsibility of individuals . . . [A]ll the wisdom to which you & I respond tells us that this great aim cannot be achieved by a U.S. self-contained either economically or ideologically. America has no chance . . . of developing the good life as we see it unless there is at least a roughly corresponding development (instead of denial and disintegration) in *some* of the rest of the world. And this does not mean to me . . . that we must go dashing off declaring war on Hitler or Hirohito or anybody else tomorrow or the next day. But it does mean that the stakes of American civilization (*not* prosperity only) are world-wide stakes. . . . The American people do not know this.

You and I know it. . . . So it is up to you and me to do our part to tell the American people that this is really so. . . .

. . . To no one else could I say with the same assurance of understanding: by God, what a job we've done! Only you & I know all the *unspectacular* headaches—& mistakes! . . .

Selah! God knows what may happen before we meet. . . .

Luce met Clare in Paris, spent a week there talking with French leaders, then went over to barrage-ballooned London, where they stayed as always at Claridge's, a place that satisfied their mutual demand for the best and most prestigious and was only a block from the embassy ruled by the isolationist Joseph Kennedy. Kennedy said the British were as good as licked. "I told him I could not match him argument-for-argument," Luce later recalled. "I could only tell him I did not *believe* they would be, and so I prayed." It seemed that these two power-seeking men were willing to give each other a push. Kennedy had recently been flattered in a second Time cover story ("grinning, cussing Joe Kennedy, known and loved by millions of English-speaking men"). The ambassador had coaxed Luce to write the preface to *Why England Slept,* by his twenty-three-year-old son John—an expansion of the young man's Harvard senior thesis on England's failure to prepare for war, to be published later in the year. Luce was impressed by Kennedy's charming second son. He might have been unwilling to write the preface had he known that the ambassador had first approached Harold Laski, Laski having declined on the ground that he felt it "the book of an immature mind; that if it hadn't been written by the son of a very rich man, he wouldn't have found a publisher."

As for Clare, she was exasperated that in the face of all the British disaster the nation could still stomach the same prime minister, writing, "It was a shocking thing to me that long after Mr. Hitler had blown Mr. Chamberlain's *Pax Umbrellica* inside out, they still let him hold the twisted framework over their heads for protection." The Luces talked with generals, press lords and peers. They spent a weekend at Lady Astor's magnificent Cliveden, where appeasement was no longer in vogue. They made arrangements for audiences with Queen Wilhelmina and King Leopold and flew to Holland May 7.

In contrast to the blaze of spring tulip fields, there were sudden dark rumors that the Germans were coming. The Luces attended dinners with Dutch leaders arranged by American Minister George Gordon, but because of the uneasiness the queen did not see them. On May 9 they went on to Brussels and stayed in the top-floor suite of the American embassy presided over by the rich lawyer John Cudahy.

Luce soon had that peculiar good fortune so often yearned for by newspapermen—physical presence at the scene of great and dangerous events—though in his case it was perhaps less luck than his insistence on such constant search for events that he could scarcely avoid occasional collisions with them. At 5:25 next morning a maid rushed in shrieking *"Les Allemands!"* Hearing

planes, the Luces leaped from their beds. "We were at the window looking down into the street when we heard a tremendous explosion," Luce said later. "The house across the street collapsed. The sirens began to blow."

Their appointment with King Leopold was at ten, but the king had other duties that morning. The two Luces were alike in a disregard for danger which they would demonstrate repeatedly. Some forty people had already been killed in the air raids. Ambassador Cudahy urged them to leave immediately, but they insisted on staying for an embassy dinner that evening. By then the bombs were fewer and quite distant, evidently hitting the airport. Luce had cabled the home office in part:

> Your special correspondent, Clare Boothe, is sending Billings a brief eyewitness account of the first day of the German's grand attack on the Western world. I hope Life can use it this week as a signed item in a lead story. . . . [It was given subsidiary position.] If you were here today, remembering 1914, you would be sad but also you would be plenty, plenty mad. The word Boche is the only word used on the streets today to describe the enemy, and no other word would sound right. I deeply wish all priggish, pious pacifists could be here today.

In the morning they hired a car and headed for Paris, passing refugees in carts, bicycles and haywagons—then British troops singing as they marched northward to meet the Germans. They passed a symbol now ironic, the monument to the dead at Vimy Ridge. In Paris they found many bejeweled residents of the Ritz terrified. Perhaps their terror was no worse than that which would be shown by any nationals in such a situation, but Luce felt the special contempt he held for a nation whose government, like the Literary Digest, had failed to measure up to its competition. The believer in heroes looked vainly for them in crumbling France—for men who had the courage, conviction and style to rally a demoralized people. The believer in aristocracy perhaps blamed it on the erosions of the Popular Front, though England's Tories had done little better. But now at the last moment England had produced a hero, Churchill having just become prime minister. Luce, scanning the horizon for heroes, took some comfort in a statement of sympathy for the invaded countries by the Pope, and shock and anger expressed by President Roosevelt. A cable he sent home made clear his impatience with anyone thinking America had nothing to do with this war:

> The remarks of Roosevelt and the Pope sound wonderful here. I am practically prepared to become both a Catholic and a Third Termer unless the opposition offers some small degree of competition. Unless the others move awful fast, it looks like Davenport's man [Willkie] is the only Republican who can get this [Luce's] homecoming vote.
>
> Sober and long experienced observers say it is utterly irrelevant to discuss right and wrong in connection with the present German regime. The simple fact is that the Germans will stop at nothing to get what they want and there is utterly no evidence that they want anything less than all they can get by the most

ruthless means. Whether or not they bomb civilians is similarly irrelevant, because they will not waste ammunition if it serves no purpose, and they will not hesitate to destroy every woman and child in Belgium if they can gain thereby . . . [T]he United States is indulging in complete and criminal folly unless it proceeds at once to build every single military airplane it can possibly make in the next six months. Never mind who uses them, never mind who pays, but for God's sake, make them. Similarly, all possible military equipment of every sort should be ordered at once, regardless of cost.

If Life and Time fail to sell this idea now, it probably won't matter much what these estimable publications say in years to come. . . . The Germans have one weapon greater than all their army and that is the blindness and stultification of those in every country who are too fat to fight.

XVI

1. THE WILLKIE-LUCE LEAGUE

Luce came home, the columnist Jay Franklin said, "like a bat out of Flanders with a demand for national unity." He reached New York alone May 20, his venturesome wife remaining behind to stay with the Kennedys and see more of Europe's convulsions. Luce's heady patriotism and politics revolved around his conception of what he called the American Proposition (Clare shortened it to Amprop), in which he saw the nation as destined to spread freedom and prosperity around the world. He came shouting, like Paul Revere, that America must wake up. The born competitor knew that America must compete— quickly—with Hitler. Two days after his return he made his first nationwide broadcast over NBC: ". . . *if* Great Britain and France fail, we know that we and we only among the great powers are left to defend the democratic faith throughout the world. . . . We have to prepare ourselves to meet force with force—to meet force with *superior* force." He sounded the warning over the Columbia network: "If we deal with the Third Reich on a basis of appeasement of any kind, it will follow as sure as night follows day that we will pay for it . . . in the bloody end of all *our* democracy. We must deal with Hitler as with an enemy. . . ."

As he would in later crises, he seemed impatient for America to go in and solve it, angering isolationists. Senator Burton K. Wheeler referred to his speeches as "really advocating that we get into the war."

He was implementing the *Rex* letter, telling the American people what he knew and they did not. He gave up on Thomas E. Dewey and Senator Taft as Republican candidates because they dodged the war issue, and came out for Willkie, the anti-isolationist, the viewer of America as part of the world. Life frankly beat the drum for Willkie, Fortune published Willkie's article "We

176

The People," as Joseph Barnes noted, "accompanied by what was practically a nomination of him by the Luce editorial board," and Davenport resigned to become Willkie's right-hand man. Still, when Luce went to the Republican convention in Philadelphia in June, Willkie was a very dark horse. His nomination on the sixth ballot was a surprise which the Lucepress cheered, and Luce won the suspicion of the isolationist Republican Old Guard who disliked the Johnny-come-lately Willkie's internationalism and former Democratic allegiance.

Thereafter Luce became a trusted Willkie adviser. No one—not even his father—dared walk into Luce's penthouse office unannounced, but Willkie did so repeatedly without injury. "He looked like a big bear," Miss Thrasher recalled. "He'd come in about 6:30, say good evening to me and walk right in to Mr. Luce's office. Mr. Willkie would put his feet up on one side of the desk and Mr. Luce would put his feet up on the other and tell me, 'You can go home now.' I have no idea how long they talked."

When John Kennedy's book *Why England Slept* was published August 1, Luce's foreword stressed one of the reasons Kennedy gave for Britain's failure to prepare: "A boxer cannot work himself into proper psychological and physical condition for a fight that he seriously believes will never come off." Now, said Luce, America had the same trouble. We had to *believe* war was coming, but so far neither of the candidates seemed to believe it, not even Luce's candidate:

> [Mr. Roosevelt] can't believe we are ever going to fight. Otherwise how can he so glibly guarantee that we will not need to sacrifice one tiniest bit of our "social gains." . . . Mr. Willkie may reasonably be pardoned [on political grounds] for presenting himself to the Republican Convention as a prime keep-out-of-war man. . . . But all his genius of personality and industrial management will be bitter ashes in our mouths if Mr. Willkie goes forth to prepare for a war which he leads us to believe isn't really ever going to happen.

Young Kennedy came in to chat with Luce, brightening the office with his Irish smile, charming Miss Thrasher by giving her an autographed copy of the book, being granted a few minutes of Luce's time because he was Joe Kennedy's son.

"Mr. Luce was very anxious for Mr. Willkie to be elected," Miss Thrasher recalled in great understatement. Luce longed to become Secretary of State, a position for which he felt himself to have special qualifications which it is unlikely that he concealed from Willkie. While his journalist-propagandist status was as questionable as ever, his call for national dedication was one the administration itself would adopt, and none too soon. Confidentially Luce warned his senior men that it was their "journalistic duty" to sound the danger signal, to "cultivate the Martial Spirit" and to be "savage and ferocious in our criticism of all delay and bungling." He visited Secretary of State Hull to argue for the transfer of over-age destroyers to the hard-pressed British, and

later urged this on the President himself. Luce's hearing was deteriorating—a handicap he perhaps mentioned obliquely in his rather grandiose memorandum:

> After dinner Prex and I have a private talk in the Oval Room. My big question is, has he or has he not made up his mind about sending destroyers to Great Britain. I understand him to say definitely that "it's out" . . .

Not long thereafter, the destroyer deal was made. Meanwhile, National Affairs Editor Matthews aroused the Lucean ire. Although Matthews opposed a third term and was nominally for Willkie, he did not share Luce's propagandist audacity. The inexperienced and impulsive Republican candidate made errors that Time reported just as if he had been a Democrat. The canny President made few, and Time in some issues reached an approximation of fair political reporting. It was all very well for Time to praise Willkie's personality and courage and to describe him as "the hardest-hitting extemporaneous day-by-day debater of public issues whom the Republicans have had for a candidate since Roosevelt I." But when the same issue said some Republican professionals feared that Willkie was muffing his opportunities and might be "only a fatter, louder Alf Landon," Luce exploded. Felix Belair, Time's new Washington man, had suffered the jeers of other newsmen because of the magazine's pro-Willkieism. He showed his misunderstanding of Luce, who of course had no wish to be objective, when he observed that the story "did more to clinch Time Inc.'s reputation as an objective publishing house than any other recent development."

Matthews, who was working sixty hours or more a week, recalled: "Luce called me up at home to complain, in a long, rambling, furious diatribe . . . When I got a chance to speak I told him, with equal fury, that if he ever again called me at home on a Wednesday . . . I would resign on the spot . . . Wednesday was the one day I had with my family, it was a sacred day, and was never to be trespassed on again. He apologized handsomely . . ."

Luce thereafter reserved his complaining for the other six days, but Matthews stood him off as no other editor ever did. Time later reported Willkie's splitting of an infinitive, told of crowds booing him in Michigan and elsewhere, and said he seemed to promise rather a lot when he said, "I pledge a new world."

Now and then Luce would get a Willkie speech idea in the small hours and would telephone it to Miss Thrasher at her West 73rd Street home through the Time switchboard. She would take the Elevated through the night to the T-L Building, where she would give the information to the Willkie campaign train on Luce's private wire. She might get home at four, but she would be at work at 8:30, not minding it at all because "it was all so exciting." Clare, returned from Europe, took the stump in reply when Dorothy Thompson switched her support in October from Willkie to Roosevelt. The two women at times forgot their candidates in the heat of their own contest. Because Miss

1. Vestigial wings seem visible on the baby Henry Luce, first-born of missionaries in China. Below, at three, the forceful tycoon is in the ascendant.

2. Mother Luce with young Harry, Emmavail, Elisabeth (seated) and baby Sheldon.

3. Rev. Henry Winters Luce (seen in later life) was red-headed, dedicated, sometimes tactless enough to discompose his seniors.

4. Level, challenging gaze marks young Luce (standing, extreme left) with classmates at Chefoo School, where he upheld America in a preponderantly British atmosphere.

5. The collegian shavetail Luce (left) appears below in his guise as managing editor of the Yale Daily News. He is to left of Chairman Briton Hadden, seated in center, with staff. Hadden, the biggest man on campus, would retain that status as Luce's partner in magazine enterprise.

6. The beautiful and charming Lila Luce, who tried to slow down her driving husband, wrote him, "I am going to kidnap you and take you to some leafy solitude . . . to laugh." Not laughter but typical Luce intensity is conspicuous at right.

7. Divorce was in the offing when Daniel Longwell carried a romantic Luce message to Clare Brokaw (shown with daughter Ann) in Salzburg, far from New York gossip.

8. The jovial but Napoleonic Hadden rather upstaged his partner Luce from the beginning. Their growing estrangement was solved tragically by Hadden's death.

9. Archibald MacLeish was first to protest Time's manipulation of news. Laird S. Goldsborough (below, right) was storm center of the staff ideological warfare.

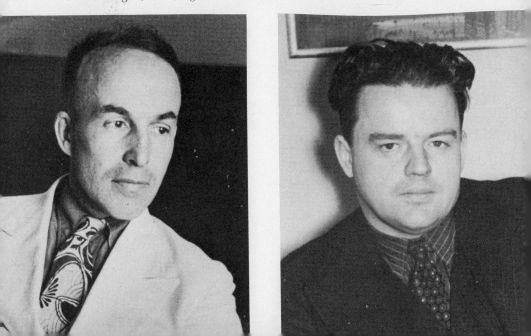

10. The talented John Shaw Billings became Luce's editorial chieftain, responsible for Time, Life and Fortune.

11. Ralph Ingersoll (below). His opposition to Luce ended his Time Inc. career. T. S. Matthews (below, right) also fought Luce and was later ingeniously jettisoned.

12. At Mepkin, Jo Davidson fashions bust of Luce. Below, the propulsive tycoon exhibits most dazzling smile ever photographed of his usually serious countenance.

13. In the famous courtroom confrontation Whittaker Chambers stands (left) to identify Alger Hiss (standing, right). Below: Close-up of reformed Communist Chambers.

14. John Hersey (left), a Luce favorite, fell out with him over news slanting. Allen Grover (right) found a European tour with the Boss an exhausting experience.

15. Luce in China with Theodore White, another favorite soon to be thrown overboard.

16. The liberal Eric Hodgins (left) deplored the ascendancy of Goldy and then Chambers. C. D. Jackson (right) ate crow for Life before Hollywood right-wingers.

17. Roy Alexander (below) survived as the Boss's companion on three long tours.

18. The "miracle editor" and his Congresswoman second wife in pastoral Connecticut.

19. In his heyday—striking if not handsome, attractive to women, flinty of eye.

20. Wendell Willkie would probably have named Luce his Secretary of State. Below Chiang Kai-shek and Madame were promoted to stardom in the laudatory Lucepress

21. Tsingtao journalists fawn over the revered visitor (center) in 1945. Below: With
H. H. Kung he dedicates propagandist China House he founded in New York.

22. Luce and his ensign son Hank meet by chance in mid-Pacific.

23. Congresswoman Luce acknowledges ovation for "GI Jim" speech.

Thompson had visited the Maginot Line a few weeks after Clare and had been permitted to fire a gun, Clare called her "the Molly Pitcher of the Maginot Line," attributed her switch to "hysteria" and said, "I was the first American woman to be taken on an official conducted tour of the Maginot Line. Dorothy Thompson was the second—and last." Miss Thompson replied:

> Miss Boothe is the Body by Fisher in this campaign. She is the Brenda Frazier of the Great Crusade. She has torn herself loose from the Stork Club to serve her country in this serious hour. . . . I have met the ladies of café society who save nations in their time of crisis, and I have visited the nations they have saved. . . .

Near the campaign's end, Life, after its heavy Willkie bias, showed how effective a truly impartial journalism could have been by publishing "The Case Against Willkie" by Bruce Bliven, and "The Case Against Roosevelt" by Robert Moses. Luce topped it off with a signed editorial emphasizing the importance of the canvass, declaring the non-voter to be "a traitor to the Republic" and adding, "never knowingly will I shake hands with him or sit down to a meal with him." E. B. White complained in the New Yorker that this put him in a fix: Bliven's argument made a vote for Willkie out of the question, Moses' arraignment of Roosevelt ruled him out as well, and now Luce, who had made it impossible for him to vote, called him a traitor for not voting. It troubled White, too, that at dinner parties he and Luce could not eat together. "One of us could be placed at a small table by himself and served separately," he supposed.

Luce, heedless of E. B. White, knew his work was in vain when the Fortune Poll predicted that Roosevelt would get 55 percent of the vote.

"Miss Thrasher," he said, "I don't want you to be too disappointed. Mr. Willkie is not going to be elected."

After the election, Roosevelt, who had been annoyed throughout the campaign by Time's fictionizations, let off steam by writing a long, long letter of complaint to Luce. In it he listed literally scores of errors, one by one, paragraph by paragraph. He knew of course that many of them were not mistake-errors but examples of Time's policy of clever and often malicious invention. He wrote that he felt it in the public interest that journalism should "conform to a reasonable extent with facts." He felt that journalism based on "misrepresentation" and "deliberate falsehoods" would in the end have a destructive effect on the democracy, and "I hate to see an educated group of people doing things to their country which their very education, in the better sense of the word, should keep them from doing."

There was much, much more in the letter. In the end he withheld it and instead had his assistant Lowell Mellett send a shorter letter of protest. Luce, believing it to be only from Mellett, replied with a defense of Time which was passed on to the President. "It is a slippery reply," Roosevelt wrote in part in a memo to Mellett.

2. THE AMERICAN CENTURY

Willkie's defeat condemned Luce to four more years of Roosevelt, four more years of exclusion from the political center of power though still commanding acknowledged journalistic power. Perhaps his own hopes for the Presidency had ebbed. The magnetism and bravura so vibrant in men like Churchill, Hitler and Roosevelt, which was transmitted almost like an electric shock to the people, was entirely lacking in his dour, withdrawn nature. Briton Hadden had had it. Ironically, Clare had a large share of it, luxuriating in the spotlight, so exhilarated by her researches in Europe and her feeling of crowd response while speaking for Willkie that a political career looked more than ever attractive.

Henry R. Luce did not have enough of it.

Nevertheless he was not one to underestimate his weight. The spirit of the *Rex* letter emerged in an idea which he first tried out as a public speech in three widely separated cities—Pasadena, Tulsa and Pittsburgh—before he published it in Life in a signed editorial titled "The American Century." In addition to its appearance in his own magazine, reaching perhaps a dozen million readers, he promoted it at great expense in full-page newspaper advertisements all over the country and by mailing copies of it to hundreds of leaders of thought. He had put hard study into it. He felt it to be, as it was, an important statement in a field with which he was always as much concerned as if he had been Secretary of State—the field of national purpose and long-range policy, the field of Amprop.

The United States was already in the war for all practical purposes, he wrote, and had better set its goals. The notion that we were entering the conflict to save the English was far short of the mark. That we would hope to do, but our main purpose was to establish American dominance in the world, to realize that "the complete opportunity of leadership is *ours*." Seven years of Roosevelt had failed to make democracy produce prosperity on a narrow nationalistic basis. We must win the war and make it work on a world basis. Our "free enterprise" system had to spread to prosper: "We know perfectly well that there is not the slightest chance of anything faintly resembling a free economic system prevailing in this country if it prevails nowhere else." °

So a triumphant America had to behave like a leader or fail. She had to push, spread, take charge. She had to keep open the world's seaways and airways "for ourselves and our friends" in order to expand free economic enter-

---

° In his insistence on the necessity to spread "free enterprise" internationally for our own profit, Luce was saying here, as in the *Rex* letter, something similar to what Professor Schlesinger so sharply censured Professor Chomsky for alleging incorrectly that President Truman had said.

prise. Military power was essential. Luce was frank in saying that this military-economic expansion would add pecuniary profit to the spread of American "ideals":

> The vision of America as the principal guarantor of the freedom of the seas, the vision of America as the dynamic leader of world trade, has within it the possibilities of such enormous human progress as to stagger the imagination. Let us not be staggered by it. Let us rise to its tremendous possibilities. Our thinking of world trade today is in ridiculously small terms. For example, we think of Asia as being worth only a few hundred millions a year to us. Actually, in the decades to come, Asia will be worth to us exactly zero—or else it will be worth to us four, five, ten billions of dollars a year.

Hence America should be generous with food and with technological help, but only for friendly nations. Prophetically he warned that there would be forces of "Tyranny" opposing the establishment of the "American Century" —a reference to the Communism he did not name, the controlling animosity of his life. Here came a striking passage whose violence he concealed by euphemism. He predicted a deadly and possibly prolonged postwar struggle between America and her tyrannical enemies:

> Nor need we assume that war can be abolished. All that it is necessary to feel— and to feel deeply—is that terrific forces of magnetic attraction and repulsion will operate as between every large group of human beings on this planet. Large sections of the human family may be effectively organized into opposition to each other. Tyrannies may require a large amount of living space. But Freedom requires and will require a far greater living space than Tyranny. Peace cannot endure unless it prevails over a very large part of the world.

For all her idealism, he made plain, America must be ruthless in carrying out her destiny:

> [We must] accept whole-heartedly our duty and our opportunity as the most powerful and vital nation in the world and in consequence to exert upon the world the full impact of our influence, for such purposes as we see fit and by such means as we see fit.

That was hard talk, which he repeated:

> It is the manifest duty of this country to undertake to feed all the people of the world who as a result of this worldwide collapse of civilization are hungry and destitute—all of them, that is, whom we can from time to time reach consistently with a very tough attitude toward all hostile governments.

Luce's "American Century," so reminiscent of his oration at Yale twenty-one years earlier, seemed also the 1941 version of Beveridge, singing the praises of an America so good and great that it must have no qualms about playing sahib. America must be first in the world. The capitalism which Roosevelt had shackled into failure in the nation would succeed gloriously if

spread internationally under American auspices. With the war won, the world and its riches would be up for grabs. America and her friends must grab it. He made it clear that our "constitutional democracy" would need change to meet the demands of a new age:

> Clearly a revolutionary epoch signifies great changes, great adjustments. And this is only one reason why it is really so foolish for people to worry about our "constitutional democracy" without worrying or, better, thinking hard about the world revolution. For only as we go out to meet and solve for our time the problems of the world revolution, can we know how to re-establish our constitutional democracy for another 50 or 100 years.

Implicit in this was his long impatience with an American constitutionalism he felt in need of overhaul more than ever because of the challenge of world war and world revolution. The exact shape of Luce's "new order" was necessarily vague in its details but not in its fundamental principles. The American Century was a capitalist century. It was a militarist century. It was a century of General Motors, Standard Oil, Pan-Am—and of Time-Life-Fortune—entrenched in Asia and Africa with the protection of American military power. In writing of an Asia worth ten billions to the United States, he would be accused of being more interested in good profits than in good neighbors. His slant was so strikingly that of the capitalist pushing for world markets that Vice President Henry A. Wallace sought to counter it with a later speech, "The Century of the Common Man," and Max Lerner with an essay, "The People's Century." Religionists found no love-thy-neighbor feeling in Luce's proposal. Harold Bosley in the Christian Century was disturbed by what he felt to be an exaltation of "political tyranny and economic monopoly" by a prominent Presbyterian layman: "Henry Luce's 'American Century' ideal is ruthlessly plain-spoken and entirely devoid of a single Christian insight into the nature of a Christian society." Norman Thomas assailed Luce's "nakedness of imperial ambition. The English-speaking nations are to police in God's name such places as we think necessary for our advantage, doing justice, as that British Nazi poet, Rudyard Kipling, told us was our duty, to the 'lesser breeds without the law.'" Freda Kirchwey let Luce have it in The Nation under the heading "Luce Thinking":

> Sounds nice, doesn't it? But at the same time doesn't it also sound faintly reminiscent? Echoes ring in the ears. Ghosts wander the corridor of the brain. "Manifest destiny." "Anglo-Saxon justice." "The white man's burden." . . . [This] brand of imperialism should be investigated by the Federal Trade Commission and a cease-and-desist order issued before the public can be poisoned.

The response to the editorial upset Luce. In it he had followed his old resolution to shun sentimentality and treat humanity as he felt it was. No eminent person commended "The American Century." Dorothy Thompson, who praised it in her newspaper column, seemed to be his most famous supporter.

Most liberals attacked it, and the conservatives who would normally have applauded his aggressive drive for world trade were mostly Republican isolationists wanting no "Roosevelt war."

But if "The American Century" was dated in its evocation of gunboat diplomacy, it would prove in time that the old was ever new and would vindicate its prescience in its outline of the strategy of the Cold War. Luce's prescription would be followed closely in America's postwar foreign policy. Just as he urged, America would give technical, economic and military aid to nations felt to be friendly, would take a "very tough attitude toward all hostile governments" and would build a huge military establishment to keep the sea and air lanes open. But something was fated to go wrong with the American Century. Luce would live to see and recognize only the beginnings of it.

3. LIKE A KING

On May 8, 1941, the Luces landed in Chungking after the grueling air journey from San Francisco. Luce was climbing another Matterhorn, carrying into a new phase of operations a global mission that would preoccupy him for years. In his magazines he had been plugging the heroic resistance to the Japanese offered by the Chinese under Chiang Kai-shek. He had also given invaluable personal help to B. A. Garside in the formation of United China Relief, which would raise millions in America.

Garside, a one-time missionary in China and a friend of Luce's father, had solicited Luce's help. There had been a tangle of eight different agencies appealing for specialized aid to China—the Fund for Christian Colleges, the American Bureau for Medical Aid to China, the Committee for Chinese War Orphans and five others. Garside had worked to combine them into one large organization which would eliminate competition and considerable overhead and would distribute money more equitably in China. Luce had agreed to contribute $60,000 and to coax a group of business leaders to become board members and supporters of the united agency. But Garside found that none of the eight groups wanted to lose its own identity and each attached crippling qualifications to its willingness to do so. When he reported on this, Luce blew up.

"You haven't got it pulled together," he snapped. "I can't ask these men to serve on the board under such conditions and I can't give a substantial contribution to an organization that won't work."

Garside agreed because "you didn't argue with Harry Luce," and left in discouragement. An hour or two later, Miss Thrasher called him and said Luce wanted to see him. He hurried back to find Luce much softened.

"This is too important to drop, B. A.," he said. "We've got to make it work."

He sent two Time publicity men, Otis Swift and Douglas Auchincloss, to

Garside along with four secretaries. Their skillful promotion, along with Luce's own pressure, finally got the eight groups to merge into United China Relief. Luce then persuaded Thomas W. Lamont, Paul Hoffman, Wendell Willkie, David Selznick and a half-dozen others of equal stature (including himself) to become board members. Luce also sent out a letter of personal appeal to all Time subscribers which alone brought in some $240,000 to UCR.

Hence by now Luce was probably the white man most important to the survival of hard-pressed Nationalist China. The good offices recognized by T. V. Soong during Luce's 1932 visit had swelled to a steady barrage of TLF publicity calculated to win sympathy and aid both from the American government and people. Luce had embarked on a triply grandiose mission: to make China Christian, to make her victorious over the Japanese and the Communists, and to make her part of the American Century. This was not the sort of project normally undertaken by a man in Rockefeller Center in behalf of a half billion Asians. It was something he could never have hoped to achieve without possession of the world's most powerful private propaganda arm.

The Chinese landscape seen from the plane had stimulated the poet in him, causing him to write:

> As the sun comes up and the clouds clear we look down upon a land of intricate and fairy-like beauty. It is the land of the terraces of rice paddies and the land of thousands and thousands of hills, each hill a separate thing, rising with surprising steepness and falling off quickly to make room for the valley and the next hill, and each hill terraced nearly to its top with rice paddies of infinitely varied shapes, some square, some round, but mostly like the sliver shape of the new moon, shapes within shapes until all but the wooded hill or mountain top is full. It is the landscape which might have been dreamed by a child of pure imagination.

Understandably, the Luces were met by a group of respectful Chinese officials including Hollington Tong, vice-minister of information, China's first American-trained newsman, a graduate of the University of Missouri and Columbia University. They were also met by Time's stringer in Chungking, Theodore H. White, wearing shorts and a sun helmet.

"Harry was majestic," White recalled. "He carried himself like a king, and had more power than most kings."

White (Harvard '38) had majored in Chinese history and graduated with honors on a newsboy's scholarship. He had gone immediately to China to prepare himself for teaching. In Chungking he landed a part-time job with the government Ministry of Information. A few weeks later John Hersey of Time had visited Chungking looking for a stringer and had hired the engaging Bostonian. White was overjoyed to discover that his occasional dispatches were published with little change. In one of them he was named as the correspondent—the first Time foreign man to get even such a one-shot byline. White wrote in a manner which Luce above all could appreciate, showing the sym-

pathy of one who loved China and was moved by the pounding the Chinese were taking.

"This famous New York publisher liked my copy," he said later. "What an intoxicating experience for a kid not long out of college!"

He waited on the Luces during their thirteen-day visit. They stayed at the handsome home of Dr. H. H. Kung, head of the civil government, whose wife was the eldest Soong sister. Both Luces were excited rather than alarmed by the almost daily Japanese air raids which left heaps of rubble helter-skelter and killed scores of Chinese. They dutifully took to the underground shelters which had been dug to accommodate the city's whole expanded population. That the Chinese got only a trickle of help from America, were never much above the starvation level and were being bombed by Japanese who still received shiploads of scrap metal from the United States did not sit well with the Luces. Perhaps they were surprised to learn that so far Chiang had received less help from America than from the Japanese-fearing Russians.

Inevitably they visited United States Ambassador Nelson Johnson (a 1939 Time cover subject) at the embassy across the river. Luce had a two-hour talk with the British ambassador, Sir Archibald Clark Kerr, whom he described as "not only the most charming white man in China but also, in the opinion of many, the ablest diplomat." The couple were the honored guests of Foreign Minister Wang Chung-hui, of Mayor K. C. Wu and his wife. Luce, interested as always in Yenching University, whose Peking buildings were now occupied by the Japanese, addressed a gathering of the considerable number of alumni White rounded up. Luce was feted by Dr. Kung at a dinner attended by the minister of war, General Ho, and the head of China's scarcely perceptible navy, Admiral Shen. T. V. Soong was in Washington, trying with little luck to get American planes with which to oppose the Japanese strikes. By special permission of Chiang Kai-shek, the Luces took a wild journey to the quiescent infantry front by plane, train, automobile and Mongolian pony, as Clare snapped pictures with a camera whose operation she had mastered with characteristic close and determined study. But the crowning point was tea with Madame and Generalissimo Chiang, whom Luce described as "the greatest ruler Asia has seen since Emperor Kang Hsi 250 years ago."

The Luces were greeted by the dynamic and theatrical Madame, after which the slim Gimo, clad in khaki, made his entrance. It was a great moment for Luce. ". . . [Y]ou got the feeling that there was no person in the room except the man who had just entered it so quietly," he wrote. Chiang was hospitable, as indeed he should have been. With Madame interpreting, Luce produced a gift for him—a portfolio of photographs, gathered by Life, of him, Madame and the leading men of his Nationalist government. "He grinned from ear to ear," Luce observed, "and was as pleased as a boy with the pictures of himself and Madame." Madame herself impressed him almost equally because of her glowing tribute to Mrs. Luce's beauty. While the two women were fated never to be mutually admiring, perhaps because of competing

queenliness, Luce was exultant over the visit. If in the Gimo's eyes he was an instrument of aid for China, it was a fair exchange since the Gimo was Luce's instrument in his own triple mission.

A bomb had destroyed Madame's pantry and along with it her store of cigarettes. The Luces had brought along an enormous supply, knowing of the shortage there. They replenished Madame's supply, having already left many cartons at the press hostel where White and other correspondents lived. The Chiangs' gift to Clare was a magnificent pair of Chinese silk pajamas, and to Luce a jade Tang horse. "An hour later we left," Luce wrote, "knowing that we had made the acquaintance of two people, a man and a woman, who, out of all the millions now living, will be remembered for centuries and centuries."

But from the ambassadors, White and others, he learned that the Chungking government was painfully inefficient, that urgent business waited weeks to get done because everything depended on the personal attention of Chiang or Dr. Kung. Furthermore, Chiang's Kuomintang ruling party was accused of corruption and tyranny, and criticism was growing. On leaving, Luce took a liberty that did him credit. He intended to step up his already powerful campaign for American aid to China, and he wanted it to be well used. He left a letter of thanks for Chiang containing a chiding which, however gentle, was something rarely heard by the Gimo. He mentioned the inefficiency and the criticism and went on:

> Your speech to the Kuomintang headquarters some weeks ago calling for reform was much admired in America, but does not seem to have been taken very seriously here. If a drastic reform in the attitude of some sections of the Kuomintang is possible, it would seem to be desirable at once. I am told that the best young men and women dislike both the Communist and Kuomintang parties and feel politically homeless.

He ended by expressing his appreciation of the difficulties and with renewed assertions of gratitude. He had already put White on regular salary and told him, "You're going with us." He planned to make use in New York of the writer's specialized knowledge. White, after two hungry and harried years in Chungking, was delighted.

"Henry Luce Roused to Enthusiasm," headlined the Hong Kong Sunday Herald. Stopping at Manila on the homeward flight, the Luces stayed with American High Commissioner Francis B. Sayre and Luce spoke in behalf of China to a businessmen's group in Baguio. He met General Douglas MacArthur, field marshal of the Philippine army and a believer in his own Amprop, a man who made the same crashing impact on him as had Chiang. After the long island-hopping trip to San Francisco, both Luces addressed the influential Commonwealth Club, lauding China's courageous battle and urging American aid. Reaching New York, Luce told reporters his journey was "the greatest trip I have ever made in my life," told of China's need for help and

said, "General Chiang Kai-shek is a magnificent leader." He hurried to Washington and conferred with Presidential Assistant Lauchlin Currie, who was charged with expediting aid to China, and with Reconstruction Finance Corporation Chairman Jesse Jones. He also arranged interviews with Secretary Hull, Secretary of the Navy Frank Knox, Secretary of the Treasury Henry Morgenthau and War Secretary Henry L. Stimson—all, no doubt, in China's behalf.

On June 22 came news that should have sent him into a jig. The Nazis suddenly attacked the Russians along a 2000-mile front. Luce put Marshal Semyon Timoshenko on the cover of Time, which welcomed this diversion of German might away from England and hoped that the Russians could hold out much longer than the few weeks the Nazis thought the job would take. Not *too* long, however, though Time did not say that. Perhaps Luce, even more than most American anti-Communists, cheered it as God's own retribution against both sides and heaved a sigh of relief that at any rate the Russian evil would at last—if a little late—be crushed by the Nazi evil, as he and so many others had counted on for years. But he kept his mind on America's duty, as Time's punchy account showed:

> Like two vast prehistoric monsters lifting themselves out of the swamp, half-blind and savage, the two great totalitarian powers of the world now tore at each other's throats. But the time gained was no gain unless urgent use was made of it. No good use would be made of it if the U.S., pleased to see Nazism fighting Communism, relaxed its defense efforts.

In Time and Life, leading non-interventionists including Charles and Anne Lindbergh, Senator Bennett Champ Clark and General Robert E. Wood were treated with skilled ferocity. Even Luce's good friend ex-Ambassador Kennedy was described by Life as "defeatist about Britain, in favor of a quick peace." The three isolationist publishers, Colonel Robert R. McCormick of the Chicago Tribune and his cousins Joseph M. Patterson of the New York Daily News and Mrs. Eleanor "Cissy" Patterson of the Washington Times-Herald were designated by Time as "the Three Furies" who "ground out their daily gripes at the risks involved in the Administration's policy of trying to stop Hitler." Luce wanted America to get into the war. One issue of the cinematic March of Time, "Uncle Sam—Nonbelligerent," lampooned the isolationist Senator Wheeler and, said a leftist critic, "assumes that everyone in the United States but a few appeasers favors war." The radio March of Time raised labor's hackles by dramatizing strikes which slowed production of tanks and other arms. There was a steady sniping at the Washington bureaucracy which could not seem to achieve efficiency. Every arm of the organization executed Luce's order to "cultivate the Martial Spirit" and to be "savage and ferocious" with bunglers.

Never was China forgotten. The striking face of Madame Chiang appeared on the cover of Life for June 30. Inside was Luce's own 10,000-word account

of his visit and his observations of Chinese heroism and need, illustrated with the pictures taken by Clare. Chiang having been on Time's cover to the point of satiety, his General Chen Cheng appeared there along with a story by Theodore White on the unvarying Luce themes: China's heroism, China's importance to the defense of America and her urgent need. White was commissioned by Luce to do a series of four articles on China for Fortune conveying the same message in detail. Luce himself spoke over CBS in behalf of United China Relief, saying with perhaps excessive confidence, "The imperial Japanese army has been stopped cold in its tracks . . . China's army is the outstanding creation of a very great leader of men—Chiang Kai-shek." He spoke similarly to audiences in New York, Buffalo, Flint, Los Angeles and points between. As B. A. Garside said, "When Harry Luce put his mind to something, things got done."

Young White, lonely in New York, was invited out for weekends to the Luce Greenwich estate. "They made me completely at home," he said. "I'd meet famous people there—John Gunther, Walter Duranty, Sir William Wiseman, the jet set of the Forties."

4. FOR THIS HOUR AMERICA WAS MADE

Luce had perfected his policy of cultivating important people, learning from them and skillfully making them contribute to his power and success. His use of the Time cover story (and of Life and Fortune in a different way) was brilliant, double-acting, self-propelling. Even among intellectuals who tended to sneer at the magazine, to appear on Time's cover had become a national and international cachet of distinction. There was no great difficulty in finding people willing to endure this notoriety. The magazine's regular cover artists, Ernest Hamlin Baker, Artzybasheff and Boris Chaliapin, did a profitable business on the side painting Timelike portraits of individuals who sought to give the impression that they *had* appeared on the cover. People invited to the Luces' were apt to break any engagement and neglect affairs of state or of the soul, to accept. Once arrived, they were on their mettle to be scintillating and informative.

In the case of those few who became subjects of cover stories, a strange thing happened. These people usually found Time's stories about them inaccurate in detail and powerfully slanted to give the subject a newspeg or a souped-up interest calculated to promote the Boss's ideas and to sell magazines. Yet, with few exceptions, they were so delighted at entering this hall of fame that they were still friendly and still useful as sources of information, so that Time profited at both ends, coming and going. Furthermore, the important friends of cover subjects, equally anxious for entrance, would go to considerable lengths to be obliging to Time. Luce would have deserved recognition as a master of public relations on the basis of his development and

exploitation of the cover story alone. He played cleverly on this human long-ing. As one guest at the Greenwich house noted, "Ranged on tables are count-less photographs of the great and near-great the Luces have known."

On Sunday, December 7, 1941, the gathering at The House included Vin-cent Sheean, Ambassador to Moscow Laurence Steinhardt, Dr. Lin Yutang, Virginia Cowles, Margaret Case, and Joseph Thorndike of Life. Twenty-two people sat down to luncheon at 2:30. The Luces had a rule that meals must not be interrupted by telephone calls. One came at dessert time, however, im-portant enough so that the butler brought the message on a tray to Clare at table. She glanced at it. She tapped her glass with her spoon for attention.

"All isolationists and appeasers, please listen," she said. "The Japanese have bombed Pearl Harbor."

There was a hubbub of gasps, exclamations and demands for details. Only one of the guests kept his place amid a general rush for the radio and the tele-phones. Dr. Lin apologized for finishing his dessert: "You see, this is all so very expected." Mrs. Luce took the trouble to send roses to the isolationist Cissy Patterson with a card: "Hiyi: How do you like everything now?"

Luce was immediately on the wire to New York. Life, which had gone to press the night before, would be dead without news of the attack. His chauffeur got him to Rockefeller Center in less than an hour. The presses in Chicago were stopped while he supervised the remaking of the seven lead pages and of revising the next issue of Time, which would go to press in thirty-six hours. It was one of those times when the alert, driving Boss had the unanimous admiration of his staff. He allotted a couple of precious minutes to telephone his father in Haverford. For all his shock, Rev. Henry Luce found in the news the same cheer that his son did. Japan was now at war with both China and the United States, meaning that China and America were allied as they never had been before. "We will now all see," the old man said, "what we mean to China and China means to us."

That same night, Dr. Luce died in his sleep at the age of seventy-three. To Theodore White, who expressed condolences, Luce replied calmly, "It was wonderful that he lived long enough to see America and China as allies." The Japanese attack was a providential aid to Luce's own grand plans for Chris-tianizing and Americanizing China at a speed hitherto undreamed of. His edi-torial in Life expressed shame for America's past irresolution along with a call to arms as stirring as the born fighter could make it:

> This is the day of wrath. It is also the day of hope. . . . For this hour America was made. Uniquely among the nations, America was created out of the hopes of mankind and dedicated to the fulfillment of those hopes. It is for this reason that we accept only two alternatives—either to die in the smoking ruins of a to-tally destroyed America or else to justify forever the faith of our fathers and the hopes of mankind.

Only two weeks before Pearl Harbor, President Roosevelt had taken a pub-

lic swipe at Time for its report of the bibulosity of President Pedro Aguirre Cerda of Chile, head of South America's only Popular Front government. Whether or not in reflection of Luce's dislike of all popular fronts, Time said of Aguirre in a three-paragraph account: "He spent more and more time with the red wine he cultivates." The angry Chilean government demanded an official apology. Aguirre's death a few days later added to the American embarrassment. When Roosevelt made a formal apology to Chile, he seized the opportunity to denounce Time and to give his news-conference listeners the unusual privilege of quoting him directly, saying:

> . . . [T]he government of the United States has been forced to apologize to the government of Chile for an article written in Time magazine—a disgusting lie which appeared in that magazine. . . . [W]e are informed by our ambassador that this article was a notable contribution to Nazi propaganda against the United States. . . .

Luce, the "savage and ferocious critic," showed again, as he had at the time of the New Yorker parody, that he could dish it out much better than he could take it. The President, speckled with scar tissue after years of Time's cunning punches, had drawn a little blood for once himself. Luce's cry of pain emerged in the form of a public statement in which he made no apology and characterized Roosevelt's remarks as "unwarranted by the facts and unwise as an attack on a free and honest press."

But now, with the nation at war, he put away resentment and wrote the President pledging that "the dearest wish of all of us [at Time Inc.] is to tell the story of absolute victory under your leadership." He added a personal note in his own bold hand:

> . . . The drubbing you handed out to Time—before Dec. 7—was as tough a wallop as I ever had to take. If it will help you any to win the war, I can take worse ones. Go to it! And God bless you.

XVII

1. AMERICA FIRST

Early in February 1942, Clare, again a Life correspondent, left by air on the long trip to India by way of Brazil and Africa. On February 16, Luce went to New Haven to make the principal speech at the sixty-fourth annual banquet of the Yale Daily News. Although he had been back at Yale scores of times since graduation, this was an especially important occasion—the first time he had spoken to the News men since the dear days when he and Hadden ran the paper. He had been asked to "explain the war."

The time for explanations was past, he told them. Now was the time for action performed in faith. "Reason has been the Maginot Line behind which Western civilization retired. . . . Night has descended. The hour has struck for action and more action." Reason was obviously on our side, he said, but it was more appropriate to summon the eternal verities of virtue, honor and duty, and all that Yalemen had to know in this war was that they were fighting "For God, for Country and for Yale."

Although he received polite applause, he did not quite get away with it. At the same time, Life was on sale with another of those stirring and imperialist Luce appeals for American leadership in the war and in the "American peace" that must follow it.

Under the heading "America First," Seth Taft wrote an editorial in the News: "There's no point in being soft-shirt or mealy-mouthed about what Mr. Luce proposed Monday night . . . about what Mr. Luce has proposed in his editorials in Life . . . His doctrine is America First throughout the world, Manifest Destiny, Yankee imperialism." And in Luce's old Yale Lit, John G. Gardner's editorial denounced his "harangue against Reason" and his enlistment of religion in a scheme for "world conquest."

191

W. A. Swanberg

By the time these shafts were aimed at him he was out of range in London, only to come within range of Cassandra again, who wrote:

> His papers are "slick," and he faithfully murders the English language in one of them every Monday morning. He is responsible for creating . . . a style of writing that moves with the smooth grace of a man riding a bicycle with hexagonal wheels. Mr. Luce is given to publishing his own signed editorial pronouncements that are reminiscent of an Archbishop giving a service in a super-cinema.

He was treated more respectfully by the Daily Express and the Evening Standard, both owned by his friend Beaverbrook (who had been on Time's cover in 1938 and again in 1940), the Standard describing him as "a very different type from his brilliant, witty wife, Clare Boothe. He is a serious man with an enormous respect for facts; that is where the success of his magazines lies." The Express told of his whirlwind visits to Glasgow, Birmingham, Liverpool and other centers to see aircraft factories and other war plants.

By this time Clare was in Cairo. London was different since the Kennedys had left, but one can be sure that Luce walked the same block from Claridge's and pumped information out of Ambassador John G. Winant. His mission was to discover England's condition, mood and war aims other than mere survival. As a businessman and politician it struck him as mad that any nation could enter such an ordeal without knowing clearly what it hoped to accomplish.

Time now had a London bureau on Dean Street headed temporarily by young Stephen Laird, who had to face the fusillade of questions Luce fired at his staff people whenever he was on tour. The Minister of Information, Brendan Bracken, presented him to the press, the Manchester Guardian writing, "Mr. Luce . . . is not a patch on Miss Clare Boothe, his playwright wife, as a witty, lively, outspoken victim for an interview."

The terrible *Luftwaffe* blitz was over, but the blackout was dense, the food awful and the Germans were poised across the Channel. Luce, walking in the ruins of Coventry Cathedral, admiring British courage, was vexed about British vagueness about Socialism creeping in, and above all about war aims. "Willing and eager to die," he wrote in his report, "—but for what?" He found the Russians high in the people's esteem: "Soviet Russia has saved them. . . . Soviet Russia is immensely popular. By comparison, their cousin country of America is scarcely noticed . . ." The Soviet, far from collapsing in a few weeks, was putting up such a furious resistance that Luce was torn between admiration and loathing, writing, "Russia has shown a greatness and ferocity of will and conviction equal to, if not greater than, the vaunted fanaticism of the Hun."

He returned to New York and soon flew to California to lunch with Donald Douglas in Santa Monica, visit four bomber plants and compare their efficiency with England's. He gave thought to his wife's contemplated campaign for Congress and to a squabble he and his publications were having

with the McCormick-Patterson press which, if no longer isolationist, was so bitterly critical of administration war policies as to make Luce think them foot-dragging. He favored Roosevelt's war efforts, only wanting more of them and faster. The Chicago Tribune replied to animadversions in Time and Life by pointing out that Luce, though still (at forty-four) of combat age, "has not gone into the armed services." The Tribune thereafter called him "Henry R. (White Feather) Luce."

Meanwhile, Clare had reached Lashio, Burma, where she interviewed General Stilwell and had a lucky meeting with the Chiangs, who had flown down to confer with the general. Perhaps out of regard for her political ambitions, she had no objection to the first person singular and did not slight her own place in the confidence of the great. "Madame Chiang read me a bitter article that she had written," she wrote for Life. ". . . Chiang once said to me that Madame was worth ten divisions to China. . . . I ate dinner with the Gissimo, Hollington Tong and Madame. . . . I had a talk with handsome, blue-eyed, crisp-mustached General Alexander. . . . I talked with big, handsome, able, dark, young Governor of Rangoon Sir Reginald Dorman Smith." One of her stops was Kunming, where she interviewed General Claire Chennault of the Flying Tigers. Doubtless seeking his pilots' own accounts of their experiences, she talked quite late one night with a group of them. This came to the attention of a Chennault staff officer, Paul Frillman, who recorded, "I was awakened . . . by noise and laughter from the pilots' bar. I blearily struggled into my old robe and made my way there. The commotion centered around an attractive blonde in a well-tailored version of Churchill's air-raid suit . . . She was charming everyone, and it was a great party, but I saw some pilots who were slated for a dawn mission, only a few hours away.

" 'It's late and I'm afraid the lady should go,' I said. . . .

" 'But don't you see who she is?' several asked.

" 'I don't care if she's the Queen of England,' I said. 'It's time to go.' That ended the party.

"At breakfast I saw her sitting next to Chennault, who called me over and introduced me. 'This is Clare Boothe Luce,' he said.

" 'We've met,' she snapped with as heavy a frost as Stilwell's."

She was home late in April, loving the excitement of foreign correspondence and wanting more of it. Her dispatches were printed at great length in Life, with photographs showing her with the noted people she wrote about, but were excluded from Time. John Hersey one day walked into Gottfried's office to find Luce there, urging Gottfried and Matthews to use one of her dispatches with a byline in FN. Gottfried and Matthews were adamant against it, and Luce, with the occasional editorial humility that could be so winning, finally bowed to their judgment. Roy Alexander opened the door at that moment and the doorknob struck Luce a hard blow in the kidney, so that he left both in physical and mental discomfort.

Clare's stepfather, Dr. Austin, who had only recently died, had represented

the preponderantly wealthy Connecticut district in which Greenwich was located, from 1938 to 1940, when he had lost narrowly in the Democratic landslide that overwhelmed Willkie. The Luces were legal residents of Greenwich although they spent little time there. "Harry urged me to run," she recalled. Although at times he could be angry with her, he was perhaps impressed by the political insights she had shown, usually but not always in agreement with his own. On the surface there was generosity in his promotion of the wife whose press clippings were so much superior to his and who had weapons he lacked for attaining public office. He evidently understood that her need for activity and power was as demanding as his own. Possibly the thought of part-time freedom from the wife who could out-talk and out-quip him was not totally undesirable.

He queried his New York editors, to find them almost unanimously opposed to her candidacy. There was outright hostility toward her on the part of some members of the staff, perhaps because she had sometimes called them "Harry's little people" and because the matter of publicizing her always presented journalistic problems. These problems were enlarged by Luce's own utter insensitivity toward the journalistic ideal of independence. Belair, his Washington man, was also opposed, pointing out that for Time to report her doings as a Congresswoman would strain the credulity of its readers.

"No," Luce replied in perfect seriousness, "because whatever Time prints will be believed because it is in Time."

The Republican nomination was hers for the asking. Luce assigned his assistant, Wesley Bailey, to be her undercover campaign manager, it being hoped that it would not become known that a Time Inc. man was involved. Her opponent was Democratic Congressman Leroy Downs, a Norwalk newspaper publisher. She campaigned vigorously, making 116 speeches from Greenwich to Danbury to Bridgeport, soliciting workers' votes on her promise of sympathy for labor and showing her union card in the Dramatists' Guild. She tickled the Tories by attacking Roosevelt for fighting a "soft war" and for waste, such as $100,000 in musical instruments given to the WPA in West Virginia. "Nero needed only one fiddle to play while Rome was burning," she said in speeches. She always wore a fresh rose in the lapel of her tailored suit. She referred to Downs as a "rubber stamp" and a "faceless man," to which he replied that while he was not at all faceless, his face was admittedly the less beautiful of the two. She attended a communion breakfast of Polish women in Stamford, found them icy toward her—a non-Catholic who lived most of the time at the Waldorf, in the South or God only knew where in the world—but thawed them by saying that she was the last American woman out of Warsaw before Poland was inundated by the Nazis. She won handily with a plurality of 6400 votes. Time, in a story about her campaign, forgot entirely to mention her opponent's name.

She retained Edward L. Bernays to advise her on her public-relations approach to Congress. Talking with her at the Waldorf apartment, Bernays was

aware of her beauty, intelligence and "provocative presence," writing, "I understood why Harry had fallen in love with her."

"Mr. Bernays," she told him, "I can't get anything about myself in Time." Luce, who was present, permitted them to talk privately. "But he kept pacing the floor outside," Bernays recalled, "back and forth, and now and then he'd come in. It seemed impossible for him to relax."

2. ANOTHER GOLDSBOROUGH

The astonishing Russian defeat of the Nazis' best at Stalingrad and the mighty westward drive that followed, gave Luce nightmares. America, he felt, must not permit Russia to win the war. America must win it first. It was neither patriotic nor politic to speak out against Russia. In his second venture into global editorializing in Life—the one which had aroused protest at Yale —he threw up a cloud of ambiguity in his efforts to alert the nation:

> [America's war] is war against the cleavage of mankind into Right and Left which, tearing Europe asunder, made Hitler's victories possible. It is war against the hidden civil war which, raging throughout the world, weakened the structure of nations until much of their national identity had been lost before Hitler overwhelmed them. . . . It is war against . . . the setting of group against group. . . .

He was saying circuitously that the real enemy was Russia and Communism. To let Russia win the war against Hitler might mean that Russia would emerge as the world's mightiest power and wreck America's opportunity to dictate the peace:

> . . . [I]f [anyone] expects the Russians or the British or any other people to win this war for us, he is inviting defeat for America—the most dreadful defeat that any nation ever suffered. This is America's war and America must win it. . . . [T]he *imperative of victory* is American leadership. America must be first in the work of farm and factory. America must be first in the fields of battle—and on sea and in the air. America must be first in the councils of war and America must be first in the policy of the world.

America's moral and political superiority invested in her the right to reorganize the world according to her own design:

> Because America alone among the nations of the earth was founded on ideas and ideals which transcend class and caste and racial and occupational differences, America alone can provide the pattern for the future.

Freda Kirchwey was even more critical than before, writing, "his whole cult of American superiority is no whit less revolting than the Nordic myth that provides the moral sanction for Hitler's brutal aggressions." Luce, in his ideological struggles, evidently missed his old friend Goldsborough. Goldy,

after his sabbatical on full salary, had been put in charge of Time's quite minor Science department, had disliked it and eventually left to join the Office of Strategic Services. Luce found another Goldsborough in Whittaker Chambers.

Chambers was short, chunky, powerful and untidy, his necktie always twisted, his dark baggy suit littered with cigarette ashes. He had bright blue eyes and his serious corn-fed face at rare times could light up in a friendly smile. Matthews, who hired him as a book reviewer, was impressed by his intellectual background, his capacity for hard work and his dramatic writing style. Everyone was struck by his conspiratorial air. Luce had had a good impression of Chambers from the time in 1939 when he joined Time and for a brief period did cinema reviews. "Who reviewed *Grapes of Wrath*?" Luce asked one week when he happened to be editing. Chambers said he had. "It's the best cinema review ever in Time," Luce said, adding that he and Clare had seen the première of the movie and their appreciation of it had been greatly enhanced by Chambers's review.

Young Sam Welles, a newcomer who was moved in as Chambers's assistant when the latter was in charge of book reviews, was baffled by the older man who seemed kindly enough but seldom spoke to him except about the books they reviewed and never, never, did what was commonly expected at Time when two men occupied the same office, namely, propose that they lunch together. Welles at last became irked enough at this to reverse the usual procedure and ask the senior man to lunch. Chambers seemed so upset by the suggestion, and so evasive, that Welles was spurred by curiosity to press the idea, and Chambers agreed with what seemed great reluctance. With Chambers in the lead, saying little, they boarded the Sixth Avenue subway and got off at Macy's. Chambers led Welles all the way across Macy's ground floor to the Seventh Avenue side, where they took an escalator to the second floor. There they walked across to the Sixth Avenue side, Chambers looking at none of the merchandise but trotting smartly ahead. They then took an escalator to the third floor, repeated the process up to the fourth, then took an elevator down to the first floor, where they emerged on the Sixth Avenue side and Chambers said, "Let's eat in the Longchamps in the Empire State." They hurried over there and had lunch, Welles trying earnestly to make conversation, Chambers replying in monosyllables. It was only over coffee that Chambers suddenly relaxed and began to talk in a most friendly and charming way. A few days later the deeply puzzled Welles got up courage to ask Chambers what his game was. Chambers explained that he had been a Communist courier and had quit the Party in revulsion over the Stalin purges, and as a result was being followed by Party avengers seeking to kill him. A likely way was to take a man to lunch and poison him, sometimes through an ally in the restaurant. Hence Chambers avoided eating with anyone he did not know. He had taken the elaborate route through Macy's to throw off other shadows, and had not been

sure of Welles himself until coffee arrived, by which time, he said, "I knew you were too ingenuous to be a Commie." He showed Welles the pistol he carried in an inner holster. Thereafter, Chambers and Welles were good friends, and Welles never found him anything but truthful, though others at Time would later claim him to be either overimaginative or a liar.

"He was so bitterly anti-Communist and anti-Stalin," Matthews remarked, "that we were careful not to give him books to review bearing on those topics."

Now, in 1944, he was still furtive, armed and brilliant. "He saw himself as a Dostoevskian character, fated by destiny to play an important role," said John Barkham, who worked with him. "In his pocket he carried a miniature score of Beethoven's Ninth Symphony. He said that the scherzo of that symphony was one of the mightiest works ever conceived by the mind of man."

He always worked behind a locked office door—sometimes slept in his office and shaved in the washroom. In a restaurant he was careful to sit with his back to the wall so that he could see the door. Timen took sides, some thinking him a genius who had risen above youthful political follies, others believing him in some part a fake and poseur, perhaps a little crazy. At this time, when the brutalities of Soviet Russia had been obscured by her magnificent stand against the Nazis, the anti-Chambers clique included many liberals who looked forward to postwar peace and coexistence with a reformed and friendly Russia.

This was scarcely Luce's view of the matter. When he again ran across the Chambers he had first known only as a fine reviewer, and discovered that he was a former Communist who had come to loathe Communism, there was established a firm rapport between the two men. An important element in that rapport was the extraordinarily close relationship—almost a special arrangement—each had with God.

3. GLOBALONEY

It seemed that the whole world was looking forward to the Congressional debut of the remarkable lady from Connecticut. One could not be with her long before sensing the proportions of her ambition. As the Washington writer Maxine Davis put it, "Mrs. Luce has a consuming ambition, a will to power, great power. No personal satisfaction is enough. Nothing less than the power to direct the destinies of nations will ever be enough."

Since the Presidency was beyond her sex, the Senate and the Vice Presidency would have to do. The range of her view and the plenitude of her self-confidence was not far from equaling that of her husband, who was pressing buttons to save China, out-gun Russia and ready the world for the American Century. If it was true, as Scott Fitzgerald had observed, that the very rich

were different, people consumed by ambition had their own earmarks. Luce, for one, had a habit that annoyed Matthews (and others), small in itself but perhaps revelatory:

> [He invariably appropriated] any matches or packages of cigarets within his reach, no matter whose they were. . . . I am sure this was only absent-mindedness; all the same, it seemed to me another form of rudeness, an unawareness of other people. I suppose he must have had a strict upbringing as a child, but I sometimes wondered if he hadn't also learned in his mission compound a lordly disregard for servants and underlings.

On her part, Clare, as Miss Davis noted in an article paying tribute to her courage and industry, "is not a cozy woman, a warm woman." She was addicted to bizarre classical allusions, rhymes and puns which at their best were irresistible and at their worst seemed no more than labored self-advertisement. Speaking to the Women's National Press Club, whose members were about to question her, she said that she felt "on the spot tonight—on the spot *qui mal y pense.*"

Surprisingly, this keen, talented woman, so anxious to make a grand entrance into national politics, stumbled onto the political stage and then muffed her lines. She offended Republican Leader Joseph W. Martin by using her husband's influence to arrange a speedy meeting with Democratic Speaker Sam Rayburn. She affronted her own constituents in Danbury, the hat-making city, by permitting herself to be photographed hatless on the Capitol steps. An interview she gave the New Yorker in which she lamented her inability to get a cook and the difficulties she was having with an inept maid was hardly politic amid wartime sacrifices and shortages. Her prompt request for appointment to the high-and-mighty Foreign Affairs Committee made eyebrows rise, membership in this council usually being the reward of seniority after faithful labors. When she was invited to the President's traditional White House supper for new Representatives—a purely social function, no politics allowed—she sent him a 1200-word reply listing issues she wished to discuss with him including "the people's long delayed fury against the swollen and wasteful Washington bureaucracies." Presidential Press Secretary Stephen Early informed her coldly that she was out of bounds. Roosevelt himself handled the situation by saying just two words to her in the crush—"How's Henry?"—then turning to the next freshman.

Her maiden speech was historic. She labored over it at her apartment at the Wardman Park Hotel among pictures of her husband, her daughter, young "Hank" Luce (now at Yale), Peter Paul (now at Brooks School), and two of General MacArthur, along with two parakeets and a cocker spaniel named Speaker. She delivered it on the late afternoon of February 9, 1943, at a time when the House was usually almost empty. Now it was well filled by Congressmen eager to get an eyeful and earful of the gentlewoman from Connecticut. Speaking on the subject of "America's Destiny in the Air," she aimed her

main attack at Vice President Wallace because of his call for international postwar freedom of the airways, though she also criticized Roosevelt, Stalin and Churchill. She was not ready to relinquish American sovereignty of her airspace. She could see, as she put it, "the air liner *Queen Elizabeth* put in, the *Stalin Iron Cruiser*, the *Wilhelmina Flying Dutchman*, the *Flying De Gaulle* . . . But shall I scan, like Sister Anne, the skies in vain, searching for the shape of an American clipper against the clouds?" The snapper produced a sensation:

> Much of what Mr. Wallace calls his global thinking is, no matter how you slice it, still globaloney. Mr. Wallace's warp of sense and his woof of nonsense is very tricky cloth out of which to cut the pattern of a postwar world.

The Timism "globaloney" made front pages all over the country in newspapers whose inner-page editorials often criticized the cheapness of the wisecrack. Some accused her of isolationism—quite incorrectly, since both she and her husband were firm internationalists as long as the world was reorganized on properly Lucean and American terms. There was some resentment against a freshman Congresswoman, enjoined by tradition to be seen and not heard, who leaped at the Vice President's throat only a month after her arrival. Time gave her and her speech a hefty three columns, mostly approving, whereas Fortune bravely called it "ill mannered." "Well," Eleanor Roosevelt commented, "do we want world peace or not?"

Despite her poor beginning, she was smarter and more aware of the issues than most Congressmen. She was assigned to the prestigious Military Affairs Committee. She had five secretaries. She did, it was said, have an unfortunate habit of name-dropping, as another Washington observer noticed: "Congressmen . . . were antagonized when the freshman in their midst drove home a point by 'But Winston Churchill told me,' or 'Mr. Hoover says that . . .' Later she stopped this."

What with her prodigious activity, her daughter's access to her was limited. Ann, now an eighteen-year-old sophomore at Stanford University in California, was said to have been upset once on arriving home from school to find only a chauffeur meeting her at the airport. Now and then during vacation the girl would wander over to Rockefeller Center to see her stepfather, but he was generally too busy to give her more than a moment. His assistant Wesley Bailey was occasionally deputized to take Ann to lunch at the Louis XIV or the Rainbow Room, finding an air of wistfulness about her. The situation was sometimes similar when Luce's sons visited them in Greenwich. Once, when Peter Paul returned after a weekend there, his mother asked if he had had a good time. Not particularly, he replied. The opera singer Lily Pons, a Senator and two governors had been among the guests, so he had seen little of his father.

4. THE MIGHTY MISSIMO

Nine days after Globaloney, another proud woman, the recently arrived Madame Chiang, spoke in the same chamber. Luce—through Time, Life, Fortune and both the radio and cinema MOT, plus the enormous publicity he had engineered for United China Relief and the hundreds of influential business and professional men all over the country whom he had lured into it—had been the greatest factor in raising the Gissimo and "Missimo" from the status of being unknown to the American public into household names brushed with the gilt of heroism and glamour. Theodore White, back in Chungking, was sending rousing dispatches about the Chinese which got the best display. Annalee Jacoby was Time's second correspondent in that remote city where only the biggest newspapers had even one. Life photographers Margaret Bourke-White, Carl Mydans and others had sent back hundreds of pictures of China at war. Clare's Life dispatches from Burma and China had further helped to educate American readers. Both Luce and Clare had made many speeches in behalf of China and the Chiangs, some of them reaching large radio audiences. The Luce publicity promoted the Chinese as full-fledged members of the Grand Alliance, with Chiang on the same footing as Roosevelt, Churchill and Stalin. He had strengthened the hand of Dr. Soong and the Chinese commission begging more Lend-Lease help in Washington, and had in turn encouraged the faltering Chinese back home to hang on a little longer against the Japanese.

Indeed, the publicity job Luce performed gratis for the Chiangs must rank as the greatest of its kind. Again (as with his exploitation of Time covers), it alone would place him as one of the most exalted of public relations practitioners, a man who could easily have made his fortune in that field or in advertising had he preferred. There was a standing joke at Time Inc. that Luce, Roosevelt, Churchill, Stalin (and of course Chiang) should have a summit conference so that Luce could tell the rest of them how to finish off the war and reorder the world. So far, the publicity he gave the Chinese, while heavily slanted, was effective allied war propaganda. The Gimo, who had valued the Missimo at ten divisions, must have known that the Lucepress influence was worth much more. Significantly, when Madame arrived (in an American Stratoliner which had been sent to China to pick her up) and was met by Harry Hopkins, she carried a copy of Life containing an attack on British policy which she said had led to the loss of Burma. Hopkins wrote, "She wanted me particularly to read that article as being her point of view."

Madame did not reflect any of the Chinese destitution for which she was so eloquent a pleader. The richness and variety of her dress were dazzling. When she went to New York for treatment of a skin trouble, she took over the entire twelfth floor of the Harkness Pavilion for herself and entourage, en-

suring privacy. She brought her own silk sheets, which were changed daily. When she was a White House guest, she annoyed Mrs. Roosevelt by her queenly habit of clapping her hands when she wished a household employee, as she did in China. She startled the President, when he asked what would be done in China if miners struck as they were doing in the United States, by drawing a hand across her throat.

Her speech before Congress got a full-page photograph in Life, a personal tribute (". . . this beautiful woman, clad in black and ornamented with flawless jade") and a full-page editorial pep-talk urging Americans to support her plea for greater war aid and stressing in italics a Luce prophecy: *For the fact is that the U.S. will need China in the future just as much as China needs the U.S. now.*

Time not only reproved Roosevelt for niggardliness toward China but for complacency about China's plight. Life's reporter Frank McNaughton let out all the stops in his account of Madame's separate appearances before House and Senate:

> Mme. Chiang's three hours at the Washington Capitol . . . are inevitably a part of U.S. history. . . . It was a sight such as Senators will talk about for years. . . . She had all the art of the greatest of divas. . . . Senators, without exception, said they had never heard anything like [her speech]. Many said they never expected to hear anything like it again. It was almost as though a modern Sappho had charmed them with emerald phrases and her own pearly beauty. . . . House members were stunned at her command of English . . . her calm assurance and her stage presence. Congressmen were wholly captivated by her personality, amazed by her presence, dizzied by her oratorical ability. . . . The most famous woman in the world. . . . If the Generalissimo could take the Japs as Madame took Congress, the war in the Pacific would be over in the bat of an eyelash. . . .

After discussions with President Roosevelt, she arrived in New York to be gathered into the arms of the Luce publicity apparatus. Bailey and other Luce assistants had worked for weeks to make her the center of a series of banquets and mass meetings in New York, Chicago and Los Angeles which would give her person and her message maximum exposure. Luce aimed to help both her causes to the utmost—her appeal for more military aid and more public donations to United China Relief. John D. Rockefeller, Jr., had consented to be chairman of the Citizens' Committee to Welcome Madame Chiang Kai-shek, a committee composed of 270 influential and fashionable New Yorkers, Luce himself being content to be called "co-chairman" although he was the wheel behind it all. Madame, who always insisted on the best hotel in whatever city she happened to be visiting, took a large suite at the Waldorf a few floors below the Luce suite.

She was the honored guest at a dinner at the Waldorf on March 2 immediately preceding her appearance at a mass rally at Madison Square Garden. Madame's face was on the cover of the March 1 Time, then on sale. In addi-

tion to Rockefeller, the sixty guests honoring Madame at the dinner (and subsequent mass rally) included Wendell Willkie, General Henry H. Arnold, Dr. T. V. Soong, Paul G. Hoffman (now a Time director and head of UCR), David Dubinsky and Governor Thomas E. Dewey of New York plus the governors of New Jersey, Pennsylvania, Connecticut, Massachusetts, Rhode Island, Maine, Vermont and New Hampshire, with their wives.

As the dinner got under way and the Missimo did not appear, an emissary was sent to her suite. He returned to say that she was indisposed and would not attend the dinner—an embarrassing contretemps since the whole shebang was in her honor. The women were especially anxious to meet this rara avis from the Orient. There were hurried consultations between the Luce staff and Madame's staff as the *tournedos sautés aux champignons* grew cold. She was adamant. She would address the Garden rally but could not attend the dinner. There was a feeling, perhaps unjustified, that the trouble was simply Madame's famous temperament and that a five-minute appearance at the dinner would have done her no harm.

Later, when she left for Chicago, the local UCR committee had scored a coup by getting half a floor of the Palmer House free for her and her entourage. But her nephew, who arrived in advance to complete arrangements, was dubious. Is it the best hotel? he inquired. An excellent hotel, he was told— perhaps not quite the most fashionable, but luxurious, unexceptionable and *free*, a saving of several thousands of dollars for China.

The nephew shook his head. Money was no object, he said. Madame must have the best, which he had heard was the Drake. So the Drake it was, and UCR did not save the several thousands. Madame refused to listen to the UCR representatives who accompanied her on the tour and essayed to advise her on American attitudes. She knew American attitudes, she said, having graduated from Wellesley. She neglected to thank Paul Hoffman for the mighty effort which UCR had made that year under his leadership, raising $7 million. The organization's Chicago officials were embarrassed because during her stay there the Missimo seemed to wear a different and more opulent fur coat every day, whereas it would have helped the money-raising if she had worn simple clothing. At that same time, Chiang's troops in China were unpaid and gaunt from malnutrition; the famine in Honan had reached such proportions that all dogs had long since been eaten, peasants were dying like flies (the dead would total two million) and it was unsafe to ride a horse into the province because starving people would slash at it.

Madame Chiang went on to Los Angeles, where her expensive tastes were taken as a matter of course. On Luce's and Hoffman's urging, David O. Selznick had arranged suitable homage. There was (to mention only a small part of the varied activities) a great banquet at the Ambassador and a monstrous gathering at the Hollywood Bowl at which the Committee to Receive Madame Chiang included Mary Pickford (who carried the special bouquet), Rita Hayworth, Marlene Dietrich, Ingrid Bergman, Ginger Rogers, Shirley

Temple and twelve other equally illustrious actresses. Madame Chiang's escorts included the governor, the mayor, two generals and an admiral, introductory remarks were made by Spencer Tracy and Henry Fonda, "The Madame Chiang Kai-shek March," composed for the occasion by Herbert Stothart, was played by the Los Angeles Philharmonic Orchestra and the Combined Services Bands, and a Methodist bishop managed to squeeze in an invocation before a "symphonic narrative" about China brought Walter Huston and Edward G. Robinson into the scene, followed at last by Madame herself. The lavish eight-page program for the show, printed in two colors with expensive artwork on heavy cream-colored stock, obviously represented a sum that would have alleviated some of the Honan hunger and dutifully, like screen credits, gave commendation to seventeen staff people who organized the event ending with the greatest commendation of all, "Arranged and Supervised by David O. Selznick."

XVIII

1. SEE ME ABOUT HITLER

Luce the editor maintained a balance between approval and terror, praise and damnation, that stimulated his men to the same paroxysms of effort they had once given their colleges. Give him an idea and he was aflame with interest. Stand up to him in argument on an "open" issue, give him as good as he gave, and he accorded respect. Let him walk all over you and you were dead. The trick was to compete with him and make him like it. He kept crowding, pushing, snarling, putting one on the defensive. It was like getting into a cage with a tiger, but exciting if one came out alive.

One could win an occasional battle with him provided it was understood that one was at Luce's mercy and could not win the war. Some thought that the liberal slants that occasionally got into the magazines had nothing to do with editors' arguments but were Luce's foxy concessions to Time's considerable number of liberal readers. The fact that he could on rare occasion succumb to a liberal point of view or a liking for a liberal politician combined with his ardent internationalism to anger the mossback-isolationist-reactionary typified by Colonel McCormick of the Chicago Tribune. McCormick, sometimes joined by his cousins in New York and Washington, complimented Luce by regarding him with suspicion and the feeling that he was, of all things, inclined to the left and occasionally taken in by the Communists. The caveman columnist Westbrook Pegler had similar suspicions, abetted by Luce's employment of "radicals," as Pegler described all liberals, and the fact that Congresswoman Luce had a mind of her own and a working-class constituency that sometimes let her vote with the Democrats. Perhaps Luce's stand was better illustrated by the reply he was said to have made when asked why he had so many liberals on the staff: "For some goddam reason Republicans can't write."

His treatment of advertisers had what seemed an expedient ambivalence. When not curbed by wartime stringencies he held annual meetings of his space salesmen at plush resorts such as Shawnee-on-Delaware or White Sulphur Springs and gave them speeches (often so overlong that his golf-minded captive audience fidgeted or slept) to inspire them to sell more linage. But his constant pitch to his editors was the absolute supremacy of editorial matter and the absolute subordination of advertising. He talked tough to his editors and said no magazine was worth its salt unless it lost an advertising contract every month or so. Fortune's offending of the Matson Line has been noted. A similar incident occurred when John Dos Passos wrote a Fortune article about the Timken roller-bearing town contrasting the elegant homes of the executives on the hill with the shacks of the workers near the factory below. Timken was so angry that Fortune was barred from its advertising schedules —a sizable loss.

Luce made it a point to crow over these rare examples to the editorial staff and to the ad salesmen. It made them all feel cocky and spread talk in the trade that here was a publisher so confoundedly successful that he could insult advertisers and still fill his pages with everything from Ivory Soap to Chevrolet. This doubtless was in part a ploy, for in general he treated advertisers reverently and an account was handled like precious jewels. Liberals and leftists on the staff were angered by Time's pro-industry handling of industrial and labor news, which was one of the reasons why Luce's old friend Stephen Vincent Benét ended up by "disliking intensely many of the principles on which Time operated."

There was the case of Time's story in the Medicine department under the heading of "Constipation." It featured "jolly, talkative" Dr. Harold Herbert Aaron, who called bran "a material unsuited for human consumption [which] should be relegated to the barn." Worse than being merely useless, he said, it was downright harmful, sometimes obstructing the intestine.

This came as a shock to the W. K. Kellogg Company, heavy advertisers of their All-Bran and other cereals. The Kellogg ads disappeared from Time. There were conferences between Time and Kellogg people. Three weeks later Time's Medicine section featured a piece headed "Bran Booster" about the research conducted by Dr. Bernard Fantus at the University of Illinois. Dr. Fantus swore by bran. He had fed it to a hundred students experimentally and was so reassured that he ate it daily himself and recommended it generally. The Kellogg advertising resumed in Time. One suspects that Luce did not believe in overdoing the alienation of advertisers.

While Luce's memos were sometimes corrosive, they were usually thoughtful, and on rare occasions warm. Once, after he had taken over temporarily as managing editor, he sent benevolent word to the whole editorial staff:

What with Thanksgiving, a rusty Managing Editor and seven inches of snow, I'm afraid the issue of Time we put out last week was far from being a very good

issue. In fact, it may be terrible. But anyway I'd like you to know that I greatly enjoyed the work and hope to do my part better this week.

I have no particular discoveries to report—except one, namely, the distinct impression that the present Time staff is an abler and more talented staff than any I have previously known.

For a man almost without verbal humor, his scribbling of "Eh?" on the margin where a writer had used an obviously mistaken word was amusing. His one-liner to Grover, "Allen—see me about Hitler," testified to his problem-solving ability. Sometimes his memos could combine wit with a dash of menace, as when he wrote Hodgins and a few others about new ideas for Fortune:

> As you may recall we had a couple of sessions a couple of months ago regarding a basic pattern or patterns for Fortune. We also had a dinner. It was all, I am sure, good fun. But did it serve no other purpose? In short, is nothing to come of it? . . .
>
> The seasons come, the seasons go; the earth is green or white with snow.
>
> If no one else wants to lay down a constitution for Fortune, I will. But this is fair-warning that if I get to it first, the Luce-Schlieffen plan will be carried out with unprecedented frightfulness.
>
> Where'er upon life's seas we sail, for God, for country and for Yale.

His anxiety to get top-echelon men to leave their desks for occasional stimulating trips (at company expense) led to a memo to his publishers and managing editors just before the war:

> The most important place for Publishers and Managing Editors to be is on the job—i.e. as near as possible to copy and printing presses.
>
> The next most important place for them to be is all over the place—i.e. all over the world.
>
> At the present time, no senior Time Inc.er seems to be at large.

When enlistments and the draft created a manpower problem, he wrote, "I suggest that it is something like a duty for every member of the staff not to get sick." To the proposal that Life join with Simon & Schuster in getting rights to the postwar writings of Winston Churchill, he responded, "In general my idea would be to *grab everything*—just being sure we get the roast beef & not the leavings." They later got a whole side of beef with very few leavings. On the question of expanding Time's Paris bureau, he was cautiously approving: "Now my notion is not to pay them an aggregate of many thousands of dollars a year (plus fabulous expense accounts) merely to drink coffee on the boulevards and to communicate to us from time to time their meditations on the smell of the chestnut trees."

A question discussed furtively was: Who would be the Old Man's successor? True, he was only forty-five and full of pep and vinegar, but he had talked so insistently about "handing over the company" when he was forty or forty-five that some believed him. That refrain was less heard now, with the

war leaving the company in the hands of fossils in their forties. Still, Time was marching on, as Westbrook Van Voorhees said so portentously on MOT. Luce's oldest son was still only a kid at Yale. The "old masters" who might logically assume command—Billings, Gottfried, Matthews, Hodgins—were themselves in their forties.*

The smart money was on John Hersey, who had had the Boss's eye almost from the start. Hersey had done excellent reporting from the Pacific and had moved up the masthead. His *Into the Valley* had been well received, giving him the cachet of a writer who could make it on his own outside the organization. He had of course been a guest of the Luces many times. (The number of times a person was a Luce guest was counted very gravely by the ambitious men in the T-L Building.) It was now felt by many insiders that the increasingly hard-bitten Luce was incapable of real affection for anything but Time Inc. and the growing power it gave him; but he did seem to have an astringent fondness for the China-born writer whose background so nearly matched his own.

But the liberal Hersey was sensing disillusionment. The remarkable organization Luce had built was not all glamour, prestige and high pay. Blood was flowing in the T-L Building. Luce was becoming more rigid in his judgments. There was also his incessant habit of pitting men against each other in order to get more out of them. Before Ingersoll's departure, his swift rise had been a challenge and a threat to the man second only to Luce himself, Roy Larsen. Even the publishers and managing editors of each of the three magazines were on an equal basis of power, and although one was concerned mainly with editorial content and the other with business operations, there was often fierce competition between them. Promotions of importance were made not only on a basis of past good work but also after a couple of candidates had fought for the job. Since they knew they were fighting for the job, a kind of jungle savagery sometimes resulted. Although both Hearst and Pulitzer had made use of the practice, and it was far from unknown in other fields, Luce had sharpened it to a deadly edge.

Undercover conflicts were fought over every junior and senior editorship but were especially ferocious around the managing editorship of Time—the best-paid "news" job (under Luce's) in the world. Luce in 1939 had made certain of a sanguinary struggle by appointing not one but three managing editors—Gottfried, Matthews and Norris. Although Gottfried was the senior man, he could feel the hot breath of the others until the situation was resolved by the naming of Matthews to sole possession in 1943 and the shifting of the other two. At Life, Daniel Longwell, Wilson Hicks, Joseph Thorndike, Jr., C. D. Jackson and Edward K. Thompson had been placed in varying degrees of

---

* John Martin had left the company. Sheldon Luce was in the Army and would not return to Time Inc.

high-level confrontation. Fortune had its own Luce-refereed duels involving Russell Davenport, Eric Hodgins, Ralph D. Paine and others.

This Lucean practice was sometimes called Roosevelting, because the President shuffled men around into similar positions of tension, but was more often known at TLF as Chinese Checkers. The only mogul who was seldom if ever thrust into a Chinese Checkers game was Billings, still top man on the money-coining Life. Luce, it was believed, was fascinated by him because Billings succeeded in restricting Luce's communication with him to a minimum. Billings, who managed to be at once aloof and agreeable, kept his family life strictly separate from Time Inc. and somehow achieved a measure of privacy even on the job. Otherwise, the various Time departments were in continuous Balkan war. There were particularly bitter feuds between NA and FN. Individually Timen fought for a higher place on the masthead, which meant not only more money but a bigger office with one more window. Nowhere did windows convey such a message of status. Hence the prevailing mood at Time Inc. was exactly what Luce wanted it to be—one of extreme tension and competition, with an attendant high incidence of emotional and digestive disorder. One Timan who moved to the Herald Tribune discovered that the offices, washrooms and working conditions there were atrocious by comparison but that there was a wonderful serenity at the Tribune because no one seemed to be cutting his neighbor's throat. The ink-stained members of the newspaper press eyed Luce and his chromium-trimmed, tweedy kingdom with mixed envy, alarm and contempt. Stories made the rounds about him, some apocryphal: that Luce liked the ladies; that Luce ended a policy discussion with his editors by saying, "I want all you men to keep an open mind on this question until I make up my mind how we'll decide it."

When any of his men blew in from abroad, Luce could hardly wait to talk with them. On Walter Graebner's arrival from his London post, Miss Thrasher informed him that he was having lunch with Luce and sent the same command (in the form of a request) to Hersey. They dined very well at the Drake on Park Avenue as Luce cross-examined Graebner about the situation in England and Hersey barely got a word in. Around two, long after the dishes had been taken away, Luce looked at his watch and snapped, "Where the hell's the head waiter? They haven't even taken our orders." Graebner and Hersey had to inform him that he had eaten without being aware of it.

That steak and potatoes could slide down his gullet unperceived, and that he could unconsciously appropriate other people's cigarettes were equal manifestations of the ego reserved for matters of greatness. Godless Russia was much on his mind. On March 11, 1943, he addressed 976 of his New York employees at the Waldorf in celebration of Time's twentieth anniversary. After recounting the old story of how he and Hadden had founded Time, he got down to his fears, refraining from naming the enemy who was actually our ally but not hiding his hope that Time would have a role in saving the country and the world:

Only if America is deeply and truly loved by her children, only so can America rise to her full greatness. Only by rising to the very heights of greatness can America save herself. And only if America achieves salvation for herself, only so can America, in any sense whatever, save the world. . . . [May it] be said of us that Time was the servant of the servants of America.

2. CELESTIAL INTERROGATIONS

Luce's hatred of Roosevelt reached its zenith when he found himself barred from all war theaters. His plan to tour the Pacific in 1943 was foiled when his application, approved by the War Department, was overruled by the President. Correspondents could go, but not publishers. Although Roy Alexander was certain that the prohibition was aimed at Colonel McCormick of the Chicago Tribune, Luce was positive it was a personal affront to him.

Certainly the President was unaware of the condition of tension and unbearable curiosity which Luce could alleviate only by taking a trip. Since he had to go somewhere, he left by train in April on a Southern tour whose every detail was arranged, as always, by his office. His first stop was the antebellum mansion of John Billings across the Savannah River from Augusta, Georgia. Billings had warned him to come via the Atlantic Coast Line, which stopped at Beech Island near the Billings estate. Someone at Time had erred, for Luce came instead on the Southern Railway. When he demanded to get off at Beech Island, he was angered by the conductor's reply that since the train did not even go through Beech Island it could not stop there. It did, however, stop at Augusta, where Billings caught up with him. Luce greeted him and said, "Now take me to the state capitol." He was surprised on being informed that the capitol was at Atlanta, 160 miles west.

Luce was a pleasant guest except for a slight awkwardness at dinner when he brought up the inevitable subject of China. Billings's aged uncle, Judge Henry Hammond, one of those at the table, made the mistake of inquiring facetiously whether China was worth saving. The judge's penalty was a long, careful Luce lecture on China's great worth to the civilized world, its terrible travail at the hands of the Japanese and America's shameful failure to help China as much as she should be helped.

According to plan, William Howland, the courtly head of Time's Atlanta bureau, arrived next day by car with his friend Ralph McGill, then assistant editor of the Atlanta Constitution, who wanted to meet Luce. The three men headed for Atlanta, after first stopping at the Hammond pond to see two black swans which the judge had presented to Luce. Howland got out to stir up the swans so that Luce could see them in action. He got more action than he expected, for the swans surprised him by instant attack, pecking him angrily as he hurried back to the car. Luce laughed slightly—the only time Howland ever saw him laugh—while McGill was bent double with laughter.

With Howland driving, Luce got on well with the amiable McGill in the back seat. McGill discovered that to be a companion of Luce could mean the loss of one's identity as a person and his re-establishment as a bureau of information, a victim of what was known in the T-L Building as the Celestial Interrogation. It was Luce's first visit to Georgia. He asked McGill a thousand questions, ranging as always from the sublime to the ridiculous—from penetrating questions about Southern journalism and politics to: "I see we're in McDuffie County. Why do they call it McDuffie County?" McGill told him why.

In Atlanta, Luce put up at the Biltmore and dressed for a dinner which Howland had arranged at the swank Piedmont Driving Club. It was typical of the affairs which Luce came more and more to expect while traveling—a gathering, always in the most expensive surroundings, of personages whom Luce could ply with questions. It became known among Time people as the Prandial Interrogation.

The guests, in addition to Howland and his wife, included the young liberal Governor Ellis Arnall and his wife, the economist Dr. Malcolm Bryan and his wife, and a widowed Georgia judge who had made some unusual decisions. The Negro maître d'hôtel at the club warned Howland, "The judge is not in good shape." The judge indeed was drunk. Luce, however, was so engrossed in conversation with the Arnalls and Bryans—especially Mrs. Arnall, who looked particularly dashing in a low-cut gown—that he hardly spoke to the judge. Howland, worried that his Presbyterian chief might be angry about the judge's condition, was grateful to Mrs. Arnall for attracting Luce's admiring attention. The maître d'hôtel kept giving the judge coffee to bring him around, but at one point he suggested loudly, "Tell Mr. Luce about the nigger problem," without getting a rise out of the guest from New York.

After the Interrogation, as the Howlands escorted Luce back to his hotel, he inquired, "Wasn't the judge a little peculiar?" Howland agreed that the judge was an eccentric man.

XIX

1. EARLY FROST

In 1943, when America and Russia were on warmer terms than they had been since the 1917 revolution, Luce cautiously began the Cold War. By then, the Red juggernaut was driving the Nazis back across scorched Russia and the emergence of the Soviet as a postwar rival of the United States could be foreseen. Luce of course never trusted the Russians, who could be expected to oppose his American Century. Their godlessness alone made it impossible for him to view them with anything but revulsion, and it would soon become apparent that Roosevelt could be attacked through them and his policies toward them. Politics aside, Luce was honestly fearful that America was in danger of being taken in by Russia. One of the indicators was a Fortune poll which found that 81 percent of Americans thought the United States should work with Russia as equal partners in the coming peace.

It would be over Luce's dead body that the U.S. permit itself to be treated by any country—even England, much less Russia—as an equal partner after the war. America must be number one, top dog, the boss in the world.

The question of American-Soviet relations has since become so colored by emotion and propaganda on both sides that it is difficult to say whether postwar comity would have been attainable even with the most earnest mutual effort. The background of Stalin was scarcely reassuring. Nevertheless, earnest effort was essential, the only civilized course. There is a question whether Luce believed this, since his mistrust was so deep and since Russia represented not only the Antichrist but the only military, propagandist and economic force likely to compete with America for control of the postwar world. As a businessman, he wanted to get the Russians to sign on the dotted line about their intentions. Early in 1943—more than two years before the end of

211

the war and sixteen months before the Russian plea for a second front in Europe had been answered—Time reflected the Lucean suspicion:

> The central problem was Russia. . . . [U]nless a general and open agreement is reached soon on joint postwar policies, the Allies' present comradeship in arms may turn into a barracks brawl. . . . Russia holds too many trumps to be finessed in the game of politics . . . [I]f the partners in war do not lay their cards on the table soon, there will be the devil to pay.

Luce believed literally in the devil. Rather than quoting middle-of-the-road journals which were elated over the Soviet military advances and the prospects for accommodation with Russia, Time quoted the Red-baiting New York Daily News: "Stalin will accomplish what Hitler tried to do—dominate all Europe. The effect of all this on us will be to leave us in as much danger from Europe as we were before this war." Time dared to utter the terrible thought:

> The peace-loving nations of the world, which had tragically demonstrated their inability to head off World Wars I & II, again showed signs of an inability to head off World War III.

The Soviet Union, suffering terribly despite her military recovery, her heartland laid waste, had perhaps earned some right to her own suspicions that the Anglo-Americans were in no hurry to save her with a second front. The Roosevelt administration was working to maintain Allied unity and to arrange discussions with Stalin. The amazing Russian resurgence after Stalingrad was the joyous subject of American headlines and radio commentators, repeated over millions of dinner tables. To Luce, all this represented danger. His problem was to arouse Americans to the Russian menace, as he saw it, without causing popular indignation and loss of circulation. In March he published an issue of Life devoted entirely to the U.S.S.R., cover to cover. More respectful than critical, it was yet significant in managing to swing emphasis away from the Russian as a brave warrior and ally to the Russian as a world revolutionist and postwar threat, aided by Lend-Lease and not very grateful.

Luce was pleased by the Cairo Conference in the fall—the first and only one of the gatherings of the great to be attended by Chiang Kai-shek. Madame was there too, impressing correspondents with her "extremely chic costumes." But the Teheran declaration signed shortly thereafter by Roosevelt, Stalin and Churchill was attacked in Life for its vagueness. "If it can be believed," said Life dubiously, "it solves everything; if it cannot, it is a colossal fraud." The declaration merely affirmed in general terms the unity of the three leaders in war and their determination to attain a postwar "world family of democratic nations" in which all peoples "may live free lives untouched by tyranny and according to . . . their own consciences." Life inquired, "Are the Russians really dedicated to 'free lives' and the elimination of tyranny? The word 'conscience' is not exactly a Marxian word."

On the day after Christmas, Luce left to join his wife, who was on a national speaking tour, in California. After a stay at Palm Springs, where they were joined by Ann Brokaw, they went to San Francisco, where Clare had booked several speeches and they could continue their visit with Ann. Now nineteen, she was a senior majoring in social science and an excellent student. On January 11, Luce caught a morning plane for New York. Ann had lunch with her mother in San Francisco, then returned to Palo Alto in the car of a Stanford University friend, Virginia Lee Hobbs. In Palo Alto, their open convertible was struck by a car coming out of a side street. Miss Hobbs, who was driving, was slightly hurt. Ann, thrown from the car against a tree, was killed.

Luce flew back to San Francisco, where messages of condolence were coming in from the Churchills, the Chiangs, the Beaverbrooks and others. It was decided that Ann, after a memorial service at Stanford, should be buried at Mepkin, which had been virtually unused during the war. The Luces returned with the body, stopping en route in Washington, where Luce, in writing the obituary for Time's Milestones, identified Ann as "the daughter of Mr. and Mrs. Henry Luce." When Belair of the Washington bureau mentioned that she had not been his daughter, he replied it must go in that way anyway. If he was saddened, Clare was in almost suicidal despair. He gave his assistant Bailey $1500 in cash with instructions to take charge of all arrangements for the funeral. Bailey even selected the burial spot, a grassy glade from which the river could be seen through liveoaks.

2. ENLARGING CATEGORY THREE

As 1944 came in, Luce bought a 12½ percent interest in NBC's Blue Network, a hookup of more than a hundred radio stations all over the country, for some $800,000. This expansion of what was already the world's largest communications empire caused no general alarm. Professor Carl S. Friedrich, a Harvard specialist in public opinion and propaganda, expressed mild concern over this concentration of opinion-making power in Luce's hands. The editor of the little Smethport, Pennsylvania, Union—a labor paper—took it more seriously, writing, "[Luce] is the most dangerous man in America."

Luce was highly sensitive to the public reaction to his radio expansion, perhaps fearing criticism on the ground that he was showing monopolistic tendencies. Time clerks studied the press and radio reaction and reported to him, also noting the press mention of Congresswoman Luce (which was small) in connection with news of his enlarged holdings. Mrs. Luce began making occasional speeches over the Blue Network, and Time began a second radio "news" program, "Time Views the News," over the same hookup. Since Luce now had more money than he knew what to do with, and he was always more interested in power, it seems likely that power was the important factor in the purchase. Coming up were two momentous events whose outcome he wanted

to influence, the shaping of the postwar world and the 1944 Presidential election, not to mention his own wife's bid for re-election. In mid-1944 his propaganda holdings were as follows:

> Time, with a domestic weekly circulation of 1,160,000; it also printed special editions for the classroom, for Canada, Pony editions for service people in Europe and Asia, Air Express editions for Mexico and South America, and special editions for other foreign countries printed in Sweden, Australia, Persia, Egypt and India; and a V-mail edition for the U.S. Navy. All were in English, but Time planned a German-language edition to be sold in Germany after that country's defeat.
>
> Life, with a weekly circulation of 4,000,000 in America and some 317,000 abroad.
>
> Fortune had a monthly circulation of 170,000, and Architectural Forum 40,000.
>
> Radio March of Time was heard weekly by an estimated 18,000,000 in America.
>
> Time Views the News was heard daily by an audience not yet estimated but in the millions.
>
> Cinema March of Time appeared every four weeks in 10,000 American and foreign theaters.
>
> United China Relief, which Luce had helped found and finance and of which he was the real boss, was an organization powerful in propaganda. He had recently bought a handsome East 65th Street town house and altered it to establish China House, a center for Chinese exchange students and also for propaganda.
>
> Lastly, Luce was planning a new monthly magazine aimed at intellectuals.

The assumption that each copy of his magazines was read by an average of more than four persons, if true, would multiply circulation figures as far as propaganda impact is concerned. Although this would be reduced by some duplication of Time and Life readers and of radio and theater audiences, a Luce opinion, message, point of view or slant promoted through all his outlets would be likely to reach *at least a third and perhaps considerably more of the total literate adult population of the country.* The enormous leverage this afforded in shaping public opinion—especially when propaganda was skillfully hidden in the news—was obvious. Perhaps it was a move aimed at blocking criticism before it became serious when Luce established and financed the Commission of Inquiry on Freedom of the Press, a group to be selected by his friend (Yale '22) President Robert M. Hutchins of the University of Chicago, which would spend more than two years in its investigation. The commission's findings would be interesting since Luce's concept of a free press included the freedom of Luce or anyone else to pursue an undeclared if not secret molding of opinion. While he would defend this concept to his dying day, he did admit the possibility that single control of a large percentage of the communications media might constitute a problem.

Andrei Gromyko, the Soviet ambassador in Washington, was also aware of a problem, the problem of the rising hostility of the Lucepress toward Russia. He asked an unnamed member of Time's fourteen-man Washington staff, "Who makes the policy on Russia for Time Inc. magazines?" The writer hedged, giving the impression that there was no central policy-maker and that policies were dictated by events. When this got back to Luce, he was irate. A memo went out to all editorial and public relations people:

> . . . Time Inc. does have policies and is not at all ashamed of having them, or of what they are. The earliest prospectus for Time the Weekly Newsmagazine admitted to bias and we have never since that time submitted to any emasculating operation. No one can read our magazines without knowing that our policy toward Fascism or other authoritarian political forms is one of everlasting condemnation. . . . The chief editorial policymaker for Time Inc. is Henry R. Luce—and that is no secret which we attempt to conceal from the outside world.

Gromyko, to quote an inelegancy of the day, hadn't seen nothing yet. Luce was discovering an affinity for former Communists or fellow travelers who had turned right. To Whittaker Chambers, already high in his regard, he added Willi Schlamm and William C. Bullitt. Schlamm was a reformed Communist, a refugee from Austria who had become a writer for Fortune. Neither Chambers nor Schlamm became well known to Luce until they were already in his employ. Bullitt, on the other hand, had the mystic Yale credentials, had entertained the Luces in Paris and had in turn been entertained by them. Hated by conservatives when he first went overboard on Russia, he was now hated by liberals and leftists because he had turned so violently against the Soviet. After the fall of France, Bullitt had returned to Washington as an assistant to the Secretary of the Navy, but he had his eye on the job of Undersecretary of State Sumner Welles. He had urged the President to demand postwar concessions from the Soviet Union on the threat that the United States would otherwise switch its whole strategy to the defeat of Japan first. Luce may also have entertained Japan-first thoughts as a blow to Russia. Roosevelt rejected the Bullitt idea. Later, rumors flooded Washington to the effect that Welles had made advances to a Negro porter on a train, and Roosevelt had to let the valuable but vulnerable Welles go. Far from getting the job, however, Bullitt was fired by the President when he was told that it was Bullitt who had spread the rumors. Luce of course knew of this through his Washington bureau. Bullitt would become an occasional Luce correspondent on assignments liberal Timen called "Red-wrecking."

Luce's infatuation with the small, clever, black-haired Schlamm began in part because Schlamm could answer questions like an oracle. His continental background and experience with European Communism gave his question-answering special timeliness in view of Luce's fear that Stalin would communize Europe. Many of the senior staff regarded Schlamm as a courtier.

215

Often with the Boss in the Penthouse, he was also a frequent Luce guest at the Waldorf and at Greenwich. Schlamm was advance thinker and organizer for Luce's projected "brain" magazine, known scornfully in the building as Brow because of its highbrow aims. Chambers, who also had Luce's ear and his admiration as an intellectual and writer, was untidy and not fully house-broken but was often in the Penthouse and occasionally Luce's companion in coffee-break sessions he liked to hold in a drugstore across the street.

Chambers, who had been elevated to take charge of Time's book review section, had found a way to get his anti-Russian slant into the magazine. At first, as he later described it, "I never missed an opportunity to jab at Communism in my stories." He now realized his control over one of Time's hidden editorial pages because in reviewing books one could comment on the whole spectrum of news. His earlier efforts had come out of the meat grinder much altered because his bias was too obvious. As he put it:

> I began to see that the kind of sniping that I had been doing was shallow . . . It seemed to me that I had a more important task to do, one that was peculiarly mine. It was not to attack Communism frontally. It was to clarify, on the basis of news, the religious and moral position that made Communism evil.

This was what Luce had been doing for two decades. After his temporary suspension of the campaign, he was resuming it by indirection as Chambers was doing in Books. He boosted Chambers into the editorship of the entire back of the book—thirteen sections including Books. "This was my first association with Luce," Chambers recalled, "with whom . . . I came to feel a bond of common editorial and journalistic intuition, and, more important, a common religious concern . . . [H]e is an intensely religious man." A true fanatic, Chambers had his troubles among Time's liberals, whom he detested as unwitting fellow travelers and who hated him as cordially. He had tried unsuccessfully to get one of them fired as a "Red," a charge found to be untrue. He had many enemies in the building and felt that they were conspiring against him, but he was as sure as Luce of God's favor. "I cannot really be beaten," he told a researcher, "because on my side is a Power."

On his side was another power—Luce. In August, the current FN editor, John Osborne, was sent to Europe as a correspondent. Whether or not this was done to make room for Chambers, Whittaker Chambers became Time's Foreign News editor. The man whose prejudice had formerly barred him from so much as reviewing books on Soviet or Communist subjects was now in charge of mighty FN with its influence over four or five millions of readers in the U.S. and many abroad. The climate of hostility, always chill around FN and NA, began to freeze with Chambers's elevation. But the move was agreeable to the apolitical Managing Editor Matthews, who liked Chambers and admired his writing. Chambers, who had been aiming for FN all along, was elated, later writing:

> The tacit ban on [my] editing or writing of Soviet or Communist news had at last been broken. My assignment sent a shiver through most of Time's staff,

where my views were well known and detested with a ferocity that I did not believe possible until I was at grips with it. With my first few Foreign News sections, the shiver turned into a shudder.

Luce gave FN to Chambers on a two-month tryout basis. Evidently the shivers and shudders were wanted, for he stayed. There seems no question that his promotion signaled a new Luce propaganda drive against Russia. Its central theme appeared in a long, long Life editorial article, "The World From Rome." It was under the byline of Bullitt, but there were some who thought its apocalyptic periods had the sound of Chambers's retouching. With the Anglo-American armies now liberating Paris and rolling across France toward Russian armies fighting through Poland and the Balkans, the moment when two conflicting philosophies of government must either find some accommodation or plunge the world into disaster, seemed not far distant. The majority in the West viewed the coming meeting jubilantly, never doubting that accommodation was possible. Bullitt, on the contrary, contemplated the collapse of the Nazis with dread. Bullitt, said Life, had written the piece after he was "granted interviews with well-informed and authoritative personages, among them Pope Pius XII," suggesting that he was actually reflecting the views of the Pope and these unnamed personages. Bullitt himself hinted that he spoke for the Pope as well as for Western civilization:

It is but natural . . . [that] the Vatican should take the long view of events and strive to understand, and make understood, the deep tides that move the nations. And from the Vatican spreads throughout Rome, quietly and naturally, a comprehension of each new event in the world picture. What is that picture as seen from Rome?

Bullitt ticked off his points, paragraph by paragraph, page by page:

It is an old picture . . . a picture of western Europe and Western civilization threatened by hordes of invaders from the East. . . . Great Britain alone will not be strong enough to stop the threat from the East. . . . [T]he Romans are by no means sure that we [the U.S.] recognize our own interests. . . . [N]ine of the 15 members of the so-called Polish Committee of National Liberation set up by the Soviet government are Communists. . . . The Italians . . . look beyond the end of the fighting with little hope and much fear because they are afraid that the withdrawal of American and British forces . . . will leave them at the mercy of the Soviet Union. . . . The Romans . . . fear that in the end Moscow, in the form of Tito, will be installed on their eastern frontier. . . . They are even more frightened by the prospect that their northern neighbor, Austria, may fall under the control of Moscow. . . . The Romans know Hitler, and they have heard him swear that if Germany should face defeat he would pull down the pillars of Western civilization on the heads of the Allies . . . by having Himmler turn over Germany at the moment of collapse to the Communists. . . .

. . . A sad joke going the rounds in Rome gives the spirit of their hope: What is an optimist? A man who believes that the third world war will begin in about 15 years between the Soviet Union and western Europe backed by Great Brit-

ain and the U.S. What is a pessimist? A man who believes that western Europe, Great Britain and the U.S. will not dare to fight. That is as far as Roman optimism dares to go, since the Italians feel that failure of the U.S. and Great Britain to stand strongly for independence for all the states of Europe has made certain a new world war. . . .

The deepest moral issue of the modern world—the issue of man as a son of God with an immortal soul, an end in himself, against man as a chemical compound, the tool of an omnipotent state, an end in itself—may thus be fought out in Italy. . . .

This was shocking stuff to the 81 percent of the people who, according to Elmo Roper's Fortune Poll, saw Americans and Russians settling their problems at the peace table. The 81 percent was composed of a large proportion of people in whom three years of wartime collaboration with the Soviet had dissolved suspicion, and a smaller second category who were aware of the East-West chasm but confident that good will and patient negotiation would bridge it. Category Three, of which both Luce and Bullitt were members, thought the chasm unbridgeable and that the West must either turn on Russia immediately or stand guard over her permanently. Luce was determined to enlarge Category Three, which represented only 19 percent of the people. In an effort so obviously unpopular, he had avoided identifying himself with the article. Interestingly, it had been preceded in June by a similar though milder article in Fortune by Charles J. V. Murphy, "The British Look at Russia," which may have been a dry run. It employed the same technique, arousing American suspicions of "the bear that walks like a man" by dwelling on growing British doubts.

The protest over the Life piece was immediate. As it admitted in a later issue, the article "evoked a deluge of letters, mostly denunciatory." Pravda, itself not known for strict truth, said that it contained thirty lies, that Bullitt was a discredited politician known for his "anti-Soviet idea," and "The choice of the . . . article by Life magazine seems strange in the light of all this." The complaining letters from readers could perhaps be best summarized by a sentence in one from Lee Grant: "The article . . . may do more harm than you or anyone else can ever measure." This was a majority sentiment—that Life had ripped open wounds almost healed, sown suspicion at home and in Russia and inflicted serious hurt to the cause of peace. "It is the first time," Max Lerner wrote in a passion in PM, "that anyone with a veneer of respectability, in a respectable paper, has uttered a direct call for a war between England and America on one side and Russia on the other." The Bullitt piece was denounced in an open letter to Luce whose signers ranged from Dr. Albert Einstein and Bishop Arthur W. Moulton to Serge Koussevitzky and Professor Ralph Barton Perry of Harvard.

The Bullitt article was also an attack on Roosevelt policy. More than a year earlier, the President had asked Sumner Welles to protest formally any articles in Time, Life or Fortune that "hurt the Good Neighbor policy . . . or

tend to promote disunity among any of the United Nations." Since then Roosevelt had assailed Drew Pearson for writing in his newspaper column that Cordell Hull "long has been anti-Russian" and saying over the radio that Hull's chief assistants felt the same way. Hull had called in Gromyko to give him official repudiation of the Pearson talk. The Life article, not merely "tending to promote" Allied disunity but demanding it, was an incendiarism alongside which Time's little indecorum about the Chilean president's wine-bibbing was picayune. Yet it seems to have escaped official censure, the President perhaps deciding that the best answer to this direct challenge would be to remove Mrs. Luce from Congress, which he essayed to do.

3. LUCES vs ROOSEVELTS

Eleanor Roosevelt and her secretary, Malvina "Tommy" Thompson, had gone to see *The Women* together. "After we left," the First Lady later told Beatrice Blackmar Gould, ". . . Tommy and I asked each other if we ourselves had ever known any women like the women in the play. We agreed that we had known *one*."

Perhaps there was a touch of malice in the emphasis on the last word and the assumption that any numskull would know whom she meant. The antipathy between the Luces and Roosevelts was multiplied because of its mutuality. Luce had come to have serious suspicions that Mrs. Roosevelt was tainted with Communist subversion and the fourth-term issue made him livid against the President who had already kept him out of central political power for twelve years.

Hence the combined Luce efforts against the Democrats in 1944 were massive. Political commentators all over the country had given amazed attention to the lady from Connecticut who blended beauty with brains, money and the power of her husband's magazine, radio and cinema properties. Although the more desiccated Republicans had not forgiven the Luce plunge for Willkie in 1940, the party knew that in the Luces it had a power combination it would be foolish not to exploit. Most first-term Congressmen were lucky to get within earshot of the stage at the party's national convention. Mrs. Luce, who stayed with her husband at Madame Chiang's favorite, the Drake Hotel in Chicago, was a featured speaker. Luce, looking cool in a white suit, read the Chicago Tribune while other speakers including his Waldorf neighbor Herbert Hoover droned on, but "he dropped his newspaper and listened, rapt," when his spouse came to the rostrum. This was when she gave her famous speech apostrophizing "GI Jim and GI Joe," suggesting that Democratic bungling had caused excessive battle casualties:

Who is GI Jim? Ask rather, who *was* GI Jim. He was Joe's pal, his buddy, his brother. Jim was the fellow who lived next door to you. . . . Jim did not com-

plain too much about his government. . . . Jim figured that anybody can make mistakes. . . . If Jim could stand here and talk to you he might say, "Listen, folks, the past wasn't perfect. But skip it. Get on with the business of making this old world better." . . . And this we will do, for Jim's sake.

While the New Yorker commented that the speech "made it difficult to keep anything on our stomach for twenty-four hours," the Lucepress began giving sympathetic attention to the Republican candidate, Thomas E. Dewey. Life sent photographers to his country place at Pawling to snap him popping cherries into his mouth and posing with his family, making a five-page spread with glowing captions. In September Luce flew to London for a quick tour, England evidently not being considered a "war zone" although a few V-1's were still falling and the first V-2's just arriving. With him was the Life writer Noel Busch—one of the company Old Guard, having started with Time in 1927—who was returning there as a correspondent. Busch, who always got along well with Luce, enjoyed him particularly during his short stay. They went to a movie together in the blackout, then on to Lord Beaverbrook's by bus, where Luce penetrated a large gathering to get at Beaverbrook and pester him with questions about war and politics so insistently that the Beaver became impatient and Luce actually amused. "Harry seemed to enjoy the whole adventure," Busch recalled.

In Life, Raymond L. Buell asked, "Should Liberals Vote for Dewey?" and answered with a resounding three-page Yes. Another Life declared that the fourth-term issue alone was enough reason to "turn the rascals out." Both Life and Time favored pictures of Roosevelt (who at sixty-two indeed had only six months to live) looking sag-jowled and feeble and plugged the theme of debility: "His thinning hair was pasted flat," said Time. ". . . the sallowness of his cheeks showed, and the heavy lines on his face . . . [H]e looked tired. . . . [W]hether or not the President had answered the questions about his health . . . would not be known until Election Day. . . . [H]is weary face looked seamed and haggard." It suggested that the old tosspot was now too creaky for his usual hidden liquor and his chainsmoking.

Dewey, aglow with health and political principle, seemed to touch neither alcohol nor tobacco:

> Tom Dewey had a field day with a hatful of hapless Administration quotes. . . . Republicans everywhere were heartened by the stiffness of his mustached upper lip. . . . [H]is fame as the fearless young prosecutor was secure . . . rapid success story, from small-town editor's son to governor of the biggest state. . . . [H]e was cool, precise, tough-minded. . . . A crisp, vigorous young man . . . who had perfect stage presence. . . . He was the only candidate discussing the issues. . . . Tom Dewey had learned discipline as a boy in Owosso. (Given a tricycle, he was told that, if he fell off, he would lose the tricycle for a year. He did, and the tricycle went into the Dewey cellar for a year.) . . . Tom Dewey kept punching. . . . Tom Dewey stayed on the attack. . . . Tom Dewey quickened his attack. . . .

Time harped on a new note, a suggestion that Roosevelt was not a true-blue American:

> He brushed off Earl Browder. . . . Earl Browder and his enthusiastic Communist support for Term IV. . . . Perhaps Franklin Roosevelt doesn't like the Communists, said Dewey, but look how they like him . . . the left-wing support for Franklin Roosevelt from P.A.C. and the Communists. . . . Roosevelt's disavowal of Communist support. . . . Tom Dewey explained why . . . the Communists are supporting Mr. Roosevelt.

In Connecticut, Congresswoman Luce's opponent was Margaret E. Connors, a Bridgeport attorney, who said that Mrs. Luce did not represent her district but the interests of "Time, Life, Fortune, Inc.," adding, "If she didn't have the backing she does, she would not be as dangerous as I think she is." Mrs. Luce wrote several pieces for the Hearst press and in one of them, as Walter Winchell put it, she "gleefully colyumed . . . that Bill Bullitt's article in Life would give FDR the hotfoot." Asserting her role as a national rather than only a state figure, she spoke in eight cities from Boston to St. Louis, sometimes to nationwide audiences over the Blue Network. She had financial support from at least one moderate, Luce's occasional tennis opponent William Benton (Yale '21). Of Roosevelt she said in Chicago, "He is the only American President who ever lied us into a war because he did not have the courage to lead us into it. . . . The shame of Pearl Harbor was Mr. Roosevelt's shame." The administration fought back in this bitterest of campaigns. Henry Wallace, Harold Ickes, Orson Welles, Clifton Fadiman and others Mrs. Luce called "the whole Broadway-Browder axis" spoke in Connecticut against her. Falling in with Time on the Communist issue, she called Ickes "that prodigious bureaucrat with the soul of a meat ax and the mind of a commissar" and suggested that the Democrats had been "taken over by the Communists and the Fellow Travelers . . ." There was credible talk that in the T-L Building some of "Harry's little people" had sent contributions to her opponent, Miss Connors.

To friends she remarked that famous men had their distinctive gesture: "Churchill has his V sign, Hitler his upraised arm, and Roosevelt . . . ?" She moistened a finger and held it aloft for the wind. Her warmest supporter, the Bridgeport Post, commented archly, "at times she is positively cruel." Winchell, feuding with Time because of its continued disparagement of him, wrote that a "Repubiggie" had told Dewey, "You'd better mute Clare Luce. She'll cost you a lot of votes." To which Dewey was said to have replied, "That's funny. My wife told me the same thing." The leftish PM crowed in disclosing that Mrs. Luce had sought the support of Sidney Hillman's Political Action Committee which both she and Luce had condemned, and bristled when she then said the P.A.C. had marked her for defeat, adding, "If my head rolls in the basket at the election, surely it's a more American head than Mr. Hillman's." Did she perhaps consider Hillman less American because he was a Jew, born in Lithuania? PM demanded.

Things were getting hotter on both sides. Mrs. Luce was also critical of Roosevelt's running mate, Senator Harry S. Truman, and Mrs. Truman, who was on his office payroll—something he frankly admitted, saying, "A Senator can't get along on $10,000 a year. After all, we're just poor folks." Truman said angrily to a newspaperman, "The way she talked about my wife—well, if she were a man, I would have done something about it."

The President himself, en route to Boston, stopped his special train in Bridgeport and addressed a station throng for five minutes, his arm around Miss Connors. It was not enough for her when the votes were in. While Roosevelt was beating Dewey handily, Clare Luce squeaked out victory by 2000 votes. Time gave her a two-column send-off that did not mention Miss Connors, a picture with the caption, *"To factory girls a heroine,"* and said, "in two years Clare Luce had risen from the position of an interesting novelty—a good-looking Congresswoman—to an eminence as a main target of the Roosevelt Administration." Time said that Roosevelt, having trouble with the voting machine at Hyde Park, snapped, "The God damn thing won't work." Ministerial and lay groups from all parts of the country raised enough of an uproar so that the President had to assure the nation that although he had permitted himself a little "damn," he had not used the Lord's name with it.

After the election, the formidable Evalyn Walsh McLean gave a great party in Washington for the Trumans and was displeased when the Luces appeared. As General Harry Vaughan recalled it, Mrs. McLean confronted them at the door, told them they had not been invited and said, "I'm going to ask you to leave," which the Luces did. Soon Clare was off with a group of Congressmen to appraise the European war—a mission that got her a two-page spread in Life showing her clad fetchingly in parka and galoshes and referring to her as "the attention-getter of the party." Luce meanwhile gave the sermon on December 10 at the Immanuel Church in Hartford where his parents had been members during their stay there. Speaking on "The World's Need for the Church," he took as his text Luke 2:52: "And Jesus increased in wisdom and stature, and in favor with God and man."

XX

1. THE CHAMBERS WAR

In Time, Whittaker Chambers supported what he termed Bullitt's "flesh-creeping look at postwar Europe" and called the attacking Lerner a leftist who "echoed Pravda." This guilt-by-association tactic was coming into heavy use and would become a gauge of the ferocity of the issue that ultimately would divide the United States and wound it more than any outside enemy. Time did not carry the tactic in both directions, for the Bullitt piece was such an echo of Goebbels's propaganda line that the Nazi radio hailed the Life article as "proof that the Americans now saw the futility of the war, the emptiness of victory, and the truth of the National Socialist philosophy."

Life itself declared defiantly, "the fact that Mr. Bullitt was a Russophobe was no secret even before the publication of his article." But it was the Weekly Newsmagazine that did the steadiest work in enlarging Category Three. John Barkham, a newcomer to the home office and to FN, observed that Chambers's editing was drastic. Older hands at Time, including men as high in the organization as Eric Hodgins and Allen Grover, grew disturbed at what was happening.

The war and its demands had forced Time to build an extensive network of correspondents in all parts of the world. The "rewrite-sheet" days were theoretically over. Among these men were Walter Graebner in London, Charles Wertenbaker in Paris, John Hersey in Moscow, John Osborne in Rome and Theodore White in Chungking. Graebner and Wertenbaker had small staffs under them in London and Paris. These men were sending cables to New York which wound up on Chambers's desk. A clever editor could of course change the tone of a cable or story by merely cutting a few words here and there, a little jugglery or transposition, a change of context, a slanted headline or subhead, the addition or changing of words in the editing or—most of all—

by rewriting completely. "Chambers thought nothing of tossing a whole story out the window and rewriting it from beginning to end," Barkham recalled.

Time's foreign news, every word of it edited by Chambers and much of it actually written by him, became a weekly outpouring of anti-Soviet propaganda. To the usual tricks of adjectivization, emphasis and suppression were added the special Chambers gifts: flashes of wry humor, melodrama, historical parallels, classical allusions and flights of the imagination. He was subtler than his famous predecessor, Goldsborough. Soon office boys, researchers, writers, senior editors and executives picked sides in what became known as the Chambers War.

The members of the peace, or anti-Chambers, faction were generally agreed that this was both a great and a delicate moment in history. It seemed to them that for the first time in many years the sweet dream of world peace might be within realization. It was so entrancing a prospect and yet so difficult of realization because of old suspicions on both the Soviet and American sides that it required the utmost effort to be fair, to be friendly. The dream had to be nurtured. Its essential was a belief in good will, which had been growing on both sides. Now, they felt, Chambers was turning the dream into a nightmare with his vengefulness and distortion.

Chambers and his coterie, which included Luce, regarded this kind of thinking as sentimental hogwash. They had no faith in a Soviet whose Marxian doctrines and past history indeed were enough to chill the blood and whose policies in Poland had scarcely been reassuring.

Quite aside from the question of which group was right lay the question of the morality of the manipulation of the news to favor either side. Luce, who had manipulated the news constantly when there was no visible danger to the republic, was now certain that such a danger faced his American Century. The correspondents themselves were startled when they saw what was happening to their dispatches. Graebner in London cabled Luce directly about his concern over the twisting of his cables from their original meaning. Hersey in Moscow cabled Matthews:

> Several recent copies of Time have just reached me. In all honor I must report to you that I do not like the tone of many Foreign News stories. I need not itemize: You know what I mean. . . . For this week, and until I cool off, I shall abstain from corresponding with Foreign News. . . .

Chambers became an object of such detestation in T-L that the pistol he packed may have been a necessary precaution. The faction loyal to him was smaller but equally impassioned. Time's closet door swung open, disclosing the house skeleton. By November the hatred was so virulent that Luce had to take action. He ordered Billings, who had recently been made editorial director of all publications, to circularize the correspondents as to their feelings about the use Chambers made of their material. Billings's report read in part:

> . . . they are all convinced that Chambers edits Foreign News into a pattern. Though not one correspondent says it in so many words, they all plainly feel

that that pattern is that World Communism (i.e. Russia) is in a world conspiracy to attain world power. Our correspondents obviously disagree with this pattern, unanimously reporting Russia as a peace-loving nation . . . Chambers, in turn, regards our correspondents as naïve or ignorant about the workings of world Communism . . .

Wertenbaker had pointed out specific "distortions of what we believe to be the truth." Graebner listed instances of exaggeration and distortion, sometimes amplified by the use of provocative headlines, indicating "a definite attempt to ram home to the readers that Russia is a hell of a big problem." Osborne cited two stories that were "glaringly off base," mentioned an example of "lifting isolated facts from a cable without accepting the cable's general tone and underlying idea," and another story in which "the parts were right, the sum was wrong." Hersey charged "editorial bias" that was "grossly unfair" and "actually vicious," and that most of the passages used from his cables were "torn from the context . . . and put into [the] new context of Time's editorial bias."

Although none of this seemed to place the FN editor in a good light, Luce decided that it really did when one considered the whole picture. Perhaps his settlement of the dispute in January was not free from disingenuousness. There was a strong suspicion among the aggrieved correspondents that the whole "investigation" had been cooked up by Luce exactly after the manner of a Presidential commission appointed to mollify complainers while continuing the practices complained of. He complimented the correspondents for their good work, but most of all he endorsed the work of Chambers, which the correspondents had unanimously questioned. Chambers, he wrote, had been vindicated by events:

In general, in 1944, the Foreign News Department wished to convey the information that even in that part of the world misnamed the United Nations, things were not going very well. The posture of events in January 1945 seems to have confirmed Editor Chambers about as fully as a news-editor is ever confirmed. . . . Let there be no doubt or misunderstanding that we are all above all concerned with giving a true account of contemporary human happenings. . . . There remains only one real question between any of us as to the so-called Russian problem, and that is the relation between the Kremlin and Communist trends or activities throughout the world. I have just been told, in a highly confidential manner, that Stalin is, after all, a Communist. I am also somewhat less confidentially informed that the Pope is a Christian. Some will say: what does it matter in either case? And what does it matter that Hersey advises me that he, John Hersey, is a Democrat? Well, I cannot say for sure just what these pieces of information signify, but one must respect the data in each case. A good Foreign News Editor, while guarding against the prejudices arising from his own convictions, will not ignore the circumstance that the Pope is a Christian and Stalin a Communist and Hersey, God bless him, a Democrat.

W. A. Swanberg

2. THE CHINESE PUZZLE

In Europe, Congresswoman Luce met generals including Eisenhower, Patton and Mark Clark, each of whom had been on Time's cover, developing what one of her biographers called an "inevitable" rapport with Patton because they had "just the same all-out, neck-or-nothing will to victory, and the same ruthless, logical type of mind that cuts through the layers of soft thinking to the hard realities of what must be done." John Hersey's *A Bell for Adano*, recently published, had depicted a ruthlessly logical American general who enjoyed tormenting peasants and shooting their donkeys. The Congresswoman spent Christmas near the Italian front. She was home to celebrate New Year's with Luce in Greenwich, then was off to Washington for the opening of Congress.

In February, six lower-echelon reporters on the Time-Life Washington staff resigned "over disagreement with the Luce editorial policy." Wilder Hobson, a Time senior editor opposed to Whittaker Chambers, was transferred to Fortune at his own request.

On March 5 Clare was off to Italy again for two months at the request of Field Marshal Sir Harold Alexander, who wanted her to witness and publicize Anglo-American cooperation in Italy. Luce had taken a smaller apartment at the Waldorf to "lessen the echo," it was said by Timen who had shivered during visits there not only because of its lack of homelike touches but Luce's total unawareness of the lack. Often alone, he would invite men like Billings, Alexander or Matthews to lunch or dinner, usually on short notice. Dinner would be at one of his six New York clubs—Union, River, Racquet, Brook, Cloud and Yale. He was having political trouble with two of his favorites, Hersey and White.

White had become increasingly disenchanted by the galloping inhumanity and corruption of the Chiang regime. His account of the Honan famine had been cut and edited sharply in Time to remove mention of the government's callousness and inefficiency, and his ensuing dispatches were more heavily edited to lighten or remove information unflattering to Chiang. White protested by mail and in the spring of 1944 he flew to New York and took up the argument with Luce by memo and a few personal talks. White declared that the Chiang government was rotten to the core, that the people knew it and were deserting. Luce thought the corruption hardly surprising considering the difficulties faced for so long by the Nationalists. But to his credit, he did entertain some doubt. He sent a confidential memo to his top men saying that he was considering the possibility of a change in his China policy. He permitted White to write an article for Life on the deterioration of the Kuomintang, which apparently was only altered in the conclusion and which stressed the American duty to support the regime that seemed so insupportable. But Luce

reconsidered and decided that a corrupt Chiang was better than the growing Communist menace, which he identified with Russia.

When White returned to Chungking that summer, the Japanese were attacking and the Chinese giving ground with little struggle. General Stilwell had all but given up on the slippery Chiang. American money and supplies were enriching Kuomintang grafters while the Japanese advanced. There was persistent talk that Madame Chiang's sister, consort of Luce's friend Daddy Kung, got a commission on all planes purchased, and that she and Madame Chiang had "raked in huge profits from speculation in silver . . ." Some American observers thought the personal financial interests of Kung and T. V. Soong, both millionaires, were incompatible with their governmental positions.

In the fall, Chiang's troops crumbled and most of the Eastern front was lost. Roosevelt, looking on China as the springboard for the coming American attack on the Japanese islands, was appalled. His cable to Chiang urging that Stilwell be put in command of all Chinese troops so wounded the Gimo that he demanded Stilwell's recall. The President, impatient but deciding at length that he had no choice but to go along with Chiang, yielded on October 19. Stilwell's withdrawal brought the Chinese pot to a boil, raising the fundamental question of whether American policy there was sound.

To White it was the worst of errors that the fabled Stilwell, the American military man who best knew Chiang and the whole complex situation, should be sacrificed to the unsavory regime which America supported. White was in accord with Stilwell's belief that the blank check America was giving the Nationalists encouraged their corruption and reduced their military effort, and that if aid were given to other Chinese groups fighting the Japanese—several war lords and the Communists—the effect on Chiang would be salutary. In this they were joined by several Foreign Service officers in China. One of them, John S. Service, observed that Chiang's survival depended on U.S. support, that American dealings with him continued on the "unrealistic assumption that he is China . . . It is time for the sake of the war and also for our future interests in China that we take a more realistic line . . ."

White, convinced that the problem badly needed an airing, wrote a careful account of the facts as he saw them for Time and got it through the Chiang censorship by sending it to the United States on Stilwell's own plane.

The story never appeared. There was a Time cover story on Stilwell, the man in the news, but it was written by Whittaker Chambers. Taking a line opposite from White's, it criticized Stilwell for inability to cooperate with Chiang, censured the Roosevelt administration for bungling the whole problem and painted the Gimo as the defender of civilization in China, the victim of repeated American blunders:

> As usual Chungking, not the U.S. or Yenan, was criticized for the Stilwell incident. . . . [I]f Chiang Kai-shek were compelled to collaborate with Yenan on

Yenan's terms, or if he were forced to lift his military blockade of the Chinese Communist area, a Communist China might soon replace Chungking. And unlike Chungking, a Communist China (with its 450 million people) would turn to Russia (with its 200 million people) rather than to the U.S. (with its 130 million) as an international collaborator.

Now a front-page New York Times story by Brooks Atkinson, just back from China, described Chiang as "bewildered and alarmed by the rapidity with which China is falling apart" rather than a focus of political unity:

> The decision to relieve General Stilwell represents the political triumph of a moribund, anti-democratic regime that is more concerned with maintaining its political supremacy than in driving the Japanese out of China. America is now committed . . . to support a regime that has become increasingly unpopular and distrusted in China, that maintains three secret police services and concentration camps for political prisoners, that stifles free speech and resists democratic forces. . . . The Chinese Communists . . . have good armies that are now fighting guerrilla warfare against the Japanese in North China. . . . The Generalissimo regards these armies as the chief threat to his supremacy . . .

Richard Watts, Jr., on leave from the New York Herald Tribune and serving in China with the American OWI—a friend of White's—remarked on what happened to White's dispatch:

> Time saw fit to ignore the information sent it by a correspondent of the highest reliability. . . . Obviously, it is Mr. Luce's business if he wants to defend his chosen Chinese party at all cost . . . My only point is that it does tend to destroy any reputation his publications may have for objectivity when they toss aside the careful, factual reporting of one of their ablest correspondents because it does not happen to fit in with the political line of the boss. That would be all right if Time were frankly a journal of opinion, but that is not what it presumes to be. Its insistence is that it is a news magazine with a passion for getting at the facts.

White learned of the suppression of his story not from the home office but through a Domei broadcast from Tokyo. "Harry saw Chiang as the only hope for China," he said later, "and I saw Chiang as China's greatest enemy." Still loyal to the man who had been so generous and encouraging, he wrote Luce a twenty-six-page letter protesting the Stilwell story and explaining the situation. Luce, unconvinced but still valuing him as a correspondent, made what developed into an odd sort of bargain. An exclusive story about the Chinese Communists in their remote bastion would be a journalistic coup. He gave White permission to fly to Yenan and to observe and confer with Mao's people.

Here White found a different kind of dictatorship. The Yenan claim that they were "democratic" was based on Communist postulates absurd to an American, but there was no laughing off the unity and strength of the Yenan Reds. Harassed by Chiang's forces and without aid from either Russia or the

United States, they had made it on their own and fought the Japanese effectively. It appeared that Stalin had long suspected them of being Trotskyites, called them "margarine Communists" and given them nothing. Obviously proud of their independence, they were enthusiastic about the American drive across the Pacific against the Japanese and hopeful that the Americans would understand that (in their opinion) Chiang did not represent China. Occasional official American visitors had been struck by the confidence, the air of discipline and dedication at Yenan, so refreshing after the Chungking decay. White wrote a story sympathetic to the Communists which was published in Life and was supposed to balance the Stilwell story in Time. He could see that civil war was inevitable in China—an idea Luce disputed—and when he persisted in this theme in his dispatches, he received instructions from New York to avoid further comment on politics and confine himself to reporting the military developments.

Thereafter, Chambers was in full command. Time, said the critic A. J. Liebling, was much like a waiter captain who meets the customer at the smörgåsbord table, insists on helping him make a selection and then heaps the plate with items the management has a particular interest in serving.

"At Time, Inc.," Liebling wrote, "you are likely to get a bit of Chiang Kaishek out of the deep freeze with every meal."

3. *GHOSTS ON THE ROOF*

In February 1945, as the Yalta conference ended with amicable announcements concealing the details of the Big Three agreements, Whittaker Chambers wrote a fairy tale he called "The Ghosts on the Roof." It depicted the late Czar Nicholas II and his murdered family alighting as apparitions on the roof of the palace where Roosevelt conferred with Stalin and Churchill, carrying on an excited dialog as they peered through holes in the shingling at the three statesmen.

It would fill two printed pages. Time did not sacrifice two pages even in peacetime, much less the paper-scarce time of war, except for a message of great importance. This was admittedly pure fancy. Chambers showed it to a couple of friends in FN. It made their eyes pop. He gave it to Managing Editor Matthews, who was responsible for every word in Time. Matthews saw that it was clever, readable, a tour de force. But it went further into fabrication than even Time was wont to go, and he could feel heat. He showed it to a couple of his editors, who all but burned their fingers on it. Finally he showed it to Luce, who read it with keenest interest.

It is necessary to guess at Luce's motivation, but a fair surmise seems attainable. He saw instantly that it was strong propaganda against the Soviet Union. But he had a delicate situation on his hands. Liberals, Rooseveltites, Russophiles and peaceniks on the staff were already seething over what they

regarded as unfair slanting of the news. They blamed this on Luce as well as Chambers. Luce wanted to publish "Ghosts" but he did not want to be blamed for it.

"He gave it back to me," Matthews recalled, "and said that it was my decision whether to run it."

The story of the Chambers piece meanwhile had traversed every corridor and cubicle of Time's editorial offices on the twenty-eighth and twenty-ninth floors. Almost everybody took sides. The Rooseveltite faction, anxious to give the coming United Nations conference at San Francisco every chance of success, was bitterly opposed to it. They felt it was bad enough to have Chambers twist and distort genuine dispatches coming from real-life Time correspondents in Europe and Asia without permitting him to create propaganda fairy stories. When it was seen every week what Chambers could do to fact, the things that he might do with fiction would boggle the mind. Only a few people on the two floors had actually read "Ghosts," but the essence and slant of it were passed by word of mouth. The minority of Republicans, religionists and "realists" who said that Marxism was self-proclaimed world revolution respecting nothing but force, cheered it. Hard words passed. The situation had overtones of grotesquerie—grown men and women muttering, cursing, laughing, quarreling, even getting drunk, about a fairy tale. "Ghosts" had become a symbol to both sides. By now Matthews had missed Time's February 27 deadline and had to hold over the piece—and the decision—for the March 5 issue. Thus the tension rose as editors discussed the crisis with their wives and friends. The Democrat John Hersey, back from Moscow, was among those who earnestly urged Matthews to throw the story away. Chambers smoked his pipe and said nothing.

For Matthews to reject a piece so topical and entertaining because of political considerations that meant little to him probably would have seemed, in his own mind, pusillanimous. His uncertainty about journalism and his own role in it was evident in his memoirs:

> Is journalism really necessary? and is it actually trying to inform people about what is going on in the world—or just trying to sell them a bill of goods? . . . [I]t seemed to me that journalism was actually doing both at the same time. . . . Journalism was really a part of the entertainment business.

This did not sound like a Zenger or a Pulitzer. Matthews seemed not to have defined clearly in his own mind the role of journalism as the guardian of honesty and democracy that made the integrity of the editor not merely important but crucial. He published "The Ghosts on the Roof" in the March 5, 1945, issue of Time, pages 36 and 37.

It was ironic anti-Soviet propaganda written in Chambers's Dostoievskian vein. Its ghostly characters commented enthusiastically about Stalin's territorial aggrandizement and predicted that he would "settle the old score with Chiang Kai-shek" as he proceeded in his program of gobbling the world. The

wraith of Nicholas II was so admiring of Stalin's appropriation of areas Muscovy had sought vainly for centuries under the monarchy that he had been converted: "I became a Marxist," he said.

"Ghosts" brought Luce's Cold War more into the open and underlined the odd role of Matthews. For him to be managing editor of America's most politically oriented and propagandist "newsmagazine" was as if Scott Fitzgerald were Secretary of State. His memoirs show his occasional awareness that Luce was a propagandist, unfair in his presentation of the news. They also suggest that this awareness was often lost in his continuing effort to shake off the remnants of Hadden's collegiate Timestyle and make the magazine's "news" presentation adult and polished. There was, too, the deadening effect of habit which George Orwell would soon describe. Matthews, now a sixteen-year man, was used to Time propaganda. Just as Soviet editors and citizens later became so accustomed to Pravda's talk of "bloodsucking imperialists" and the whole Russian repertoire of propagandist jargon that it was actually accepted as news, so did the editors and readers of Time become numbed to its artifices and inventions. Matthews had long since lost the sense of shock with which some Time stories affected men of the outside press. On the other hand, he had none of the fear of Luce that paralyzed other editors. He could and did go into Luce's Penthouse to demand and get an apology for an insulting memo. Other editors whose blood was curdled by the TLF political bias wished either that they had Matthews's fearlessness (and his millions) or that Matthews had a touch of political savvy and journalistic vision.

The Time device of using an unidentified and often imaginary character who is quoted as expressing opinions Time wanted to express, has been noted. It is necessary and perhaps not unfair to use the same device here in a character called Old Timemployee. He represents a number of former Lucepress people and a few still employed there who remember the Chambers War, have opinions about it, but would rather not be quoted directly. What Old Timemployee thinks and says here naturally has to be a consensus, not necessarily accurate or agreed on every detail, possibly prejudiced in some ways, but representing a point of view.

Luce occasionally called Matthews "the grammarian," a nickname he loathed, in ironic allusion to his political shortcomings. But Old Timemployee suspected that although Matthews's lack of depth in this field could sometimes exasperate Luce, in the long run it was useful to him, permitting him to push his anti-Roosevelt and anti-Soviet feelings to lengths that would have offended a managing editor of well-defined and opposite political loyalties. Anti-Sovietism had to be pushed with delicacy during this interval before the Cold War officially started.

The shifting of Whittaker Chambers into FN, Old Timemployee thought, was a strategy too perfect to be accidental. He had the bias Luce wanted, the subtlety and skill and the contempt for mere evanescent fact which he manipulated into what he regarded as long-run truth. It was also good strategy to

have Matthews as managing editor—the only person other than Luce who would check Chambers's copy—instead of someone of political sensitivity. Eric Hodgins, who had been troubled by Luce's long sponsorship of Goldsborough, was even more appalled by Chambers, whom he considered more dangerous. Hodgins later lamented how Luce had repeated his error, "once again reposing trust in Time's Foreign News editor, by then, God help us, Whittaker Chambers, whose brilliant deviousness made Goldsborough look like Oliver Optic."

Old Timemployee, knowing that Luce had a deviousness of his own that made Oliver Optic look like Gene Stratton Porter, was convinced that he chose Chambers with his eyes wide open as his ideal instrument for enlarging Category Three, just as he leaned on Schlamm and Bullitt for their special gifts. Normally Luce ran his shop as he wanted to, moving his men around as he wished and letting the chips fall where they might. Now he was walking on eggs because Time was so understaffed that employees worked overtime as a matter of course. He sent occasional memos asking each employee to guard his health and assuring him that things would be better when the servicemen returned to their posts. It would have been possible for as few as a dozen editors, if they became disgruntled enough to quit, to endanger the whole operation.

Hence, to prevent disaffection, the elevation of Chambers to FN was made to look like routine instead of foxy policy. And Luce had made what appeared outwardly to be a careful investigation of Chambers when complaints rose to a dangerous level. He had not only cleared Chambers and extolled him but he had also complimented everyone else involved. He had smoothed the waters.

So Old Timemployee and his friends felt they were being had. They were full of the peace idea and anxious to give it a fair chance. There was fear that Luce's dog-eat-dog spirit of competition, carried to its ultimate conclusion, meant war for world hegemony. As for religion, bless us all, said Old Timemployee, Luce and Chambers made much of America's Christianity and their own special insights into the heavenly kingdom as opposed to the Soviet denial of God. But it did seem that the Christian virtues of tolerance and charity were almost as hard to find in Time's Penthouse as in the Kremlin.

"Some of our group were imaginative people," Old Timemployee said. "They conjured up a picture of Luce's God. He wore a GOP button, smoked Muriel cigars and drank Mount Vernon whisky as advertised in Life, drove a Buick, carried a bazooka, wore a helmet and exhaled fire and brimstone at Moscow. And some of us were even sure that he had a forked tail."

XXI

1. THE AMERICAN FRONTIER

On March 19, Luce had an off-the-record talk with Secretary of State Edward Stettinius about Roosevelt, Stalin, Yalta and plans for the United Nations. His notes registered opinions and observations: that Roosevelt had conceded too much at the conference and asked too little of Stalin in return; that Stalin's "straightforward" insistence on a sphere of influence in Eastern Europe might have been acceptable if Roosevelt and Churchill had won a sphere of their own in return; that Stettinius said the President was placing his faith in the United Nations; and that Luce feared that Russia would communize all of Europe unless American aid was sent speedily to save Germany and points west. Stettinius, soon to leave the Cabinet, agreed with Luce that Roosevelt was guilty of "double talk" in his breezy assurance that such things as spheres of influence had been barred in the Yalta agreements.

At the same time, Life urged that the successor to the Dies Committee keep a sharp eye for American Communists:

> . . . there is something peculiarly American about the impulse that starts an investigation of un-American activities. . . . [O]ne basic tenet of Americanism is that ends never justify means. . . . The Communist Party . . . has no scruples about means and . . . its first loyalty is to the national interest of a foreign (however friendly) power. The Communists operate through numerous and ever-changing "fronts," from labor groups to sharecropper rallies. . . . [The Committee's aim should not be] to persecute, but to expose and identify [and to do a] good labeling job.

The Lucepress would often justify means by ends, as in the case of Chiang, but decry this comfortable device in others. Also at this same time, sixty-nine-year-old Maxim Litvinov, going into retirement in Moscow, was shaking his

233

head over East-West relations. "The situation is developing badly," he told an American reporter. "First, the Western Powers make a mistake and rub us the wrong way. Then we make a mistake and rub you the wrong way." Ten days later, on April 12, Roosevelt was dead at Warm Springs. The great United Nations happy family which he had intended to launch with his own charm and prestige would have to be inaugurated by others. Soon Molotov and his Soviet negotiators arrived in America, said Time, and sat "hour after hour, staring glumly at their navels" when things did not go to their liking. The Americans and British would have to be tough with them.

As if to prove that it was indeed Roosevelt who had barred Luce from the combat zones, he was given clearance for the Pacific by President Truman, the Nazis having surrendered May 8. He reacted like an object hurled by a catapult. He picked the jovial Roy Alexander, now running Time's "U.S. at War" department, as his companion. ("Luce always figured you should be ready to go around the world with him on a day's notice," Alexander observed.) The hostile New York Daily News snapped, "Henry Luce, the poison-pen publisher, was off to China the moment his wife, Clare Boothe Luce, returned from a prolonged tour of Europe." He would not get quite to China this time. After a stop at the San Francisco Conference where forty-six nations were devising a charter for their peace-making organization, he and Alexander took off May 19 and in five weeks visited the Philippines, Guam, Iwo Jima, Saipan, Kwajalein and Hawaii, flying in assorted aircraft and becoming the Navy's guest for a time on an aircraft carrier.

Alexander found Luce a dynamic and fidgety companion—up at 5:00 A.M. on the flat-top, eager to see the planes take off, to talk to the captain, the crew. He never relaxed. If all else failed he would lasso Alexander into a game of gin rummy. Along the way, finding himself by astonishing chance near the destroyer in which twenty-year-old Ensign Hank Luce was serving, Luce managed a five-minute chat with the son he seldom saw on dry land. His scrutiny of the Navy in action was translated into story ideas with which he bombarded Billings by mail or cable:

> We should have in Life and Time stories on the civilian Reserve officers. I think that more than 80% of all officers in this vast Navy are civilian reservists. . . . Pending my return . . . I suggest the following items rate consideration: [naming six subjects for Time or Life articles].

He could get a note of menace into an otherwise unremarkable cable, as when he ordered the deployment of more photographers to the Pacific and ended, "I hope this will all be attended to by the time I return; otherwise our domestic peace is liable to be disturbed." And there were frequent flourishes of his American pride and American patriotism which so often blared into American spread-eagleism:

> We are now fueling at sea—"we" being a more powerful collection of fighting ships than had ever been assembled before in the world's history up to a year

ago. . . . In the last year or two the U.S. Navy has conquered some 20,000,000 miles of ocean (check figure). . . . The American frontier is no longer Malibu Beach; the American frontier is a line Okinawa–Manila—and it will never be moved back from there. . . . Americans have a very acute sense of where their "home" is; from now on their home is a continent *and* the ocean that covers nearly half the globe. This is the political geography for the next round of the human drama. . . .

In one cable he ventured a prediction that proved him more expert than the top military experts, who estimated that it would take more than another year to beat Japan. The atomic bomb, not yet tested, was an unknown quantity. The dwindling of Chiang's military credibility had darkened the picture ominously. It was believed that the Japanese islands would have to be invaded—a bloody operation that would cost endless thousands of American lives. This calculation, and the disappointment in Chiang, had been factors in Roosevelt's concessions to Stalin at Yalta, gaining the promise of Russian help in the task of subduing the Japanese. Luce did not *want* Russian help there. If possible he wanted to keep the Red Army out of the Far East, which he meant to establish as an American sphere of influence. On the basis of a few weeks' observation west of San Francisco, and although he evidently knew nothing as yet about the atomic bomb, he felt sure that the American chiefs of staff were mistaken. He cabled Billings:

> In the tentative opinion of your special correspondent, Japan can be made to sue for peace within two or three months if the American Government uses the proper combination of political and military strategy. . . .

He was back in San Francisco June 20. While Alexander went on to New York, Luce flew to Washington to talk with Navy Secretary James V. Forrestal and also, for the first time, with President Truman. He wanted to tell the President that the Japanese had little left with which to defend their islands. For some reason—he could at times be inarticulate—he did not get his message clearly across to Truman, who would scarcely have been inclined to prefer his opinion to that of his military chiefs. Luce also visited Congresswoman Luce after a long separation. The two were ideologically agreeable, as Time indicated under the heading "Congresswoman v. Russia":

> Since her return from an eight-week visit to Europe . . . Connecticut's Congresswoman Clare Boothe Luce has sent many a verbal slingshot at Communist Russia. Over the radio and in articles in the Hearst press she has pounded away at the thesis that Russia, as the strongest power in Europe, is rapidly communizing the continent. In a series in the Congressional Record she discussed all the small countries in Russia's orbit, detailed the Communist influence in their present governments. Her conclusion: "This cannot long remain two worlds as it is today—the world of totalitarianism and the world of liberty. Indeed, as our conflict with Nazi totalitarianism proved, these two worlds are doomed to come into conflict. . . ."

The efforts of both Luces to enlarge Category Three were well known in Moscow. Pravda's most noted propagandist, David Zaslavsky, wrote of the "planned hysterics of Mrs. Luce," said "the honorable lady does not like us," described her as "Goebbels' unconsoled political widow," and said that she had presented a resolution in Congress decrying the "sins" of Yalta and had declared in speeches that the Soviet would "swallow all China" as well as the Balkans. The Soviet railway workers' journal accused her of trying to frighten Americans by giving them false pictures of Communism. Another Pravda commentator, Boris Izaakov, said she had "waged a personal little war on Hitler's side against the Soviet and the American people." His remarks, also broadcast over Moscow radio, included the charge that she was "both a victim and promoter of hysteria." As for Luce, in addition to the notice taken of him by Gromyko, he was lectured by Andrei Vishinsky and also by the Daily Worker and the New Masses, which headlined, "Luce Plans the Next War."

Although none of these persons or publications was precisely unbiased, both Luces felt it necessary to be ready for the "next war"—a phrase recurring more frequently in Time and Life—and the Congresswoman was urging the use of mines and caves as shelters since it was evident that Russia and others would soon solve the atomic riddle. People around Luce noticed that the war—or was it advancing middle age?—had reduced that flexibility which, though limited, had been so charming, his ability occasionally to see another point of view. Although those who knew him best realized that he was able to adapt his religion to his quest for power, it seemed not without cost. Matthews, Grover and others noticed that he had occasional assaults of conscience that were visible facially. This perceptible inner turmoil was a striking quality, combined as it was with the growing arrogance and severity, the hardening of the chill blue eyes. There was speculation as to what was eating him. Some felt that he needed a psychiatrist, while Wertenbaker, now back from Europe, had a wild theory that all he needed was a rip-snorting affair with a lady liberal in politics and persuasive of manner.

There was a theory that he was bottled up inside, so guarded and secretive that he deprived himself of the normal therapeutic experience of confiding in someone. Matthews was so puzzled by him that he arranged a luncheon with Luce's sister Mrs. Moore, who was very close to him and who resembled him greatly except that she had the warmth her brother lacked. Explaining that an understanding of Luce would be mutually helpful if he was to work for him the rest of his life, Matthews asked Mrs. Moore if she could unfold the riddle of his character. "But Mrs. Moore seemed as puzzled as I was," he recalled.

Luce's mother's disapproval of his divorce and remarriage, and of his worldly way of business and of life, was hurtful, and he could be sharp with her. When she arrived in New York for one of her infrequent visits she did not always stay in the Luce Waldorf suite but sometimes at the quiet New Weston Hotel on Madison Avenue. On one such visit she was invited to dine with Luce at the Waldorf but found the prospect unnerving enough to make an ex-

cuse and to dine instead with an old friend. She let her son know that she was worried about his immortal soul. She was aware that the Presbyterian clergy was not unanimously admiring of him. His status as the managing director of the world's largest liquor-advertising medium did not sit well, nor did his Broadway methods of promotion. Some clergymen felt him excessively war-like and disliked his publications as materialistic and unreliable. One promi-nent Presbyterian who sometimes served with Luce on national church com-missions found that Luce was valued in the church as a source of money and publicity but that many of the clergy thought him unprincipled. This man knew Luce and the Presbyterian inner circle well enough to know that Luce was aware of this feeling toward him and that it caused him anguish.

The atom bombs dropped at Hiroshima and Nagasaki impressed Luce as proof of American technological leadership, a shattering demonstration to the Kremlin that for a time at least America was the greatest power in the world. His excitement over such world events never seemed to interrupt his business thought. To his top executives he laid out a proposition, three days after Hiro-shima, requiring their expert forecast as to how quickly they could accept a "commitment" to make Life magazine so attractive that it would sell 5,200,000 copies, with increased advertising rates.

Before leaving for China in the fall of 1945, he had made plain to his edi-tors his feelings about the idea of sharing atomic secrets with Russia.

Luce's first postwar visit to China has been narrated in Chapter I. He had been enveloped in the euphoric glow of conscious American super-power, soon after the A-bombs had knocked out Japan. While there, it will be re-called, he met Mao, met Chou, but talked at length only with the Kuomintang elite and American officers in a half-dozen cities. His insulation from opposing views was perhaps inevitable. Yet it seemed a classic example of Luce-in-the-cocoon, the true believer banishing the dissidents. Theodore White, whose appraisal of China would largely be borne out by history, had returned to New York. He was replaced by William Gray and John Walker, able writers but new in China, both well informed of the Luce propaganda line. It appears that Luce had largely closed his mind against any thought that China's prob-lems would not now be solved by Chiang, with American help, and had shut himself off from information and opinions running counter to this theory. He was entering on a period of confusion and error which would be in some part responsible for China's and America's greatest postwar disaster.

2. TAKE DRASTIC MEASURES

When Theodore White returned to New York in the fall, John Hersey had gone to the Orient on an unusual arrangement permitting him to write for the New Yorker as well as for Life. Both young men had been first inspired and then disillusioned by Luce. White immediately took a six-months' leave to

write a book about his experiences in China, with Annalee Jacoby as co-author. Only once or twice during the interval did he see Luce, who was chilly, feeling that his former protégé had been seduced by Communist propaganda.

In December, Whittaker Chambers, who had been writing about two-thirds of FN himself, often getting little sleep, had a heart attack. Max Ways, an able Baltimorean who had won Luce's confidence in only a year on the staff, took over FN. Indeed, Chambers's rule in that department had caused such animosity and disruption that when he returned after recovering he was given other writing duties in addition to the post of special adviser to Luce on Communist matters, and the Chambers War de-escalated.

Luce, overjoyed in his certainty of Chiang's victory, was less happy about his wife's conversion to Catholicism. Shaken by her daughter's death, she had ultimately taken five months of instruction from Monsignor Fulton J. Sheen, the priest already known for his conversion of several famous people. Before long, in the manner of one wishing to help others with similar burdens, she would relate in McCall's magazine that the experience had elevated her spirit and had also given her increased moral ammunition against Communists because of their denial of "personal sin." And Luce would soon prove his ecumenism in approving his wife's conversion and attending an occasional mass with her, so that the rumor swept the T-L Building that Himself (as he was sometimes called behind his back) was taking instruction. Matthews scoffed at it: "The day Harry Luce turns Roman Catholic I'll look out of my window and see streams of pigs flying past."

Complaints rose in England when Walter Graebner dickered with Churchill and secured first publication rights for Life of secret wartime speeches he had made before the Commons. "What goes on here?" asked the London World Press News. "Do the British people have to get speeches made by a British Prime Minister to the British House of Commons from an American magazine?" They did, because Graebner had got there first with the most and the speeches were judged to be Churchill's property. The outcry had hardly subsided when Luce flew to Europe with a dozen other editors and publishers including General Julius Ochs Adler of the New York Times, Gardner Cowles of Look and Robert Fuoss of the Saturday Evening Post as four-week guests of the War Department to inspect bomb damage and the military government in Germany and Austria. The group ate together and traded off bunking with each other, so Fuoss became well acquainted with Luce. He found him astonishingly naïve and "inquisitive to the point of total annoyance." These were the incessant questions that tormented Luce underlings because they feared their subsequent careers might hinge on the speed and excellence of their replies. To Fuoss, Luce also confided one of his business principles, saying, "The way to get the best man for a job is to let two men compete for it."

While he was away, Congresswoman Luce was puzzling David Lilienthal

of TVA at a luncheon at Marquis Childs's, saying to Lilienthal, "You are the only living New Dealer—I underline *living*—who is still popular," and talking about spiritualism and socialism. "At times [she has] that gift for the clever and cutting phrase," Lilienthal wrote, "at other times extraordinarily obtuse . . . She has a weird kind of mysticism. This is very bad in men; in women, who have power—of money, beauty, wit and political talent (she has all of them)—it can become even worse. She can be very amusing and clever—as when imitating people, like . . . [the] Ambassador of Brazil, or silly Lady Astor. . . . I thought at a certain juncture that she was just a plain phony . . . But she isn't a phony. . . . [S]ince she is a member of the House Military Affairs Committee and the wife of the editor of Time-Life, etc., I more or less did what was expected of me. . . ."

Luce meanwhile saw films of the German concentration camps, consulted in Munich with Professor Ludwig Erhard, dined with Justice Robert Jackson at Nuremberg and observed in his notes that Europe's problems revolved around "the hideousness of defeated Nazi Germany and the similar hideousness of victorious Soviet Russia." He thought the Roosevelt-Truman agreements with Stalin not merely blameworthy but knavish, mentioning twice in the same paragraph "the crimes of Yalta and Potsdam." He wrote, with the assurance that could startle even his top men, "I now have a German policy for America." His policy was to strengthen Germany as a democratic defender against Russia. It would first be necessary to take summary steps which he discussed dispassionately:

> Initially, for a year or two, take drastic measure[s] to destroy the Nazi government and system. Kill a number of people. Heavily penalize a number of more people. This job ought to be completed within a very few months from date.

Though distressed that England had gone Laborite, at any rate "Mr. Attlee's anchor is Christianity," Luce saw a trend for "the European-Christian tradition of decency and freedom." As he concluded this trip, he met by chance a woman who would try to change his horizons as a journalist.

3. PUBLIC ENEMY NUMBER ONE

Boston-born Mary Bancroft had lived in Europe for ten years, having married and then divorced a Swiss banker, her second husband. Daughter of the publisher of the Wall Street Journal, educated in private schools, during the war she had worked under Allen Dulles, chief of the Office of Strategic Services mission in Switzerland and had dealt with international spies as part of her routine. She had studied and worked with Carl G. Jung, a circumstance that increased her frankness and dislike for intellectual evasion and self-deception. To these qualities were added an active social conscience, an informed concern about America and its postwar role, a literary gift and a rich

sense of humor. She was forty-two, six years younger than Luce, and had resumed her maiden name. She spoke fluent German and French. She was devoted to her two children by her Bostonian first husband, a son and a daughter.

Late in April, the harried young vice consul at the American consulate in Zurich telephoned her about a group of VIP's, all journalists, whom the War Department had been flying around Germany. They were due in Zurich that evening. The consulate was expected to see to their comfort. He mentioned their names and asked her help in greeting and entertaining them. Luce's name aroused her interest because of her disapproval of his magazines. As she later recalled:

> I had some strong reservations about the Luce publications. I had discovered that Time and Life were actually used to teach [Europeans] what life in the United States was like, and I was not sure that Henry Luce was aware of his responsibilities. I first made this discovery when talking to groups of French school children from the south of France who had come to Switzerland during the war years. In a question-and-answer period I would get questions like: "I read in Time (pronounced 'Teem') that the Americans are using planes to sow wheat in Texas. Is this method being used in other states with other grains?" A little girl of ten had said she wished "Teem" would tell her what the Americans thought of *"le problème Alsace-Lorraine."* I felt that if Luce was the missionary I had been told he was, he had better pay more attention to the accuracy of his Foreign Affairs section of Time. . . . I loathed "Timese" and disapproved of opinion in unsigned articles. I felt that Time, and to a certain extent Life—and to a lesser degree Fortune—were twisting the truth, often in subtle ways and again not so subtly . . .

Mrs. Bancroft joined the vice consul and a knot of members of the American colony in a reception room of the luxurious Hotel Baur au Lac, a place redolent of expensive perfume and Havanas. She noted that Luce had a gait that suggested self-consciousness queerly mingled with aggressiveness and even pugnacity. Introduced to him, she led with a smiling pugnacity of her own: "So there you are, Public Enemy Number One!"

Astonished, he grinned, protested and stuttered something like, "Public Enemy Number One! Me? Now why do you say that?"

As they sat together over cocktails, he remarked that this was no way to talk to "the man who invented the American Century." She began giving him her "strong opinions" about his magazines, continuing as they sat down to dinner. The Luce Prandial Interrogation was somewhat reversed, for she held the floor fully as much as he did. He sputtered, denied but listened. As she later described it:

> . . . I found myself becoming less and less interested in trying to stop journalistic corruption . . . and more and more startled by the recognition that this man was so shy, so unsure as to whether he was really "right," so quick to see what had been bugging me . . . It was at this time I realized how the element

in which he felt most at home was power, and how that controlled so much, if not all, of his thinking—if not his feelings. Yet strangely enough on that very first evening I decided that Harry was . . . perhaps not so much kind as compassionate. I know I felt that here was someone I could say anything to—absolutely anything that came into my head—and I wouldn't be hurt in any way as a result.

She was aware, too, of his tactlessness. He shouted across the table to General Adler of the Times, jerking his thumb at her, "Doesn't she remind you of Dorothy Thompson?" and turned to Mrs. Bancroft, noting her nettlement, and said, "She's very famous, you know." She was not flattered either by the thumb or the comparison, thinking Dorothy Thompson an excessively opinionated woman who had once interviewed Hitler and decided he was harmless, a mere pimple on the face of Europe.

Mary Bancroft would continue to astonish, outrage and fascinate Luce throughout fifteen years of friendship. Leaving Zurich the next morning, he took leave of his American companions. In Frankfurt, according to schedule, he was met by Raimund von Hofmannsthal of his London office. The polished and jovial Von Hofmannsthal, son of the Austrian poet, had worked in the advertising department of the New York office of Time for several years and had been a special friend of the Luces there. Married to the beautiful Lady Elizabeth Paget, familiar with several languages, he was at home in London and continental society and would become on many Luce visits a combination of companion, translator, chauffeur, major-domo and social fixer. Von Hofmannsthal was not surprised that Luce did not smile or appear at all pleased to see him. His demeanor was often cool and preoccupied. They flew to Vienna, where Von Hofmannsthal was thoroughly at home and where Luce warmed up, grasping his arm and saying with surprising affection, "Now we are together." Staying at the Bristol, they attended several official functions and one huge champagne gala which Luce asked Von Hofmannsthal to arrange at the hotel and which was enlivened by public officials, actors and actresses at their gayest, with music and dancing, all paid for by the American publisher. After visiting a nearby Nazi prison camp, they went by car to Switzerland, Luce talking about China and occasionally asking rapid-fire questions. Eying one lovely mountain view, he said, "We have bigger mountains than those in America. Why are these more beautiful?"

Von Hofmannsthal thought furiously. An interesting if not definitive answer was expected. "Because the beauty here is man-made," he said. "Even mountain slopes are farmed in Austria."

Luce jotted this down in his notebook and later used it in a speech.

Wartime scarcities lingered and they were unable to get dinner. Luce was in a sour mood when they reached the Swiss border at Feldkirch toward 9:00 P.M. When the border guard found something questionable about Luce's passport and there was a slight delay, Luce went white with rage. He said through gritted teeth that he would grab the fool's stamp and stamp the passport him-

241

self. Von Hofmannsthal, actually fearful that Luce in his rage might get them into trouble, was relieved when the guard let them pass at that moment.

In Zurich, while Von Hofmannsthal cooled his heels, Mary Bancroft was surprised to get a telephone call from Luce saying he was in town again wanting to "look around a bit more." He took her to lunch and then to dinner two days in a row. She had further opportunity to explain her objection to the Lucepress propaganda, so different from the Neue Zürcher Zeitung and the Swiss press in general.

Liking his willingness to listen to her (though he made no explanation or defense of his "news" presentation), she also listened to him and gained some understanding of his values. Quite opposite from being ascetic, they were frankly oriented to worldly success. Success seemed honestly to him the proper criterion for judging people, books, art, products or nations. He was puzzled when she said this was by no means necessarily so. His enjoyment in talking with a woman who disagreed with him fundamentally, who patiently pointed out what she believed to be his misconceptions, who had not a particle of the fear and flunkyism felt by some of his editors, was indicated by his prolongation of it. When she helped him select a watch, she discovered that he took it for granted that the costliest watch was the best.

> I do not remember how the conversation went [she recalled], but I remember the intensity of it—both in the store and for hours afterward when he'd keep coming back to the subject. Wasn't the most expensive thing the best? And if not, why not? And when was this true and when wasn't it? And from there we'd get into Adam Smith and Karl Marx and I don't know who else. I kept saying, "Listen, it doesn't really matter. You said you wanted the best watch, and the man in the store thought you meant the one that was best as a watch—a watch to keep accurate time." Well, why wasn't the best watch the most expensive? "Because it didn't have diamonds around it." But why hadn't the salesman pointed that out? "Because he didn't think you were such a fool you couldn't see the diamonds and realize that was the reason." "Are you telling me I'm a fool?" "In this instance, YES." "H'mmm," and a grin spread over his face. "So you think I'm a fool." "I didn't say that. I said 'In this instance.' " "Never mind that . . . Take the proposition: Is the most expensive the best? Or, if you will, is the best the most expensive?" "No, the best is the *least* expensive in the long run." "In watches?" "No, stupid, in *everything*."

Luce seemed delighted to be addressed in this summary way. She felt that to him, "having anyone talk to him in such a way was a display of a kind of affection that he felt a great need for and seldom found, particularly since he had become a 'tycoon.' " When he left Zurich he told her how much he had enjoyed their conversation and that it must continue. Switzerland was still on wartime rationing, and after his departure she received a note containing the meal coupons he had not used.

Luce was back home in May and ready next to address himself to the problems of Asia. But first he had to settle the question of Theodore White, who

had finished his book with Mrs. Jacoby, *Thunder Out of China,* and was ready for reassignment. White knew that Luce would not want him in China, and when Wertenbaker, now chief of correspondents, suggested the Moscow post, White was delighted. But Luce called in White and said, as White recalled it later, "I'm not sure you're the man for Moscow. It seems to me that you and Hersey have been using Time for your own personal advancement." Later he sent word through Wertenbaker that unless White agreed to accept whatever assignment was given him, there was no place for him. White, in resentment, left the company.

Meanwhile, Francis Brown had come over from the New York Times organization as a senior editor of Time and was given the Religion department as one of his responsibilities. Brown was summoned to a Prandial Interrogation. One might have a luncheon appointment of long standing or of critical importance but one was expected to cancel it when Miss Thrasher called at 11:30 and said Mr. Luce would like to have lunch with one. Over the soup, Luce asked the inevitable question: "How are you going to handle Religion?" Brown, who was something of an agnostic, took a deep breath and said diplomatically that it was an important human phenomenon that he hoped to treat with dignity and discrimination. Luce banged the table, saying, "Yes, and we want to make it goddam *interesting* too." In several luncheons with Luce, Brown noticed with amusement that he always ordered a dessert called a Frozen Smile.

Still nurturing his dream of vacationing at Tsingtao and watching from that vantage point the rebirth of China under Chiang, Luce had written Wesley Bailey in Shanghai:

> . . . will you please proceed to Tsingtao and get me a house for July and August. . . . The house need not be swank; it needs only to be comfortable. Three or four bedrooms, living room, dining room and something to serve as library or study. I presume there will be no great difficulty in getting adequate servants.

Bailey, astonished at Luce's conception of China as a place miraculously restored to order after the shattering war, wrote that it was impossible:

> . . . the water situation in the area is acute . . . the Navy has requisitioned 200 of the best houses in the area for the officers and families of the Seventh Fleet . . . good servants are not to be had. . .

Luce would get to China nevertheless—doubtless would have even had he not been under the impression that the Gimo extended him an invitation. John R. Beal of Time's Washington staff had gone there earlier as a member of the mission of General George C. Marshall, sent by President Truman to mediate the quarrels between Chiang's Nationalists and the Communists and to foster the formation of a coalition government. Before leaving, Beal had talked with Luce who, it is safe to say, advised him about the situation in China. Arriving in Nanking, Beal met Chiang, who inquired courteously

about Luce and said in a general way that he and Mrs. Luce would be welcome any time. He was surprised when the literal-minded Luce interpreted this as an invitation. Business was good too, causing Luce to send out an exhilarating fiat:

> Time as everyone seems to agree is a damn good magazine these days—and consistently so.
>
> On looking over the personnel cards today I was struck by the relatively low level of salaries paid to writers. In my judgment at least $20,000 of raises must be made as of July 1st to ten or twelve writers. . . . Time has the most promising staff in years. It is the opposite of being over-paid.

Lest anyone think the Boss was going soft, he took a look at the Washington staff and issued a contrary decree:

> In Washington, Time has twenty-nine people and Life has seven. That is at least two too many. I would hope that Time could be reduced quickly by four or five people and Life by one or two.

With his wife in Congress, Luce on several occasions called Oliver Jensen, editor of Life's Entertainment department, took him to dinner and accompanied him to private film screenings. It seemed evident that he was hungry for human companionship. Jensen, a man with a strong vein of humor, found that Luce enjoyed a political joke provided it was signaled in advance and he knew a joke was coming. He felt the Boss's basic motivation good—that he had facets of liberalism and was interested in more than money. Indeed the jovial Jensen got the distinct impression that Luce came to suspect him of being insufficiently serious, even frivolous, in the face of momentous world problems. One night, after Luce accompanied Jensen and James Agee to a movie, he told them with a burst of enthusiasm, "I know a great place for a nightcap." It turned out to be a dreary Childs restaurant on Lexington Avenue behind the Waldorf where there was no liquor to be had and Luce chattered contentedly over sandwiches and cocoa. In July 1946 Luce vacationed in Snowville, New Hampshire, with Willi Schlamm as his companion. Schlamm was still working on the projected intellectuals' magazine, Brow, planning to use anti-Communist material by Arthur Koestler and others as well as a wide range of general articles. One unforeseen difficulty was that the intellectual establishment seemed unfairly monopolized by liberals who would laugh at any overt linking of Luce with intellectuality. It had seriously been proposed by one Time executive that Brow be published in another city and the Luce sponsorship hidden in order to obviate that threat. Doubtless Luce and Schlamm talked about Brow. On returning, Luce learned that an alert American Legion post had discovered a man believed to have Communist sympathies in a minor writing post at Time, and that the writer had left the company voluntarily to write a novel. Luce issued a memo:

> . . . . Well, maybe I never made myself sufficiently specific. Maybe the only way I can make myself understood is to try to imitate a cavalry sergeant. Here

'tis: I do not want any Communist sympathizers working for Time Inc. I hope
that statement is plain enough for the record for the time being.

Actually, as even Whittaker Chambers agreed, the organization by then
had been cleared of Communists but problems of ideology still thickened the
air. When Max Ways went on vacation, it caused a near uprising on the part
of staff liberals when Chambers, known by some of them as the Resident
Fascist, filled in as FN editor. The problem continued to preoccupy Congresswoman Luce, who had recently been baptized at St. Patrick's Cathedral in
New York by Monsignor Sheen and had received her first Holy Communion.
She wrote the Herald Tribune that war against Russia seemed inevitable because America was a "Christian country" and the Soviet Union was a "godless
country" which would try to impose its godlessness on us by "force and violence."

4. HOW TO MAKE IGLOOS

When Wesley Bailey returned to New York for reassignment, he was thrust
into the Deep Freeze, a Time institution so seldom used that he was not even
aware of it. He was given a cubicle on the twenty-eighth floor with nothing to
do. His former position as Luce's personal assistant had been filled, and Clare
had decided not to run for Congress in the fall, but he looked forward to
other duties. He was still unassigned and biting his nails a month later, entertaining the theory that Luce might be irked over his arguments against printing Life in China, or even over his failure to find a suitable villa at Tsingtao.
His paychecks continued but the cubicle became a lonely place as he worked
crossword puzzles, read every word in every newspaper, and all the latest
books. "I read *I Can Get It for You Wholesale* in one day," he recalled. At last
he heard that a few other former Timen had been given the same Deep
Freeze treatment. It was a procedure followed in the case of employees who
had done work too good to permit them to be fired out of hand. It was expected that they would ultimately get the point and resign. Bailey did so and
went to work for Cosmopolitan magazine, still feeling loyalty to Luce and
blaming himself to some degree for not having "sold" himself to Luce in some
new promotional capacity.

He left in good company. White had recently decamped, and in August
Luce was shocked to see that *Hiroshima*, John Hersey's narrative of six persons who had survived the Bomb, was published in the New Yorker, which
devoted an entire issue to it. It created a sensation. Newspapers in America
and various parts of the world reprinted it, people everywhere discussed it, it
was read over the radio, it was quickly published as a book, and Hersey's already considerable fame was further enhanced. Like *A Bell for Adano*, it was
the work of a man whose compassion could cross national boundaries into

enemy country. It looked on the Bomb not as an inspiring example of American might but as a cataclysm bringing all humanity together in sympathy for its own inhumanity. This was a sentimental view to Luce. But chiefly he was outraged at what he regarded as disloyalty, even though *Hiroshima* was something the Lucepress would never have touched. Hersey's picture was not merely turned to the wall but removed outright from the Penthouse. Within the space of a few weeks Luce had become estranged from two of his most talented and most favored young journalists.

At almost the same time, the White-Jacoby book *Thunder Out of China* was selected by the Book-of-the-Month Club. It contained the appraisals of General Stilwell, Chiang's regime and the Communists which White had not been able to get into Time and Life because of the opposition of Luce and Chambers. Luce now placed White on his list of fellow travelers. It was the beginning of the irrational rejection of unpleasant fact, and the irrational suspicion of those who clung to fact even when unpleasant, which would come to full flower in McCarthyism.

In September Luce flew to San Francisco for a duty near his heart. He addressed four hundred Protestant missionaries about to sail to China into Christian disaster he might have foreseen had he paid more attention to White and General Stilwell. He congratulated them on their opportunity, saying, "Missionaries today are more rightly esteemed than ever before in history. . . . The missionary goes to China today with a new reason for hope—the existence of a Christian Church of China." Five weeks later he took with him Roy Alexander and Robert Elson, head of his China-lobbying Washington bureau, on a flight to China in a plane provided by Assistant Secretary of the Air Force Stuart Symington (Yale '23)—a private use of government facilities that would be criticized with special vehemence by the Chicago Tribune. (Symington would soon appear on Time's cover as if in compensation.) Stopping again in San Francisco, Luce wrote Mary Bancroft (whom he had earlier cabled), urging her to come to America so they could continue their conversation. Elson and Alexander, primed for a Fisherman's Wharf feast, got a Luce drugstore counter quickie instead.

Arriving in Shanghai October 26, he was driven to Nanking and paid homage by the Nationalist oligarchs he had supported so loyally. Alexander and Elson went on to Peking, Luce having generously insisted that they see Yenching University and the Luce Pavilion there at his expense. The anti-Chiang but non-Communist Shanghai paper Hsin Min Wan Pao greeted Luce with an appraisal gaining exotic flavor in translation:

> Why is it that publisher Luce should be so warmly welcomed? . . . The three big magazines that Luce owned, Life has a circulation of over 4 million subscriptions, while Time has about one million and 200 thousands, and Fortune has 170 to 180 thousands subscription. Moreover, the March of Time screen production made by his company was record 13 rolls every year. All these films were being shown in 8000 cinema halls in America and 3000 others in countries

outside the United States. There is no second publisher who could have a big business such as that of Mr. Luce. . . .

Even those who paid very little attention to the present hardship of the Chinese press circles, it is very clear to them that the best-sell magazines among the book market in China today are Time and Life. . . . The free flooding in the selling market of these two magazines is indeed admirable and envied by the bad-shaped home magazines.

Being so big in its scope . . . Luce's business as well as his work could really be interpreted as important as that of a propaganda minister in any country. Views and opinions that appeared in his magazines are naturally drawn to attention in America or in foreign countries.

Although Luce's Time and Life have declared themselves as the two objective reporting magazines, the cultural and political circles in America have long had the comment on these two magazines' "objective attitude" as hypocritical. . . .

Luce met General Marshall, who had now spent ten months in Nanking trying to bring the two sides together, finding them both suspicious and intransigent. Marshall's job was made the harder by anti-Communist Congressmen back home who shouted for all-out aid to Chiang—sentiments duly reported to Chiang and not inclined to make him more moderate, and at the same time tending to increase Mao's suspicions that the Americans were not really mediating but were taking Chiang's side. On October 5 Marshall had cabled President Truman that his usefulness had ended and his recall would be appropriate. Dim hope, however, had risen again and he would stay another two months. Dr. John Leighton Stuart was now American ambassador, so Luce's prestige could scarcely have been higher either with the American or Nationalist officialdom. He was feted by the T. V. Soongs at a banquet of abalone, chicken and crushed bamboo and pigeon eggs. With Soong he was the honored dinner guest of the Gimo and Madame. K. C. Wu, Chiang's mayor of Shanghai, was his host at another dinner. He was eulogized again at a dinner given by Minister of Information Peng Hseueh-pei. On October 31, Chiang's sixtieth birthday, Luce was accorded a signal honor. Along with General and Mrs. Marshall, he rode with Chiang and Madame in the Gimo's bullet-proof Cadillac and then in the Gimo's private train to a lakeside spot where they picnicked together.

The Marshall mission, of course, mediated between Chiang and Mao with the understanding that Chiang would be boss. In Chiang, the United States saw an ally against Russia but was opting for a "landlord's government" even then being abandoned by the Chinese masses. Just as Luce had turned against Theodore White, so the administration had rejected the appraisals of its own China experts and of General Stilwell, who had foreseen a long Chinese bloodletting. "We ought to get out—now," Stilwell had written fourteen months before this Luce visit to China.

Luce, who would later bitterly condemn the Marshall mission and Ameri-

ca's whole China policy, seemed to support the policy as long as he believed that in any case Chiang would come out on top. To the outsider this appeared likely even though Marshall's mediation was getting nowhere, truces were being broken and there had been intermittent war for three months, for Chiang's forces far outnumbered and outgunned the Communists and seemed to be winning. Luce had originally written Marshall to wish him well in China. Now, if Chiang won the whole prize by force of arms, it would surely have seemed to Luce a better solution than successful mediation that left the Communists with some voice in the government, if a minor one, and an accepted standing in the country.

Ambassador Stuart, himself a former missionary, was linked by loyalty and sentiment to the "Christian" Chiang although inwardly appalled by Nationalist tyranny. An interested observer was young John F. Melby of the embassy staff, one of those Foreign Service officers who made it their business to look, listen and learn as much as possible about what was going on in the country among all factions. He knew that the Communists, far from being defeated, were an efficient and formidable force growing steadily because of popular despair over Nationalist decay.

"It can . . . be argued," he observed apropos of Luce and Stuart, ". . . that the missionary movement has had more influence in shaping American attitudes toward China than any other single factor; and it paid handsome dividends to the Kuomintang."

The Nationalists had sent armies into North China where the Communists were strongest—moves that seemed superficially successful but which really represented a dangerous overextension. The Timan John Beal, although of course an all-out Chiang man, could see that the Boss was naïve in his assumption that the war was as good as won. Luce was also the victim of an unwavering belief in his superior understanding which caused some Timen to speculate that you could drop him down among Eskimos and he would immediately tell them how to make igloos. As Beal wrote, "Luce dominated the conversation after dinner, as he has at all these Chinese functions . . ." He got it into his head, and in that circle no one disputed him, that the Communists were all but beaten. On October 31, when Alexander and Elson returned from Peking, Ambassador Stuart gave a dinner for Luce at which all the Timen were present, including White's replacement, William Gray. Their talk of certain victory astonished Melby, who noted in his diary:

> The conversation was incredibly unreal. The remarks of the Time-Life people nearly convinced me I have been right as to what the new line will be—the problem has been solved, there are only scattered groups of bandits left, and they don't amount to much. It is, I think, the beginning of the blackout.

Melby was aware of Time's influence, adding:

> One of the more unfortunate determinants of the American image around the world over the years has been Time with its enormous audience both in and

outside the United States . . . Although it has seldom been possible to question its factual accuracy [sic], it has been a frightening example of how the news can be "managed" by discreet selection of facts and the use of adjectives. . . . There has long been an impression that Time was the mouthpiece of Washington. . . .

Luce, Elson and Alexander returned via Shanghai, where they dined with John S. Potter, father of young Hank Luce's fiancée, a wealthy banker and real estate man who had offices in the Bank of China Building on the Bund and a home on Park Avenue in New York. Although Potter in a sense was a fugleman of Luce's American Century, he was so fed up with Nationalist rottenness that he growled, "I'd be happy if the Communists won and cleaned up the mess." Alexander later recalled, "Harry didn't quite go through the ceiling. He tried to be polite to the father of his future daughter-in-law. But he made it plain to Potter that if he thought things were bad now, they would be far worse if the Communists should ever gain control."

As the Americans left Shanghai, the newspaper Hsin Min Wan Pao said good-bye:

> Mr. Henry Luce . . . has hurriedly left for Tokyo after having visited his friends in China. . . . All through his sojourn here, he never came in contact with the common people, nor had he anything to do with the daily life of the masses. If he were to discuss the "Chinese problem" in his magazines on the basis of his observations, he would . . . just help to add a bit of misunderstanding to Sino-American relations.

He avoided the Tokyo masses as well. He dined with his two aides at the American embassy as the guest of General MacArthur who, since Luce had first met him in the Philippines in 1941 had been a heroic figure in Time. He had been a Time cover subject in 1941, 1942, 1944 and most recently in 1945. ("MacArthur had the qualifications . . . confident, at ease, urbane, witty and analytical . . . he was the man for the job [in Japan], there could be no further argument . . . his deeds had spoken.") The general could not complain about *that* treatment. He was, as he should have been, a cordial host. His entire agreement that Chiang was the man to save China did him no harm in Luce's estimation. When Luce said that he and his companions would like to talk to the prime minister, MacArthur was not loath to demonstrate the power of the conqueror. "Wouldn't you rather see the emperor?" he asked. Indeed they would. The three spoke to Hirohito through an interpreter at the royal palace, with Luce doing most of the talking. He framed one blunt question: "How does it feel to be mortal after having been a god for so long?" The interpreter evidently thought it best not to relay that one to an emperor already suffering from a reduction in circumstances.

XXII

1. THE CHINA LOBBY

That summer, the Luces, disturbed by a small private airfield near their Greenwich place, sold it for $220,000 and bought for about the same price a seventy-acre estate near Ridgefield, Connecticut, fifty miles from New York. Its Georgian red-brick house had twenty-eight rooms and would prolong the servant problem which had always beset them. They were nearer Weston, where the Moores had a summer place, so they could easily exchange visits with Luce's sister and brother-in-law. Their many Chinese possessions were accented by such touches as bamboo curtain rods but were set against a modern background featuring the growing Luce collection of paintings. Clare's office was in beige and blue, Luce's in the red-white-and-black combination used in the Life covers, and there was a fine reference library in the basement. Called Sugar Hill, the place was handsome and luxurious rather than glittering with the magnificence Luce could have afforded—the home of a couple too busy to put down roots, the home of a man still conscious of the value of a dollar and opposed to vulgar display.

Always, as in Greenwich, there was an elaborate jigsaw puzzle ready on a table to safeguard him against an idle quarter hour. Simultaneously he worked on political puzzles in Asia and Europe and planned the defeat of the Democrats in 1948 and his own ascension to the inner-circle power that had been denied him so long. MacLeish had observed that one of Luce's great strengths was his naïveté, his innocent refusal to see any bounds to his success. In business this had worked splendidly since Hadden's death because of his exceptional skill. In the more complex and unpredictable game of politics he was less successful. In his maneuvers in China, which he promoted with the loudest national voice, he was not quite the expert his birth and his certitude led many to believe.

250

Whittaker Chambers's prediction that Stalin would "settle the old score with Chiang" proved mistaken. On the contrary, Stalin had kept his promise and dealt with the Nationalists as the recognized government of China—a terrible blow to the Chinese Communists whom he mistrusted. The treaty he made with Chiang at the war's end seemed anything but outrageous to Life at the time, for the magazine praised it as a "great victory for common sense" and declared that "the present prospects of China are a vindication of American policy in Asia for almost 50 years." These were words that the Lucepress would later eat. The treaty, which came as a consequence of Stalin's agreements with Roosevelt at Yalta, had indeed given Stalin concessions in China in return for Soviet military help against Japan which proved unnecessary. The Russian armies in Manchuria had done the Chinese Communists more harm than good. While they had permitted the Chinese to take over some areas liberated from the Japanese and had let them appropriate Japanese arms, the Russians had looted Manchuria of almost a billion dollars' worth of Japanese machinery and armament which the Maoists had hoped to appropriate for themselves. The Communists were left with more blame than praise for Stalin. The dogma of monolithic world Communism, which Luce had propagandized for so long, was scarcely credible here.

The Maoists, some of whom had long made their homes in the caves of Yenan, were strangers to the chicken-and-abalone galas of the Kuomintang. Their friendliness toward the Americans had been turned to bitter hatred by the heavy American aid to Chiang.

"The character of the problem of Asia is always the same," Mao told the New York Times reporter Foster Hailey. ". . . United States monopoly wants to rule the world, including England. . . . United States policy is now against the interests and the will of the Chinese people." Hailey scouted the widespread belief that the Communists were Stalin's puppets:

> The civil war in China . . . has been depicted by many as a struggle primarily between the United States and Soviet Russia. That is nonsense. There is no question at all that United States support made it possible for Chiang Kai-shek to wage war on the Communists as long as he did. There is no creditable evidence I have seen or heard of, that Soviet Russia has given any large-scale support to the Chinese Communists beyond abandoning to them the Japanese arms and ammunition that were taken from the 1,000,000 Japanese soldiers that were captured by the Russian Army . . . The Russian Army took out of Manchuria much war-potential equipment . . . that would have made the Chinese Communist task much easier . . .

One American missionary wrote of the disillusionment of the clergy in Chiang and of Protestant leaders who complained to Chiang about government "corruption and apparent lack of interest in the welfare of the people," who thereafter "continued to suffer the displeasure of Chiang . . ." Ambassador Stuart himself, after the cause was lost and his own lifework had been obliterated, reflected:

W. A. Swanberg

And yet this [Kuomintang] party almost from the time it came into power had tolerated among its officials of all grades graft and greed, idleness and inefficiency, nepotism and factional rivalries . . . These evils had become more pronounced after V-J Day in the attempts to crush Communism by a combination of military strength and secret police. The government had steadily been losing popular support and even respect. . . . In painful contrast the Communist party was free from private graft, officers and men lived very much together, simply and industriously, severely disciplined, thoroughly indoctrinated.

In January 1947 General Marshall gave up after a fruitless year and returned to Washington to become Secretary of State. He knew that he had been used, that neither side had ever really given up its determination to exterminate the other. Chiang's troops had reached their highwater mark, spread in pockets in the North against the counsel of American military advisers still aiding them, and highly vulnerable. Chiang, with Luce's muscular help, was appealing for more American aid. On Luce's recent visit to China, the foxy Soong had queried him closely about the possibilities of Republican resurgence in the next elections, evidently on the theory that the Republicans would distribute more money and arms to Chiang than the Democrats. As Melby in the Nanking embassy saw it, "Soong and entourage are dancing around like a bunch of small boys who have to go to the bathroom. They are using every known dodge to get our money—though they must know by now that any loans will not make the slightest difference."

Luce now saw the most grandiose project of his lifetime in danger of ruin. Wrapped up in the ruin was not only the fate of China and of Christianity and the Asian hegemony of the United States but also his own peace of mind and reputation. Chiang-in-China was to have been the crowning of a decade and a half of planning in the Chrysler Building and Rockefeller Center and of countless thousands of words of Lucepress propaganda. The nightmare rise of Mao-in-China brought a powerful Luce counter-strategy. For one thing, his China Institute of America, founded as a haven for Chinese students, now was registered (with Luce as trustee) as a foreign agent working for the Nationalists. It was said that members of Luce's Washington bureau were beating a path between their office and the Chinese embassy presided over by Dr. Wellington Koo. The newsman Robert S. Allen devoted part of a broadcast to the increasingly powerful China Lobby of which Luce and the attorney Thomas Corcoran (whom Time had once skewered as a shifty New Dealer) were the visible headmen:

> The House Appropriations Committee is secretly investigating one of the most brazen lobbyist pressure drives that Washington has seen in years. Aim of this pressure drive was a $60,000,000 raid on the U.S. Treasury in the guise of more aid to the Chiang Kai-shek government in China. The U.S. has already loaned and given to the Chinese government over six [sic] billion dollars. . . .
> . . . [T]he Chiang Kai-shek raid is unique. It's the first time that a foreign government has openly lobbied to tap the U.S. till. . . . During the past week

252

the capital literally swarmed with Chinese lobbyists. The State Department estimates that there are over 200 agents of Chiang Kai-shek now in the U.S. lobbying and propagandizing for more American millions. . . .

One of the most remarkable aspects of this remarkable foreign raid . . . is the fact that it's being masterminded by certain well-known Americans. They are a strange group of allies. On the extreme right is Henry Luce, ultraconservative publisher . . . And on the left is Tommy Corcoran . . . once a bitter enemy of Luce. But now Luce and Corcoran are working hand in glove to get more American millions for Chiang Kai-shek.

Luce has been propagandizing and agitating for another two-billion-dollar U.S. handout for Chiang for a long time. . . . And in Washington practically the whole Luce bureau has been working full blast as part of the Chiang lobby. . .

Months earlier Life had featured the aggressive Presbyterian layman John Foster Dulles's two-part denunciation of Russia for aiming to conquer the world. Dulles was expected to be the next Republican Secretary of State. Now Life attacked the career men in State who were "all so cautious and wooden" in their opposition to entangling America further in what had become a Chinese civil war of huge proportions. "Our Chinese policy has been one of mere temporizing and is now demonstrably bankrupt," Life said. The word "war" recurred incessantly in its editorials and features. One of them stripping U.S. foreign policy down to two essentials: ". . . 1) to prevent the next war; 2) to win it."

Luce exchanged letters and occasional visits with Navy Secretary James Forrestal—once his guest at Mepkin—who was obsessed with the Communist threat and made his office a clearinghouse for anti-Communist information and efforts. Forrestal exchanged similar information with many others including Luce's friends Cardinal Spellman and Monsignor Sheen, and also with J. Edgar Hoover. The Secretary had commissioned a Smith College professor to make a special study of Soviet Communism which argued that if "a true Communist could destroy the United States by pushing a button, he would do so," and that, barring unlikely circumstances, ultimate conflict was inevitable. Luce was one of those who received a copy. Forrestal also sent out copies of Arthur Koestler's gripping story of Communist brainwash and torture, Darkness at Noon—a book that would later be reissued by Time Inc. Like Luce, Forrestal now believed the Marshall policy in China to be disastrous and that more aid should be given Chiang. The two men agreed on the need for a greatly enlarged military budget. Fortune published an article, "The Arms We Need," based almost entirely on Forrestal's figures and urging that "the only way to avoid having American foreign policy dominated by crisis is to live in crisis—prepared for war."

When Forrestal's nearness to a breakdown became apparent to those close to him, Time smelled a plot, saying "he had been marked as the victim of one of the biggest headhunts in the history of Washington politics."

Luce also continued his partiality for reclaimed radicals—men once intoxi-

cated with Communism and now as immoderate in the other direction. This time it was James Burnham, the ex-Trotskyite whose *The Struggle for the World* was the first of the mailed-fist shockers to bring the American Century into martial postwar focus and to call for fast U.S. preparation not only for war with Russia but for assertion of world leadership. Life published a condensation of the book with enormous promotion, and Time gave it a big play, with a picture of Burnham captioned "Too true for comfort." It was "chilling" stuff, Time conceded, and would be attacked as "Fascist war-mongering," adding, "Only one defense of Burnham's book can be made: it is—appallingly—true."

Through his Washington bureau Luce tried strenuously for an audience so that he could press his China policy on President Truman in person. He had sought vainly to see him immediately after returning from China. If Truman by this time had managed to forgive the Luce slurs on Bess, he could not have been happy about the TLF animadversions on his stewardship. Elson, Time's tactful Washington bureau head, was sent to consult Presidential Secretary Charles Ross about Luce's wish for a hearing. Ross was amiable without committing the President. Evidently in response to Elson's suggestion, he said he had already urged the President to read Burnham's *The Struggle for the World*, which Luce was actively promoting. Ross said he felt the President's views on China were now quite similar to Luce's and that he agreed with Luce in another respect—that a successful U.S. policy must be based on sound morality, and the trouble with the Russians was that they had no morality.

Luce was going at his usual breakneck speed. In January 1947 he had spent several days at the Time-sponsored Cleveland Forum, a huge conclave of foreign and American statesmen and dignitaries designed to promote Time Inc. and American business as well as to persuade Americans to think big in American Century terms. He made a speech in Syracuse, another in Philadelphia, journeyed to Chicago on business and in May flew to Brazil—his first trip to South America—as the guest of Oswaldo Aranha, president of the UN General Assembly. He came back urging exploitation such as a Life picture story about Sao Paolo and predictably finding "one of the greatest and most irresistible personalities I have ever encountered," this time in Aranha. Soon he was making a speech in Scranton, telling his late father's townsmen mistakenly that "[the] war between Soviet Russian Communism and non-Communism is being fought right now in China," adding, "Some day, somehow, we've got to go back there and put the situation in order. I pray God it may not be necessary to do so with force of arms." It was safe to say that by now, in large part due to his own efforts, Category Three contained a majority of the American people.

Hurrying back to New York, he got into his cutaway and stock two days later and went to his son's wedding to brunette Patricia Potter at Lu Shan, now after twelve years a mansion surrounded by horticultural splendor. One

of the officiating pastors was Rev. George Buttrick of Luce's own Madison Avenue Presbyterian Church—a divine with whom Luce liked to discuss theology but for whom his opinion was impaired because Dr. Buttrick was a pacifist. One of the many guests was Luce's favorite writer-philosopher, eighty-six-year-old Dr. Alfred North Whitehead. When one woman guest felt faint because of the heat, and Dr. Whitehead was called to revive her, he did so by explaining that he was only a Doctor of Philosophy.

Luce highly approved of the lovely bride, who had lived a part of her life in China and had attended Bryn Mawr. This was one of those rare occasions when he was brought together with his whole "first family." Peter Paul Luce —now a student at M.I.T.—was one of the ushers, Lila was radiant, the Severinghauses and Moores were there in a body and old Mrs. Luce struggled with a hearing aid. The occasion was not monopolized by Senators, governors or prime ministers. After the ceremony and the champagne, the music began and Luce danced with Lila for the first time in twelve years. John Billings, who was one of the guests, observed that this was the high point of the day second only to the wedding itself. Everybody applauded the strikingly handsome couple who had experienced separate vicissitudes, the mother and father of the bridegroom.

2. "FEARFULLY IRRESPONSIBLE JOURNALISM"

A young Iowan named Merle Miller came back from army service in Europe heartily sick of war and believing that men of good will should work for peace. An excellent writer, he landed with Time and did very well. He inhabited one of the smaller cubicles, attended the weekly teas given by Managing Editor Matthews for the editorial staff and kept his eye peeled for material for a novel that was taking shape in his mind. Soon he discovered that Time was slanted, unfair, dishonest. He was not instructed to write dishonestly but he came to understand osmotically what was expected. As he later described it:

> No one ever ordered anyone to write anything . . . in a certain way, except, possibly, in the heat of an election campaign. But if you were bright—and you didn't remain on the staff long unless you were—you soon understood the rules.

He described an instance of how this worked out in practice:

> I was attempting that day to write a story that would imply that the Czechs who had once been such gentle lovers of what the news magazine referred to as quote Western civilization unquote were no longer either quite so gentle or so friendly. I hoped in the story to be half-way honest and at the same time to get the story I wrote past the blue pencil of my immediate editor as well as the managing editor.

And another:

> My assignment was to write a story about Yugoslavia, which would point up, subtly but understandably, the remarkable physical resemblance between Mar-

shal Tito and Hermann Goering, would remind the reader that the similarity was political and social as well, and finally the fact that, now that the war had ended, the readers of the news magazine must be prepared to realize that not all our wartime allies would be our peacetime friends. . . . The Yugoslav story went well, had precisely the right number of inverted sentences, just enough innuendo, exactly the correct amount of what, while it could not be proved, read just as well as fact and in many ways better.

Miller quit Time in disgust. He soon came out with a very good novel, *That Winter*, from which these excerpts are taken and in which he limned the Time fakery with the devastating verisimilitude of one who had been there. The book sold very well—so well that Luce, who lacked time to read it, asked Daniel Longwell to appraise it for him. Longwell, the former Doubleday bookman, marked the pages Luce might be interested in and noted that while Time appeared as background, it was not the book's central theme. Nothing to worry about.

Miller, who was later an editor of Harper's and then the Saturday Review, was sufficiently disturbed by his encounter with massive misinformation and manipulation of public attitudes that he spoke against it when he got a chance. In one public lecture he attacked the imposture of Reader's Digest, noted that the New Republic was now so biased that it never criticized the Soviet Union, and paid his respects to his former employer, Time:

> It's edited brilliantly, is well written, but is dishonestly written. It is extremely unified in that every single story carries the slant of the editor, Henry Luce. On the other hand, Time's competitor, Newsweek, is honest. It gives bylines whenever the material is editorially written so that you know it is the opinion of the writer.

So Miller joined that small group of TLF people concerned enough with integrity to quit the plush Rockefeller Center offices, the big salaries, the profit-sharing and the prestige. His gesture against journalistic fraudulence was inevitably a pea-shooter against granite. Probably Managing Editor Matthews did not even hear the rattle against his fortification. In his preoccupation with style he sometimes warred with the researchers whose duty was to keep Time "factual." There were sixty of these capable young women, required by unwritten law to have pretty legs and by a rule in the book of their boss, Senior Editor Content Peckham, to wear sheer silk stockings and to keep the seams straight. When a writer was assigned to a story, a researcher still gathered all the facts for him. Since she was in supposed factual command and he merely the rendering artist, she went over his finished copy word for word. She penciled a dot over each correct word. If she found a word she could not dot, it was the writer's supposed duty to correct it.

In its promotion, Time made much of this arduous and expensive search for truth. It helped make the editorial cost of Time $1.48 a printed word, against less than a dime a word for most newspapers. But the system was honored as

often in the breach as in the observance. To one researcher who offered a dictionary to prove a point, Matthews said, "Webster is the work of human hands." He once told his assembled writers, "Now, look, let's not take these researchers too seriously." There was a continuing battle between writers and researchers that helped to add up to that $1.48 a word. The writer's purpose was to get as tall a story by the bothersome girl as he could, while her hope was to keep him somewhere within the bounds of plausibility if not truth. In the case of particularly masterful writers carried away by their subject, the researcher system served their fictional impulses rather than factuality, much as some government agencies founded to protect the consumer ended up by swindling him. It cannot be said, for example, that any researcher with penciled dots rescued Whittaker Chambers or Laird Goldsborough from error.

Never did the character and wishes of the Boss trickle down more certainly to the staff and become more manifest in the finished product. It was well known, though not openly discussed, that his aim was not mere fact but was entertainment that assured rising circulation, which in turn assured rising power in his propaganda, which to him represented the final truth.

Matthews himself brushed aside a researcher in Time's Medicine department, Beka Doherty, in his determined effort for a good story. It was a cover about the psychiatrist Dr. William C. Menninger which had already been revised eight times when he got his hands on it. Although this was late Monday night and checking copy had been turned in, after which (said the rules) no major changes could be made, Matthews saw room for great improvement. He began playing with it himself. He made more and more changes as he went along, such as defining Freudianism as "European smutlety" and describing the mentally ill as people lacking the moral character to face their problems. Miss Doherty protested, as the rules ordered her to. But, she said:

> Matthews refused to see me, refused to discuss the matter further with the senior editor or the writer, who were both miserably in the middle. The thing was only solved when I threw a fit of temperament which everybody said was perfectly justified, because Matthews' version of the story would have brought ridicule to the magazine, on the writer, and myself personally, would have choked off effectively all the medical sources we had been at such pains to build up, would have caused acute pain to all the mental patients who read Time . . . and last (and least) would have seriously misrepresented the facts.

Attention should be paid to the parenthetical "and least." Daily newspapers were prone to make typos and even errors of fact in producing several editions a day against imperious deadlines. Time, with a week between deadlines, made few typos but oozed with the inaccurate or misleading (quite aside from propaganda) because of the constant effort to improve on fact and make a "good story." Time's slurs, taunts and gibes were often inserted just to jazz things up. Time lacked the restraining influence felt by the editor of a

257

daily newspaper who knows that a sizable percentage of his readers can check personally on the accuracy of most stories. Time's story about Paducah was believed by readers in all other places, and the reader in Dubuque was not disillusioned until Time carried a story about Dubuque, when he would say, "They got that wrong."

When the editor of the new magazine Fact scouted around for people who disliked Time, he was all but trampled in the rush. Ralph Ingersoll, who knew a good deal about Time, said, "The way to tell a successful lie is to include enough truth in it to make it believable—and Time is the most successful liar of our times." Dwight Macdonald, another ex-insider, said, "The degree of credence one gives to Time is inverse to one's degree of knowledge of the situation being reported on." Tallulah Bankhead said, "Dirt is too clean a word for Time." Eugene Burdick deplored Time's "dishonest tactics," Mary McCarthy its "falsifications," and Igor Stravinsky found this level of reporting even in one of the specialized departments: "Every music column I have read in Time has been distorted and inaccurate." The critic Eric Bentley found manipulation to be its worst vice: "More pervasive than Time's outright errors is the misuse of the truth." Bertrand Russell wrote, "I consider Time to be scurrilous and I know, with respect to my own work, utterly shameless in its willingness to distort."

George Horace Lorimer, who found fourteen important factual errors in Time's four-hundred-word piece about his career, was kinder; he simply wrote Time, listing the errors but not asking for a published correction, which of course he did not get.

News manipulation was sheer policy, Time's way of life, performed as a matter of office routine. It often resulted in entertaining trivia harmful chiefly in its corruption of gimmick-seeking editors and writers and its general and pervasive debasing of truth. When Time did a roundup story on the alleged emphasis of country weeklies on bucolic interests rather than the 1946 election, it followed the slant at all costs. It often skipped front-page election stories in the weeklies and quoted inside squibs concerning hog sales, fishing excursions and Ladies' Aid meetings "which came," it said, "smudgily from flatbed presses in the nation's small towns." Country editors complained about this misrepresentation. The sage Henry Beetle Hough of the Vineyard Gazette in Massachusetts observed that "the facts were twisted to suit the point of view of the Time editor, and the whole picture . . . was narrow and distorted." Hough's reproving editorial read in part:

> Ah, neighbor, which comes cockily from the many stories of an expensive skyscraper in Rockefeller Center, it is not clear printing which makes words shine or endure, and it isn't always clipped or polished rhetoric. No, no! Plain speech, honest, forthright, and possibly well-smudged, makes better reading in heaven and even in some nearer places than a good deal of well turned mechanical patter.

Bernard De Voto, who had commented on Life's strategic use of the "rapidly slipping chemise," was so enraged at Time's despoiling of William Vogt's book on conservation and ecology, *Road to Survival*, that he took four pages in Harper's to excoriate it. This was one of those instances where "the degree of credence was inverse to the degree of knowledge," for De Voto knew something about conservation and had read the book. De Voto did not seem to realize that a researcher had checked every word. He noted Time's "sweeping misrepresentations of Mr. Vogt's book," which it accomplished "by making him and people of like opinion say what in fact they have never said, by attributing to them ideas which they do not in fact hold, by derisive epithets, by citing as demonstrated facts what are really limited hypotheses or mere wild guesses . . . by ignoring the issues and the evidence, and by assertions for which no support is given and none exists." De Voto observed that Time felt that the author was "against industry"—an attitude that aroused Time's best infighting as the defender of industry. De Voto was shaken not by the kind of inaccuracy one could forgive but by the evidently deliberate misinformation and deception of the reader. "I have no space to discuss the harm [the article] has done," he wrote. "I merely remark that it is fearfully irresponsible journalism."

Most knowledgeable and cynical of all were newspapermen in New York, Washington and elsewhere who actually saw the raw news come in over the wires and then saw how it was gimmicked by Time. Not far behind was a growing number of college journalism or politics classes whose instructors and students saw what was happening, and where Time was studied regularly as a horrible example of the distortion and coloration of news, among them Dartmouth, Hunter College, the University of Missouri and Iowa State College. The Southern California Daily Trojan observed, "Henry Luce's publications have made slanting the news a science—so much so that one can hardly read a single article in Time, for example, without coming upon some outright attempt to influence one's thinking." At Dartmouth's "Great Issues" course, Time's distortions, errors and misrepresentations were listed, along with corrections, on panels mounted before the class.

Factuality aside, Matthews had raised Time's literary quality noticeably. If the "smutlety" sort of gag was still a trifle overdone, Time nevertheless was so easy to read that some read it for entertainment rather than information, just as others bought the New Yorker solely for its cartoons and the Reader's Digest for its jokes. Time's propaganda came through in any case. True, some thought the Lucepress rather worldly for such a religious man as Luce. This topic came up when ex-Congresswoman Luce, forgetting in her earnest crusade her servant problem, her three homes and her jewel collection, wrote the New York Herald Tribune criticizing the "materialism" of Communism.

This startled the critic Lewis Galantiere who, without reference to Mrs. Luce's own possessions, had thought that Time, Life and Fortune, with their full-page display ads of limousines, liquors and cosmetics, had a worldly color-

ation. It was one thing, too, to run straight advertising and another to run so-called textual matter designed to tie in with advertisements either specifically or generally. Galantiere had recently been riveted to his chair by a four-page Life text (not advertising) feature purporting to give "an honest representation of the dream of most United States families." Its first double-page photograph showed a new and handsome house, a stationwagon, television set, power mower, washing machine, bath towels, refrigerator and other useful gadgets including a $48,500 helicopter. On the next two pages were given "a woman's dream," which included a $595 lace dressing gown and a $330,000 diamond-and-emerald necklace, and "a man's dream" filled with expensive sporting equipment. Fanciful as all this looked, Life said, "it is based on the hard statistics of consumer demand and manufacturers' unfilled orders."

Galantiere, not at all interested in defending Communism, still felt that Mrs. Luce did not have to go to Russia to find the mundane. He wrote the Herald Tribune to say that he "had been struck (as Mrs. Luce doubtless was) by the unrelieved materialism of [Life's] view of the American people."

When Luce saw *Death of a Salesman* and talked about it later to a friend, the friend noticed that he did not entertain the thought that the play's theme might have direct application to him. But like Willy Loman, the success-worshiping protagonist in Arthur Miller's play, Luce was not immune to occasional inward wrestlings. His mother continued to let him know that she worried about his soul. And Mary Bancroft's visit to America in 1947 brought him together in expensive restaurants with a woman he found both delightful and stimulating but whose suspicions of his magazines and his motivations put him on the defensive. She seemed to read every line in his publications, to place them alongside facts known to her through other channels, and to compare them in ways not flattering to Time Inc. Mrs. Bancroft sailed on the *Mauretania* in October to find aboard the handsome Virginian, Charles Wertenbaker, whose disagreements with the Luce-Chambers ideology had recently caused him to leave Time in a final though friendly separation. He was rejoining his wife in France, where he would finish a novel. Mrs. Bancroft had enjoyed his *Write Sorrow on the Earth*, and since she was also writing a novel, and they were equally fascinated by Luce's complexities, they had much to talk about. Their conversation aboard the liner came near impelling Mary to send Luce a cable: "Now you've got all that money and power, don't you think you might begin to try to do a little good?" but she decided against it and later included the same suggestion in a letter. Wertenbaker, planning a later novel whose central character would be a newsmagazine tycoon, and who still felt that what Luce needed for his political improvement was a tempestuous affair with a lady as liberal philosophically as she was romantically, insisted that it was her duty to ensnare him. She already had him so bewitched, he said, that he would follow her to the ends of the earth and she had only to be reasonably receptive. He used as a basis for this judgment the fact that she had already received some rather long, handwritten letters from Luce.

Under all this badinage the two agreed that there was more than mere political wrongheadedness in Luce's course. They thought that Luce, with such capacities for journalistic greatness, was instead using his journalism more and more to promote his own personal and political power. After leaving the boat, the two would carry on a long correspondence about the progress of their respective novels in which further discussions of Luce would appear. Wertenbaker, who had covered combat during the war, put her friendship with Luce in military terms. Addressing her first as "Corporal," he gradually raised her rank to reward what he saw as progress in her campaign of entrapment. Mrs. Bancroft, delighted by Wertenbaker's amusing and witty letters, went along with the jest. Many years later when she finally told Luce about this "game" she and Wertenbaker had played, he seemed to enjoy the thought that he had figured in what he chose to regard as "a sort of Noel Cowardish thing."

3. TROUBLE WITH THE DOTS

Luce's rejection of the evaluation of the American press for which he had put up $200,000 three years earlier, caused astonishment. A few in his own organization unkindly suggested (not to him) that he had felt subconsciously that the evaluators would automatically skip him on the theory that a burglar does not alert the police, or that the least the Committee on the Freedom of the Press could do would be to give a clean bill of health to the fellow who paid their expenses. When the commission had required $15,000 more to finish their work, he bowed out and his friend William Benton of Encyclopaedia Britannica supplied this final sum.

The commission's preliminary report, "A Free and Responsible Press," found that press freedom was indeed in danger. Among the general criticisms were some applicable to the Lucepress: the increasing concentration of press power in the hands of a few, and the use of the press for propaganda. In many specific ways the report castigated the kind of journalism constantly employed in Time, Life and Fortune, without of course naming them:

> "The first requirement is that the media should be accurate. They should not lie." ". . . Giant units [of the press] can and should assume the duty of publishing significant ideas contrary to their own . . ." "[The press] ought to identify the sources of its facts, opinions, and arguments so that the reader . . . can judge them. . . . Identification of source is necessary in a free society."

Time gave virtually no bylines and seldom identified its sources. As has been seen, it was famous for its ability to find unidentified politicians or bystanders who would make statements on news events providing the very point of view Time sought to promote, usually in memorable language. Time's ability to find such unidentified people even in the days when its only sources had been the newspapers which themselves could not find them, had been a

source of wonder to the working press. Newspapermen called Time's unidentified witness the Delphic Oracle or Disembodied Voice and got a kick out of going through an issue to count the Voices. Time seldom was able to find unidentified persons to make statements with which Time disagreed. To knowing readers (but not the unknowing) the unidentified commentator's mask came away rather easily and he was discovered to be the propagandist voice of Time. He was ubiquitous—always present at historic events, never escaping Time's reporter and always willing to be quoted if not named. When Jan Masaryk fell to his death in Prague, sure enough there was an unnamed Czech peasant woman leaning over a balustrade in the palace, an on-the-spot witness who told Time, "The damned, damned Communists killed him. They are worse than the Nazis."

The commission told how news could (but should not) be slanted and distorted:

> . . . If the Chinese appear in a succession [of scenes] as sinister drug addicts and militarists, an image of China is built which needs to be balanced by another. If the Negro appears . . . only as a servant . . . the image of the Negro . . . is distorted. The plugging of special color and "hate" words . . . such words as "ruthless," "confused," "bureaucratic"—performs inevitably the same image-making function.

This could be construed as criticism of Time's methods of image-building and adjectivization. But still worse was to come:

> Of equal importance with reportorial accuracy are the identification of fact as fact and opinion as opinion, and their separation, so far as possible. This is necessary all the way from the reporter's file, up through the copy and makeup desks and editorial offices, to the final, published product.

Perhaps this was what made Luce throw up his hands and disavow the commission he had founded. "Impartiality is often an impediment to truth," he protested. "Time will not allow the stuffed dummy of impartiality to stand in the way of telling the truth as it sees it." He added strangely, "The commission is, in fact, complaining about the worst sections of the press, and to them it administers some well-deserved rebukes."

Luce's friend Dr. Hutchins, chairman of the commission, said, "It is inconceivable to me that Henry Luce would disagree with the general conclusions of the report." But Walter Lippmann was one of the few who lauded it. The commission urged the creation of a privately endowed agency, independent of both government and the press, to report annually on the press's performance. Luce was joined in rejection by the vast majority of the newspaper press, which disliked having even an independent body, with no power other than publicity, looking over its shoulder.

In 1948, Time's twenty-fifth anniversary was celebrated with a special twelve-page "biography" of the magazine written mostly by Max Ways, who

had proved so able a man that his salary had skyrocketed and he was often called on by Luce to debate with him domestic and world problems. The suggestion of some critics that money had something to do with the Luce attitudes did not of course mean that his top men were insincere and motivated only, if at all, by cupidity. Some of them had been taking liberties with the news so long that it seemed as natural as for a chef to season a goulash. There were old-timers and newcomers, though perhaps not many, who truly believed in what they were doing. This was obviously the case with the strapping, intellectual Ways, whose sensitivity to news manipulation had not been dulled gradually. He had joined up as a forty-year-old newsman heavily experienced on the Baltimore Sun and Philadelphia Record to whom Time's facile shaping of events must have come as a sudden revelation rather than a slow and crippling disease.

Clearly he approved of Time, for the twelve-page biography was almost an unbroken hosanna. True, his admission that Time performed a certain processing or coloring of the news did not come until the very end of the appreciation, a point only the more determined readers would reach. He suggested that the additives Time combined with the news were not at all an imposition on the reader who might have thought he was getting unadulterated news, since there was no such thing as unadulterated news. There was no mention of the possibility that the additives were calculated to influence readers who might reach different conclusions if left to their own judgment, or that there might be something deceptive in all this. On the contrary, the additives reflected Time's concern over national and world events and its hope to instill the same care into its readers:

> The shortest or the longest news story is the result of selection. The selection is not, and cannot be, "scientific" or "objective." It is made by human beings. . . . The myth of "objective journalism" reached its height about 1938–39, before the Hitler-Stalin pact, before the sharp cleavage of war reminded the Western world that the famed "two sides of a question" are not always, or even often, equal. . . .
>
> Time in the 1930s was reporting the facts about Germany, for example, in a way that clearly showed Time's working hypothesis: that the Nazi Party was very bad medicine. It reports the Communist Party today against the background of a similar hypothesis. . . .
>
> Time's prospectus promised that "no article would be written to prove any special case." It tries hard to keep that promise. . . . Time is not dispassionate about news. It cares about what's going on in the world, and it hopes that its readers care. . . . Fairness is Time's goal.

One of Time's researchers seemed to have been careless with a great many of her dots. Ways had not been with Time during the Thirties or he would have known that the magazine in those years coddled the Nazis, not to mention glorifying Mussolini and Franco and hovering around the edges of anti-Semitism. It was littered then, as it still was, with articles written to prove

special cases. And if Time's ideal really was fairness, it could not reasonably be said that the ideal had often been reached. To some, such as Andrew Mellon, Wendell Willkie, J. Pierpont Morgan, Thomas E. Dewey, Neville Chamberlain, Pius XII, General MacArthur, General Patton, Chiang Kai-shek and all the Soongs, it had been fair—really more than fair. But in all candor it had to be said that Time had not been fair to others such as Léon Blum, Maxim Litvinov, Manuel Azaña, Haile Selassie, Hugh Johnson, Rexford Tugwell, Franklin Roosevelt, or to William Vogt and his book *Road to Survival*, to name only a few. Indeed some of these persons and many others had been treated not with the accidental unfairness that gets by in the deadline rush but with deliberate, vicious, repeated and prolonged unfairness.

What was revealed here about a newsmagazine staffed with sixty researchers which, on its twenty-fifth birthday, could make so many errors about its own recent and easily explored past?

There was revealed at least such a lack of liaison between the word-dotting researchers and the creators of Time's finished copy as to raise doubt of the system's validity. Some more effective control of the word-dotting seemed to be in order. The problem was to get the dots over the right words. Still the system, with all its inadequacies, was persevered in. As Time moved into its second quarter-century, it still placed implicit faith in the dots.

XXIII

1. THE AUSPICIOUS STAR

In December 1947 Chinese Ambassador Wellington Koo visited New York with a whole bagful of decorations which he conferred on Luce, Thomas W. Lamont, John D. Rockefeller, Jr., Paul Hoffman and others useful to Chiang Kai-shek. Around Luce's neck Dr. Koo hung the Special Cravat of the Order of the Auspicious Star. The retiring president of United Service to China (United China Relief's postwar name), former Governor Charles Edison of New Jersey, received an award one notch higher, the Grand Order of the Auspicious Star. It was taking nothing away from Governor Edison to say that no one in either hemisphere deserved more acclaim from Chiang than Luce. In Time alone, that infallible barometer, Chiang had set a record by appearing on the cover six times and was soon to be honored there for the seventh. To many Timen it came under the heading of "Harry's mania."

The Lucepress demands for more aid to Chiang had reached a crescendo when William C. Bullitt went to China to investigate the situation for Life. In Nanking, where General Wedemeyer had followed General Marshall and was giving Chiang military advice he often ignored, Bullitt ran into John Melby at the U.S. embassy. "Like most others he is appalled by what he has seen and heard," Melby wrote in his diary. "He keeps muttering, 'Someone has not been telling the truth.' "

Although Bullitt smelled the Kuomintang corruption, it would not do for him to show his wry face. His article in Life, titled "A Report to the American People on China," was ballyhooed by full-page ads in dozens of newspapers —always the sign of a high-powered Luce propaganda effort. It gave a partisan account of the background of the civil war, blaming Roosevelt for "betraying" Chiang, whom it glorified as a man who "bulks larger than any living American." It conveyed the idea that China was *not* in civil war, that the

265

threat was purely external, that the Chinese Communists were mere agents of Stalin. Whether Bullitt himself knew that this was not so, as a propagandist he knew it was the only line to take. The war-weary American public would never allow the country to be drawn into a Chinese factional bloodletting. The chances were better that it would defend China against Stalin. Bullitt was so aware of the tendency of money and materials to vanish in the hands of Chiang's friends and relatives that to his recommended program for saving the Gimo with $1,350 million more in American money he added eighteen suggestions for Nationalist reform and the dispatch of General MacArthur to supervise the whole operation. His plan would commit America to heavy and open military intervention in the civil war.

Perhaps it was these suggestions, which really amounted to an indictment of the Gimo who was yet so highly praised, and the thought of the Gimo being subordinate to MacArthur, which caused the decision that Luce should get only the Special Cravat. Yet he kept lobbying all the harder for more help for Chiang. Twice in ten months Time made Secretary of State Marshall its cover subject, in both cases less for the purpose of laudation than for warning and for the application of political pressure about China. Admitting that he had his points, Time asked that rhetorical question that always placed a public official in doubt before the public: "But is Marshall big enough for the gigantic task ahead of him?"

Not unless he pitched in for Chiang, Time warned, arguing against the theory that the U.S. should wash its hands of the Nationalist crowd "on the ground that some of its leaders were crooks." It seemed to come out for American support of virtually any government as long as it was anti-Communist, assailing the "holier-than-thou attitude that the U.S. could only associate itself with simon-pure, double-distilled democrats conforming to the strictest tenets of the Anglo-Saxon moral code."

By now the China Lobby was an amorphous group, preponderantly Republican, boosting Chiang for reasons of anti-Communism and also as an issue against the Democrats. Luce was easily the lobby's most powerful member through sheer force of propaganda. With him were people ranging from Alfred Kohlberg, a wealthy importer of Chinese lace whose interests were in part commercial, to Congressman Walter Judd of Minnesota, a former medical missionary in China. The pressure was enormous, as Eric Sevareid said in a newscast:

> Unless the Senate changes things, Republican Representative Judd of Minnesota and publisher Henry Luce have won their fight to get more military help to Chiang Kai-shek in China. It was inevitable that the great prestige of Secretary Marshall would come a cropper on some issues some time, but the curious thing is that he has failed to win his case on this issue of China's military needs, a topic on which he has been regarded as the government's number one expert.

One Washington mystery was why Republican Senator Arthur Vanden-

berg, chairman of the Foreign Relations Committee, suddenly withdrew the committee's report excoriating the Chiang regime for "corruption and incompetence" in favor of a revised report much gentler with Chiang. There was speculation that Luce might be behind it, one of the rumors being that if Vandenberg did not get the Presidential nomination that summer he would quit the Senate and become editor of Fortune at $60,000 a year.

The China Lobby had already begun a course of calculated vengefulness against Chiang-doubters in the State Department. John Carter Vincent, one of the early Old China Hands in the Foreign Service to become disillusioned with Chiang, and who had since become chief of the State Department's Office of Far Eastern Affairs, was under such fire that he was relieved of that office and sent to Switzerland as minister to remove him as a target. The embargo on the shipment of munitions to Chiang was lifted. Chiang got 230 American planes, and American Marines withdrawing from North China left hundreds of tons of munitions to the Nationalist soldiers, who were beginning to show more interest in looting than fighting. The administration recommended financial support to Chiang less than the Luce-Bullitt demands. Yet Congress shaved it down, still voting a healthy $400 million in economic and military aid which justified the Chinese embassy entertainments in Washington and the Auspicious Stars. In Fortune, a thoroughly misleading apologia for Chiang and attack on Democratic policy was followed by steady propaganda in Life and Time, the latter assailing Truman for his "half-a-loaf" policy, although Congress itself had cut the loaf. It attacked Marshall for his insistence that money could not save Chiang unless he won back the public with democratic concessions.

"You can't win guerrilla warfare with the people against you," Marshall said. Like most of the professional China hands in the Foreign Service, he thought the Chiang government doomed because it would not or could not reform and was becoming totally dependent on American aid.

Luce, whose postwar experience in China was as nothing compared with Marshall's solid year of talk with both sides in the civil strife, had moved far toward his belief in money *plus* outright American military intervention. His magazines must have been the most influential single factor in enlisting some American legislators and much of the public in a belief that was quite mistaken—a mistaken belief that would cause enormous national turmoil—the belief that we were shortchanging Chiang in comparison with massive Russian help erroneously thought to be given the Chinese Communists.

There was concern among liberals on Time's staff, one of whom left an unsigned statement on Billings's desk:

> The Time writers do not share the Management's enthusiasm for the Republican Party. There are five or six admitted Republicans on the staff. There may be a few Republican fellow travelers. The writers are not Democrats either. The overwhelming majority were supporters of Franklin Roosevelt and are waiting for some political group which will continue his work. . . .

Practically all (perhaps all) the writers dislike Communism. But many feel that some of the anti-Communist material which has appeared in Time has been unfair, undignified and dishonest. They do not like to see Time descend to the Communist propaganda level by using semantics, unproved rumors, and hate and fear appeals.

Most of the writers believe that much of the outcry against Communism comes from pressure-groups which are as undemocratic as the Communists . . . they do not applaud alliances with these groups. . . . Most writers extend their feeling about Communism to the foreign field. But they hate to see Time condone (as it has) objectionable foreign parties and governments just because they are anti-Communist. They feel that this policy is not only morally wrong but dangerous and ineffective. . . . The religious propaganda that gets into Time makes them writhe. . . .

In the midst of all this, the rumors of intrigue that invariably circulate with special spite about wealthy people with churchly connections did not pass over Luce. They were given a fillip by the publication in 1948 of the novel *The Great Ones* by Ralph McAllister Ingersoll. As Lewis Gannett observed, one could not read the book "without being aware that the author is the same Ralph Ingersoll who . . . from 1930 to 1935 [was] managing editor of Harry Luce's 'Fortune,' from 1935 to 1936 general manager of Mr. Luce's combined enterprises, and from 1937 to 1939 publisher of 'Time.' " The novel's unlovable protagonist, Sturges Strong, not very bright but insatiably curious and hard-working at Yale, joins his far more gifted classmate Allen Bishop in founding a newsmagazine and carries it on skillfully after Bishop quarrels with him and leaves. He divorces his first wife to marry a famous and predatory beauty. He founds a new magazine so successful that advertising rates had been set too low and he narrowly escapes ruin before becoming more successful than ever. When his new wife seeks control of the magazine, he fends her off but lets her go abroad as a special correspondent, interviewing generals and foreign leaders—intervals during which Strong carries on affairs with other women.

In Orville Prescott's opinion, "What Mr. Ingersoll has done is to take two of the most prominent persons in the literary-publishing world and rearrange their lives for the purposes of cheap and vulgar fiction." His observation that the book was "an affront to good taste and literary ethics" was echoed by Gannett, who admitted "having had a kind of low fun reading it myself" but thought it raised "large questions of the ethics of spite writing and publishing."

2. THE LITTLE OLD VOTER

In addition to influencing policy, Luce was pulling strings to elect a President in 1948 and perhaps to get into the Cabinet himself. The scuttlebutt said

that he was sponsor of a scheme to make Vandenberg the Republican nominee (and certain victor) by promising to give Governor James H. Duff of Pennsylvania "a powerful buildup in his publications" if Duff would swing Pennsylvania's delegates to Vandenberg. Duff would then be given the Vice Presidential post and Luce would at last achieve his dream of becoming Secretary of State. Governor Duff, son of a Presbyterian clergyman, did indeed appear on Time's cover, with the warmest kind of appreciation inside the magazine, in the issue appearing the very day the delegates were assembling in Philadelphia for the convention. Many of the newcomers were seen reading intently the publication whose red border framed the sturdy-looking likeness of the governor. No doubt about it, it gave the Vandenberg-boosting Duff the treatment:

> . . . Strapping affable redhead. . . . Friendly, outspoken six-footer . . . rugged frame and electric blue-grey eyes. . . . Big Jim had come up . . . his roots were deep in Pennsylvania history. One of his ancestors was a member of William Penn's Council . . . unpretentious and homespun. . . . His rear was secure. . . . Key man, Keystone State. . . . Jim Duff would move into the firing line with his rifle cocked. . . .

Ex-Congresswoman Luce, who had been in Hollywood writing the script for *Come to the Stable* and had spoken to many Catholic groups, perhaps had not given up hope for the Senate or something better. She was a convention speaker and Luce a mere listener. Sure enough, she gave a strong plug for Vandenberg, far stronger than her commendation for Dewey and others. "Clare was a sight to see as she stood on tiptoe in her black suede flatties," wrote Dorothy Kilgallen, "and railed against 'the troubadours of trouble' and the 'crooners of catastrophe.' " She called Henry Wallace, whom she had once accused of Globaloney, "Stalin's Mortimer Snerd." She blistered both FDR and Truman with such gusto that the New York Sun headlined, "Mrs. Luce Roasts Democratic Party to a Turn." One of her points was that both Presidents "got along fine" with Stalin. "Good old Joe," she said, "of course they liked him. Didn't they give him all Eastern Europe, Manchuria, the Kuriles, North China, coalitions in Poland, Yugoslavia and Czechoslovakia?"

The commentator Raymond Walsh discerned the obvious: "The Republican Party . . . evidently plans to come to the aid of the Chiang regime on a larger scale than the Truman administration has. This policy is due to the influence of Mr. Henry Luce . . ."

The Chinese embassy people and Chiang himself took a sharp interest in the proceedings, naturally favoring the Vandenberg candidacy which, with Luce as Secretary of State, would solve many of their problems. Nevertheless, when Dewey was nominated they fell into line like loyal Republicans. Luce's mocking friend in Switzerland, Mary Bancroft, did not think highly of the political company he was keeping. She referred derisively to "that great liberal and socialistic-minded fellow, Bill Bullitt, and that unassuming little blonde

Communist, Tom Dewey." Luce never knew quite how to take this lively lady whose raillery seemed calculated to puncture his pomposity and yet whose kindliness he treasured. She went on to challenge one of his firmest beliefs:

> Do you remember on that day when we lunched together and you forgot to eat that clam, you said to me that if the human race was ever going to work out a way of life or of living together they were going to work it out in the U.S.A. and then you went on with a lot of nonsense about how the U.S.A. was o.k. because everything worked and New York got itself fed? Well, the Swiss have worked out a way of life and if we would just learn everything they know and run our country as they run theirs—you'd have it—your human race living together as human life was meant to be lived. . . . I've been here now only four days [after her trip to America]. I don't know who has raped who in Massachusetts or who has murdered who in the rest of the country nor do I know the ins and outs of Benny Meyers' love life, but I do know what is going on in the rest of the world and I only have to read a newspaper of four pages with NO ADVERTISING in order to do so. Furthermore, in case you think this statement un-American . . . one of the four-page papers I can read . . . is the Paris edition of the New York Herald Tribune.

Luce was victimized also by Westbrook Pegler, who gave Mrs. Luce credit for "scratching Harry Truman's eyes out with tinted claws" but who had an animosity caused in part by an implausible theory brought on by the confessions of Whittaker Chambers: that Luce was soft on Communists in his organization:

> China-Boy Henry Luce gotta lotta money. China-Boy lives in swell hotel, tippy-top Waldorf-Astoria. Gotta full dress suit, gotta tuxedo, plug hat, fur collar, gotta No. 2 wife. Missy Luce velly plitty lady, makee talkee, plenty savvy. Henry Luce plenty big shot. Chucks his weight around. . . .
>
> China-Boy Henry born Shantung, speakee Chinee, catchee Chinee name.
>
> In Chinese Henry Luce called Fuey Pi-yu, pronounced as it sounds. Your nose knows what it means. Fuey Pi-yu means Henry Luce.
>
> Long time ago, Fuey Pi-yu came stateside to go to college. (Boola-Boola! Yale! Rah!) Never went out for football but got his letters in fan tan, mah jong and Chinese checkers. Sometime Fuey Pi-yu invented Timestyle, a nervous disease of the typewriter. . . . Life . . . began publishing pictures which persistently pressed toward absolute nakedness. . . . Life . . . began whipping and zipping around the place like a Peeping Tom's dream. It was such a peculiar interest, this picking bits of lint off the female carcass, this nagging at a loose string of womanhood's union suit and winding it on a stick until the poor girl was almost stark naked, that people wondered and wondered.
>
> It seemed that someone very influential at Life had a slant. As though the boss had just found out something.
>
> Well, as the years went on, Fuey Pi-yu made just more money than he ever suspected the existence of. As he got richer and richer he began to sense, by the feel of people and current history, that an American, with all his money and his

peculiar principles and vanity . . . could become a kingmaker. He could put men in fear of him by dirty slurs. If he could make a President of the United States, that would be the next thing to making a King. . . .

After Mr. Willkie died, Pi-yu scanned the field and set a trap for Sen. Arthur H. Vandenberg. . . . If Henry Pi-yu could have put over Vandenberg he would have expected to be Secretary of State. He can't ever hope to be President because he was born in China. . . .

Recently a backslid Bolshevik named Whittaker Chambers turned up in . . . Washington.

To put it in Timestyle: "Fat-faced, vapid senior editor of Time Magazine, New York smear sheet of Fuey-Pi-yu . . ." Chambers confessed he had been a Communist Party courier and the Kremlin's contact man with officials of the State Department. . . .

Luce, who scarcely needed reminding of the international Communist menace, had the Chambers-Hiss case on his mind as he carried Dewey's banner in his magazines. If being reproached by Pegler for "dirty slurs" was an arresting experience, it had to be said that Luce did not deal kindly with Truman during the campaign, especially since he was the sure loser. As Time saw the President:

Harry Truman got sore. His talk was tougher than ever. His speeches were folksy but their well-hammered themes were fear and self-interest. . . . At a midnight stop . . . he interrupted his blistering attack on Congress to scold and silence a group of noisy boys. . . . In San Francisco and Oakland he was bitterly disappointed by unenthusiastic audiences . . . But Candidate Truman was most infuriated by Candidate Tom Dewey's refusal to take his bait and get into a slugging match with him. . . .

[Meanwhile] Harry Truman had to make some kind of show of being President. . . . Truman's unbroken fealty to the Kansas City machine bossed by his great & good friend, the late, great-bellied Tom J. Pendergast. . . . There was not much left to the presidential campaign except counting the votes. . . . But Truman strategists hoped that their candidate still had a Sunday punch which would knock Tom Dewey off his high pedestal and force him to fight on Truman's level. . . . [When Truman] damned the 80th Congress and the Taft-Hartley law, nobody seemed really to care or to listen.

The campaign came soon after the Weekly Newsmagazine's anniversary mention of Time's fairness, its endeavor to avoid articles proving any special case, and its compassion about the news. Its compassion for the good-as-elected Dewey was evident even though Dulles was slated to be his Secretary of State:

San Francisco received him with open arms. An audience of 9,000 interrupted him 32 times with applause. . . . Tom Dewey had observed one salient fact. At every whistle stop and cattle crossing, the line that invariably drew loud applause was an attack on Communists in the Government. . . . Dewey cried: "The tragic fact is that all too often our own Government . . . seems to have so

far lost faith in our system of free opportunity as to encourage this Communist advance, not hinder it." . . . Tom Dewey was obviously gaining in confidence . . . He seemed less like a candidate bidding for votes and more like a statesman speaking not only for his party but for his country. . . . [He called for] "an end to the tragic neglect of our ancient friend and ally, China." . . .

A Life feature, "The Truman Train Stumbles West," listed the President's poor crowds and speechmaking bobbles. In Shanghai and other Chinese cities, Life noted, Chiang partisans were carrying Dewey-for-President signs—the first time an American election had so gripped the Nationalist interest. But the Chiang forces to the north were so rapidly crumbling before the Communists that one New York commentator described the situation ironically:

> . . . Mr. Dewey is supported by men—for example, Henry Luce of Time, Life and Fortune—men who are aggressive supporters of the military intervention policies of Generals Wedemeyer and Chennault. . . . [But] while Mr. Dewey has been running for the Presidency, Chiang has been running from the Communists, and it now looks as though Chiang would run to the ocean before Dewey manages to get to the Potomac.

Perhaps it was an omen that on the night before the election, thieves stole $20,000 in jewelry from the Luce Waldorf apartment. On election night at the biggest NBC television studio in Radio City, Life had the props ready to make victory visually memorable: a huge and expensive model of the White House rigged with a treadmill. The treadmill would be turned on electronically when the Dewey win became official and would show huge cardboard elephants marching in the door. TLF faces went incredulous as the night wore on in gathering electoral astonishment. The treadmill was never turned on because no one had furnished donkeys. The story of the unused elephants —one of those amusing human-interest oddities prized by editors—did not make either Time or Life. It furnished two entertaining columns for Time's competitor, Newsweek, and some outrageous fun in the New Yorker. Time essayed a stiff upper lip:

> The little old voter fooled everybody. . . . But politics is a show. Harry Truman, with his mistakes and his impulses and his earnestness, had turned out to be an interesting personality. He had often ranted like a demagogue. . . . [But] Harry Truman was now absolute boss of a resurgent Democratic Party.

In France, Wertenbaker wrote Mary Bancroft in humorous vein, admitting astonishment at Truman's election, aware that Luce had suffered more than astonishment, and venturing a political prediction fated to be confuted:

> The foe [Luce] has suffered a crushing defeat. . . . Except for short periods of reaction, such as '45–'48, and always barring a coup, I don't think there is any more room in our country for what he thinks he stands for. One man [Theodore White] told him about China, and left, and I tried to tell him about Spain. Why don't you tell him about himself?

272

To Luce it was catastrophic. Sixteen years of dedicated labor in the Republican vineyards—a bumper crop all ready for the picking—and the Dewey blight had ruined every grape.

A few weeks later he had recovered enough to write Mrs. Bancroft, albeit in a vein still reflecting shock. Like many in America, he wrote, she was deluded by malign forces in a time of political decay. But while he condemned the illusions which misled her and the American majority, he praised her spirit and ended on a note of warm affection.

3. USING THE DEVIL

A large part of the Bancroft side of the Bancroft-Luce correspondence leveled explicit criticism at the Lucepress for misinformation, quasi-information, fictionization and a general lack of the sense of responsibility expected of the world's most influential journalist. While Luce, on his side, sometimes expounded his political principles, not once did he discuss or defend his journalistic tactics. He seemed to avoid the subject. He did not so avoid it in talks with his editors, who were at his mercy as Mrs. Bancroft was not. He adjured them to take a stand, saying that mere fact without interpretation was empty, an evasion of duty.

If the $215,000 Hutchins commission of twelve famous specialists had failed to convince Luce that his journalism could stand correction, it was perhaps fantastic for the lady in Zurich to think she might reform him. Yet she was no tyro, having written frequently for American magazines and for a number of Swiss newspapers, including the Neue Zürcher Zeitung and Die Weltwoche. She read voraciously, was well informed about American and European affairs, and her OSS experience had schooled her in the ways of propaganda and the manipulation of power.

But her outstanding qualification was honesty, an unerring eye for the phony, the half-true, the misleading. At times in her letters she took the artful line that propaganda got into his magazines because he could not watch them closely enough:

> . . . It seemed to me that there is such a divergence between what you really think and Time and Life, that it is a serious matter. . . . When I talk to you you throw out an idea—as an idea—something which is but an idea to you—and you have thousands of ideas—but your subordinates get hold of this idea and somehow believe in it. Since it is an idea and you had it, I should imagine that you enjoyed watching it become flesh and blood or at least printer's ink after which, because of the circulation and influence of [your] publications, said idea enters into the minds of people and does become flesh and blood with a life of its own. Yet it seems to me that in some ways all this is but a kind of trial balloon to you—and while in other times this is O.K. and interesting and instructive and comparatively harmless, right now it is deathly serious. . . .

She worried about the exploitation of mere crowd-pleasing "ideas":

> The other evening at [a cocktail party] I listened to [a Time editor] talking
> . . . it suddenly occurred to me that what I had overheard was him carrying the
> torch and believing in or kidding himself that he believed in just one idea of
> yours which . . . was but a small part of the world picture. . . . This dance of
> ideas seems to me a dangerous thing—the results touching on the frivolous. . . .
> It strikes me that it is the fractional part of your thought which is danger-
> ous . . .

Luce had perfected a method of propaganda that was to Pravda as a thousand flashing rapiers were to a clumsy bludgeon. In the end both methods had
the same effect, leading the public in the direction Stalin, on the one hand,
and Luce, on the other, wanted them to go. Mrs. Bancroft called it "this business of using the devil to fight the devil," and pointed out that it might be a
problem to see that "the user does not become possessed by the devil." She
worked unremittingly for the reform of Public Enemy Number One, trying to
transform him into the public benefactor she felt he should be, stunning him
at times with occult observations:

> . . . I don't love you for your mind, Harry, really I don't—much as this thought
> may insult you. 'Tis your soul I love. And I bet you don't even know what it
> looks like. It is blue, Harry. Quite light blue and there is a lot of white fog in the
> valleys of it. . . . If you don't believe me, the next time you are at a dinner
> party, turn to your dinner partner and ask apropos of nothing: "What is the
> color of my soul?" And see if I am not right.

She worked at intervals on his soul because of the contradiction she found
between his professions and his deeds. She proposed that he accept the Biblical injunction to "renounce the world," give away his wealth and become a
saint:

> I wondered if perhaps I couldn't find a worthwhile outlet for my talents
> . . . by forming some kind of international organization with headquarters at
> Geneva in connection with your soul . . . There is a fairly large group who feels
> that your soul is in danger. These people want you to put on bedroom slippers
> and quiet down; they want you to do little instead of big things. They want you
> to get interested in a butterfly or a mouse. They want you to take up with a fat,
> ill-dressed, noble, spiritual, but not necessarily stupid woman. As near as I can
> make out, the ideal woman for the purpose would be a cross between Mme.
> Curie, Pilar of "For Whom the Bell Tolls" and Mother Machree.

She was constantly reminded, she wrote him, of the power and responsibilities of his magazines, as when she rode in a Zurich bus and heard an English-
woman say, "All that I know, I learn from Time, Life and Reader's Digest."
This was as nothing compared with the millions of Americans who could say
that of Time and Life (let the proper proprietors worry about Reader's Digest). She picked on one of those swashbuckling imperialist articles in Time,

ripped out the page and sent it to Luce with eight statements or arguments marked. She disputed either the facts or the conclusions or both in all eight, one of them being Time's complaint that American business was not spreading into Europe as aggressively as it should. This, she wrote, "strikes me as simply not true. I think only of . . . Coca-Cola [which is] waging terrific war with the Swiss, which has reached even to debates in the Swiss parliament." Nor did she agree with Time's statement that ". . . the U.S. has not and cannot have a 'master race' complex or a 'lawgiver' complex." "I have heard the exact opposite opinion in Europe," she wrote. "Americans there, for instance, particularly in Germany, behave and talk exactly like a 'master race'—are often referred to as 'having caught the illness from the Nazis.' "

She expended prodigious effort in trying to blow away that white fog from his lovely soft blue soul. She felt him bristling with slogans and clichés about capitalism, and was annoyed at TLF's habit of linking "America" and "free enterprise" as if they were God and Jesus:

> Why won't somebody explain very simply so my elevator man to say nothing of myself will understand what the hell the capitalistic system is—not just "free enterprise"—but what it is and just how it is abused. The lack of so many people being able to see clearly on this issue which the Communists hammer at, creates . . . a tremendous undertow and drag . . . Communists are always whispering "This is an economic fight" and the words of all "rich men" become automatically suspect . . .

She resented, on a visit to this country, the Lucepress assumption of American superiority and America's "mission" to spread its superiority over the world:

> You know, Harry, if I were an editor I would save my ardor & my crusades for within the U.S.A.—and just do educational stuff abroad—and by educational I mean things like the great religions, etc.—anything that makes people [in America] realize other people think, feel & *are* different & have a right to be so. I could go on & on & on about ardor & crusades for "the enlightenment of mankind" *here* in the U.S.A. & I think to do it *here* is the only way to do it *there*. You know—lead by *example*—"Look Homeward Angel"—"People in Glass Houses"—all that stuff. You know, Harry, there is a premise with which I disagree as an editor—I disapprove of telling Americans how wonderful they are and for the following reasons:
> 1. It drives the really wonderful Americans crazy for really wonderful people know just how wonderful they are *not*.
> 2. It makes all the smug horrible ones & the ignorant ones more smug & insufferable than ever . . .
> As an editor you can look at America two ways:
> 1. The most wonderful, wonderful, wonderful place in the world full of the most wonderful, wonderful, wonderful people who because they are so wonderful can ride forth to throw their weight where I as an editor think is right.

2. A great country that can still be a lot greater. . . . we can't be moralizing at others 'til we moralize a bit at ourselves.

And she challenged that complacent phrase, "the American way of life":

. . . Before God I have no idea whatsoever what "the American way of life" is and I want to know myself—for myself—and so I can answer that absolutely incessant question from Europeans. I have found no Americans who can define it —and everyone I ask begins to giggle when I ask the question.

Wertenbaker, in the south of France, delighted by what he chose to regard as the approaching success of their "campaign," spurred her on by mail: "Attack him frontally. Disperse his center, roll up his flanks, and demand his unconditional surrender."

4. THE CHURCH AND THE PENTAGON

If Vandenberg had been nominated and elected, and his reputed choice as Secretary of State had been given his head, there seems little doubt that American billions would have been followed into China by American soldiers and in all probability by morally justified atomic bombs. In later years, in a statement evidently representing his maturest thought, Luce wrote that Chiang had not been given a chance, that, "as I am in a position to testify— the great mass of the Chinese people were not yearning for land reform or anything else," and that what the United States should have done was to "give full support to Chiang, including the use of American troops."

The newspaper Hsin Min Wan Pao would not have been alone in questioning his authority on the matter of what the "great mass" in China wanted or did not want. It appears that to Luce it was largely a simple religious-moral question, perfectly apparent that the godless Communists had no more justification in the eyes of man than of God, and that complex considerations of statecraft could not affect this. Had he lived in the time of the Crusades, Luce would surely have elbowed aside Count Raymond of Toulouse as leader of the first one. Yet it was perhaps tragic in its long-run effect on America that the Dewey-Warren ticket was not elected. The Democrats had been in power too long, Republican desperation and hatred were getting out of hand and if the Republicans had taken over the problem of China and grappled with it successfully or not the issue of McCarthyism might not have arisen.

To Luce, on top of the 1948 election disaster, his American-Century dream was turning into a nightmare in the realm he considered his own, China. At the same time, his mother was dying of cancer at the Severinghaus home in Haverford. A secretary made three appointments for him to visit her but he broke all of them on the score of the press of business. Knowing as he did that she was not entirely approving of his course and had some fears for his soul, perhaps he blanched at the thought of a final interview. She died on Novem-

ber 6 at the age of seventy-seven, only a few days after that catastrophic election.

After attending the funeral near Utica, he went on to Milwaukee where he startled the United Council of Church Women by urging them to collaborate closely with the Pentagon in making war decisions against the Soviet evil:

> . . . I believe that once the Church has accepted its responsibility, it will be in a position to make its voice clear and strong so that the war-making power of our nation is put under Christian judgment, Christian restraint—and the courage of Christian conviction. . . . This is fundamental but I believe the Church can then go even further and lay down principles as to how we fight. In order to do this—is it hopelessly visionary?—I see the great leaders of our Church sitting down with our top military men and viewing them not as the enemies of society but as men who as much as any layman desire to do the right as God gives them to see the right.

He could hardly have been more frighteningly specific about his sense of religious-moral crusade and his linking of American policies with his own view of religion. The news headlines must have struck him like blows. Eric Sevareid, for example, commented on the dispatch of William Bullitt to China once more, this time representing the Republican-controlled watchdog committee examining foreign spending—an idea some thought to be Luce's, or at least inspired by the Bullitt piece in Life:

> This mission can only result in a report, Congressional speeches, and pressure from the Luce publications, all insisting on heavy American expenditures to keep Chiang Kai-shek's government from complete collapse. Chiang now has his back to the wall, politically as well as militarily. There are food riots in his capital city of Nanking now. Mobs are roaming the streets there and in Hankow and Shanghai. Foreigners are beginning to pour out of those cities. Strikes are spreading as hunger and fear are spreading.

The rosy latter-day speculations about the benefits that might have derived if America had stood clear of the Chinese civil war and had given early recognition and aid to the Mao regime include the possibilities that neither the Korean nor Vietnam wars would have occurred, that the Soviet-Chinese split would have taken place far earlier and that America would be the unquestioned world leader with unblemished moral reputation. One need not accept this picture, but it can scarcely be rejected out of hand in toto.

In December, Madame Chiang visited Washington again in a last desperate bid for more American millions. The glitter of her 1943 image had faded and the press treated her with the offhand attention given the representative of a lost cause. By now she was so inseparably linked with Luce that a WOR newscast said, "Henry Luce and former Ambassador William Bullitt are said to be behind Madame Chiang Kai-shek's fund-raising mission here." And Walter Winchell, still feuding with Time, announced, "Madame Chiang Kaishek is seeking an estate in Conn., near the Henry (Time) Luces. Just in case

her husband's regime falls." Life's full-length picture of Madame showed her in a silk gown with open-toed high-heeled pumps and a sumptuous beaver coat. ". . . it was impossible to say," Life commented bitterly, "whether her smile was hope or merely bravery."

5. EIGHTY-FOUR IMPORTANT PEOPLE

When Winston Churchill reached New York in March 1949, after being feted in Washington, he lodged with his friend Bernard Baruch but was otherwise appropriated by Luce, who had become his chief literary employer and had made him rich. Luce arranged (and paid for) not one but two great private dinners for him. The first, at the Ritz-Carlton, was attended by 220 distinguished people from all professions, not forgetting a group of TLF's biggest advertisers and the admen who handled their accounts. Probably Churchill had no idea that his prestige was helping Lucepress space salesmen to sell advertising.

The second, four days later at the Union Club on Park Avenue, was an intimate affair with only nineteen guests, all of them TLF editors and writers except Churchill himself. It was said that there were Time-Lifers who would have sold their immortal souls for invitations. Attendance was at once a tip-off on the current pecking order and a reward for good work, while the non-attendance of some indicated their occupancy of the Luce doghouse or, as it was called, being "strategically diminished" by the Boss. A couple of those being diminished this time were Noel Busch and John Davenport, both of whom had attended a Luce dinner for Churchill during his 1946 visit.

Tension rose as the upper editorial echelon awaited the selection of the seventeen (besides Churchill and Luce) who would attend. About a few members of Luce's inner Cabinet—Billings, Matthews, Alexander and Longwell—there was never any doubt, but around the fringes there was bound to be either joy or tragedy. Billings, long since installed as Luce's editorial prime minister, sweated over the choice with the Boss, and it was done. Churchill at the table was flanked by the Messrs. Ways and Osborne, regarded as Luce's foreign minister and minister of war respectively, both familiar with London and with British politics. Directly across from him was Luce, flanked by Matthews and John K. Jessup. At the last moment, to the displeasure of some of the others, Luce decided that a place must be made for Willi Schlamm. Schlamm had not fought his way up the ladder like the rest and was regarded as a backscratcher. His name being German for "mud," there were occasional witticisms, one of them being, "Harry is stuck in the mud."

Luce, the blunderer in parlor social contact, was at his best in the formalities of a stated program. He made a graceful little speech, to which Churchill responded with his rumbling eloquence. The great man relaxed later over brandy and cigars, admitted that he had enjoyed the repast and

said, "My tastes are simple. I like only the best." The editors attending would not soon forget the occasion, nor could they forget that Luce was one of the few men in the world who could summon such gatherings. To his whole organization, even down to the telephone girls, it was a reflected triumph, one of those items of prestige that made TLF an exciting and "glamorous" place to work, and among the fringe editors left out there was perhaps the determination to execute such brilliant manipulation of the news that they could not be skipped next time.

To Luce himself, the greatest of promoters, the dinners (the small one cost him $1087.46, the big one almost $7000) were part of his calculated program of lion-hunting, of using the great not only for information and political leverage but to shed glory and profit on his organization and himself.

In April he and Allen Grover flew to Europe for more lion-hunting and (it almost seemed) to formulate American policy for combating Communism. But if he planned his journey as a Secretary of State would on a tour of exploration and inquiry, he worked harder than any Secretary of State. So did Grover, who served not only as Undersecretary but also, being at home in international society, as *chef de protocol* and arbiter of when Luce should or should not wear dress, something he was always uncertain about.

The overriding issue was the progress of Western Europe in combating Communism. One Lucean defect was growing: his impatience with people who could not grasp the logic and necessity of the solutions he prescribed.

The two envoys were scheduled to visit Rome, Milan, Geneva, Zurich, Vienna, Brussels, Paris and London. The journey was smoothed by advance planning by subordinates including clockwork precision of transportation, hotel reservations and VIP interviews at each stop. On this tour Luce had interviews, often at luncheon or dinner, with eighty-four important people, not counting Mrs. Bancroft in Zurich who had an importance of her own. They included (to name a few of the best known) Pope Pius XII, President Luigi Einaudi and Prime Minister Alcide de Gasperi of Italy, Prime Minister Paul-Henri Spaak of Belgium, President Vincent Auriol and Prime Minister Henri Queuille of France, General Charles de Gaulle (who had already appeared on Time's cover), General deLattre de Tassigny (who very soon would), Jean Monnet (later), the Duke and Duchess of Windsor (she had made it, not he), Winston Churchill (repeatedly), and Lords Beaverbrook (twice), Camrose and Kemsley. Luce made it a point on his journeys to list all the important people he had seen by name and title and pass it on to his executives along with his report on his discoveries. Few had any doubt that he took an ingenuous pleasure in publicizing his meetings with the great. He frankly bragged about it at his annual TLF advertising meetings. Part of his own prestige, he knew, was money. His huge payments to Churchill and the Duke of Windsor for their writings had made world headlines.

Time's Rome bureau chief, Charles Jones, never recovered his standing with Luce because he failed to meet him at the airport. The Presbyterian

Luce negotiated a firm defensive alliance with the Pope (a good friend of Cardinal Spellman's) against the common Soviet foe. Premier de Gasperi had already appeared on Time's cover as a reward for his resourceful battle to prevent a takeover by the Italian Communists. Grover, sitting with Luce during his interviews, was literally exhausted after one day of solid talk ended at six when the editor of Osservatore Romano left their suite at the Excelsior Hotel following his report to the Americans.

"Al!" said Luce. "We have two hours until dinner. How'll we make use of the time?"

During one dinner in Rome, Luce's curiosity was intrigued beyond measure by two Italian gentlemen at a nearby table who leaned toward each other as they talked with great earnestness. "Al, what are those men talking about?" he asked—a question Grover could not answer.

In Milan, with Cambridge-educated William Rospigliosi of Time's Rome bureau as interpreter, Luce conferred with officials and industrialists, then was delighted by the color and activity of the local fair. But his mood darkened when they dined. He had heard of the festive cake of the area, *panettone,* and had Rospigliosi order some. The waiter shook his head. They had none. Luce was incensed. This, he told Grover and Rospigliosi, was a regional specialty, something of which they should be proud, something they should never be without, especially during the time of the fair. The fact that they did not have it indicated a lack of efficiency or national pride or both. The missing *panettone* seemed to affect him as strongly as an error of state. As they left, Luce commanded Rospigliosi to tell the manager that this was no way to give visiting foreigners a good impression of Milan.

Charles Wertenbaker, having heard from Mrs. Bancroft of Luce's coming visit, held to his military design. He sent an urgent one-word telegram to "Colonel Mary Bancroft": "Attack." Her promotion to a colonelcy was a measure of the importance he attached to the skirmish, but it was one she had to decline. The relations between her and Luce, by mutual agreement, were always on a firm level of platonic-intellectual correctness, and to make it official when they met this time in Zurich, Grover was in the offing as chaperon. After their stay, the two Timen went to the airport to discover that their plane for Vienna would be delayed because of bad weather in Austria. Luce could not stand delay. "Is there a plane going somewhere right now?" he asked. There was one leaving immediately for Amsterdam. To Amsterdam they went, crossing Vienna off the itinerary and managing on short notice to have interviews with eight Dutch functionaries including the minister of finance, the *chef de cabinet* and the editor of Rotterdam's biggest daily newspaper.

In Paris, Time's bureau chief Andre Laguerre was Luce's companion in a call on President Auriol. Auriol had taken offense at Time's criticism of French colonialism in Indochina and, as Luce described it, "Monsieur Auriol sat me down in front of his presidential desk and in his native Gasconese gave

me a tongue-lashing for the best part of an hour." Laguerre later arranged a dinner for Luce and a group of personages at Le Berkeley restaurant, famous for its soufflé. The dinner was crowned by the entrance of the dessert chef carrying the soufflé, accompanied by the manager himself to confer special status. Luce, who had chosen this moment to make an informal speech to his guests, kept right on talking. The faces of the dessert chef, the manager and all the guests fell along with the expiring soufflé. When it was served, flat as shoeleather, only Luce was unaware of the culinary crime he had committed.

Much as Luce despised General Marshall for his failure in China, he generously gave *le plan Marshall* credit for holding the line in Europe. His report gave a special laurel to Italy, where "Communists have been totally ejected from the police force . . ."

In London, where he had a seven-room suite at Claridge's, he received kindly treatment from Beaverbrook's papers (as the Beaver always received in Time). The Daily Express called him "Vigorous, nonstop magnate Luce," warmly recalling his wartime service to England, while the Evening Standard noted, "He married one of the most beautiful women in the United States," adding, "He works incessantly; every luncheon is a business luncheon, almost every dinner is an occasion for entertaining politicians and statesmen." He took time for a hurried trip to Oxford, visiting hallowed "Ch. Ch." and taking tea with Lord David Cecil and Sir Hubert Henderson.

In London he had earlier played Chinese checkers with Walter Graebner and John Osborne. Graebner had been "boosted" to the directing of all European news from his London vantage point, while Osborne moved into his old post as head of the London bureau. Graebner thereafter found that he had virtually no new duties and that Osborne had taken over the old ones. Whenever Luce came to London, he saw that Graebner and Osborne visited him separately, never together. Now Eric Gibbs headed the London bureau but the situation was the same. What saved Graebner (who later solved the situation by becoming a prosperous London advertising man) was his continuing negotiations with Churchill for publication of his further writings, during which the old war-horse became friendly. He always sent his letters to Luce through Graebner, after first asking Graebner to read them. Luce never sent Graebner copies of his letters to Churchill, but Churchill always saw that Graebner got a copy at once. Graebner, who accompanied Luce on a couple of his visits to Churchill, found the press lord of Rockefeller Center so overawed by the masterful Briton that he was all but mute and very uneasy. It was the same in Zurich when Mrs. Bancroft introduced him to her friend Prince Constantine of Liechtenstein (whom he carefully included on his list of VIP's interviewed). At lunch the prince had to carry the conversation while Luce fidgeted, smoked and was visibly ill at ease. Although Liechtenstein's statistics were much less impressive than Time Inc.'s (population 12,000, no army, a nine-man police force), Prince Constantine, cousin of the ruling Fürst in whose veins flowed the blood of the Hapsburgs, aroused a particularly bad

case of social malaise. There was nothing to cross-examine the prince about. No power to be wielded or harnessed. Mrs. Bancroft was amazed at the extent to which the tycoon was intimidated by nothing more than grace and charm. Churchill's Anglo-American ancestry was matchless in its own way, and she came to understand that Luce actually had a grudging respect for Franklin Roosevelt's family tree even though he usually disparaged the tree by calling the late President "that son of a bitch."

6. THE "LOSS" OF CHINA

In China, Chiang's final rout was humiliating. General Wedemeyer had said that the Gimo's soldiers could hold the Yangtze with broomsticks if they wished. They melted away. "Why," asked Senator Tom Connally, chairman of the Senate Foreign Relations Committee, "if he is a generalissimo doesn't he generalize?" The Nationalist government disintegrated and a group of Chiang's generals skipped with $30 million in U.S. aid money. The defeat was not one of lost battle but lost leadership. Chiang, once a great leader but always a warlord, had been disowned by his people. Months earlier, General David Barr, chief of the American military advisers to Chiang, reported to Washington:

> . . . The military situation has deteriorated to the point where only the active participation of United States troops could effect a remedy. . . . No battle has been lost since my arrival due to a lack of ammunition or equipment. [The Nationalist] debacles in my opinion can all be attributed to the world's worst leadership . . . the complete ineptness of high military leaders and the widespread corruption and dishonesty throughout the armed forces . . . [He recommended withdrawal of the U.S. Military Advisory Group in China.]

Chiang's remaining forces fled to Formosa where, after slaughtering some 20,000 Taiwanese, they established a dictatorship. Here Chiang declared himself to be still the true leader of the people on the mainland who had repudiated him. On October 1, 1949, the Mandate of Heaven settled on the Communists (who theoretically disbelieved in heaven) as they formally inaugurated their government in Peking. The Russians, who had been studiously correct and could easily have recognized them earlier, waited until the very end before switching their diplomatic recognition from Chiang to Mao. Russian recognition was quickly followed by that of other nations, some friendly to the United States but following a course of international realism which this country now eschewed.

Luce's mien, as Matthews noted, was a bank of thunderclouds. By evidence available even then, he was totally mistaken in the area he considered as much his specialty as the Holy See was by Pius XII. The half-billion Chinese would have to go their own way forsaking God, the Soongs and the China

Lobby. The idea that the United States could dictate China's form of government seemed an extension of the old missionary-and-gunboat attitude. The Truman administration desisted from further interventionist effort to prop ruin.

The "loss of China" was a shock to America in some part because the Lucepress had given America a biased and misleading picture of personalities and events there. The Luce publications, because of his background and his preoccupation with China, were widely regarded as authoritative. The China Lobby which denounced the administration's China policy had no feasible alternative to offer.

The charges about the "loss of China" and the "crime of Yalta"—both led by Luce before being taken up by partisan extremists and even middle-roaders—were nurtured into noisy life by Republicans out of power since 1933 and rendered desperate by Truman's 1948 victory. One can imagine Luce seething on receiving the following request from the lady in Switzerland:

> I wish . . . you would explain to me about the immense mass of negative Chiang Kai-shek stuff that has accumulated in my mind over the past 20 years— based on reading & on-the-spot reporting *not* from liberals. I still can't make out why, *if* his government were not both corrupt & impotent, it fell.

XXIV

1. TIME MARXES ON

The Chambers-Hiss case occurred at a time when its shock value brought a great, though dangerous, political benefit to Luce and the Republicans. Chambers's skills, since his shift from FN, had made him indispensable in handling tricky cultural or religious subjects for Time or Life. Almost invariably he got anti-Communist propaganda into them. One of his recent assignments for Life, done at Luce's suggestion, was "The Devil," a long and clever sketch of the Fiend which made plain his presence on the side of the malign forces favoring Communism and threatening what the Lucepress always called Western Civilization. Chambers was a $23,000-a-year man, emotionally and pietistically close to Luce. It was at one of their drugstore coffee chats that he informed Luce that he had been called to testify as an admitted ex-Communist before the House Committee on Un-American Activities and suggested that because of the adverse publicity, Luce would not want him as an editor any longer.

"Nonsense," Luce replied. "Testifying is a simple patriotic duty." °

According to Chambers himself—a man not addicted to simple truth—Luce sometime later took him and a third man, a European whom Chambers hid under the fictitious name of Smetana, to dinner. Chambers told them that Mrs. Philip Jessup, wife of the Truman-appointed delegate to the United Nations, had been trying to "get me off Time" and went on, "Luce was baffled by the implacable clamor of the most enlightened people against me. 'By any Marxian pattern of how classes behave,' he said, 'the upper classes should be

---

° This and following quotations are from *Witness*, by Whittaker Chambers (Random House, N.Y. 1952).

for you and the lower classes should be against you. But it is the upper class that is most violent against you. How do you explain that?'

" 'You don't understand the class structure of American society,' said Smetana, 'or you would not ask such a question. In the United States, the working class are Democrats. The middle class are Republicans. The upper class are Communists.' "

This kind of straight-faced simplism was as characteristic of Chambers as it was of Luce and the Lucepress. Was Smetana a real person—perhaps Schlamm?—or just one of those handy phantoms—a Disembodied Voice—Chambers and Time ushered before the reader for the purpose of making propagandist points? Chambers's account continued:

> When Smetana presently rose to go, I started to leave with him. Luce drew me back. Alone, we sat facing each other across a low table. Neither of us said anything. He studied my face for some time as if he were trying to read the limits of my strength. "The pity of it is," he said at last, "that two men [Chambers and Hiss], able men, are destroying each other in this way." I said: "That is what history does to men in periods like ours."
>
> There was another heavy pause. I knew that there must be something that Luce wanted to tell me or ask me, but I was too weary to help him. Suddenly he said, "I've been reading about the young man born blind." . . . Apologetically I said, "I haven't read Time for the last two weeks."
>
> "No, no," Luce said impatiently. "I mean the young man born blind. It's in the eighth or ninth chapter of St. John. They brought Our Lord a young man who had been blind from birth and asked Him one of those catch questions: 'Whose is the sin, this man's or his parents', that he be born blind?' Our Lord took some clay and wet it with saliva and placed it on the blind man's eyes so that they opened and he could see. Then Our Lord gave an answer, not one of His clever answers, but a direct, simple answer. He said: 'Neither this man sinned nor his parents, but that the works of God should be made manifest in him.' "
>
> Slowly, there sank into my mind the tremendous thing that Luce was saying to me, and the realization that he had brought me there so that he could say those words of understanding kindness. He was saying: "You are the young man born blind. All you had to offer God was your blindness that through the action of your recovered sight, His works might be made manifest."
>
> In the depths of the Hiss case, in grief, weakness and despair, the words that Luce had repeated to me came back to strengthen me.

Chambers resisted any inclination he might have had to play down his own role in this drama of history. He did not recognize the tests of truth observed by ordinary men. His career with the Communists as well as with Time Inc. had shown him to be as imbued with historic mission as Luce, without the slightest doubt of his authority and indeed his sacred duty to revise mere fact into a higher truth. As for Luce, his show of sympathy for both men—Hiss as well as Chambers—was one of those rare flashes of warmth that could be so winning. To the journalist and power-seeker in him, the Chambers-Hiss case

was unmatched in the scope it offered for propaganda. It was divinely constructed to please God and help the Republicans. It had side drama which, with apocalyptic interpretation, could be ballooned into motifs enhancing the central theme. Hiss, the accused Communist spy, had been a functionary with Roosevelt's entourage at Yalta. He had been secretary of the San Francisco Conference which drafted the United Nations charter. He was a friend of Secretary of State Acheson, who had been a law partner of Hiss's brother Donald and who was a constant Luce target because he had allegedly quit on Chiang.

The Lucepress had long since given over its praise for the treaty Stalin gave Chiang's China as a result of the Yalta agreements. It had become a Republican article of faith that Yalta was a Rooseveltian-Democratic crime. There was a united Republican effort to stress Hiss's presence at Yalta and make his role appear more important than it was. The same was true of Hiss's more responsible position at San Francisco. And the Republican propaganda possibilities in the Acheson-Hiss friendship, what with the increasingly malevolent use of guilt by association, were obvious.

Luce joined his party in an effort to portray Alger Hiss as the logical fruit of the Democratic administrations which had been in power since 1933 and which had allegedly been soft on Communism and had sold out China to the Russians. The British observer Alistair Cooke, amazed at American political violence, wrote:

> If we [the United States] are now baited in every direction by the Russians, it does not satisfy Americans to say that this is the turn of history. It must mean that somebody entrusted with our welfare betrayed us or blundered. A nation with a religious trust in progress simply cannot admit that even when the best is done, hard times may follow. In such a nation no man's honor is above suspicion.

James Bell of Time was assigned to provide all-out coverage of the Hiss case during both trials. His intensive day-by-day account, running to as much as 7000 words a day, was not for publication but for the information of Luce and others in the front office, and also served as the grist from which Duncan Norton-Taylor, who was then National Affairs editor, would grind his weekly Time account.

When Chambers testified that he had been a Communist courier dealing with Hiss, and Walter Winchell began a delighted campaign of suggestion in the Hearst press that Time had been "run" by a Communist, Chambers became an embarrassment. Luce had known that Chambers was a former Communist but not that he had been an active member of a spy network. His resignation was hastily accepted, but Luce made a generous settlement on him.

"Gee Whittaker!" said Winchell in his column. "Time Marxes on." He repeatedly said that Chambers had "edited" Time instead of being one of six senior editors working under a managing editor who in turn worked under

Luce: "Timemag . . . was edited all these years by Whittaker Chambers, self-confessed Communist, accused perjurer and Russian spy! Time botches on!" The report that the Soviet spy Vladimir Gubitchev would be deported back to Russia brought the Winchell comment, "Too bad. He would've made a wonderful Senior Editor at Time." He inquired, "How can we get the Communists out of the State Dep't when we can't get them out of Time Mag's editorial dept?" All this was in reply to a steady Lucepress disparagement of the Hearst press and of Winchell himself. In one month he made forty-seven such derisive remarks concerning Luce or Time and their Communist editor-writer, all of them reported on by a Time factotum set to watch him. When Winchell mistakenly reported that Luce had donated $50,000 to the Republican Party, he received a chilly letter from Allen Grover informing him that this amounted to an accusation that Luce had violated the Hatch Act which put a $5000 limit on donations. Winchell made a quick correction in his column.

The Lucepress coverage of the trial scarcely achieved its ideal of fairness. Life ran one two-page feature by Bell devoted solely to ridiculing the psychiatrist Carl Binger, a witness who had described Chambers as a "psychopathic personality," even to the extent of running an unflattering picture of Dr. Binger with the caption, "Psychiatrist Binger assumes professional air." Time likewise derided Binger and presented the federal prosecutor, Thomas Murphy, as the guardian of national virtue. Both Time and Life referred with constant affection to him as "Tom Murphy," as they had to Tom Dewey. They did not report Tom Murphy's embarrassment when he attacked Dr. Philip Jessup, who had supported Hiss's reputation, as a member of such subversive groups as the Institute of Pacific Relations, and discovered from the defense attorney (who got no friendly nickname treatment) that other subversives in that organization were Newton Baker, President Gerard Swope of General Electric and, of all people, Henry Luce. Time assiduously placed Hiss at the President's side at Yalta (". . . an adviser to Franklin Roosevelt at Yalta." ". . . at Yalta, he sat at Franklin Roosevelt's shoulder"). Time made evident in subtly non-libelous ways its belief in Hiss's guilt long before he was convicted.

After the verdict, reporters swarmed around Acheson. The Secretary, contemptuous of the methods of the attackers, was man rather than diplomat when he responded not with the expected bromide but with his famous statement in which he pointed out that Hiss's case was under appeal and therefore still before the courts, that "I do not intend to turn my back on Alger Hiss," and gave his reason in a reference to the Bible. Time stretched the facts visibly when it reported that "Acheson went to the defense" of Hiss. It said a "roar of indignation rose from Capitol Hill" and listed roars from a group headed by Congressman Richard Nixon, the young Californian who had given his political career a momentous boost by his ardent pursuit of Hiss, and who called Acheson's statement "disgusting." Time urged its readers not to make

the error of believing that only Alger Hiss had been on trial but that Hiss, in some manner not clearly defined, blighted all the Democrats:

> Within a span of six hours one day last week, the case of the U.S. *v.* Alger Hiss became a major political issue . . . [To] defend Acheson was to defend Alger Hiss. . . . Acheson, borrowing a scandal from the Roosevelt Administration, had hung Hiss so tightly around the Truman Administration's neck that it would be next to impossible to shake him off.

The anti-Communist crusade was already so disfigured by hysteria and expediency that it drove some thoughtful people into fellow-traveling postures simply out of indignation, Samuel Grafton wrote after Life had published a new Communist exposé, running the photographs of fifty alleged American Communists or Comsymps. Between the two great parties, the Communist issue had taken on the overtones of emotion and religion which both Luce and Chambers saw in it and which would militate against a rational American policy toward it. Both parties were "against" Communism. But for years they would quarrel bitterly about the reality and sincerity of their againstness. From this time on, the question of defining the nature of correct Againstness, and of analyzing politicians for their possession of this exact degree of Againstness, and their past records on the question of Againstness and also the records of their friends and associates, and even of disagreement among experts on how some people stood in Againstness, would take precedence over more constructive political pursuits.

Three weeks after Hiss's conviction, that pioneer of Lucepress Againstness, Laird Goldsborough, now forty-seven, plunged to his death from his ninth-floor office in the Time-Life Building, wearing overcoat, rubbers, Homburg hat and gold-mounted cane. In his pocket was a note giving his Fifth Avenue home address and asking that his wife be notified. After his wartime service with the OSS he had since used the rented office as a free-lance writer for Reader's Digest and other magazines. His falling body struck a pedestrian a glancing blow, lighting near the building entrance Luce used. Myron Weiss, Goldy's old associate, recalled that he had had a gothic imagination and might not have been free from a wish to dramatize his death in the mind of his former employer and friend. Luce, who had been generous to him, was shaken. The tragedy weighed on his conscience and he talked about it occasionally with Max Ways, one of Goldsborough's FN successors, wondering whether he had let Goldy down.

2. GOD HAS HIS TV ON YOU

When Mary Bancroft read Whittaker Chambers's account in the Saturday Evening Post containing his grandiloquent "letter to his children," she wrote

Luce, "I felt I was swimming in swill." Chambers was, she felt as a long student and friend of Jung, "emotionally ill," a man writing "statements in . . . maudlin prose which simply are not true":

> . . . I think [Chambers] does more harm than good and I think he makes thousands of people who, but for him, would not even question Hiss's guilt, send up secret prayers to Heaven that Hiss somehow will be cleared—or what is even worse, say to themselves: "Well, all I know is, *I* would rather live in slavery under Alger Hiss, than in freedom beside Whittaker Chambers. . . . To me he is as dangerous as an individual as Germany is as a nation . . . he mucks up the whole issue and I am disgusted with the Satevepost for giving him all that space . . . what is happening is that Chambers is making [some people] swing toward Alger Hiss in dangerous ways. . . . I wish Mrs. Roosevelt had "caught" Alger Hiss—and the FBI had "caught" Chambers—then the two issues would never have become melted together in their present dangerous way. . . .
>
> I think every time Chambers opens his mouth—verbally or on paper, in any way—he does harm to Western Civilization.

She had faith in her ability to "enlighten" Luce. She poked fun at him when he thought of running for the Senate. While Hiss was on trial, and Clare withdrew from the Connecticut race after being considered a contender, Luce was strongly tempted and his name was in headlines for some days. Some of his colleagues urged him against it, and Mary could not check her amusement at the thought of Candidate Luce attending rallies, shaking hands and kissing babies, nor did he seem likely to retain any last vestige of journalistic open-mindedness if elected. It was not these considerations, however, but a poll showing him very unlikely to win that caused his withdrawal.

More and more in his speeches he was taking the almost explicit stand that America as God's nation must be ready to destroy that work of the devil, Soviet Russia. On February 18, 1950, he traveled to Harrisburg to honor the "strapping affable redhead" Governor Duff in a speech ironically billed as a plea for tolerance. America, he said, was founded in reverence for God and the moral law:

> It is precisely this article of faith that is most relentlessly attacked by Soviet Communism. . . . We are in very great trouble today, we and the whole of mankind. The organized form of that trouble is easy to name. It is Soviet Communism.

He quoted his venerated Teddy Roosevelt, who had said that peace was of no value "unless it comes as the handmaid of righteousness," Luce adding, "We shall be prepared to sacrifice" for American ideals that "can only be known by faith."

Two days later, exhausted by work, the Chambers-Hiss ordeal, the sniping of Walter Winchell, the nail-biting about the Senate, the loss of China and his pervasive fear and hatred of world Communism, he boarded a train alone for Charleston. He read Mary's last letter and reread some earlier ones as he

rolled southward. Reaching his destination, Yeaman's Hall Club near Charleston, he wrote her an eight-page letter—remarkable for him.

He had been thinking about her, he wrote as he reread her letters, which he found fascinating. But he was provoked by her appraisal of the Hiss-Chambers case. She might have been kinder, he thought, since Chambers was a former associate of his and was undergoing a fierce ordeal—as Hiss was also, he added. Luce said his enemies were all on Hiss's side, not to mention some deluded friends, and he thought it amusing to find Mary joining the choir of sentimental unreason headed by Eleanor Roosevelt. Some day, he went on, she would have to explain why she could be so unexcited about Communism, brutal and bestial as it was. And, in a sudden plunge into despair, he said she ought to write and instruct him as to what he was to do with the rest of his life.

He admitted that a part of the reason for that unhappy question was her derision at the idea of his becoming a Senator. It hurt him to have his friends regard the thought as ludicrous. Obviously he had been terribly disappointed by the outcome—perhaps his last chance for the political office for which he longed. He finished his eight-page letter, had a martini and a lone dinner at the club, then returned to his suite and wrote her a four-page letter to add to the first. Again he mentioned that, in their political disputes, she could be unintentionally wounding. But again he ended on a note forgiving and affectionate.

Clare arrived at the club next day to do some writing. The Luces had given up Mepkin in 1949, selling all but the central 3000 acres and the buildings, which they gave to the Catholic Church for the use of Trappist monks. The monks, who maintained themselves by their own labor, soon had altered the Stone-designed glass-fronted dwellings into cell-like cubicles and a chapel. They cared for the grave of Ann Brokaw and for that of Clare's mother, who had also been killed in an automobile accident in her late sixties and buried there. It was Clare's intention to join them there when she died.

Luce relaxed (if such a restless man could ever be said to relax) at golf, sightseeing and reading. When he heard that Billy Graham was preaching in Columbia, relaxation was over. His bureau chief in Atlanta, William Howland, was summoned to Charleston by plane. As Luce and Howland got into Clare's long Roadmaster, Clare said, "Harry, be sure not to drive; you don't even have your license with you." But no sooner were they on the way to Columbia than Luce took the wheel and Howland hung on for dear life for some forty miles as the car seemed destined for the ditch with every belated steering correction Luce made. Howland, knowing that Luce would enjoy it, had arranged for them to join Governor Strom Thurmond at dinner. They dined with the Thurmonds at the governor's mansion, where Luce was impressed by the efficiency of the Negro servants and was startled to discover that they were "trusties" from the state prison, one of them a convicted murderer. After hearing Graham's service along with the Thurmonds at the nearby audi-

torium ("God has his TV on you every minute," Graham shouted. "Are you ready?"), they picked up the evangelist and returned to the governor's mansion, where Luce and Graham discussed theology animatedly until after midnight, with not even the governor managing to get in more than an occasional word.

After being the governor's overnight guests, the two Timen drove back to Charleston, Howland again going through the knuckle-whitening ordeal of moving over while Luce practiced driving. As they wheeled southward in fearful zigzags, a siren sounded behind them and Luce pulled over to the side with difficulty. He was questioned by State Highway Patrolman T. J. Jackson:

"You been drinking?"

"No."

"Let's see your license."

"Well—I left it home in Connecticut."

"What's your name, Bub?"

"Henry R. Luce."

"What's the 'R' stand for?"

"Robinson."

Released on payment of ten dollars' bond, Luce relinquished the wheel and said very little as they drove to Charleston. Always the editor despite all, however, he did instruct Howland to get a story on Graham, which appeared a fortnight later in different forms in both Time and Life.

His Harrisburg speech, reprinted with minor changes in The Christian Century under the title, "Moral Law in a Reeling World," received ten angry attacks and no praise in the correspondence pages of a later issue. The Rev. A. J. Muste reminded him that in appropriating the "moral law" for America he had forgotten a cardinal point in that law—to have regard for the "beam in our own eye." Another reader thought Luce's readiness to resort to military force hardly Christlike, that Roosevelt was the man who boasted about "taking" Panama, and "what haunts me is that this whole attitude smacks very much of Hitler." The rest assailed The Christian Century for presuming that "America's greatest liquor advertiser" could claim moral authority on any subject, much less international affairs, one writing, " 'Moral Law in a Reeling World' is an apt title for the address by Henry R. Luce. As I turn the pages of Life, Time and Fortune I wonder whether anyone is doing more to send the peoples of the world reeling to destruction . . . ."

The Christian Century reached Mary Bancroft in Zurich, who read it and sent it on to Wertenbaker at Ciboure. Wertenbaker replied:

> I sympathize with your reaction to that speech. After reading it and retaining my lunch, I looked hard at the picture and I said to myself, said I: "That man is really sick." . . . Talking morals to men in stiff shirtfronts undoubtedly contributed to the illness . . . I was sorry to see that face because it has been hurt by a good many things, many of them avoidable and some reparable.

W. A. Swanberg

3. THE POWERS OF EVIL

The "exhausted" Luce resumed his compulsive activity the moment exhaustion receded. A speech in Bridgeport, another in Hartford, one in New Haven. Then, on May 25, 1950, a solo trip to Europe where, after picking up Andre Laguerre in Paris, he visited Frankfurt, Bonn, Düsseldorf, Berlin, and reached Munich June 2.

He had cajoled Mary Bancroft into meeting him at Munich. Wertenbaker, having heard from her about the coming reunion with Luce, addressed her as "Mme. General" and counseled impetuosity. However, Laguerre filled the office of chaperon at the Hotel Drei Könige. She noticed again, as she had at the time of Luce's visit with Grover, that whenever he was accompanied by a subordinate he had a majestic disinclination to bother with the details of paying tradesmen and hotelkeepers. He preferred to have his companion, in this case Laguerre, act as equerry and be ready with the wallet.

In the morning, she and Laguerre were having breakfast in the dining room when Luce joined them, scowling. He continued to be disagreeable until Laguerre made an excuse and left. "You and Laguerre seem to have a lot to talk about," he said. "I trust I'll learn how you've settled the affairs of the world." But he brightened up later because of a luncheon with leading businessmen that had been arranged for him. That night, after cocktails and dinner, Luce and Mary went to a carpenters' ball at a huge beerhall.

". . . Harry danced and flirted with the carpenters' wives, the livelier and more buxom the better," Mrs. Bancroft recalled, "while I hopped about with carpenters who assured me they had fought only on the Eastern front, never against Americans and never even 'im Westen.' . . . The only time I thought Harry had any fun was at that dance, and there he was really a way I never saw him except there—quite coarse, if you can imagine it, sort of tickling a squealing, plump carpenter's wife, a Tugboat Annie type, and ordering more and more beer and talking quite fluent German as he got more and more beer into him. He was really almost 'natural' that evening, and quite 'physical,' tickling and pawing, but never—interestingly enough—dancing with me. I was a 'mind' on this trip, and so he treated me."

The next day he was off with Laguerre for Strasbourg and Paris, making a speech at the World Organization for Brotherhood luncheon in Paris, where he let his listeners know that his brotherhood did not extend to "our enemies and those who are neutral against us." Returning to New York, he was on the job for two months before he flew to Denver to meet Clare, who was addressing a seminar at Aspen. He also checked Time's Denver bureau under Barron Beshoar. Beshoar had made dry runs to brief himself on scenes and buildings the "question machine" would ask about. He did well as he rode in from the airport with Luce until the Boss pointed at a large excavation which

Beshoar had neglected to investigate. "Harry," Beshoar said grimly, "that's a hole in the ground." Mrs. Luce meanwhile was telling reporters that U.S.-Soviet differences had no more than a fifty-fifty chance for peaceful settlement. "We may as well settle down on a total war-footing now," she was quoted as saying. "We should build up our strength and force a backdown in Kremlin policy."

Returning to New York, Luce decided on a "Sabbatical" of six months to a year for "travel and study," which Time's board of directors, heavily under his thumb, granted. There is some evidence that the forlorn "what-am-I-supposed-to-do-with-my-life" mood was not entirely dispelled. Action and adventure and important people, if not unfailing antidotes for the horrors, were the best he knew. He left by air for Rome November 3, continued eastward and bounced back from a severe fever in Istanbul by taking sulfa. He had allotted himself a fortnight to investigate Turkey, Iran, Iraq and Lebanon. His central problem was Iran, a scene of friction with Russia since the war. Its northern province of Azerbaijan had been occupied by Soviet, British and American troops during the war to assure a flow of Persian oil after the German destruction of Soviet oilfields. The Russians had stayed on and fomented sentiment for a regional government for Azerbaijan which would of course ultimately have become a part of the U.S.S.R. They had withdrawn after being condemned in the United Nations Security Council. The United States had swiftly moved in with loans and military and technical advisers.

The problem was to bolster the anti-Communist Shah, who had formidable opposition in his own country. Luce was checking on the Truman-Acheson policy of containing Russia, fearful that the fellows who had lost China would lose Iran too.

One of his first criteria for judging a nation's worthiness was its attitude toward his own. Turkey, whose modernization he had admired under the great Ataturk—one of his heroes—stood well here. "The Turks—at least the upperclass Turks," he wrote Billings, "really seem to feel that they have an affinity with America . . ." Because of his fever and his brief stay there, the most important personages he saw were a former foreign minister and the Turkish chief of staff. He took the trouble, as always, to check on Time's local stringer and found him good. Reaching Teheran, he called on Ambassador Henry Grady and was quickly surrounded by eminence. In Iran, as prearranged, he was in the hands of Max Thornburg, a former California Standard Oil executive, later petroleum adviser to the State Department and now a $72,000-a-year oil consultant for the Shah and a good Presbyterian.

"This afternoon a huge cocktail party is being given for me," Luce wrote. "Tomorrow I have an audience with the Shah in the morning and dinner with the Prime Minister at night." Next day he noted that "200 people turned up" at the party, "including . . . practically the entire government." The power of Time Inc. was not unknown in Persia. Luce was pleased that the Shah Riza Pahlevi gave him a ninety-minute audience. The Shah was under both inter-

nal and Soviet pressure because of the presence of a small U.S. military mission and a smaller group of American police specialists who were training Persia's gendarmerie. The military mission had helped to organize the army and to re-equip it with American arms. The Russians charged that Iran had been converted into an American military base on her border. There had been armed incidents on the Azerbaijan frontier, the Shah himself had been wounded by a would-be assassin the previous year, and he had outlawed Persia's Communist Tudeh party.

In return for his difficulties in behalf of anti-Communism, he expected a huge loan, far bigger than the State Department thought realistic. The Shah was doing a little pressuring of his own. Only ten days before Luce's arrival, a Soviet-Iranian trade agreement was announced, and at the very moment Luce was talking with the monarch, his government was ending the Persian-language broadcasts of the Voice of America. It was clear that he got his point across to Luce, who wrote in his report of the conversation:

> . . . [W]e have failed to convey either to H.I.M. or to his people any idea that we, the U.S., are serious about Persia. And perhaps we aren't. If we aren't, then it's worse than folly . . . Much better an honest "isolationist" like Taft than an irresponsible (if not worse) internationalist like Acheson. The *bad* internationalists will be the ruin of both America and the world.

Luce was delighted when Thornburg, who waited for him during his long audience, asked jocularly if he was taking over the royal job. In the English-speaking prime minister, General Ali Razmara, who was a national hero for his part in defeating separatism in Azerbaijan, Luce found the greatness he usually encountered on his journeys, writing Billings, ". . . the ablest man in Persia—a man in a class by himself . . . outstandingly able. . . . A prime candidate for a cover." Iran being under martial law, Luce received from Razmara a *laissez-passer*. With Thornburg as companion, he was flown to Tabriz, the mile-high metropolis of Azerbaijan, where they set out by car, with an escorting officer-interpreter leading in a jeep, for the Soviet border. As always, Luce wrote a travelog containing interesting observations and brimming with his boyish delight in such adventures. The roads were ghastly, the scenery much like Wyoming until they reached the border, where snow-covered Transcaucasian peaks pink in the sunset caused him to write, "This is one place where the Iron Curtain is breath-takingly beautiful." Iranian soldiers were posted there—Soviet soldiers across the river. One has a picture of Luce, his blue eyes icy, straining to glimpse his enemy and God's across the way. He wrote:

> Here for 100 miles south and 200 or more miles north is the debatable land between Asia and an indiscriminate place called Russia . . . here in spectacular scenery, the line is momentarily drawn . . . against the powers of evil . . .

In Tabriz they stayed overnight with the American consul. At the Ameri-

can Presbyterian mission in the same city, Luce praised these spreaders of the Word ("How very, very admirable!") and was pleased to find a nurse at the mission who had, a few years earlier, been a member of his own Madison Avenue Presbyterian Church and of course had heard of him. The old senior missionary told him that it was perhaps not quite as difficult to make converts as in the years before the war, when any Moslem who became a Christian stood an excellent chance of being murdered.

Going on, Luce and Thornburg had tea with the governor general of Azerbaijan. They passed camel caravans. (Passing one long donkey caravan, Luce could not restrain his curiosity and had the officer-interpreter stop and ask where they were going. They were en route to Baghdad to visit the Golden Mosque and other Moslem shrines—something that stuck in Luce's mind.) Driving eastward to Ardebil, they saw the Caspian and an international bridge crossing into Russia:

> When we came to the bridge, the colonel said that if we wouldn't talk any English, he would take us on the bridge. In the middle of the bridge was a high ironwork fence. This was literally the Iron Curtain. There we stood for a moment brooding and then turned back.

Had Hadden been living, he doubtless would have shouted, "Look out, Harry, you'll drop Iran." There was indeed a bit of the boy on the burning deck along with the Napoleon in Luce. With Thornburg he stayed overnight with a Persian major whose servant gave them vodka and turkey. They visited the mosque in Ardebil. They got stuck while crossing a stream and were soaked. Five days of this and they were back in Teheran, where the delighted Luce left for Baghdad and Beirut.

"On the basis," he wrote, "of a two-day rather low-pressure visit to Baghdad, I will not put myself forward as an expert on Iraq." Still, he was a quick observer and his tendency toward instant expertise was strong. "The main points about Iraq are quickly stated," he wrote. "The first point is about Jews and the second is about Nationhood." He was astonished at the Arab feeling against the Jews and against America as being on the side of the Jews, and he was indignant at the plight of the Arab refugees. "The Jews of America are always making a great hubbub about humanitarianism—the really great thing for the Jews of America to do would be to raise a fund of $1,000,000,000 to take care of the refugee Arabs whom they banished out of their homeland. Time Inc. would undoubtedly suffer Jewish reprisals if we took up the subject vigorously, but there is evidently need of some courage in this matter. . . . And in any case America—including American Jews—ought to be told at how great a price of American good-will Zion has been purchased."

This was one of those rare moments when he showed genuine sympathy for human beings. The warmth for humanity simply as humanity, quite separate from his usual concentration on power, was so unexpected and appealing as to underline its gradual disappearance from his consideration.

I am glad I came into [Beirut] from the East. When one flies over the last couple of hundred miles of the Syria desert and over the last mountain range, one breathes suddenly the air of a different world—the Mediterranean, partly Christian, modern world.

It angered him that the French had arranged it so that one had to have a degree from the Jesuit college in Beirut in order to qualify for the civil service. "This college is supported by the atheistic government of France—France being in turn supported by the U.S." His patriotism was always near the surface: ". . . [L]et me revert now to the deep feeling of pride which as an American we may have in Beirut University. Today, of course, it is a prime U.S. asset in the great game of world politics."

He attended the American embassy's Thanksgiving reception—coffee and cake, no liquor out of deference to the many missionaries there. Reaching Rome, he told William Rospigliosi that he had sensed an upsurge of Moslem nationalist or spiritual feeling and that he must talk with the Vatican specialist on the subject. That would be Eugene Cardinal Tisserand, an acknowledged authority on the Arab world. The cardinal was skeptical when Rospigliosi arranged the meeting and Luce told him his impression. Did Mr. Luce speak Arabic? No? Well, one could not learn much in those countries speaking only French. Luce had to admit that his French, too, was almost nonexistent. Cardinal Tisserand did not precisely say so, but he made it evident that a man who knew no Arabic and little French, had spent only a fortnight in those countries and had never been there before, was hardly in a position to say that there was an upsurge of anything.

Nevertheless, as Rospigliosi later noted, Luce was right, as shown by the Arab revival that soon burst out under Nasser. Luck? Many of Luce's colleagues believed he sometimes had a sixth sense about news in the making, although he was sometimes terribly wrong. When he reached New York December 1, Mary Bancroft had already arrived there to market her first novel. He took her to dinner and smoked furiously as they debated such questions as: Were the Republicans justified in branding well-meaning Democrats as Communists or fellow travelers? And was there not a possibility that these tactics would damage the Western civilization they were supposed to preserve?

4. SUCCESS IS HIS ELEMENT

Mary Bancroft, startled by the savagery of anti-Communism in America, wrote her old friend Dr. Carl Jung in Switzerland:

. . . Thanks to the fact that my family owned—and still own—"The Wall Street Journal"—and are in the Social Register and belong to the so-called upper classes, I am free of the suspicion of being a Communist. But almost ev-

eryone who expresses a liberal view or says a kind word for Tolstoi is in danger of being reported to the Federal Bureau of Investigation. A Communist witch hunt of truly incredible proportions is in full swing. However, I have several Communist friends and many Left Wing friends and they suspect me of being a "Fascist." You must be either a Communist or a Fascist. If you say you are a democrat, you are regarded as hiding your true feelings. . . .

Another thing that struck me was how much on the defensive everyone was. I would say, "These are pretty flowers." "Do you have better flowers in Europe?" someone would inevitably snap back. Everything American must be the best and must be recognized as such. A truck in the American Legion parade carried a sign "America—Love Her or Leave Her." And I was extremely careful to say I lived in Switzerland simply because I had a good job here—but if I got just as good a job in the U.S. I would return at once. Otherwise I feared being turned over to the un-American Activities Committee.

This was written months before Representative Nixon had told Congress that the Roosevelt and Truman administrations had not only permitted the government to become honeycombed with Communist spies but had failed to combat them even when aware of their presence. It was almost two years before Senator Joseph R. McCarthy was heard from.

A prime reason for Luce's later reputation as a mugwumpish Republican who could steer his party in benign directions was his alleged powerful opposition to McCarthy. A study of the Lucepress and Luce's own memos during McCarthy's four most fearsome years suggests an interesting reason for this misconception: The Lucepress itself, after McCarthy had turned from an exclusive preoccupation with Democratic "betrayal" to Communism and had begun to embarrass Republicans including President Eisenhower, began to dig into the Senator cautiously. At intervals in later years it propagandized itself as having "fought" McCarthy. With equal success it propagandized itself as having pitched into Hitler and Mussolini, to whom it had given steady aid and comfort, and it also propagandized itself as having attacked the Munich treaty which at the time won its sympathy, just as it later belittled the Chamberlain who at the time of Munich had been Time's cover boy.

The Lucepress's own retrospective morality and judgment was unimpeachable. Actually, it gave McCarthy more support than opposition throughout his career. In Luce's lifelong campaign to alert the nation against Communism, McCarthy for all his crudity was an effective successor to Chambers and Bullitt. The Senator, however, became an issue of such hot controversy that an editor so preoccupied with circulation had to approach him with care. "Half my readers are Democrats," Luce often said, not wanting to lose one of them. As one observer put it with only slight exaggeration, "Mr. Luce had a genius for reading the public temper. He wasn't about to stomp McCarthyism until he was certain that witch-hunting was no longer popular among his readers." A McCarthy biographer saw it from the Senator's side: "During this period [after almost two years of McCarthy] Joe had nothing but warm praise for Henry Luce . . ."

This was not because the Lucepress praised McCarthy—something it did only a few times—but because the two were shooting at the same targets and because the Lucepress dignified the McCarthy operations by reporting them deadpan long after the Senator became a palpable national disgrace. For example:

> Could Republican Senator Joseph R. McCarthy be stopped? After three tries, administration strategists were beginning to despair. Neither anguished denials of Communism in the State Department nor vitriolic attacks on McCarthy and his witnesses could quiet the uproar the Wisconsin Senator had caused.

The question of fairness was probably irrelevant to Luce since he felt the Republic to be in danger, as he did almost permanently after the war. His religion inevitably entered in also. He believed that preachers entirely lacking in distinction but burning with faith could sometimes be chosen by God to utter great revelations. From there it was a short step to the acceptance of a demagogue like McCarthy or a dissembler like Chiang as instruments of the Lord. The occasional zigzags of the Lucepress on McCarthy suggested also a Lucean ambivalence as to the best political use to be made of the Senator whose first sensational charges were so patently incredible that it appeared that McCarthy, instead of aiding Againstness, would make it look ridiculous. Luce preferred Richard Nixon, the smart young man on the make who was sketching a more plausible picture of the back-street Democrat-Communist liaison. McCarthy's pyramiding of lies seemed visibly absurd, a threat to Nixon's campaign of insinuation. In this early view of McCarthy, Life ran a worried editorial denouncing the "pro-Soviet" policies under the Democrats but denouncing also the McCarthy style of attack as a threat to national unity:

> The danger of Communism is real. And we shall not cease to urge greater efforts in fighting Communism until it is licked. But there is a right way and a wrong way to fight Communism. . . . It is wrong when all officials of a vital arm of government—the State Department at the moment—are subjected to virulent and indiscriminate suspicion. . . . The past cannot be undone. We Americans desperately need to pull ourselves together to wage really effective political warfare against Soviet Communism—now.

Astonishingly, McCarthy, instead of being squashed by the Senate, kept shouting and demonstrated a powerful public following. The Lucepress then retreated into its largely noncommittal reportage for almost a year and a half, only occasionally beating the Senator with a feather. It slighted the courageous effort of Luce's friend, Senator Benton of Connecticut, to take action against him in the Senate. The Luce sixth sense about news was generally more valid in sensing the psychic state of his readers—their readiness to follow some new political turn suggested in his magazines—than in outright political prophecy. It was, as Mary Bancroft described it, like a surfboarder judging the crest of the wave.

Luce and His Empire

The pragmatist Luce was watching the waves. His memos and letters showed his knowledge of McCarthy's extravagance along with recognition of the Senator's great service in spreading the anti-Communist gospel and charging a Democrat-Communist linkage as responsible for the fate of China. Luce also had his eye on Nixon. The young man was with the China Lobby all the way. Chambers liked Nixon, who had worked so dramatically for the conviction of Hiss. There were wheels within wheels here, for Luce admired Chambers and was thinking of taking him back when things quieted down and Walter Winchell might be expected to drop his tired attacks. Once when Luce returned from Washington in a Time plane, he landed at the sandlot airport at Westminster, Maryland, where a chauffeur-driven limousine waited to take him to Chambers's nearby farm. It would have been remarkable of them not to discuss the recently ended trial and the young California Congressman who had, so to speak, taken the tarnished Timan under his wing and made him presentable for public credibility.

(Unknown to Luce, Mrs. Bancroft had given samples of his handwriting to Dr. Oskar Schlag, who lectured on graphology at the University of Zurich. In Switzerland, graphology was taken seriously. Dr. Schlag knew only that the subject was an American, fifty-three years old. Judging from his report, one might feel graphology underrated in the United States. "The writer is an extremely self-willed personality," the 1200-word analysis began. "He is original and many-sided, highly gifted and very skillful in practical and organizational matters . . . He has sensitive antennae for the atmosphere around him . . . Success is his natural element. He needs it as a fish needs water." And the professor got down to details more directly related to Luce's involvement in American politics: "He will favor people who have won his affection or who have understood how to steal into his heart, for he does not possess a well-balanced judgment of people . . .")

Luce had blown such a monsoon of propaganda ever since the recall of General Stilwell as to envelop America in a steamy climate perfect for McCarthyist cultures. The Hearst press had helped, and the McCormick press too, as well as some independent papers even to the furiously right-wing Union Leader in Manchester, New Hampshire, but no American had so established himself in the public and official mind as the owner-manager of correct American policy toward China as Luce.

America's foreign policy had been bipartisan and successfully anti-Communist in Europe, but in China it had lost bipartisanship abruptly when it became apparent that Chiang's leaky junk was sinking. The Lucepress had shrieked in pain and fury against the Democrats ever since, with others taking up the cry. The American public in general, vague about China except for a blind confidence that China was a dear friend, was so shocked at the discovery that China was no longer a friend—indeed might now be a friend of Russia—as to seek scapegoats. Luce furnished them. Probably more than any

other single force, the Lucepress channeled the groping and disorganized emotions of American distress into McCarthyism.

Luce, like McCarthy, called down curses on the head of Dean Acheson, Marshall's successor. Unlike Marshall, whose seamed face suggested all the homespun American qualities, Acheson's glinty eye, upswept mustache and suavity matched the striped pants his job often obliged him to wear and matched also the Yale-plus-Harvard background so suspect to Middle America.

Also, Acheson dropped those three unguarded remarks that were (like Truman's assertion that the charges against Hiss were a "red herring") twistable and which were seized on and paraded before the public endlessly by the Lucepress. One was his statement that he would not turn his back on Alger Hiss. Another occurred after Chiang fell and Acheson said the State Department would "let the dust settle" before formulating a new policy, which could be construed as indifference and inaction instead of the reasonable caution it was meant to denote. A third occurred during a public speech when he neglected to include South Korea specifically within the U.S. defense perimeter, an omission which many felt caused the Communist invasion of that country. The Lucepress was unconscionable in its repetition of Acheson's refusal to turn his back, Acheson letting the dust settle and Acheson forgetting South Korea. Time and Life nagged about that unturning Acheson back as if it implied Communist sympathies or treason. They kept it up despite protests such as that of the New York Post: "If Life views Acheson's statements on Hiss as covert expressions of sympathy for Communism, Life really knows better."

Of course Life knew better. It was using a McCarthy tactic—the steady build-up of suspicion around a public servant for political purposes. When that master of the smear, Westbrook Pegler, called Luce "the master smearer of his time," he spoke truly if without sufficient self-examination. With Time's circulation almost two million, and Life's more than five million, and with each of them attacking Acheson almost on a weekly basis, the Secretary was under the most withering fire since FDR himself. For fifteen years Acheson had been a fellow of the Yale Corporation, an honor Luce still coveted and which may have aggravated the choler of a man so enamored of recognition. With help from other partisan publications, Time and Life so bemused the public about Acheson's crimes that his old friend and fellow member of the Corporation, Republican Senator Robert Taft, felt constrained to tell him that they had better keep separate during an academic affair in New Haven, lest they be photographed together to the Senator's political embarrassment. Later in the day, when they met in what seemed a safely remote corner, Taft relaxed and shook Acheson's hand—then froze as popping flashbulbs proved the corner unsafe after all.

In Washington, Representative Albert P. Morano, Clare's former political manager who had succeeded her as Congressman from her district, urged

President Truman to dismiss Acheson and "appoint former Representative Clare Boothe Luce as his successor." Clare was informed of this in Hollywood, where she was writing a screenplay about Pontius Pilate, whom she described as the "arch appeaser of all time." She agreed heartily that a new Secretary of State was needed but neither affirmed nor denied her own availability.

Luce still watched the waves. In the fall of 1951, a year and a half after the Wheeling speech—by which time McCarthy had questioned General Marshall's patriotism and talked of "20 years of treason"—he decided that the country was ready to turn against the Senator. His September 10 memo to Life editorialist Jessup said it was time to hit McCarthy with careful aim. The Lucepress thereupon took its most courageous stand. A Life editorial roasted Senator Taft for his link-up with McCarthy, called on him to "renounce and repudiate" the connection and went on:

> The cumulative debasement of U.S. politics has gone far enough. Somebody must forego the pleasure of further groin-and-eyeball fighting. . . . The nation owes no debt to Joe McCarthy.

This was followed by a less forthright four-page Time review of McCarthy's Democratic-treason campaign (his picture on the cover was captioned "Demagogue McCarthy") stressing the point that while his methods were wrong, his aim was good. The Senator was tossed a few posies (". . . an ingratiating and friendly fellow. . . . Joe was liked and respected in college, liked and respected in the Marines, liked and respected in his home town. . . . He dotes on children . . .") but was described as a politician in danger of discrediting a good cause:

> He bored in, hitting low blow after low blow. . . . No regard for fair play, no scruple for exact truth hampers Joe's political course. If his accusations destroy reputations, if they subvert the principle that a man is innocent until proved guilty, he is oblivious. Joe, immersed in the joy of battle, does not even seem to realize the gravity of his own charges.

Then the intimation that readers must not make the mistake of discounting Joe's cause because Joe went at it roughly, and the danger the cause was already suffering because liberals were turning Joe's performance to their own advantage:

> . . . [The] nation . . . had finally learned . . . that it was locked in a life-or-death struggle with world Communism. . . . When McCarthy first spoke up, Hiss, whose case Truman had called "a red herring," had just been convicted, and Acheson had declared: "I do not intend to turn my back on Alger Hiss." The U.S. people had just begun to realize fully the malevolence of the enemy they faced. Abroad, the West had suffered a grievous setback in the loss of China to Communism. The public, quite correctly, thought that someone must be to blame. . . .

Some have argued that McCarthy's end justifies his methods. This argument seems to assume that lies are required to fight Communist lies. Experience proves, however, that what the anti-Communist fight needs is truth, carefully arrived at and presented with all the scrupulous regard for decency and the rights of man of which the democratic world is capable. This is the Western world's greatest asset in the struggle against Communism, and those who condone McCarthy are throwing that asset away. As the New York Times put the case: "He has been of no use whatever in enabling us to distinguish among sinners, fools and patriots, except in the purely negative sense that many of us have begun to suspect that there must be some good, however small, in anybody who has aroused Senator McCarthy's ire."

This, Time said, was the real McCarthy threat—the misuse and distortion of his campaign by unprincipled Democrats:

> A very practical danger lies in this inevitable, negative reaction to McCarthy. The Administration supporters have gradually come to see that they could make capital out of "McCarthyism." If anybody criticizes the judgment of any State Department official . . . the cry of "McCarthyism" is raised.

The lesson for good Americans was clear, said Time:

> More than Joe McCarthy went into the making of McCarthyism. It would never have become a force if mistakes of policy had not led the U.S. into a position that alarms the public. . . . Some of the sentries of the republic were asleep after the war—and some are still drowsy. The finding that they were not traitors does not answer the charge that they were bad sentries.

McCarthy replied by denouncing Time for "degenerate lying" and by writing franked letters to many of the biggest Lucepress advertisers urging that they stop giving business to the magazines which were smearing him and paralleling Communist attacks on him. At Time Inc., where Luce's ability to sense the public mood was regarded as uncanny, it was seen that for once he was wrong. McCarthy was not on the skids but seemed more popular and powerful than ever. His attack was the kind that would have been expected to bring Luce out in full battle. Instead, the Lucepress withdrew to a safe distance. It played the issue very cautiously as the weeks went on, avoiding any suggestion that Joe might be dangerous, now and then slapping his wrist or patting his back and taking the general line that McCarthy was a needed balance against Truman's softness on Communism.

5. GOD IN THE ELEVATOR

It seemed implausible that the President who had sat beside Churchill at Fulton and had promulgated the Truman Doctrine and the Marshall Plan could reasonably be accused of insufficient Againstness. Yet the Republicans had succeeded so well that when Truman issued the Loyalty Order that put

more than two million federal employees under FBI scrutiny, he was quoted as saying, "That should take the Communist smear off the Democratic Party." But the Democrats never seemed able to achieve the all-encompassing Againstness defined by Nixon, McCarthy and Luce. The Hiss case and the turn in China plus the war in Korea had put them on the defensive again. A new sign of the retreat of the Truman-Acheson forces before the McCarthyite onslaught came when Dean Rusk, now Assistant Secretary of State for Far Eastern Affairs, spoke at the anniversary dinner of Luce's China Institute. He gave the first firm administration support to Chiang, saying:

> We do not recognize the authorities in Peiping for what they pretend to be. The Peiping regime may be a colonial Russian government—a Slavic Manchukuo on a larger scale. It is not the government of China. It does not pass the first test. It is not Chinese. . . . We recognize the national government of the Republic of China [Chiang, holding only Taiwan], even though the territory under its control is severely restricted. . . . That government will continue to receive important aid and assistance from the United States.

Doubtless this pronouncement, made in Luce's presence, showed the administration's recognition of the desirability of appeasing the powerful propagandist as well as the body politic. Luce, who presided, commended Rusk for his "strong and vigorous statement." Vigor aside, the statement was not only mistaken but was a mistake appalling in its consequences.

Dr. Schlag had found religion central to Luce's personality, writing, "[He cultivates] a kind of private *Mystik* which has a remarkable background . . . it draws its dynamism largely from a kind of consciousness of mission in which the strongly egotistical, narcissistic tendencies are mingled in genuine fulfillment. At the same time, it is an earthy and private religion which we encounter here . . ."

For years at Time there had been amusement or shoulder-shrugging at Luce's habit of riding up the elevator alone to his Penthouse. Jokes by the dozen had been made about it, including the charge that he was guilty of the ultimate Jim Crowism, refusing to ride not only with members of other races but with any race at all. It had been more seriously ascribed to shyness, ego or his need for three minutes of quiet before the day seized him. Few had ascribed it to God. This was a secret he confided to only a few persons. He prayed to God every morning as he ascended thirty-six floors toward heaven. He wanted no interruption. The necessary elevator operator had his back to him and knew better than to utter a word, although he did not know that if he spoke he would break into Luce's silent colloquy with the Almighty.

So there was, in a way Dr. Schlag had scarcely divined, a private quality to Luce's religion, even a quality of eliteness. The thirty-six-floor prayer was repeated when he went down at the day's end, and before he retired he invariably prayed on his knees. This routine reflected a deeply felt closeness to God. Some of his executives, without knowledge of the elevator prayers, noted this

celestial propinquity. The feeling of these observers that Luce seemed more privy to God's designs than others, may have been a correct evaluation of the demeanor resulting from this special elevator arrangement. Some of the less reverent called Luce's often confident opinions "God-Agreement."

There were many problems to be solved, for the Presbyterian General Assembly as well as the Christian Beacon had recently condemned his magazines for their liquor advertising, the hierarchy suspected him of the cloven hoof and the Christian Century critics called him a sinner. But his speeches and memos indicated that he received a large part of his divine counsel on foreign policy, especially the policy toward Communism. He had read Arthur Koestler's *Darkness at Noon*, with its chilling depiction of Communist godlessness and inhumanity, the state as an absolute end, the individual as a nonentity, stripped of decency and dignity by a secular philosophical principle. He had been moved to sympathy by the disaster visited even at a distance by this Communist absolute on Chambers and Hiss. To the godless State-Absolutism of Communism it was natural for Luce to oppose the God-and-Freedom Absolute which he saw in America. The God-Agreement of such an innately aggressive man produced a kind of religion in which the temperate and pacific were swept away by the jingoistic and militaristic—the church-in-the-Pentagon.

Not for him the gentle preachments of peace, compromise, negotiation and conciliation. Not for him the verse in Matthew about turning the other cheek. Luce could look up from the Bible snorting fire and brimstone. He could emerge from church at a full gallop with both six-guns spitting, Bowie knife ready for close quarters.

Samples of his God-Agreement appeared in an astonishing memo he sent to Matthews, whom he was planning to fire. The Episcopal Matthews, for all his political irresolution, saw Luce's error in his appraisal of China and understood that it was an error of faith over reality, a flat rejection of hard fact opposing him. As Matthews described it:

> . . . Long before China's defection—or kidnapping, from his point of view—into Communism, he must have misunderstood China just as badly as his hero Chiang Kai-shek did. . . . [O]n this one issue alone he went beyond the bounds of reason. At the climax he pitted his faith in the China he had known against the present facts reported by his principal correspondents on the scene; it was a heavy responsibility for a journalist to take, but he took it. When the facts were against him and he was proved wrong before the world, he had to have a villain, someone who could be held responsible for "losing" China to the enemy, and his villain was ready to hand; the Democratic administration in general, Roosevelt and Acheson in particular.

Matthews sent Luce a memo asking blunt questions about his attitude on McCarthyism, Communism and the loss of China. Luce's astonishing reply seemed consciously to uphold faith over fact and to relegate logic to subsidiary importance:

Your questions regarding my sentiments on Communism, etc., are good questions which have to be answered. They are also somewhat "infuriating." Any similarity between you and Mrs. Roosevelt is strictly coincidental, but I suppose what is "infuriating" is the tough persistence of individual points of view. Men today [as] in times past cultivate the illusion that we "think"—that we try to think "objectively," that we try to "reason together." But again and again it turns out that we are born a little liberal or a little conservative or a Buddhist or a Methodist. The only thing which seems to change opinion is *Event*. On the day before Pearl Harbor, William Randolph Hearst printed a long signed editorial praising the Japanese as "our" only good friends in Asia; two days later they were of course "dirty little bastards." . . .

In London in 1940, Ambassador Kennedy was sure the British would be defeated; I told him I could not match him argument-for-argument, I could only tell him I did not *believe* they would be, and so I prayed.

All this confirms the essential truth, as I read it, of the Bible,—especially the Old Testament, which, however, was not annuled [*sic*] but fulfilled by the New. That truth is that men cannot achieve wisdom by their own efforts, nor goodness. Only a great Event can change man—an event in their personal life (Nicodemus had to be born again) or their collective life (The Assyrians coming down like the wolf on the fold).

However, there still seems to be some "cosmic demand" that we should exercise our best judgements [*sic*], reason together, etc.

With this rather necessary preamble, I turn to your questions.

First of all, I dismiss your Question Three by saying I do not know how many Americans agree [with me] that the U.S. is "reaping the fruits of a disastrous policy" and this question is of very secondary interest. The right question is: "Is it so?" I say it is. For me, personally, if not as an Editor, I and one other man whose judgement I respect are a majority. And the truth will be made plain by wrath if not by reason. But it is precisely because it is our job to help the truth prevail by reason that I am constrained to answer your other questions.

1) "Should we be anti-anti-anti-Communist?" Yes. The Ship of Public Opinion, or of Man's Emotion, is always lurching to one side or another. . . . In my judgement as a skipper, Public Opinion, especially among the Upper Middle Class (much of our audience) has lurched to anti-McCarthyism. So we need to counter that lurch.

2) How do you "fight" Communism—in the U.S., except as McCarthy "fights it"? You do it in two ways among others:

    a) As Nixon has fought it (or as Judge Medina, or Tom Murphy did)

    b) By asking such intelligent editors as T.S.M. to keep awake when they read such things as Playwrite [*sic*] Miller wrote in the New York Times.

    c) About China. . . . I will tell you the sense in which we "had" [China]. We had in the sense that never in human history did our great (and racially different) country have such a good name in another country as the U.S.A. had in China. In a sense the "good will" toward the U.S. in China was "too good" to be true—but there it was. The hard pragmatic matter is that (to anticipate the second half of your question) a

305

government "friendly" to the U.S. might now be ruling in China which would completely alter the "balance of power" situation in the world, and, with this totally different "balance," there would be some sense in the Acheson-Kennan "containment" policy.

Might have been? Unless you believe in the absolute inevitability of history—fatalistically determined and with no objective room for "free will" or human "responsibility"—then nothing *had* to be the way it was, and anything might have been at least somewhat different. That is the purely logical argument.

But the reason I believe China did not *have* to go Communist was because I was there in 1945, and I trust my judgement *as a reporter.* (It troubles me that you don't!) My judgement in this reportorial matter is disagreed with by Lattimore and Teddy White, but on the other hand it is supported by others like Gruin. As for people like White, they *seemed* (honestly or dishonestly) to favor the Marshall Plan in China— but that certainly failed, and darn quickly. . . .

Luce's reference to McCarthyism suggests that he watched it much as a fireman inspects a boiler gauge and wanted the pressure to go neither too high nor too low. It had subsided a bit and needed rekindling. In his aggressiveness and strangely secular anti-secularism he found an echo in young William Buckley (Yale '50, Daily News, Bones), whose *God and Man at Yale* attacked Yale's depravity as shown by its declining interest in religion and its encouragement of points of view including anti-clerical and anti-capitalist ones. Luce, who was three decades and many elevator rides ahead of Buckley in religious experience, had for years urged collegiate and national glorification of God and free enterprise. One of his complaints about the Committee on the Freedom of the Press had been its failure to acknowledge explicitly the press's "responsibility to God."

But foremost was Luce's introduction of God-Agreement into world dialectics. In his singularly literal religiosity, he believed not only that God had founded America as a global beacon of freedom, but that in some manner America was justified or even ordained to spread this freedom around the world. It seems likely that the fate of China and the threat of Soviet Russia had combined with his undying American Century ardor to emerge more insistently than ever into the John Foster Dulles theme of America's divine mission to liberate the world.

6. IMPLEMENTING GOD-AGREEMENT

Few Americans seem to have been so imbued with a sense of global mission as Luce, or so confident of the nation's capacity to fulfill it. One hazard in establishing such close ties with God and capitalism was the tendency to exclude other gods and brush aside other beliefs. He moved into attitudes more

religiously aggressive as the Korean war increased his indignation. In spirit he was years ahead of the Dulles argument that the Truman "containment" of Communism was an evasion of the American mission and that the Communist countries must ultimately be set free. Luce sounded this theme with slight variations in speech after speech in 1951 and 1952. In San Antonio he preceded his talk with an interview about the McCarthy issue in which he said civil liberties were in no danger:

I do not approve of Senator McCarthy's methods. However, the democratic process always fosters movements which go a little too strong one way or another. There is always a counter-cry, though, and in this case the counter-cry to McCarthy is McCarthyism. . . . I think the Chambers-Hiss case will be important in the coming election. Chambers' witness to the dangers of Communism was probably the biggest single factor in making people take Communist infiltration seriously. . . . If you find even one Red under the bed—or in the State Department—you disqualify the validity of the term "witch-hunt."

At Trinity University in that city he got down to the nation's mission: "The greatest prophecy of our time is the prophecy of Communism, much greater because truer in its hideous falseness than Hitler. . . . It is for America to proclaim the new age—the Age of Hope based on man's amazing capacities and God's infinite Providence."

"The office of America is to liberate," he told the students at Lafayette College, where, along with Dr. Norman Vincent Peale, he was awarded an honorary doctorate.

". . . [A]ll of us here tonight are resolved, I am sure," he said at St. George's Society in New York, "that we shall not give up our mission to restore decent order and liberty in the world."

"I come before you . . . as a man with a mission," he said in Philadelphia, and quoted Oswaldo Aranha: " 'The United States which has disintegrated the atom has the duty now to integrate the world.' "

In Cincinnati: ". . . America, we alone, save for a few small nations, we alone enjoy life, liberty and the pursuit of happiness and are called upon, in such a world, to help to establish those conditions of freedom and order under which men may enjoy life, liberty and the pursuit of happiness. Yes, America has greatness thrust upon her."

At the College of Idaho, a Presbyterian institution which granted him the degree of Doctor of Humanities, he said: "God rules the world. . . . In His Providence, He calls this nation now to be a principal instrument of His will on earth."

In Dallas, speaking to a gathering of lawyers, he found an American flaw. He rebuked the late Justice Oliver Wendell Holmes, who he conceded was a great man but for his appalling agnostic philosophy, which must be wiped off the slate:

I submit to you today that we ought to believe what is true, and that the truth is that we live in a moral universe, that the laws of this country and of any coun-

try *are* invalid and will be in fact inoperative except as they conform to a moral order which is universal in time and space. Holmes held that what I have just said is untrue, irrelevant and even dangerous.

I submit to you further that you as lawyers have one urgent task more important than all others—to reverse Mr. Justice Holmes—and to do so for the sake of The Law itself, for the sake of the American people, and for the sake of our own individual peace of mind.

But some Americans felt that Holmes represented a freedom from a kind of thought control that seemed essential to Luce's peace of mind. Dr. Frank Kingdon spoke up against thought control:

This is a belief that Mr. Luce certainly has a right to hold. . . . But he is not satisfied with this. He wants it made the official American faith. . . . I want to point out the danger in this assertion that any particular religious philosophy or philosophical creed is American to a degree that others are not. . . . Not only Justice Holmes, but Robert G. Ingersoll, Mark Twain, and William James might find themselves unable to accept Mr. Luce's dogma of Americanism. . . . We have gone far in restricting civil liberties in these recent days. Far gone as we are, there is still enough of our ancient liberty left to withstand any effort by any man or any group to fasten upon us any religious dogma as a test of patriotism.

By this time Luce had reverted to his main theme in a speech to the Buffalo Chamber of Commerce. Whether or not his blizzard of speeches reflected a hope to be included in the next Republican administration, he was a man with a mission and he had long since discovered a great satisfaction in making public addresses and had grown skillful at it. He told the Buffalonians: "The American mission is to help to establish Freedom and Order in the world. Any definition short of that is certainly false and probably dishonest. . . . No nation can be allowed to exercise authority in the world which, for any reason, cannot or will not provide basic civil rights to its own people."

A local editorialist noted his "magnificent self-assurance":

Frankly, we were more impressed by that last than by his definition of America's mission in the world. The establishment of freedom and order in any given jurisdiction is, in a very fundamental way, the function of a government. To claim it as our mission to execute that function on a global basis is to suggest nothing less than giving the American Government a global jurisdiction. That, to put it mildly, is a rather broad rendering of the American mandate. Not to mention the fact that there are one or two governments in the world, still fancying themselves as sovereign, which might not approve the assumption of a global jurisdiction by us.

Life, whose editorial line was closely supervised by Luce, was mobilizing the nation for battle against Russia in frequent editorials and feature articles. It accused Acheson of an Againstness so laggard that he sought to maintain peace with the Soviet, saying that he seemed "to assume . . . a point at which accommodation, if not formal agreement with Soviet Communism would be

possible." This was not possible, said Life although Russia now had the Bomb. "There can be no compromise . . . which can enable the two worlds to live their lives in separate peace."

After the start of the Korean war, despite occasional ambivalent moments of pause, Life's jingoist tone was uppermost. It assailed the administration for letting "clichés become the basis of thinking on foreign policy." In subsequent issues it began biting the bullet: "The prospect is war. World War III was never closer. . . . At last we know our enemy. . . . [W]ar with Communist China does not necessarily entail involvement with its mass armies." ". . . [W]ar to the finish, war NOW." "The enemy of the free world is implacably determined to destroy the free world. . . . There can be no compromise and no agreement with Soviet Communism." Life asked, "Does it make sense to use the Bomb on the Soviet Union now?" and urged serious discussion of the question as it professed willingness to take on *both* Russia and China:

> In view of the declared enmity of Communist China and the declared purpose of Communist China to seize and dominate all Asia, Life sees no choice but to acknowledge the existence of war with Red China and to set about its defeat, in full awareness that this course will probably involve war with the Soviet Union as well.

Life seemed to count out the Truman administration and annex the reins of government itself in an editorial ultimatum to "the Kremlin gang":

> Our terms for coexistence are . . . very flat. The Communist imperialism and totalitarianism of the Stalin regime are intolerable. They must be replaced and their sign and seal, the Iron Curtain, removed. . . . [F]reedom under law is *everybody's right and America's mission.* . . . The U.S. has minimum requirements in Russia, but they are irreducible and mandatory: liberation.

Among its many editorials and articles discussing war with Russia and/or China, Life published an exhaustive two-part text-and-photograph analysis of "The War We May Fight," declaring that America could win by a strategy Life could of course disclose only in part. "We can stop the Russian steamroller in Europe with the strategic idea of 'spider-web' defense, imaginative airborne tactics and modern weapons," said the blurb. Life's spiderweb defense consisted in part of Allied "redoubts" in Norway, Denmark and the German Alps from which the main Red drive into Germany could be flanked and at the same time pummeled from the air with tactical atomic weapons. The article increased the impression of the imminence of war by lapsing from the conditional into the future tense:

> Eisenhower himself will direct operations in the Central Area: Western Germany, France and the Low Countries. Here . . . the West's fortune will depend on its ability to hold two crucial anchor positions: in the north, the Danish peninsula, with its base in Schleswig-Holstein; and in southern Germany, the Alpine redoubt where Hitler had planned to make his last stand. . . . The

ground armies thus will serve as the anvil against which the Red Army can be pinned while strategic air power, from its bases around the Soviet periphery, swings its sledgehammer.

Again, in one italicized paragraph, Life made clear its certainty about the inevitability of East-West confrontation, saying the sooner the better:

> *Someday, a president of the U.S. will have to take a fighting stand against Communism somewhere west of California. It will be better to do it today than tomorrow. It would have been better to do it yesterday than today. And a lot better day before yesterday.*

The Lucepress saw danger that Red China would topple dominoes in Asia. One of them, it felt, was quivering even then—Indochina, where only the French kept it from falling into the hands of what Life called "Ho Chi Minh's gangsters." Life turned that fateful corner at full speed in a long appraisal of Indochina in which Bao Dai was termed the "respected" ruler, French military stamina was extolled but readers were warned that "[the French] urgently need arms from the U.S. and the clear-cut support of American policy makers." Life stressed the domino theory almost three years before Eisenhower entered the White House, saying we must not make the mistake we made with Chiang, abandoning him because of presumed failings:

> . . . [T]he first political fact of life about Indo-China today is that the French army alone is keeping Indo-China out of Communist hands. That also means that it is the only strong shield for the weak governments of Burma, Thailand and Indonesia. That, in turn, marks it as the only serious barrier between Communism and the gates of India . . .

XXV

1. THE MAN IS GREAT

For the true believers, the mere existence of another group professing a different ideology is threatening because it suggests that their own may be wrong. An atheistic society that survives and prospers is, by this very fact, a threat to a theistic one, and vice versa. The mutual sense of threat is sharply increased if each of the rival ideologies requires its adherents to convert or destroy believers in the other, as has been true in the past of Islam and Christianity and, more recently, capitalism and Communism.

—*Dr. Jerome D. Frank*

When General MacArthur disputed American policy in the Far East and President Truman recalled him, Luce's reaction was predictable. MacArthur, who appreciated Chiang, hated Communists and wanted to attack the Chinese Reds, had been Time's cover man six times, his last appearance having been the occasion of a memorable tribute:

Inside the Dai Ichi Building, once the heart of a Japanese insurance empire, bleary-eyed staff officers looked up from stacks of paper, whispered proudly, "God, the man is great." General Almond, his chief of staff, said straight out, "He's the greatest man alive." And reverent Air Force General George E. Stratemeyer put it as strongly as it could be put . . . : "He's the greatest man in history."

MacArthur now made his seventh cover appearance, coming abreast of Chiang Kai-shek. He was also on the cover of Life and, it seemed, distributed almost throughout the magazine, corncob pipe, trenchcoat, battered cap and all. Time and Life rode the crest of the public adulation that surrounded the general on his return home—what some called the Second Coming. Luce was

311

among those few who visited him when he stayed briefly at the Waldorf, a group conspicuously right of center including Colonel McCormick of the Chicago Tribune, William Randolph Hearst, Jr. and Cardinal Spellman. Time and Life agreed that the President had a *right* to recall MacArthur and stressed that this was not the point at all. The point was, not who had the authority but who had the best program for America and the world? MacArthur, said Life and the Weekly Newsmagazine.

MacArthur had "the humility to believe in God," as Life saw it; ". . . for him it is impossible to divorce policy and action from moral principle." Senator McCarthy agreed, calling the President a "son of a bitch" in a Milwaukee speech. Senator Jenner of Indiana blamed Communists in the administration for the general's recall. Time gave its own perspective:

> Seldom has a more unpopular man fired a more popular one. Douglas MacArthur was the personification of the big man, with the many admirers who look to a great man for leadership . . . Harry Truman was almost a professional little man . . .

Time's own Tokyo bureau disagreed with the Boss. Its members threw a great "liberation from MacArthur" party which was enthusiastically joined by MacArthur aides relieved at the departure of the imperious general. Time in New York generously paid the bill for the bacchanalia while the Lucepress for five successive weeks covered the tumult and the Senate hearings, played up MacArthur's "There is no substitute for victory" and belittled the "professional little man's" argument: "We are trying to prevent a third world war." Luce seemed to regard this effort as evasive and pusillanimous. "You may not like him," he told the Lifeman Emmet John Hughes about MacArthur, "but he meets the test of greatness. . . . Whatever ground he stands on, it is *his*."

Thereafter he would deplore the American failure to bomb beyond the Yalu, to get after the Chinese Communists and to put Chiang back on the mainland, and would ascribe the American troubles in Asia to a refusal to face up to the problem as MacArthur did. He would lose confidence in General Omar Bradley, the chairman, and the rest of the Joint Chiefs of Staff because of their support of the Truman rather than the MacArthur view. The general's conviction of American invincibility and world mission was at one with Luce's as, in the Senate Office Building, he called for all-out battle against world Communism:

> I believe we should defend every place from Communism. I believe we can. . . . I have confidence in us. . . . I don't admit that we can't hold Communism wherever it shows its head.

There was no shilly-shallying here, none of those niggling doubts about jurisdiction or sovereignty. The reservations felt by Senator J. William Fulbright represented the kind of thinking Luce regarded as defeatist. Fulbright said he was opposed to Communism but was disturbed by the general's

theory that Communism anywhere and everywhere was our enemy. He had thought that Communism became a matter of international concern only when it destroyed world order by aggression.

"In that concept, Senator," the general snapped in nine words that Luce must have cheered, "I disagree with you completely."

From Zurich Luce received outrageous sentiments from an admirer of Harry Truman:

> I had thought of flying home, wearing a dress on which was stencilled "I'm just wild about Harry." . . . I hope you don't mind, Harry, that for the moment I am more in love with the President of the United States than with you. . . . I *am* just wild about Harry, that other Harry. I listened breathlessly to his speech rebroadcast over the American Forces Network—and swooned with delight when he said "blongs" (belongs). . . . If MacArthur, before Congress, dares to say one word against Dean Acheson or Harry Truman, I shall turn my concentrated hate, now reposing on Governor Tom Schmooey, against him. . . . I only hope that the whole MacArthur brawl doesn't lead to civil war between his supporters and those of Truman with the Russians being forced to intervene on the side of Truman. . . . I am very busy watering the pansies in my window box and working on my second novel.

Writing from Ridgefield, Luce could not refrain in his reply from saying that during the MacArthur fortnight he had had three letters from General Eisenhower. He asked how a person of such abilities and achievements as she could embrace such atrocious political beliefs. And his next letter declared angrily that in the MacArthur quarrel he was a gladiator in the arena whereas she was a mere spectator in the grandstand throwing ripe vegetables at him. He admitted that it irked him that she disagreed so heartily with his politics and he wished that she could assume a more neutral attitude. Although her barbs obviously stung him, he closed on a placatory note and pleaded that for all their differences they must nurture their friendship, which was important to him. This seemed evident enough, for it was unusual for him to accept such disagreement with anything like good grace—a point Dr. Schlag, the graphologist, had touched on:

> It will not always be easy to get along with him; he does not recoil from arbitrary behavior if he is convinced he is in the right; self-willed but also stubborn, the twisting of circumstances and facts are not unknown to him and when he is angry (which ought not to be exactly seldom) he can stage a formidable scene. . . . In the background of his personality are jammed up a mass of aggressions.

He was indeed indulging a mass of aggressions and staging a formidable scene over China. The Lucepress, which had long antedated McCarthy in these aggressions, fell in with the Senator in his baseless suspicions and charges leveled against a group of highly competent Foreign Service officers formerly based in China. Most notable were the charges against Owen Lattimore, the Johns Hopkins professor who had worked for the State Department

in the Far East and for a time had been Chiang's adviser. Lattimore, like his colleagues, had made the mistake of being essentially right about what was happening in China. The Lucepress treatment of Lattimore was in the best McCarthy tradition, questioning his loyalty in headlines ("WAS LATTIMORE A COMMUNIST?") and denouncing his thinking and his policies as dangerous if not traitorous (". . . more dangerous than a carload of spies"). Others, including John Paton Davies, John Carter Vincent and John Service, would find their careers ruined and their peace of mind and reputations damaged by continuing attacks and investigations abetted by the Lucepress. W. Walton Butterworth, who had also failed to see the divinity of Chiang while he was American chargé in Nanking, escaped suspicion of treason but was drummed out of his job as head of Far Eastern Affairs and replaced by a man to Luce's liking, Dean Rusk.

But the man who logged the greatest total of denunciatory Lucepress wordage was, of course, Acheson. At least one Old Timemployee was convinced that Luce's animus toward Acheson, strong enough on the China count alone, was inflamed not only by Acheson's membership in the Yale Corporation but by his possession of a social polish the fidgety Luce envied, and by a conviction that Acheson was coolly ignoring him. The thought that the Secretary was beyond his power to punish was infuriating. The publication of the White Paper in which the State Department explained (not without an element of the self-serving) the sad denouement of the Chinese drama, occasioned two bitter pages in Time blaming on Acheson what Acheson and his Eastern experts, as well as Theodore White, preferred to blame on inevitable forces of history. Luce always referred to it as "the Whitewash Paper." Time charged, "As far back as 1944 one [American] embassy report flatly declared the Communists were 'the force destined to control China.' " If this seemed treason to Luce and McCarthy, it seemed more like sound observation to those who felt that China's course could not be dictated by outsiders.

Readers of the Lucepress doubtless believed Acheson at the very least a fellow traveler instead of a determined anti-Communist aggressively surrounding Russia with American "containment" forces. The Hearst and McCormick papers were Luce's loudest allies in attacking Acheson. Life repeatedly demanded the Secretary's resignation, sometimes in language worthy of McCarthy:

> It was Acheson who was Truman's chief adviser on basic policy, and Acheson was also Truman's chief alibi-ist. It was Acheson . . . who befriended Alger Hiss and was mixed up with the Owen Lattimore crowd in the State Department who stupidly or deliberately played into Communist hands in Asia. . . . Acheson would not only have let Formosa go to the Communists, he might have recognized the Communist government of China, if he could have got away with it—and he still might.

Luce could not peer into the future and see that it would be one of his most

loyal associates in Againstness, Richard Nixon, who would make the first move in the direction of friendship toward Communist China. While Life used the meat-ax on Acheson for its estimated 18 million readers, Time's experts at denigration exercised their more subtle skills on that magazine's better educated audience of some six millions. By now, Time's effrontery in calling itself a newsmagazine had attracted the attention of the journalist-investigator Ben Bagdikian, who observed:

> It is typical of Time's political reporting that the political world is generally divided into the forces of evil and the forces of virtue. If a political figure is a devil in Time's perdition—he helps an elderly lady across the street just to impress the neighbors. If he is a political angel—floating in Time's heaven—his hand at the aged elbow is evidence of an innate kindness. . . . While Time was not alone in characterizing Acheson as a menace, it was perhaps the most sophisticated and effective organ in destroying public confidence in Acheson. It did this not so much with rational argument and fact, as with the tone words added in Rockefeller Center.

Tone words were evident in its second cover-story assault on the Secretary of State:

> . . . The familiar bony face, the hawk nose, the mustache, the Homburg. . . . Demands that he resign. . . . What people thought of Dean Gooderham Acheson ranged from the proposition that he was a fellow traveler, or a wool-brained sower of "weeds of jackassery," or an abysmally uncomprehending man, or an appeaser, or a warmonger who was taking the U.S. into a world war, to the warm if not so audible defense that he was a great Secretary of State. . . . [C]harges that the State Department had housed party-liners and homosexuals had obviously stuck . . . tall, elegant and unruffled . . . he tried not to listen to the criticisms . . . his blue, slightly protuberant eyes studied the state of his foreign policy. It was not a very encouraging study. . . . To what extent was Acheson to blame . . . ? . . . two basic errors. . . . [T]o what extent was Acheson to blame for Mistake No. 1 . . . ? . . . Acheson . . . sometimes spokesman for a "liberal" group . . . (which included, among others, Alger Hiss) had held various attitudes toward Russia, none of them unfriendly. . . . Chiang was abandoned to his enemies. . . . Acheson . . . gingerly . . . "wait until the dust settles" . . . disastrous phrases. . . . so-called White Paper. . . . to provide Acheson's State Department with an alibi. . . . undermined Chiang, aided Mao. . . . Acheson's State Department continued hopefully to stroke the fur of the Red leader, Mao Tse-tung. . . . "the China mistake." . . . Asia, on which he had turned his back. . . . Dean Acheson deserved to be judged. . . . The case against Dean Acheson . . . the fatal flaw. . . . disastrously failed in Asia . . . the old animus against Chiang Kai-shek . . . symbol of a mistake. . . . minimizing Asia. . . . crucial state of hesitation. . . . Acheson . . . punctilious and polite . . . his hem-hawing, tiptoeing fellow conferees. . . . Has Dean Acheson become a national danger? . . . either Dean Acheson must go, or . . .

Time got in not only the direct reference to Acheson's noted refusal to turn

his back on Hiss, but two indirect ones: "he might have preferred to turn his back on the East," and "Asia, on which he had turned his back." Condemning McCarthy's crude attacks on the Secretary, Time succeeded in disfiguring him more artfully. In tone-word contrast was Time's cover story about Luce's fellow Republican-Presbyterian John Foster Dulles, negotiator of the peace treaty with Japan who was gunning for Acheson's job after the next election:

> A tall, sunburned man . . . with a trim, grey-haired woman . . . made for the airport waiting room. No one recognized Mr. and Mrs. John Foster Dulles as they . . . sat down at the lunch counter and ordered ice-cream sodas . . . vanilla soda . . . the world struggle for freedom . . . he himself had translated the Dulles words into the Dulles deed: the Japanese Treaty. . . . brought it off almost single-handed. . . . "Christ teaches us," replied Dulles, "that nothing is unforgivable." . . . unaffected remark . . . (said an awed friend) . . . "the greatest piece of mental machinery I have ever known." . . . Protestant hymns. . . . Young Foster . . . read *Pilgrim's Progress* . . . could swim the 2½ miles across Henderson Bay. . . . graduated a Phi Beta Kappa and valedictorian. . . . career went steadily upwards. . . . Great ideals. . . . one of the highest-paid lawyers in the country . . . director in 15 corporations. . . . large, cheerful family dinners. . . . He had servants to minister to him. . . . But he needed something more. Dulles . . . found it in a mission. . . . Dulles' committee proclaimed: there is a moral order which is revealed in Jesus Christ; the U.S. must lead the other nations into a political mechanism which will uphold that morality. Vengeance must be laid aside. . . . peaceful means . . . an end to exploitation of colonials. . . . diplomacy with morality . . . he wrote one of the first analyses of the true motives of atheistic Russian Communism. . . . Russia sharply protested . . . but Dulles had seized the initiative. . . . Dulles contrived a lawyer's compromise. . . . sincerity. . . . Dulles carried on his crusade. . . . Against the 50% chance of failure, Lawyer Dulles stacked the lessons taught him by history and the lessons he had learned in church.

Of the Acheson story, 74 percent was negative and derogatory. Dulles received 100 percent approval, the most vicious thing said about him being that he had a "graceless" writing style. But from the beginning, the man with the hawk nose, bony face, protuberant eyes and the Homburg lost the votes of Time-readers to the tall, idealistic, sunburned man with the attractive wife who indulged unnoticed (except by ubiquitous Time) in that most appealingly American of temptations, vanilla ice-cream sodas.

2. TWO PRESBYTERIANS

The two Presbyterians, Luce and Dulles, would cause suspense and even terror in ensuing years because of their determination to reshape the world as closely as possible after the pattern of American moral transcendence. Both had had the good fortune of discovering that their religion and their politics

were complementary. The top-lofty Dulles, son of a Presbyterian clergyman, seriously traced his ancestry back to Charlemagne and lacked Luce's winning qualities of boyishness. Although Luce was a far better public speaker, both tended to dwell heavily on American righteousness. One of Dulles's favorite sayings was, "Moral force is the only force that can accomplish great things in the world."

These incivilities of self-righteousness were testimony of a Calvinist background which surfaced in them both like some genetic flaw. As Professor Nicholas Spykman of Yale had observed, "The heritage of seventeenth-century Puritanism is responsible for one of the characteristic features of our [American] approach to international relations. . . . It makes our people feel called upon to express moral judgments about the foreign policies of others . . ." These same moral judgments in aggressive personalities emerged in the American sense of world mission and destiny. Time, in writing about Dulles, might as well have been writing about Luce when it said, "there is a moral order which is revealed in Jesus Christ; the U.S. must lead the other nations into a political mechanism which will uphold that morality." And Dulles, writing in Luce's Life, where he was often a welcome contributor, could have been speaking for Luce as well as himself when he emphasized America's international mission:

> There is a moral or natural law not made by man which . . . has been trampled on by the Soviet rulers, and for that violation they can and should be made to pay. . . . [Our] liberty [is] not alone for the people of this country, but hope to all the world . . . We have always been, as we always should be, the despair of the oppressor and the hope of the oppressed. We have, however, never been a militaristic people. . . . Our dedication is to peace . . . those enduring principles that are our priceless spiritual heritage. They befit our nation in its majestic role today—at once the guardian and the servant of the hopes of all who love freedom.

One observer of Dulles's impregnable nationalistic self-satisfaction, William Miller, wrote in a passage as applicable to Luce that "the exercise of those Puritan muscles on absolute right and wrong can leave a man unable to bend, to see how right and wrong may look from the very different position of, say, a Nehru." Both Presbyterians were men of great mental vigor who sank to narrowest parochialism in the area where the molten materials of their religion, patriotism and politics fused into one great cold and flinty mass.

Such ferociously aggressive men were uncomfortable with ideological competition or even with any Againstness less marked than or differing from their own, and their reaction was to suppress or crush it. When either Luce or Dulles started talking about "America's priceless spiritual heritage" or "the hopes of all who love freedom," lesser nations had reason to become uneasy. The two were the outstanding exponents of the repudiation of the Truman principle of containing Communism in favor of the Republican battle cry of

"liberation." Just as Luce's explication of this had brought uneasiness to the Buffalo editorialist, so the constant dinning of the liberation idea in the Lucepress gave the shakes to European allies and to America's thoughtful The Reporter, which complained:

> . . . The words of Time and Life are even more dangerous than those of the irresponsible right-wing fringe. In their peculiar obsession with the fortunes of Chiang Kai-shek they have not only discredited the State Department but attacked the whole plan of containment. Whether we like it or not, most of the anti-Communist world has put its faith and hope into the containment of Russia as the only alternative to total war or Communist slavery. These nations have endorsed that policy as a contract with the United States, and they must be severely shaken by attempts such as Life's to throw the shadow of Hiss and the insinuation of Lattimore (whom no court has found guilty and who has been cleared by the Senate Investigating Committee) over their chosen strategy.

The repudiation of containment, in addition to its purely political motivation in attacking a Democratic doctrine, was in part a result of Luce's conviction that the idea of exercising patience, waiting and holding in the hope that Russia would in time rise above the Stalinist horror and join the family of nations, was illusory and defeatist. Patience was never his forte. As he put it in his Harrisburg speech:

> "Peace"—this is Theodore Roosevelt speaking—"Peace is generally good in itself, but it is never the highest good unless it comes as the handmaid of righteousness; and it becomes a very evil thing if it serves merely as a mask for cowardice and sloth, or as an instrument to further the ends of despotism or anarchy." That is a clear statement of the moral law as applied to peace and international politics. And what could be more truly and profoundly American?

The two Presbyterians had a disconcerting readiness to discuss and entertain the thought of nuclear war, an attitude apparently reflecting their religious and moral certainties. Life, as has been seen, sponsored a public discussion on whether the Bomb should be used on Russia at once, and also pronounced itself ready for war with both Russia and China—a conflict certain to be nuclear. Luce seems never to have met directly the purely military argument that all-out support of Chiang would have required sending millions of American soldiers to China unless nuclear weapons were used. Life's statement that "war with Communist China does not necessarily entail involvement with its mass armies" evidently referred to the employment of nuclear weapons.

In Luce's case there was involved also the element of embarrassment over his "wrongness" about China, plain frustration and hot temper. He had become convinced that all Communists were dirty fighters and must be fought on their own vicious terms. He was already scanning the globe for some Christian hero who knew how to "handle" the Reds. ". . . [T]he U.S. must acquire a policy that will save Southeast Asia from the clutch of Commu-

nism," Life instructed the Truman administration. When Churchill sent General Sir Gerald Templer to Malaya to put down the native-and-Chinese Communist insurrection there, and he made progress by using ferocity not always printable, Time applauded. Templer was honored with a Time cover story in which the Communists were assumed to have only ignoble aims and their leader was described with the expected pejoratives ("Chin Peng, slight, 31, pimply-faced, fanatical . . ."). Templer was lauded as the "smiling tiger" in an account of guerrilla warfare similar to that in Indochina, a formidable fighter for God:

> . . . [D]eceptively fragile-looking, tough soldier. . . . bayonet-fighting champion. . . . firm to the point of ruthlessness . . . an austere, stiff-backed autocrat in uniform . . . a bit of a dandy . . . connoisseur of claret. . . . The basic fact about the war in Malaya is the jungle. . . . Communist sympathizers. . . . "You can't deal with a plague of mosquitoes by swatting each individual insect." . . . a dirty little war. . . . Civil servants learned to fear Templer's thin-lipped, tigerish sneer. Asians loved it when he looked a prevaricating Asian politician in the eye and said: "You're a stinker." . . . cut the rice ration. . . . In London, Templer's [methods] provoked a storm. . . . But Templer kept on being tough, regardless. Soon his toughness began to tell. . . . In his air-conditioned office in King's House, he plotted daring innovations in guerrilla warfare: . . . poison spray to clear the roadsides of ambush areas. . . . Templer's success. . . . terrorists had been killed. . . . [T]he reporter from the Communist Daily Worker asked him if his collective punishment policy was not the same as that used by the Nazis. Templer's lip curled into a smile like a soundless snarl. . . .

Time readers, bearing in mind other Lucepress accounts, were not likely to put this story down without reflecting that one thing America needed was to get rid of ineffectives like General Bradley and replace them with tigers like Templer who exterminated Reds like mosquitoes.

XXVI

1. SIZING UP EISENHOWER

A foreign policy that takes for its standard the active hostility to a world-wide political movement, such as Jacobinism, liberalism, or Communism, confuses the sphere of philosophic or moral judgment with the realm of political action, and for this reason it is bound to fail.

—*Hans J. Morgenthau*

On January 22, 1952, the *Queen Mary* sailed for England with Winston Churchill aboard. Perhaps this was why Luce took a stateroom instead of his usual time-saving plane. Churchill, to Luce's relief, was prime minister again after the Tory resurgence. Luce, in his capacity as unofficial surveyor-general of the anti-Communist military-industrial alliance, was not sure he was satisfied with England's contribution. The Labor government had upset him with its quick recognition of Communist China and what he called its "complacency" about the Communist threat. He was sincerely concerned about building a world anti-Communist military organization. American money as well as American military power had helped save Europe—a debt he did not forget. His American-Century tendency to regard all Western European nations as debtor nations and American satellites was implicit in the peremptory tone of a Life editorial:

> Item: European defense has to get out of the planning stage and become something that will check a Red attack. Item: France and Italy must wake up from their smug tolerance of their enormous Communist parties. Item: Germany must be made able to contribute to the common cause. Item: Europe must have more integration along the lines of the Schuman plan.

Churchill was one of the few whom he did not dare address in such arbi-

trary terms. One can only guess that Luce was gingerly with the great man and did not read him lessons in anti-Communism. Luce's purpose, in addition to testing the muscle of the Atlantic community, was to talk with one of its chief muscle-builders, General Eisenhower in Paris, about the Republican Presidential nomination. He also hoped to see that unnerving dialectician, Mary Bancroft, to whom he had written to ask if she might have dinner with him in Paris in February. He joked about his visit with Eisenhower, of whom she had a low opinion, and said he would be disappointed if she could not join him for one of those interminable dinner-discussions in the City of Light.

He gave a fortnight to his own London bureau, now headed by Laguerre; to political socializing with the aid of the fashionable Von Hofmannsthals, and to a personal appraisal of Britain's industrial potential as America's ally. With one of his London aides he spent three grueling days in Lancashire, inspecting factories in Billingham, Wilton and Manchester, seeing the Manchester docks from a launch on the ship canal and paying a courtesy call on Lord Mayor Collingson, telling him, "The size and concentration of [the city's] industry is colossal." He made no secret of the reasons for his interest, the London Observer (which called him "one of the most powerful men in America") noting:

> Events since the war, especially the collapse of China . . . have convinced Luce that America cannot keep the peace of the world unaided. This trip appears to have strengthened his support for some sort of Atlantic Union, a policy which accords with his support of General Eisenhower for the Presidency.

Equally important to him as his appraisal of industrial strength was his estimate of Britain's Againstness. To his role as the leading American propagandist for anti-Communism, he had added that of inspector of the standing of America's allies in the same doctrine. While the new Churchill government, with Eden as Foreign Secretary, would of course improve on the Attlee softness, he was not at all satisfied that it would improve enough. Time's next issue would have an Anthony Eden cover story designed as a warning to Britain as well as to America on this score. Luce conferred with Laguerre on this and cabled the New York office that criticism of Eden would have to be muted because "I am in the middle of serious investigation of the British position and have not yet arrived at any conclusions."

For all that, Time found Eden's Againstness inadequate. He and Churchill, after six years out of office, were "dismayingly out of touch with many of the facts of international life." They were too willing to see a possibility of negotiation with the Soviet:

> Eden . . . [was] full of conventional diplomacy. Was the gap too wide between East & West? Let there be small agreements with the Soviets, and upon them trust might be built. In that way, though still wary of each other, East and West might come to live together in peace, if not in harmony. It was the familiar British formula: adjustments, not solutions.

321

The death of George VI during Luce's stay was another example of news awaiting his arrival before it occurred. He cabled Billings:

> Death of the king and succession of the queen is one of the most profoundly moving events since the surrender on the Missouri and I trust there will be no lack of sympathetic imagination in the treatment of this subject in both Time and Life.

It was an illustration of his susceptibility to power as well as the drama of history, likening the transfer of power from deceased king to young queen to the transfer of power from old Japan to the young United States. He followed with a long cable of instructions on the handling of the cover story on Queen Elizabeth II, then crossed to Paris and talked with Eisenhower, whom he had previously met both at Columbia University and in Europe and with whom he had had some correspondence. The general, long the cynosure of President-makers, had been studiously dodging visiting politicians and, when he could not dodge them, talking only about the weather. One of Eisenhower's closest advisers was Luce's good friend Paul Hoffman, now administrator of the Marshall Plan. Also, it was axiomatic that a person who had been a Time cover subject never really got over it. Ike had adorned the cover six times, once as Man of the Year. After this immortalization the general could no more have turned Luce away than he could have brushed off an angel appearing in a pillar of fire. It is safe to say that the two talked of other things than the weather. Indeed, since Luce had already virtually decided on Eisenhower as his candidate, it seems possible that his visit was not only a courtesy call and final appraisal but also intended to let Ike have a good look at *him*, the general's benefactor, who might not be above wanting some reward after the election.

When he later had a five-hour dinner with Mary, she felt that he talked about Eisenhower less with the excitement of a hot partisan than the businesslike attitude of a producer who has found the star for his great film. She felt that he wanted badly to be one of those few who could drop in at the White House, be welcomed and be regarded as the President's friend and unofficial adviser—a standing he had never had.

She could scarcely be impartial here, however, for her daughter, Mary Jane Badger, was engaged to marry Senator Taft's fourth son, Horace, the two having met when young Taft took graduate work in Zurich. If it had to be a Republican President, Mary was for the Senator. In a subsequent letter to Luce, she praised Eisenhower with tongue in cheek, using one of those metaphors that jolted him:

> . . . One of Ike's great strengths is that he is a soldier who doesn't like or want war—doesn't need it for his "performance," like some others, including Montgomery and deLattre. Now this fact—this differentiation—gives him great strength. It's like a whore who believes in chastity . . .

Before leaving Paris, Luce stopped in at the apartment of Theodore White,

24. Manfred Gottfried and Roy E. Larsen in powwow with the balding editor-in-chief.

25. Mary Bancroft, long a friend, essayed to rectify Luce's politics *and* journalism.

26. Dean Acheson became a target of Lucepress vilification.

27. Luce presents President Truman—hardly a favorite—with his Time cover portrait.

28. General Marshall, too, suffered a long TLF bombardment.

29. But General MacArthur's dashing impetuosity inspired purplest Lucepress prose.

30. Below, Luce in Taiwan in 1952 inspects Chiang army training for the "back to the mainland" chimera. At right, he puffs cigarette as he and Timen listen to his friend Lord Beaverbrook, one of many newsmakers who addressed the editorial staff.

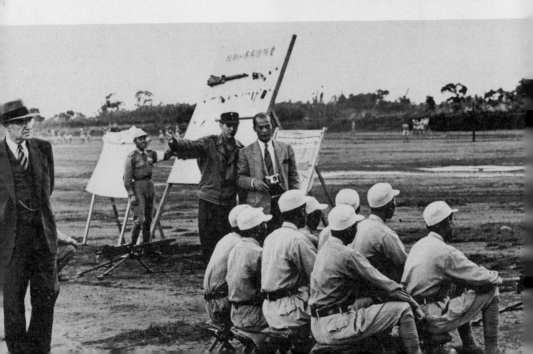

31. On 1952 round-the-world swing, Luce visits Indochina front with U.S. Ambassador Heath (black hat) and French General Gonzales de Linares. The American editor, in his report, said there should be little further difficulty in winning war. Heath (and Luce himself) would later be aggrieved by a Life story on Indochina.

32. Flanked by Churchill, Dewey and other bigwigs, Luce presides at the Ritz Hotel jamboree—one of three he promoted for the Briton, his most famous Life writer.

33. Madam Ambassador Luce chats with group including President Eisenhower and her nominal boss, Secretary Dulles (glasses).

34. Adlai Stevenson, so mistreated by Luce-press innuendo, was classified by Mrs. Bancroft as a cultivated man. Luce, she said with shattering frankness, was not.

35. Cardinal Spellman and Luce with the Vietnamese they both backed, Ngo Dinh Diem.

36. Nasser (seen with Luce) was a Lucean hero who fell, became a "son of a bitch."

37. Mrs. Luce, backed by husband, said the hostile Sen. Wayne Morse had been kicked in the head by a horse—her way of abandoning further effort to become American Ambassador to Brazil.

38. Chiang and his powerful eulogist had enormous effect on policies toward Asia.

39. Young Sen. John F. Kennedy, Presidential candidate, before addressing assembled Timen. At left is John K. Jessup. Otto Fuerbringer is in rear between Luce and Kennedy, and Thomas Griffith (face turned) is beyond Kennedy's other shoulder. "I like Luce," JFK remarked after the meeting, feeling him similar to his own father.

Drawing by Richard Decker; © 1962. The New Yorker Magazine, Inc.

40. The littlewig who dreamed of becoming a bigwig
was invariably seized by this glorious fantasy.

41. "My favorite queen," Frederika of Greece, with daughter and American admirer.

42. Time's fortieth anniversary party in 1963 jammed the Waldorf ballroom (below) with 1700 guests including 300 who had appeared on Time's cover. Speakers included Vice President Johnson, Secretary of State Rusk and Dr. Paul Tillich. Each cover subject had his "cover" flashed on screen above stage as he was introduced. It was publicity high-water mark for Luce, seen on rostrum (above, left to right) with Secretary Rusk, Treasury Secretary Douglas Dillon, Clare and the ubiquitous Cardinal Spellman. Dr. Tillich's warning seemed little heeded.

43. Forever talking with VIPs, Luce here counsels the attentive President Johnson.

44. Below, squeezing out Charles S. Rhyne, he makes a point to a future President.

45. Here he expounds to dictator Tito, whom he incautiously denominated a "hero."

46. The grizzled Boss, after 41 years, handed over his Editor-in-Chief title to Hedley Donovan. Thereafter, in "retirement," he still worked like a horse for his magazines, praised God, raised church funds, extolled peace, supported war.

now a news-service correspondent there. They had not met since their bitter parting in 1945. Since then, Time in 1948 had given White a swipe in commenting on his magazine account of the Stilwell episode, noting "his warm regard for the Chinese Communists," and Luce, in a 1949 interview in St. Louis, had unkindly gone out of his way to say, "Teddy went all the way over to the side of the Communists in China." Now, however, Luce was "entirely pleasant," as White recalled it. Not a word was spoken about China. Luce, always after able writers, may have begun to view White as too gifted a man to lose because of political differences.

On his return to New York February 16, he gave his usual private-luncheon lecture on things done, people seen and decisions made to a group of seventeen executives of whom fourteen were editorial men, only Larsen and Charles Stillman representing the business office and Howard Black the delegate for the advertising department. Doubtless much of it had to do with plans to nominate and elect Eisenhower. Although Senator Taft was a fellow Bonesman, he was not the internationalist Luce demanded, was politically far too mature to take any instruction from Luce, and besides, Luce felt Ike more of a sure winner. Thereafter in the Lucepress, Eisenhower appeared more and more the American demigod.

This was one of those years when Luce seemed to be going and coming so rapidly as to almost meet himself. After a four-day sojourn in South Carolina, he left in April with Clare for a three-week tour of Spain, where their activities included "dinner with a half-dozen prominent Spaniards and their ladies" and visits to monasteries, wineries and beaches, ending with three days in Paris. Here, one suspects, the two President-makers visited Eisenhower together. On their return, Luce spent three weeks at home in Ridgefield, then went to Yellowstone Park to make a speech. Before the year was over he would visit Chicago for the Republican National Convention, Cleveland for a speech, Texas for a speech, Grand Rapids for a speech, the Far East to visit eight countries, and return via Europe in time to spend the last week of the year in the Bahamas at the snuggery of Lord Beaverbrook.

Meanwhile, Clare was in politics again up to her pretty knees, advancing the Eisenhower cause in a Hartford speech in which she dismissed Taft as a loser and warned: ". . . the defeat of Eisenhower at Chicago would be taken by European Communists as the signal that America was going home [meaning "isolationist"]. It would give Stalin the only real political victory he has had in Europe since the formation of SHAPE under Eisenhower."

When she and Luce arrived at the Drake Hotel in Chicago a few days later for the convention, they ran into Elmo Roper, the pollster who for many years had conducted the Fortune survey and was a good friend. But Luce had had a recent political disagreement with Roper and passed him by without a greeting. Later he got over his pet and they talked amiably at one of the many party sessions. Clare this time was a delegate from Connecticut and not a convention speaker, possibly because of some Republican superstition about

her speech at the 1948 convention in which she had pronounced Truman finished. Young Henry Luce III, now a Time Washington correspondent, was there, covering Taft headquarters. (The other son, Peter Paul, had worked briefly for the company in 1949, decided that journalism was not for him and gone into other business.) Taft's campaign manager was none other than Luce's old Yale classmate and Cleveland friend, David Ingalls. It was said that Ingalls never forgave Luce for his desertion of their brother Bonesman and Time's destructive treatment of him.

2. THE NIXON CRISIS

During Luce's absence in Europe, Matthews had run a cover story on his Princeton classmate and good friend Adlai Stevenson, governor of Illinois. It was so complimentary to Stevenson even to the handsome Chaliapin cover painting and the cover line that when the Boss returned he was called on by at least one concerned and conservative senior editor who pointed out that Stevenson not only was a Democrat but might be nominated for the Presidency. Luce, who had already been maneuvering to oust Matthews, undoubtedly was pressed by greater urgency as Stevenson loomed as the likely candidate. To have the formidable Matthews as managing editor, seeking to boost Stevenson while Luce endeavored to hurl him into outer darkness in favor of the Republican candidate, preferably Eisenhower, would never do. Even yet he had regard for Matthews, a valued man for twenty-three years, and although he was so wealthy that his hefty Time salary was almost entirely swallowed by taxes, Luce still hated to fire people and could not bring himself to discharge an old colleague outright.

As he prepared to dislodge him by deviation, Whittaker Chambers's book *Witness* came up for review. Matthews selected Sam Welles, still a good friend of Chambers's and believed to understand him better than most, to write the review. Welles, who was now Time's chief correspondent in Canada, traveled down from the Yukon, where he had been working on a story, in order to get instructions and to interview Chambers. The book was of course a stirrer of hot controversy in its approach to the problem of Communism. Matthews said to Welles, who was a fellow Princetonian and Episcopalian, "Sam, this is a tricky business. I think you and I should pray over it—should go to early communion together over it." They met next morning and went to the Church of St. Mary the Virgin on 47th Street, where they prayed that Welles's review would be a worthy one, then breakfasted together at Schrafft's on 51st Street. Here they met Roy Alexander, who had just come from communion at St. Patrick's Cathedral. Hence Welles's thoroughgoing and laudatory review, which was blurbed on the cover, "Chambers v. Hiss," and filled the whole book section, could not rightly have suffered from any divine displeasure over lack of consultation.

Luce, taking Matthews to lunch one day, told him that he had *already* moved Alexander into his job as managing editor. So, he asked, what were they going to do with Matthews? Matthews, astonished, replied that this seemed to be Luce's problem. He did not construe it for what it was, an invitation to resign. Luce, unhappy that his meaning had been missed, launched into further obliquity. He gave Matthews the title of editor, moving himself theoretically out of the post but retaining, of course, all authority. Matthews found his own authority limited to the supervision of cover stories. The climax came when the rising National Affairs writer Otto Fuerbringer, whose conservative politics were a joy to Luce, wrote a second cover story about Stevenson after his nomination. Matthews, who disapproved of Fuerbringer in any case, exploded when he found the story to be disparaging and to include such information as the incident in Stevenson's childhood when he and a cousin were playing with a gun, it discharged and the cousin was killed. Matthews suspected an implication that Stevenson's effect on American government might be as damaging. The story was unfair, he said, and the shooting tragedy was not germane and must come out. He and Fuerbringer argued about it for an hour, with Alexander as unavailing referee. Matthews finally called Luce about it. Luce summoned the two, heard the argument and said the shooting incident should be removed.

But the rest of the story remained largely as it was, and Stevenson was saved from the shooting scrape only to be maimed thereafter by Time's hatchet. As Matthews wrote later, from then on "there was no holding Time. The distortions, suppressions and slanting of its political 'news' seemed to me to pass the bounds of politics and to commit an offense against the ethics of journalism." Time, however, had been committing these same offenses during most of Matthews's editorship. For Matthews, who had been in the saddle during the two heavily slanted Dewey campaigns, had sponsored the FN distortions of Whittaker Chambers and published his "Ghosts on the Roof," to exhibit sudden journalistic virtue in behalf of Stevenson suggested that journalistic ethics had not taken priority in his mind until his good friend was involved.

Still he did not resign. Now it was the popular Alexander, a favorite of Luce's, a top man for thirteen years who could handle any department, a good Catholic sharing Luce's feeling about Communism, who took over. As to propaganda, Alexander followed the easy Luce line that objectivity was a myth, that there was no such thing as objective journalism except in the stock market quotations. In any case, the staff was making the necessary adjustment to the hardening Luce attitudes, Kronenberger writing, "imperceptibly but surely the atmosphere of Time began to change. . . . [O]ne of the things wrong with [the] staff was its being more royalist than the king."

One danger Time had to guard against was too-obvious propaganda. Its readership being literate, there was the risk of offending even Republicans who resented having the news manipulated, heroes puffed and villains hissed.

But Luce was so determined to bring Republican victory this time that he accepted the risk and pushed propaganda a shade farther than before. Time's Eisenhower bias offended Taft Republicans long before the convention eliminated the Ohioan. It also offended Mary Bancroft, who was visiting in America. She felt that Luce's support of Eisenhower was based on expediency and on his desire for a President who would accommodate his own yearning for behind-the-scenes power. In May, Mary and Luce had dinner at the home of mutual friends. Mary, whose satire could be devastating, lampooned the Time-Life-Eisenhower infatuation until Luce grew white with rage and their host, seeing the danger signs, repeatedly touched her toe under the table in warning. Luce shouted at her. She shouted back.

When Luce took her home later in his limousine, he apologized after a fashion, said that she could be annoying beyond endurance and that at any rate he was slightly comforted by the fact that she had lost her temper too.

The complaints of Taft supporters were so bitter that Time's Letters department analyzed them. It was discovered that by August, nine weeks before the election, more than 1500 readers had written to Time—more than double those during the 1948 race—about its political coverage. Sixty-two were angry enough to cancel their subscriptions outright, and fifty-five vowed that they would not renew. Time's steady build-up of Eisenhower for five months before the election involved the sculpturing of many thousands of words, of which the following give an idea:

> They saw Ike, and they liked what they saw . . . amazingly good campaigner.
> . . . strong, vigorous manner of speech . . . innate kindliness and modesty. . . .
> They liked Ike . . . he made them proud. . . . the Kansans cheered. . . . great
> humility and clarity. . . . He nudged Mamie. . . . [H]e grabbed Mamie and
> hugged her. . . . force, sincerity and spontaneity . . . fine performance. . . .
> Ike's natural warmth . . . delighted reporters. . . . Eisenhower charm . . .
> glowing enthusiasts. . . . Ike had certainly struck a spark. . . . A great American
> soldier disclosed political greatness. . . . "godless Communism" had con-
> quered vast areas of the world. . . . Ike was in his element. . . . The crowd
> loved it . . . they stopped him with cheers and yells of "Go to it!" "Attaboy!" a
> total of 61 times. . . . high school bands playing John Philip Sousa. . . . Hun-
> dreds swarmed over Eisenhower's car. . . . Eisenhower denounced defeatism
> . . . cleanse the Government from top to bottom of subversives. . . . a man of
> unique experience . . .

Stevenson's cover story carried the suspicious blurb, "Does he make sense to the American people?" The inside copy suggested that he did not. Time, which had praised his work against corruption when he was governor of Illinois, now said, "He has never so much as slapped the wrist of the Cook County Democratic organization, the most corrupt and powerful of existing big-city machines . . ." It dramatized Eisenhower's confabulations with European heads of state, while Stevenson was treated as a late-comer:

> Stevenson had not yet set the Eastern woods afire. . . . Standard Democratic
> formula. . . . bitter terms . . . growing anger. . . . Stevenson was thrown on

the defensive. . . . Stevenson set out to explain. . . . Ten months ago, Stevenson was not even a name in the national consciousness. . . . nervous laughter. . . . unfitted for the job. . . . Can Stevenson refreshen the Fair Deal? . . . a Washington operator. . . . a man who feels that there are two sides to most questions. . . . crowds were small, far smaller than Eisenhower's. . . . did not rouse his audience. . . . Was he making any sense . . . ? . . . Stevenson tried desperately. . . . Stevenson would have to face the facts of life . . . Stevenson swallowed manfully. . . . Does Adlai Stevenson, and what he stands for, make sense to the American people?

Time's twenty-one pictures of Ike showed him at his smiling or earnest best. Of its thirteen photographs of Stevenson, more than half showed him with mouth open, grimacing or otherwise unappealing. Luce meanwhile aided the cause by lending C. D. Jackson and the young Life writer Emmet Hughes to the Eisenhower campaign as speechwriters.

While Democratic Vice Presidential candidate John Sparkman was ridiculed as a Southern connoisseur of cough drops, Eisenhower's running mate Richard Nixon got a rousing cover story:

. . . [G]ood-looking, dark-haired young man with a manner both aggressive and modest . . . He seemed to have everything . . . an attractive family, a good war record, deep sincerity and religious faith. . . . bright student. . . . worked his way through Whittier College. . . . taught Sunday school. . . . patriotic. . . . was under bombardment. . . . rarely takes a drink. . . . one of the most effective harriers of Communism. . . . hard worker. . . . Back home in Whittier . . . the folks were confident.

But President Truman, campaigning for Stevenson, received stern interpretation in the Newsmagazine:

Harry Truman's weird charges. . . . Upon Dwight Eisenhower he poured his most reckless abuse. . . . Trumanism. . . . Harry Truman's attempt to swing Jewish and Catholic votes. . . . Truman tactics. . . . Truman's attempted character-assassination. . . . Truman's rabble-rousing. . . . Harry Truman had done his demagogic best . . .

If Ike had a flaw, Time suggested, it was his failure to come right out and applaud Nixon for his anti-Communist work: ". . . Eisenhower has not yet made an explicit recognition of the priceless service to their country rendered by men who justly damaged the reputations of people who really were Communists, *e.g.*, his running mate, Senator Nixon." It appeared that Time and Life were viewing the young Californian as a protégé, a possible eventual successor to Eisenhower, who was already sixty-two. The Lucepress had not mentioned the lengths to which Nixon and his California associates had gone in their efforts to pin Red labels on the Democrat Jerry Voorhis, whom he defeated for Congress, and on the Democrat Helen Gahagan Douglas, who was denominated the Pink Lady and whom he defeated for the Senate. Nixon employed the same tactics in this campaign. He was, as in the case of the Pink

Lady tag, expert in the framing and intoning of suggestions of turpitude in language which, when minutely examined, was not libelous. He retold on television the story of the Hiss case. He repeated the statements of J. Edgar Hoover about the Communist peril and said, "Mr. Stevenson has never expressed any indignation over what Hiss has done." But Luce and the whole Republican party faced a crisis when the New York Post broke the story of the Nixon fund of $18,000 collected by a group of wealthy constituents in California who might not be above wanting some return for their money.

Nixon's first counterattack was that the story was a "Communist smear." The gibes of hecklers and the reaction of the Republican hierarchy made it plain that this would not suffice. With the Republicans mounting a furious attack on "Truman corruption," the discovery of the Nixon fund seemed disastrous to Eisenhower and the Republican press. The bellwether New York Herald Tribune expressed the party's dismay and its fear that the disclosure might defeat the Eisenhower ticket unless, as it recommended, Nixon withdraw and be replaced by a candidate without such embarrassment.

Luce faced the horrid prospect that again, as in 1948, the Republicans might lose through a fluke. He was loyal to the young anti-Communist who really represented his policies better than Eisenhower did. Time did not succumb to the widespread Republican panic. It used two and a half pages to put the event in cooler perspective and place the most generous construction on it. Admitting that Nixon had erred in keeping the fund secret, it listed four extenuating circumstances which, when scrutinized, did not extenuate: That most Congressmen had to supplement their small salaries by lecturing, drawing on their private wealth or some such device; that Nixon purportedly had never handled any of the money himself; that the contributors "resembled a *Who's Who* of Southern California business," and that they "were all ardent admirers of Nixon." Eisenhower's jittery staff, Time complained, "compounded and magnified the problem" instead of taking it in stride. In its September 29 issue it said, "One reason for secrecy [in the fund] was that Nixon's people wanted to avoid a factional clash with the Warrenites." In its October 6 issue it said, "The fund was not really secret at all."

Nixon's whole political career hung in the balance when he made his "Checkers" television appearance with his wife in a dramatic account of his modest scale of life, his mortgages and Mrs. Nixon's "Republican cloth coat." Time hailed it as a triumphant vindication, noting his statement that regardless of what happened, "I'm going to campaign up and down America until we drive the crooks and the Communists . . . out of Washington." Time said, "he had made one of the most dramatically successful speeches in the history of U.S. politics," "he had established himself as a man of integrity and courage . . . he had changed from a liability to his party to a shining asset." The muckraking Drew Pearson thought otherwise, writing that the $18,000 represented "gratitude expressed in the form of campaign contributions for favors done and votes cast while he served in Congress"; that the collector of

the fund had been aided by Nixon in his efforts to get a $500,000 tax refund, and that among those who contributed were fifteen oilmen and eleven real estate executives who "had had heavy stakes in legislation on which Nixon had voted," and that Nixon had voted down the line in their interests.

Life gave Nixon seven pages and forty pictures titled "Nixon Fights, Wins and Weeps," mentioning his "pathos and candor," the "heart-warming ovation" he received and the "tears in Mamie's eyes" on witnessing "this tremendous drama." Both candidates, it declared, emerged stronger than ever: "Nixon . . . had established himself as a new force in the party with a prestige seldom enjoyed by a vice presidential candidate . . ." Ike's handling of the case was "much more than just lucky," he deserved "the credit due to any top commander for the happy outcome of the Nixon affair," and his "command decision" dispelled any lingering doubt of his executive ability.

To one angry reader who wrote, "I know you boys are trying to sell Ike to the voters . . . but what kind of a 'fair coverage' ratio do you call this week's maneuver of 6 and ⅔ pages Ike and ⅓ page Stevenson?" Life replied that editorially it did indeed support the Republicans but that in "factual reporting" it simply hoped to achieve "interesting and complete coverage."

The gimmickry of the Nixon performance was matched by that of the Lucepress whose powerful support was so important a factor in his hairbreadth escape from political ruin. Somehow, in all the excitement, Luce had time to dine with Mary Bancroft, and she had flowers and a letter from him when she sailed for Europe on October 18.

"Of course I would have to be in the middle of the Atlantic when Truman called the Republicans Nazis," she wrote. ". . . Only the Republicans *aren't* Nazis. . . . What it is, as I see it, is that the microbes of the disease are there —the open wound in the American psyche . . ." And she could not resist teasing him:

> You said something about being puzzled as to why certain people didn't "respect" you. . . . I thought of what *I* respect you for: I respect you for having made money. Now think that one over. . . . I'm not awed by people who *have* money—but I am awed by people who make it. And you did make it, didn't you? You didn't either inherit or steal it.

Down to election day, the Lucepress brought up all its guns in electioneering more partisan than had ever been seen even in that forum of bias. There were incessant reminders of Acheson's unturned back, and suggestions that Stevenson was surrounded by subversives in the persons of such as Arthur Schlesinger, Jr., James Wechsler and Willard Wirtz. There were accusations that he was so lost as to have suggested the possibility of parleys with Russia. There were savageries such as Life's charge that Stevenson was aligned with the "Acheson faction" which "watched the victories of Mao with feelings ranging from complacence to connivance." The faction, it said, included also Eleanor Roosevelt, Philip Jessup, John Service and Owen Lattimore, all of

whom were abused in language implying treason. "On the periphery of this faction," said Life, "one finds the trail of Alger Hiss."

Meanwhile, Luce, upset by Mary's suggestion that McCarthy might do in America what Hitler had done in Germany, cabled to reproach her for the shocking idea that Americans were like Europeans and could follow such a pattern.

3. RUBBING THEIR NOSES IN IT

Ten days after the Eisenhower-Nixon landslide, Luce gave a dinner at the Union Club for the entire Time staff even down to assistant editors and researchers. He knew that Matthews's resentment at Time's neglect of the "ethics of journalism" was shared by many liberals on the staff and perhaps even by some Republicans. In his speech (he was the only speaker) he mentioned his awareness of the tension on the twenty-eighth and twenty-ninth floors. He was triumphant over the election. But Time's closet door was opened wider than it had been since the Chambers War, the skeleton visible to all but the blind. Considering the wounded feelings in the staff, some thought he would speak in the tone of hard-boiled placation that he could sometimes adopt.

However, from the dais the editors he saw drew salaries ranging from $10,000 to $50,000 a year—well-fed and well-tailored people whose feelings had not been sufficiently wounded to make them take the recourse always available to them, namely, quitting and going to work somewhere else where they could be ethically content but could not afford servants, vacations in Hawaii and private schools for their children. Not surprisingly, Luce could not entertain too much respect for this kind of ethics. Rather than placating his listeners, he addressed them quite arrogantly. He was boss, he said. There was no job tenure at Time:

> I suppose that most of you, or many of you, take Time rather for granted . . . take your paychecks for granted. . . . But I think an old-timer, a real old-timer, can never *quite* get used to the fact that we don't have to worry too much about Time's still being in existence a little while. . . . So I introduce myself to you first of all as an old-timer. And then secondly, I introduce myself to you as your boss. Whether or not I'm the father of Time or of Time Incers . . . I am literally your boss.

His talk was swaggering enough to raise the question of whether he had taken an extra cocktail. It seems more likely that he was speaking advisedly to malcontents he wanted to put in their place. Matthews sat near him, his face graven in stone. He spoke from compressed notes rather than a completed script, which always made him ramble. One listener, Sam Welles, noted that Luce kept twisting at a jacket button. When he came to the closet door, far from closing it, he swept it wide open:

> Now we are *for* objectivity. That may surprise some of you. . . . There is objective truth in the universe. Ours is a universe of law. In this universe there is

scientific truth and there is moral truth. . . . Majorities do not make truth. Intellectual facts do not make truth. . . . [W]hat is the objectivity we are against? The alleged journalistic objectivity. . . . a claim that a writer presents facts without applying any value judgment to them. That is modern usage—and that is strictly a phony. It is that that I had to renounce and denounce. So when we say the hell with objectivity, this is what we are talking about. . . . Now this does not mean that value judgments are bad. . . . Quite on the contrary. It means that 75% of the business of recognizing, selecting and organizing facts is having a correct value judgment. And that is just as true for the Associated Press or the United Press as it is for Time, whether or not they have the intelligence to recognize it. . . . The phrase "dignity of man" expresses a value judgment, or to go to another century, "Give me liberty or give me death" expresses a value judgment.

He said that the American press—even Time itself—shared guilt in the loss of China to the Communists and the ensuing murders of some 14 millions by them, because the press had given the correct objective fact that the Chiang regime was corrupt and had failed to give the more vital value judgment that, corrupt as it was, it was infinitely to be preferred over the Communists:

American journalism was very much implicated in that mistake. . . . I think we might all of us take a vow tonight that God help us, we will not be again an accessory before the fact to the murder of mankind.

He did not go into the question of why Time had approved when Chiang's forces won and slaughtered the Communists in 1927 and again in 1934 during the Long March, or why the value judgment would have been approving of a similar murder of mankind if Chiang had won in 1949 and decimated his enemies, or why his slaughter of the Taiwanese was acceptable. He did not touch on why he was specially qualified to render value judgments for the nation and the world. Like the Communists, he based his reasoning on moral absolutes which could not be questioned, as when he advocated the banishment of Holmes because "we ought to believe what is true."

But his most important lapse was in passing over the question of how he was authorized to make value judgments that were not open and acknowledged but were hidden, unknown to his readers but affecting their impressions and their votes—the value judgments that made Eisenhower appear heroic, Stevenson ridiculous, Nixon "sincere" and Truman evocative of disgust.

Matthews and other resentful listeners knew that one person's value judgment differed from another's—that in short, value judgment was nothing more than opinion or prejudice. It came down again to Time being a magazine of opinion and persuasion masquerading as a newsmagazine. The word for opinion masquerading as news, aimed at controlling the reader's thought and molding his ideology, was propaganda in the totalitarian sense of that word. It was propaganda whether done by the late Voelkischer Beobachter, Pravda or Time. This masquerade involved deception of the reader. The Boss

did not discuss the kind of value judgment which commissioned him to deceive his readers, nor did he touch on the broader question of whether Americans who were so deceived were really members of what he liked to call "the free world" and were the inheritors and beneficiaries of the "liberty and freedom" which he exalted in his speeches. In his distinguished audience there were men and women who could have upheld the proposition that "liberty and freedom" implied an electorate that was informed rather than deceived and controlled. They could have argued that in exact proportion to the extent that the electorate was no longer informed but was deceived and controlled, its liberty and freedom were gone and they were slaves of the reigning value judgment. And they could have finished by declaring that anyone who deceived and controlled the public in this way was—far from being a guardian of liberty and freedom—the deadliest enemy of liberty and freedom.

No one in the audience, however, did so.

One must guess at Luce's reply to such an argument, but the guess seems a safe one: World Communism regimented its masses by propaganda, and world capitalism had no choice but to do the same or be overwhelmed. If it was coming to the crunch—an Armageddon between Fascism and Communism—there was no doubt which side he chose. Time had attacked the New York Times for printing Harrison Salisbury's Moscow dispatches under an italicized precede warning that the dispatches, like all news out of Russia, had to pass Soviet censors. While Salisbury had reported that Russia was "armed to the teeth," he had also noted that the "cleaning, painting and construction" in Moscow and the increasing manufacture of pots and pans suggested no immediate Kremlin plan for war. Time, whose line had it that the Kremlin *was* planning war, objected to this dissemination of Soviet "propaganda" and the folly of "every U.S. newspaper which still pursues the never-never-land ideal of 'objectivity.' " Salisbury had not got the proper value judgments through the censors, Time said, condemning news without value judgments:

> In simpler days there was probably no particular harm for readers (if no particular benefit) in the broadside scattering of "facts" without interpretation or perspective. But . . . that day [is] past.

Perhaps these thoughts entered the minds of Matthews and other Time exponents of journalistic ethics as Luce's speech continued. If he left things unsaid about the shaping of news, he left no doubt about the cause Time served, over and above the essential cause of financial success:

> . . . that is the cause of America. For me that is the categorical, moral imperative . . . I mean America in relation to the world, the whole world of mortal men in the 1950s. . . . Toynbee regarded America as simply a peripheral part of European civilization. I regard America as a special dispensation under Providence.

His coat button, so long twisted, came off and rolled to the floor. This categorical imperative was Luce's fundamental value judgment. It reflected a patriotism so astonishing in its vehemence that some of his editors thought it inspiring, some felt it sophomoric and Mrs. Bancroft—whose own patriotism was as deep as it was thoughtful—called it maudlin. Listeners had passed written questions to Luce which he undertook to answer at the end of the speech. A couple came from dissidents who sought to soften Time's "news" bias by the inclusion of signed columns, or of an editorial page. Luce rejected both. He read off the final question:

> "Do you think Time's reputation for fairness and/or objectivity suffered seriously during the recent Presidential campaign?" I can't quite make out about that. I suppose the important word here is the adverb "seriously." I think it suffered some. I don't think it suffered seriously. In fact, I don't think it suffered seriously at all. But I'm not sure about that. I haven't been around the country. I haven't done my own private Gallup poll on that . . . I can assure you that among Republicans it is not generally regarded that Time showed any lack of objectivity. After all, you know, we were making a hell of a pitch for Democratic votes, and even the Democrats who didn't vote for Eisenhower we still love, and we want all of them in 1956. So after I see a few more Democrats, I can answer that for myself. . . .

It is difficult to resist the impression that Luce was frankly making a joke of the dissidents, rubbing their noses in his power. The next question resulted from the rumor that he might take an office in the Eisenhower administration: "Will you continue to serve as Time's editor-in-chief?"

> Well, you know, I told you I was your boss. I guess that means I could fire any of you. I don't know anybody around here that's got a contract, have they, Roy [Alexander]? So I could fire any of you. . . . But I don't know anybody who can fire me. Sometimes I wish there were. Well, as long as I don't get fired, I propose to serve as Time's editor-in-chief. . . .

4. VALUE JUDGMENTS IN ASIA

Although it was believed a foregone conclusion that John Foster Dulles would become Eisenhower's Secretary of State, and Luce greatly admired Dulles's moral outlook on foreign policy, perhaps he still had a lingering hope to edge out his fellow Presbyterian. Luce's ambivalence at times could be Jesuitical and he could argue both sides of a question with what seemed equal sincerity and logic. In any case, young Emmet Hughes, the Lifeman who had been loaned to Eisenhower as a speech writer and of whom Luce had become fond, was summoned to the Penthouse shortly after the election. Luce showed him a letter he had written to Eisenhower's close friend and adviser, General Lucius Clay, urging that the President-elect choose the untried Thomas E. Dewey for State.

"Tom might make a better Secretary than Foster," Luce said.

Hughes was amazed. In subsequent reflection he was unable to understand Luce's switch or to bring himself to believe it might be a Luce maneuver to toss the State appointment up in the air in the hope that it might light on him.

Luce was off for Tokyo two days after his Union Club talk, on a grueling five-week tour around the globe on which he would survey the Far East from his own TLF primacy and would report directly to President-elect Eisenhower. While Dulles's attitude toward the Far East seemed in tune with his own, Luce was never able to trust others with global problems. Despite Time's heroic appraisals of Eisenhower, in all candor he had little confidence in Ike as a statesman.

One might disagree with Luce's politics and yet admire the persistence and energy with which he advanced them. At the risk of becoming boring on the subject of the Far East (which he often was), he was determined to make certain that the incoming administration knew of his special authority in that field, understood the Luce Far Eastern policy and followed it. At his own great effort and expense he was about to lay out a course which the United States would follow substantially for many years with calamitous results, and which might not have been followed so closely but for his advice.

His itinerary would have tested an athlete, much less a fifty-four-year-old chainsmoker: San Francisco, Honolulu, Tokyo, Seoul, Tokyo, Taipei, Hong Kong, Manila, Singapore, Jakarta, Singapore, Saigon, Singapore, London, and back to New York. The oddly unreal Luce foreign-tour scenario was repeated in all its detail: the advance planning, the conferences with VIPs ranging from heads of state to ambassadors, generals and admirals, the ending of conferences to dash for a plane for the next conference, the discussions in which concern for The People in all their millions never seemed high on the agenda, the rigidity of all this guaranteed by Luce's fixed opinions which he appeared more anxious to verify than to test. On his 1949 European tour of state he had listed eighty-four VIPs with whom he had met and talked. This time he listed only thirty-eight by name, dozens of others being mentioned in passing by their titles. But among the thirty-eight were nine heads of state and one emperor, a roster of eminence perhaps not quite equaled in the earlier tour. Certainly some of the leaders he met believed that this decisive and authoritative man, somewhat deaf, treated with such respect by all American officials and by his own local correspondents, held some high, if unofficial, position in the American government.

He was greeted enthusiastically by Syngman Rhee in Korea, that "free world" leader whose autocracy was growing embarrassing. Much had changed since the war years when Rhee had haunted the T-L Building to solicit the kind of Luce support Chiang was getting. Luce had been forced to shelve the idea that "free world" leaders must permit freedom and to fall back on the line that the cause of anti-Communism justified toughness of method.

Again, as on all his tours, Lucepress publicity strengthened his hand. Rhee had been honored by a Time cover story explaining him to Americans with correct value judgments, and he would soon be the cover-hero again. Recent Time cover stories lauding Generals Mark Clark and James Van Fleet, and Time's support of the military against all comers, perhaps was a factor in their thoroughly respectful reception of the visitor. Although Luce was in Korea only three days, his discussions inspired a memo to Billings which he headed, "What to Do About Korea." Its burden was that what must be done was to destroy the Communist enemy, which he said could be done at what he described as a relatively moderate cost in American casualties—about 40,000. His casual employment of these figures, along with such suggestions as the merging of the church and the Pentagon, seemed to affirm that he viewed the clash with Communism as a religious war as well as one for world primacy.

After visiting the prime minister of Japan and spending Thanksgiving in Tokyo, Luce went on to Taiwan. The smiling Chiang and his dynamic Madame feted the journalist who had poured American dollars into their coffers, fought for them in adversity and had seen them through to a considerable if more modest grandeur in Taiwan. "Give us the tools," Chiang said, "and we will finish the job of reconquering Red China." Luce was photographed with Chiang and was honored by a parade of "battle-ready troops" for his inspection.

It was true that Chiang no longer led in total number of Time cover stories. Three Eisenhower cover stories in 1952 had put the general ahead of the Gimo nine to seven. But the Chiangs, kept posted by their Washington embassy, knew of Luce's bitter battle against Acheson and of Luce's indoctrination of the incoming administration and the American people in the matter of support for Chiang. Praise for him had appeared and was appearing in almost every issue of Time, Life and Fortune. Luce's emissary John Osborne had visited Taiwan and, in a full-page dispatch to Time fairly foaming with rage, had denounced Truman and Acheson for their "blind and stubborn" failure to give the Gimo military support regarded as adequate. The Lucepress displayed constant ingenuity in aiding Chiang. For example, an Artzybasheff Time cover showing Mao followed by hordes of locusts had, along with the text enlarging on the depiction of the Communist leader as a plague, been almost as good as a Gimo cover.

All this had involved an inner struggle for Luce, who ordinarily respected only success. Chiang had failed on the mainland. Luce's dilemma had been resolved by Chiang's dependable anti-Communism and his iron-handed success in ruling the unfortunate and resentful Formosans whose island he had invaded. Moreover, he was now convinced that Chiang was gaining strength that would actually enable him to cross to the mainland and redeem it from the usurping Reds. Luce, who was also gathering material for a signed article on the Far East for Life, expressed in one memo a confidence in the Gimo that was wisely excised from his Life account:

After Chiang Kai-shek has landed and maintained himself for three months on
the mainland, the Communist menace to Asia will be finished and the whole of
Asia will turn anti-Communist.

This astonishing appraisal seemed to qualify him more for the role of Old
Testament prophet than for Secretary of State. It would prove to be not only
terribly mistaken about Chiang but to embrace monumental errors about the
force of Communism in Asia—errors that Theodore White and such China
hands as John Paton Davies and John Carter Vincent had fruitlessly warned
against. Yet Luce and Dean Rusk, who had described the Mao regime as non-
Chinese, a Russian puppet, a "Slavic Manchukuo," were voicing what became official theory and which Dulles embraced so heartily that for years he
would seek methods for fomenting the revolt against Mao which was believed
inevitable. Luce, in his Life piece, would so repeatedly stress the "moral,"
"Christian" and "religious" sponsorship for his anti-Communist crusade that
Mary Bancroft in Zurich, after reading it, would comment on the unusual
literalness of his beliefs:

> I wonder if perhaps one basic misunderstanding which short-circuits our—
> yours & mine—communications *politically* isn't that I simply can't understand
> how any intelligent person can think the Christian religion is *true*. . . . I can &
> do separate religion & *thought-intellect* completely.

Luce could not. If it was true, as he had told the Time*men* at the Union Club,
that Chiang had been skimped in the value judgment, he was repairing the injury. His article in Life would prove to be a series of rectified value judgments, picturing Chiang as "a devout Methodist" as was his "beautiful lady,"
and stressing that America at long last had "developed a world-wide policy of
anti-Communism" in which Chiang was a most valued ally even if the Democrats seemed unaware of it. Luce also turned his thoughts to military strategy.
He envisioned Chiang's forces as the center of a three-pronged assault on
mainland China, the other two being in Korea and Indochina.

When he went on to Manila he was inevitably attracted by the hard-fisted
defense secretary, Ramon Magsaysay, because of his sanguinary warfare
against the Communist-allied Hukbalahap rebels. Already Time had rewarded Magsaysay ("a national hero") with a cover story depicting him, like
Sir Gerald Templer, as a fellow who knew how to handle Reds. Luce set in
motion arrangements for Life to pay Magsaysay $5000 for an article ex-
plaining his success in suppressing Communists and to give him every aid in
his campaign to succeed Elpidio Quirino as president in the 1953 elections.
The Philippine government was even more corrupt than Chiang's and the lot
of the people was abysmal, but the important thing there, as elsewhere, was
anti-Communism.

In Jakarta Luce was so impressed by the charming, Princeton-educated at-
taché Walter Guzzardi, Jr., who escorted him around in the absence of Ambassador Merle Cochran, that he made a note to hire Guzzardi away from the

government. Next stop, Saigon. Here Luce spent two days with the American ambassador, Donald Heath, and hit on a method of winning the Indochinese war—a victory that had eluded the French for six years while France was being bled white. Now it was America's war as well. The insufficiently anti-Communist Truman administration, perhaps in part due to the demands of Time and Life, had arranged to foot most of the bills while France continued the fighting against Ho Chi Minh's Vietnamese. Thus Truman, exhorted by Luce, became the first of five American Presidents involved in Vietnam—an involvement still existing at this writing, nineteen years later. A French plan then was to train an indigenous army that could handle the situation so that the *poilus* could leave—an effort duplicated many years later by the Americans under the name of Vietnamization.

Ho's Vietnamese had been American allies. They had fought the Japanese and Vichy French during the war and by its end had won control of most of the countryside. In September 1945 the Vietnamese had promulgated a Declaration of Independence, written for Ho, which began with a tribute to the United States, a country then much admired in Vietnam:

"All men are created equal. They are endowed by their Creator with certain inalienable rights; among these are Life, Liberty and the pursuit of Happiness."

This immortal statement was made in the Declaration of Independence of the United States of America in 1776. In a broader sense, this means: All the peoples have a right to live, to be happy and free.

But humiliated France at war's end was determined to regain her "empire," and the Potsdam conferees (including anti-imperialist Russia) decided that Indochina was still the property of France. Returning French troops drove the new government from Saigon. After an uneasy armistice during which Ho's party won a national election and the Republic of Vietnam was framed to continue "within the French Union"—that is, as a colony—fighting began again and blood was still flowing when Luce arrived.

Luce knew that the French had exploited Vietnam's people and resources in the ruthless colonial tradition. He was, despite his American Century dreams, against colonialism *per se*. He was in favor of national self-determination and independence. The Vietnamese deserved freedom after almost a century of French rule. The French had set up a puppet government in the south under Bao Dai (who had been on Time's cover in 1950) which was itself a model of cynicism and corruption.

Luce knew all this. In fact, he had every reason to favor the Vietnamese struggle for freedom except for the value judgment which his publications had been so instrumental in building into an American religion—that Communism was a monolithic world conspiracy, and that Communism anywhere was therefore an enemy. Despite the strong evidence that Ho was a determined nationalist and nobody's stooge, he was indubitably a Communist.

"The Emperor [Bao Dai]," Luce wrote, "was pleasantly polite but he gave

me nothing to be enthusiastic about." Ambassador Heath escorted him on a visit to the puppet prime minister, then a quick journey to the front. Luce recorded in his notes:

> The war can be won—and quite speedily—provided that the political climate is changed . . . and provided, of course, that the Chinese don't come in full scale. . . . Or, if they do come in, it will be quite as convenient for us to destroy Chinese Communist armies in Indochina as anywhere else. . . . The clearing out of guerrillas is a messy business but this can be done any time the pressure in the North is not too severe.

This appraisal after forty-eight hours seemed to belittle the French, who had given the war intense thought for six years without finding an easy solution. Luce also seemed rash in his estimate of the ease of "clearing out guerrillas" and in challenging Mao's half billion to land battle—a battle which his use of the pronoun "us" made it appear that he had joined personally with his country. Always alert for Time ideas, he cabled Billings:

> Please get started cover painting Admiral Radford with background indicating vast Pacific and Far Eastern area. Had excellent visit with jungle and delta war and keenly anticipate reunion New York.

Then, giving a day and a half to Singapore, as he described it, "After all these encounters I flew in 33 hours, 8,000 miles from Singapore to London to dine at 10 Downing Street with Winston Churchill and his principal crony, Lord Camrose."

If he was not gray with fatigue as he dined with the prime minister, he was superhuman. It is a reasonable guess that he gave Churchill a report on his Far Eastern talks and urged, despite England's recognition of Mao, that she take a more active role in America's world anti-Communist crusade. While Churchill cordially detested Communists and liked to say, "their blood flows green," he was, along with most Europeans, able to take a less evangelical and more realistic attitude toward them—a posture that was becoming an annoyance to Luce.

There was talk in London that Luce, because of his aid to Eisenhower, would succeed Walter S. Gifford as ambassador to the Court of St. James's—a job he would surely have prized. "One man who would like to be Ambassador is Henry Luce," said the London Daily Mirror without qualification. A night's sleep and he was off for New York, where he saw Eisenhower forty-eight hours after alighting.

He talked to the President-elect fresh from a world tour highlighted by discussions with many important figures and climaxed by dinner with Churchill. Winthrop Aldrich had meanwhile been designated ambassador to England. Clare had called on Eisenhower November 28, during Luce's absence but with his knowledge. He offered her, she later said, the Secretaryship of Labor —a post she thought unsuited to her talents. When he offered her the ambassadorship at Rome, she accepted on condition that Luce help her.

338

XXVII

1. MORALITY, HO!

After two decades of Democratic rule, the Eisenhower administration rolled in on a powerful tide of piety strangely foaming with aggressiveness. First place in the inaugural parade was given to a creation called "God's float," bearing the legends "Freedom of Worship" and "In God We Trust"—public notice of the Republican affiliation with the Almighty. The aggressiveness was supplied less by the General-of-the-Army President than by his pipe-smoking Secretary of State, a prayerful man with a mission identical with the Luce mission: to see America liberate the world. At times Dulles's excessive enthusiasm about this irked the President. It was all very well to attack the Democratic policy of containment of Communism in campaign oratory and to go them one better with a gospel of liberation. Eisenhower wanted it understood that this business of "liberation" did not mean that we were going over there to do it by force—something Dulles seemed to forget at times.

"[Dulles's] policies have a religious motivation," Life explained to America. ". . . he is trying to put U.S. policy back on an explicitly moral basis . . ."

In Los Angeles the Rev. James Miller offered a prayer beginning, "Now that virtue has been restored to high places . . ."

Immediately after taking office, Dulles appeared on television to warn the nation of the threat of Communist envelopment. Pointing to a huge map behind him which showed the great mass of Russia and China in black, he told how, under the Democrats, the Communists had in seven years increased their might from a control over 200 million people to 800 millions, "and they're hard at work to get control of other parts of the world." His dry lawyer's voice painted a picture of creeping terror, of the enemy sneaking around the American flanks: "The Soviet Communists are carrying out a policy which they call encirclement. . . . They said they didn't want to start an open war

against us until they get such overwhelming power that the results will not be in doubt . . ." He warned that if the Russians "largely completed their encirclement of the United States," they would gobble us up.

As he spoke, the United States had bases in Okinawa, Saudi Arabia, Turkey, Libya, Morocco and England, and would soon complete one in Spain, from all of which it could deliver nuclear bombs to Russia and/or China. It had military alliances with fourteen European countries. It would soon arrange military cooperation with Iraq and Iran. It was about to complete military-defense alliances with Australia, the Philippines, Thailand and Pakistan. American military forces were in Korea and Japan, and the United States was supporting the French in Indochina. America recognized Chiang on Taiwan as "China" and soon would heap armaments on the Chiang 600,000-man army, a hundred miles from Red China.

America was being encircled? There was semantic confusion here perhaps wilder than that depicted in Orwell, comical in its Orwellian way and filled with the same undercurrent of terror. The terror arose from the reversal of meaning and the annihilation of logic. American words were departing from sense. If American leaders could actually believe such things, then there was no limit to what Americans might say and do in defense of what they believed. The fact that it was a lay religious leader who uttered the words about encirclement added to the paradox. And if the Lucepress claim that it had 40 million readers was correct, then these 40 million were well preconditioned to listen to Dulles with serious attention.

The predictions of Orwell came to strange realization in the person of the multimillionaire Presbyterian elder in the television studio pointing gravely at the map, showing millions of Americans how they were being encircled.

Nor was the Weekly Newsmagazine free from the Orwellian in its praise for the Dulles lecture and Dulles's aim to create in other peoples "such a love and respect for freedom that they can never really be absorbed by the despotism, the totalitarian dictatorship of the Communist world," and Time's conclusion: "Already, the Eisenhower-Dulles approach had begun to pay off."

The President joined a Presbyterian church. Cabinet meetings began with prayer, one Washington joke ending, "Damn it, we forgot the opening prayer." Government men had Bible breakfasts, special church services, prayer groups and a "Back to God" crusade that suggested that there had been slippage. Life magazine, in an article about the President's religion, noted heavy attendance at Senate and House prayer groups. Only the great and near great gained entry to the prayer breakfast of the International Council of Christian Laymen, where ham and eggs preceded a New Testament reading by Vice President Nixon and the singing of hymns. Dulles, Luce's only rival in the perception of America's special position as moral counsel for the world (he would compile a grand total of more than fifty speeches and articles on the subject) spoke at this time on "The Power of Moral Forces."

America, he said, had that power: "I can assure you that your President, your Cabinet, your Congress, recognize the priority of spiritual forces."

The piety that settled over the Potomac and spread like a contagion over the land seemed a protective reaction against godless Communism and a self-congratulatory closing of ranks among the faithful. J. Edgar Hoover put it bluntly: "Since Communists are anti-God, encourage your child to be active in the church." Vice President Nixon said in his earnest way, "Among the great privileges that we enjoy is the privilege of hearing President Eisenhower pray at the beginning of his inauguration. That could not happen in half the world today."

Meanwhile, Bishop Sheen, who had ushered Mrs. Luce into the church and had played tennis with Luce at the swank River Club, was now the television priest whose handsomeness and suavity had rocketed him in the ratings as he assured Americans of their blessed advantage over Communists. Sheen's boss and Luce's good friend Cardinal Spellman worked incessantly to put down Communists in the Far East, but had no more respect for the Russian variety of Communists, whom he called, "God-hating, lustful beasts masquerading as men." Luce's closest Catholic friend and debating companion, the Jesuit Father John Courtney Murray, was more scholarly in his analysis of the American "moral function" of justice as opposed to the Marxist social function, vesting all rights in the state. Billy Graham and Dr. Norman Vincent Peale, both friends of Luce's, had enormously successful radio-television programs in which they spread the gospel of an America which, for all its little transgressions, had a God on its side not permitted beyond the Oder-Neisse line. None of these men seemed sufficiently enwrapped in universal love to escape all of the implications of the words of Richard Hofstadter:

Religion, for many individuals or groups, may be an expression of serene belief, personal peace, and charity of mind. But for more militant spirits it may also be a source or an outlet for animosities. There is a militant type of mind to which the hostilities involved in any human situation seem to be its most interesting or valuable aspect; some individuals live by hatred as a kind of creed . . .

Probably most Americans, if asked to name the one who most nearly combined the function of founder and most effective long-term promoter of national anti-Communism and religious-moral superiority, would have named someone like Spellman or Dulles. This would have done a great injustice to Luce. He had worked at it longer and harder and more influentially—and in his odd way, more quietly, week after week for twenty-nine years—than anyone else in sight. The national build-up of sizzling simplism and zealotry was exemplified in the virile American talk of Mike Hammer in Mickey Spillane's *One Lonely Night*, which sold three million copies: "I killed more people tonight than I have fingers on my hands. I shot them in cold blood and enjoyed every minute of it. . . . They were Commies, Lee. They were red sons-of-bitches who should have died long ago. . . . They never thought there were

people like me in this country. They figured us all to be as soft as horse manure and just as stupid."

2. TWISTING THE LEG

Mrs. Luce, to whom Luce referred in his letters as "The Ambassador," sailed for Naples with her husband-adviser and his sister, Mrs. Moore, April 14, 1953. Luce, seemingly made of steel wires, had gone at full speed except for one brief holiday since his swing around the world. Along with Arthur Hays Sulzberger and General Adler of the New York Times, he had lunched at the Bernard Baruch home in New York with Churchill, the subject this time being the forthcoming sixth volume of his memoirs, to be published both by Life and the Times. It was Luce's second prandial meeting with Churchill, on different continents, in hardly more than a fortnight. ("Why should anyone who lunches with Churchill even have to *open* a letter from me?" Mary Bancroft wrote with less humility than humor.) He had attended the inauguration and several inaugural parties including one at the home of Philip Graham. With his top staff men he had lunched in the private Time dining room with Ambassador Abba Eban of Israel—another in the endless series of Luce-sponsored luncheons with newsmakers and news-explainers. He had flown to Oregon to address a press gathering on the need for high ideals in newspapering, returning too late to attend the swearing-in of his wife by Chief Justice Fred Vinson with Secretary Dulles beaming approval.

The death of Stalin and the succession of Malenkov filled two successive issues of Time with ominous adjectival material. Luce had fired burst after burst of memos admonitory, suggestive or approving to bolster the magazines against his absence, though he would be back briefly in June. He congratulated Alexander on a cover story about Thornton Wilder except for its lack of real point: "The horse having run beautifully through fields and over brooks balked at the big hurdle." To FN Editor Thomas Griffith he addressed a suggestion for a special Time section on Europe with the preamble:

> Europe—what a great word! And how great the cycles through which it has traveled since the Bull took the lady for that memorable ride through the surf!

Meanwhile the Democratic Hearst columnist Frank Conniff voiced a partisan complaint even though speaking from a journalistic rostrum hardly known for impartiality:

> Time Magazine . . . has already earned ranking as the house-organ of the Republican Administration. And I do mean the house-organ. I mean, the thing is out there explaining, apologizing, and interpreting the various Republican moves in a way that might make a discerning reader nauseous. . . . I gather from the pages of Time Magazine that a new race of geniuses has descended on Washington. . . . Clare Boothe Luce. . . . This is the best possible Ambassador for Italy?

The ambassador-designate had thrown plenty of dead cats and was now getting them back from both sides of the Atlantic. The job ahead of her was formidable. There were great dissimilarities between U.S. anti-Communist tactics in Italy and the Far East. The Cold War having reached its sustained pitch, the U.S. was exerting financial and political pressure to keep Italy's minority but powerful Communist party from gaining control. In any case it backed an honest and honorable man, the Christian Democrat Alcide de Gasperi, who was working manfully to solve the country's grievous problems, which included 2,500,000 unemployed. Almost $3 billion in American aid had poured in. The earlier Ambassadors James Dunn and Ellsworth Bunker had let it be known in discreet and gentle terms that a Communist victory would diminish or stop the flow. This was the sort of suggestion that had to be made with tact rather than the twisting of the Italian arm, or leg. Mrs. Luce's record of strident anti-Communism and the opinion of some friends that tact was a quality unknown to her, raised the question of whether she was equipped to get maximum political mileage out of American aid to Italy. Since her husband and adviser was as emotional in his anti-Communism and, if it were possible, even less versed in tact, there were grounds for doubting that the American embassy in Rome would serve either of the two countries as well as it should.

There was a nonpartisan conviction in Italy that while women were unsurpassed as mothers, sopranos and mistresses, important political posts were exclusively the province of men—an axiom that persuaded many Italians that America had downgraded Italy's importance in sending an *ambasciatrice*. "What do you think we are, Luxembourg?" a lesser Italian official had inquired. Italian Communists of course despised Mrs. Luce. She was referred to in Communist quarters as "a comic-opera ambassador" and as "a kind of superannuated canasta player." The monarchist paper Candido featured a picture of the Stars and Stripes edged with frilly lace. Another paper ran a picture of the actress Claire Luce, who was no relation, playing Cleopatra in seductive deshabille, identifying her as the new ambassador and bringing consternation to Pope Pius XII.

In 1948 Mrs. Luce and Joseph P. Kennedy had helped raise $2 million from American donors to help de Gasperi defeat the Communists. Still in power, he faced elections in June in which it was feared that his majority might dwindle. Hence the new ambassador faced an early crisis. She was serious about her job, determined to succeed at it. After a long session of writing which had been less successful than her earlier work, her political ambitions had returned and it seemed evident that she hoped to move even higher than this considerable eminence.

Luce's personal assistant, Edward C. Finch, had been sent on ahead with Margaret Quimby, the blonde and learned top researcher for Time, to prepare a place for the Boss. Luce, never sensitive about keeping his magazines clear of other interests, had been persuaded that he must have an office en-

tirely separate both from the embassy and Rome's Time bureau. This would help allay suspicion on the part of other news organizations and officials that he and his bureau had a pipeline of inside information from his ambassador wife, to the disadvantage of others. When Luce arrived, his personal office was ready—six rooms on the Corso d'Italia overlooking the Villa Borghese cypresses, a staff of six and a Lancia and driver. It was on the fourth floor, but Italian elevators were so slow that there would be time for quick prayer. Billings was running the New York shop in his absence, but Luce would keep in close touch and would be in New York half the time.

He lived with his wife in the government-owned, seventeenth-century Villa Taverna, a scant mile away across the park on the Viale Rossini. A lovely building with extensive gardens and a staff of eighteen servants, it had cost the U.S. $840,000 in 1948. Into it the Luces moved a large part of their expanded collection of paintings, including works by Delacroix, Manet, Renoir, Degas, Pissarro, Rouault, plus canvases by Churchill and Noel Coward. Time's Rome bureau was a ten-minute walk to the south of Luce's office. The American embassy was ten minutes farther south, the spacious Villa Margherita on the Via Veneto.

Social invitations to the Luces would be addressed, "Ambassador and Mr. Luce." Since as ambassador she had precedence over every other American in Italy, and as plain Mr. Luce he had no precedence at all, there were immediate crises in protocol. Should the lady sit at the head of the table and her husband a kilometer away? It was solved when the Italian government gave Luce the honorary rank of minister. He professed satisfaction, saying, "I sit down among the young and pretty girls." Nonexistent was his own sense of protocol. Finch caught him putting on a soft business shirt to wear with his Prince Albert while accompanying Clare to the Quirinale for the highly formal rite of her presentation of her credentials to President Luigi Einaudi.

"Harry, you can't wear that," Finch protested.

"Why not? Why not?" he demanded in his repetitive way. It turned out that he had forgotten to bring a stiff shirt and thought the soft one quite adequate. He accepted the loan of Finch's shirt and remarked afterward that it was true, every man there had worn a boiled shirt.

Clare was in charge of all U.S. government operations in Italy—the embassy, the Mutual Security Agency, the military advisory group, eight consulates and nine information centers. She was top boss over 1150 Americans and Italians. She took possession of a vast desk in the embassy's splendid Louis XV room, with the American flag to her right and her ambassadorial flag to her left—forty-eight stars on a blue background which she was entitled to fly from any warship in which she sailed. As a "political" ambassador she would be watched sharply by the career people in the embassy. As a person in the public eye whose opinions were moving rightward, she would be scrutinized by liberals back home.

There had of course been rumors and speculation about a cooling of the re-

lationship between the Luces. The ambassadorship was an instance of a mutuality rare to them. For much of their seventeen years of married life they had done things separately—one might almost say in rivalry. Now they were working at something together, at least for a part of the "half the time" that Luce agreed to give Rome. He was proud of her position, conscious of its difficulties and anxious to help. Indeed he was jealous of her prerogatives, reproving an American admiral who forgot that her rank entitled her to sit on the right side of the rear seat in the officer's limousine. It seemed to mark a new beginning for the Luces, perhaps implying an agreement that they had been too much divided and would give togetherness a try for four years, the ambassadorial term usually expected. If that was so, it was also true that Luce had long wanted to study Italy at leisure instead of on the fly, and now, as a dedicated sightseer and world problem-solver, Communist-threatened Rome was at his doorstep and all Europe was nearby.

Three weeks in one place was about all he could stand without exploding. In three weeks he abandoned his duties as assistant ambassador and hurried to London in his guise as Secretary of State *pro tempore* to put Churchill and the British right vis-à-vis the U.S. Clement Attlee had made critical mention of Senator McCarthy in the Commons. In the Commons, too, Churchill had gone so far as to imply willingness that Red China enter the UN after a settlement of the Korean war—an idea Luce as well as Dulles would fight to the death. On May 21 Churchill lunched with the American publisher who had enriched him and to whom Churchill still hoped to sell more of his writings— a business connection perhaps not politically influential on either side. Significantly, Luce privately scoffed at Churchill's qualifications in Far Eastern diplomacy. A cable from London bureau chief Laguerre gave New York the gist:

> Luce lunched with Churchill yesterday, and afterwards said he had found his host very reassuring. Luce felt that Churchill has at last taken the trouble to learn some of the facts about the Far East. This is quite a recent development. . . . Churchill disclaimed responsibility for Attlee's speech last week. . . . On the possibility of Big Four talks, Churchill emphasized that things might or might not have taken a turn in Russia. We ought to know about those people, he repeated. It would be wrong to pass up any opportunity to probe present intentions in Moscow. Luce did not get the impression that Churchill wanted to make any concessions. . . . Luce was relieved to find that Churchill seemed to have no illusions about Mao's regime or Red China's real feelings toward the West. [Churchill agreed that] it was a "matter of American honor" that in no circumstances should Formosa be surrendered to the Reds, before or after a settlement. Luce's feeling was that Churchill's general position on the Far East was by no means as bad as might have been feared. He thought this was a good time for Washington and London to get together on these practical matters. . . . Their conversation was naturally private.

Luce also talked with T. S. Matthews who was working in London on an illusory project of starting and heading a British edition of Time. This Lucean

hocus-pocus had been devised in order to get Matthews away from New York and to swish him out of the organization. Luce returned to Rome to help the ambassador fight the Communist enemy there.

Clare was aware of her weakness for seizing the limelight and for speaking hastily and for effect. She was determined to correct them. On her desk was a motto: "*And above all, not too much zeal.—*Talleyrand."

But Talleyrand was not always at hand. Power and religious dogma were employed both by the ambassador and her husband-assistant before the June elections. Luce saw to it that the Catholic de Gasperi was Time's cover man at the moment of greatest influence, presented in heroic guise as the bulwark of Italian morality and religion. He was, Time said, Italy's representative of the same morality and "religious inspiration" as France's M.R.P. and Adenauer's Christian Democracy in West Germany. Italian Communists were likened by Time to wolves slashing at "the shaky-legged colt of Italian democracy."

This was a propagandist oversimplification, since the Communists, whatever their Soviet connections, as Luigi Barzini observed, were "also the largest and most powerful labor party, the only one which actively defends the workers' interests." At the same time, Mrs. Luce was discovered giving out crucifixes in La Martella, an occupation permissible for a priest but suspect when done by the American ambassador, as the Communist paper L'Unità saw things. She was under constant and inimical surveillance. Then she made a speech to the American Chamber of Commerce in Milan, saying that if the elections went the wrong way it would have "grave consequences for the intimate and friendly cooperation between Italy and the United States." Here was open meddling, said her critics. A speech she made the following night at Genoa about the extent of American aid to Italy was widely interpreted as twisting the leg a little farther. The de Gasperi government lost crucial seats both in the Chamber and Senate and went out of power in less than two months. Some declared that the leg-twisting had lost votes for the center parties. It was recalled that Signor Luce had "adopted" China, and "look what happened there." It was not an auspicious beginning either for the ambassador or her assistant.

3. YEAR OF THE SNAKE

Had Italy gone Communist, according to observers inclined to the humor of exaggeration, the ambassador and her assistant would have demanded a proclamation of martial law, called in the American Army, Navy and Air Force, and themselves manned machine guns from the Villa Taverna. The Communists, however, were far from a majority and Italy staggered along under four different premiers for the next eight months. That keen observer Luigi Barzini, becoming friendly with the Luces, decided that while the am-

bassador seemed an actress enacting Clare Boothe Luce, a coiner of epigrams and puns, she was if anything overconscientious, working long hours although she wilted in the Roman heat, concerned because she could not get the Italians to worry about themselves as much as she did.

"What can be done?" she would exclaim in desperation. "What can I, what can the government of the United States do?"

Palmiro Togliatti, the Communist leader, disparaged her, once calling her "a poor old lady" who brought Italy nothing but bad luck. It was a fine thing, she remarked, that while the government defended her against his less wounding charges, "nobody remembered to deny that I am an 'old lady.' "

Luce, having spent almost his allotted three consecutive weeks in Italy, flew to America, in part for a round of visits in Washington. He was losing no opportunity to get as close as possible to this first G.O.P. administration since his name carried national prestige. In a memo to Alexander he bewailed Eisenhower's "great mistake" in failing to fire Generals Omar Bradley and Lawton Collins from their berths in the Joint Chiefs—a reminder that he could scarcely forgive their failure to give MacArthur his head. He talked with the Vice President and liked him:

> Dick Nixon. "He's grown in the last few months," says W. Chambers. "He's invaluable in the National Security Council," says a fellow-member—being about the only one . . . who knows about the "realities of politics"—and instead of trying to wish them away, tries to fit policies to politics and vice-versa. In a short interview I was greatly impressed with this young man.

He flew back to Rome, where his wife was nervously chainsmoking filter cigarettes as she sought to encourage the formation of an Italian coalition to stand off the Communists. He gave her enough of his time and advice so that it was said that America got two ambassadors for the price of one—perhaps an appraisal more felicitous than true, since both Luces had difficulty in restraining their zeal and were said to have offended de Gasperi and other Italian leaders with efforts that were thought meddlesome.

Luce also explored Rome on the side, often getting lost in back streets. Like the ambassador, he ran his office on American hours, without the three-hour midday siesta observed by all Italians. His valued aide and social adviser, the half-American Duchessa Elena Lante della Rovere, steered him (and his wife) through intricate Roman social mazes which otherwise would have defeated him. He studied Italian with little success. As always, he could be cruel or kindly, often treating Robert Neville, head of his Rome bureau, like an errand boy but showing kindness to his own office staff. When he learned that Margaret Quimby was troubled by the heat when she went home for lunch, he gave her the use of the office car. Miss Quimby, terrified of him, found him so considerate under his formidable exterior that she later decided her fear was absurd. He would, however, appropriate her cigarettes if she left them within his reach.

His manners were still startling, seemingly the result of self-preoccupation carried to the point of insensibility to others. Dining at a restaurant with friends, he would become so absorbed in his own monolog that he would impatiently wave away the waiter who sought to take their orders. He forgot that they had come there to eat and that his companions were hungry. Once, returning to the Villa Taverna, he encountered young Shirley Potash, who had been one of Clare's assistants for several years and whom Clare had invited for a visit without thinking to inform him.

"What are you doing here?" he demanded without greetings or preliminaries.

"Clare invited me for a couple of weeks," she replied.

"Oh," he said and walked away, this being the total of the conversation. Later, however, he took her to lunch and was perfectly charming.

Visiting Bonn early in August, he subjected his local bureau chief, Frank White, to the usual fusillade of questions, was fascinated by a visit to the Henkel soap works and praised Germany because "there is no Communist Party to amount to anything in Germany." Disgusted with the endless Cabinet crises in France, he sent up prayers of thanks for Adenauer, who not only worshiped the Christian God but was forming a powerful bulwark against the infidel. "God bless him," he implored in a letter to Billings, saying it was unfortunate that America was delaying so long in rearming Germany.

His visit was spoiled by his discovery that the French were erupting over a sixteen-page feature in Life on the Indochina war whose pictures and text had been supplied by David Douglas Duncan. Titled "Year of the Snake," its theme was that "ineffective French tactics and ebbing French will" made it appear that Indochina was "all but lost to the non-Communist world." French staff officers were pictured as enjoying "bankers' hours," long siestas and carefree weekends while more and more of the country was won by Ho's Vietminh. Only in daylight was it safe to travel in most areas, the guerrillas taking over at nightfall. France, with one ineffective government following another, was pictured as seeking an excuse to get out of the war. Vietnamese soldiers, not anxious to die for France, did not fight well. American millions were being wasted there. Duncan quoted two United States officials sent to Indochina by the Mutual Security Administration as saying that huge sums earmarked as aid for the people were largely lost through inefficiency and outright grafting on the part of the French-sponsored puppet government. One of them, Dr. Malcolm Gaar, said, "I am distressed—I am embarrassed—I am often ashamed," at the failure of American aid to get through to the masses for these reasons.

The other, Herman Holiday, shook Luce by uttering the unutterable in Life. Holiday had earlier been in China and had seen the United States back Chiang despite the fact that he had lost the people. The same thing was happening all over again in Indochina, Holiday said, with France and America

supporting a government not representing the people, and, "We seem to have learned very little from our failure in China."

It was true that America had learned little. Those who had learned had been flayed by the Lucepress, then by Senators McCarthy and Nixon and all the Republicans as either traitors or incompetents. The Paris press from Figaro to L'Humanité reacted to the Life article with furious charges of "odious," "outrageous" and "despicable." The French Foreign Ministry called the Life article "defamation and slander." L'Aurore went so far as to snap at Monsieur and Madame Luce:

> As director of Life and Ambassadress in Rome, respectively, Mr. and Mrs. Luce have for a considerable time been in the habit of writing and saying anything with rather doubtful success [so translated].

There were tense cables about "Rover Boy" Duncan between Luce and Billings, and between Luce and Edward K. Thompson, managing editor of Life. Luce received an anguished letter from Ambassador Heath in Saigon, who had been his host there eight months earlier, saying in five single-spaced pages that it was not so and how could Life do this? Heath enclosed a statement by Herman Holiday saying that Duncan had not quoted him correctly. Dr. Gaar had suddenly left the government service, though it was claimed that he had left voluntarily.

Returning to Rome, Luce wrote a long letter to Billings which he tore up, as he said in a letter next day, because it was less rational than emotional. He said that the more he thought about it the more outraged he became at the Rover Boy. Duncan was admittedly a valuable man who had done excellent photo-reporting from Korea and elsewhere. Indeed, a letter from Eric Gibbs, now heading Luce's Paris bureau, said that a candid official in the French office for Indochinese affairs admitted privately that there was much truth in the Duncan story but that things were "changing." Things, as would become evident year after year, were always "changing" there.

Luce ordered that Duncan see him in Rome. Life published a hurried "correction" of the Duncan story, featuring the new French offensive under General Henri Navarre (who also became Time's cover-hero) which, it said, had already destroyed 5000 tons of Vietminh materials. It included a patriotic statement by Ambassador Heath titled "France Is Fighting the Good Fight" and saying in terms that would become well-worn over the years that the Indochinese had a great stake in the war: "independence in the community of free nations or subjugation under Communist dictatorship."

One of the more interesting of journalistic confrontations occurred on the evening of September 2 when the thirty-five-year-old, Kansas City-born Duncan sat down among orange trees in the garden of the Villa Taverna with a beetle-browed Luce. Duncan had the advantage in everything but rank, having been in Indochina eight weeks to Luce's two days and being a reporter who insisted on presenting the case not according to mythology but according

349

to his own investigation. He would be confirmed—and Luce would be re-futed—in a matter of months at Dienbienphu. He wrote a long letter to Managing Editor Thompson of Life describing the meeting:

> Mr. Luce was of the immediate opinion that my story was "defeatist" and therefore wrong. When I turned to pick up the magazine which I had brought with me, and started to say that there were some solid, constructive opinions about how the situation might be improved, he became quite indignant and said that I apparently had no desire to hear what he thought, as I, apparently, had no concern for any opinion other than my own.

Luce insisted that "great changes" had been made in Indochina and that Duncan had reported on a situation no longer prevailing. Duncan, not one easily intimidated, politely disagreed, saying he had consulted the most qualified sources, felt the story absolutely accurate and that no significant changes had taken place since. Luce, comparing Duncan's story to Acheson's "defeatism" about China, then produced one of his more ingenious rationalizations for the suppression of truth:

> Mr. Luce then pointed out that an entirely true story can be a wrong and malicious story . . . and drew a comparison between France's plight now and Britain's during 1940. He pointed out that it would have been wrong to point to the shortcomings of British colonialism at a time when the only country trying to stand against the Nazis was nearly on her knees.

There was mention of Duncan's original cable to Thompson proposing the story, in which Duncan commented that newsmen in Hanoi were betting ten to one that Life would not run such an account. Thompson had replied that Duncan had "a hell of a nerve" to predict what Thompson would or would not run. Luce suggested that this had been a sly maneuver to make Thompson rise to the bait, and inquired whether Duncan questioned Thompson's ability and desire to give straightforward reportage. Not at all, said Duncan:

> Mr. Luce then added that I must have been referring to the policy of the magazine. I agreed. He then added that I must have been referring to him. I answered "Yes." I added that it was the opinion of many reporters, myself included, that a bare-knuckle story on Indo-China would not be tolerated because of France's role as our ally . . . Mr. Luce leaned back into his garden chair, took off his glasses, and didn't say much for several minutes.

The Boss had encountered a frankness that was growing rare in the home office. Duncan observed that if he was a source of embarrassment he should be fired. That was not the answer, Luce replied, but Duncan was "not in step" with the Life organization, which created a great problem. Yet when Duncan left, still out of step, Luce had so far recovered himself—and perhaps discovered respect for a man who stood behind his work and his opinions—that he wished the young man luck. Duncan continued to work for Life (on less sensitive subjects) as did Managing Editor Thompson and Assistant Managing Editor Sidney James, who had edited the story.

But Matthews, after working in London for six months, furnishing an apartment and joining two clubs, found the Time-in-Britain project dropped, as had been the intention all along, and his career as a Timan ended. It was Luce's most complex and elaborate separation of an unwanted man, having taken a year and a half after he first decided that Matthews must go, and cost in the neighborhood of $100,000, what with Matthews's salary and expenses.

"Why did you keep me standing on tiptoe so long," Matthews cabled, "if you weren't going to kiss me?"

4. BURNING THE BOOKS

Luce, the pioneer of the China Lobby, had nurtured it into an organization of enormous influence. Its bloc in Congress included Senators McCarthy, Bridges, McCarran, Knowland, Wherry and Representative Judd, to name only a few. (Wherry had told an enthusiastic crowd, "With God's help, we will lift Shanghai up and up, ever up, until it is just like Kansas City.") Vice President Nixon and Admiral Radford were behind it. It was invariably supported by such patriotic organizations as the American Legion, the D.A.R., the AFL-CIO and the U.S. Chamber of Commerce. It was further abetted by the well-heeled Committee of One Million Against the Admission of Communist China to the United Nations, in which politicians ordinarily as opposed as Senators Dirksen and Douglas found full agreement. Luce was a charter member. The China Lobby was also backed by a third group called the American China Policy Association, one of whose members was Alfred Kohlberg, the importer of Chinese laces. Until the summer of 1951, Clare Boothe Luce had been president of this group.

Less famous workers for Chiang crowded around the Chinese embassy in Washington. Eight hundred thousand dollars allotted the embassy by Taiwan for public relations, augmented by another million dollars arranged for by Madame Chiang, enabled the hiring of expensive publicity men. Both T. V. Soong and H. H. Kung now lived in New York and were influential in the cause.

The "inside men" of the China Lobby who communicated in code by cable directly with Chiang and coordinated activities in Washington were five shrewd Chinese working out of their embassy, headed by Peter T. K. Pee and W. K. Lee—known by the younger Washington Timen as "Pee, Lee and All That." The persistent hope of these merry gentlemen was that America would go to war against Russia and Mao so that the Chiang people could ride comfortably back to power on the thermonuclear wings of World War III. One of their cables, which later fell into American hands through a Chinese code clerk, read in part, "Our hope of a world war so as to rehabilitate our country is unpalatable to the [American] people." Their program of lavish entertainment of legislators was largely supervised by their $25,000-a-year publicity

head, the American William Goodwin. Goodwin threw parties for thirsty Congressmen at the Mayflower Hotel and the Metropolitan Club in Washington and at several places in New York. In one interview he estimated that he had entertained "about 100 Congressmen a year and had converted half of them to support more aid for Nationalist China."

The Lucepress—the Lobby's most potent propagandist voice—had the help of that other Calvinist megaphone of America-first, the Reader's Digest. The Digest occasionally "digested" Lucepress propaganda on China, spreading the message among many more millions, and also carried persuasive pieces of its own, some of which over the years would be authored by Congressman Judd. As with the Lucepress, most of the Digest's readers were unaware of the tutorial slant of the pocket-sized magazine which pretended to be a literary cross-section, and in which they placed abiding faith.

The China Lobby had no trouble dictating the appointment of the new Assistant Secretary of State for the Far East—Luce's old friend Walter Robertson, whose comparative inexperience in that part of the world was redeemed by his dependable Againstness. The American refusal to recognize the Mao regime, which many other civilized nations from Sweden to Israel promptly recognized, seemed calculated to perpetuate the national ignorance about China. Some European politicians and diplomats were astonished at what seemed to them an American denial of reality and an ideology of self-righteousness which might yet make them as objectionable as the most hide-bound Marxists. The British chargé in Peking, Humphrey Trevelyan, reported that the Communist government was generally successful despite enormous problems, that Chiang was *kaput* on the mainland even as a symbol, that it was if anything more important to have representatives in a hostile than in a friendly country, and that the U.S. China policy made no sense.

It was of course the Luce China policy. One of its rituals was illustrated at a Chinese embassy formal dinner at which Senators McCarthy, Knowland and Bridges rose and joined in the shouted toast, "Back to the mainland!" The China Lobby's power was visible in the well-known reshuffle and harassment of Foreign Service China experts held responsible for what had happened, and the dismissal of some of them. The same canonical fervor created a climate in which anti-Chiang or neutral professors might go jobless, since the Lobby "put U.S. academic institutions on notice about whom they might hire as China specialists and what they might teach."

Luce was unruffled by Secretary Dulles's surrender to McCarthy, the investigations of Foreign Service people suspected of not having been "right," and the firing of the China experts John Paton Davies and John Carter Vincent. While Vincent was serving in Switzerland, a Senator McCarthy gumshoe named Charles Davis had arrived to find "Communist" evidence against him. Vincent had received a telegram signed in the name of a Swiss Communist leader, asking for a meeting. It had actually been sent by Davis, who was jailed by the Swiss for the forgery and who wrote Vincent from durance apol-

ogizing for his perfidy. This was a fair gauge of the McCarthy character, a shoddiness that began to stain the administration because of Eisenhower's retreat from the issue and Dulles's subservience to the senatorial primitive.

The Lucepress was so bitter against Vincent and all the hands who had "lost" China that Mrs. Vincent had written Luce, whom she had met at a Georgetown gathering. She protested the attacks, saying that Time saw everything in a "pro-Chiang" or "pro-Mao" light. This, she thought, was a "contrived issue," the correct one being to find what was essentially pro-American. In Luce's reply, he spoke of the "tragedy" of China which came about because of General Marshall's failure in pursuing a "hopeless" policy founded on "hideous error."

He was hardly fair in so denouncing a policy which he had supported as long as he thought it would benefit Chiang. Some of Luce's editors, in their talk of "Harry's mania," meant literally that he was not quite rational on the subject. Nadir was reached when McCarthy's two subalterns, Roy Cohn and David Schine, both twenty-seven, made their eighteen-day inspection tour of USIS posts in Europe, sniffing after Comsymps and pro-Red reading matter. European observers were amazed at the genuflexion before the two young detectives by expert veterans of the Foreign Service. It was widely believed in Europe that Senator McCarthy was more powerful than President Eisenhower—the most powerful man in America, which meant the world. The discovery by Cohn and Schine of a USIS man in Frankfurt who had "once signed a Communist Party petition," his immediate dismissal, and their discovery also of "subversive" books in the overseas libraries, are matters of dolorous memory. In this time of humiliation for the Land of the Free, jittery employees were burning or removing suspect books from many of the USIS's 285 libraries abroad. Among the books banished were those written by anyone of "radical" or unsafe opinions, including the classic sociological study *Middletown*, by the Lynds. Works by the decidedly anti-Communist cousin of the Secretary of State, Foster Rhea Dulles, were thrown out because he had urged the recognition of Red China. Also excluded were books by the leftist Rockwell Kent, detective stories by the leftist Dashiell Hammett and "books by practically anybody who was wrong on China." Secretary Dulles did not protest, nor did Luce.

Nor did the President, although millions were waiting for him to exorcise this national demon. Dodging McCarthy carefully, he could offer nothing more inspiriting in a speech at Dartmouth College than his assurance that it *was* all right to read books, and "How will we defeat Communism unless we know what it is . . . ?"

The evangelical spirit was evident when zealous anti-Communists turned their attention to "subversive" books in high school and college libraries and in bookstores, and a Senate committee and another in the House began investigating Communism in education. No administration leader spoke up, though a chorus of oppositionists including Averell Harriman denounced the vigi-

lante "ministry of fear." The McCarthyites had the headline-a-day Senator inspiring them along with a growing number of influential followers—the Chicago Tribune, the New York Daily News, the Hearst press, and such national leaders as J. Edgar Hoover and Cardinal Spellman. Time had given Hoover a laudatory cover story in which his investigations of people of suspect ideology were shown to be benign. Spellman, whose mansion behind the cathedral was perhaps a horizontal two hundred yards from Luce's Penthouse, occasionally dropped in and the two would go for a brisk walk. Luce was more in agreement with him than with his fellow Bonesman Harriman, as his publications showed. No Lucean fears came to light as the two Congressional watchdog committees summoned educators and editors suspected of unsatisfactory Againstness past or present.

Luce's friend Robert Hutchins, now head of the Ford Foundation, felt differently, saying, "Everywhere in the United States, university professors . . . are silenced by the general atmosphere of repression that prevails." Professor Henry Steele Commager of Columbia University described it as "a campaign of repression and suppression more violent, more reckless, more dangerous than any in our history," adding, "Already teachers fear to discuss certain subjects in the classroom." Bertrand Russell remarked on America's "reign of terror" caused by "policemen who have professors at their mercy." England was concerned enough about McCarthyism so that the new queen in her coronation speech made oblique reference to it in citing England's "free speech and respect for the rights of minorities." The London Economist noted that McCarthyism was "generally loathed" in Europe, while the leftish New Statesman declared, "The Hitler-McCarthy analogy is disturbingly apt." It mentioned powerful interests including "many American industrialists" and "a substantial part of American Roman Catholicism" as being in alliance with McCarthy and added:

> It is anti-Communism that binds these social forces together. It is a deep social malaise that finds the same outlet in anti-Communism as that which so many Germans found in anti-Semitism.

A Luce memo to Max Ways urged that a Timan telephone the two founders of Simon & Schuster and ask how it came about that two of their editors received prominent billing in Senator McCarran's report on "subversives." Another Luce memo gave McCarthy credit for unearthing Communism in government that the Democrats might otherwise have kept hidden. A Life editorial soothingly declared, "McCarthyism is a form of exaggerated campaign oratory"—an idea that John Carter Vincent or Owen Lattimore might have disputed—and that William Jennings Bryan and Henry A. Wallace had likewise employed McCarthyism. Luce began to lose patience when McCarthy attacked Republicans as well and hired a new ex-Communist investigator, Harvey Matusow, who charged that the Time-Life staff harbored "76 hard-core Reds." This was after Whittaker Chambers himself had pro-

nounced the staff clear of Communists and was as credible as Matusow's charge that there were 126 "dues-paying Communists" on the Sunday staff of the New York Times, which actually had a total of ninety-three employees on the Sunday staff. Luce's refusal to see in McCarthyism any threat to civil liberties was evident in a cable he sent to Thompson of Life:

> My basic feeling about the whole McCarthy thing is that its greatest damage to America is that it distracts the American people from the real problems which confront them. Prohibition occupied the minds of Americans in the twenties and the result was the world's greatest depression. McCarthy is a menace to America not because he is a menace to civil liberty as the egg heads wail but because he distracts Americans from serious consideration of the really great things they should be doing for peace and liberty throughout the world. . . . But perhaps the time has come to inquire why such expert politicians as Brownell and Nixon and Knowland and Martin and Hall and Dewey are unable to handle this critter.

Time, in one of its rare boxed editorials, conveyed the idea of McCarthy's rightness, declaring that "The specter of the U.S. in the grip of a hysterical witch hunt, of the President's cowering before McCarthy's power, bears only a specter's relation to reality." Much of McCarthy's fame, it said, came about because of the attacks on him by "the apologists for the New and Fair Deals," and it reminded its readers that "There were, in sober truth, Reds under the bed" and that "the U.S. had traitors and conspirators in the 1930s and '40s, and previously it had Benedict Arnold and Aaron Burr too." As for the book-burnings, Life agreed that some books should be purged, though not the detective stories of Hammett, and suggested that too much fuss had been made about books on both sides. Life also called on the Maryland farmer Whittaker Chambers to answer the question, "Is Academic Freedom in Danger?" in an article of some 6000 words.

Chambers, whose qualifications as a judge of academic freedom might not win unanimous respect, declared that the matter was turned upside down— that freedom of any kind was gone unless Communists were exposed. He dismissed Dr. Hutchins, Professor Commager, Bertrand Russell and their kind as "the voices of the liberal neurosis." He listed professors who took the Fifth Amendment when grilled by Congressional committees about earlier Communist affiliations and noted that Harvard and a few other colleges had brazenly kept them on their faculties anyway. Was that terror? So far, he said, only about fifty "Fifth Amendment educators" had lost their jobs, a number he thought trifling when compared with the total number of educators. He passed over the effect that the fate of the fifty might have on the freedom of the million or more still employed. There was no need for fear among honest men, he said:

> . . . At every move against Communism, liberal nerves come unglued. . . .
> The mass of Americans . . . know perfectly well that they are not living in a

reign of terror and that they seldom look behind a door for anything more frightening than an umbrella. . . . There is no evidence . . . that the congressional committees are trying to impair academic or personal freedom. . . . I have yet to see one witness called before a congressional hearing who could be called "innocent." . . .°

5. THE RIDGEFIELD MEMORANDUM

Things were getting tough enough in Europe so that the devout Adenauer's electoral victory in September 1953 inspired an exultant Luce cable from Rome urging a Life editorial by Jessup and outlining what he should say:

> It is obviously the greatest good news which the cause of freedom and of the United States has had in a long time. Without this great victory United States would not repeat not have had a single genuine collaborator in Europe for Great Britain is now waging a fierce diplomatic battle against us. This is perhaps not repeat not the time to make the point bluntly but in any case we would eye assume wish to say that unless this victory is fully exploited to achieve great upbeat in anti-Communist integration of Europe we really do not repeat not deserve another chance and probably will not repeat not get it. Editorial should not repeat not spend much time on analytical windup but should be one of earnest exhortation to Eisenhower and the American people to get cracking on dynamic foreign policy.

Getting cracking on a dynamic foreign policy meant extending God's earthly realm as Adenauer and Dulles were doing. The encouraged Luce flew back to America on the same day he sent the cable and rested briefly at Ridgefield, where he created one of the outstanding papers of his life although it was no more than five hundred words in length. His reflections there on the partnership of America and God gained immediate support and amplification from Secretary Dulles's September speech to the United Nations, which helped inspire the paper. Dulles made plain America's adherence to the moral law and voiced undying U.S. opposition to Communism. Leaders

---

° In addition to the many college professors who might disagree with Chambers's appraisal of the benignity of these probes were thirty-one grade and high school teachers in New York City alone who lost not only their jobs but in some cases their careers and reputations when they were dismissed during the Red hunt. They were not direct victims of the Congressional committees but of state laws passed as a result of the Congressional furore. They had either refused to answer questions about Communist party membership or had denied membership but had refused "to say whether they ever had been members or had known teachers who were." They suffered "humiliation and degradation," received hate letters and in some cases had difficulty finding other work. In 1967 the Supreme Court (after fifteen years) declared unconstitutional the law under which they were discharged. No restitution had yet been offered them in 1971. Most of them still asked newspapers not to print their names since it might subject them to new abuse and loss of present jobs. It is not known how many thousands of similar cases exist in other cities and states.

of other nations were growing ever more restive over the American Holy Alliance with God, perhaps feeling it hardly fair that the nation possessing so much in the way of riches and other advantages should appropriate the Almighty as well.

Luce realized the difficulties in conveying to other nations the correct idea of America's moral rectitude without seeming to be stuffy or self-righteous about it. Dulles, he thought, did such a fine job of explaining this in the UN that his Ridgefield paper was in large part a tribute to his fellow Presbyterian:

> The significance of Dulles is now clear. He is the champion of the proposition that politics (including international politics) has something to do with morals and that morals have something to do with God. This proposition is revolting to Nehru and Nehru, the atheist, has now defined the significance of Dulles by accusing him (and the whole anti-Communist effort) of possessing "an element of dogmatic fervor, resembling the old approach of bigoted religion."
>
> . . . . [A]s the attack on Dulles has been rising all over the world, it has more and more been centering on his politics of moral Right and Wrong. The French papers have been trying to get their sights on this issue. And only a couple of weeks ago, a leading German paper—yes, in Adenauer's Germany—had a long attack on Dulles as a "Puritan." With much reiteration, it deplored the Puritan streak in America.

Luce clarified the correctness of the American position and its freedom from bigotry:

> The struggle between Freedom and Communism is, at bottom, a moral issue. And any serious moral issue is, at bottom, a religious issue. This, I think, has been our feeling. This surely is the message of Whittaker Chambers. . . . The uniqueness of Abraham Lincoln lies in the fact that he made the moral issue clear. . . . Man is an ambiguous proposition. He is never wholly right. He has never any occasion whatever for self-righteousness. How therefore to put God on your banner without self-righteousness [?]. . . . We must surely support Dulles as vigorously as we can in this effort to establish a moral basis for our world politics. . . .
>
> His handling of this supremely difficult issue in his United Nations speech was, it seemed to me, excellent. In effect, he said that the moral imperative of Freedom was inherent in the consciousness of the American—not something he was inventing or enforcing. He eschewed coercion of others but equally refused to deny the moral imperatives in the American approach.

Luce's failure in humor was most noticeable when he fell back on the moral absolutes that formed the basis of his thinking. Perhaps two of the most Lucean of sentences were the one uttered in his excoriation of Justice Holmes—"I submit to you today that we ought to believe what is true"—and the climactic question in the Ridgefield paper, "How therefore to put God on your banner without self-righteousness?" His admission that man could only be partly right and had no occasion for self-righteousness did not keep God from appearing miraculously on Luce's American banner. The problem was

not whether God was on the banner. He was there, all right, and the problem was to make this plain to the world without seeming snooty about it. Luce conceded that the previous administration had tried on occasion to make America's religious-moral heritage understandable to the world, but the task had been too much for the Democrats:

> Truman like any American president spoke religiously, he also often acted morally (Korean intervention). Acheson, too, took off his hat to God. But Truman-Acheson never succeeded in putting the words and the deeds together. It can never be done anywhere near perfectly. But Dulles is making a tremendous effort to do it as well as it can be done.

For all of Dulles's good work, Luce concluded, there would continue to be benighted opposition—something the Lucepress would have to fight at the Secretary's side:

> He—and we—will get into a lot of trouble on this issue. I think we have to be companions in that trouble.

The Luce Ridgefield Memorandum, as it came to be called, charted the course of his magazines for the remainder of his life. True, it was not essentially new in its expression of the God-America relationship, which Luce had known of since childhood and which his publications had interpreted for the public since their beginning. It was nevertheless new in its flat-out definition of the relationship and its understanding of the fact that patriotic Americans, even at the risk of some trouble, would have to teach the rest of the world about it. It could be said that the God-America idea, which had already been rolling at a steady clip, gained greater speed with the release of the Memorandum and the total alliance of the two powerful Presbyterians. Its prediction that Dulles and the Lucepress would be "companions in trouble" in their crusade was not borne out in America, where God remained on the banner with little protest. The trouble arose in getting the idea across to other nations. The Weekly Newsmagazine, following the Luce line at the time of the Memorandum, pointed out the difficulties in showing the rest of the world, free as well as enslaved, its error:

> One measure of Secretary Dulles as the champion of a moral order in politics is the rising opposition to him. For weeks, the British, soaked in the politics of expediency, have been working behind the scenes to unseat Dulles. After Dulles' speech, Clement Attlee struck a public blow, professing to find "certain tendencies toward intolerance" in the U.S. approach. Attlee is still glowing from a visit to Communist Yugoslavia. No Communist sympathizer, Attlee yet feels compelled to find some good in Communism before he can cooperate with it. That is the kind of absolutism that emerges from Attlee's relativism. Dulles can do business with Tito without giving an inch in his absolute opposition to what Tito stands for.

Time also followed the Memorandum in giving the back of its hand to the intolerant Nehru:

. . . [T]he conspicuously unhumble Nehru rose in the Indian Parliament to denounce U.S. policy. He called it "a narrow approach which considers everything in terms of black or white [with an] element of dogmatic fervor, something resembling the old approach of bigoted religion."

Time mentioned the mistaken intellectual skepticism about the idea of the God-America alliance:

Many leaders in philosophy and politics either deny 1) the existence of the moral law, or 2) its relevance to politics. They recoil from what they call the "absolutism" of any political system that claims any connection with standards beyond man's capacity to repeal. They point to the thousands of arrogant and wrong-headed politicians who claimed to be the voices of God.

But the newsmagazine had value judgments to put these fears to rest. "In politics," it said, "the Christian emphasis on humility is a warning against putting God on any banner . . ."

6. SOFT-HEADED LIBERALS

. . . But surely we have not been right to create an image of ourselves as an unrealistic moralizing power, ready to risk the world's suicide to protect our own preconceptions. . . . The American religious community bears a considerable responsibility for [this], and it is a threat in the nuclear age. One might even go so far as to say we Americans are more dangerous with nuclear weapons than the Russians. Why? Because our practicality and our moralism join to make a kind of double-or-nothing psychology, and double-or-nothing is a frightening game with nuclear weapons. . . . Ironically, the idealist and the militarist join in creating the mindset that believes that "in war there is no substitute for victory." And since that world of war and force is utterly evil, entering it can only be justified by the highest, most sweeping (and most uncompromising!) moral ideals. Thus at the extreme it might even be charged that American idealism not only helps to bring on the wars it condemns but also may make them worse when they come.

—*William Lee Miller*

Life, taking stock of its unchallenged record in Againstness, pointed out that it was early in the field and had taken some lumps for it before the nation discovered how right Life was:

. . . The subject of Communism has taken up more space on this page—and in the leading articles of this magazine—than any other subject since the war.

In September 1944, nearly a year before World War II was over, Life published an article by Ambassador William C. Bullitt pointing out the postwar threat of Communism. This article brought from our readers a greater volume of hostile letters than any other serious article Life ever published.

359

Since then Life has published dozens of articles by leading authorities on the fight against Communism. Most notable perhaps have been four "key" articles by John Foster Dulles . . .

Meanwhile we have published not less than 100 editorials on the struggle against Communism. These editorials have pointed out the sheer wicked inhumanity of Communism and the wicked ideology of Communism which is the *direct* cause of its frightful inhumanity, the organized murder of at least 20 million people and the imprisoned wretchedness of hundreds of millions. Murder, Inc.? Its address is the Kremlin, Moscow. Its branch offices are every Communist cell in the world. Its traveling salesmen are men like Owen Lattimore. . . . Communism is, in our time, The Great Sin Against Humanity. We need to fight against that—together and unitedly.

Apologies are due Professor Lattimore for repeating Life's utterly scurrilous use of his name. His vindication was proof of Life's recklessness.

Emmet Hughes, the Lifeman who had been an Eisenhower speechwriter and had returned after the election (with Luce's blessing) to serve as a Presidential assistant, had, like others not obsessed with Againstness, looked on Stalin's death as an opportunity for a drive for a relaxation of the Cold War. Eisenhower himself had thought so. He had said privately, "Look, I am tired —I think everyone is tired—of just plain indictments of the Soviet regime. . . . Instead, just *one* thing matters: what have *we* got to offer the world? What are *we* ready to do to improve the chances of peace?"

It was the most logical of questions in any age, let alone a nuclear age. The unspeakable Stalin era had ended at last. The new unknown, Malenkov, made a great show of offering to solve international problems by peaceful negotiation. "At present and in the future," he said, "there is no . . . question which cannot be solved by peaceful means. This refers to relations with all states, including . . . the United States . . ." Here was an overture, something even the hard-boiled Churchill saw as an opening, saying, "It would be wrong to pass up any opportunity to probe present intentions in Moscow." Like Luce in London urging Churchill against any "concessions," Dulles opposed the idea of parleying. Time made fun of "starry-eyed Western diplomats" who "began to hear the beat of the wings of Russia's mechanized dove of peace . . ." Things were shaky in Russia, Time said, and Malenkov's talk of "the possibility of the prolonged co-existence and peaceful competition of two different systems, capitalist and socialist," was spoken only "in hopes of winning time to consolidate." Four months later, Time still saw it not as a chance to move toward peace but as "a first-class internal crisis in the Soviet empire" that should be exploited aggressively. The two Presbyterians were solid in their rectitude. The wings, whether mechanized or not, ultimately stopped beating and the Cold War grew colder.

Mary Bancroft having recently moved to New York, Luce occasionally had dinner with her, rising from his eaten-but-untasted meal to pace, smoke and talk. He liked to state a proposition and then argue it, disclosing in the debate

both the trigger speed of his thought and a curious lack of cultural perception and sensibility. His conviction was growing that Eleanor Roosevelt was consciously engaged in subversion. Two favorite subjects of discussion were God and the Greeks. He was particularly impressed by the Greek aphorism, "Character is destiny," repeated it frequently and even wrote it down on a bit of notepaper in Greek and gave it to Mrs. Bancroft, telling her it was something she should always remember.

While she never heard him laugh (indeed the only person who comes to mind who did hear him laugh was Howland during the episode of the aggressive swans), he often smiled and even chuckled during their discussions, which for him represented the utmost in enjoyment.

On January 28, 1954, he telephoned her to say good-bye. He arrived in Rome January 30 to resume his odd melange of duties. Although he enjoyed the zoo nearby in the Villa Borghese gardens, and was convinced that a polar bear there recognized him, he grew bored in a little less than the usual three weeks. Summoning the Timan James Bell from his Bonn post (Bell had spent three years in the Middle East and knew it well), he flew to Cairo with him just in time to witness the short-lived cavalry revolt against Colonel Nasser.

Luce, like a cub reporter, dashed out of the Semiramis Hotel with an interpreter to investigate the excitement. Bell, worried about his safety, was relieved when he met him hours later at the Semiramis bar. Luce's tie was askew and his face dirty but he was exultant over his talks with various street demonstrators and had got from them, he said, "some good quotes." Most of them *were* good. Bell added them to his dispatch to Rockefeller Center. Luce also talked with Colonel Nasser, who spoke English and told him something of Egypt's problems, inevitably arousing in Luce that familiar feeling that he was talking with one of the world's great men.

When Luce and Bell returned to Rome a week later, Luce could hardly wait to read the first proof of the issue of Time containing their dispatch. "They cut out my quotes," he said in deep disappointment. "Damn it, they were interesting quotes." Bell agreed, but said that was the way it was, working for Time in the field.

Clare was averaging ten hours of hard work every day, plus an official dinner party almost every night. She had no time for her adored pair of miniature poodles, Scusi and Prego. Her post was costing her husband about $100,000 annually over her $25,000 salary. Many American tourists felt it their right as taxpayers to visit the residence and talk with the ambassador. On July 4, with the aid of her unflappable, Vassar-educated social secretary, Letitia Baldrige, some 4000 Americans had enjoyed an open-house garden reception at the Villa Taverna, munching sandwiches, drinking Cokes and leaving the garden a shambles. There were perhaps compensations in the visits of the famous or wealthy—Audrey Hepburn, Henry Fonda, Elsa Maxwell, Gina Lollobrigida, Prince Bernhard, Spyros Skouras and many others. Skouras insisted that no ambassadorial residence was complete without its own movie theater. The

Luces agreed, both being movie lovers. Money was no object, but when architects appraised the building it was found to be too old and delicate for such radical changes.

Miss Baldrige was one of those persons of wit, ability and industry who got along well with the overworked and sometimes blunt ambassador. She was struck by Clare's outrageous epigrams—"Time wounds all heels," or "No good turn goes unpunished"—and by her application to duty. On the more serious problems she would sometimes pick up the phone and talk across the sea to Dulles or the President directly. Many Italians had got over their pet when they discovered that the ambassador, though indeed a woman, was in any case a famous and brilliant woman who—whatever her errors—worked very hard and went regularly to Mass.

As for the assistant ambassador, well, he was famous too. As Miss Baldrige put it, "Mr. Luce was not the quiet shy type of man who could be content to bask in the glory of his ambassadorial wife."

She was on excellent terms with him. At the time, part of the Timorganization was working on plans for the new Luce magazine Sports Illustrated, sneeringly called Muscle, Sweatsox or Jockstrap by TLF intellectuals. The search for a new journalistic enterprise had hovered for a time on the subject of fashion (which Clare had pushed enthusiastically and which Timen had feared she might appropriate), then briefly on children, and had settled firmly on sports. Luce, who was growing a little creaky for tennis and was taking up golf, had little knowledge of other sports but felt obligated to develop a nodding acquaintance with some of them. With Miss Baldrige and a couple of others from the embassy he watched *fútbol* between Rome and Naples at the vast Mussolini stadium, Foro Italico. A pouring rain did not dampen the spirits of 100,000 shrieking spectators, but Luce watched the struggle of hurtling bodies in silence as rain trickled from his hat. His speechlessness, Miss Baldrige decided, "was due to fascination, not anger," and he later gave a three-word summation: "Remarkable. Yes, remarkable."

He was as dogged in his pursuit of sports knowledgeability during the intervals he spent wifeless in New York. With Billings he held luncheons during which the SI staff was expected to hatch arresting ideas for articles. Among the suggestions were to get Churchill to write on polo and Eisenhower on golf, but one that caught Luce's fancy was the subject of Russian athletes being mere employees of the state. He was taken to sports spectacles at Madison Square Garden and Yankee Stadium by Edward Thompson, Clay Felker and other editors, drawing from them definitive explanations of the meaning of such terms as *seventh-inning stretch*, *freezing the ball* and *left hook*.

The two Luces, each in his own way, exhibited individuality which made them the talk not only of New York and Washington but of the diplomatic set in all the European capitals. According to Cyrus Sulzberger of the New York Times, Clare had "horrified" a dinner party at the recent Luxembourg meeting of ambassadors, at which many European dignitaries were guests. She said

that the editor of an American women's magazine had asked her to write a review of the new Kinsey book on the sex patterns of women. She had decided it would not be appropriate in her present position. Diners pricked up their ears, said Sulzberger, when she added that it would not take her 480 pages to demonstrate that men were unintelligent and that women, rather than being interested in sex, put up with men simply in order to have children and security.

Sulzberger, who flitted around Europe like Luce himself and knew more people and what they thought because he listened to them, was critical of both Luces. He attended a small dinner party at the Villa Taverna shortly after Luce returned from Cairo and was seated next to the ambassador. He was impressed, as everybody was, by the beauty and excellent figure that made it seem incredible that she was only a few months shy of fifty.

"But," he wrote, "this exterior conceals the most arrogant conceit and the most ruthlessly hard-boiled self-assurance it has ever been my privilege to come up against." She felt that the only way Italy could be saved from Communism was by a governmental move to the right. Sulzberger was unable to contribute to the conversation, he complained, because she maintained unbroken talk. She told of embassy problems "and her own brilliance," as Sulzberger saw it, in handling them and would say to her embassy minister, Elbridge Durbrow, "Durby, isn't that so?" at which Durbrow would agree that she had done well indeed. She was impatient with Pope Pius, saying he was old and ill, insisted on being his own Secretary of State and that things at the Vatican were in chaos. Sulzberger reported that he was unable to understand how she could learn anything about Italy since no one else got a word in. In the next room, Luce was talking with other guests including Mrs. Cavendish Cannon, wife of the ambassador to Greece. Mrs. Cannon was in the middle of a story when Luce looked at his watch and interrupted: "It is twelve o'clock. The embassy car is here waiting for you, Mrs. Cannon." There was a sudden dead silence at his rudeness and Luce "practically pushed" his guests out the door.

Luce himself was impatient with the Pope and his staff. He had the determination if not the dogmatism of the Scotch divine who in 1772 became convinced that Pope Clement XIV was the "whore of Babylon" in Revelation and could be saved only by being converted to Presbyterianism. Pushing near the Pope during a service, the Scot shouted, "O thou beast of nature with seven heads and ten horns! . . . Throw away the golden cup of abominations, and the filthiness of thy fornication!" He was led away by Swiss guards. Luce's problems with the Pontiff were different. Little could be done about the first—his conviction that for all the Pope's known anti-Communism he was not gathering and exerting all of the enormous counter-forces of the Vatican as efficiently as he should be. Certainly there were few who criticized the Pope on this score. The second concerned Luce's friend Bishop Sheen. He thought Sheen was being spoiled as America's "television priest" and that his

great abilities would be better utilized in Taiwan, where he could perhaps also keep an eye on developments for Luce. Luce had written the Pontiff urging that the bishop be transferred to Taiwan. Three weeks had passed and he had had no reply. This was not the way business was done in America. He spoke to William Rospigliosi about it. Rospigliosi pointed out that the pace of the Vatican was much slower than that of Time Inc., especially now that the Pope was so old, and counseled patience. Patience was a quality Luce had never cultivated. He had Rospigliosi arrange an interview with Monsignor Giovanni Montini, who represented the Pope in such matters. Rospigliosi, who went along as interpreter, found it embarrassing because Luce seemed to think there was an obligation for the Pope to comply with his request, whereas there was no such obligation.

"Ask him what's being done about it," Luce said. Rospigliosi asked Montini and had to reply that nothing was being done.

"Ask him why not," Luce snapped. He was irate when he left, saying to Rospigliosi, "That fellow will never be Pope." Here he was wrong, for Montini would later become Pope Paul VI.

When the prominent Harvardmen and friends of Roy Larsen, Paul Cabot and Thomas S. Lamont visited Rome with their wives and dined with Luce, trouble brewed when Cabot pronounced Dean Acheson one of the greatest of American Secretaries of State. The Luce protests grew even more explosive when Cabot gave his opinion that Alger Hiss was probably innocent and that Senator McCarthy might spell the end of American liberty. Luce, as he admitted in a letter to Billings, became very rude and there was an hour-long argument during which Luce said he feared Commies much less than he feared soft-headed liberals.

As the guardian angel of Taiwan, Luce was upset by a very long confidential letter from K. C. Wu describing the lengths to which, he said, the Chiang dictatorship had gone. Wu, who had been governor of the island and had sought to institute democratic reforms, had, he said, been blocked at every turn by the Gimo and his son, Chiang Ching-kuo. As Wu saw it, the old ideas which had brought such disaster on the mainland were now prevailing in Taiwan. There were now four branches of the Gimo's secret police actively operating, all opposition had been crushed by terror, and Wu had resigned his post when he found himself stripped of power. Soon thereafter, he wrote, an attempt had been made to murder him by tampering with the steering mechanism of his automobile in the hope that it would seem an accident. He had at length been permitted to leave Taiwan with his wife but had been refused permission to take his fifteen-year-old son with him. The son was now being held as a hostage while Wu lectured in the United States to make his living.

Wu had let part of the story out to the American press. It threatened to strain the credibility of the Luce-Dulles depiction of Chiang as the hope for a free China and to furnish nasty propaganda for the Chinese Communists. Luce sent the letter back to Billings with instructions that it be relayed to

James Shepley, head of Time's Washington bureau. Shepley was to consult with those firm friends of Chiang, Vice President Nixon, Assistant Secretary of State Walter Robertson, JCS Chairman Admiral Arthur Radford and Congressman Judd.

Nixon turned out to be out of the city. Robertson, Radford and Judd assured the Timan that their faith in Chiang was unbroken, their collective opinion being that a little totalitarianism seemed to be essential in the Far East and that K. C. Wu was the victim of an overactive imagination. Time had been unable to kill the story since the softened version which Wu had disclosed had appeared in the newspapers. Time ran three careful paragraphs on page 41 declaring that Wu had left Taiwan "for his health (asthma)" and playing it down as a minor disagreement. The scandal blew over and Chiang of course continued to receive American aid and recognition as the personification of the real and democratic China.

By the time Shepley had talked with the officials, Luce was spending three days in Paris, then to London for two days and dinner with Churchill, coming out of 10 Downing Street at midnight with Sir Winston's first manuscript on the *History of the English-Speaking Peoples* for Life. He was usually kind to Beaverbrook's reporters, but he was quite churlish to a Yorkshire Post man who called on him at Claridge's, saying, "I don't want to give interviews. I am a newspaper man myself. My job is to collect news, not to give it out."

XXVIII

1. MASSIVE RETALIATION

As the French neared defeat in Indochina, Eisenhower rejected the urging of Dulles, Nixon and Radford that they be given direct American military support. French Premier Pierre Mendès-France, who had taken office with the promise to end the unpopular war, became an object of Lucean disgust. Before returning to Europe, Luce had had private talks with ten administration officials including the President, Vice President Nixon (two hours) and Dulles. From Rome he had gone to Geneva, where Dulles, Molotov, Eden, Chou En-lai, Mendès and many diplomats from Southeast Asia sought to settle the problems of that part of the world. Luce, the perennial witness of great events and great men, perennially influencing them when he could, dined in Geneva with Timan John Beal and Assistant Secretary Robertson, who echoed Luce's sentiments in calling the French defeat at Dienbienphu one of the worst days in American history.

The Luce line had been steady since 1950, when Life said, "the U.S. must acquire a policy that will save Southeast Asia from the clutch of Communism." Indeed Luce, in his aggressive willingness to commit American military power in Asia, was ahead of anyone in the administration with the possible exception of his fellow Presbyterian. The Lucepress now emitted weekly trumpet-blasts of anger at what was happening there. Life warned that the hope of "freedom" would "depend on America's willingness to take full part" in defending it, and even permitted a breath of criticism of Eisenhower by describing his attitude as one of "indecision." It deplored the failure of America and Britain to "agree to fight for Indochina" and it called for greater American military spending.

Luce was fed up with the French, fed up with the English for supporting France in her desire to end the war, fed up with the thought of another Com-

munist victory. Like Chiang Kai-shek, he was even unhappy that the Western nations had given Communist China the added stature of recognition at the conference. Time's account of the results of the Geneva talks, with France to clear out and with Vietnam's government to be decided by general elections, was a classic in value judgments preempting the news. Mendès-France and Eden, who backed him, were sketched in the rhetoric of contempt. Chou was depicted as a barbaric conqueror who, "like a great khan bestowing gold upon some worthy vassal," presented Mendès with Chinese silks. Time described Chou as having "the eyes of a man who could kill," while Life did better with a long article citing "sources Life considers absolutely trustworthy" in suggesting that Chou years earlier had "wiped out the entire family of a political enemy."

The Newsmagazine talked of "defeatism," of "disorganized, confused, divided Western delegations" and said one great mistake made by the West had been in counting "postwar France as a great power." It lamented that "the U.S. had plainly shown no enthusiasm to get involved in Indochina," and that "the whole of Indochina might have been saved if the free world had long ago plainly showed its determination to save it." It ran one of its more dramatic Chapin maps, showing China inhabited by a huge octopus, one of whose tentacles gripped Indochina while others stretched out menacingly toward the Philippines, Indonesia, Burma and India.

For the first time in twenty-three years the world was without a shooting war. Even Molotov stopped glowering long enough to say that Geneva showed there was no dispute that could not be solved by negotiation. The Malenkov regime continued its conciliatory talk, which Life denounced as an "illusion" and mourned that the "ground of freedom lies cracked and gullied as though from some great moral drought." The glowering was done by Dulles, furious at the British for pushing the Geneva solution. He had refused to shake Chou's hand at Geneva and had quit the conference when the news came about Dienbienphu, with all its implications, leaving subordinates to handle what had become a losing parley if one supported the likes of Bao Dai.

The world's two most powerful Presbyterians grew more belligerent in 1954, Dulles enunciating his policy of "massive retaliation" and Luce joining him in scanning the world for allies who were not afraid to fight. Both churchmen were individuals of enormous ego and skill, lacking humor and flexibility, aggressive, suspicious, Puritanical, Machiavellian, specializing in the language of truculence. Both insisted on regarding China and Russia as an eternal Communist monolith and hence, rather than finding methods to divide them, continually pushed them together. Both were obsessed by Red China and seriously mistaken in their conviction that the Mao regime did not have popular support, Dulles still putting much thought on methods whereby he might reactivate the Chinese civil war. Both yearned to "save" Indochina. Both were so certain of America's moral rectitude that they regarded neutrals such as Nehru (an unbeliever) almost as enemies. Both felt it essential to watch and

suppress Eisenhower's peaceful tendencies. Dulles, with the wholehearted support of the Lucepress, had been able to thwart the President's early hope to find a thaw in East-West relations.

The two Presbyterians were the toughest rocket-rattlers of the time. Life magazine was as frank as always in its search for friendly gunslingers, giving up on France as hopelessly chaotic and on England as having lost the old holy fire:

> . . . [W]hat allies can [we] count on? . . . In Asia the South Koreans and Nationalist Chinese . . . in Europe the Turks and the Greeks. To them could safely be added Pakistan, Adenauer's Germany and Magsaysay's Philippines . . . they are staunch against Communism and unafraid to risk war.

One London commentator wished that Luce had followed his early resolve to retire by age forty so that "we would have been spared the naïve and insulting editorials in Time and Life disparaging Britain as an 'unreliable ally,' " and pointed out that America had been several years behind Britain in becoming a reliable ally in the last two wars. In Washington, when the President forgot to ask Agriculture Secretary Ezra Benson to give the opening prayer at a Cabinet meeting, it was Dulles who reminded him, on which Eisenhower agreed: ". . . I really need all the help we can get from *up there* this morning." And at the end of the year it was John Foster Dulles who was Time's Man of the Year, honored for his efforts to free America from encirclement, for securing agreement for the rearming of Germany, for completing the Southeast Asia Treaty Organization composed of eight nations aligned against Communism, and for a mutual defense treaty between the United States and Chiang Kai-shek. Time, praising the "skill and force" which he had shown in "dealing with the Communists," went on:

> With one sharp stroke after another, he stripped the Communists naked of the pretense that they really wanted peace at anything less than their own outrageous price. If millions remained deluded by the "soft" Malenkov line, that was not the fault of Dulles, who rescued other millions from gullibility. . . . Dulles [did not] try to veil the free world's grim dependence on massive atomic retaliation.

2. MY FAVORITE QUEEN

Luce had snatched Walter Guzzardi away from the Foreign Service to serve as his right hand in Rome. Working for Luce, Guzzardi discovered, was at once exciting and dangerous, like walking a tightrope or membership in a police bomb squad. One had to accept him on his own terms, to accommodate instantly to his quirks, but he was stimulating in his constant flow of ideas, his outrageous manners and kingly bearing. He took a liking to Guzzardi, which indeed was essential because if he did not you had better find a career elsewhere.

He was as ready as ever to permit dinner companions to become his lecture audience. Once Guzzardi lunched with Luce and a couple of Italian businessmen and went through what became routine—the Italians beckoning a waiter and Luce waving the waiter away with ferocious gestures as he developed his arguments, the waiter retreating uncertainly to a middle distance, the Italians growing hungry and impatient, and Luce talking, talking. Finally Guzzardi, pitying Luce's companions, broke in, saying, "Harry, the gentlemen would like to eat." Luce seized a menu offering a long listing of culinary delights, glared at it, snarled *"Haricots verts!"*—evidently the first item he noticed— and resumed his monolog. He ordered no main dish. He was surely the only patron who had ever had luncheon consisting of green beans and chocolate cake.

His own clock-watching punctuality and impatience at even a moment's delay made the supervising of any arrangements involving the conjunction of Luce and other people at a given time an ordeal, especially if the uncertainties of transportation entered in. On one occasion Luce wished to present the Pope with a handsome leather album of photographs which a Life photographer had taken of the Pontiff presiding over a gathering of children. It was decided to make an occasion of it—to take along the staff of Luce's own office and a part of the staff of the Time bureau to witness the presentation. The appointment was made with the Pope for 11:00 A.M. Guzzardi sweated over the problem of getting a dozen people from two different offices in two cars to the Vatican at the same precise moment. The cars set out on time, but there was still the matter of Roman traffic. Luce, riding in his limousine with Guzzardi, was happily asking questions, some of which Guzzardi could not answer— questions of the compulsive type such as, "Walter, in that building over there, why is one window higher than another?"

Guzzardi's relief was extreme when the troupe reached the Vatican together and were escorted inside to an ornate chamber where Pius XII would see them. Now a new peril arose. The Pope was late—five minutes, ten minutes. Luce got up and began pacing the floor, his brow thunderous. "God damn it, Walter," he growled, "where the hell's the Pope?" Luckily the Pontiff arrived and the tension dissolved as Luce presented him with the album, then leaned over his shoulder and interrupted him as a Pope should never be interrupted, pointing out the appealing faces caught by Life's cameraman.

Luce found most of his Italian friends in the big-business sector, including the tycoons of Fiat, Olivetti and Montecatini. Impatient with the nation's slow recovery, he blamed it in part on socialism and said that Italy's problems could be solved immediately with good capitalist business practice and hard work. Meanwhile the ambassador had worked with English and other representatives and had been instrumental in bringing about a satisfactory settlement of the Trieste question which had kept Italy and Yugoslavia at loggerheads. Italians were so pleased that even some politicians who had once

denounced her for meddling now praised her. People seldom viewed her neutrally but either liked or disliked her intensely. Her admiring biographer said that her embassy minister Elbridge Durbrow was expressing the opinion of her whole staff when he said he admired her for her intelligence, her open mind and sense of humor. The persnickety Sulzberger, although he had talked with her again and found her "quite interesting," later talked with James Riddleberger, American ambassador to Yugoslavia, who said he had received a different opinion from Durbrow. According to Riddleberger (as Sulzberger had it), Durbrow claimed he had all he could do to keep her from acting as a sort of ambassador-in-charge-of-Europe and from sending instructions to Ambassadors Aldrich, Dillon and Riddleberger.

While her conversational brilliance was generally conceded, some thought she lacked discretion and talked too much for an ambassador. According to Sulzberger again, General Alfred Gruenther thought her indiscreet, for example, in saying that Churchill was planning to retire and had so told her husband. A generally friendly article about her in Look said, "As a diplomat, Clare Luce tries too hard and talks too much." "I don't talk too much," she insisted, "but I'm widely misquoted." Sulzberger, who kept trading gossip with everyone in Europe, said there were opinions among other American diplomats in Europe that the State Department kowtowed to her because of the power of her husband's magazines, Ambassador Douglas Dillon in Paris saying, "She hasn't got anything except Time, Life and Fortune." There were rumors that she sought the ambassadorship in London or in Paris, or that she wanted a Cabinet post. Naturally, rumors flew about such a beautiful, gifted and controversial lady. Prime Minister Churchill, who enjoyed her company and had encouraged her to take up painting, had told Luce, doubtless in jest, that she should be moved from Rome to Paris "because she can do more harm there."

What with Luce's influence in electing Eisenhower, Clare's closeness to the administration, the great respect for the Luce political power held by other American ambassadors in Europe and the seriousness with which the Luce-press took its role as international interpreter of America, it was no wonder that foreign government circles and royalty often regarded the Luces and the magazines as, if not precisely an arm of the United States government, something very close to it. It was helpful for a foreign government to be favorably viewed by the Lucepress. It was bad to be unfavorably viewed. An earlier Time cover story about pretty, German-born Queen Frederika of Greece had been complimentary to her, King Paul and to Greece itself as a member of NATO. Now the Luces were accorded an unusual honor—dinner, the two of them alone, with the king and queen at the Greek embassy in Rome. Luce's vaunted democracy implied no dislike of royalty. The evening lasted until 12:45 and, as he put it, "both of them more than lived up to the rave notices they have received." Luce thereafter referred to Frederika as "my favorite queen," and they would meet again.

"If you want to see Clare Luce's back hair rise," noted one interviewer, "mention Communism." She had weakened the Italian Communists somewhat by effecting a policy of denying American contracts to Italian firms under the domination of Communist unions. Like Luce, she had a sharp sense of public relations. When de Gasperi died, she cut short an American holiday to fly back for the funeral, thus forcing diplomats of other nations to come in from the beaches. When an Italian airliner suffered a disastrous crash in New York, she canceled a reservation with an American line and switched to L.A.I.—a sign of confidence noticed gratefully in Italy. She traveled from Italy's toe to its thigh, visiting a town damaged by floods, a regional fair, a pasta factory, always getting headlines, praised by friendly observers as a lady with a great heart and accused by the hostile as seeking publicity and higher office. Asked by a reporter if it was a disadvantage for an ambassador to be a woman, she replied, "I couldn't possibly tell you. I have never been a man."

Her old friend and still her successor in Congress, Albert P. Morano, was singing her praises in the House. On one holiday in New York, Luce had given her a party at River House attended by many Lucepress editors. Max Gissen, Time's head bookman, commented to Luce that American-Italian relations seemed to have improved, and Luce gestured toward his wife, saying, "That's Clare's work." Gissen thought this a propitious moment to suggest a Time cover story about Alberto Moravia, leading up to it with talk of Italian novelists. "The trouble with the Italian novelists," Luce said, "is that they don't understand Italians"—a remark that left Gissen speechless, and Moravia never made it.

According to the captious Reporter magazine, the ambassador was at times unable to keep her prejudices from interfering with her diplomacy, as when Eleanor Roosevelt spent four days in Rome. Mrs. Luce invited about forty guests to meet Mrs. Roosevelt at an elaborate luncheon, the magazine said. Most of them were from the embassy. None of the many Italians anxious to meet the widow of a President who had become a figure of world fame on her own, was invited. Said the Reporter:

> According to people present, however, the luncheon turned out to be a triumph for Mrs. Roosevelt. The guests, particularly the younger ones, were so taken with her, so anxious to hear her talk, that the ambassador had no choice but to let the party go on and on, while looking nervously at her watch.

Yet she could respond instantly to situations of inherent humor, if one could believe that teller of tales, Art Buchwald. Later, in Paris, she waited an unexpectedly long interval in front of the Ritz for her car, which was delayed in traffic. A unit for the American production of *Love in the Afternoon* was shooting a night scene of the Ritz, and an assistant asked her to move on:

> Madame Ambassador decided to test the right of a private citizen to stand in front of her hotel and refused to budge.
> The assistant asked if she spoke English and she shook her head. French? She

371

shook her head again. Then he brought someone over who spoke Spanish and
the ambassador replied in German. They found someone who spoke German
and she answered in Italian.

At last the director came over and said: "You look familiar. You speak English?" [No answer.]

Then the director whispered to one of his assistants.

"What's the name of this old actress?"

That ended the joke for the ambassador, who thereupon walked into the
lobby. It was, she later said, the first time in four years that she had been
"asked to step out of a picture instead of into one."

3. THE AMBASSADOR IS POISONED

When the Eisenhower administration released blood-chilling information
about the new H-bomb, the Lucepress urged maximum exploitation of it, accusing those who opposed it of "hand-wringing" and saying that it was the
H-bomb that made possible the Dulles policy of " 'massive retaliation' against
further Communist acts of aggression." Soon afterward, it strongly favored
the finding that the nuclear scientist J. Robert Oppenheimer should no longer be trusted with classified information. And although it was getting fed up
with Senator McCarthy as a growing embarrassment to the Republicans, it
approved his endless hunt for Reds and congratulated him for "investigative
achievement" when, among other things, he discovered that the Army promoted a "dental officer while his loyalty was seriously in question." The
Lucepress joined the attacks that drove Charles Chaplin out of the country.

A new kind of full-page advertisement on the part of war-armament builders, who always identified themselves as "defense" industries, was appearing
in the Lucepress. Typical was one by the United Aircraft Corporation which
asked for engineers and carried the message that American air power would
prevent war if kept at a sufficiently high level.

When the ten-year-old secrets of Yalta were finally let out of the bag, Time
seized on the opportunity to publish a six-page special Yalta section emphasizing once more Luce's undying hatred of FDR. His administration was exco-
riated for its failure to understand that "democracy and Communism would
not blend" and for failing to adopt the hard line necessary. "WE MUST BE
TOUGHER," said a Time headline quoting an official with whom it agreed.
Meanwhile Life, after publishing a dozen-odd articles by or about Dulles, invariably stressing the moral hard line, had come to be regarded as almost
official in its intimacy with the Secretary. Now, in Life, Dulles topped his earlier talk about "liberation," "rollback" and "massive retaliation" with a long
article blurbed on the cover: "THREE TIMES AT BRINK OF WAR: HOW DULLES
GAMBLED AND WON." The article, by James Shepley, lauded Dulles's "liberation of Communism" principle after the Democrats' "negative theory of con-

tainment." It purported to show how Dulles had averted war by putting the hard line into practice, including the threatened use of atomic bombs in connection with Korea, Indochina and Taiwan. A central paragraph read:

> Always, of course, there has been and continues to be risk. Says Dulles, "You have to take chances for peace, just as you must take chances in war. Some say that we were brought to the verge of war. Of course we were brought to the verge of war. The ability to get to the verge without getting into war is the necessary art. If you try to run away from it, if you are scared to go to the brink, you are lost. We've had to look it squarely in the face—on the question of enlarging the Korean war, on the question of getting into the Indochina war, on the question of Formosa. We walked to the brink and we looked it in the face. We took strong action."

A hurricane of controversy struck the moment the magazine went on sale. Every editor, columnist and television commentator had firm opinions about Dulles's brinkmanship. The large majority were not sure they enjoyed the spectacle of Dulles balancing himself on the nuclear precipice on three separate occasions and letting Americans know long after the fact, through the medium of Life, that they might have been on the verge of extinction. Nor were they keen about his description of this game as an "art." There seemed a bravado about the Dulles performance hardly measuring up to the high seriousness expected of a Secretary of State in dealing with these solemn issues. Adlai Stevenson demanded that President Eisenhower, just recovered from a heart attack, repudiate or oust Dulles. The British Foreign Office flatly disavowed statements in the article referring to them. London newspapers called Dulles "an edgy gambler" and noted that "if this is an art, it is the most terrifying one we ever encountered . . . Mr. Dulles would make anyone's hair stand on end . . . this terrible doctrine will shock the United States."

The President admitted that there might be some "unfortunate expressions" in the article. Dulles, discomfited, tried to disclaim the way in which the opinions were attributed to him. Shepley, still head of Time's Washington bureau, had interviewed Dulles for the article along with John Beal and Charles J. V. Murphy, and Beal had taken a tape recorder with him. While it was true that the Lucepress reputation for accuracy was not high, it appeared that the fault lay more with Dulles, whom even Shepley regarded as a publicity-seeker, than with Life. Luce tried to mitigate Dulles's embarrassment by making a public statement which was less apology for the article than praise for it. He thought the blurb might be a trifle inflammatory, said that nuances might have been lost when the article was cut for publication, then wheeled around and vigorously defended Dulles and the article itself, managing to suggest that Dulles's and Life's critics were un-American, adding:

> . . . [T]here is nothing in Secretary Dulles' words which is contrary to common sense. For the secretary is stating in vivid terms the perils of appeasement which should be understood by free men everywhere.

While the nation and the world were getting a better understanding of the rigors of Presbyterian diplomacy, Ambassador Luce was leaving her post in Rome under the strangest of circumstances. She had lost weight, had trouble with her teeth, lost several brushfuls of her slightly graying blonde hair, and felt ill enough so that she found it difficult to keep up her stiff ambassadorial pace. Once, as she was leaving for a formal dinner, her maid Gretel protested that she had lipstick on her teeth. "Gretel," she replied, "the important thing nowadays is not whether I've got lipstick on my teeth but rather have I got teeth."

In May 1956, exhausted, she returned to New York for a medical checkup. While she was gone, her spouse assumed some of her social chores. He escorted the visiting Harry Trumans around Rome, showing them the Colosseum, Forum and Capitoline Hill with such verve that Mrs. Truman had to leave the men to their sightseeing while she returned to her hotel to rest. Although it could not be said that Luce had been enthusiastic about Truman as President, he did thoroughly approve of his challenges to the Soviet as in the Marshall Plan and Truman Doctrine. That night the Trumans were guests at the Villa Taverna, where Truman (who did not entirely approve of the Luces either) played Paderewski's "Minuet" on the piano while a parcel of American and Italian diplomats looked on and former President Luigi Einaudi was one of the listeners.

Luce headed homeward a week later via London, where the Von Hofmannsthals had him as a dinner guest along with a sizable group of Tories including Prime Minister Eden, Lord John Hope and Julian Amery. Luce staggered Mrs. Von Hofmannsthal by arriving on foot from Claridge's an hour early while she was working furiously in preparation for the gathering. "I thought we could just sit and talk before the rest of them came," he said. After dinner, Luce, who had once again talked with Nasser and was bursting with admiration for him, told this entirely antipathetic group of the Egyptian's greatness. Eden kept his temper though his foot was swinging. Amery could finally stand Luce's encomiums no longer. He managed to get the floor —not an easy feat once Luce had it—and expounded the opposite line, that Nasser was an unscrupulous dictator and a menace to the peace. Luce, growing angry, said, seeming to have appropriated Dulles's office for the moment, "You are forcing the United States to choose between Nasser and England."

Amery nodded. "Yes."

The calm answer made Luce so furious that he got his coat and plunged out the door without a farewell as the other guests stared. He did not apologize later. The Spectator published a burlesque of his visit, referring to him as "testy, Nasser-infatuated Luce." Arriving in New York, he said his wife was suffering from chronic enteritis but that he was confident she would recover full health in six weeks. Some of the more cynical observers calculated that six

weeks would give her time to appraise the political situation, look for a more important assignment or run for office.

The "dump Nixon" movement had been under way since February, when the President announced that he would be a candidate again but refused to discuss Nixon's role. Eisenhower's serious heart attack naturally sharpened interest in the qualifications of the person who would succeed him should he die. Some Democratic votes would be needed to re-elect him. The Nixon record of vilification—in 1952 he had talked of "Adlai the appeaser . . . who got a Ph.D. from Dean Acheson's College of Cowardly Communist Containment"—had won him unanimous hatred among the Democrats. The President himself thought it would be best for him to settle for a post in the Cabinet.

Some thought that the ambitious Clare Boothe Luce sought the job. Her friend Randolph Churchill wrote, "If it had been decided to dump Mr. Nixon from the ticket she would have been very glad to have stepped into the breach. The vice presidency has often been the stepping stone to the White House. And short of being Pope of Rome there is probably no other job which Mrs. Luce would more willingly discharge than that of President of the United States."

In July, when Eisenhower's running mate was still in doubt and the convention loomed, Time splashed a full-page story headed "Arsenic for the Ambassador," telling how she had been slowly poisoned in Rome. When tests showed traces of arsenic in her body, said Time, CIA investigators had been called in to find out who was poisoning her. Long investigation had brought the oddest of solutions: She had been poisoned not by Communists but by her bedroom ceiling. Dust containing arsenate of lead had drizzled constantly but invisibly from the twenty-five-year-old paint, to be inhaled by the ambassador and ingested with her morning coffee.

The story made headlines all over America and in Europe and would of course have been good political publicity had that been intended. Some critics suggested that this was what was intended. There was something touching about the lovely ambassador becoming a victim of unseen poison as she toiled loyally for her country. There was a quarrel of experts over the possibility of such poisoning. Francis Scofield, an American paint scientist, said that since the turn of the century paints contained too small an amount of arsenate of lead to produce such a result. Dr. Robert Kehoe, an authority on poisoning but not on paint, declared that such poisoning was possible.

Not so the malicious publication Le Ore of Italy, which called the story "ridiculous" although "It has everything: a beautiful woman—herself a novel-writer, the suspicion of a plot to poison her with arsenic, a mysterious boudoir in a 17th century Italian villa, trimmings of politics and espionage service, and, finally, a journalistic triumph for the weekly magazine Time which, incidentally, is owned by Ambassador Luce's husband . . ."

Le Ore cited another American expert, Joseph Battleyn, who said such poisoning was impossible, as did Signor Ambrosi, owner of one of Italy's oldest paint firms. Ambrosi was quoted as calling the story "nonsense." Le Ore declared that the paint had produced no such effect on the previous ambassadors Dunn and Bunker, "who, together with their respective wives, had stayed in the same villa and slept in the same room."

In the end, the ambassador had been publicized as never before, the public was left in some confusion, but Richard Nixon was the running mate after all.

4. "OH, HARRY," SPAKE THE LORD

The propriety of the Luce exaltation of Nasser and the Luce renunciation of the Von Hofmannsthal party were suddenly brought into question when Nasser did two things no Lucean hero could do and stay in his niche: (1) recognized Red China and (2) carried on friendly negotiations with the Soviet Union. Secretary Dulles decided that Nasser, whom he had tried to lure away from his neutrality between the capitalist and Communist worlds, was moving even farther away from American morality and closer to Communist sin. Dulles publicly rebuked Nasser by suddenly withdrawing the American offer to help finance the Aswan Dam, a move that startled the world. The Weekly Newsmagazine commended the Secretary for a "victory for the West," "a gambit that took the breath of professionals for its daring" and won praise for its "instinctive rightness"—an appraisal that would not be borne out.

For once Luce moved away from world crises instead of jumping into the middle of them. He had come home from Italy not long before the English-French-Israeli attack on Suez and the almost simultaneous Russian crushing of the Hungarian revolt. He returned to Rome after the American election and gave a reception at the Villa Taverna for Hungarian diplomats and refugees, the ambassador, only partly recovered, giving him center stage for this function. Hungarians attending would remember his kindness and sympathy for their cause, and the Life editorials applauding Hungarian heroism and the special fifty-cent story of the gallant but doomed struggle published by Life, the profits going to Hungary.

But there were questions about the American policy of "liberation" which had been so powerfully advanced by Dulles and publicized by Luce. It seemed that when the crisis came, and a satellite country sought to liberate itself, Uncle Sam looked the other way and proposed resolutions in the United Nations. The American-operated Radio Free Europe had encouraged satellite peoples to revolt, and when they did revolt they were left to be slaughtered by Russian tanks. Indeed, Hungary showed what a hollow thing the "liberation" policy was, and after that neither the Secretary of State nor his journalistic eulogist talked so warmly about liberation.

Meanwhile, Luce seized opportunities while in New York to have dinner

and debate with Mary Bancroft. He had a terrible cigarette cough, and she urged him to cut down on smoking. She also urged him to cultivate a modest break from his tenacious Republicanism, and she made fun of Eisenhower. Luce's deafness was now quite severe and he was still too vain to wear an electrical aid, so that their conversation was carried on in shouts as Luce paced the floor, sat down, got up again to pace the floor, smoking incessantly —a debate they continued more quietly by mail.

> . . . You said you were sorry for me [she wrote] that I couldn't rejoice that Ei-senhower had turned out to be such a good man . . . My error in judgment about Eisenhower came from not realizing what an unworldly man he was and what a "soft" one. . . . I am very glad he's been adequate to riding along like a football hero on the shoulders of his supporters without falling off and getting trampled to death. But the French have a saying, "Il faut voir la fin."

Eisenhower aside, there was the question of Luce himself. In countless hours of argument she had come up repeatedly against his capacity for ration-alization, for twisting logic to his needs. It mystified her that a man so ob-sessed with God could be so self-deceptive in his journalistic activities, as if he thought he could con God as he seemed to be conning himself. The two of them had often discussed the ultimate confrontation with God and the theory that each person must render a satisfactory accounting of the gifts and abili-ties given him. In her opinion, God would see through him instantly:

> If I never saw you display full knowledge of certain characteristics of yours which at other moments you pretend you don't have, I wouldn't pick on you as I sometimes do. . . . The Lord gave you a Fine Mind . . . And he gave you the ability to get money and power. . . . I think that you ought to be in Fear and Trembling about this one aspect of matters. I could imagine the fol-lowing dialogue when the ultimate account is rendered: "Well, Harry" (this is the Lord speaking.) "How about it? I know you got all that money and power. How could you help it when I gave you that ability? But what *use* did you make of 'em after you got 'em?" At this point Harry begins to pace about, thumbs in vest pockets, watch chain getting an occasional flip. And the Lord has to listen to quite a lot of explanations and expositions interlarded with quite a few philo-sophical quotes. Then Lord speaks: "Oh, Harry, Harry! I gave you a better mind than that. It's OK with the money—you did fine on that. But the power? Re-member, my boy, I have been reading all your thoughts these past years and I know too the impulses of your heart."
>
> You see, Harry, it never occurs to me that the Lord doesn't know everything that goes on inside of all of us—and within every living creature. I imagine you don't look at things that way. I guess what I am trying to tell you is that on many occasions you have in my presence revealed . . . your full awareness of factors, forces, facts that when it suits your purposes you behave as if you re-garded as nonexistent. I wouldn't mind if this was just a cover-up. What exas-perates me is that you actually seem to drop them out of your consciousness. And it's such a ghastly waste of time and energy coping with you when you do it.

377

The Luces had contributed $60,000 for the re-election of Eisenhower. Time and Life covered the election with innovative adjectivism. Time publicized the information that Senator Estes Kefauver, the Democratic candidate for Vice President, perspired so heavily that he always carried an extra shirt with him. So far as is known, this was a journalistic milestone, a point never before brought up about a candidate for national office. Certainly no mention was made of the Eisenhower or Nixon perspiration. Time was consistently unkind to Kefauver, mentioning that his handshake was "limp but not clammy," satirizing the classical name of his mother, Phredonia, ridiculing his much-publicized investigation of crime and his "poor-mouthed Southern drawl," describing his "tedious habit of shaking one hand after another, looking at its owner with glazed, unseeing eyes, hardly hearing himself mouth some meaningless banality," and pointing to alleged left-wing tendencies. It interpreted him as "gliding along like an imperturbable praying mantis, just showing his sympathy." Time made spectacularly invidious talk about his technique in pitching manure at the very beginning of the Kefauver cover story:

> On his farm in Platte County, Mo., a friend of Estes Kefauver sat musing about why he likes the Senator from Tennessee. "I think," said Missouri's cattle-raising Democratic Representative William Hull Jr., "that he is the type of fellow who, if he was out campaigning and came across a farmer pitching manure, would take off his coat, grab another pitchfork and start to work." This week, pitchfork in hand, Vice-Presidential Nominee Kefauver was all set to start work on the key part of his Democratic campaign job . . . with a soft pitch of faith, hope and parity.

Eisenhower was pictured throughout in heroic proportions, miraculous in his return to glowing health, and Stevenson as a sorry third-rater whose reservations about H-bomb brinkmanship might be of left-wing origin. The President apparently had the effect of inspiring betterment among his friends, for Time had pictured the jovial George E. Allen during the previous administration as Truman's "croniest crony" who was "all the more remarkable because, to the naked eye, he is a clown." Now, "the President [Eisenhower] chatted quietly with golfing companion George E. Allen, Washington lawyer and friend of Presidents."

Time's emphasis on Kefauver's oddities doubtless reflected a real fear that the unpopular Nixon would hurt the ticket and a desire to suggest that his Democratic opponent was if anything worse. The United Automobile Workers' publication Ammunition became so exercised over Time's interpretation of the candidates that it devoted most of a whole issue to it. It was incensed at the glorification of Nixon, who had been warned by the Republican hierarchy to keep his speeches on a "higher level" than heretofore and evidently was trying to do so but could not help lapsing occasionally into allusions calculated to arouse suspicion of treason such as a return to the linking of Stevenson with Hiss. Time's account of Nixon's "triumphant" tour of Manila showed the superiority of the Nixon handshake over the limp Kefauver grip:

From the moment Nixon and his wife emerged from a MATS Constellation at Manila's airport, the Vice-President generated friendship. He shook hands held out from the cordoned crowd, relied with effect on his California Spanish, three times halted his white Cadillac on the drive to Magsaysay's residence to shake hands. Secret Service men blanched, but Filipinos loved it.

Ammunition commented:

> See? And it's all done with words. The Nixon handshake is even brave; it does things in far-off places that make Secret Service men turn white under the keen eyes of trained Time reporters who have made a special study of the skin tones of fearful Americans in the tropics.

Time also stressed the Nixon courage in speaking at Salt Lake City despite illness: "Nixon gripped the sides of his lectern to keep himself erect. Photographers edged forward, setting their cameras to picture the Vice-President at his moment of collapse. . . . But somehow Nixon made it . . ." Mary Bancroft was unsympathetic, noting, "Poor Richard Nixon. He just got sick being good. I hope he stays good. He is a catastrophe—politically—when he is good. Just no good at all." Elsewhere she instructed Luce on "quality merchandise" and "punk merchandise" in politics:

> You've got to look at his [Nixon's] voting record . . . Then there were his hatchetmen's anonymous calls—telephone calls—in both the Helen Gahagan Douglas and Voorhis campaigns—the fact he has never *done* anything—not held a job as governor, general, etc.—that he is simply "sellable"—I'm not putting all this in the right language—I'm just saying the trouble is he's a plastic not a basic material . . .

In the end, of course, the two men she designated as a football hero and a plastic material were elected in a landslide. Ammunition, which conceded that it presented the labor point of view and thought that Time and Life should honestly say who *they* represented, used forty pages to document the unfairness of Time, Life and Newsweek. It found that the latter, biased though it was, could not match either the prejudice or the virtuosity of the Lucepress, to which it applied an adjectival treatment which was, on careful thought, very near to exact truth:

> . . . [Luce] is clamorous in defense of the "free press." Yet, his magazines are masterpieces of bias. They are snide, shabby, smartalecky, sneering, and, above all, slick. They snigger rather than laugh. They rarely strike but often stab. They are mean-spirited and vindictive. They are unctuous and patronizing.

The Democratic Digest ran an exposure of Time's bias titled, "Time the weekly WHAT?" Ben Bagdikian observed:

> Time's treatment of the campaign in 1956 was so consistently biased that it would be reasonable to label it campaign literature. . . . Nor need one be pro-Democratic or anti-Republican to question the ethics of such political reporting

in a publication that tells the reader he is getting news in "Time, The Weekly Newsmagazine."

But the best six-word appraisal of Time appeared on page 3 of Ammunition—better even than Time's own twenty-fifth anniversary self-appraisal that "Time is not dispassionate about news. It cares about what's going on in the world, and it hopes that its readers care. Time [seeks] a truthful summation. . . . Fairness is Time's goal." As Ammunition put it: "This is news? This is hokum . . ."

XXIX

1. THE LUCEPRESS POLLUTION

Time today is the gratuitous sneer and the open mouth of shocked belief, it is the wisecrack of Madison Avenue and the maxim of Main Street, it is the mouthpiece of the Republican Party and the spokesman for the American People, it is the leer of Hollywood bed-talk and the clasped hands of Presbyterian piety.
—The New York Post

America was on the verge of a mortal crisis involving public confidence in its institutions—that confidence without which the nation was nothing. It was the hoariest of chestnuts, so often repeated as to be forgotten or ignored, that a modicum of larceny in government could be endured as long as the people knew they had a reasonably honest and independent press to hold it up to shame. Ideally the press, in all its honest diversity, *was* the electorate in its endless scrutiny and judgment of the elected.

Ultimately, a large part of the public would be shocked by the discovery that its greatest press lord, controlling its most popular and respected "news" publications, was neither honest nor independent but was allied with certain politicians and certain ideologies which he advanced by deception. In the Weekly Newsmagazine, American journalism saw a new and precedent-shattering development: the formation and careful instruction of a gifted staff in the skillful perversion of the news.

It had all happened with the gradualness and imperceptibility of the pollution of air, water and soil occurring at the same time. The Lucepress was permeating the atmosphere with an informational smog so expertly generated that for a time the only smarting eyes and protesting lungs seemed those of a few discerning Democrats, radicals, collegians and labor leaders. The public at large seemed at first to be inhaling it virtually unawares. As Luce neared

381

sixty, he had some 12,000 employees aiding him in the production of smog in his thirty-three-story Rockefeller Center building and his scores of other worldwide offices and plants, and he was planning to expand into a new forty-seven-story building nearby where more people could generate more smog.

With few exceptions, even those employees directly involved in producing the smog had no overpowering sense of betrayal. They had been initiated gradually into the rites of news-manipulation. They had been lectured by the Boss, with persuasion compounded of his powerful personality and high salaries, on the absurdity of those news organs which tried to be objective, and on the moral obligation to "take a stand," to formulate value judgments, to atone for those millions of Chinese murdered by objectivity.

He never told them outright that the value judgments must be cleverly concealed. This had been implicit since the time when he edited copy himself, and they *were*, most of them, cleverly concealed. The little wisps and tendrils wove their smoky way into meanings, crept into phrases and jokes, obscured faces and motives, shifted highlights so that the benign could appear evil and vice versa, and at times swirled into thick enough clouds to obliterate the view of large political designs. Plenty of Timen developed ulcers or consulted analysts. But there was little real guilt, for a reason which perhaps most of all testified to the virtuosity of the Boss.

It was simply that by employing new techniques he had made the pollution of news not only respectable but admired. He had grounded his whole enterprise in the Ivy League. He had glorified the Establishment. He had created a smart new fashion of "reporting." He had clung to the church, smitten the ungodly and atheistic, addressed religious and civic groups, waved the flag, embraced academe, conferred with the mighty, and had received uncounted honors in America and other countries. He had further won over many of his own people by a seeming sincerity of principle. It was of course a moral lift to have confidence that he believed implicitly in what he was doing, even if what he was doing was devious and dangerous.

Hearst, whose propagandizing of news was minor in extent and in influence compared with Luce's, had not won respectability and indeed had not really tried. He had been happy with his castles, his Marion Davies and his circle of movie stars, and with a certain rough-hewn honesty he had not put on churchly or academic airs. His product appeared on smudgy newsprint and was read largely by blue-collar people. Although his propaganda in his later years had been much like Luce's, he was generally regarded as non-respectable by the upper-middle and ruling classes who swore by Luce.

Propagandists have always wielded power by exploiting a universal human foible: the naïve belief (existing to a considerable degree even in the most sophisticated) that what is printed or uttered authoritatively must be true or contain some truth. This belief, controlling to some extent even when the publication is known to be biased, is immensely magnified when the publication is believed to be accurate and objective—that is, dealing in news rather

than propaganda. A rule of propaganda as old as mankind is that the insertion of a special-interest promotion in a vehicle believed to exclude special interests is of extraordinary value. Hence the manufacturers of a new synthetic who would spend thousands to advertise it in the then popular Saturday Evening Post would even more handsomely reward a public-relations man who succeeded in getting laudatory mention of the product into an editorial article in the Post, or in the newspapers. The reader would discount the advertisement to a large extent as propaganda, but would accept the article as news and therefore true.

Since the war, Luce, the eternal seeker of power, had achieved it more and more by the cleverness of his concealment of increasing amounts of propaganda in his publications, which were not generally known to be propagandist. The manipulative corruption of the Lucepress worked on two levels—the readership which was deprived of honest information, and the politicians of the administration who were well aware of the manipulation and knew themselves to be in debt to Luce. He built an elaborate facade of rationalization around his deception of the public, its underpinning consisting of the ridicule of objectivity as a myth. He had corollary tactics, one of them an insistence that news was often so complex that it was impossible to give all sides.

"Do you imply that there are always two sides to a question?" he demanded of an interviewer from Editor & Publisher. "Are there not more likely to be three sides or 30 sides? If I should answer that a man ought to speak and print the truth as he sees it, would you consider that to be a pretty good starting point . . . ?"

It would indeed, as long as he conceded that "the truth as he saw it" was opinion, not news or fact, and that he should in all conscience tell his readers that they were getting opinion. Luce could get testy when pressed by outsiders on this ground.

"I am a Protestant, a Republican and a free-enterpriser," he snapped at one of them, "which means I am biased in favor of God, Eisenhower and the stockholders of Time Inc.—and if anybody who objects doesn't know this by now, why the hell are they still spending 35 cents for the magazine?"

This was perhaps as close to a justification as he could get—let the buyer beware—since Time was neither the newsmagazine it purported to be nor a magazine of open opinion. The whole secret of its power lay in its concealed opinion—i.e., propaganda. Astonishingly, most readers believed the Lucepress dispensed news rather than propaganda. Even the small percentage who knew perfectly well they were reading propaganda—and those who regarded Time simply as a Republican organ—were falling into the propagandist trap when they felt easily able to discount it. The knowing reader could spot the obvious adjectival twists, the visible laudations and denigrations (and would be influenced to some degree, despite all his assurance, even by them). He was less likely to note the many extremely subtle touches of propaganda—the quiet little mood word, the nuance, the Disembodied Voice, the descrip-

tive that seemed innocent but was not. And he missed entirely the facts that were suppressed, the "facts" that were exaggerated, the emphasis of some items in places of prominence such as headlines, leads or picture captions, or their soft-pedaling in one line between the ads on page 49. Nor could he know when the editors had splashed propaganda with prominence of position and extra length. And few were aware of the extent to which they were influenced by photographs which showed a smile or a scowl, a neatly pressed suit or a rumpled shirt that perhaps even showed perspiration.

In fact, the Lucepress propagandists were experts, and any reader, no matter how alert, would come away with some of the ideas they sought to implant.

When a democratic majority votes or acts on a basis of manipulated information, it necessarily becomes a manipulated majority and a manipulated government. The Lucepress threat would have been mitigated had there been equal propaganda exerted by the opposition. But the Lucepress had *no hidden-propaganda opposition.*° The influence exerted on its 40 million weekly readers had no counterpart on the other side. On the contrary, its success had produced two thriving competitors on the same political side of the street, Newsweek and U.S. News & World Report, both big except in comparison with Time. Neither was yet as cleverly fictional as Time, but like Time they looked back on the week's news with their own bias, which also favored the Republican establishment. The combined propagandist influence of the three was enormous, as Bagdikian observed, because of the skill of presentation:

> [The newsmagazines] have arisen in the present form only in this generation, a generation unprepared for the special forms of influence which the newsmagazines use. In many respects this influence is comparable to modern advertising techniques of depth probing and psychological motivation. By using many of these methods in the presentation of news interpretation, the newsmagazines are influencing a generation of middle-class voters who are extremely sensitive to conventional bias in newspaper stories but almost totally unaware of the new techniques in newsmagazines.

Time, alone of them all, was working on its second generation. Old Timers had been reading the magazine for well over thirty years, old Lifers for more than twenty. All were presumably well indoctrinated with a robotized, self-righteous patriotism that included an automatic and undiscriminating hatred of Communism instead of the understanding of Communism that intelligent foreign relations would require. Time's impact was increased by its widespread use in high-school current events courses slanting young minds with bias, misinformation and a pushbutton hatred of Communism that usually carried into maturity.

° Such liberal publications as the New Republic, The Nation and The Reporter not only had minuscule circulations in comparison with the Lucepress but honestly made known their character as journals of opinion and comment, not newsmagazines.

Time's readability, its occasional insights and its guarantee of entertainment on almost every page had made it something near a national habit, or addiction. It could on occasion make even a radical stand up and cheer with a devastating portrayal of a reactionary or small-minded politician. It had so warred on the egregious Senator Bilbo of Mississippi as the "worst man in the Senate" that Bilbo had declared Luce to be a "nigger lover." It could run an excellent feature on the eight most expendable men in the Senate, impaling four Democrats and four Republicans with near-impartiality. It never failed to pass along the latest and best wisecracks. Its writing at times could be splendid. As for Life, trivial as it often was, it had some of the best news photography in the world. And while it was true, as Dwight Macdonald said, that it ran eight pages of Renoirs next to a roller-skating horse so that the reader got the impression that Renoir and the horse were of equal eminence, it had to be added that at any rate the magazine did not exclude Renoir in favor of the horse.

It was this skill in technique, this air of excitement, this entertainment, this "instruction," this occasionally demonstrated capacity for fairness, that brought in the millions of customers who tripped and fell painlessly into the propagandist net.

2. TRUTH UP THE CHIMNEY

The most articulate opposition to the Luce program of brainwashing came from two women, Mary Bancroft and Laura Z. Hobson. Mrs. Hobson had recently returned to Time as a consultant in promotion. She could see that the magazine was a fraud—a fact which made her promotion work painfully disingenuous—and was pondering the touchy business of pointing this out to Luce. In the interim she had written several novels, one of them the best-selling *Gentlemen's Agreement.* Her salary at Time was huge, and she was one of the few who could get into Luce's Penthouse and be sure of a careful hearing. She liked him personally. She did not go so far as to subscribe to the feeling of some liberals that he was a Fascist or proto-Fascist although she detested his constant mobilizing-for-war against the Communists and wished that he could develop a more balanced attitude.

Since she was working for Luce, she did not have the full freedom of criticism enjoyed by Mrs. Bancroft. Both of them had noticed Luce's unawareness of back-street aspects of America he never encountered. Once in a taxi with Mrs. Hobson, he had suddenly turned and said, "Poverty is ended in America, real poverty, poverty as Dickens described it," and had swept aside her sharp disagreement by a method he often used, namely, by ignoring her and continuing his exposition. Once to Mrs. Bancroft in her apartment he had said, "Now that poverty is finished in America, the country can turn to other

problems." When she protested that this was not so, he accused her of falling for the bleeding-heart nonsense of Mrs. Roosevelt.

The American press, in the main, clung to the folklore that the press must not criticize the press, and let Luce alone. This was true although the Luce-press manipulation of news made editors of the old tradition writhe. New York then had two powerful newspapers, the Republican Herald Tribune and the liberal Times, which separated news and opinion with something approaching scrupulosity. Both had national influence. Both were painfully aware of the Lucepress distortions. But the new owner of the Tribune, John Hay Whitney, like the headmen of the Times, Adler and Sulzberger, was a friend of the Luces. With only minor exceptions the Times and the Tribune hewed to the rules of the game. They raised no finger against Luce, nor did any paper of national influence except for the occasional fusillades of the Chicago Tribune. That "newspaper," whose own news was unconscionably slanted, was infuriated among other things by Luce's long-disavowed Commission on the Freedom of the Press. It took the odd line that he was inclined toward Communism.

The brilliant Bagdikian analysis had appeared in the Providence Journal, a Republican paper favoring Eisenhower, before it was published in the small-circulation New Republic. When Milton S. Gwirtzman, a Harvard senior, wrote an article for the Crimson in 1955 listing some of Time's most egregious Republicanisms, part of it was picked up by the news services and quoted in many newspapers. When the columnist John Crosby permitted himself some animadversions, they were less on the subject of propaganda than mere accuracy. They were inspired by the actor Alec Guinness's disgust at the misrepresentation in Time's cover story about him. "It's absolute rubbish," Guinness said. "From the cover picture to the story, it wasn't me at all. There are ten, 15 or 20 inaccuracies in it. There is no trace of the truth at all. They've even got my son's name and age wrong. Amazing how wrong a magazine with such a reputation for research can be." Crosby reflected:

> Well, it's not so amazing. Time is a flagrant example of publication by committee rather than by responsible individuals and by the time legmen, researchers, editors and writers get through pushing the facts around and making them conform to style rules, policy and individual bias, the truth has fled up the chimney. Guinness is simply saying publicly what many people have said privately for years.
>
> Time has got so august, so all-powerful and so obsessed with being readable that it has forgotten how to write a simple news story. Time once quoted me as having said something I didn't say and then, to compound the felony, got someone else to comment on what I hadn't said to start out with. It takes a very rich and very enterprising magazine to do that.

There was a point that Crosby missed—or perhaps he felt he could not go that far in press criticism. It was that the underlying purpose of Time's com-

mittee-and-meatgrinder system seemed to be to simplify and facilitate the doctoring of the news. As far as is known, this purpose was never openly stated. It apparently was not originally so intended. As a practical matter, that was how it worked out. No news publication was so error-ridden over the years as Time on the committee system. The system had long, long since proved ineffectual in its original purpose of ensuring accuracy. Time's retention of it suggested appreciation for a method permitting convenient departure from the truth. In that upside-down world it was the writers most gifted in fictionization (*vide* Goldsborough and Chambers) who were most highly paid, and it was those who felt responsibility to fact (such as Hersey, White and Merle Miller) who were called to account and moved elsewhere. Mary Bancroft kept unloading hints, writing Luce:

> I've at last thought of something I'm *for* instead of *against*—brace yourself. Integrity! . . . [This is the] age of the advertiser, the word, & Instant Recognition —this age of that little cancerous approach, the gimmick . . . If the American Peepul fall victim to the word, operating via the gimmick, we're lost.

Loss of integrity, she added, was identical with corruption, "And what annoys me most is corruption under the guise of respectability." But not once did the lover of debate permit that formidably logical lady to draw him into a discussion or justification of his propaganda, perhaps realizing that this was one debate he would inevitably lose.

The Democratic New York Post ran a ten-part examination of Time and Luce that suggested vividly the victory of propaganda and cleverness over honesty. But such candid appraisals were the exceptions. For the rest, the Lucepress had no opposition, and no analysis of its methods reached its bemused readers. There was that rich yarn about the man who read Time and the New York Times and who told a friend, "I'm quitting the Times. It's a liar. I've been checking it against Time." No one was blowing the whistle on the Lucepress. There was no agency to protect either the electorate or the elected against it. On the contrary, new garlands were forever being laid on the founder's brow. Although he had failed to realize membership in the Yale Corporation, he had been awarded honorary degrees by eleven well-known colleges. Many of their citations were similar to that of Colgate University, whose president told him, "you have strikingly demonstrated for our times the compatibility and the virtue of responsible journalism in a free society." Perhaps it was time to question the competence and responsibility of educators who could thus institutionalize the gimmick.

Realistically, was it too late? The gimmick was so thoroughly institutionalized that the upper- and middle-echelon people at the Lucepress were the recipients of honorary degrees themselves. The work of flavoring and manipulating the news and deriding and bespattering the Boss's targets became a kind of game. The gag about Kefauver and his pitchfork was regarded as the richest piece of writing to come out of the shop in years, a mark for younger

fellows in NA to pitch at. No writer seems to have resigned because an unusually honest and dedicated politician had been unfairly treated. To editors trained from the beginning in this journalism of irresponsibility, it had become as much a part of their lives as the production of Westerns by Hollywood cowboys and the creation of television cosmetics commercials by advertising specialists.

There was power too, the power of the Boss filtering down through the mighty handful of managing editors and assistant managing editors and publishers and assistant publishers, the larger but still powerful ranks of senior editors, star writers and bureau chiefs, and down to the literally hundreds of associate editors, contributing editors, domestic and foreign correspondents. Each of them carried and used his formidable splinter of the power of the biggest "news"-publishing combine on earth. All of them traveled first class and stayed at the best hotels. When stocky Thomas Griffith traveled the world as Foreign News editor of Time, he noted the deference and respect accorded him by prime ministers, foreign ministers and other officials who were autocrats in their own lands. He was, after all, Luce's personal representative, the Foreign Minister of Time, with pipelines to Washington and every other capital—far more powerful than most foreign ministers who had only one small nation as bailiwick.

A fraction of the power drifted down even to young TLF rookie writers a few years out of college, who became speakers heard with respect by business, religious or educational groups.

There were, of course, occasional doubts and twinges at 30 Rockefeller Plaza. A few who could not stand the fraudulence of NA and FN got out from under by transferring to such back-of-the-book departments as Cinema or Business, where the gimmickry was not dictated weekly from on high and in any case could not start a world war. There were those who soothed their consciences with secretive efforts to tone down excess, regarding themselves as counter-agents, doing good when they got away with it and still drawing that wonderful salary. But this was risky business and, according to Penn Kimball, who worked for Time, it seldom succeeded or lasted long.

"The ones who cracked under the strain," said Kimball, "were the ones who were somehow trying to beat the system, the ones who thought: 'Now if I could just slip a sentence in that would say this.' Then they'd settle for 'If I could just get this one word in.' Finally they'd settle for the feeling: 'Well, anyway, I prevented them from saying certain things . . .'"

Kimball moved over to Collier's. Another Time writer saved *his* peace of mind through a flight of fancy, imagining himself to be an advertising copywriter. As such, his own views were irrelevant and Time was the client, always right. "I see my assignments," he said, "in these terms: This is the angle, this is the product, and we want to sell it to this particular audience."

In the inverted world of Time, he was not indulging his imagination but was seeing things in coldest reality. He *was* an advertising copywriter. Time

was his client, infallibly correct. He *was* selling the product to the upper-middle-class market. His rationalization merely eased his contrition over his role in such humbuggery by removing him from journalism, where one was expected to exercise responsibility, to advertising, where everybody understood that there was no responsibility at all.

It would be axiomatic that the example of the Lucepress as at once the least accurate and responsible and the world's most smashingly successful, would hardly tend to elevate the national journalistic level. To its shortcomings as a journalistic inspirer and its fundamental deception of the reader could be added specific propaganda feats which turned out to be baneful for America and the world. A strong case could be made that America's disastrous Asian policy after 1949 was in large part due to years of Lucepress propaganda. One of the very few who ever taxed Luce to his face for Machiavellianism was Dr. Eugene Carson Blake, Stated Clerk of the Presbyterian Church. At a meeting of church leaders in a Time conference room, Dr. Blake, in front of the others, denounced Luce as a Christian of questionable sincerity. In what must have been his humblest moment, Luce agreed that his Christianity could be improved and the meeting went on.

XXX

1. CADILLACS OR FREEDOM?

The shattering surprise of the Soviet Sputniks caught technology-proud America lagging in a field it had thought its own. Luce and the whole nation were as stunned as if Russian H-bombs were certain to rain down from above, as indeed many expected. There was sudden criticism of Eisenhower and his chip shots. Life mirrored the Boss's profound anxiety in a special Sputnik issue which actually suggested that the President had better get a move on and must have paralyzed its 20 million readers with fear, from its exhortatory editorial ("Since there may be a war, Americans will back every step the President has proposed . . .") to its exhortatory article, "Arguing the Case for Being Panicky." It assailed American complacency and said the crisis dictated a national renunciation of trivialities and a solemn dedication to serious purpose:

> What, then, should we do? Just this: we should each decide what we really want most in the world. . . . What do we want most? A Cadillac? A color television set? Lower income taxes?—Or to live in freedom?

Inevitably, in the same thick issue was a three-page advertisement for the 1958 Cadillac, in four colors with a background of gold, along with nineteen other full pages of automobile ads, several television ads and a kaleidoscopic offering of stern American necessities ranging from Revlon's Red Caviar Lipstick ("a soft-spoken scarlet") to Lady Borden's Holiday Bisque Tortoni Ice Cream and Miss Clairol's hair coloring ("so natural only her hairdresser knows for sure!"). The advertising-free Nation snapped, "Life, clearly, knows what it wants: freedom *and* the Cadillac account." Lucius Beebe, the transplanted Eastern philosopher, a fervent Communist-hater, let go with both pearl-handled pistols in his Virginia City Territorial Enterprise:

Luce and His Empire

For a quarter of a century . . . the most powerful single influence on American taste and its social destinies has probably been Life Magazine. . . . [It] has risen to a position of affluence shared by no periodical in the English-speaking world. Publicity and promotion . . . have been within its gift or refusal to a degree that has made its editors a great deal more powerful than the Federal Government . . .

In recent months, however, Life has suddenly become aware of the facts of life . . . It admits in a hair-raising signed article . . . that the Russians are so far ahead of us in everything that the days of the American Republic are numbered, and very correctly attributes this state of things to the fact that Americans vastly prefer TV comedians, Cadillacs and pro football to the dreary precautions of staying alive.

Yet it is difficult to remember when . . . Life has not devoted its most mature and effective enthusiasm to promoting what it now deplores. It has lavished billions of dollars worth of space on rutting Texas cowboys with mandolins and criminal sideburns, on creating television comedians, on the mammary glands of Italian actresses, on Detroit motor car designers, on Hollywood starlets . . . all the things it now, in the shadow of Judgment Day, is busy renouncing. It is hard to name a cheap, vulgar or meretricious aspect of the American chromium pigsty that has not received priceless publicity and implicit approval from the most influential periodical in the history of printing. . . .

Yet even while it . . . admits that the American eagle is a gone goose, Life has no least or slightest intention of itself renouncing the things that have accomplished the end of its own world. . . . In the identical pages in which Life urges Americans to take the true measure of the disaster that has befallen us and to make a choice between Cadillacs and survival, it pushes the fortunes of a Negro musical comedy on Broadway and carries advertising layouts for a nest of Detroit-made motor cars that would turn the stomach of a Texan. Like Rome and Babylon . . . the barbarians when they come will find America bogged down in an undulant sea of female bosoms in the most expensive full color halftones in Life.

It is problematical if, when the Russians take over, they will suppress or continue Life. It has been by indirection and complacency a powerful agency in the undoing of the United States; on the other hand the things it has glorified could be the end of the Russians themselves if permitted to stay around. The American people, however, in this final contingency, will have the satisfaction of knowing that they have been washed up once and for all in the very best dynaflow, rotary motion, jet propelled, low fuel consumption, no laundress-red hands washing machine. As advertised in Life.

Life and all the Luce publications continued to exempt themselves from the Spartan measures they urged on the country. Those who expected Time, Life, Fortune and Sports Illustrated to set a patriotic example by ending their frivolities and getting down to save-America bedrock with articles devoted to physical fitness and advertisements limited to muscle-builders, ammunition and survival kits were mistaken. Life kept right on with sprightly articles and picture layouts on society gatherings and Broadway spectacles while SI gave

serious attention to the Boston Celtics professional basketball team, the most exciting ski slopes and the prospects for the New York Yankees. Nor was there any change in advertising, which continued to stress the 1958 automobiles, golf clubs, brassieres and deodorants and was particularly heavy on Old Granddad, Gordon's gin and Ronrico rum, as if to suggest that these might be the only real alleviatives. Months passed, giving time for the alteration of advertising and editorial schedules, but there was no significant change. By summer the Sputnik scare was pretty well over, it seemed that the Russians were biding their time about vaporizing us, and Life's cameras were turned on beach beauties and resort wear while SI went in for surfboarding and the heavyweight boxer Floyd Patterson.

But if the Sputniks had not yet incinerated America or reformed the Luce-press hedonism, they had so alarmed Luce as to produce an astonishing result —unmistakable, if short-lived, criticism in his magazines of Eisenhower's relaxed conduct of office. As Stewart Alsop noted, it was "as though the Osservatore Romano had suddenly attacked the Pope." For America to be second in anything, particularly armaments, was insupportable. Vacationing in Phoenix a few weeks later, the Luces had as their guests the Nixons. One may be sure that the Vice President heard a great deal about the Sputniks and America's need for total effort, even at the expense of Cadillacs.

2. RALLY ROUND THE FLAG

When Mrs. Luce had finished her term as ambassador, she rested at the swank and strictly feminine Maine Chance spa of Elizabeth Arden in Phoenix. Luce, joining her there, stayed at the Arizona Biltmore Hotel and played its private golf course, which was surrounded by handsome residences. They took a fancy to the former Tommy Manville villa near the fifteenth green, a rambling, six-bedroom place of pink stucco and tile roof surrounding a loggia, and bought it for $250,000.

In January 1958 Laura Hobson was invited by the Luces to spend a few days with them there. Luce, who had been in Arizona but had returned for a few weeks of work and a speech at the University of Pennsylvania advocating hurried construction of bomb shelters, flew back with her but preferred to sit by himself and read, as he usually did. When they changed planes at Chicago, he confided that he was reading Max Shulman's *Rally Round the Flag, Boys* and was unable to understand it because of the slang and gags. It worried him to miss the point. She told him she would prepare a glossary for him. As they flew on to Phoenix, separated again, she glanced back and saw Luce slump sideways in his seat, apparently ill, his face ashen. She hurried back, bent over him and asked what was wrong. He seemed hardly able to speak. A stewardess came running with aspirin and a glass of water and he revived quickly, saying he was all right and making it plain he wanted no more talk about it.

They were met at the Phoenix airport by the Luce chauffeur of many years, Arthur Little—the only family employee who had not created a problem by quitting. There was dinner for four that evening—the two Luces, Mrs. Hobson and Herbert Goren, who was beginning a column on bridge for Sports Illustrated—and they played bridge after dinner. Luce had earlier decided in his headlong way to take up bridge. Always a believer in experts, he had then summoned the expert Goren to Phoenix for a weekend to teach him the game. Such speed of instruction was beyond even Goren, who described his manner of play: "When Harry picks up a hand, he goes into a trance. The best time to play with him is when you're dead tired, because you can always take a nap while Harry counts his points. I think he would be a better player if he wasn't so awfully afraid of making a mistake. He's too proud."

Goren said "proud"; others would have said "competitive." Luce hated to lose at anything. He was proud as the four played on this occasion, and Mrs. Hobson thought him normal except that he said little—a gross abnormality that could have been caused by his concentration on the cards. It was not until five days later, on February 5, that he was seized by a severe heart attack and rushed by ambulance to St. Joseph's Hospital. Clare, who rode in the ambulance, was standing in the hospital corridor, talking with a nun, when Mrs. Hobson arrived. She embraced Mrs. Hobson, wept and said, "My life would be over if anything happened to Harry."

Luce's son Henry and brother-in-law Maurice Moore flew out immediately. News of his heart attack, it was felt, might affect Time stock adversely, so it was reported that he had suffered from influenza that developed into pneumonia. For decades he had been running like a racehorse, operating under constant tension, taking too many sleeping pills and absorbing the smoke of a million cigarettes, and he was nearly sixty. He was released after eighteen days, claiming to be ready to slow down but fingering a cigarette as he left. He stayed in Phoenix for six weeks, then returned to work at what seemed the briskest of canters if not quite a full gallop.

The Sputniks had exacerbated the anti-Communism in him which had been doing quite well as it was. The old evangelical absolutism seemed blended as always with his American-Century thrust for power, the hymns of his childhood driving him in his manhood:

> Can we, whose souls are lighted
> With wisdom from on high,
> Can we to men benighted
> The lamp of life deny?

Since he had always started with the premise of Communist evil, and kept reminding America of its mission to free the world, it was hard to see anything but military confrontation at the end of that road. His anti-Communism was expressed in militarism—"Onward, Christian Soldiers"—to the exclusion of efforts to understand the aspirations of other nations or any real search for

accommodation. How could one compromise with the devil? In talking with friends, he could veer from a decided, if intuitive, opinion that the Russians would not attack to a sudden certainty that they were about to vaporize America and Time Inc. His magazines, however, hewed to the bad-guy enemy idea and the need for bristling armament. In his speeches now he was urging two measures which on their faces seemed broadly humanitarian rather than concerned centrally with the war on Communism. One was the promotion of the rule of law on a worldwide basis, the other the elimination of American tariffs and the formation of a free-world economic union. Both, under their innocent facades, advanced the same old principles. On the theory that Russia and China were lawless, the organization of nations adhering to codified law, American style, would strengthen the anti-Communist cause in one realm as economic pressure would in another. Speaking at Yale in April, he urged these two "giant steps" and emphasized that America faced "the test of survival."

Secretary Dulles, with Calvinist certainty equal to Luce's, continued his stony view of the world crisis as a problem of alliances and armaments, neglecting the civilized processes of diplomacy. When the Chinese proposed increased contacts and invited fifteen U.S. newsmen to visit the mainland, Dulles reiterated the ban on all travel to China and denied passports to the newsmen. This narrow-spirited attitude aroused some American criticism—even Luce, to his credit, protested the ban—and Dulles finally permitted the validation of a few passports. But he would not guarantee reciprocity for Chinese newsmen here, and the offended Chinese withdrew their invitations. An opportunity for thaw was turned away. The Chinese-Russian hostility toward each other grew, but the Dulles policies kept these two most populous of the world's nations united in enmity toward the United States.

Dulles had Luce's enthusiastic support in his steps to vitiate the Geneva agreement, prevent the Vietnamese elections and to take over the "protective" part of the role formerly played by the French. American millions now went to Ngo Dinh Diem in Saigon for the purpose of keeping Vietnam split in two and founding a firm anti-Communist regime in the south. Diem was spending many of the millions to bribe opposition leaders. Direct American involvement in Vietnam had begun, much of it in shady maneuvers justified on the ground of desperate necessity to maintain an anti-Communist foothold in Indochina. Had we not "lost China" by our failure to act aggressively enough? We must not lose Indochina. This was by no means a purely Republican concept but had strong support from leading Democrats, and no strong opposition. So far had the defeat of Chiang, the outraged Luce reaction, the growth of McCarthyism and the fear of being classed with the "appeasers" come to dominate American policy.

The Luces had attended Dulles's sixty-eighth birthday party in Washington along with the President and Mrs. Eisenhower and members of the Cabinet—his last before he was stricken with cancer. The Dulles freeze toward Red

China would outlive him by many years, as would the American moral-religious intervention in Vietnam. When Meyer Kestnbaum, a special assistant to the President, urged that Red China be recognized by this country and admitted to the United Nations if it made certain policy changes, Senator Bridges said Kestnbaum's "usefulness is about over." Senator Knowland, so firm for Chiang that he was known as "the Senator from Formosa," agreed. When the (Protestant) National Council of Churches advocated recognition of China and her admission to the world body, there was an outcry from secular, Catholic and opposing Protestant groups, dark talk of the Council being in the hands of Communists, and a hostile report in Time stressing critics who spoke of "misguided judgment" and "betrayal beyond belief."

Chief among those who would have been betrayed was Chiang, whose ambassador to the United Nations, Dr. Tsiang Ting-fu, had recently employed an American public relations firm, the Hamilton Wright Organization, to extend the work of the China Lobby. The Chiang group was paying Wright a $300,000 annual fee for four years on his agreement to secure Chiang at least $2,500,000 a year worth of publicity in the news and entertainment media. The purpose of the propaganda, of course, was to influence American public opinion to continue and enlarge the subsidization of Chiang along with the non-recognition of Mao's half-billion. Thereafter, Chiang propaganda disguised as news and written by Wright employees was circulated all over America by such well-known organizations as the New York Herald Tribune Syndicate and the North American Newspaper Alliance. The upright Senator Paul Douglas of Illinois, a believer in Chiang, was later embarrassed when he discovered that a pro-Chiang piece written at the Wright stable, and to which Wright had coaxed him to attach his name as author, had been financed by Chiang. In all probability it was American money used by Chiang to wheedle more American money. As one investigator, Philip Horton, described it:

> Money is the most important and fascinating of the many fascinating characters in the China Lobby—a character capable of endless disguises. It is everywhere. In a massive stream it flowed from the United States to China. It has returned in large amounts to the United States via numberless channels to create more millions, more propaganda, more aid, more private corruption, and more public confusion.

Mary Bancroft was able to joke, though with an edge of sarcasm, at the clutch of myths, prejudices, slogans and clichés which ruled American policy —the implicit belief in technological superiority, the self-righteousness, the anti-intellectualism, the zealously inculcated belief in the Communist devil. She wrote Luce sarcastically, as if speaking for the average American and his naïve faith in the Eisenhower father figure:

> But although the horrid suspicions have occurred to us—briefly—that Daddy may be sick, a bit too self-indulgent sportwise, and possibly even stupid—still generals are great and mysterious figures with specialized minds and with those

horrible Russians eyeing us so ferociously we certainly do need a very, very great general for how else, except through fighting, do you protect yourself? Certainly not by improving or educating yourself. That's ridiculous. Who needs education when they've got know-how? Stalin is perfectly horrible. He's little. He's pock-marked. He actually talked to that man who was really almost dead at Yalta where we were betrayed by Alger Hiss who was educated. Besides, Stalin sat in a little gold chair at Potsdam after dinner and had the Missouri Waltz played to him by you know whom and who connived with George Marshall and that Yale man [Acheson] to lose us China. . . . everyone knows [Stalin] once robbed a bank. Stalin personally killed twenty-seven million farmers. . . . He's not just insane like poor Hitler. He's really evil. And then—Bang!—he dies. Our mortal enemy shouldn't die. The Devil is immortal. And who takes his place? Jackie Gleason [Malenkov]? Not exactly. But still isn't everyone supposed to love a fat man? Still J. Edgar Hoover, that Virgin Mary in pants, says we must go on hating and we must watch out. . . . And then . . . the fat boy succeeded by roly poly in that double-breasted gray flannel suit . . . up goes Sputnik and . . . Daddy blew up with it—for Daddy should have known, Daddy should have prevented it. . . .

The gnashing of the Luce teeth must have been feral. Nor could he have been happier over the next, in which she commented on Vice President Nixon's insistence on continuing his South American tour despite the stones hurled at him by angry citizens, and noting the strong survival of McCarthyism:

. . . All of a sudden it seems to me that we've taken an unnoticed jump forward on the "thing" that went underground when Joe McC. fell from grace—in other words we are more—speaking of us collectively as a people—like the Germans than we were then. And by this I mean we seem to be losing touch with reality—if people are reality—thinking everyone who is against us is a Communist, imagining that if we only explain ourselves, we will be loved and admired. . . .

This disconcerting drumfire perhaps made him appreciate all the more his tolerant first wife, with whom he had kept on the best of terms. Before she left for Europe in 1958, he wrote her with true warmth:

Dear Lila—You very kindly said that you would do an errand for me in Rome or Venice. This is the errand: get me a present for me to give to you—something that you'd like to have. This would give me great pleasure. (Enclosed herewith —the wherewithal)

I hope this errand will add to the joy of travel and to the drama of Rome & Italy.

With every good wish and all affection, Harry

3. THE PUBLIC BE DAMNED

In March 1959, some 10,000 Bolivians, enraged at a Time story, stoned the American embassy in La Paz, burned copies of Time along with the American

flag and rioted until two of their number were killed. Time had quoted an un-named U.S. embassy official as saying that America had spent $129 million in Bolivia without effect, adding jocularly that the only solution was to "abolish Bolivia and let its neighbors divide the country and its problems among them-selves." The Bolivian Cabinet met to consider measures to restore order, while hundreds of Americans were evacuated to an army camp for their own safety. The Bolivian ambassador in Washington called on Secretary of State Herter to express concern over the article. American embassy people in La Paz denied having made the statement "quoted" by Time. Luce issued a statement regretting the violence but admitting no Time error.

At the World Press Congress then meeting in Columbia, Missouri, John T. O'Rourke, editor of the Washington Daily News, read a cable from a Latin American editor indignant about the Time story. O'Rourke called on Time to identify "the strangely anonymous joking official whose remarks, if made, caused the riot." He said that both he and John Knight, publisher of the Knight newspapers, had been victims of false reporting in Time and had met others who had had similar experiences. There was a painful awareness among newsmen of Time's trick of unloading a wisecrack or an opinion by as-cribing it to an unidentified person. There were many kinds of fiction, O'Rourke said—why not news fiction? "It is nice," he added, "to escape once a week from mundane reality and gaze at the wild, improbable place around me through Time's kaleidoscopically colored glasses." These and further re-marks reflecting on Time's reliability won him applause from his audience of newsmen suggesting a general agreement with him. Foreign Minister Victor Andrade of Bolivia, less humorous, was asking what steps the U.S. govern-ment would take "if it proves that the statement attributed to an American official was forged by the magazine."

Meanwhile, the President had nominated Clare for the post of ambassador to Brazil. She made plans for the move to Rio, where Luce would also operate part-time from his own office as he had in Rome. She received unexpectedly severe opposition from the maverick Senator Wayne Morse of Oregon, who had been handled roughly by Time on two counts: he opposed Dulles's poli-cies and he had switched from the Republican to the Democratic party. Morse did not think that Time's Bolivian story was a good omen for successful diplomacy in South America. He brought up the matter of Mrs. Luce's speech in Milan, calling it "meddling" in Italian politics. He attacked her speech dur-ing the 1944 Presidential campaign when she said Roosevelt was "the only American President who ever lied us into a war because he did not have the political courage to lead us into it"—a remark she now said that she regret-ted. He accused her of "instability" and of "extreme partisanship" in Italy, mentioning also her "relationship to Time, Life and Fortune" and the "inter-twining of Luce policy and Eisenhower policy in conducting the vital affairs of the United States."

Ex-President Truman, who had sold his memoirs to Life for a reputed

$600,000, chimed in from Missouri with an intentional confusion of gender: "What a nice thing it is to have Mr. Clare Boothe Luce in the grease in Bolivia. He spent a lot of time trying to put me in the grease but never succeeded."

Senator Dirksen, deprecating Morse's resurrection of an eleven-year-old speech made by Mrs. Luce, said, "Why thrash old hay or beat an old bag of bones?" Senator Humphrey jumped up, twinkling. "I must rise to the defense of the lady," he said. Dirksen hastened to make himself clear: "I am referring to the old bag of political bones, these old canards."

After all the fuss, she was confirmed 79 to 11. She immediately gave the following statement to the Associated Press:

> I am grateful for the overwhelming vote of confirmation in the Senate. We must now wait until the dirt settles [obviously a reference to the famous Acheson remark about the "dust" settling]. My difficulties, of course, go some years back when Senator Wayne Morse was kicked in the head by a horse.

It was not the statement of a diplomat who intended to keep her job. Morse snarled that this proved what he had said about instability. Luce now issued a long statement charging that Morse had destroyed her opportunity for usefulness in Brazil, that much of the attack was really aimed at him (Luce) and his publications and that he had asked his wife to resign. It turned out that Morse had gone to unusual lengths, having telephoned her New York physician to ask if she had been under psychiatric care. He replied that he could not give out such information without her permission. When she promptly gave her permission, he replied that she was not and had not been under such care. Senator Stephen M. Young of Ohio, a Democrat who had voted against her, went to his anthology to add to the uproar, reading into the record a bit of verse by the Victorian poet Sir William Watson:

> . . . In truthful numbers be she sung,
> The Woman with the Serpent's Tongue;
> Ambitious from her natal hour
> And scheming all her life for power;
> With little left of seemly pride;
> With venomed fangs she cannot hide;
> Burnt up within by that strange soul
> She cannot slake or yet control;
> Malignant-lipped, unkind, unsweet;
> Past all example indiscreet—
> The Woman with the Serpent's Tongue.
>
> To think that such as she can mar
> Names that among the noblest are!
> That hands like hers can touch the springs
> That move who knows what men and things!
> That on her will their fates have hung!
> The Woman with the Serpent's Tongue.

Luce and His Empire

Although the President defended her, praised her work in Italy and urged her to take the Brazilian assignment, Mrs. Luce resigned.

Soon thereafter, Laura Hobson hit Luce with a sixteen-page memo telling him that Time was really pretty bad—bad enough to stultify her promotion work. It had *lost* seven-tenths of one percent in circulation—the first loss after many years of unbroken advances. Meanwhile, Newsweek and U.S. News had gained (though still of course far behind Time). She didn't think Time's trouble was the competition, nor did she think its trouble was Ben Bagdikian or Milton Gwirtzman. She thought Time's trouble was Time.

After twenty years of the Democrats, Eisenhower had come in and, as she put it, "Time was in love, and one's maturity often is reckoned by the way one handles love." She did not think that Time (for which one could read "Luce") had handled the affair maturely. She had not been with the company at the time of Luce's 1952 Union Club lecture to the staff on the impossibility of objectivity and the necessity of value judgments but she had heard about it and knew the whole pitch. She had also read closely Time's twenty-fifth anniversary restatement of purpose with its dismissal of objectivity and its proud assertion of "care" for the news, and she knew *that* pitch too. She had noted that John Hay Whitney of the Herald Tribune had recently picked a Democrat for his top editor and had announced publicly, "The paper will continue its policy of complete objectivity in its news columns and of independent Republicanism on its editorial page." *That* was honest. She had been shocked when she read Jacques Barzun's best-selling *House of Intellect* and found that Barzun had called Time "misinformation trimmed with insults." (Barzun had gone a good deal further than that in his outrage over a Time story about Nietzsche, writing in very small part, "More dull error could not be compressed into so few words.") Luce's two favorite rationalizations for his "news" policies made her bristle—rationalizations which had been taken up by some of the editors. One was his assertion that since he "invented" the newsmagazine, he naturally set the rules. The other was that a news weekly was not accountable to the standards set for a daily paper. She dared to pick them apart:

> Not for a minute can I believe it would be acceptable, for example, to Bagdikian, Barzun . . . or Whitney, [to say] that since Time invented the newsmagazine, it knew better than anybody else what the ground rules of newsmagazines should be. . . . To me, that's the same as saying, "the public be damned," and I think the time is long since gone when Time could say anything like that.

If it was true, she suggested, that a news weekly was a different breed of cat from a news daily and was absolved from the responsibilities of a newspaper, this interesting secret should be divulged to Time's readers. Most of them took the word "newsmagazine" literally. Time, she urged, could repair its good name by doing one of two things: by treating the news without bias, or by admitting the bias, announcing itself as a Republican magazine and changing its name to Time, The Weekly.

The Hobson memorandum might have become the basis for Time's declaration of maturity and responsibility but for a factor which Mrs. Hobson either misunderstood or could not bring herself to mention. On page 15 she wrote, "Isn't it the true intent of Time, today as always, to help people keep informed . . . ?"

Well, the answer to that was No. Luce was not and never could be a newsman dispensing information. He always was and always would be a propagandist with a mission. The memo so hurt him that he never mentioned it to her although they met and talked on other subjects. Time did not change. Time marched on.

4. WELCOME, KHRUSHCHEV

The American people must learn not to react automatically with horror at the mere mention of the word Communist.

—Sir Denis Brogan

The news-spectacular of 1959 was the American tour of the man Mrs. Bancroft had called "roly-poly in a double-breasted suit." Premier Khrushchev paid his historic visit at the invitation of President Eisenhower—an offense to the Calvinist ghost of Dulles. Eisenhower felt the need to reassure that sizable part of the population who felt, as did the Lucepress, that Khrushchev had horns. "What we are talking about now," he said soothingly, "is finding some little bridge, some little avenue yet unexplored, through which we can possibly move toward a better situation."

But after a dozen years of nerve-jangling Cold War, many Americans applauded the President's willingness to meet the premier even if Khrushchev was—as he was—undignified, impulsive and boorish between his bursts of almost equally startling good nature. Russia was a fact of life even if she was an invention of the devil. Khrushchev was indubitably an improvement over Stalin. Whatever damage was done to American morals by this mingling with the godless Bolshevist might be well sacrificed in the effort to avert holocaust. It would have seemed to American advantage, once "roly-poly" was invited, to smother the bloody memories of Hungary and Poland and treat the visitor with courtesy and good will. But the Lucepress, which bore so large a share of responsibility for that considerable body of citizens feeling automatic hatred for the Soviet, recoiled like a virgin at the approach of a rapist.

Life had one excellent report of a meeting between Khrushchev and a group of American business and professional leaders at the home of Averell Harriman, written by Harriman himself. Cool and measured, it showed the great gulf between Soviet and American thinking and the effort that would be required on both sides to bridge it, but it did not treat the effort as both useless and immoral as the Lucepress otherwise invariably did. Coming from a

man experienced in both Soviet and American wiles, it had an indispensable blend of realism and good will and showed what responsible journalism could do in informing the public about the gravest problem of the age.

Alas, almost all the rest of the heavy Time and Life coverage was conspicuously lacking both in courtesy and good will and was in fact simply a bigger helping of its usual smörgåsbord of propaganda. Time, a chip on its shoulder, mentioned the premier's "ice-cold bullet eyes" and called his tour "not so much a move to reduce world tension as a historic and tireless one-man campaign to cajole, flatter, wheedle, shame, threaten and defy the U.S. into changing its way of looking at the world." Life, telling of the careful security precautions that were taken, said that Russia had hinted that World War III might be the result if Khrushchev were hurt. Life's welcome was expressed in an editorial:

> The world's Number One Communist comes to America in a blaze of nightmare portents, stained with blood, promising peace and shooting rockets toward the moon. . . . [He] has already scored a propaganda victory by getting here. . . . His profound and dangerous Communist illusions about America will not be eradicated . . . we can act natural, with the common civility due any guest. . . . When he repeats his tired truisms about the need for peace, no response is needed. If he cracks peasant jokes, we need not disguise the fact that we like comedians. . . . U.S. capital goods could be all too useful to the terrible Russian war machine. . . . [But] let's all listen—just in case Mr. K. budges a bit. . . .

A one-page Life appraisal by John Osborne used the terms "cold calculation," "repellent," "hard view" and "ominous message" and managed to mention twice the famous Khrushchev phrase "we will bury you" without his explanation of its metaphorical meaning. The Lucepress coverage of Khrushchev was studded with ingenious variations on the "burial" theme just as mention of Acheson had once involved self-propelled reference to his unturned back. There was also a clear Life purpose to snap and use the most unflattering pictures possible of a man who could have used a little flattery. A huge rear-view shot of the bull-necked premier staring at the Lincoln Memorial carried a caption suggestive of Lincoln's freeing of the slaves as opposed to Russia's enslavement of the people. Trickiest of all was a photograph of Khrushchev calling his dog, the beast, its tail lowered, looking timid and fearful, the caption reading, "Like several million people, his dog Arbat gets the word from Khrushchev—and reacts."

The malevolence of that picture and caption would itself have undone elaborate coverage otherwise favorable.

The Lucepress trampled on the uncounted millions in America and the rest of the world who saw this meeting between East and West as a miracle in itself and yearned for the additional miracle of a moving together, if ever so slightly, of the two great disputants, each possessing armaments which alone made rational dialog imperative. But when Khrushchev, after his Camp

David talks with Eisenhower, appeared at his most affable and persuasive on nationwide television, admitted the difficulties in bringing about agreement, went so far as to liken the Socialistic system to Christianity, and ended in fuzzy English, "Good-bye, good luck, friends!" the electronic medium defeated the churlish Lucepress. When he left, the Americans in euphoria over the possibilities of *détente* certainly outnumbered those who spurned *détente* as appeasement.

During the Fifties, Emmet John Hughes had been regarded by many Timen (not without some disapproval) as the successor of White and Hersey as Luce's white-haired boy. There was strong speculation that he might even be tapped as Luce's editorial successor, Henry Luce III being younger and lacking experience. Hughes, like White and Hersey before him, was liberal in politics. Luce, having more than his quota of down-the-line political supporters in the staff, admired spirit and difference of opinion as long as they remained circumspect in debate and of course obedient in editorial policy.

After Hughes returned from his second assignment as an Eisenhower adviser and became head of Time's foreign correspondents, the relationship grew particularly close for such a loner as Luce. There were wheels within wheels here too, for Hughes was a close friend of Richard Clurman, a Time editor who had married Shirley Potash, the young lady of the unforgettable "What are you doing here?" scene at the Villa Taverna, and Mrs. Luce looked on Mrs. Clurman almost as a daughter. The Luces had attended the Clurman wedding, performed by a rabbi, and Luce had been fascinated by this new experience, a wedding ceremony unlike any he had previously witnessed. Also, Hughes, a strong Catholic, was a close friend of Luce's close friend Father Murray. Once Hughes and Murray, playing golf with Luce at the Ridgefield course, watched him address the ball with the ferocity and the will to win with which he addressed everything.

"You are looking," said Murray in a normal tone which Luce would have heard but for his deafness, "at the only man I know who can *will* a golf ball two hundred yards."

Oddly, while Time mourned the death of John Foster Dulles ("a missionary for peace in the cause of freedom. . . . the clear, stern conscience of freedom"), Hughes was finishing a book with the prophetic title *America the Vincible*, attacking the Dulles policies Luce had always admired. Among the Dulles (and Luce) canons Hughes assailed were the notion that a division of nations is necessarily between good and evil, and that a free society is inherently strong while a tyranny is inherently weak. Most of all he faulted Dulles for his evasion of all Russian proposals for peace talks and his refusal to initiate proposals of his own. Luce had long known of Hughes's opposition to Dulles and did not seem to hold it against him. The book received a moderately friendly review in Time, though Hughes, like any author, thought it could have been a great deal more appreciative.

At this same time, Luce himself for the second time in his life became the

subject of comment by gossip columnists suggesting that his marriage, which had sailed through all sorts of weather for twenty-three years, might be tossing in the storm of a new romance. A year earlier, at the request of Lord Beaverbrook, he had hired the Beaver's pretty, brunette twenty-four-year-old granddaughter, Lady Jean Campbell, as a publicist for Life. Now he (and Mrs. Luce and Lady Jean) received the unwelcome attentions of a free-swinging free press in the rumor department which Time had always exploited with such piquance. When Luce returned from a September trip to London, Oxford and Paris, Hearst's attentive Cholly Knickerbocker reported hearing rumors from Europe "that the powerful publisher has admitted to intimate friends that he and his wife intend to separate," going on:

> Luce has often been seen in the company of the lovely Lady Jean Campbell, daughter of the Duke of Argyll. . . . While some friends explain this as a purely platonic friendship, the frequent meetings of Luce and Lady Campbell have certainly added fuel to rift rumors. Mr. Luce himself, however, denies the stories. When I reached him at his Ridgefield, Conn., home, where he was spending the weekend with his wife, and asked him to comment on the reports, he replied:
> "Clare and I are here together. It is all very premature, to say the least."
> Then, after a pause, he added, "There is nothing to it at all."

Readers could perhaps pay no more serious heed to Cholly Knickerbocker than to the Timan who investigated Estes Kefauver's inclination to perspire, or the Lifeman who wrote the captions under the Khrushchev pictures. Still, there was a special idiom used by gossip columnists in their efforts to get meanings across to readers without inviting lawsuits. And if Luce had been quoted correctly in using the word "premature," it did not seem the remark of a man anxious to quell the rumor once and for all. Mrs. Luce herself was said to have disposed of the talk with one of those imaginative bits of repartee in which no one could match her—that if Luce married Lady Jean, "Then I would marry Lord Beaverbrook and become my husband's grandmother."

The gossipists could not drop the subject. As the Luces were about to leave for Phoenix, Suzy of the New York Daily Mirror mentioned in passing that the couple "are trying to quiet the separation rumbles." And Mrs. Luce, on returning from Phoenix a few days later to occupy their new forty-first-floor Waldorf Towers apartment, was queried by Nancy Randolph of the Daily News and was reported as saying, "So help me heaven, there's nothing to it. I've already denied it. Harry has denied it. It's just too bad we have to keep on saying so."

Lady Jean was the daughter of the Duke of Argyll by his first marriage to a daughter of Lord Beaverbrook. Her father's ancestral residence was Inverary Castle in the Western Highlands. To say that gossip flew at the T-L Building is to understate. Editors who could speculate that Luce was anything but immune to ancestral castles and titles of nobility even when unconnected with

beauty, had to admit that all they knew was what they read in the papers. Although such gossip had always been of great interest to the Lucepress, now and then being ballooned into a great sensation as in the case of King Edward VIII, and the current Luce question would have seemed of legitimate interest at least to the editor of the People department, there seems no apparent record that Luce was queried about it and certainly there was no story about it in the Lucepress.

Lady Jean returned from Europe a few days later and was immediately waylaid by the society editor of the World-Telegram, who reported that she "turned somewhat pale" when informed of the recent talk and quoted her as saying: ". . . as for these astonishing rumors, I am reminded of the inscription over the gate to the beautiful flower garden of St. Andrew's University in Scotland. It's by an anonymous sage, circa 1720, and carved in stone it reads, 'They have said; they will say; let them be saying.' "

One of the last words that "they" said came from the Luces' friend Elsa Maxwell, who a month later gave one of her moneyed-set parties at Trader Vic's and commented in her column, "I was happy that Henry Luce of Life and Time could come with his beautiful Clare. This rather scotches rumors of impending separation that recently beset these two. Clare sat at my table with the Albas, Ali Khan, Don Jose Felix de Lequerica and his wife, Count and Countess Motrico . . ."

5. TO MAKE MEN FREE

Early in 1960, TLF moved into its new forty-seven-story building, another unit of Rockefeller Center at Sixth Avenue and 50th Street. There had been several ceremonies in connection with this, the earliest being the groundbreaking, at which Luce and Nelson Rockefeller manned jackhammers for a minute or so. Luce, the man who had difficulty turning on a television set, seemed defeated by the jackhammer, the watching Time archivist Lillian Owens explaining Rockefeller's superior technique on the ground of experience: "After all, he's broken ground for a dozen buildings in the Center." Although the finished building was not wholly utilitarian, the dollar-conscious Luce had cut down on some lavish touches suggested by the TLF art director, Francis Brennan, and others. One of the architects had urged a great lobby dominated by murals by the modernist Fritz Glarner, reminding Luce of what an example the Sistine Chapel had been in history.

"That Pope [Sixtus IV]," said the pragmatist Luce, "was not a very good one but he knew his business. Michelangelo's paintings promoted the Pope's business. Now, that Glarner does nothing for my business." Only one Glarner mural was used, and there was no effort to make the lobby rival the Sistine Chapel.

Louis Kronenberger, still drama critic, after several years without a word

with the Boss was summoned to the prandial presence to discuss an article, and noticed a difference:

> . . . By now, when he expressed an opinion or came forth with an idea, he clearly expected to be agreed with; and should agreement be less than total, he was honestly surprised. There was nothing of the dictator involved, only of the sovereign—of, say, Queen Victoria. I felt sure there still survived in Time Inc. people who would agree or disagree with him, but I was surer still of a large standing army of heel-clicking opportunistic yes-men, or of striding, pompous, yea-sayers.

Emmet Hughes noticed that Luce's interest in opposing points of view dwindled, that he no longer hired new people who disagreed with him. The young Catholic thought that the aging Presbyterian tried to think in Christian terms but succeeded least of all in his human relations. It seemed to Hughes, who felt affection as well as deference for the Boss and was properly appreciative of the special kindliness bestowed on him, that Luce's roughshod treatment of TLF people was not the result of ruthlessness but of an innate lack of capacity for understanding other human beings. It was as if this was a quality missing in his original makeup rather than deliberately cast off by the hardening tycoon. Some old-Timers disagreed, saying he had been more human in the earlier days. There was a school of thought believing that Luce, always egocentric, had at some point along the way to power deliberately suppressed the undersized complement of warmth and sympathy with which he had been originally equipped, regarding it as weakness, sentimentality, an obstacle to true greatness. He had of course renounced sentimentality as a schoolboy. He knew he was considered hard. One of the things found in his desk after he died was a quotation from Van Wyck Brooks's *Opinions of Oliver Allston*:

> The life of the heart thrives when people are hard-headed, while the tender-minded play into the hands of the tough in heart. When people's heads are soft, their hearts grow hard. It is the tough-minded who achieve the hopes and aims of the tender in heart.

So his toughness was only for the greater good. True, he carried it a little far. He could bully an editor unmercifully, and an idea could make him leap for joy while a human problem left him unmoved. But in the T-L Building he had already won a legendary status that seemed to exempt him from the judgments visited on ordinary men. He was the Founder, the great mystery, the power in residence, at his desk eight or ten hours a day unless he was traveling, excitedly involved with the world whether right or wrong, on first-name terms with scores of his editors, the magician who with a word could send you to Hong Kong or give you a $10,000 raise, the only man in the world who had asked Emperor Hirohito how it felt to abdicate heaven, or to interrupt the Pope, or to praise Nasser to Anthony Eden. Such a man could perhaps be for-

given a little wrongheadedness. There were men in his employ who felt him seriously mistaken—not without evil—who were yet under the spell of his peculiar boyish magnetism and his excellent salaries. Reinhold Niebuhr, once a Luce favorite, had declined from grace as Toynbee had because he could not descry with Luce's clarity the American flag draped around God. As Niebuhr put it:

> His piety consists of reverence for his missionary father, but he has this conflict: a tremendous will to power, side by side with his piety. I heard him deliver a speech once in which he cited "those who believe in God above all and those who believe in America above all." It was an extraordinary combination of piety and America First.

He was playing Chinese checkers with his old skill, the two most important pieces on the board now being Sidney James, editor of the money-losing Sports Illustrated, and Andre Laguerre, moved in as his assistant. Laguerre, expert in foreign news, had no special interest in sports. But he was the kind who could never easily be an assistant to anyone except perhaps Luce himself, so the struggle for supremacy between James and Laguerre became itself a week-after-week Time Inc. sporting event with a large if discreet audience, some placing bets. Luce continued to invite important newsmakers to lunch with his editors, some of the most recent having been Field Marshal Montgomery, Golda Meir, Ludwig Erhard and King Hussein. This excellent practice sometimes deteriorated in value when the buttinsky Boss interrupted the guest to place a long and elaborate question or to make an interpolation, both of which tended in his hands to become speeches relegating the guest to audience status. Noel Busch, who was fond of him, had dinner with him at the Racquet Club in order to convey an important message. But Busch had written a book about Adlai Stevenson and Luce kept questioning him about aspects of Stevenson. Busch wanted to resign and discuss the terms of leaving. A half-dozen times he began, "Harry—" but Luce would frame another fifteen-minute question. It was not until near dinner's end that Busch got his point across, upon which Luce was most understanding and generous in his terms.

As the staff took possession of the new building, Roy Alexander ended his long tenure as managing editor of Time and Luce emphasized his growing appreciation of political agreeability by moving the arch-conservative Otto Fuerbringer into the job. Fuerbringer (Harvard '32), the tall, crusty son of a Missouri Lutheran seminary official, was a driver and a martinet. Both his toughness and Toryism were suggested by two of his many nicknames: the Iron Chancellor and Otto Fingerbanger. Emmet Hughes, disagreeing totally with Fuerbringer's politics, resigned although Luce urged him to stay. One Timan had noticed that when Clare had retired from Congress, Luce himself had written the story for Time "to avoid putting any writer on the spot." The Luce account glowed with such praise that Fuerbringer, then National Affairs

editor, sent it back to him. Luce toned it down a bit but once again Fuer-bringer bounced it back at him and it was not until the fourth version that Fuerbringer approved it. As the Timan put it, "Otto had sensed instinctively that Luce would admire him for it."

The next assignment of Alexander, now elevated to the less demanding office of editor, was to accompany the Boss on a world tour. The fiction that Luce had suffered from pneumonia in Phoenix was still maintained, though Alexander noted that Luce's New York physician was a heart specialist. Dur-ing their first stop, Paris, in April, Alexander received a letter from Clare warning him that Luce had been advised against overactivity, loss of sleep and excess of any kind, and that he found it hard to follow such advice. He did indeed and there was little that Alexander could do about it. En route to Rome they made stops at Düsseldorf, Bonn, Zurich, and Geneva, meeting with Time personnel, American diplomats and foreign politicians and busi-nessmen at every stop. "It was lunch and dinner every day," Alexander re-called, "black tie every night."

It was while they were in Rome that the U-2 spy plane was shot down in Russia and the Eisenhower administration made its grotesque series of errors in handling the matter. The fact that this was only eleven days before the President was to meet in Paris with Khrushchev, de Gaulle and Macmillan in a conference with some possible hope of easing the Cold War made the over-flight at this time seem an obvious blunder. Then, in quick succession, the ad-ministration lied about the plane and was caught in the lie; the President about-faced, admitted and justified the spy flights a few days after Khru-shchev in Moscow had given him an opportunity to deny personal knowledge of them; Presidential Press Secretary James A. Hagerty denied reports that the U-2 flights had been suspended; and the President himself contradicted Hagerty's denial, saying that the flights—a few days earlier described as "vital" to American security—were ended permanently. Khrushchev, tramp-ling over the wreckage of American dignity, ended the summit conference forever with a volley of guttersnipe invective. A chance for civilized discus-sion had been lost. Luce, totally suspicious of the infidel, was relieved rather than disappointed. In a later talk to his editorial staff he jested about the shat-tered summit meeting:

> The "summit"—I won't say they weren't interested [in Europe], but this was all settled . . . there was unanimous understanding that at the "summit" nothing would happen . . . which was what should happen—which was nothing. Every-body was sure nothing would happen. The only mistake they made, of course, was they didn't figure out how it was going to be that nothing happened. I guess Mr. Khrushchev had to figure that out.

Time explained that the conference would have been "unproductive" any-way and that the world was "bored" with it even before it started.

In Beirut, Luce told a gathering of professors, "I used to like Nasser, but I

don't like him any more," not mentioning Nasser's warmup toward the Russians as the cause. (He later told his editors, "The United States saved his neck, the son-of-a-bitch"). In New Delhi he addressed the Press Club and, said a local paper, his activities with Alexander hardly indicated cardiac worries: "Their programme was tight . . . : appointments with Dr. Radhakrishnan, Mr. Morarji Desai, ambassadors, businessmen, top American and Indian Government officials; dinners with Indian editors, columnists and cultural leaders; a tour of the Delhi Cloth Mills and a look at other industries." Rising at three or four in the morning to catch planes had not slowed the Boss down. His barking of orders to hotel help was reminiscent of the British Raj. In Bangkok he and Alexander dined with the prime minister and other officials and ran the legs off the local Time correspondent, who was a Thai. "Harry used him as interpreter," Alexander recalled, "running in and out of temples, talking with priests, always giving them a five-dollar bill, asking about the attitude of the people. Our Bangkok man said, 'This man will drive me crazy.' "

In Taipei they dined in state with the Chiangs and Luce was treated with the pomp and deference that he loved and had truly earned. In eleven years the fiction that he had created—that Chiang and his 14 millions on Taiwan were China and that Mao and his half-billion on the mainland were temporary usurpers—had become firmest American policy. Luce and Alexander inspected Chiang's air force, largely supplied by American funds which Chiang was pulling strings to augment.

The travelers reached New York May 28, having been gone five weeks. In Chinese checkers, Luce had decided for Laguerre, who became managing editor of SI while James was kicked comfortably upstairs to the publisher's office. As for the larger conflict, he had become impatient with the slow progress of the Cold War. You either won or you lost; you didn't just coast. Traveling to Washington to tell the Senate so, he first stopped with his bureau chief Shepley in Vice President Nixon's office for a chat about the Presidential sweepstakes coming up. Nixon, who thought that young Senator Kennedy had the Democratic nomination bagged, called in Senator Lyndon Johnson to join the conversation. Johnson, running hard, recalled things he had done to promote Kennedy and said that the Kennedy family now sought to embarrass his campaign for the nomination in ways that included spreading rumors that Johnson had had a recent serious heart attack which, in view of the grave attack he had had in 1955, made him seem a bad Presidential risk.

Luce, after lunching with Nixon, told the Senate Subcommittee on National Policy Machinery that coexistence with Russia seemed impossible, that the United States must dedicate itself to effort and sacrifice to win the Cold War rather than merely continuing it and that it would be a good idea for the Senate to proclaim this as the nation's goal. He urged increased defense appropriations, a huge fall-out shelter program and a diplomatic drive to extend the rule of law in international affairs. (His campaign for the "rule of law," as will be seen, became largely a euphemism for friendship with any government

that would oppose "lawless" Communism.) He admitted that a stepped-up Cold War which the Soviets saw themselves losing might well turn into a hot war, for which we must be ready. America's mission, he still said, was "to make men free":

> Our national purpose must be to promote, by every honest means, the establishment of constitutional governments—that is, governments which respond to man's dream of freedom by giving them freedom under law. By our successful progress toward this goal we shall win the cold war.

The Nation, always suspicious of him, was not certain that he was not deliberately aiming to bring on hot war:

> Does Mr. Luce really believe that anything short of the extirpation of Communism can make the world safe for his brand of capitalism? If so, what is his prescription for victory? We wish Mr. Luce would lay it on the line.

He seemed to have trouble laying it on the line to himself. Sometimes apparently confident that war could be avoided, he was subject to sudden intimations of holocaust. Once, having a glass of bourbon with Robert Hutchins and William Benton at the latter's suite in the Savoy Plaza, he had an odd answer when Benton asked why he persisted in wasting time and money on that losing venture, Sports Illustrated. "I think the world is going to blow up in seven years," he said. "The public is entitled to a good time during those seven years." He said it in utmost seriousness, and a sudden shift in the conversation prevented any search into his meaning. Again, having dinner with Laura Z. Hobson, he asked, "Laura, are we going to have nuclear war this year or not?" When she expressed hopeful skepticism, his face grew very grim and he said, "From what the Rand Corporation says, I think we'd better get ready."

XXXI

1. MAY THE BEST ANTI-COMMUNIST WIN

On the climactic night of the 1960 Democratic Convention in Los Angeles, Joseph P. Kennedy arrived for dinner at the Luce apartment at the Waldorf where Luce and his son Henry had been watching on television the nomination of John F. Kennedy. The profane Joe did not stint his praise for his son nor his belief in his worthiness of support by the Lucepress. When Luce said he assumed the young man would take a liberal stance in domestic policy, Kennedy broke in, "Harry, you know goddamn well that no son of mine could ever be a goddamn liberal." Tut-tut, Luce said—as a Democrat he had to make liberal gestures domestically, and this would not be held against him. "But if Jack shows any signs of going soft on Communism (in foreign policy) —then we would clobber him."

"Well, you don't have to worry about that," Kennedy said. The two Luces then had the unusual experience of sitting with the father as, sometimes highly excited and puffing at a cigar, he saw his son on the screen delivering his acceptance speech.

(After the election, Luce would make practical use of this in a pep talk to his assembled advertising salesmen, describing the television evening with Joe Kennedy and stressing that important Luce connections of this kind contributed to the prestige of the company and to the stature of each ad salesman, who could confront the most august client with the conviction that he was at least as important as the client.)

Senator Kennedy, painfully aware of what the Lucepress had done to Stevenson and Kefauver in 1956, came respectfully to lunch with Luce and his editors at the new building. Luce had liked him ever since he wrote the preface to Kennedy's book. However, he had built up Nixon with five venerative cover stories since the last election ("one of the busiest, most useful and most

influential men in Washington. . . . Ike turns to Nixon and says, 'Dick, you take over.' ") For good measure he had devoted a cover story to Mrs. Nixon ("poise and aplomb. . . . stamina and courage . . . one of the U.S.'s most remarkable women . . . a public figure in her own right"). He was not about to become a Democrat even for the likable likes of John F. Kennedy, but he did not want to destroy Kennedy as he had destroyed Stevenson. There was also the recollection of Laura Hobson's nasty memo along with the incredible fact that Time had sagged a tiny bit, perhaps because the value judgments had been too visible. Life, too, was losing ads to television, and what with SI still in the red the magazine profits were not quite as lush as heretofore.

An entirely new factor was the existence of one of those ideas which gripped Luce from time to time like a python and which he sought to consummate in public policy. This was the idea he had aired to the Senate committee, the idea of winning the Cold War. Whether or not he ever defined the exact terms of such a victory, here was an opportunity to emphasize the need for the triumph to both candidates and the whole American electorate. That he would support Nixon was felt to be as sure as his advocacy of the Deity. He surprised everybody. He denied a published report that he favored Nixon.

"Mr. Luce has in no sense of the word come out for Richard M. Nixon," said the New York Times, quoting a Luce spokesman, "and neither has any of the Time, Inc., publications. Mr. Luce has the highest regard for the two candidates, both of whom he has known for a long time."

What was this? Was the old hardshell going soft? The other shoe dropped a week later in a Life editorial headed, " 'Life' Is For Whom?":

> Mr. Luce is proud of having written the foreword to the book Jack Kennedy wrote in 1940 when he was 23 years old. Since then Senator Kennedy has justified Mr. Luce's high opinion of his ability. There is another man of that same generation who has done more for the nation and the world—Richard M. Nixon. . . .
>
> Life, on its editorial page, will come out either for Nixon or for Kennedy. Ever since last January Life has made it very clear as to *how* it would arrive at its choice. We began by listing the major issues. . . . Especially on the world scene, in the struggle with Communism.

This was at once Luce's sharpest propaganda ploy and his method of getting the most leverage out of his journalistic power. He set bait for both candidates, both of whom desperately wanted his support but would not know his choice until mid-October. It assured that Nixon and Kennedy—each already safely anti-Communist—would stress anti-Communism harder in order to win the coveted endorsement. It made more than ever certain that anti-Communism, already solidly bipartisan, would be the reigning principle of policy no matter who was elected. It would further reduce the waning influence of the few remaining anti-anti-Communists and of those legislators who saw that automatic anti-Communism could cover vast unwisdom and

could get the country involved in odd places. It would also subject the electorate—already thoroughly indoctrinated in anti-Communism—to whatever additional persuasion was needed to make its anti-Communism utterly automatic and unintelligent, a condition of national brainwash that would accept without complaint the ruthless steps Luce felt essential in Asia.

There was every indication during the campaign that Senator Kennedy had taken very seriously the Luce warning about "softness on Communism" relayed by the elder Kennedy and repeated so insistently by Life. It would not have to be a particularly close election for the powerful Lucepress to make the difference between defeat and victory. Kennedy leaped into the fray with an evident determination to prove that his Againstness was if anything better than Nixon's. Some moderates thought he overdid it a trifle. He hurled defiance at Khrushchev, urged a colder Cold War, deplored the Eisenhower "missile gap" and blamed the President for losing Cuba, as Luce and McCarthy had blamed Truman for losing China. When Nixon ripped into him for his "appeasing" suggestion the previous spring that the U.S. might have expressed regret over the U-2, Kennedy (who now undoubtedly regretted his regret) came back strong for more Minuteman and Polaris missiles to "advance the cause of freedom." His pitch for national "vigor," to get the nation "moving again," to multiply armaments, to shoot the moon, to spread American liberties, seemed aimed at impressing, among others, Henry R. Luce.

A fortuitous factor at Time was the aneurism suffered by Managing Editor Fuerbringer, who had little respect for Democrats, and his temporary replacement by his middle-roading deputy, Thomas Griffith. Griffith saw to it that the candidates were nicknamed Dick and Jack with apparently equal affection, and were treated with something very near impartiality—a posture that must have had them both gasping with apprehension as they waited week after week to see Luce's thumb go up or down.

But when it came to anti-Communism, Kennedy could not match the superb credentials of Nixon, who had inherited and tidied up the mantle of McCarthy and had built his career on the concept. Kennedy had made errors along the way. He had failed to see that Quemoy and Matsu were vital, whereas Nixon had been willing to fight for every inch of those islands. Nixon had a clear edge also in his veneration of Chiang and of Dulles, as well as in his hatred of Mao. Nixon had been right along with Dulles in urging the laggard Eisenhower to give direct military support to the crumbling French in Indochina. He had also taken the clear stand, as Time earlier put it, that "the U.S. must not even talk about recognizing Red China," and he was as firm in barring Red China from the UN. He was hot for more aid to South Vietnam, he was opposed to appeasing the neutralist Nehru, he spoke darkly about Communist subversion in the United States, and to top it off he had been stoned and spat on by Communists while visiting in South America, an experience so far denied Kennedy.

When one added up the qualifications there was no contest. The ax finally

fell on Kennedy in a double-barreled Life editorial favoring Nixon both in domestic and foreign policy. It was not only Kennedy himself, Life said, but the friends he traveled with. Some of the Democrats showed "gullibility about Communism in particular," and such outstanding Democrats as Chester Bowles and Adlai Stevenson were accused of being afraid "that we are 'dragging our feet' on disarmament, and . . . that we may be neglecting some other avenue of accommodation with Khrushchev." Two other Democrats, Senators Fulbright and Morse, seemed defeatist in saying that Red China could not be kept out of the UN forever.

Chester Bowles, who was Kennedy's foreign-policy adviser, had been a millstone around the candidate's neck as far as Luce was concerned. Bowles had written for the magazine Foreign Affairs an article that challenged the folklore still accepting Chiang as China and urging a reappraisal of China policy. He had advocated that the United States give up its "exposed position" on Quemoy and Matsu, possibly influencing Kennedy's opinion on this issue. Life commented:

> Kennedy's attempt to surrender Quemoy and Matsu is, we hope, the last sigh of the illusion that peace can be secured either by the "nonprovocation" of Communism (nothing provokes a Communist like nonprovocation) or by dividing up the world with the masters of Moscow and Peking. Communism recognizes no boundaries to its ambition, and neither can freedom. . . . With Nixon and Lodge in charge of U.S. world policy, we shall feel both safer and more hopeful in the enlarging struggle.

Certainly the Time-Life swing to Nixon saved the Vice President from the clear defeat he would otherwise have suffered as a result of his poor showing in the great television debate. Looking at it the other way, had the Lucepress attacked Kennedy as it had attacked Stevenson, it seems safe to say that Nixon would have been elected. By a strange twist of fate, Luce in all probability had put a Democrat in the White House.

The narrowness of his victory shocked Kennedy and made it evident that he would have to proceed more carefully than if he had won a clear mandate. He was so grateful to Luce for the considerate treatment given him by Time —and by Life as well until the very end of the campaign—that he asked William Benton if Luce might not be converted to become a Democrat. Benton replied, "The answer to your question is an unequivocal 'No.'" Kennedy, who had been ready to move for a change in America's China policy, apparently took the Luce criticism on this score to heart. The importance of the liberal Bowles in the new administration, in any case, sank. Rusk became Secretary of State, Bowles was named Undersecretary, and as Bowles related it, Kennedy asked him when he came up for confirmation "to play down the differences between my ideas about China and the generally accepted wisdom generated by the partisans of Chiang Kai-shek." The State Department Far Eastern bureau and other cautious advisers warned that any thaw toward Mao would mean political disaster.

Indeed, Kennedy's extreme sensitivity to the press would only be exceeded by that of his two successors. The Luce Asian policy influenced the new administration from the start. Kennedy got into immediate trouble with Luce (and with most Americans) when the Bay of Pigs invasion of Cuba by anti-Castro Cubans, planned by the CIA under Eisenhower, was allowed to fizzle without air support. The existence of Fidel Castro only ninety miles from Florida gave Luce nightmares without moving him to the slightest sympathy for Khrushchev and Mao, surrounded as they were by American bases. Time and Life attacked Kennedy's indecision and Fortune dropped a blockbuster, a long story about the fiasco by Charles J. V. Murphy so devastatingly critical that Kennedy felt he could not let it pass.° He sent General Maxwell Taylor, chairman of the Joint Chiefs of Staff, to New York to talk to Luce and correct what he claimed to be errors in the Murphy piece. The President told a news conference that the Fortune article was "the most inaccurate of all the articles that have appeared on Cuba," and he privately regarded the author as "particularly biased and hostile."

Luce came back from Phoenix imbued with the kind of ardor usually reserved for all-out war. Several passages in Kennedy's inaugural seemed to reiterate Luce's favorite proposition that "America's mission is to make men free." The President had said: "We shall pay any price, bear any burden, meet any hardship, support any friends, oppose any foe to assure the survival and success of liberty." Those were free-swinging words, to be sure. Luce felt that patriotism now required every individual and every business organization—especially Time Inc.—to take the anti-Communist pledge with the high solemnity of a religious vow. Speaking to his executives in the sporty auditorium of the new building, he touched on the responsibilities of a free press and went on:

> In Life's series on National Purpose the most clear-cut, the most forthright statement of national purpose was . . . that we must decide to *win* the Cold War. . . . Tonight, at this moment, I will speak of "we" as meaning simply we of Time Inc. And I propose to you that we of Time Inc. now register in our minds and wills that from here on out the dominant aim of Time Inc. shall be the defeat of the Communist movement throughout the world. . . .
>
> Now of course we . . . do not have the means to wage war as Francis Drake did. . . . However, unlike the 16th century, ours *is* an age of journalism—and at least on that battleground we can do some service. . . . Every individual and every organization in the land can strike a blow for Liberty and against Communism—now. . . . And to repeat, the climax of the struggle with Communism will come—soon. It has begun and, in all probability, by 1965 we shall either

---

° Luce had read advance proofs of the article in Phoenix. He found it so censorious that he sent word back to Duncan Norton-Taylor, managing editor of Fortune, not to run it. Norton-Taylor was in a predicament: he had nothing else to substitute for the Murphy article. So he toned it down considerably and ran it, and never heard further from Luce about it.

have negotiated our own surrender or Communism will have become a disrupted, discredited and disintegrating force. . . . For the first time America has a Capital E-Enemy—huge, brainy, implacable, our self-avowed Enemy. "We will bury you," he says. Adding—it won't hurt much.

Gentlemen, I say the time has come to make it hurt. . . . And to begin to make the Enemy hurt—and hurt bad. There is a grimness in this determination. . . . Before us lie the greatest prospects of human achievement—a truly Golden Age. The way must be cleared. . . . A clear and irrevocable determination to clear the way for Liberty and Progress, must be made sometime, somewhere, by somebody. . . . I propose that the determination be made now, that it be made here, and that it be made by the editors and managers of Time Inc.

Although the humor faction at Time had dwindled under Fuerbringer, there was some sub rosa suggestion that Luce's declaration of war should be disclosed to the public and made official through the dispatch of a note from Time's Foreign News editor handed by Time's chief correspondent in Moscow to Foreign Minister Gromyko.

The Luces meanwhile had sold the huge cooperative apartment at River House which they had owned since their marriage but had used rarely as they occupied a succession of suites at the Waldorf. They moved to a smaller but still grand apartment, all on one floor, at 960 Fifth Avenue, near 74th Street. It was near the galleries and museums and across from the park, where Luce liked to walk, his head down as always, so deep in thought that the park's beauty seemed unnoticed and he might as well have been in the Bowery. He had also attended the forty-fifth reunion of his class at Hotchkiss School, an affair that must have brought a rush of memories even to the man who always looked ahead—those misty days of The King, of Hadden and Sudler, of the dear Literary Monthly that had really got him started in journalism. (Hotchkiss now had a spirit not without secularity, as its Alumni News would later show in commenting on Luce: "One million dollars [income] before taxes!") Then, in the breakneck Luce style, to Washington for two days, Phoenix for four days, Tucson for two days, back to New York on June 1 and on June 12 aboard Air France with Clare for Paris. Two Luce dinners with members of the Paris staff, then by air to Milan for a staff-arranged dinner with Italian friends. By car to Turin and a tour of the huge Fiat plant (owned by the Luce friends the Agnellis) and the workers' school, followed by an afternoon at the local exposition, another grand dinner (how sad that Luce seldom tasted his food!), a night's sleep, then an air hop back to Milan, a change of planes and another hop to Venice. There they met the William Bentons that very afternoon at the Royal Danieli, had a night's rest and were off next day on Benton's chartered yacht, the *Flying Clipper*. Among the guests were George Kennan, now ambassador to Yugoslavia, and Mrs. Kennan; the Ladies' Home Journal editorial team of Bruce and Beatrice Blackmar Gould, and the savant of contract bridge, Goren.

Benton, as kinetic as Luce but extremely sociable, a raconteur with a sense

of humor, was not above needling the solemn Luce. He was one of those in tune with Clare, admiring her beauty, wit and grasp of world affairs. Less so the Goulds who, however impressed by her abilities, found flaws in her social technique: "Her undeniable arts might have landed her almost anywhere, except that once in a while, the perfected mechanism went slightly awry, the voice became thin and the goal too obvious." As for her husband: "Henry, absorbed in books and papers, was silent much of the time, but when he spoke his comments were pithy and stimulating." Luce was fussing over a revision of his preface for John Kennedy's *While England Slept*, which was to appear in a revised edition. "Why," Benton inquired, "did you, Harry Luce, ever do a preface for Jack Kennedy?" Luce looked up, replied in one word, "Joe," and went on writing.

The Kennans and Goulds left the party at Dubrovnik, while Paul Hoffman, now a United Nations official, joined them in Crete. There was a set of Benton's latest *Britannica* aboard. Luce and Benton "read up" on the points of interest every night, and next morning would go out examining ruins. Hoffman enjoyed one set of ruins but thereafter left them to Luce and Benton, astonished at their incessant curiosity and energy. Benton noted that the Luce who could so easily be gruff and rude was at his best toward Clare, that he "crowded attentions on her." The Daily News's Nancy Randolph who, along with other gossipists, had been watching the Luces closely, came up with the same message. She would soon report that Luce gave his wife "a three-strand pearl necklace with a big winky-twinkly diamond clasp" and that things appeared "serene" again "in spite of those horrid reports of many months ago."

The Luces caught a plane home from Istanbul after almost a month of cruising—the longest they had been together continuously since their honeymoon. On his return to New York July 17, the sixty-three-year-old cardiac outpatient spent a day in Washington (where he pressed on Secretary of State Rusk his international "rule of law" idea), two days in St. Louis for a speech on the same subject, two days in Martha's Vineyard, a weekend on Long Island and three days in Bermuda before reaching Gettysburg August 30 for an interview with ex-President Eisenhower. Appearing under the Luce byline in Life a week later, it got across the idea as kindly as possible that Ike's hope for agreement with Khrushchev had been founded on ignorance of Communism's reality. It stressed the Communist "intention to dominate the entire world," wrote off the Eisenhower-Khrushchev "spirit of Camp David" as an "illusion" and declared that "we must oppose what is morally wrong in Communist actions and we must be faithful to our own moral obligations."

2. PROFILES IN COURAGE

"During the 1950's," Undersecretary of State Chester Bowles later reflected, "Jack Kennedy often expressed to me the view that American pol-

icy in regard to China was unrealistic . . ." But Kennedy was lunching occasionally with Luce now and had grown more cautious. Dean Rusk was the archangel of foreign policy, repressing Bowles regularly. Yet when Bowles sought to open a useful American window on both Red China and Russia by recognizing the new buffer state, Mongolia, Kennedy and Rusk were with him. It would be well to have a diplomatic mission there to reduce American ignorance of what was going on.

But first the State Department's own Far Eastern bureau opposed the idea on the ground that it would be construed as a softening of our position against China. ("This, of course, was my intention," the rash Bowles later admitted.) Then the China Lobby, joined by the Committee of One Million Against the Admission of Red China to the United Nations, assailed the idea.

That did it. The move was dropped. Bowles in fact became an embarrassment to the administration because he had the courage to oppose Luce and the China Lobby, and he was later removed to a safe distance from Washington by being named ambassador to India.

Kennedy had told his ambassador to the UN, Adlai Stevenson, "You have the hardest thing in the world to sell. It really doesn't make any sense—the idea that Taiwan represents China. [But if] we lose this fight, if Red China comes into the United Nations during our first year in town, your first year and mine, they'll run us both out."

It was moonshine; the President knew it was moonshine, but he would never have dared say so publicly and felt forced to continue leading the nation on a policy of moonshine because an American majority had been inculcated with the belief that it was not only *not* moonshine but was true, patriotic and blessed in heaven.

Henry Steele Commager observed, "The arguments that were invoked to justify religious wars and religious persecution in past centuries are invoked now to justify sleepless hostility to Communism—even preventive war. . . . [F]or years we have heard, and not from extremists alone, that the struggle between Democracy and Communism is the struggle between Light and Darkness, Good and Evil, and that the moral distinction is an absolute one."

Commager sounded like a man who had been reading the Lucepress. There was no question that Norman Cousins, editor of the Saturday Review, had been reading Time when he protested that it had called distinguished people who questioned American nuclear policy "dupes of the enemies of liberty," had used the "spillover technique by which one name on a list is made to stain all the others," had dealt in "damaging catch-phrases" and had made it appear that the National Committee for a Sane Nuclear Policy "was advocating a policy of surrender."

Oddly, Cousins wrote as if these were new tactics employed by Time, rather than hallowed Time devices new only in their enunciation by the Iron Chancellor.

The irrationalities of anti-Communism were expected from such Funda-

mentalist spellbinders as Rev. Carl McIntire, the deposed Presbyterian right-winger of New Jersey. The audience of the Lucepress, on the whole better educated than McIntire's, would have scoffed at his weekly rantings. Yet they accepted some of the same basic arguments appearing in the more "respect-able" rhetoric of the Lucepress, one of them being the conviction that America's heavenly connections were unequaled by those of other countries—an intrinsically totalitarian proposition always at the bottom of the Luce rationalizations. Appalled though he was by the prospect of thermonuclear war, Luce felt that it must be faced. "It's what people call the unthinkable," he said to his pastor at the Madison Avenue Presbyterian Church, Dr. David C. Read. "Well, people had better think of the unthinkable." Always suscep-tible to the latest "expert" who came along, he was enormously relieved when he read Herman Kahn's *On Thermonuclear War* and was assured that the ho-locaust would by no means wipe out America. He told an audience at New York's University Club:

> It could happen. Let's learn to think that terrible thought. Then let's learn to think a novel thought—that civilization could survive such a war, provided we start now to do the necessary things. . . . I suggest that a general theory cov-ering our activity would contain these two propositions: First, that order must be established in the world—a global order, a *new* order. Second, that the major responsibility for bringing about this order rests upon the United States. . . . [T]ake the best-loved phrase of do-nothing diplomacy—"non-interference in in-ternal affairs." This has long since become anachronistic nonsense. . . . we must *rediscover* a truth about power. A nation that is formed out of a belief in liberty under law—for others as well as for itself—need not be timorous about asserting its Authority. It need not be laggard in backing its Authority, as necessary, with power.

He was at pains to demolish the fallacy that interference in other countries was improper on the part of a nation as morally upright as the United States. At lunch with the President, Luce urged a firm reaffirmation of the Monroe Doctrine—an idea Kennedy thought "a little out of date." A Time cover story on President Monroe said it was not at all out of date and advocated the inva-sion of Cuba. In the case of Vietnam, as James Reston remarked, "Henry Luce is publicizing the hard line and glorifying intervention as a noble princi-ple." Luce enunciated the principle in a speech at Westminster College in Missouri:

> . . . [I]f we want to take a real step forward into the actual modern world, then we will insist that our diplomats give up this archaic cant about not interfering in the internal affairs of other nations. We must indeed make careful distinc-tions . . . We may say, for example, that we should not interfere by military force. Well, of course we are at this moment interfering in Vietnam with a four-star general, 7,000 troops and millions of logistical supplies. . . . Certainly we need to make distinctions but it has become quite clear that we cannot rule out the use of force in every case.

3. CHRISTIANS, TO ARMS!

Despite Eisenhower's unfortunate trafficking with Khrushchev—something done literally over Dulles's dead body—Luce knew that the Birchers were wrong in calling both of them Communists. Life and Time carried critical articles about the John Birch Society. A later issue of Life in a brief news item poked fun at the Australian physician-turned-Redbaiter Frederick C. Schwarz, who operated a "School of Anti-Communism," saying, "Schwarz preaches doomsday by Communism in 1973 unless every American starts distrusting his neighbor as a possible Communist or 'comsymp.' . . . Schwarz . . . landed in this country with $10 in his pocket in 1953, but he has built the 'crusade' into a $500,000 business."

Life caught a tartar in Schwarz. The Australian had originally been discovered in Sydney by the touring Rev. Carl McIntire, who had an unerring eye for excellence in anti-Communism, and persuaded him that he was needed in America. In California, already a state with a vested interest in military production, Schwarz had surrounded himself with a drove of Communist-haters, including Patrick Frawley, head of Technicolor, and his colleague George Murphy, the actor who would later become a United States Senator. Two of his associates were former FBI agents, W. Cleon Skousen and Herbert Philbrick. Philbrick, it was said, waved a copy of Life before the faithful and said, "Whoever pulled that sleazy stunt is working for the Communist criminal conspiracy."

It seems impossible to pass by without a respectful pause a statement linking Luce or any of his works with the "Communist criminal conspiracy."

So heated were the passions aroused by Schwarz that when two clergymen conducted an anti-Schwarz rally, both of their homes were damaged by bombs while they were at the rally. California Attorney General Stanley Mosk, who had bravely described the John Birch Society as an organization of "retired military officers and little old ladies in tennis shoes," took off against Schwarz's Christian Crusade as "patriotism for profit," saying that in ninety days in Los Angeles alone it grossed $311,253 and netted $214,737. That was not far from a million in profit a year—pretty fancy going, he said.

When Life, even in a two-paragraph squib, spoke disrespectfully of the organization, it was deriding something bigger than it may have realized—a group with an influential following whose displeasure could mean a loss of advertising revenue, and this with Life badly feeling the competition of television advertising.

Frawley and Schwarz flew to New York to protest personally to Luce. There was also an angry reader reaction, much of it from California. A few weeks later, on October 16, 1961, Schwarz produced the greatest anti-Red extravaganza yet seen, advertised as "Hollywood's Answer to Communism."

Before an audience of 15,000 at the Hollywood Bowl, a Boy Scout troop presented the colors, everybody sang "God Bless America," and Schwarz and his faculty gave instruction in hatred that was carried over the entire Coast by a network of thirty-five television outlets. On the stage sat many film personalities, including John Wayne, James Stewart and Roy Rogers. One of the special speakers was Senator Thomas J. Dodd of Connecticut, himself a former FBI man with the superpatriotic ardor nurtured by that organization, who demanded "total victory" against Communism. Another was Congressman Judd, the warhorse of the China Lobby and a fellow member with Luce of what was known by cynical liberals as the "John Foster Dulles Memorial Society."

Least happy of the speakers was C. D. Jackson, publisher of Life, who had flown the breadth of the nation to eat crow before the 15,000 and the estimated seven million television viewers:

> It is a great privilege to be with you tonight because it affords me an opportunity to align Life magazine in a very personal way with a number of stalwart fighters . . . against the first implacable foe our country has ever had—imperial, aggressive Communism. . . . Knowledge is power. . . .
>
> You have with you a man who has dedicated his life to helping disseminate that knowledge [about Communism] and therefore to helping endow our nation with that power. That man is Dr. Fred Schwarz and, like all dedicated men, he will be subject to oversimplified misinterpretation. I know that you are not interested in how that happened, but I hope you will be interested in my statement that I believe we were wrong and that I am profoundly sorry.

The Life capitulation was the most impressive victory of the Christian Crusaders to date. Senator Barry Goldwater commended Life for its "greatness" in confessing error, as did the National Review and a few Hearst columnists. The San Fernando Valley Sun, on the other hand, described a subsequent Beverly Hills party attended by George Murphy at which "Mr. Murphy told with relish how he had made Henry Luce 'come crawling to him on his hands and knees'" in the person of Jackson, and that he had accomplished this by persuading "three large Life advertisers either to threaten or actually withdraw their advertising from Life." The heretical Reporter magazine remarked on how Life's editorials usually called on Americans to exhibit determination and courage in behalf of national survival:

> Scarcely a week goes by in which either an individual or an entire population is not urged to reaffirm some ancient principle and, if need be, to march in its name over the edge of the nearest precipice. Sad to say, events of the past few weeks have raised some doubts in our mind as to whether Life is ready to take the plunge along with its loyal readers. . . . Maybe we missed the point of all those editorials about courage.

"Hollywood's Answer" was videotaped and shown on television stations throughout the country, so that Jackson's recantation for Life got maximum

nationwide exposure. The popularity of the show augmented a trend already in the making, causing an advertising dope sheet, the Insider's Newsletter, to observe that anti-Communism was "the hottest commodity on the mass-media market." Some 250 different radio and television anti-Communism shows were in the works, from "The Red Report" to "Communism: World-wide." All of them sold soap, cornflakes and other merchandise to Americans between chilling fictional demonstrations of Communist villainy and betrayal. From the first little anti-Communist barbs in Time in the Twenties to the anti-Communist triumvirate of TLF in the Thirties and the full-throated Time Inc. Againstness in the postwar years, a great national industry and art form had grown.

Two weeks after Jackson's humiliation, Luce arrived in Los Angeles to receive, along with Ralph McGill and Walter Cronkite, an achievement award from a University of Southern California alumni group. It was not one of Luce's great moments. Naturally he was asked whether he had ordered Jackson to apologize for Life.

"It was his own idea," Luce said. "He is one of the most important experts in ideological warfare." (Jackson had served in psychological warfare during World War II.) Luce praised Dr. Schwarz's book on the evils of Communism and also the value of anti-Communist schools because "to know your enemy is a good thing."

Cronkite took a different tack, remarking that there were pressures on the news media to give greater publicity to anti-Communism, and that he had received many protests from Southern California about his documentary called *The Red Face of China*. "If you say anything good about a Red country," he said, "you are perforce Red." McGill added, "We have got the thing [Communism] well in hand," urged a more "positive approach" and raised a warning at that time little heard—that "super-patriotism" would turn Americans in suspicion against Americans.

A similar thought had struck the columnist John Crosby as he mused over the Schwarz-Jackson spectacle which Luce had permitted if not specifically ordered his subordinate to invest with the Life-Luce seal of approval:

> My great objection to Communism is, as Bertrand Russell has so acutely pointed out, that it is based on hatred not on love. . . . The great tragedy is that the Soviets are pushing us into their image—hatred and monolithism. We are becoming a hating society, not a loving one. The lunatics, which we thought we had successfully buried with Sen. McCarthy, are with us again . . . Again we find the haters in California . . . staging a monster three-hour concentration of pure venom on television (sponsored yet) in which the patriots suggested again and again that the United States was largely peopled by traitors.

4. PASS THE AMMUNITION

One of the hundreds of guests at Life's twenty-fifth birthday party was John K. Galbraith, who had worked briefly for Fortune. A special television

show Life presented touching on changes during the quarter-century, he thought "incredibly awful," but the dinner at the T-L Building was good. He shared Luce's table with the Duke and Duchess of Windsor, Mrs. William Randolph Hearst, Jr., Perle Mesta and the John D. Rockefellers III. The slant of the program made him sense "a considerable need to sell Life," as he put it, and he asked himself, "I wonder if all is well?"

It could have been better. Ten years earlier Life was king of the field, two million ahead of Look and the Saturday Evening Post in circulation and fat with ads. Now it was thinner and its seven million circulation was approximated by each of the other two. All three had inflated their circulation figures by practically paying people to subscribe—a practice at which advertisers looked down their noses. Life had recouped handsomely through its massive promotion of books which it published by the ton for popular consumption. Time was holding its lead and SI was finally coming out of the red.

The Boss was mellowing a trifle in areas unconnected with his ideological freeze, although he was as tense as ever, would blow up over a wasted split-second and could bite one's nose off if crossed. After addressing his private secretary as "Miss Thrasher" or "Miss T" for twenty-seven years, he called her successor, young Gloria Mariano, "Gloria" from the start. While she maintained a healthy respect for his crotchets, she was stimulated by his rapid-fire brain, thought her job was "like going to college every day," and like others felt a real affection for him. Once when she had laryngitis he ordered, "Gargle with warm water and salt." One quickly learned not to say such things as "Nice day," for he would whirl and snap, "Why do you say that?" He had two or three Bibles in his desk and never traveled without one in his briefcase.

Mrs. Elsa Wardell, a Fortune researcher, had been selected for her ability and tact to be Luce's aide in researching material for his speeches. "Mr. Luce prefers that ladies do not talk," Allen Grover warned her. Finding the same grammatical error in four successive drafts of one of his speeches despite her repeated notation of the error, she wrote on the fourth draft, "It sounds silly to say this." That brought a Luce summons and a steely declaration, "I don't like to be called silly." But he relented immediately when she said, "That was the only way I could get your attention." It *had* got his attention and had proved its efficacy. However, when she spoke up about his habitual misquotation of a line from Emerson, he snapped, "I like my way better," and that was that. Emerson stood corrected. His personal assistant, Mrs. Emeline Edwards, a former Time writer, had been tested for the position by Himself. Who was president of General Motors? Of Ford? Which countries were in the European Common Market? Etcetera. She passed, but discovered that every day with Luce was a test of sorts, for he liked to pick her up on points of fact. Once, during a bad week which was climaxed when she gave him the wrong name for the Italian foreign minister, she exclaimed, "I just wish you'd be wrong once!" "It must be irritating," he agreed a trifle smugly.

A concept that fascinated Luce-the-debater and which he often discussed with Max Ways and Father Murray was the American national purpose or public philosophy. Many intellectuals agreed that the aims and ideals so clearly in mind in the early Republic had been lost as the people pursued luxuries and shunned complexities which were vital to their existence. The public philosophy—that individual-becoming-mass feeling toward the nation and its responsibilities as well as its benefits—far from being an abstraction, would soon emerge as the most practical and crucial of questions. The nation was on the verge of disruptive conflict among factions ranging from a largely older group believing in God, material success and anti-Communism, to a largely younger group rejecting all three, and many shades of belief between the extremes. The quarrel, of which Luce would see only the beginning phases, would expose a fearful American fragmentation which he appears to have underestimated.

Earnest public beliefs, and general agreement in these beliefs, were of course essential for mere security, much less greatness. Germany under Hitler had shaken the world because it believed for the time in his ideology. A corruption of Marxism, in which only the state was free, had attained despotic power in Russia and might gain more in Red China with the deifying of Mao. By contrast, some critics said, the American public philosophy—its belief in the essential freedoms, rights and responsibilities of the individual combined into a system of social justice—had been lost somewhere between the built-in bar, the double garage and the swimming pool.

It was easy to see how a struggle would end between a nation whose people believed fiercely in its philosophy and a nation fat and confused. Those exhortatory Life editorials urging the populace to march over the nearest precipice in defense of principle had been Luce's remedy—the missionary voice of his late father multiplied by the immense Lucepress circulation. He preached an America emancipated by technology, reveling in the "good life" of luxury made possible by free enterprise, yet intelligent, informed, responsible—an America of endless materialism smiled on by God. Despite his occasional strictures in inter-office memos that "It is not permissible to put God on our banner," God was never off Luce's American banner. God was in his speeches, he acknowledged God as the founder of the concept of American liberty, God had a part in his recent interview with Eisenhower, God formed the basis of his anti-Communism, God lay behind his talk of the "anachronistic nonsense" of non-interference in other nations, God had been his and Dulles's partner in the conduct of America's "moral" foreign policy and the threat of "massive retaliation." It seemed as impossible for him to curb his excessive intimacy with his heavenly ally since childhood, with whom he still communed in his private elevator, as for the early Puritans to refrain from believing Indians to be instruments of Satan and praising the "Providence of God" that sent three hundred Pequots into a trap "for the divine slaughter by the hand of the English."

W. A. Swanberg

There was a growing belief among younger people that selfishness and mediocrity lay behind any such American exclusivity in God-Agreement and that a respectable God would scarcely be so chauvinistic. Many collegians—that group which thirty years earlier had thought Time so smart, so modern—now moved toward the view that Luce was the greatest square and cornball of his whole generation. When he spoke to the students at Brandeis University, and one of them asked why Time was called a newsmagazine when it editorialized so heavily, he had the nerve—despite that acid memo from Laura Z. Hobson—to reply that since he had invented the term he was privileged to define it as he wished. This did not wash in that nest of sophistication. One of his listeners, Michael Charles, covered the speech for the student newspaper as if he were a music critic commenting on "a new work composed and arranged by Mr. Henry Luce." He found Luce's rendition of American culture and America's gifts to the world discordant:

> Luce's opus bore a faint resemblance to the Tristan of R. Wagner, in that the entire work was a series of unresolved chords. . . . The overture . . . introduced the leitmotif of Time, Life and Fortune. It was atonal. . . . There were two major themes, the world theme and the Good Life theme. . . . Not since the days of Attila the Hun has any people concerned itself with the rest of mankind the way Americans do. The United States has troops and missile bases all over the world . . . American economic aid is also unparalleled. The Marshall Plan, the World Bank, Point Four and Green Stamps all show the deep concern of American people for their foreign neighbors. . . . Taken in its totality, Luce's work was no landmark, or hallmark or even watermark. Though not informative, it was interesting to those who had seats; my legs got very tired.

Surely Luce had never been treated with such amused contempt, nor had his "Americanism" been so ridiculed. The review demonstrated a well-advanced segment of student thought whose public philosophy was revolutionary in its rejection of the praise-God-and-pass-the-ammunition spirit still so prevalent among the Luces, the John Waynes and the Walter Judds. The old unity of public philosophy was shattering. The existence of strongly opposed public philosophies within the nation was an omen of national conflict.

Luce, who had thought himself the advance agent of a new world, must have been jolted as the realization grew on him that in some quarters he was regarded as Methuselah. Certainly he felt that his own magazines, in their eternal interpretation of America and the world, had enriched the public philosophy. His "American Century" and similar essays, as well as the contributions of Dulles, William Ernest Hocking, Walter Lippmann and many others, had aimed at clarifying and directing the national purpose. He had demanded that his editors give it serious thought and had encouraged Max Ways to delve so deeply into the subject that Ways's work emerged as a full-length book. He had put Father Murray on the cover of Time on his publication of a similar work. The national purpose was Luce's prime concern. He had fea-

424

tured discussions of it in four successive issues of Life. Leading and shaping public opinion on these themes had always been his passion, and it must have troubled him that his success had been far from complete.

5. SHY AND GUARDED

Luce agreed entirely with Billy Graham that there was nothing blessed about failure. His cult of success encompassed the whole spectrum of his thought. Just as he worked for more corporate profit and was busy raising millions for a huge and visibly successful Presbyterian church edifice in Washington, so he exhorted the nation to build and buy more automobiles, develop more patriotism, to work harder for a bigger GNP, a bigger military establishment and the best and most strategically located supply of H-bombs.

"I like Luce," John F. Kennedy had said after that first lunch with him and his editors. "He is like a cricket, always chirping away. After all, he made a lot of money through his own individual enterprise so he naturally thinks that individual enterprise can do everything. I don't mind people like that. They have earned the right to talk that way. . . . But what I can't stand are all the people around Luce who automatically agree with everything he has to say."

In the fall of 1961, Luce had dinner with his sister and brother-in-law, the Moores, then took off with his Bible for the World Council of Churches Assembly at New Delhi. Stopping in Paris at the Ritz as always, he dined with the T-L staff there and had lunch with Jean Monnet, who could not have refused him had he wanted to, having just appeared on Time's cover. Monnet was a hero because of his role in the Common Market and Western European solidarity against Communism. A twelve-hour flight then dropped Luce at New Delhi at 3:00 A.M. But there was a five-man T-L deputation, including Charles Mohr, to meet him and escort him to his vast suite at the Ashoka Hotel, and the very next day (a Sunday!) Mohr gave a cocktail party for him at the hotel. This had been arranged in advance to permit Luce to meet immediately some of the interesting people who would be there. Many Protestant leaders, including Billy Graham (who had been Luce's guest at a Time editors' luncheon a few months earlier, had made the cover back in 1954 and was highly approved of by the Boss) were in New Delhi.

Luce was impressed by the Nebraska-born Mohr, whom he had known when he was Time's White House correspondent. The Life correspondent Donald Burke, who had been with the magazine twenty-three years, was another of the troupe covering this confusing and hard-to-report assemblage. Several times, perhaps because Burke was an old Lifer dating back to the early days under Billings and a charming fellow originally from Waterbury, Luce telephoned him in the evening and asked him up for a drink. On such occasions the Boss could be appealingly human and democratic in a way inconceivable of, say, Hearst or McCormick. Burke noticed again Luce's ma-

chine-gun bursts of talk, his terribly nervous manner of handling his cigarette, his finger-drumming on the nearest available surface. He was immensely curious as to what would emerge from the council. Near its end, though Luce did not ask to see his copy, Burke knew that he wanted to and showed it to him. Reading it, Luce disagreed equably, saying he did not think Burke had answered the question of the assembly's results. Burke argued that there was no clear answer to that and his copy remained unchanged; but Luce, as always, wanted to give the reader simple and understandable answers even when there were no simple and understandable answers.

An astonishment to him was a rumor he heard while away from New Delhi that Governor Rockefeller's pending divorce had been announced—a front-page story that would surely affect the governor's political future. He rushed back to Delhi to find that it was true and that his own brother-in-law Tex Moore was Rockefeller's attorney. Moore had known of it while dining with Luce, but the lawyer-client relationship had kept him silent.

Luce took time to lunch with the new American ambassador, the same Galbraith who had once worked for him and who would soon be on Time's cover. The others at the luncheon were Harvard President Nathan Pusey and his wife (Pusey had long since made the cover) and the Maharajah of Mysore, who was fated never to appear there. Galbraith, a denizen of another political world, took him by plane and elephant to see Jaipur and Amber Palace. That was spectacular, and yet the increasingly religious Luce spoke most fervently later of the "many splendid sermons" given at New Delhi and wished that millions might have been there to hear them.

On the death of Dr. Hu Shih, who had so strongly supported Chiang, Thornton Wilder was invited by Luce to a meeting at the China Institute to honor the late scholar. Wilder, whose career had touched Luce's in three widely separated places—Chefoo School, Yale and Rome—regretted that he had seen him only rarely since college, usually at noisy reunions where there was no chance for quiet talk. He believed, with Charles Lamb, that "one should keep one's friendships in repair," but Luce was too busy. Wilder had once admired much in Luce. Time's cover story on Wilder had been laudatory if not wholly accurate. Now the writer had no sympathy for his old classmate's China policies, found him "shy and guarded" and yet like a bulldozer in his despotic need to command people and events.

Invited to the meeting only as a guest, Wilder attended simply out of regard for Luce, since he knew little of Dr. Hu. After Wilder got to the meeting, as he recalled it, "To my surprise I discovered that I had been assigned the role of concluding speaker on the program. I heard Harry introduce me as an old friend of Dr. Hu Shih. I spoke—to the best of my knowledge—of Dr. Hu Shih's work as a scholar and reformer of the Chinese language. I did not tell the audience (nor Harry until the close of the meeting) that I had never met Dr. Hu Shih."

6. THE BIRDS AND THE KITTENS

Mrs. Bancroft felt that the reason she and Luce got along was that they made friendly intellectual contact—and got through to each other—on any subject that interested him at the moment, from politics, journalism, religion, or the Greeks, to death. This was something he found impossible with most people, and he admitted a great loneliness. His shyness and the guardedness Wilder and others noticed, combining oddly with his bulldozer qualities, deprived him of any sure technique for developing more than superficial acquaintanceship, and he had hundreds of acquaintances. His way of cross-examining someone in whom he was interested usually left that person feeling that he was being picked over for ideas, harvested like a cornfield, rather than being regarded as a fellow human being. Some Lucepress editors believed his long friendship with Father Murray was less a friendship in the usual sense than an endless series of intellectual duels about religious and social abstractions between two men who enjoyed dueling, and that Luce always came out of the swordplay with new thrusts to try on *them*, the editors.

His letters to Mrs. Bancroft manifested his affection, as did his countenancing of arguments from her which not only contradicted his beliefs but not infrequently poked fun at them—something no one else could do. She got away with this because he knew she had the greatest respect for his talents and his power—such respect that she spent much time and effort in trying to turn them in more constructive directions.

She believed that his loneliness came about because of an ego so insecure that he feared to give anything of himself away lest he not get it back, feared to risk any release of affection and substituted the drive for power. "Love and power are mutually exclusive," she wrote him once. But he sometimes needed such things explained, as in the case of the price of watches, which she undertook to do:

> The other day in the zoo, the keeper of the camels wanted to give M. J. [her daughter] two little kittens to bring home, for unless he found someone to take them away, the director of the zoo would make him give them—still living, although doped—to the "big birds." Now if you take birds as a symbol of thoughts and ideas—as they are taken symbolically in so many primitive cultures and by analysts in dreams—and raise them to "big birds"—i.e. "big ideas"—and take the kittens as symbols of feelings and the human heart—you get what as I see it is going on all the time. The key to the situation is the role of the keeper. Whose side is he on? In this instance he was for the kittens against the birds. I see you, Harry, as a kind of keeper. And naturally I get all wrought up when I feel you are on the side of the birds—particularly the big birds.

While this kind of instruction fascinated him, there was little evidence that

427

it changed him. Once, when talking of his oppressive sense of loneliness, he asked seriously if she would leave him $1000 in her will, a gesture which would give him a needed sense of being cared for and remembered. It was typical of his materialism and lack of feeling for objects of beauty or sentiment that he should mention money instead of, say, a painting or bibelot. His discovery earlier that objects of art were collected by tycoons and were regarded by them as important as well as valuable had launched him into the collecting of paintings with the help of Francis Brennan and the Grovers, Mrs. Grover being a painter and her husband having a keen eye for art.

He worked for understanding, visited the museums and studied paintings, but he never attained any real appreciation of art, any personalized vision. He was impressed by the "success" of the artist or the fame of the painting, missing the thrill of the enchanted beholder. He bought a Van Gogh, a valuable canvas which, however, departed enough from the usual Van Gogh style so that some friends commented that it did not look quite like Van Gogh. These comments made him lose faith in the picture and he ordered it sold. Although he was delighted to be named a trustee of the Metropolitan Museum, and served conscientiously, his contribution was diminished by his limitations in understanding. The same was true of books, for he still favored best-sellers. "He couldn't seem to see what the difference was between *War and Peace* and *The Caine Mutiny*," Mrs. Bancroft observed, "except that he'd enjoyed reading *The Caine Mutiny* more."

When an artist or a work of art became news, however, they came into his domain and he knew how they should be covered for maximum reader interest. This contrast of brilliant perception and impenetrable obtuseness could be both fascinating and maddening. He seemed at times to conceive of the American way of life as that land of Cockaigne inhabited by the handsome people pictured in the Life ads, those people who were so well-dressed and happy, surrounded by American-made luxuries. In one conversation with Mary Bancroft, they took up the question of what constituted a cultivated man. She named several persons, including Adlai Stevenson, as being in her opinion cultivated. Luce asked bluntly if he—Luce himself—was cultivated. She replied that she thought not. It was a mark of the friendly frankness of their relationship that he was not angry but was ready to debate the question. There ensued a long discussion of cultivation in which he took the stand that being cultivated implied being "ineffectual," but in the end he conceded in a winning display of humility that he was not cultivated, that he wished he were but that "I don't have time."

She felt that one of the things that impaired his cultivation was his worship of success, which sprang from his work ethic, his religion and his pragmatism. She implored him to have an occasional Time cover story depart from the usual preoccupation with success in merchandising, politicking or military enterprises and devote itself to some magnificent failure, someone who had aimed nobly without hitting the mark. This, however, violated his basic be-

liefs. He was a trifle irked that she had no doubt whatever that he would carry the long-time money-loser Sports Illustrated to ultimate financial success because, as she reasoned, $ucce$$ was his thing, the thing he always succeeded at.

She was interested in the contrast between his considerable knowledge of theology and his somewhat childlike mental conception of the Deity, whose likeness seemed to range from the kindly, bearded De Lawd of *Green Pastures* to the granite sternness of a figure on Mount Rushmore. In their frequent discussions of death, they touched not only on the mien of God and His expectations but also on the attitude of the mortal not yet embraced by death but facing it. The fighter Luce did not feel it required that a Christian should accept death with resignation and surrender. He was delighted when he ran across Dylan Thomas's poem on the theme, and recited its nineteen lines to her from memory. The first three read:

> Do not go gentle into that good night,
> Old age should burn and rave at close of day;
> Rage, rage against the dying of the light.

He did not expect death for a long time, but when it approached he meant to fight back.

XXXII

1. AMBIGUITY IN PERFECTION

The tendency to claim God as an ally for our partisan values and ends is . . .
the source of all religious fanaticism.
                                                    —*Reinhold Niebuhr*

The President's special counsel, Theodore Sorensen, described Time as "in
John Kennedy's opinion consistently slanted, unfair and inaccurate in its
treatment of the Presidency, highly readable but highly misleading." Kennedy
thought that Time's White House correspondent, Hugh Sidey, sent in accurate and friendly dispatches but that they were rewritten in New York with
hostile tones at the behest of Managing Editor Fuerbringer, unknown to
Luce. While it was true that Luce no longer watched every word in his magazines, he did not miss many of them, he was sympathetic with the Iron Chancellor's politics and it is doubtful that the managing editor worked in many
digs not approved by the Boss. Luce always defended him, saying, "I know
you don't like Otto, but I think he's a goddamned good editor."

The Lucepress was applying every available ounce of Lucepressure to
shape and toughen the Presidential policy. Those little tricks of denigration
could hurt a chief executive as sensitive to the press as Kennedy, so aware
that he had been elected with a popular plurality of one-tenth of one percent.
The Lucepressure was always there—the praise, the warning, the reproof, the
urging—even in stories substantially friendly. The line was undeviatingly
hard—the fruit of Luce's announcement to his editors that Time Inc. must
resolve to win the Cold War. Bowles had been cast overboard, and there is no
telling how much the pressure had to do with it, and whether Kennedy
knuckled under ever so slightly in other ways to the author of his preface.

In making Kennedy its Man of the Year, Time patted his back for jettison-

ing Bowles ("the wrong man"), for talking tough to Gromyko and for strengthening American "military might around the world," but castigated him for "downgrading Laos" and warned him of "the marauding forces of Communism on every front in every part of the world." Elsewhere, Time needled him about Castro and the Soviet arms build-up, urging an invasion of Cuba. Life did the same, one of its articles being by Clare Boothe Luce, who wrote that what was at stake in Cuba was "the question not only of American prestige but of American survival." Both Time and Life glowed with praise for the President when he issued his ultimatum to Khrushchev on Cuba, Time saying, "Generations to come may well count John Kennedy's resolve as one of the decisive moments of the 20th century," Life burbling in its excitement, "Nikita Khrushchev had monstrously miscalculated the American spirit and will. His hand was called." A Life editorial called it "a major turning point in the 17-year Cold War. . . . In sharp contrast to frustration in Vietnam, murkiness in Laos and stalemate in Berlin, this was action with honor . . ." There was the familiar competitive toughness, the insistence that this was a matter of power, not simply a question of the balancing of "rights":

> In some quarters it has been fashionable to argue that action against a Soviet base in Cuba would jeopardize our right to NATO bases in Turkey. This is nonsensical reasoning. The Russians never conceded our "right" to bases in Turkey (or Spain, or North Africa). They tolerated them because the consequences of going after them were too obvious. . . . [The editorial continued:] We might be fighting again by the time this issue of Life is in your hands. . . .

Time explained that a mere mathematical comparison of military bases was meaningless because of America's strictly moral use of them as opposed to Soviet immorality. It quoted, of all people, Chiang Kai-shek's UN ambassador as saying, "A revolver in the hands of a gangster is not the same thing as a revolver in the top drawer of a peaceful citizen." Time, agreeing, made plain the benevolence of American militarism:

> . . . [T]here is an enormous moral difference between U.S. and Russian objectives. . . . The contrast between the Communist record and the U.S. record since 1945 is vivid enough for all to see. . . . The U.S. bases, such as those in Turkey, have helped to keep the peace since World War II, while the Russian bases in Cuba threatened to upset the peace. The Russian bases were intended to further conquest and domination, while U.S. bases were erected to preserve freedom. The difference should have been obvious to all.

John Foster Dulles could not have said it better. Unquestionably the U.S. did enjoy a world moral advantage over a Russia whose brutality in Hungary was well remembered, but it was a bank credit that could be overdrawn. A week later there was no war, Khrushchev had backed down and Life saw hope that this "indicated a disposition to *win* the Cold War." It warned: "Foreigners who do not understand our political system—*e.g.* Nikita Khrushchev—this is proof that the system is still in good shape." It said "we are

standing by our moral commitments" in Berlin, urged that we must "disman-
tle not only the missile bases but the [Castro] regime," and called for more
American help to India in its border battle with Red China. Although Nehru
had been stupid in his neutralism, he was now learning the facts of life, all the
fronts against Communism were vital and "that is why the U.S. must be on
India's side." Time declared that Russia had more missiles aimed at Western
Europe than the U.S. had aimed at Russia from bases in Britain, Italy and
Turkey (not counting other foreign bases in range of Russia where missiles
were readily deployable, and the many SAC bases and the movable Polaris
submarines based in Scotland). The two contending nations were now on a
basis of aimed missiles awaiting the pushbutton, each possessing nuclear
power that could destroy the other.

A few months later, there was an interesting seasoning of Luce authoritarianism in his remarks to his staff in marking Time's fortieth birthday:

> Time believes. . . . Time's value-judgments run through all the fields of en-
> deavor. . . . The founding of this country was, as I believe, a Providential
> occurrence. . . . only a virtuous people can be free. . . . America's mission of
> liberty [is] not only for this country but for the world. . . . [T]he whole concept
> of the American Proposition requires [Time] to exist. It requires a free press—
> and more, a free and responsible press. . . .

One possessing the code would realize that what he was saying was that
Time was now slanting the news everywhere rather than just in national and
world affairs, and that only a morally slanted press was a responsible press.
Time's talents and its power were demonstrated again in May 1963 when it
threw its greatest wingding, its fortieth birthday party, celebrated this time
for public promotion rather than staff esprit de corps.

To some less sophisticated foreign statesmen, this function must have bolstered an impression that Time Inc., rather than being a corporate publishing
house, was an official arm of the U.S. government—perhaps a combination of
the State and Defense departments with Commerce thrown in. Luce, brilliant
as always in promotion, spurred his vast organization to paroxysms of effort to
make this an unparalleled occasion, which indeed it became. The idea was to
build the revel around a guest list composed of surviving individuals who had
appeared on Time covers since the beginning in 1923.

Not the villains, of course. Khrushchev, Mao and Nasser were not invited,
nor were other more easily accessible people who might lack accord with the
spirit of the occasion—Dean Acheson, Senator Morse and Fidel Castro among
them—nor the Space Ship, the U.S. Taxpayer or the Derby winner Native
Dancer, all cover subjects. Since there had been more than 2000 covers in
Time's forty years, and it was necessary to restrict the cover-hero guest list to
three hundred, there was picking and choosing. Still, Luce insisted that it be
democratic and representative. Among the guests were not only such China-
Lobbyists as T. V. Soong, Cardinal Spellman and DeWitt Wallace, but not a

few with whom he had disagreed ferociously in policy or politics—Adlai Stevenson, Henry Wallace, Norman Thomas and James A. Farley among them.

Who among these sometimes touchy people would get the best seats? Content Peckham, placed in charge of protocol, took much of her instruction from the State Department. Expense was disregarded. The affair, held at the Waldorf May 6, was an enormous corporate success even if (or really *because*) it dramatized the growing governmental subservience to publicity, the withering of a sense of separation between officialdom and the promotional side of the press. It might have been better for powerful officials of the current administration to have remained aloof, or at least to enjoy the champagne and the *filet de boeuf au foie gras* with *sauce Périgueux* without taking part in the program. The cozy mingling of government with a private propagandist seeking to influence that government was inappropriate even though the propagandist was fanatically well-intentioned. Perhaps it was asking too much for politicians to remain in the background when the Lucepress had seen to it that representatives of 160 publications and news agencies were on hand and that films were made that would be shown by all major U.S. television networks and newsreel companies as well as television and radio coverage in England, France, Germany, Japan, Radio Free Europe, the Armed Forces Network and the Voice of America.

Clare, in turquoise "embellished with a perfection of emeralds and diamonds," greeted Elsa Maxwell with a kiss, saying, "You and I, we never made it, darling," meaning, of course, the Time cover. And Luce, reveling in this occasion which so visually marked the peak of his success and power, introduced his wife to the throng of 1700 in the ballroom: "One who has never been on the cover of Time for a very . . . poor reason—she married the Editor-in-Chief."

The President, represented by his youngest brother, the Senator from Massachusetts, sent a telegram which Luce read to the crowd and which read in part: "Every great magazine is the lengthened shadow of its editor. . . . Henry R. Luce has shown himself one of the creative editors of our age. . . . Like most Americans I don't always agree with Time, but I always read it." Vice President Lyndon Johnson spoke briefly: ". . . Many of us owe Harry Luce a very great debt for being the first publisher to select magazine cover models on a basis other than beauty. . . . A good many of us would have been shot or sent to remote exile if we lived in other parts of the globe, so it seems to me that those of us who have been brought together here tonight owe a great debt of gratitude to our nation and its determination to preserve freedom for us all." He was followed by Secretary of State Rusk, whose 1951 speech at the Luce-endowed China Institute about the Mao government not being Chinese was an appraisal still, twelve years later, not grasped by some 700 million Chinese. The Calvinist son of a Presbyterian preacher, he was as one with Luce and the late John Foster Dulles in his assurance that morality

and American aims were identical. He had just returned from a mission to Pakistan concerning armaments. He said in part:

> I have known Harry Luce in many different ways, as an individual, as a publisher. There are two ideas to which I know he is deeply attached, which seem to me to be central to our relations with other countries. . . . The first is the notion of law. The law which does not enslave but liberates. . . . Secondly, this underlying and fundamental difference between a world of coercion and a world of freedom.

The most serious speaker was the German-born, seventy-six-year-old University of Chicago theologian, Dr. Paul J. Tillich, once a target of Nazi thought control. He seemed to discover in this well-fed and bejeweled assemblage more self-approbation than self-examination, a simplistic hero-villain concept and a tendency toward easy slogans. After his congratulatory opening remarks, Tillich fired blunt sentences, some even aimed at his host, having to do with the "ambiguity of perfection":

> An awareness of the ambiguity of our achievements is alive in those who know that the American form of democracy, though preferable to most other present political methods, is not the end of the ways of historical providence. . . . [Here Dr. Tillich permitted himself a quiet assault on the American complacency which assumed that everything American was unambiguously right and that those disagreeing—even though it be all the rest of the world—were unambiguously reprehensible. This, he said, was folly—all the more so when it inspired hate-filled propaganda. He felt it the duty of statesmen and of the powerful magazines to correct this self-righteous and dangerous view. Indeed, his remarks here seemed so directly applicable to Luce and his publications that Time's editors excised them from that magazine's account of the event and they must be paraphrased here. He went on:] The negative forces of our one-dimensional culture are extremely strong. . . . And I believe that it is the duty of all those who speak for our time—including Time Magazine—to help with passion and wisdom. . . .

Some 110 bottles of gin and similar quantities of Scotch whisky and other beverages had gone down 1700 hatches in addition to the champagne, and there seemed no general awareness that the white-haired theologian was doing a little shooting at "negative forces," "our one-dimensional culture" and dangerous propaganda. Did Luce, with his splendid rationalizing powers, realize that he had been pinked? Perhaps he did not hear every word, and in any case it was a busy function lasting far into the night, since the spotlight was turned on each of the cover people in order and a few words said about each. He had a whale of a time, waving excitedly at Miss Peckham, grabbing Miss Mariano and introducing her to the Vice President and to Governor William Scranton of Pennsylvania. He turned to Bernhard Auer, publisher of Time, who was verging on exhaustion after weeks of intensive work for this occasion and barked, "Bernie, we'll start right now getting ready to do this again for Time's fiftieth."

2. PARKINSON'S COROLLARY

You know, old-time newspapermen who wanted us to remember as kids the ephemeral nature of our work used to remind us that yesterday's newspaper wraps today's garbage. I think it is Mr. Luce's unique contribution to American journalism that he placed into the hands of the people yesterday's newspaper and today's garbage homogenized into one neat package.

—*Herbert Lawrence Block (Herblock)*

Lucepress people of all political hues were resentful and defensive about outside criticism. Even the few remaining liberals, hemmed in though they were by the rising tide of Lucean reaction and regarded somewhat as traitors by outside liberals, rallied against it. Not only were they swayed by Luce's odd magnetism and pious fervor but also by a corollary of Parkinson's Law:

Daily work in any established routine subject to outside attack will, to those involved in it, assume an appearance of normality and legitimacy at a speed influenced by its profitability.

Although Emmet Hughes had flouted the law and was now a columnist for Newsweek, he and Luce were still good friends—or so he thought until his book *The Ordeal of Power* was published in 1963. They had talked about the book, Luce knew it would be critical of Eisenhower and in view of his fairly calm reception of Hughes's earlier assault on Dulles there seemed no occasion to think that the new book would move him to more than a few passing expletives.

But Time's review was long and savage. It attacked Hughes as a great man's "valet" who had taken the job under the false pretense of political loyalty and had spent his time jotting secret notes of political confidences and "offering the President advice about how to run the world." Elsewhere *Ordeal* got a warm reception as an absorbing if controversial summation of the experiences near the summit of an idealistic young intellectual who felt that the Eisenhower administration had missed every boat sailing off in the direction of peace. The President himself, wanting peace, the book suggested, had lacked the high resolve and the political savvy to drive for it, had fallen into the years of brinkmanship with Dulles, and after Dulles's death had botched his one great effort at negotiation with Khrushchev. *Ordeal* was in large part a reflection of Hughes's disillusion with an Eisenhower he had admired, and still did, but whom he found lacking in the highest capacities of the Presidential office at a time in history when those capacities were desperately needed. Implicit in his book was the conviction that Russia's leaders might be anxious for honest agreement and a reduction of tensions, or in any case that it would cost the U.S. little to *test* their honesty.

Aside from the merit of Hughes's judgments was the question of the sanctity of White House conversations. Eisenhower had developed a liking for his young aide and had talked frankly with him in what may have been an assumption that it would go no farther. The total effort of Eisenhower's press secretary, James Hagerty, for example, had been to shield the President, prevent the publication of any views or statements other than those of policy. In fact, when President Kennedy read *Ordeal* he said, "I hope that no one around here is writing that kind of book." But Hughes had joined the White House staff on an entirely different basis. He had been on loan to the President for a time and had published his book after that Presidency was over. He would not permit his admiration and respect for Eisenhower to impede his transmission of what he regarded as essential facts about a public office accountable to the public in a world where ignorance and errors could be fatal.

When Hughes learned that a more moderate review of his book had been sent back by Luce with a request for more vinegar, he knew that the understanding he thought he had with his former boss had somehow dissolved. This seemed confirmed when Time subsequently ran three comments in its Letters department attacking Hughes and his book. Hughes wrote a protesting letter to Luce, now in Phoenix, containing an inadmissible note of anger. He got no reply. Father Murray, the close friend of them both, agreed that Time's notice was unfair, reviewing the author more than the book. Later, when Murray visited Luce in Phoenix, he told him that he had not done well by "our friend Emmet." Luce angrily said, "I won't discuss it," but finally was coaxed by the Jesuit to elaborate a trifle.

"I read only the first thirty pages," he said in substance, "and that was enough. It showed that Emmet wasn't telling the truth. It didn't mention that he went to Washington because I arranged it."

That was all he would say. Apparently a large part of his resentment stemmed from the lack of acknowledgment of his influence in the matter—the protégé's failure to credit his sponsor. Some weeks later, when the two met at a gathering at the Clurman home in New York, Luce ignored Hughes's proffered hand, turned his back on him and cut him dead. The break was final.

It was really not surprising that Luce should be angered by criticism of his own favorite statesmen and policies by a young man who had in the bargain gone over to a competing publisher. But at sixty-five he was settling into a disposition to appreciate the growing number of sycophants around him. The sycophant had developed a technique of agreeing with the Boss and flattering him but offering just the right amount of occasional argument—giving in at just the right moment and with the properly admiring acknowledgment of defeat—to make himself appear honest. There were those who, after studying Luce for years, had elevated this process to a fine art and had grown rich. But there were also those who merely feared him, his power over their lives and his ossifying opinions. When Theodore White, now a free-lance writer who

had come around to writing frequently for Life, wrote a piece about Governor Scranton, largely praising him, he talked with several editors who had read the article. Their lips were locked. None of them would comment pro or con until Luce himself had read it, not wishing to advance an opinion with which he might disagree. After he read it and liked it, these editors shook White's hand and agreed that *they* liked it too. These were the cautious who knew that Luce's permission of contrary opinion could be fickle and could vary according to one's fluctuating personal standing with him. By now he was thornier but could still exert some of the elusive attraction which Stephen Longstreet noted in a hard-nosed appraisal of Luce based on Longstreet's earlier stint with Time:

> He was not at all the evil man most people thought him. He was, as he saw it, God's classmate, and any slanting or twisting of journalism was for God and Yale. We knew him as a lonely, unhappy sort of fellow, who felt that the world was not taking his advice. He had little use for the staff that had sold out to him for good, and he sensed he could never hold the high office he wanted. . . . He was not at all a journalist; for he had no interest in presenting the news fairly, or in full. His publications have little merit, or much contact with reality. He wanted it that way, for he himself was remote and felt little comfort with the ordinary citizens he bamboozled. We liked him very much, and lunch with him was always good.

Yet he enjoyed Clurman's company although aware that Clurman disagreed with him politically—even about sacred China—since Clurman did not press this. And Thomas Griffith even got away with writing a book of some liberal leaning by making due obeisance to Parkinson's Corollary and with a diplomatic recognition of Luce which Hughes had neglected. His book, *The Waist-High Culture*, found measured fault with American spread-eagleism and other concepts treasured by Luce without, of course, identifying them as Lucean concepts. But he spent many pages in approval of Time and Luce along with an ingenious defense of Time's value judgments without touching on the deceptive and propagandist nature of slanted news. And he topped an interesting analysis of Luce with an observation that must have delighted the prestige-loving Boss: "If this were England he would have been Lord Luce of Rockefeller Plaza . . ." Luce (although it could not be guaranteed that he read the whole book) read *that*, all right, and sent Griffith a charming note of appreciation.

3. A SCRAP IS NOT ARMAGEDDON

If the Luces had given up hope of being President and Vice President, politics was still meat and drink to them both. Clare, whose epigrams were sometimes reported in Time but who seldom got a Life assignment, was writing a

column for the Herald Tribune and contributing occasionally to other magazines. Politically she had moved farther to the right than Luce, but her views were not always predictable. The two agreed in general in their public pronouncements about the Vietnam war.

Both in his speeches and in his Lucepress propaganda line, Luce pushed his belief that Vietnam offered one more chance for the American Century which had been repulsed in China. He was ultimately joined by people of both major parties—some of them influenced by the Lucepress and by Luce's own stature as an Asia expert—who saw the dominoes teetering. He was of course years ahead of most of them. President Eisenhower had reluctantly acceded to the enormous China-Lobby pressure which had backed the American overturn of the Geneva agreements and installed Ngo Dinh Diem in Saigon. In addition to Dulles, among Luce's friends pushing for the rescue of South Vietnam were William C. Bullitt, Cardinal Spellman and Joseph P. Kennedy. But liberals such as Senators Mike Mansfield and Paul Douglas were as convinced. To say that without Luce and the Lucepress there would have been no China Lobby, no Senator McCarthy, no national hysteria over the "loss of China" and no growing bipartisan fear in America of an Asian Communism that had to be "stopped" would be excessive. But Luce and his press abetted and enlarged all these symptoms. And it seems not impossible that without his power (or if his power had been used wisely) the American countermoves against Communism might have been diplomatic and successful rather than military and disastrous.

Among the many other questions that the Vietnam issue would pose were (1) how long it would take the nation to discover that the involvement was a tragic error, and (2) to what extent the Lucepress was responsible for concealing the error and hence delaying the discovery. What with Luce's strong influence in the American involvement and his endless demand for more and deeper involvement, he would not be in a comfortable position to admit, after accumulating catastrophe, that it had all been an unfortunate miscalculation. Time and Life had early canonized Diem as a "tough miracle man" and had praised the efficiencies of his brother, Ngo Dinh Nhu and that beauteous spitfire Vietnamese counterpart of Madame Chiang, Madame Nhu. There was little notice of the ambiguity of perfection. As with Chiang, the Lucepress soft-pedaled Diem's totalitarian rule, secret-police terror and systematic jailing, torture and murder of political opponents. Indeed, as Luce continued his fund drive for the Presbyterian church, his "free world" encompassed men, women and practices fit to curdle the blood and the "dirty war" once pushed by the French was dirtier than ever.

When Madame Nhu, the Catholic "Dragon Lady" who had scoffed at the self-immolating Buddhist monks as having "barbecued" themselves, arrived in New York, she was the luncheon guest of Luce and his fascinated editors. Clare, the Catholic and feminist, attacked Madame Nhu's critics in an article in the National Review with the arresting title "The Lady *Is* for Burning."

What was happening in Vietnam, she wrote, was much like what had happened to the Chiangs in China before the State Department "pulled the rug from under them" and allowed a Communist takeover. To the charge that the Diem family was nepotist she replied that President Kennedy had "put Bobby in control of our secret police—the FBI," and had "engineered" the election to the Senate of his younger brother Edward. America's prestige and even security, she wrote, seemed to rest on the great power Madame Nhu held in "the pale pink palm of her exquisite little hand," and her mission was to convince Americans that South Vietnam was winning the war but would probably lose it "if she and her family are undermined and thrown to the left-wing wolves." Yet, the article said, she was met by discourteous American interviewers, whereas Khrushchev had been "treated like a public hero." As for the suicide monks, in Mrs. Luce's opinion they had gained face for their temple and sainthood for themselves. "For at least three of the monks who were over age seventy," she wrote, "that must have seemed a rather good deal."

Walter Winchell chattered, "[Madame Nhu's] best friends in U.S. publishing circles are Henry Luce and his wife Clare. The latter used her magazine connections to plead Mme. Nhu's 'side of it' and also made speeches in her behalf, etc. But when it came to make a deal with a publication Mme. Nhu sold her memoirs to Luce competitors."

For all that, the Luces stood by her. In a Los Angeles speech Clare said that for seventeen years (which of course included Eisenhower and Dulles) America had followed a policy of peaceful coexistence and had eschewed force against Communism even when force would have been prudent. The American people wanted to stop Communism but didn't want to get hurt in so doing. Only three men, she said, had had the courage to act decisively against Communism: Churchill, Truman and de Gaulle. Again at the University of Utah she inquired whether there was something devitalizing about American wealth which caused a failure to act to "prevent Russian domination of the world." "We have had as a nation," she said, "a false morality about force. We have not understood as a people the diplomatic or political uses of force."

Both Luces deplored the American failure to give all-out support to the Diem-Nhu family, who understood the diplomatic and political uses of force. Luce's typical impatience at America's hesitancy about using its God-given military power had once been wonderfully expressed in a Life editorial headline, "A Scrap is not Armageddon." To Managing Editor Fuerbringer also, the Vietnam war was holy. Strange alterations were being made in dispatches from Saigon. It had long been the despairing hope of Time's Asian correspondents to prevent Luce's bias from causing preposterous error in the New York rewrites of their dispatches. Stanley Karnow, the chief correspondent for Southeast Asia, had left the organization because of these frustrations and had joined the Saturday Evening Post. He had been replaced by Charles Mohr. The tendency of Time-New York to tamper with dispatches from

Time-Saigon in order to make American military participation look more glamorous and successful became known to other newsmen there. As David Halberstam, the New York Times man in Saigon, noted, "to a large extent [Time's executives] see it not just as a magazine of reporting, but as an instrument of policy making." The situation was like that in 1944–45 when Luce supported Whittaker Chambers in the junking of dispatches from foreign correspondents and the creation of the correct scenario in New York. A. J. Liebling observed that Luce had many foreign correspondents, some of them good ones, "but he has never been able to bring himself to believe them unless they tell him what he already thinks."

His Saigon men, Charles Mohr and Merton Perry, were not sending him the expected goodies any more than Theodore White or John Hersey once had. The basis of the disagreement was the matter of the Vietnam tunnel. Luce and Fuerbringer wanted light, good clear light, at the end of the tunnel. Indeed, Luce and Fuerbringer preferred to eliminate the tunnel as far as practicable. On the contrary, Mohr and Perry's already long tunnel kept getting longer, so that the glitter of American victory was lost in the dimness. Luce's frustration was compounded by his belief in energetic prosecution and quick results in any undertaking. Eleven years earlier, on his first trip to Saigon, he had observed that the elimination of guerrilla pockets would be a simple matter, and a year after that he had admonished David Duncan for his unconstructive attitude in Life. Mohr and Perry were similarly unconstructive. They cabled that the war was going badly and that neither the Diem government nor the U.S. brass was leveling with the press. Halberstam wrote:

> . . . Charley Mohr . . . would argue for tougher coverage on Vietnam. Instead his editors, who had lunched with Secretary McNamara and other Pentagon officials . . . would explain patiently to Mohr that he understood only a portion of the big picture. And Time's coverage—paralleling the official version—would continue.

For almost a year these Timen disputed the changing and gilding of their dispatches by the New York office to conform to the Luce-Fuerbringer-Pentagon win-the-war line. Luce said to Richard Clurman, his chief of correspondents, "When President Kennedy doesn't know what's going on in Vietnam, he sends McNamara to find out. I'm sending you to find out about this business." Clurman, known to be sympathetic with the correspondents, visited Saigon, talked with Mohr and Perry and came back leaving them somewhat reassured.

But the New York script-surgery was as drastic as ever. Mohr was further incensed when Time's cover story on Madame Nhu, of which he was the author, underwent substantive changes in New York. His lead, which had begun, "Vietnam is a graveyard of lost hopes," had of course vanished, Madame's glamour and patriotism were stressed and her baneful influence on the country played down. Hard on that, a Mohr dispatch saying bluntly that the

war was being lost was rewritten in New York in tones of optimism about the improved fighting qualities of ARVN. This was followed by an angry, Fuerbringer-inspired piece in Time's Press section, censuring the whole kit and kaboodle of the Saigon press corps, including Time's own. Their dispatches might as well be "printed in Vietnamese" for all the sense they made, said Time. They hung around the Hotel Caravelle's eighth-floor bar, pooling their pessimism. They were prejudiced against Diem and the Nhus and biased in favor of the Buddhists (who, Luce and Time suspected, favored the Communists or at the very least were playing into their hands). They were *defeatist*: "[They] seem reluctant to give splash treatment to anything that smacks of military victory . . ." said the three-column dressing-down. "When there is a defeat, the color is rich and flowing . . ."

Mohr and Perry thereupon resigned. Luce did not know Perry but liked Mohr, who had given him that jolly cocktail party in Delhi and was known to be a first-rate man except for his peculiarity about Vietnam. But despite the efforts he made through Clurman, Mohr and Perry were not to be soothed, Mohr joining the New York Times and Perry, Newsweek.

Next thing, Diem and his brother Nhu had been kidnapped and murdered, with the Kennedy administration admitting only to having created an atmosphere welcoming a change. Now General Duong Van Minh had taken charge —the first of a series of revolving-door rulers who would increasingly undermine American dignity and credibility. "Press the War in Vietnam," urged Life, getting grimly behind Minh on the theory that at any rate he seemed as anti-Communist as Diem. Three weeks later President Kennedy arrived in Dallas to find full-page ads in the local papers accusing him of pro-Communist acts and to become more than ever aware, a few hours before he was killed, of the fanaticism abroad in the land.

4. *LYNDON JOHNSON CALLING*

Luce, in Phoenix, soon received a telephone call from the new President, who said he just wanted to pay his respects. "Tell Lyndon hello for me," Clare said to Luce, who did so. "She's the sweetest little woman I ever served with in Congress," Johnson said. The gesture, showing his shrewd appraisal of the Luce vanity and yearning for recognition, became an important ingredient in Luce's general approval of Johnson despite the Texan's obnoxious party affiliation. Another was an early invitation to the White House, where Luce, for all his many previous visits with earlier occupants, still gloried in the thrill of talking with the President of the United States. Soon Luce seemed to be grooming Secretary McNamara for Vice President on the Democratic ticket, impressed with a business brilliance he felt was being translated into government. London's backbiting Cassandra erupted over the cloying quality of the Luce praise for McNamara or anyone else he sought to advance:

W. A. Swanberg

When American politicians come under the "Henry Luce Seal of Good Statesmanship," they are treated to a fixed pattern of intolerable printed smarm in Time and Life. The pattern of this oleaginous praise is always the same. The hero (who is also the victim) has to measure up to a rigid set of Luce requirements for the perfect political man.

Cassandra listed them. He must be good-looking (Time said McNamara had "hazel eyes" and "chiselled features"), married (McNamara was), have children (he had three) and love them (McNamara, said Time, during the week of fierce tension over Cuba, "stole home for a few hours to help his 12-year-old son Robert Craig with his homework"). He must enjoy the approved arts (the Secretary went for Beethoven, Brahms and Bartók), must utter sentiments showing his disregard for mere money (Time had him opting for "public responsibility" and "public service") and he must like the open air ("His hobby," said Time, "is mountain climbing practiced on family vacations in the High Sierras").

"There MUST be some devil," Cassandra protested, "there MUST be some blessed salt of cussedness on the top or in the heart of Luce's imaginary disgusting cream pie."

In April 1964, the sixty-six-year-old Luce, who had once said Time Inc. was a young man's organization and he would step aside at forty or forty-five, did make a gesture at stepping aside. He took the title of Editorial Chairman while Hedley Donovan succeeded to the time-honored Luce title of Editor-in-Chief of all publications. By the early standards, Donovan himself was old and failing, being forty-nine. A tall Minnesotan and a Phi Beta Kappa graduate of the state university, he was a Rhodes Scholar who had studied history at Oxford. He had been a Timan nineteen years, rising to the managing editorship of Fortune before being tapped as the editorial heir apparent.

It was the occasion of a vast company dinner at the New York Hilton (after all those extravaganzas at the Waldorf) at which Donovan was hailed but the real guest of honor was nobody in the world but Henry Robinson Luce. His high forehead now ran far back before it encountered a fringe of gray-white hair, but the blue eyes were still steely under their intimidating porcupine brows and he was still erect and of a slimness fit to shame some of his slumping and pot-bellied younger executives. He had never said a word about his heart, and none of the others, though they knew it had once felled him, had ever dared to mention it to him.

His pioneer associate Roy Larsen, oldest of the Old Bolsheviks of Time (jokesters called Time Inc. "Larsenic and Old Luce") introduced him to the crowd as "the most successful man I have ever known," perhaps aware of some of the irony in his words. It was an evening of nostalgia, with Timen present from places like Nairobi and Hong Kong as well as from the T-L skyscraper two blocks down Sixth Avenue. It was an evening of wonderment too, and speculation. What an organization had grown from that improbable con-

junction of Hadden and Luce back in 1922! Think of the millions upon millions created by Luce on the strength of ideas! How many American statesmen and foreign potentates had angled for his support? How many Time Inc. hearts had been exultant, and how many broken, by the judgments made by the brain behind those chill blue eyes—judgments that meant advancement or rejection?

One did not have to like the man to be impressed. There was an ovation that was surely genuine as Luce rose to give a graceful speech during which a few listeners who had given long odds on their wager that he would not fail to touch on his obsession, won their money when he mourned the Red takeover in China and Eastern Europe. The old reprobate was still playing Chinese checkers with groups of his executives. Donovan's elevation marked his winning of a particularly long and tense game. But certainly there were few among the audience—even among those who feared or disliked the Boss— who would not concede that he had built the corporation with an incredibly skillful if ruthless hand and had made a mark on history, however that mark might be judged. Parkinson's Corollary was in full operation. It was hardly possible to love Luce, since he extended little love to anyone else and had few real friends, only acquaintances and subordinates. Still it was impossible not to respect his abilities over and above the endearing one of paying high salaries and profit-sharing, and it is doubtful that many of his auditors saw in him a personification of some of the things wrong with America.

But after the party was over, the question remained: Was he really quitting? Was he really handing over the editorial control that came closest to being the love of his life?

Not really. An election was coming up. Herbert Mayes, editor of McCall's, for which Clare wrote a column, put an interesting question to Luce: "But if the editors now decide to support candidate A for President, and you are for candidate B, which candidate will the magazines support?"

"That's simple," Luce replied after an interval Mayes estimated at a tenth of a second. "They will support candidate B."

XXXIII

1. THE CRACK IN THE MONOLITH

After years of screaming at Luce, Clare finally persuaded him to get a hearing aid. He got the type hidden within eyeglasses, which posed its own problem. Associates unaware of the change still automatically raised their voices until he snapped (just as he used to say "Speak up!"), "You don't have to shout."

Angry people still questioned the credibility of his magazines. Catholic Bishop Albert Zuroweste of Illinois wrote to complain in detail about Time's account of the Second Vatican Council, which he described as "distorted," "misleading" and "a colorful fabric of fact and fancy." Time did not publish his letter. Assistant Secretary of Defense Arthur Sylvester wrote that he was "appalled" at the way Life, as he claimed, had edited and distorted the meaning of letters from an American pilot in Vietnam in its effort to show that the Air Force was being supplied with obsolescent equipment. A Canadian investigator found Time's five-page report on Cuba thoroughly unreliable. Time's sensational story about a "widespread homosexual underworld" in Boise, Idaho, involving some of the city's "most prominent men," caused a newsman to make an investigation which was, said the San Francisco Examiner, "extremely unflattering to Time as an agent of truth." Time's cover story on Cardinal Cushing caused His Eminence to issue a public statement deploring "a false image of me" and two Catholic publications to cite "almost incredible errors of fact" and "editorializing in the guise of explanation." The Nation inquired, "If people read Time because they are indulging their taste for fiction, why don't they simply read novels?" The Columbia Journalism Review, canvassing 203 Washington correspondents, found that on the question of "fairness and reliability" Time was given nine votes to Newsweek's seventy-five and U.S. News's sixty-six, but that many of the newsmen thought that to ex-

444

pect these qualities in any newsmagazine was naïve and gave such answers as "Are you kidding?"

The critic A. J. Liebling thought the most puzzling thing about Time was how men of integrity could work for it. Picking at factual errors in the Weekly Newsmagazine, he said, was "like faulting a dog for not dancing well. After all, dogs aren't *supposed* to dance."

The Lucepress weakness for painting events in Vietnam with tints of rose was a subject of jokes among newspaper journalists, but there was that unwritten law that the press must not criticize the press. Bravely did the editor of the Arapahoe Herald (weekly circulation 4530) of Littleton, Colorado, flout the law in a long editorial reading in part:

> Among journalists [Time] is known as the "Weekly Fiction Magazine," but among the nation's executives it is the bible. . . . When Time's own correspondents wrote that South Vietnam was losing the war, Time's New York editors re-wrote the story to prove that our side was winning. For that's the way Henry Luce wanted it. . . . Probably the best picture of events is supplied by the New York Times each Sunday. The "News in Review" is compiled by six competent men and can be read in 40 minutes. The drug store in Woodlawn has the Sunday issue flown in each Monday and sells it for 50¢. This is more expensive than Time's fiction, and it's not nearly as much fun to read.
>
> But then again maybe you would like the truth for a change.

The publication of T. S. Matthews's memoirs caused Luce some embarrassment. When he was questioned on a WABC program by Howard K. Smith, he seemed unprepared for Smith's references to the Matthews book and his replies were not entirely coherent:

> SMITH: I want to quote to you something that . . . Tom Matthews said in a book, "The distortions, suppressions and slanting of its political 'news' seemed to me to pass the bounds of politics and to commit an offense against the ethics of journalism." What do you say to that, sir?
>
> LUCE: Well, I am trying to think what Tom Matthews would like me to say. And, if you don't mind, thinking of Tom, I will let that one go by.
>
> SMITH: Well, what about the criticisms . . . that Time's unfair?
>
> LUCE: They aren't true—they aren't true. The answer to that is that we have . . . I don't know how many Time readers—10,000,000 anyway—certainly 4,000,000 who are paid readers, regular readers. . . . But the proof is the fact that they continue to read it and renew at a phenomenal rate.

Odd as that sounded, it was logically related to Luce's theory that best-sellers must be great books and that success was proof of virtue.

While the great respect shown Luce by Presidents Kennedy and Johnson proved that all Democrats did not wear horns, and he was eager to exert power regardless of the political preference of the White House occupant, he was a strong backer of Governor Scranton's Presidential boom early in 1964. Scranton was not only a Republican but was a brother-in-law of Time Inc.'s

president James A. Linen, and Linen was a grandson of a Scranton Presbyterian who had helped Luce's parents get to China. Clare was all for Barry Goldwater, and in fact gave a seconding speech at the San Francisco convention where he became the Republican nominee. An interesting factor was that Goldwater was a Phoenix neighbor and friend who had occasionally dined and played bridge with the Luces. "He lives across the golf course and up the hill from me," Luce said.

His preoccupation with politics could prevail even in his rare conversations with children, who usually baffled him. At a dinner party at the Clurmans' he talked with the hosts' bright young son Mike. "Who's President?" he asked. "Lyndon Johnson," Mike replied readily. "Who's Secretary of State?" The boy pondered but came up with the answer: "Dean Rusk." "Who is Secretary of Defense?" Serious thought, then: "Walter Cronkite." Mrs. Clurman thought it killing but Luce immediately lost interest and turned away deadpan, the boy having flunked the test. Among the Clurman guests were the Abba Ebans, the Theodore Whites, the Norman Podhoretzes and the playwright Edward Albee—an intellectual gathering so much to Luce's liking that he stayed until 2:30 A.M., at one point asking, "How can people drink so much and still keep going at parties?" He got Albee in a corner and grilled him for two hours with the usual district-attorney intensity, exhausting him. One of his questions was, "Why can't you write a play about an admirable subject? Why not a play about Paul Hoffman, for example?" Next day he sent Mrs. Clurman roses.

After the conventions, Luce seems to have kept silent about his own Presidential preference. Henry Luce III, who now headed Research and Development for Time Inc., felt that his father carefully avoided mentioning his choice out of consideration for Hedley Donovan, who as editor-in-chief would take a stand for Life, the only one of the original three magazines with an admitted editorial page. (It would be embarrassing for Donovan, one surmises, if Luce announced for candidate B first.)

One night when both Luces, father and son, were riding with their wives through Central Park on their way to the theater, Clare spoke enthusiastically of Goldwater and asked Hank Luce point-blank, "Who are you for?"

"I'm for Johnson," he replied. He was certain that his father maintained strict silence, and in fact he never did know how his father voted. Johnson continued to butter up Luce, having him to the White House for a private dinner. For all Luce's susceptibility to such attentions, and his gratitude for them, it is unimaginable that he forgot his life mission. Certainly he asked the President carefully and specifically about Southeast Asia. And certainly Johnson told him not a whit less—and probably much more—than he had told Henry Cabot Lodge shortly after Kennedy's murder: "I am not going to be the President who saw Southeast Asia go the way China went." For the Asian policies of Secretary Rusk, the disciple of Dulles, and the Whiz-Kid Secretary

McNamara, Luce could find no quarrel except that more beef was needed in Vietnam.

The Goldwater issue which so badly divided the Republican party also divided the Luce family. The political heavens fell as the once unbudgeably Republican New York Herald Tribune came out for Johnson and dropped Mrs. Luce's column, reportedly because of her enthusiasm for Goldwater. The switch of the Tribune, for which Luce had a WASPish esteem, certainly influenced him, as did the revolt of virtually the whole Eastern Republican establishment against Goldwater, and the latter's speeches, sometimes incoherent and sometimes reckless, hardly served his cause. The Goldwater charge that Johnson was "soft on Communism" was worthy of the Birchers, describing as it did a man whose Againstness was ironclad. There apparently were weeks of Lucean soul-searching. A two-part Life article putting Johnson's wealth at $14 million and showing clearly that political influence did no harm in its amassing, indicated the usual Republican loyalty running into August.

2. NAKED WOMEN ON DECK

It was at this very time that the Tonkin Gulf incident furnished the opportunity for Johnson to address the nation over television, to launch the first U.S. air attacks on North Vietnam, to get an almost unanimous if unintended Senate carte blanche for war and, not least, to make certain that Goldwater would be routed. Life and Time hailed both the bombing and the carte blanche. Until then the public interest in the Asian involvement had been marginal, confused and more worried than ardent. The Lucepress seemed to join the administration in regarding the nebulous nocturnal affray off the coast as something that could be inflated into the sinking-of-the-*Maine* kind of affront to the flag that would galvanize the nation into bellicosity. It appears that the Pentagon made use of the Lucepress, which seemed delighted at the arrangement. Life published an extravaganza headlined "From the Files of Naval Intelligence," which was "pieced together by Life correspondent Bill Wise with the help of U.S. Navy Intelligence and the Department of Defense." The story as Life pieced it together was colorful in the extreme and fit to arouse patriotic indignation. It showed the enemy PT boats coming recklessly at the American destroyers with searchlights ablaze, "peppering the ships" with 37-millimeter fire, "keeping heads on the U.S. craft low." The account, however, had a judicious smattering of official cables leaked to the Lucepress which supported the theme of unprovoked attack.

Time made American Admiral Ulysses S. Grant Sharp its cover-hero. It enveloped the Gulf affair, already enhanced by the imaginative touches of the administration, in some of its most fanciful prose:

> The night glowed eerily with the nightmarish glare of air-dropped flares and
> boats' searchlights. For 3½ hours the small boats attacked in pass after pass. Ten

enemy torpedoes sizzled through the water. Each time the skippers, tracking the fish by radar [*sic*], maneuvered to evade them. Gunfire and gun smells and shouts stung the air. Two of the enemy boats went down. Then, at 1:30 A.M., the remaining PTs ended the fight, roared off through the black night to the north.

As to the number of PT boats, Secretary McNamara had said, "It was a night attack. We can't be certain. . . . I would say between three and six boats were engaged in the attack . . ." Time, correcting the Secretary, said there were "at least six" of them. Afterward, the blunt Radarman James Stankevitz of the *Maddox*, who had witnessed the "battle," would refer to the Time-Life coverage with incredulity:

> I couldn't believe it, the way they blew that story out of proportion. It was something out of Male Magazine, the way they described that "battle." All we needed were naked women running up and down the deck. We were disgusted, because it just wasn't true.

Senator Morse would later denounce the Pentagon leaking of selective confidential information to Life, adding that Life was "gullible" in accepting it.° But since the Lucepress seemed at one with the administration in seeking to arouse public emotion, perhaps it was less "used" than given special favors. Time also trumpeted a fanfare for Johnson:

> [The bombing] won instantaneous, widespread support for the President . . . Editorial pages throughout the country blossomed with a rare chorus of approval. . . . At week's end the U.S. forces around the world stood alert. And behind them stood their nation.

Behind them also—and behind LBJ—stood Time Inc. The theory was that Luce no longer ordered but only gave suggestions to Donovan. In September, when Life forgot about the source of that $14 million and came out strongly for Johnson (who would be Time's next Man of the Year), there was a suspicion that Himself had made an emphatic suggestion to his editor-in-chief. By then the G.O.P. scow had sprung such fearful leaks that it was every man for himself and many respectable Republicans were jumping for their lives. The shock of this Lucean shift to a Democrat was diminished by the general panic. Other factors aside, the victory-loving Boss had no desire to commit his magazines to the support of the fellow in Davy Jones's locker, which seemed Goldwater's sure destination, and thus to lose all influence in the White House.

This was bad news to Clare, who was co-chairman of the National Citizens for Goldwater Committee and, along with other Republicans including Richard Nixon and Walter Judd, was named by Goldwater as timber for his Cabi-

---

° Joseph C. Goulden, author of *Truth Is the First Casualty*, which gives absorbing insights into the Tonkin Gulf affair, later solicited the Life correspondent Bill Wise's reaction to these opinions of Life's account, but got no response.

net. The warm praise for Johnson's policies in Time's weekly write-ups was diluted only by occasional digs at his corn pone style, which some believed to be inspired by the Iron Chancellor. Clare declared frankly that Goldwater was getting "brutally unfair" news treatment in Eastern publications including those of her husband—a statement that must have aroused mixed emotions in Adlai Stevenson and Estes Kefauver. She made no secret of the political schism in the family: "I think there's room for disagreement between Americans even if they're married."

Until this time, despite Tito and the growing signs of strain between the Soviet Union and Red China, the Lucepress had hewn to the dogma (which indeed it had pioneered) that Communism was a homogeneous and indissoluble world conspiracy. It was of course not only disloyal but politically inexpedient to question this dogma, as Chester Bowles and others had learned. Now the long quarrel between the two huge Communist states became violently public as Khrushchev and Mao traded insults. The exploded myth of monolithicity, though believed by some to dictate a change in American foreign policy based on the myth, was discovered by the administration and its supporters to make no real difference. It was perhaps human not to want to confess errors of such monstrous proportions, which might suggest that the American adventure in Vietnam was mistaken, especially when it was felt that more muscle there would quickly lay the specter of America's first lost war regardless of the logic of the war.

So, too, with that other myth, so long nurtured by Luce, that Chiang and his 14 million unhappy Formosans were China. The regard for Chiang as a world hero and great liberator, waiting only the right moment to cross to the mainland and take over, had been propagandized into American folklore. A few brave men including Senators Fulbright and Mansfield suggested that the Communist quarrel made imperative a whole new appraisal of policy, and the Saturday Evening Post even urged the recognition of Mao, but these voices were shouted down.

"It seemed to a few of us," said Old Timemployee, "that America's foreign policy was being dictated by Harry Luce, Dr. Schwarz, Mike Hammer and Chiang. But there weren't many of us left at Time who felt that way."

There was no sign that Luce's mind had been changed in any way by the Russo-Chinese split. Only a few weeks earlier, Life had reiterated the hardnosed Luce policy of offering to defend "freedom" anywhere (except in Taiwan) and had assailed de Gaulle for recognizing Mao, ending:

When France withdrew [from Indochina] in abject defeat ten years ago, it was the U.S. that kept the whole area from going Communist. Our policy has not failed and we should not act as though it had. On the contrary, we should seize this opportunity to reaffirm our position: that we are determined to defend any Southeast Asian nation which is willing to fight for its independence.

Time now declared it had known all along about Communist differences

("Contrary to its reputation, Communism has never been a 'monolith' ") and said the split really made no visible difference inasmuch as all Communism was evil anyway:

> All Communists, no matter of what stripe, will share the aim of defeating capitalism. . . . The West, which for many years underestimated the importance of the split, should not now overestimate it. . . . Obviously the West for the present has nothing to fear from the split, and perhaps something to gain. But just about the only sure thing is that the split, as such, will never solve the West's own problems, or preserve peace, or assure freedom.

Luce himself, in a speech in Dallas, condemned Senator Fulbright's "fantastic discourse on mythology" and Senator Mansfield's speech "suggesting, if we heard him correctly, that we should abandon Vietnam which happens now to be our main troublesome entanglement in the cause of human freedom." He touched on the recent death of General MacArthur, praising his doctrine of total victory in Korea and China: "If we had achieved victory, if we had properly defeated the Red Chinese, the state of the world would be different today."

It was his ordinarily hard-lining wife who uttered incredible words of appeasement. Speaking at St. John's University in Brooklyn, where she was awarded an honorary degree, Mrs. Luce actually proposed that the United States consider a thaw with Red China, telling the graduating class with great prescience:

> . . . [Y]our generation will know nothing but endless war in the Orient [unless tensions are relaxed]. . . . The ways of peace—aid and trade to the Chinese people—must be explored. . . . Let us be no less ready and no more afraid than our allies to discuss ways of relaxing tensions with Mao Tse-tung than with Khrushchev. As Sir Winston Churchill said, "Jaw, jaw, is better than war, war."

Was the lady reading someone else's script by error? True, she warned that America must be ready to use the "nuclear stick" (her own ghastly phrase) on Mao if necessary. "But since the Moscow-Peking split, there are other ways, which, combined with the stick, do offer hope of stopping Chinese expansion." She suggested a wheat sale to Peking similar to the wheat deal with Russia as a conciliating move toward "far hungrier and far more desperate people" than the Russians. And she made plain her awareness of the American anti-Communist religious absolutism: "Plainly, there are no votes to be got for the White House from saying this today. But it will have to be said after November."

She deserved credit not only for airing it before November but for squarely facing world events that forced her to alter previous judgments. Lightning and thunder may have accompanied her next meeting with her spouse, but party irregularity was a game that two could play and his failure to support Goldwater made him equally impeachable. Her speech made astonished

headlines, the Sacramento Bee, under the head, "Well, I'll Be——!" recalling her earlier bedrock allegiance to Chiang-as-China and saying it was "like the National Manufacturers' Association embracing Karl Marx." It was generally agreed that she had forfeited her post in Goldwater's Cabinet.

3. A HYPOTHETICAL QUESTION

In September 1964 Luce took off for Athens with Clare and her old friend Margaret Case to attend the wedding of twenty-four-year-old King Constantine to eighteen-year-old Princess Anne-Marie of Denmark. There had been an exchange of civilities—almost a reciprocal treaty—between the Greek royal family and the lord of Lucepress. In the previous year Luce had been named a commander in the Greek Royal Order of George I. Then Queen Frederika, mother of the groom-to-be, had arrived in America early in 1964 and had been Luce's guest not once but twice—once for luncheon in Time's Tower Suite where she (backed by several aides) was questioned very politely by Luce and his editors, again for dinner at the Union Club, with thirty-six guests seated according to protocol. Perhaps never did such a professed democrat as Luce so love royalty. The wedding also furnished an opportunity to get out of the country during the last weeks of the election campaign when otherwise his temptation to interfere with Donovan would be strong. He was trying very hard to let the young man think he was running things—so much so that when he wanted to see Donovan he walked over to his office instead of issuing the old imperial summons.

The reception at the Greek royal palace called for white tie and decorations. Among the many decorations Luce could wear were those from Nationalist China, Germany, the Netherlands, and the more recent Order of Dannebrog, rank of commander, awarded him by Denmark as "the man who has set the pattern for modern journalism"—an appraisal that unfortunately contained much truth.

After the wedding ceremony, attended also by six kings, five queens and more than a hundred princes and princesses, Luce separated from his wife and Miss Case and went on to make stops of several days each at Bangkok, Saigon and Hong Kong before making his usual pilgrimage to Taiwan. His age was now added to his prestige as a reason for being met at airports by Time's highest-ranking local man, who took care of all problems including that insoluble problem of answering the many Luce questions. In Hong Kong he met his son Hank and the latter's wife, who accompanied him to Taiwan.

The moment Luce set foot on the island he was enveloped in the kind of reverential regard that might be accorded some visiting deity who could, according to his whim, inflict woe or bring happiness to Taiwan, which was a fairly accurate definition of his status. His meeting with Chiang Kai-shek—their last on this earth—was an occasion for all the pomp and splendor the

451

Gimo and Madame could amass for their greatest American friend and bene-factor. It was a meeting of two old men aged sixty-six and seventy-eight who gravely repeated to each other a fable that had long since lost meaning al-though neither of them was ready to say so. The old toast, "Back to the main-land!" was still being drunk with a shout, but the shout was a hollow one now. There was tragedy in both of them, the tragedy of men whose powerful ambi-tion had whipped them on but had tricked them out of the prize, the prize being, in Luce's terms, a Christian, Americanized China. Each had had to set-tle for something less—Chiang for Taiwan, where he luxuriated on American millions, Luce for Time Inc. and his war in Southeast Asia.

The idea of Chiang daring to cross to the mainland and pitting his forces against the regimented millions of Mao had long been absurd. Luce at last re-alized that it was absurd and was trying to adjust to the knowledge.

He stayed at the jade-encrusted imperial suite of the Grand Hotel. He was given a golden key to Taipei. He was given a Nationalist major general and rear admiral as escorts in journeys out of the city. When the Chiang-con-trolled newspapers China Post and China News tried to worm from him a promise of American support for that delightful reverie, an invasion of the mainland, he dodged them as best he could. The question, he said, was "hy-pothetical," a nice way of saying that no invasion seemed imminent or likely. He did assure his interviewers that "the prevailing attitude of the American people is pro-Republic of China and anti-Chinese Communists." The China Post cornered him with questions to which his cautious answers enabled them by dint of a little twisting to compose a headline: "Large-Scale Anti-Peiping Revolt May Bring U.S. Support, Says Luce." They did not make a headline of his most pertinent remark about the question's speculative nature: "You are not attacking the mainland tomorrow."

He called on Vice Admiral William E. Gentner, boss of the U.S. Taiwan Defense Command. He visited the $150,000 Luce Memorial Chapel at Chris-tian Tunghai University, erected in memory of his father—the Luce family's answer to the Communization of Yenching University in Peking. He in-spected the Chiang military establishment, surely aware that 80 percent of the American-subsidized Taiwan budget went to support the army.

Later, in Tokyo, he told the Foreign Correspondents' Club that the Japa-nese had tended to de-emphasize the word "Communist" when speaking of China, regarding it merely as the old China going through a dynastic change. On the contrary, he said, the central fact was that China was Communist "and something had to be done about it."

Next stop Seattle, and then New York in time to vote for whomever he voted for and see the Goldwater scow sink without a trace. In December he was back in San Francisco with Clare to take part in a televised panel discus-sion of China at the University of California. Here Clare repeated her belief that "We must soon find ways of living at peace with half the human race," but said "tragedy" would result if the UN admitted Peking and expelled Tai-

wan. Luce, seeming to forget his predilection for freedom, described Taiwan as "one of the best governed countries in the world today," remarked on its prosperity and added, "The island of Quemoy is to Asia what Berlin is to Europe." He drew a surprise attack from another panelist, Felix Greene, a British China-watcher and author of books on the Mao regime. His most recent book, *A Curtain of Ignorance*, blamed the American press for giving a totally biased and inaccurate picture of Red China.

"American newspapers and news magazines are responsible for the American public being uninformed on what is really going on inside Communist China," he said, and he turned to Luce. "There are no publications which have done more damage in American-Chinese relations than those of the gentleman now on this stage. . . . Western embassies in Peking hand around the latest copies of Time and Life to see the extraordinary things said about the country."

Luce, apt to sputter under the best of circumstances, made inarticulate sounds. Clare came to his defense, saying that he was born in China and had traveled widely there. The audience consisted of about a thousand people with a special interest in and some knowledge of American-Asian relations and of American reporting on the subject. "This spirited argument took center of the stage for a time," said one account, "and brought vigorous audience reaction—with loud and prolonged applause when Greene accused the Luce publications of being at the top of the list of distorters." "[Luce's] face was flushed, he was trembling, and his prominent dark eyebrows bristled in agitation." He offered to debate Greene elsewhere, saying he had not come prepared for "this kind of attack," adding when he was interviewed later, still furious: "I consider this an attack on myself. I am responsible for my magazines in a great measure and any attack on them is an attack on me."

That was true indeed. This was apparently the first and only time Luce was confronted publicly about the distortions of his publications. He had been so eternally praised—the Auspicious Stars, the dozen-odd honorary degrees, the medals, the congratulatory anniversary remarks by the Vice President and the Secretary of State, the invitations to the White House—that the net effect was an official and public installation of him and his journalism as American institutions.

A critic of a different kind, from within the organization, was young Andrew Kopkind, a correspondent in Time's Los Angeles bureau. He discovered that reporting was his lesser function: "First of all, I was a drummer for the largest, most powerful publishing corporation in the world." It was his opinion that the gulf most Time editorial people thought existed between them and the corporate side was fictitious, "only in their minds":

> They are company men as surely as any ad salesman. They function not as independent journalists but as operatives of an institution which is not primarily journalistic. . . . A Time reporter might as well be a junior executive at Hunt Foods or Unilever: all corporate conglomerates are essentially the same.

Luce had been frank about the writer-salesman role in a famous policy memo more than a quarter-century earlier:

> . . . [E]very single writer and every single researcher is directly in the business of trying to sell magazines. . . . Any writer who is not enthusiastic about the job of increasing our circulation *by his own writing* is here on a misunderstanding. . . . As our overhead has increased (largely in efforts to improve our products) we require more advertising than formerly to break even. . . .

His use of the word "products" to describe Time, Life and Fortune was indicative of his business orientation. The Timewriter created a news product slanted to draw the advertiser and *his* product. Time's extensive and admiring weekly Business coverage had given it a heavy readership in the paneled offices, and the frequent canonization of businessmen on the cover had entrepreneurs at all levels yearning for similar attention. To appear on the cover was the ultimate triumph of tycoonship both in prestige and profit. Even the nonconformist Cleveland industrialist Cyrus Eaton agreed that one's portrait there was priceless "but if it could be bought it would cost $20 million."

Kopkind noted that the bureau chief in Los Angeles, as elsewhere, was Time's ambassador not only to news sources but to the business and cultural power centers which generated ads. Entertaining tycoons was such an important part of his mission that—as with bureau chiefs elsewhere—he was given an enormous expense account and a residence of a grandeur appropriate for these gatherings. He was himself, as Time's ambassador, a great man. Kopkind was astonished when, as a mere beginner in L.A., he telephoned the eminent merchandising magnate Edward Carter to check a detail about his business dealings. Expecting to get the information from a subordinate, he found Carter himself on the wire saying he would come right over. "He was in my office in a flash," Kopkind recalled, unaware of the reason until an older hand told him that Carter had long hoped for immortalization on Time's cover.

The cover story about business people, or civic leaders close to business people, or politicians favorable to business people, worked merchandising wonders at the same time that it advanced the Luce precept of free enterprise:

> Over the years, coverboys and girls represent those interests with which Time Inc. will associate itself. On the simplest level, the subjects help provide advertising . . . But beyond that, they are tied into the same elite establishments as Time, and mutual back-scratching is the rule of that club.

To handle a cover story, which was done with the aid of a battery of bureau people and researchers, was a mark of prestige to a Timan, who would have a reproduction of that cover framed and hung in his office as a badge of achievement. Writers wore their cover stories as a colonel wore his battle ribbons. The man with a half-dozen or more "covers" to his credit took on heroic dimensions and was rewarded with pay hikes. This was encouraged by Luce and had long been a part of the fierce competition in the organization.

The technique of the Goodie cover (as opposed to the less frequent Baddie cover often featuring some Communist or neutral leader) was to give an impression of thorough study lightened with wit, to throw in a couple of minor depreciations (ill-tempered in the morning, roasts his subordinates) to prove Time's objectivity, and to wind up with a story making the subject feel warm all over. To this was often added the ceremony of presenting the original cover portrait to the subject, warming him a second time. Luce himself had made this presentation in the cases of such important people as Presidents Truman, Eisenhower and Kennedy, and Time executives were called on to do the honors in other cases where prestige and advertising revenue was involved.

Some Time covers featured Time advertisers with a self-propelling effect, such as Norton Hunt ("the corporate Cézanne"); Lammot du Pont Copeland, described as an American Bourbon employing fourteen gardeners and "a French chef who came to him from Lord Astor"; Lee Iococca of Ford ("hottest young man in Detroit . . . most ingenious merchandising expert . . . fertile brains"); and Conrad Hilton (" 'These hotels are examples of free enterprise that the Communists hate to see' "). It was otherwise with Mrs. Norman Otis Chandler, wife of the owner of the Los Angeles Times and also a state-university regent and the driving force in the fund-raising for and founding of the Los Angeles Music Center. Editor-in-Chief Donovan, Managing Editor Fuerbringer and their wives flew out to present her with her cover portrait, to accompany her to the full-dress opening of the Center, to announce a huge Time Inc. gift to the Center and to be photographed and publicized with Mrs. Chandler and other important Angelenos. This was part of the "mutual back-scratching" in the elite establishment which was "not primarily journalistic" and which brought in advertising revenue just as surely as if the lady dealt in canned goods. Kopkind, after three years as a Timan, rejected Parkinson's Corollary. Deciding that Time was so powerful as to "produce mass ideological manipulation, create worthless demand, and impose a whole range of values which are important to the interests of the corporation but destructive of the individual," he joined one of America's most select minorities. He quit.

XXXIV

1. THE EAGLE-SCOUT ESCALATION

The only standard by which a sound foreign policy must be informed is not moral and philosophical opposition to Communism as such, but the bearing a particular Communism in a particular country has upon the interests of the United States.

—*Hans J. Morgenthau*

The ideals of the still lusty China Lobby had an airing when Luce gave a dinner to honor Dr. Tingfu S. Tsiang, now Chiang's ambassador in Washington. Dr. Tsiang was the man who had hired the Hamilton Wright Organization to puff Chiang in America. Neither Luce nor Dr. Tsiang had much to complain about in the new President. Johnson's policies were satisfactory enough so that Luce was reported to have stocked his own bar with Cutty Sark Scotch because that was the brand served in the White House and "If it's good enough for Lyndon Johnson it's good enough for me."

Johnson, though still too hesitant about Vietnam for Luce's taste, was a more instinctive anti-Communist than Kennedy. His can-do success in manipulating a Congress which had often thwarted his predecessor was impressive, and his confidence that America could handle foreign war and domestic reform simultaneously was an echo of Luce's feeling of national invincibility. Indeed, Johnson had brought Luce to the realization that there actually was poverty in the country, and Luce was as anxious to snuff it out and create a "Great Society" as he was. Johnson's care in catering to Luce's vanity was as thoroughgoing as Luce's buttering of cover-heroes such as Hilton, Copeland and Iococca. The President's roughshod invasion of the Dominican Republic to forestall a "Communist takeover" warmed Luce's heart ("L.B.J. Was on Top of the Crisis," headlined Life) and occasioned some of the viciously

456

fictional and misleading "reporting" characteristic of Time in such circumstances. The Weekly Newsmagazine, which at times could express such fear of the enveloping enemy, occasionally took the opposite line as if to buck up the timorous:

> Everyone knows—or should—that the U.S., with its nuclear arsenal, is the mightiest nation in human history. But few people really realize the staggering dimensions of that might. . . . the destructive power possessed by the U.S. simply beggars imagination. . . . The U.S. is vastly superior to the Soviet Union in its nuclear arsenal, and it is increasing its lead every day. . . . The U.S. has nuclear weapons scattered and hidden all over the Western world. Thus, thousands of missiles and planes would definitely survive any conceivable atomic attack by the Soviets and could strike back with a barrage of missiles and bombs that could obliterate Russia or Red China.

The Lucepress threw itself bodily into the Vietnam war which a substantial part of America (including two hundred Yale professors) wanted to stop, joining the Boss in popularizing the term "isolationist" for those who preferred more constructive American activities abroad. A fortnight before the U.S. Air Force began "retaliatory" bombings in North Vietnam, he took to television to advocate such bombing in order to stop North Vietnamese aid to the Vietcong. This was two days before he addressed the annual Presbyterian Churchmen's Dinner in Washington about God and history. Admittedly it was impossible to bomb stray coolies coming down the Ho Chi Minh Trail, he said, but there were other ways to discourage that aid:

> . . . [I]n so far as we see this aid coming, we will, to use other words, "punish" by specific destruction of oil tanks and bridges and so on. . . . "Escalation" has been established in our language pretty much as a very bad word. As if you might stop a little street brawl and the next thing you know you have got atomic war. Well, this is not necessarily the meaning of escalation at all. There is a good side of escalation, too, which is you can step up your activities point by point as far as you want and then you can quit when the price gets too high. [Asked about Walter Lippmann's opinion that "We have overextended ourselves, made too many commitments in soft areas where we have no vital interests. South Vietnam is one," he replied:] Well, I think it very regrettable that Mr. Lippmann and people like that should pick up this point of view. Now the justification is something called "national interest." Well, national interest is always the phrase that isolationists or neo-isolationists hide behind. . . . I should say the national interest of the United States in this century has been and is to have a world in which we can continue development of our lives, and we cannot live in any Fortress America . . .

When the President ordered the bombing of the North after the raid on Pleiku, the decision "has served to recommit us deeply in Vietnam," said Life, "and it is a commitment that must be carried through without hesitation or confusion of purpose." It was not of course generally known at the time that leading figures in the administration had advocated a covert policy of provo-

cation in North Vietnam and that the "retaliatory" raids had been long planned. But it was already evident that the administration was being anything but candid with the public. Time, feeling that the government had been excessively patient with the enemy, thought that the restrained bombing was better than none at all, commenting, "After nothing, something. It was a long time coming." It told of "predictable" Communist protests and attacks on American embassies in various countries, and devoted an admiring cover story to General William Westmoreland, who had, it said, got his start as an Eagle Scout:

> A lean, greying six-footer . . . A bird colonel at 30 . . . the youngest major general in the Army in 1956 . . . leads by asking much of his men—and by asking even more of himself. "He's been trying to wring the 25th hour of the day out of my hide since he arrived," says one staff officer [not named]. . . . He usually works a 12-hour day. . . . "He's already been in every paddyfield in Vietnam," said an aide [also unidentified]. . . .

Millions of Americans who thought that in voting for Johnson they had voted against paddyfield-occupation, protested. The Lucepress replied with five steady propaganda points:

1. America's mission of "freedom" in Asia.
2. The villainy and perfidy of the Communist enemy.
3. The folly of statesmen such as de Gaulle, Prime Minister Harold Wilson, and U Thant, who sought to mediate.
4. The heroic dimensions of the warmakers—Johnson, Rusk, McNamara *et al.*
5. The ignorance and lack of patriotism of citizens opposing the war.

Life criticized de Gaulle's "meddling," praised America's "increased pressure" and military "beefing up" and defended the administration against intellectual war critics including two former Timen, Archibald MacLeish and John Hersey, accusing them of using "irrelevant and emotional" arguments. In a line that should have been writ large for later study, it also charged them with lack of faith: ". . . ugliest of all, they regularly imply that the Administration is withholding facts—or engaged in outright lying." Life applauded the dispatch of more troops to Vietnam and urged that they stop merely "helping" the Vietnamese and "accept more command responsibility." It attacked the "defeatist" theory that America might get "bogged down" in Vietnam, cheered the increase to 100,000 American soldiers stationed in that country and declared that Vietcong casualties were "nearly six times" ours.

The Lucepress seldom granted opponents of the war the status of patriotic and responsible citizens of a democracy but put them in categories of reprehension similar in method if not as reckless as the late Senator McCarthy. The term for them ranged from the mildness of *defeatists* to the more abrasive

Vietniks, peaceniks and *quitniks.* The term *isolationist* took on connotations of appeasement and disloyalty as well as ignorance or refusal to face the facts of global life. The quitniks and isolationists were regularly reminded that they furnished aid and comfort to the enemy. Time featured and praised McGeorge Bundy's arrogant reply to a letter from 127 professors at Washington University in St. Louis asking what American war aims were. According to Time's cover story, the Yaleman and Bonesman Bundy was illustrious:

> . . . [S]olid-gold credentials. A *summa cum laude* Yale graduate. . . . intelligent to the point of intimidation. . . . mother is related to the Lowells. . . . keen appreciation of the legitimate uses of power . . . accustomed to authority. . . . fine administrator. . . . works 12-hour days. . . . bolts his four-minute eggs. . . . from the first, he was in the thick of it. . . . awareness of the "reality of Communism."

Time heroes invariably worked at least a twelve-hour day. The Bundy story was headed "The Use of Power With a Passion for Peace," a semantic peculiarity coming directly from Luce, who used it constantly. The credibility gap was widening between the administration and the Lucepress on one hand and a majority of the academic community and the young people on the other, the latter group generally believing with Orwell that war was war and peace was peace and that the tendency to call war "peace" could be misleading. Perhaps this feeling motivated three Cornell University students to place a large poster on the Luce grounds at Ridgefield, reading, "Kill Luce . . . Our Country is Wrong Wrong Wrong"—an offense for which Luce declined to prosecute them.

". . . [T]he message of Christianity today," Luce told the churchmen in Washington, "must begin with the news that God lives and rules." He told the Memphis Bar Association, urging them to join his crusade for the international rule of law, "The predominant desire of the people and the government of the United States is Peace." But as he saw it, America had saved Europe from military and economic disaster and become the leader of the West. Now it was America's duty to modernize, legalize, democratize and technocratize the East whether the inhabitants liked it or not. "It is the West which must speak to the East out of our complex experience and faith," he told the Commonwealth Club in San Francisco. ". . . Prometheus stands for progress— onward and upward, from the dung heap to the stars! The Oriental idea is more nearly one of endless cycles of recurrence. . . . there is another thing— and, of course, I mean something fundamental—which has developed in the West and not in the East. That, quite simply, is law. There were no lawyers in India until the British came. . . . There is not a single lawyer in China today—and there never was. They had magistrates in China—and now commissars."

Echoes of Kipling often rang in his advocacy of American justice for the poet's "lesser breeds without the law." ". . . [I]t is by persistent appeal to

Law that we can most effectively confound our enemies," he declared. But he was incorrigible in his use of value judgments even in interpreting the law. He had condemned such obvious Communist violations of international law as those in Berlin and Hungary. He had backed the three prime examples of American violation (as seen by the specialist in international law, Arthur Larson), the Bay of Pigs, the Dominican intervention and Vietnam. The replacement of all commissars by lawyers was a large order, and Luce's "world peace through law" concept seemed a distant prospect visible only across rivers of the kind of blood being shed in Vietnam. Meanwhile, Time urged that America must not be intimidated by the possible intervention of Red China, saying, ". . . [I]f the U.S. backed away from the threat of Chinese intervention, it would lend powerful support to the untested notion that China is invincible." And Luce had an enthusiastic supporter in his friend, Secretary of State Rusk, who said that America's goal was simply worldwide democracy—"victory for all mankind . . . a worldwide victory for freedom."

The Lucepress, not visibly offended by the Christian use of napalm and anti-personnel horrors such as Bull-Pups, showed bursting pride in American firepower and technological ability to level forests and lay a blight on a green land in a Time cover story confidently titled, "The Turning Point in Vietnam," celebrating the big build-up of troops there:

> Today South Vietnam throbs with a pride and power, above all an *esprit.* . . . The remarkable turnabout in the war is the result of one of the swiftest, biggest military buildups in the history of warfare. Everywhere today South Vietnam bristles with the U.S. presence. Bulldozers by the hundreds carve sandy shore into vast plateaus for tent cities and airstrips. Howitzers and trucks grind through the once-empty green highlands. Wave upon wave of combat-booted Americans—lean, laconic and looking for a fight—pour ashore from armadas of troopships. Day and night, screaming jets and helicopters seek out the enemy . . . The Vietcong's once-cocky hunters have become the cowering hunted . . . the cutting edge of U.S. fire power slashes into the thickets of Communist strength. . . . Target by next summer: 280,000 [Americans in Vietnam]. . . . the largest concentration of fighting men and machinery in Southeast Asia since the French left. . . . The enemy now faces an irrevocable U.S. commitment . . . Saigon of late has had a spring in the step and a sparkle in the eye missing for years. . . . The U.S. has picked up the gauntlet. . . .

While Time grumbled that Johnson had been slow about all this ("it was almost a classic case of too little too late"), it praised him for coming around and ventured some pronouncements that would later be questioned:

"Vast, U.S.-banked civilian-aid programs are aimed at eradicating the ancient ills of disease, illiteracy and hunger."

"The U.S. presence will . . . have a beneficent impact on the countries involved."

". . . [T]here had been in the past year no fewer than 225 [American peace] negotiating approaches to Hanoi [all rejected] . . ."

"It is the Communists themselves who risk being bogged down in wars that they can neither afford nor end."

2. I'M FROM OSKALOOSA

"Do you like hearing about it when a sermon's good?" Luce asked Dr. Read as he commended his Sunday effort. "I know I like it when people say Time is good." Once in Phoenix, having heard that Dr. Read had preached about the serpent on the rock, Luce telephoned him asking eagerly that he send a copy. The verse in Proverbs commenting on four wondrous things read: "The way of an eagle in the air; the way of a serpent upon a rock; the way of a ship in the midst of the sea; and the way of a man with a maid." The eagle would surely be America, and one hardly need guess what the serpent was in Luce's mind, however he disposed of the ship at sea and the man and maid.

The Luces had sold their Ridgefield place, quitting Connecticut at last. Luce still gave about three-quarters of his time to his publications in what he called his retirement—a term which was correct in a way, as was remarked in the T-L Building, because he had previously given far more than 100 percent. He played golf, usually alone, at the Biltmore course in Phoenix, seldom breaking 50 for nine holes. A later golfer came along and discovered that the rigors of one of the most difficult sand traps had been eliminated with hard-packed sand which permitted a player to putt out of it instead of facing the tricky ordeal of blasting out.

"That's one of Mr. Luce's traps," the caddie explained, telling how Luce would burst into flame when his approach lit in a trap. ". . . He'd collar the course superintendent and demand—demand—that the offending sand trap either be filled in or else be made shallow and saucer-shaped so he could putt out of it the next time."

In Arizona he thought he found a "different kind of American." By and large he did find a more reactionary kind in this playground of the rich where, unlike the East, the prosperous were almost unanimously conservative. He stopped taking the airmailed New York Times, saying it was too expensive and it bored him. He turned to the local Arizona Republic whose far-right politics and more simplistic news treatment were more to his liking. He was a friend (in the usual Lucean sense of exchanging visits and being on amiable speaking terms) of its publisher, Eugene Pulliam, son of a Methodist clergyman and a staunch McCarthyite in his day. The Republic had attacked Life for its slighting remarks about Dr. Schwarz in Los Angeles but had extended forgiveness when C. D. Jackson made his public apology.

Clare, the swimmer who loved the sea, would have preferred a home in Hawaii. But they stayed several months a year in Phoenix, showing who was boss in that category and who had to get to Rockefeller Center in five jet

hours. Both were chainsmokers who thought of quitting but never did. While each had the prickly personality often found in highly gifted, tense and ego-centric people, Luce was the one with the volatile temper, Clare the one who (as her friends the Bentons and others felt sure) could have cut him to ribbons with deft verbal daggers any time she chose. Once while Roy Alexander vis-ited them in Phoenix, Luce exploded when she suggested getting a moder-ately expensive sprinkler system for the lawn. At times he was a nickel-nurser, refusing to authorize funds for new drapes, leaving ten-cent tips, refusing to replace his ten-year-old Chrysler. Phoenix, which had its full complement of remarkable people, recognized in the Luce couple the rarest birds of them all, a pair who had to be taken as they came. Many of those able to adjust to their imperial attitudes admired them wholeheartedly, while not a few cordially disliked them. One of the difficulties was to get a word in with either of them. The press carried occasional squibs about them, one concerning a jest said to have been made by Walter Hoving of Tiffany's. Picking up an incredibly ex-pensive vermeil cactus at his store, he said, "Henry Luce gave two of these to Clare for their house in Arizona as an anniversary gift, and I couldn't figure out whether it was because it was Arizona or because it was Clare."

That problem of the rich—especially the rich Luces—the servant problem, continued to haunt them in Phoenix as it had everywhere except in Italy. There was a quick turnover except for the indispensable chauffeur-handy-man, Arthur Little, who had been with them since 1950. Since all household bills were paid through an office in the T-L Building 3000 miles away, Phoe-nix tradespeople and household help of the Luces often had to wait for their money. As Mrs. Luce's most recent biographer, Stephen Shadegg, put it, "Like many other very wealthy people the Luces never seemed to understand that if the extra gardener hired for some seasonal work didn't collect his money at the end of the week he and his family might go hungry."

Most friends felt that the Luces, after their share of the kind of marital difficulties usually experienced by people of decided character and con-viction, were happier than they ever had been. Or the friends might amend that by saying that they were less mutually schismatic than they had been. Luce occasionally went to Mass with Clare. He gave more and more daily at-tention to his Bible. Whatever flirtations and affairs with other women which he had once indulged seemed ended. Clare wrote her monthly column for McCall's, pampered a pet myna bird and worked with skill in her magnificent studio building behind the house, at painting and mosaics. Whatever she turned her hand to, she did with some distinction. Her memory portrait of her late father showed him with a violin tucked under his chin. One she painted of Luce exhibited dewlaps he swore were exaggerated. He often read to her—anything from a whodunit to Teilhard de Chardin. The couple watched the Perry Mason series on television and occasionally saw movies. They led a busy social life, maintaining at least three separate circles of friends—the bridge players, the art-and-theater lovers and the strictly "society" group of wealth

and station. Luce, still capable of hatching stimulating ideas, could also be deadly dull when he seized on a subject in his staccato series of unfinished sentences and continued to worry it long after he had talked it into the ground. Clare sometimes openly showed her boredom, fetching her needlework and yawning over it.

Luce was hospitable to visitors in Phoenix who enunciated his own conservative beliefs. Dr. Edward Teller was a Luce house guest when he gave an interview attacking the weakness in national military security. Luce was a sponsor of a Phoenix speech by Foreign Minister Thanat Khoman of Thailand, whom he had met in Bangkok. Thanat lauded the American intervention in Vietnam, warned of "the lesson of Munich" and was praised by the local Republic as "the authentic voice of Asia." Luce inevitably was struck by qualities of greatness in Thanat, whom Fortune soon ranked with Chiang, Syngman Rhee, Diem and Magsaysay as "an unswerving anti-Communist." Now and then Luce would meet with Father Murray either in Phoenix or New York, and their firm agreement in God's immanence in the American nation's founding and continuance would serve as a starting point for the hot debate they both enjoyed.

Well before the hallucinogenic drug LSD hit the headlines, Luce was interested. One Luce house guest was Dr. Sidney Cohen of Los Angeles, who had been studying the effect of LSD on actors and other creative people. The Luces took a "trip" under Cohen's guidance. Clare reported an enhanced appreciation of colors in her paintings, while the tone-deaf Luce heard music so bewitching that he walked out into the cactus garden and conducted a phantom orchestra. He also discovered that ordinary objects such as tableware took on new dimensions of beauty. Although the Luces apparently repeated the experiment several times later, they were fortunate in having had no bad trips. Luce in fact was so impressed that he turned up in New York to present the managing editors of Time, Life and Fortune with copies of a book on psychedelic drugs along with an enthusiastic talk about the subject's story possibilities—a suggestion quickly adopted by Time and Life, the latter being the first "family" magazine to cover it. Dr. Timothy Leary, the high priest of LSD, later mentioned the Cohen-Luce experiments on a radio talk show in which he defended the drug, saying, "[Dr. Cohen has] turned on Henry Luce, he's turned on Clare Boothe Luce, he's turned on a dozen movie actors I could name. Now, why does Dr. Cohen do this, if this drug is so terrible?"

Visiting Yale in April 1966, Luce held a press conference in the handsome Yale Daily News building which was a memorial to Hadden, and criticized the earlier American correspondents in Saigon for being "excessively 'anti' the government of the day." Many Yalemen, strongly against the war, regarded him as a primordial specimen, but nevertheless he was Yale 1920 and was treated with respect. In response to that inevitable question which always had a little edge to it—was not Time as much opinion as it was fact?—he had a somewhat different answer:

"If you read a column by Reston you know you're reading Reston. . . . If you read Time you know you're reading Time."

It was a great disappointment that he had never made the Yale Corporation, but other honors kept pouring in. He accepted all comers. Williams College conferred on him an honorary doctorate of laws, which perhaps signified recognition of his continuing campaign for the "rule of law" rather than his journalism. The Honolulu Press Club honored him for "outstanding service in communications." The Magazine Publishers Association, an unexceptionably capitalist group, gave him its award for "outstanding contributions to the publishing industry," a citation whose meaning could better be understood when it was known that the previous recipient was DeWitt Wallace of Reader's Digest.

More astonishing was the Syracuse University School of Journalism's presentation to Luce of its Distinguished Service Medal. This was the first time that an institution of such size, purporting to embrace in its faculty not only an understanding but a vigilant defense of the standards of a free press, had exalted the value judgment and the gimmick. The hundreds of students witnessing the ceremony, many of whom would become teachers themselves, would presumably draw the appropriate conclusions and carry the torch of learning in the same direction.

When the Saturday Evening Post published a lively profile of Luce by John Kobler, and quoted his oft-repeated lament about having no American hometown: "I would give anything if I could say simply and casually, [I'm from] Oskaloosa, Iowa," Oskaloosa leaped to attention. Mayor Charles Russell telephoned Luce to offer him honorary citizenship. Luce, dearly loving something new and different (and loving to be fussed over), traveled to Oskaloosa to accept it and to speak at the commencement at the Quaker institution there, William Penn College. He mingled with the townspeople, chatted with them and was perfectly charming. At the commencement he told his audience that "we have to stick with this struggle [in Vietnam]," and attacked an idea taken up by more and more young people and expressed in their music, that American life was shabby and futile. This kind of thinking puzzled and alarmed him, suggesting as it did a lack of respect for the institutions and ideals for which he had fought all his life and had never questioned. Building a better society was only one of the things that could prove life's significance, he said, adding his own bred-in-the-bone belief: "Meaning was built into life in the beginning by the Creator and that meaning will endure to the end of time . . ."

3. THE REAL ENEMY IS CHINA

As the Lucepress continued its bowdlerized coverage of the war by new men in Saigon painfully aware that they must never be defeatist, Halberstam

was sending "defeatist" dispatches to the Times. Although even the Times was a trifle intimidated by the administration-and-Lucepress hostility to anything but encouraging news out of Vietnam—to purvey non-encouraging news was felt to imply dubious Againstness—the Times bucked itself up and printed the Halberstam dispatches and those of his successors on the front page instead of punishing the authors.

No slide rule could measure the effect of the Lucepressure on the continuous enlargement of the war. It was of course enormous, not only because it was again without compensating propaganda on the other side but because it was working with an administration which itself was steadily deceiving the public. Its endless propaganda affected Americans from LBJ down to humble voters in all regions. The gratification of the President and his subsidiary war makers at the applause of the Lucepress and its now 50 million weekly readers, as well as their recoil from the Lucepress's vigorous attack on any sign of weakening of the war-making will, can be imagined but not precisely weighed. Similarly, the Lucepress effect on the Senatorial questioners and opponents of the war can only be estimated. Their knowledge that their views would be presented in a manner subjecting them to contempt or ridicule could hardly have failed to make them more cautious in their criticisms and to silence them entirely on some points which they would otherwise have aired. This Lucepress ridicule must have intimidated into total silence many less courageous legislators who otherwise would have come to the support of the war-questioners. If men in Congress failed of re-election (as Senator Morse would, in part because of his opposition to the war), their ideals were of little use to the country. Wherever a hawk opposed a dove for election, the Lucepress became a useful campaign weapon in heaping contempt on the dove. Morse's ultimate defeat in Oregon was a warning of what happened to doves. The Lucepress effect in intimidating and delaying the growing public protest against the war must have been as powerful, since the identification of the war with patriotism, morality, religion and the rule of law would have its effect on those anxious not to be considered unpatriotic, immoral, irreligious or scofflaw.

In all of these ways the thought-shaping power of the Lucepress, so determined in urging the war in the first place, helped to escalate it and continue it up to the time, many years later, when it became evident to the more responsible politicians, Republican as well as Democratic, that it was a military as well as a political, economic, moral and religious disaster. How much military and civilian death and misery, how much devastation and hatred in Asia, could be laid to the value judgments? How much of the cost to America in its staggering decay of democracy, law, national unity and spirit?

No one would ever be able to answer. One has a mental picture of Luce, erect, tough, still certain of God-Agreement, flying in from Phoenix to commune with Donovan, with Fuerbringer, with other editors, about the war. Not until after he died would the Lucepress change its front diametrically,

oppose the war, and Donovan, in a belated turnabout, would admit to some error.

Now, the Lucepress shored up Johnson when his martial resolution seemed to waver. The country was in wonderful shape, said Time—"The economy is not only good but sensational . . ." Time assured the consensus-conscious President that public-opinion polls were behind him and the war. Time dramatized a Johnson so earnest in his effort to do good that his decisions came only after "interminable hours of anxious, even anguished debate." Life pictured Johnson in all his moods, and Time put him on the cover three more times in the space of fifteen months. Time interpreted the American bombing pause as a chivalric move for peace: "Never before in the 20th century has a major nation committed itself to war and then unilaterally limited its warmaking potential in hopes of negotiating a peaceful settlement." Yet "the Administration's peace offensive had yielded nothing but insults from Hanoi," and Johnson left himself open to grave censure "if it became apparent that the suspension of the air strikes against the North had endangered the success of the war," or persuaded "Hanoi and Peking that Americans have no heart for a difficult defensive [*sic*] war in Asia." Time let Hanoi have it straight:

> If it [the "peace offensive"] should fail, the burden of blame will irrevocably rest where it has always belonged—upon the heads of the Communist aggressors, for all the world to see. Then, having tried everything in every possible place, and having enlisted every nation and office that might help in the cause of peace, the U.S. can resume reluctantly—but with clear conscience—the unwelcome and unwanted prosecution of the war.

Time warned against "the trap of seeking a negotiated settlement from a position of weakness." It had long since published a Chapin diagram showing the countries of Southeast Asia as dominoes and how they would fall. It quoted Richard Nixon, now a New York lawyer, as denouncing those who wanted to "turn the Vietnamese people over to the Communists." Time, noting America's lack of home-front fervor for the war, seemed anxious to whip up a bit of it by plugging Red China's "scorn" for the United States as a "paper tiger" and belief that Americans were "incapable of combat under such [Asian] conditions." And once again, Time was ready to take on China itself—evidently an eventuality always in Luce's thoughts. The Weekly Newsmagazine deprecated the administration's feeling of "mortal peril" in the possibility of "a confrontation with Communist China." This, Time said, was an error that had come to "afflict even General Douglas MacArthur, the old hero of Inchon and champion of crossing the Yalu, who in his declining years warned Johnson never to get involved in a war on the mainland of Asia." This advice of a hero in his dotage should not be taken too seriously, Time suggested, saying that America should be alert for favorable circumstances for war with China. Under the heading, "We Will Be Far Better Off Facing the Issue," it said:

466

. . . [T]here can be no doubt whatever that China is the real enemy in Asia and the greatest threat anywhere to world peace [*sic*]. And there is room for argument that a more positive U.S. military policy toward Vietnam would be to risk a confrontation with China in the right place at the right time. . . . [T]o maintain its position in Southeast Asia, and ultimately perhaps in all Asia, the U.S. may sooner or later have to take the risk of war with China . . .

But China was still in the background, Vietnam the immediate problem. Life joined in a procession of pictorial tributes to the American presence there, emphasized the enemy's contemptuous repulse of peace proposals and attacked the "annoying clamor" of anti-war demonstrations by American "Vietniks" which it said aided world Communism and could prolong the war, and returned to the theme of the moral elevation of American war aims:

. . . [I]t is wiser and takes less bloodshed to stop a bid for world tyranny early rather than late. It is also wise as well as moral to fulfill a promise to defend a victim of attack, if you hope to promote a world of law and order in which more international promises will be kept.

Fortune kept the ball rolling with propagandist pieces such as a series by its able gray eminence of anti-Communism, Charles J. V. Murphy, who toured Southeast Asia and plugged the necessity for American support of Thailand and for an over-all American strategy founded on "an explicit and stated condition of American policy that Chinese Communist power is not going to be allowed to expand in Asia." The photogenic General Westmoreland was pictured repeatedly in Life, which called him "the Four-Star Eagle Scout" and saw in him the personification of the idealistic American motivation. Westmoreland, who had been Time's cover-hero ten months earlier, was now Man of the Year, a "jut-jawed six-footer" whose "most vehement cuss words are 'darn' and 'dad-gum,'" a man who "never smokes, drinks little" and who demanded at least a "seven-day, 60-hour week" from his aides. He was speedily followed on the cover by Secretary of State Rusk—"almost invariably at the President's side," said Time, a man whose "herculean schedule" included efforts to show "American good faith in its desire for peace in Southeast Asia." Then who should follow Rusk on the cover but the latest and least credible of the Vietnamese humanitarian leaders, Nguyen Cao Ky, Time admitting that it could be argued that he was either "the sixth or the ninth Premier in the last 18 months." Yet Time found in Ky a man of peace and law with surprising qualities of wisdom and statesmanship:

. . . Ky showed himself eloquent and honest, astute and independent, and above all a man who cared passionately about the defense and the welfare of his nation . . . he demonstrated an awareness and concern for the task of nation-building. . . . Ky has worked earnestly and hard. . . . a major military figure. . . . Ky often insists, "It is up to me and others like me to create a new society in South Vietnam." . . . "More than anything else we love peace." . . . Ky has become the closest thing to a national hero. . . . Ky has matured to his heavy responsibilities.

W. A. Swanberg

The reflections of Ky, who carried two pearl-handled pistols in his jet-black flight suit, on the delights of peace, were echoed by President Johnson (and later by President Nixon) and matched the insistent theme of peace and law in the Lucepress. Peace was the end in view, attainable only by war. The constant use of the words "peace," "freedom," "liberty" and "democracy" in the Lucepress was striking in view of their association with violence. Time now added a new organ of persuasion, the "Time Essay," which some inexact Americans thought was a special kind of news roundup. One, titled "Communism Today: A Refresher Course," advanced the theory that Communism might be more rather than less dangerous now that it was not exactly monolithic and quoted Walt Rostow on Communism. Another Essay warned Americans to take a lesson from the Bay of Pigs disaster and realize that "it is deadly to start something one is not prepared to finish." A third asked, "Is There Really Anything to Negotiate [in Vietnam]?" and answered without cavil in the second paragraph that there was not, following with six careful reasons and stressing the U.S. aim of peace and freedom.

The Weekly Newsmagazine, in its search for peace, was short-tempered with those who interfered with peace by criticizing the war which it was essential to win in order to have peace. In addition to its most frequent target, Senator Fulbright, those who felt Time's reproof included Senators Gore, McGovern, Mansfield and Gruening, Generals Matthew Ridgway and James Gavin, and George F. Kennan. Kennan, the old disciple of containment, was now regarded by Time not only as an isolationist but as an encourager of appeasement, harboring "an attitude that evokes distant echoes of Neville Chamberlain's dismissal of Hitler's plans to rape Czechoslovakia." (Time had conveniently forgotten how it had lauded Chamberlain at the time of Munich.) Time noted with satisfaction that the President was so fed up with criticism that at a formal White House dinner, "Mansfield was parked in a corner" and "Fulbright was not invited." It observed that Truman had once called Fulbright "that overeducated Oxford s.o.b.," that Fulbright spoke "to a nearly empty Senate chamber," repeated charges that his attitude "encourages the enemy," and spoke without batting an adjective of his "pleas for tolerance of repressive regimes abroad." Time, urging the Asian commitment, still had its inimitable way of smearing not only the nameless "Vietniks" and "quitniks" but also observers with decades of wise and responsible comment behind them:

> . . . [A] long, costly stalemate may well persuade more and more Americans that the pacifists and isolationists and columnists such as Walter Lippmann— not to mention Mao Tse-tung and Ho Chi Minh—were right all along in arguing that the U.S. has no business in Asia.

Such down-the-line warhawks as Senators Dodd, McGee and Dirksen basked in Lucepress commendation. Secretary McNamara won a three-column Time headline, a photograph and an encomium ("the most articulate

468

man in Washington was at his most eloquent") when he emphasized America's virtue and the fact that this very virtue caused difficulties:

> We ourselves have no territorial ambitions anywhere in the world . . . we have given other nations more than $100 billion. . . . Unfortunately the Communist governments do not share our objectives. . . . They are not inhibited by our ethical and moral standards . . .

4. CARING FOR THE NEWS

In Vietnam, American democracy and American journalism found simultaneously the ultimate proving ground of the value judgment. There had been short-term administration experiments with it along the way—Dulles's talk of being encircled by the Communists, Eisenhower's explanations of the U-2, Kennedy's communiqués about the Bay of Pigs and Johnson's intelligence about the Dominican rescue. But not until Vietnam had an American administration discovered itself to be in a great foreign involvement wherein the gradually expanding use of the value judgment proved so effective in interpreting the administration's policies and concealing the many little difficulties and confusions that might be misunderstood by the public that the value judgment had become quietly installed as the operative though unofficial government strategy.

One only had to go back to Time's fortieth birthday blowout at the Waldorf—addressed by both Johnson and Rusk—to understand that the value-judgment method of imparting news was highly esteemed in the best circles, even if Dr. Tillich had not sounded really enthusiastic. It had been tried for forty years and had not only been honored and acclaimed by the Establishment but had paid off big. While it was true that the idea of value judgments was in the public domain and that the Johnson administration had not stolen it from Time, it could not be said that Time's long experience and success with it was unknown to the administration. Furthermore, it was clear that the Lucepress did not object to the administration's borrowing of the device since it continued to heap smarm on the President and his Cabinet. Indeed the Lucepress wanted *everybody* to use it, for it kept sniping at newspapers and public officials who did not.

It would ultimately be discovered, however, that there was a law of diminishing returns in the use of value judgments when they operated over too long a period on a subject too close to deep public concern. The fulminations of Old Hatchet Face and George Schleiger, the comedy furnished by Haile Selassie and Jew Blum, and the latter-day reflections on Walter Lippmann or George Kennan could all be taken in stride. Not the growing lists of American killed and wounded—not the pictures of horror and devastation beginning to come out of Vietnam.

Those citizens beginning to doubt were kept safely ignorant of the fact that in 1965 and 1966, Secretary McNamara, his Assistant Secretary John McNaughton, Undersecretary of State George Ball and a few others in the tight little inner circle who knew the facts about the war, were also doubting. They were shocked at its unexpected cost and destruction along with their increasing presentiment that it could not be won. As honest men within the inner circle began to see the proportions of the disaster into which they had led or followed the administration—and as some worried even more about the political cost of admitting error—their doubts were still secret. The Congress as well as the people was unaware of them, and was also kept in ignorance of other vital information about the war.

The value judgment that prescribed this secrecy was one of incalculable consequence. It meant that although the error of the war was understood by some within the administration in 1965 and 1966, the voices of understanding were silenced, the trickle of blood became a river, and the war would still be raging six years later. While some newspapers had anticipated McNamara in realizing the error, were protesting the administration's policy of deception and were trying in clearly marked editorials to enlarge the already sizable part of the public aware of this, the Lucepress was on the opposite course. While McNamara was racked by doubts, Time was eulogizing him, General Westmoreland, Secretary Rusk and Marshal Ky, and Life published a long editorial by Hedley Donovan titled "The War Is Worth Winning," which Luce called "the best thing by far written on Vietnam ever."

Donovan was entitled to his editorial, which was labeled an editorial. Any honest expression of opinion, honestly labeled as opinion, was refreshing in a Lucepress so riddled with opinion masquerading as fact. This was true even though the editorial strengthened those wishing to prolong the war and tended to mute whatever inclination McNamara and his fellow doubters had to speak out, it being difficult for public officials to denounce policies which the nation's greatest propaganda medium eulogized them for supporting. Five years later—when the only question was how best to extricate the U.S. from Indochina and a majority of Lucepress readers had come around to that view —Donovan would concede that he (and/or Luce) had been wrong and would write in small part:

> One lesson, surely, is that Vietnam has been and still is too much of a President's war, first Johnson's and now Nixon's. A democracy does not fight at its best that way.

One's admiration for Donovan's handsome concession of error is dampened by his failure to note that the Lucepress fought all the way to keep it a President's war and to keep knowledge of it away from the Congress and the people. It did this not only by discrediting its own correspondents when they sought to communicate the truth rather than administration handouts. It also discredited other news organs which tried to find and publish the truth. And

470

it discredited those Congressmen—the long, long list started with Senator Fulbright—who vainly sought more information about the war, and praised the administration which denied them the information. (It could be pretty paltry in its sniping, as when the Senator said Saigon had become an "American brothel." Time snapped back that Little Rock and Hot Springs had "an abundance of whores.") Fulbright gave an interesting reply in a 1966 WCBS interview, when asked by Marvin Kalb how it happened that the U.S. seemed to be "overestimating" the threat of China which lay in the background of the Vietnam war:

> Well, I wish I knew. . . . I think it's an irrational reaction for—perhaps from the frustration and disappointment that arose at the time of Korea. And their intervention in Korea, and the question of Communism, and particularly the Democrats being soft on Communism, became a part of our domestic political dogma here. . . . The China Lobby is an extraordinarily effective organization. You have two of the strongest publications in the field, Time magazine and Life. And those publications have been hammering this away for years and years, and they convince people that this is a major threat to our security.

When the New York Times published a series of articles by a British journalist, James Cameron, about his visit to Hanoi, Time regarded the articles as vaguely subversive because Cameron quoted without comment statements made by North Vietnamese officials and, the New Republic said, "seemed to think he should have interlarded the quotes with personal disclaimers and ejaculations of disbelief, the way Dean Rusk does when citing Communists." It was the ideological echo of Time's protest when the Times first sent Harrison Salisbury to Moscow and printed his dispatches without suitable free-world exegesis and interpolation.

Now, late in 1966, Salisbury managed to get to Hanoi. His dispatches to the Times telling of widespread civilian casualties and damage to residential streets were shocking to those Americans who had been lulled by administration announcements that bombing was restricted to military and industrial targets. Time, though suggesting that the administration would have done better to acknowledge earlier that "some civilians would be killed by U.S. raids," spent more time criticizing Salisbury and the Times for "what many observers considered to be an uncritical, one-dimensional picture." Time, totally preoccupied with giving an uncritical, one-dimensional picture, wanted no other dimensions to creep in. It blamed Salisbury for "getting little more than a guided—or misguided—tour" controlled by Hanoi propagandists, and for sending out a "distorted picture" which would give the impression "that the U.S. is a big powerful nation viciously bombing a small, defenseless country into oblivion." The unsmiling accusation of "distortion" by the world's consummate master of distortion gave another chilling glimpse into the psychology of propagandist brainwash.

Life magazine, in an editorial praising the President's steady course, "Why

L.B.J. Will Continue Bombing," remarked that "even if unintentionally," reports like Salisbury's aided enemy propaganda. Some federal officials began referring to the Times as the "Hanoi Times," and Secretary Rusk said in hard tones to one Times man, "Why don't you tell your editors to ask Mr. Salisbury to go down and visit the North Vietnamese in *South* Vietnam?"

The Times, still following the code, grandly ignored Time's criticism. As always, frank appraisals of Lucepress journalism were left to non-dailies, one of them the National Catholic Reporter, whose columnist John Leo had earlier warned readers to "man your trifocals" when reading Time and commented:

> Time probably has the best corps of reporters ever assembled by a newsgathering organization, but to know many of them well is to sit through endless litanies about how their straight reportage was mangled in New York, or shaped to fit editorial conclusions that have more to do with the Luce view of reality than the actual facts. . . . Time's reportage on Vietnam is indeed a menace, but no more so than that on any nation where real or imagined Communists are engaged in a revolution. . . .

In the war which Donovan would later criticize as "a President's war," Johnson had the Lucepress at his side as the conflict became more and more the secret property of the President and his advisers and was removed from the scrutiny of the Congress, the press and the people. The administration strategy of falsehood which at last became evident to other observers was of course also evident to the Lucepress. Nothing like this had ever happened before in America on such a scale. The spectacle of the most influential organ of America's "free press" impugning other members of the fourth estate for seeking to utilize and protect that freedom was unprecedented.

In the Vietnam proving ground, the value-judgment concept both of government and journalism would come to be recognized by the more thoughtful part of the American electorate exactly for what they were—parallel drifts toward totalitarianism. The Lucepress had led, not followed, the nation into war. It had never wholeheartedly subscribed to the people's "right to know," and particularly in the area of Againstness it had always been fanatical rather than honest. A press that ridiculed objectivity, "cared for the news" in too close accord with the administration, and agreed with it in the selection and shaping of the news to be passed on to the public, was not a free press. It was the propagandist voice of one mistaken man, not elected to office, manipulating 50 million people weekly.

XXXV

1. THE MAN BEHIND THE CULTURE

In 1961 the German weekly Der Spiegel published a cover story about Luce in which a couple of paragraphs were still germane in 1966:

> No one man has, over the last two decades, more incisively shaped the image of America as seen by the rest of the world, and the Americans' image of the world, than Time and Life editor Henry Robinson Luce.
>
> Every third U.S. family buys every week a Luce-product; 94 percent of all Americans over 12 know Time. Luceferic printed products are the intellectual supplement of Coca-Cola, Marilyn Monroe and dollar diplomacy.
>
> No American without a political office—with the possible exception of Henry Ford—has had greater influence on American society. Luce (pronounced *Luhss*) was the first—between the wars—to use the term American Century. Recently, at a party on board Onassis' yacht *Christina*, Winston Churchill counted him among the seven most powerful men in the United States, and President Eisenhower, while still in office, called him "a great American."

That business of being among the seven most powerful must have interested Luce. Who in hell were the other six? He was anything but hypochondriac and seemed to have no premonition that his time was running out, but he had some leisure now and he worked on a collection of his writings which he hoped would be published. (But like other great editors, he seemed unable to view his own astonishing career editorially and to weave what should have been a wonderful story out of only one phase of it—his meetings and talks with the mighty.) In some ways he was more kindly and indulgent than of yore. When Professor Eric Goldman, who had worked briefly for Time, interviewed Luce on his "Open Mind" television program, Luce was not too full of his mission of American power to remember Goldman's book *The Crucial Decade*, and to say, "I don't know if the television allows me to say it's a hell

473

of a good book." Dr. Goldman—not the easiest man in the world to stop short—was constantly interrupted and by the end of the program had set a new record in amputated sentences, but he found Luce friendly and charming.

Now and then something astonishing would appear in Luce's magazines suggesting that he was moving in the direction of a willingness to permit Communists to inhabit the globe with American permission, as when Life editorially approved Johnson's 1966 State of the Union message:

> Although he stands pat in Vietnam, the President is flexible and conciliatory elsewhere. He even had a friendly word for a future Red China and boldly announced that "our objective is not to continue the cold war but to end it."
>
> He is proud of his two-year cultural agreement with the Soviet Union and of the fact that we shall soon exchange direct air flights with Moscow. He is proud of an increasing trade with Eastern Europe. . . . The evolutionary possibilities in Communism are a daily exhibit and challenge to our diplomacy. They are in part the happy result of our past record of firmness toward Communism, which established our credibility in Moscow and can someday do the same in Asia. This is an area to be explored with caution, but without bigotry and with the confidence in our own strength and purposes that the President so well expressed.

What had happened was that Luce was under the rosy influence of a recent trip to Eastern Europe during which he had met Marshal Tito, shaken his hand, talked with him *and discovered in this Communist a hero.* He had come right out and said in a Belgrade toast that Tito was "one of the authentic heroes of the twentieth century." Even though he was susceptible to hero-discovery on his tours, and even though Tito was an embarrassment to Brezhnev, these words were unlike Luce and they brought terrible consternation to the National Review, which editorialized, "Henry Luce is a complex man. . . . What *can* Mr. Luce have meant? . . . What Mr. Luce needs is a medium through which to reach the public."

Possibly if Luce had only met Khrushchev personally, the Cold War would have ended years earlier. The Tito incident was one of those occurring on a Time-sponsored air-and-bus tour of Hungary, Poland, Rumania, Czechoslovakia and Yugoslavia on which Luce had accompanied twenty-four American tycoons (mostly Time advertisers) ranging from President Edgar Bronfman of Seagram's to Henry Ford II. Among them the twenty-four employed 1,200,000 people and had done $33 billion in business the previous year. Time in its announcement of the tour carefully disavowed any pecuniary motives, saying that they all went "as concerned citizens eager to learn about life and politics and economics" in those countries. It named the Time contingent of Luce, Donovan and others but neglected to mention that one of the most concerned citizens making the trip was Time's advertising director, Robert C. Gordon. The power of Luce and Time Inc. was shown by the way heads of state and other important officials even in Communist Eastern Europe

jumped for them. They talked with leaders ranging from Premier Jozef Cyrankiewicz of Poland to the heroic Tito. This penetration of the Iron Curtain had not implied any relaxation of Luce's anti-Communism—simply a willingness to woo satellites and their trade away from Russia, to go along with his own advertisers' desire to get a piece of the business, and to get more of his advertisers' business.

Well, this hero-binge would surely be short. You never knew, on those rare occasions when he came forward with a halo around his head and an olive branch extended, how quickly he might dash back into church for his tommy-gun.

He was still so active and mobile that some pitied him his inability to just relax and loaf. When he was invited to New Haven by the Yale-in-China group, John Hersey, now master of Pierson College, heard of it and decided to add his own invitation. Luce was willing to bury the hatchet. He appeared at Pierson—one of the lovely quadrangles built long since his college days—and was friendly toward the novelist with whom he had broken so bitterly two decades earlier. He sat down and "discussed" with Hersey and eighteen Pierson men, to whom he recommended a fling at journalism, "whether or not you're going to be a poet or banker."

This was a peaceful confrontation between generations failing in understanding of each other, and Luce's effort was doubtless in part to bridge the gap. The old man who believed implicitly in free enterprise, in the war, in the boundless opportunity America still offered, was baffled by the skepticism of the young. His listeners were simultaneously impressed by his importance, pleased by his willingness to talk with them on this intimate basis and suspicious of the culture he not only represented but had had some share in shaping. "In Henry Luce," one of them, Roy Sussman, would write in the Pierson Sun, "[we] had been exposed to one of the most astounding successes of our era, and one of the primary powers-that-be who set the tone of our culture." His abiding faith in America and the national rectitude were not unanimously shared by his audience. "Luce's confidence and candidness reflect his strength," the Sun would say; "no matter what one thinks of his political stance, one must be impressed with the dynamism of his personality."

The current generation at Yale and elsewhere could scarcely be said to possess clear moral and intellectual transcendence over their elders. Yet there was that gulf between them. What caused it? What was really to blame for what was called "alienation"—the first large-scale confrontation between generations in American history? What was eating at the young, who were supposed to venerate the old? For one thing, perhaps most of them had grown suspicious of the big birds and sympathetic with the kittens. But surely the greatest difference between the eighteen young men and the old man talking to them was in the matter of faith—not only faith in God but faith in American institutions, American government, American leaders and American journalism. Most of the young men thought that they had been had. Hersey, in

touch with them daily, was attaining understanding of them which he would later put into a book. They were concerned with many things including what they saw as a national cash-orientation, but most of all with a truly terrifying breakdown of simple truth. The new procedure could be called deviousness, lying or fakery, or perhaps value judgments, but Hersey in his book would give it the plain descriptive term used by the collegians: bullshit. The writer for the Pierson Sun was more polite than the Brandeis collegian who commented on Luce's "atonality" and on the similar international generosity of America and Attila, but his reserve was evident. One of the questions put to Luce concerned "government 'management' of the news," the Sun continuing that Luce "replied that if the press allows government to control news, it is more the fault of the press than of the government. He added, 'If anybody's going to manage the news, we are.'"

Well, *that* could be taken in several ways. "For God, for country, and for Yale" did not mean what it used to mean. What Luce had regarded as eternal verities had undergone alteration. He knew he was a square and believed in his squareness. As the Sun continued:

> . . . Luce showed a deep interest in student attitudes toward business, making parallels between today's Yale and his Yale experience in the 1920's [*sic*]. He seemed distressed by the rejection of the business world by many of the students of today, attributing it mainly to increased affluence. Hersey remarked that this rejection of business is, in part, due to the individual's "fear of disappearing into a machine." Luce argued that this is an unreasonable fear, for the highly developed "organization does not inhibit the individual. Rather, it gives a great deal of freedom to the individual."

Some of the men at the Lucepress, not to mention Hersey himself, might question that. After the eighteen collegians had left, Luce extolled to Hersey the joys of LSD and the remarkably heightened perceptions it gave one. Hersey did not say so but thought it likely that Luce had such a powerful ego that LSD, which in others could produce hallucinations and lasting damage, in him just brought sharpened sensations. "I was glad he didn't talk about it when the boys were with us," Hersey said. "We were having a little trouble with LSD then."

Luce's yearning for membership in the Yale Corporation had never been realized, perhaps in part because of his venomous treatment of Acheson. His absolute Bulldog loyalty and willingness to address Yalemen or any other men had been acknowledged by other honors and awards such as the Yale Medal (1960). Now, four months after the encounter at Pierson College, he was at Yale again to receive his alma mater's second honorary degree. Among the ten others similarly honored was his good friend and perpetual debating companion, Father John Courtney Murray. The citation read by President Kingman Brewster, Jr., was doubtless the fruit of much thought:

> Time's march has spawned a competition which echoes the innovation Yale recognized 40 years ago with your first honorary degree. Your genius ushered in

476

a new era in mass communication. With all its risks, your zestful journalism has bolstered the capacity of the citizens of the republic to cope with domestic complications and world responsibilities. Your alma mater confers upon you the degree of doctor of laws.

"Damage" would have been a more accurate word than "risks." That Luce's journalism was often zestful, few would dispute. But when President Brewster said it "bolstered the capacity of the citizens of the republic to cope with domestic complications and world responsibilities," perhaps he choked a trifle, the opposite being the case. A more realistic appraisal had been made by President Roosevelt, whose own effect on the democracy had yet to be fully weighed, in that unsent letter to Luce written twenty-six years earlier:

. . . [I]t does bring up the question of whether . . . this form of journalistic misrepresentation is a good thing for the United States; as to whether it is not accomplishing its bit in the destruction of confidence in truth—confidence in statements—confidence in what would have been called in the old days, "civic decency." . . . [Y]our President is perfectly willing to tell you he thinks [this journalism] of serious detriment to the future of successful democracy in the United States.

Public confidence in the truth had indeed declined in an atmosphere of news pollution and official falsehood. The pitchman seemed to be driving out the newsman. In the Johnson administration and even more in the Nixon administration to follow, the Presidency had sunk and would sink to the mastery of evasion, euphemism and image. The gimmick that had proved so successful in Rockefeller Center had been enshrined in the White House, and strenuous official efforts would be made to strip the press of its feeble remaining freedom. It could hardly be said that the eighteen colleges—Yale twice—which conferred honorary degrees on Luce had shown understanding of journalism's vital role in American democracy. They had, like so many Time covers, celebrated cleverness and success and had moved the nation closer to an identification of cleverness with success.

2. MOUNT RUSHMORE

On December 26, 1966, the Richard Clurmans arrived in Phoenix for a week's stay with the Luces. They were met at the airport by Luce, who had just celebrated his sixty-eighth and last Christmas, and the chauffeur—the most important member of the Luce ménage in the preservation of family and public safety in that he kept Luce from the wheel.

Not too many weeks had passed since Luce's tour of Eastern Europe. There had been stops also in Paris and Vienna and briefings with European statesmen and American ambassadors along with the inevitable rich food and flowing bowl at every pause. It was enough to make a sixty-eight-year-old

man tired, especially since he had scarcely slowed down since. He *did* look tired, the Clurmans noticed with astonishment. Or, if not precisely tired, he looked old and wrinkled, his fringe of hair looking grayer against his desert tan.

The Luce house was festive, with some of the gifts still around the huge Christmas tree to be admired. Luce was delighted with a great sculpture his son Hank (now in charge of Time's London bureau) had sent him, which was mounted in the patio. Clare, the perfectionist, had made scores of splendid Christmas tree ornaments while Luce had read to her. She had bought white synthetic foam balls in various sizes and encrusted them intricately with ribbon, velvet and fake jewels—"imperial baubles," Luce called them. (She later gave all 168 of them to Bendel's store in New York to sell at $10 apiece for the Society for Crippled Children.)

As was usual when any executive received special Luce attention, the rest of them in New York gnawed their nails and wondered if the Boss might be cooking up something with Clurman. Luce was aware of this and probably enjoyed it as a modified version of his eternal game of Chinese checkers. Nothing was cooking. During the week between Christmas and New Year's, the Luces took the Clurmans around to meet various friends, among them the William Bentons, who also had a place in Phoenix. They played bridge at the Bentons'. Benton, a shark at cards, was still needling the inexpert Luce in his diabolical way, congratulating him in elaborate terms when he took a trick, heaping praise on him for playing a card which he had no choice but to play—treatment for which Luce had no adequate defense and which made him seethe a bit. It still irked him that Benton, a class behind him at Yale, was richer than he. This was a matter of pride, not deprivation, since the Luce holdings in Time Inc. alone were worth better than $100 million and were sufficient for his needs even if Benton had double that.

The Luces invited thirty friends to a six o'clock cocktail party to meet the Clurmans. When the bell did not ring at six sharp, the prompt Luce said anxiously to Clare, "Do you suppose no one's coming?" They all came. On New Year's Eve the Luces and Clurmans went to a benefit dance at a Phoenix club that proved unexciting enough to send them home at midnight. They switched on the television but were just too late to catch the celebration, so they had their own quick one, putting on fancy hats, having champagne, singing "Auld Lang Syne" and exchanging kisses.

No outsider ever kissed Luce except on momentous occasions. Mrs. Clurman noticed that when she gave him his 1967 kiss he rather drew back, unable to let himself go, to collaborate with frank affection.

A month later Luce flew to Santa Barbara to visit Robert Hutchins, sit in on the discussions of the Center for Democratic Institutions, and to address the students of the state university there. Hutchins—like Paul Hoffman, William Benton and Elmo Roper—was a liberal who often disagreed with Luce politically but enjoyed arguing with him and felt some fondness for him. Luce, for

all his abandonment of the kittens, was not all flint. But Hutchins's recent statement in an interview—"Mr. Luce and his magazines have more effect on the American character than the whole educational system put together"— did not sound like a joyous observation, coming from an educator.

The speech would be Luce's last—the last of his lifelong efforts involving how much thought and study, how many plane rides, how many hotel rooms, handshakes and drafty halls, never charging a fee, all in his errand of alerting America to her greatness and her world mission!

The Vietnam war which he backed was anathema to most of the students. The old fox's purpose was to make it look good to them in the long historical view, as he firmly believed it was, without antagonizing them by mention of current battle. His long training in propaganda came in handy. He told his audience that history was moving so fast that their own generation gap might be wider when they became parents: "Young people today must be prepared to find, twenty-five years from now, that the gulf between them and their children will be even greater." He put his message diplomatically in terms of a struggle of ideas in which the ideas of the enlightened and stable West, embodying progress and science, were clearly superior to the instability of the Orient and its passive concepts of ancestor worship and harmony with nature. Clearly, passivity and harmony with nature did not mean progress. The West rightly contested with nature for progress, as the Bible had said. Christianity was materialistic and justly so, he said, concerned with the well-being and dignity of the individual. "In Genesis, man is commanded to 'subdue . . . and have dominion over the earth.'" Communism, though "still a formidable enemy" politically, had nothing to offer the East because it was a pragmatic failure in "its economic incompetence and its absurd philosophy." He spoke enthusiastically of the constitutional convention in Saigon—a Western idea, aimed at bringing the Vietnamese the freedoms of the West.

He returned to the old organ note: ". . . [W]e stand for liberty under law. And that, essentially, is what the West has to say to the East." And he gave his opinion that to say this powerfully was not merely goodness on the part of the West but was downright self-preservation, since if the West could not agree on this approach to the East, it meant decline: "Well, then, that would be a sign that Western civilization approaches its end."

There were full-circle echoes here of lifelong beliefs expressed in the DeForest Oration and in the "American Century"—lifelong in large part because based on Biblical absolutism. When he spoke of the West, he thought of America as the God-anointed leader of the West. No more than ever did he intend to be totalitarian, and he always indignantly denied any "master race" concept. Since it was unthinkable to him that his God and his Bible might not represent universal truth ("we should believe what is right") he was not receptive to theories founded on other beliefs.

Young William F. Buckley came to Phoenix to dine with him and perhaps also to ask whatever *did* he mean with those complimentary remarks about

Tito. Luce and Buckley were alike in their marriage of religion and the Pentagon, but it had to be said that Buckley did not call his publication a newsmagazine. Luce said he would like to appear on Buckley's television program in the spring. He had a bone to pick with the church hierarchy because of its failure to show the proper hostility toward non-capitalist countries. As Buckley recalled it, Luce said, ". . . what I want to say is this—say it to the professional churchmen—the Council of Churches gang. Look: If you're really interested in relieving poverty, you've got an obligation to defend the system that works best at relieving poverty. See what I mean?"

Buckley and his group were a little disillusioned with Luce, doubtless in part because of his refusal to share in the Goldwater debacle, feeling that Luce was not a true crusader, that he had not given his publications sufficiently to Againstness, unaware that he had practically invented it with value judgments running back to their preschool years and had done it all so skillfully that millions of people had taken it into their bloodstreams from Time, Life and Fortune without even knowing it. To accuse Luce of failing to press a crusade was to accuse Savonarola of laxity.

In mid-February he was in New York to attend a Time directors' meeting, to wear a derby and sit on the Yale fence with President Brewster in celebration of the annual Alumni Day, and to talk politics with his editors. Prince Bernhard of the Netherlands was his luncheon guest and question target. (Fourteen years earlier, Luce had been named a commander in the Order of Orange-Nassau by the prince's wife, Queen Juliana.) Even before Bernhard was seated in the Time dining room, Luce jerked a thumb at his editors and said they had inquiries. "I'd like something to eat first," Bernhard said courageously. Food was brought him and his lunch was ingested amid a fusillade of questions about European politics.

Luce wrote affectionately to his first wife, Lila. He seemed to be visibly wearing out but without corresponding slackening of pace. Mary Bancroft, crossing Central Park, saw a man walking at some distance on a diverging path among the sycamores. He looked somehow familiar. It was Luce, whom she would have recognized instantly but for his drawn face, deep wrinkles and lusterless eyes. There was about him, she thought, the look of a man engaged by death in a struggle not yet finished but whose outcome was predictable. She was so shocked by his appearance that she did not call out at that distance but let him pass unknowing toward Fifth Avenue, where he and she lived a few blocks apart.

Luce was back in Phoenix in time to have dinner with Clare and the Elmo Ropers at the George Ullmans' in Scottsdale. Roper, though aware that Luce was aging as they all were, thought him sparkling in conversation, one topic being his concern about an American lapse into isolationism, by which he was referring to the sentiment against the war in Southeast Asia. Not until recently had internationalism required heavy weaponry. But Roper, like other

friends who talked to him during these final months, found his basic confidence in America unimpaired. Racial problems had been solved by the Civil Rights Acts, whose effective realization awaited only the solution of a few technicalities. The war was a "sticky wicket" but of course would be won. The nation, with a little good management, was on the eve of a golden age. (Certainly, Time Inc.'s 1966 gross revenue of $503 million and its current printing of more than 14 million magazines weekly had a golden hue.) Next day he and Clare were off for San Francisco, where she was to address the Commonwealth Club on the subject of the United Nations, an organization in which she had as little confidence as he.

She had worked hard on the speech as she always did, but knew that she was so critical of the UN that it ended in pessimism which, rather than make listeners applaud, would leave them wondering, "Why did I come?"

"I showed it to Harry," she recalled later, "and said it must have a note of optimism at the end. Harry said, 'Sure,' looked it over and did what came to him naturally. He wrote a last paragraph lifting it out of despond with a redemptive note." He was the can-do man, the believer in America and America's world, the preacher of universal Amprop.

A few days earlier, Judson Gooding of the San Francisco Time bureau had received the signal from Luce by telephone that they were coming. It was equivalent to pressing buttons. Gooding met them at the airport. Gooding drove them into town. Gooding answered scores of Luce questions about new buildings, business, rapid transit. Gooding deposited them at the Fairmont. In the afternoon, Gooding picked them up again and drove them to the De Young Museum in Golden Gate Park, which had a new collection of Oriental art. Gooding drove them back, stopping at the center of hippiedom, the Haight-Ashbury intersection, at Luce's request.

Luce, overflowing with curiosity about these weirdly dressed young people with the predilection for drugs, besieged Gooding with questions about them. The believer in Amprop saw here another group who were like the collegians at Brandeis and Yale and Santa Barbara in some respects—a disbelief in Amprop, a dislike of the culture and the goals of the nation, a failure of confidence, a suspicion of national fakery and a separation from the generation they thought responsible.

Such disbelief—such suspicion—was alien to him.

Another part of the signal to Gooding had been: *Arrange small dinner party, interesting people.* The Luces arrived at a private room in Ernie's restaurant to find that their dinner companions were Wallace Sterling, president of Stanford University; Ransom Cook of Wells Fargo; Haydn Williams, president of the Asia Foundation, and their wives. Cocktails, dinner with three kinds of wine, talk of education, art and world affairs, back to the Fairmont at midnight, up in the morning to breakfast and cigarettes in a suite commanding one of America's most spectacular views, a rereading of the speech, then

to the Palace Hotel, where Clare would give it at noon. Luce, who did not dodge the limelight when it was his, had an endearing way of shunning it when it shone on his wife.

"He was not like some husbands with career wives," she recalled. "Harry loved to hear me speak. He sat there and beamed just as he had in Italy."

Back to Phoenix in an afternoon plane. When they read the morning papers next day, Clare nodded. "They quote my speech. Do you know what part of it? *Your* last paragraph. Amprop has won the day."

Luce was amused and pleased. He sent Gooding a note of thanks, dispatched a memo to Donovan in New York about the situation in Rhodesia, played nine holes of golf alone with his favorite caddy, Andy Ozbut, had friends in for cocktails, then went with Clare to a dinner party at the Arizona Biltmore, getting home before midnight.

The next morning, Sunday, he was not hungry. When he canceled a golf date, Clare knew that her stoic husband was ill. He was seldom ill, and never complained when he was, so one almost had to be clairvoyant to know. She put him to bed. Dr. Hayes Caldwell—the same who had attended him during his 1958 attack and ever since—arrived to find him coughing violently. Although his blood pressure and pulse were normal, he had a slight temperature. Monday morning he was taken somewhat protestingly to St. Joseph's Hospital—an ecumenist to the last. He brushed aside Clare's effort to take his arm and walked into the hospital room unaided, taking with him a detective novel, a theological work and his well-thumbed Bible.

The Bible did not signify foreboding. He had become so attached to it that he would all but take it along on a picnic. He and Mary Bancroft had discussed God so often that she felt she understood in part his confidence in his place in God's esteem—even his ability to beguile God a trifle. Some of his editors, and some political enemies, had been impressed by his God-Agreement. His pastor, Dr. Read, had discussed the matter of faith with him and thought him sure of heaven not because of certainty of his own goodness but because of his trust in God's grace, which would transcend any shortage of good works on his part.

As for Luce himself at St. Joseph's, he appeared unperturbed, not badly ill and hence not immersed in questions of just how he would reply when the Lord said, "Well, Harry, how about it? What use did you make of your wonderful abilities?"

He underwent medical tests, with Clare standing by. In the evening he insisted that she leave this foolishness and represent them both at a dinner party to which they had been invited a week earlier. She did so but was uneasy and went home early to telephone him. He said he was fine—about to watch Perry Mason. She was too, she said. Should she come over so they could watch together?

"No," he said, "everything is going to be all right."

482

Without doubt he read his Bible and prayed before turning out his light. Shortly after 3:00 A.M. February 28, 1967, he got out of bed, went to the bathroom and shrieked, "Oh, Jesus!" so loudly that the nurse came running. He did not quite go gentle into that good night, but he was not given time to rage, dead instantly of a coronary occlusion.

AFTERWORD

Death had surprised not only Luce's relatives and editors, but the Boss himself. He had not discussed it with any sense of expectation or preparation. It was not known where he wanted to be buried until Hank Luce, reached in London, said his father had once told him. He would be buried not with his father and mother, nor in Connecticut or Phoenix, nor in the great city where Time had been born in a rookery and which it now viewed from its eminence in Rockefeller Center, but in Mepkin. The Presbyterian from China would join his "daughter" Ann and her grandmother in the shaded Carolinian glade tended by the cassocked Trappists.

A memorial service was held at the Madison Avenue Presbyterian Church and piped to throngs of employees at two auditoriums in the Time-Life Building. Time that week, for the first time ever, had Luce's challenging likeness on the cover. His spirit abided in the inner pages as well, for Time's obituary praised his journalistic "fairness": "Few journalists in his time labored harder to examine all three or 30 sides of an argument, or strove more conscientiously to see that the facts were presented fairly." Strongly liberal newspapers saluted him with obituaries more respectful than glowing, conservative ones with true feeling, but none seemed to catch his elusive essence. Willi Schlamm, who had marked the death of Senator McCarthy with an emotional tribute to him in the National Review as a man of "innocence" annihilated by the "hound-dogs of malice," wrote as illogically of Luce, "to know him was to know America." The thought-shaping power of the Lucepress was evident, for some liberal papers praised him for "fighting McCarthy" and the New York Times said soberly, "His magazines moved courageously against the late Senator Joseph R. McCarthy . . ."

Luce was buried in a private ceremony at Mepkin. No soaring monument would surmount the man who built no castles and had a thread of humility

running somewhere through the splendid fabric of his pride—only a graceful four-foot stone identical with one alongside it reserved for his widow. The Mepkin monks, far from exhibiting sorrow, startled some of the mourners by their evident joy that the great man had sloughed off the sinful world and started his journey toward the Kingdom of Heaven.

NOTES

Notes are supplied chiefly to identify persons who gave recollections or information, and to name the sources of the more important written or published quotations or opinions. The term "private source," used in a few instances, denotes information given by persons—some of them still or recently in the employ of Time Inc.—who asked not to be identified. Abbreviations used are as follows:

BP	Billings Papers	NYDN	New York Daily News
BR	Billings recorded recollec-	NYHT	New York Herald Tribune
	tions	NYJA	New York Journal-American
CBL	Clare Boothe Luce	NYP	New York Post
HRL	Henry Robinson Luce	NYT	New York Times
MB	Mary Bancroft	NYWT	New York World-Telegram
MBP	Mary Bancroft Papers	SD	Severinghaus Diary
NR	New Republic	SR	Saturday Review
NYDM	New York Daily Mirror	TA	Time Archives

Luce and His Empire

I

PAGE

1 *"Burden of sin":* Quoted in NYDM, Jan. 20, 1947.

2 *"McClure thinks":* From Oct. 6, 1945, entry in Luce diary (BP).

2 *Stilwell's verses: The Stilwell Papers* (Theodore White, ed.—Macfadden, NY 1962), 164.

3 *"Met at airport":* Luce diary, Oct. 6, 1945.

3 *White's dispatches altered:* White told author, Oct. 2, 1969.

3 *"Printing his picture":* As in Time, Sept. 10, 1945.

4 *"Stratemeyer says":* Luce diary, Oct. 6, 1945.

5 *"Poor sermon":* Luce diary, Oct. 7, 1945.

5 *"Dr. Kung recalled":* Diary entry same day.

5 *White and the Kuomintang:* Richard Watts in NR, Dec. 3, 1945.

6 *"The Republic in danger":* T. S. Matthews, *Name and Address* (Simon & Schuster, NY 1960), 274.

6 *"[W]e should realize":* Luce memo to Billings, Mar. 24, 1944 (BP).

6 *"At 57, Chiang Kai-shek":* Time, Sept. 3, 1945.

6 *Luce visits the Chiangs:* Luce diary, entry Oct. 7, 1945.

8 *Luce meets Mao Tse-tung:* Luce diary, Oct. 8, 1945.

9 *"Riding a tornado":* Bailey told author.

9 *"In a cloud of dust":* Bailey letter to wife, Oct. 9, 1945.

9 *Luce dines with Soong:* Luce diary, Oct. 9, 1945.

9 *Luce talks with Chou:* Luce diary, Oct. 11, 1945.

9 *Luce visits Chen Li-fu:* Luce diary, Oct. 9, 1945.

10 *"Presently, a truckload":* Luce diary, Oct. 11, 1945.

10 *"Grubby town":* Bailey diary, Oct. 13, 1945.

11 *"Since Marco Polo":* Bailey letter to wife, Oct. 16, 1945.

11 *"Friend of China":* Peiping Chronicle, Oct. 16, 1945 (TA).

11 *"A wee bit tight":* Bailey letter to wife, Oct. 16, 1945.

12 *"The reoccupation of China":* Luce cable to Billings, n.d.—about Oct. 7, 1945 (BP).

12 *"The city of Peking":* Luce to Billings, Oct. 20, 1945 (BP).

12 *"Notorious inefficiency":* the same.

12 *"Isn't it beautiful?":* Murphy told author.

12 *"Old German church":* Nov. 12, 1945, Luce memo to Senior List (BP).

13 *"Vastly impatient":* Bailey told author.

13 *"Incredible military power":* Nov. 12, 1945, Luce memo to Senior List.

13 *"Visited Jap hospital":* Bailey diary, Oct. 23, 1945.

13 *"He acted as host":* Bailey told author; also Gottfried told author.

14 *"Santa Claus Primus":* Luce to Bailey, Dec. 24, 1945.

II

15 *"God willing":* B. A. Garside, *One Increasing Purpose* (Revell, NY 1948), a biography of the elder Luce, 36.

PAGE

16 *Intoxicated with God:* Paul A. Varg, *Missionaries, Chinese and Diplomats* (Princeton U. Press, 1958), 52.

16 *"A million a month":* Varg, 68.

16 *"Not a few earnest men":* Robert E. Speer, *A Memorial to Horace Tracy Pitkin* (Revell, NY 1903), 67.

16 *"Dancing, cards, the theatre":* Speer, 70.

16 *"Off with his head":* Speer, 62.

16 *"Once each day":* Speer, 80.

17 *"He got hold of me":* Garside, *op. cit.,* 53.

17 *"You haven't said so":* Garside, 72.

18 *Separate cells:* Varg, *op. cit.,* 48.

19 *Protestant laymen's inquiry:* William Ernest Hocking (ed.), *Re-Thinking Missions* (Harper, NY 1932), 15–16.

19 *Pearl Buck's opinion:* Theodore F. Harris, *Pearl S. Buck* (John Day, NY 1969), 309.

20 *"The elder statesmen":* Garside, 101.

20 *President McKinley:* Ernest R. May, *Imperial Democracy* (Harcourt, NY 1961) 253.

20 *Mr. Dooley:* Quoted in May, *Imperial Democracy,* 257.

21 *"From this point of view":* Varg, *op. cit.,* 85.

21 *Senator Beveridge:* Albert K. Weinberg, *Manifest Destiny* (Johns Hopkins, Baltimore 1935), 308.

21 *"Something unhealthy":* Nathaniel Peffer, *The Far East* (U. of Michigan Press, Ann Arbor 1958), 117–18.

22 *Boxer manifesto:* Peter Fleming, *The Siege at Peking* (Harper, NY 1959), 35.

22 *The Luce escape:* Narrated to author by Emmavail Luce (Mrs. Leslie R. Severinghaus).

22 *"What days!":* Garside, *op. cit.,* 98.

23 *Mark Twain's outrage:* Marilyn Blatt Young, *The Rhetoric of Empire* (Harvard U. Press, Cambridge 1968), 193–94.

23 *Horace Pitkin estate:* Varg, *op. cit.,* 49n.

23 *Luce urges consolidation:* Garside, 100.

24 *"Delivered his own sermons":* Noted by Henry Robinson Luce's sister Elisabeth (Mrs. Maurice T. Moore), who assembled and edited HRL's family letters written through 1922 and which are herein cited as HRL Family Letters.

24 *"He has established the earth":* Noted in HRL Family Letters.

24 *"I have the globe":* Ibid.

III

26 *HRL thought she wanted to "buy" him:* Mrs. Mary Bancroft told author. William T. Hutchinson, *Cyrus Hall McCormick* (Appleton-Century, NY 1935, 2 vols.) gives the story of the McCormicks.

26 *"I am the Vine":* CBL told author.

26 *"Trudged through the rain":* Garside, *op. cit.,* 120.

27 *"My dear St. Nicholas":* St. Nicholas magazine, July 8, 1908.

28 *"The British code":* HRL told of this in a speech May 4, 1950.
28 *"Quiet, solemn, aloof":* Nym Wales, "Old China Hands," NR, April 1, 1967.
29 Letters quoted in this chapter are all from HRL Family Letters.
29 The Luce travels were narrated to author by Mrs. Severinghaus and Mrs. Moore.

IV

32 *"I deliver an oration":* This was his 283rd letter home in Mrs. Moore's compilation, written at age fifteen.
32 *Harry's tie askew:* Culbreth Sudler to author, Oct. 5, 1968.
33 *"Not for one sentimental cause":* Quoted in NYP, Jan. 14, 1965.
33 *"Matterhorn" poem:* Hotchkiss Literary Monthly, June 1916.
33 *"Oh, lights of Venice": Ibid.*
34 *"Shen-dzi" poem:* Hotchkiss Lit, Mar. 1916.
34 *Hadden's praise:* In Noel Busch, *Briton Hadden* (Farrar, Straus, NY 1949), 31.
34 *Sudler got $40:* Sudler to author Oct. 27, 1968.
34 *Cantaloupe and ice cream:* HRL later related this to Francis Brown when Dr. Brown was a senior editor at Time.
34 *"The reporting work"* and *"greatest service in journalistic work"* are from his letters Nos. 457 and 454 at age eighteen.
35 *Canby on Yale:* Henry Seidel Canby, *Alma Mater* (Farrar & Rinehart, NY 1936), 73, 75.
37 The quotation is from Owen Johnson, *Stover at Yale* (Stokes, NY 1911), 25–26.
38 *Army training at Yale:* Sudler to author, Dec. 17, 1969.
38 Perry Prentice told author about the News election.
38 *"Briton Hadden is chairman":* From Luce's letter No. 535 at age nineteen, HRL Family Letters.
39 *"Now take this down":* George Wilson Pierson, *Yale College* (Yale Press, New Haven 1952), 467n.
39 *Hadden's fake letters:* John M. Hincks told author.
40 *"Saltpeter":* Mr. Sudler's recollections covered the Camp Jackson interlude, as did Mr. Hincks's.
40 *"He had missed his war":* CBL told author.
40 *The Roosevelt editorial:* Yale Daily News, Jan. 7, 1919.
40 *"Fundamentalism isn't all":* Sudler to author, Oct. 5, 1968.
40 Canby's writing course is described in Charles A. Fenton, *Stephen Vincent Benét* (Yale Press, 1958), 84.
41 The News story about Bullitt was in the Apr. 4, 1919 issue.
41 *"Insidious soap-box orators":* The News, Apr. 24, 1919.
41 *Luce in Bones:* The News, May 16, 1919.
41 *Le Baron to Stover: Stover at Yale,* 27.
42 *"Brit Hadden . . . the big man":* HRL's letter No. 596 to his family.
42 *Kolchak story:* Yale Daily News, Oct. 30, 1919.
42 *HRL argues against Reds:* The News, Nov. 1, 1919.
42 *HRL's DeForest Oration:* Yale Class of 1920 Yearbook, 447–450.

W. A. Swanberg

V

VI

65   *"The Grotto technique":* Unidentified newsclip, TA.
65   The Hot Springs paper was the Star, n.d. (TA).
65   *"Adolphe Menjou":* Hollywood Film Daily, Oct. 16, 1927.
65   *Heyday of Mencken:* Minnesota Daily, May 15, 1929.

VII

66   *The Yale degree:* Elson, *Time Inc.,* 103.
66   *The Luces and MacLeishes in Paris:* MacLeish told author.
67   *Time in Corsica:* Mrs. Tyng told author.
67   Hadden's praise of Cleveland was in the Clevelander, June 1926 (TA).
68   *Rev. Henry Luce at Columbia:* Garside, *op. cit.,* 208.
68   *"Harry asked":* Maurice T. Moore told author.
68   *Twelve tycoons in "People":* Time, Apr. 30, 1928.
69   Editor & Publisher's two articles attacking Time were in the Nov. 3 and Nov. 17
      issues, 1928.
70   *Luce's magazine article:* in SR, Oct. 27, 1928.
72   *Luce on the tycoon:* Speech in Rochester, n.d. 1929 (TA).
72   *"Business is what we believe in":* Luce speech in Chicago, Nov. 28, 1930 (TA).
72   *The success of Mussolini: Ibid.*
72   *"America needs a moral leader":* Luce speech, Rochester, Mar. 1928.
73   *"A glacier near the top":* Lila to HRL, Aug. 24, 1928.
73   *"If this day could have been worse":* HRL to Lila, July [20], 1928.
74   *"Chicagoans go in for kidnapping":* To HRL, Apr. 12, 1928.
75   *"Hard to realize":* Lila to HRL, July 8, 1928.
76   *Mussolini on Time's cover:* Time, Aug. 6, 1923. *Stalin's "ominous past":* Time,
      Aug. 27, 1928. *"Oriental ruthlessness":* Nov. 21, 1927. *"Shabbily dressed":*
      Apr. 30, 1928. *"Speed-stunned":* Dec. 27, 1926. *Time's second Mussolini
      cover story:* July 12, 1926. *Stalin "cold-blooded":* Aug. 27, 1928. *Little public
      adulation:* Nov. 12, 1928.
76   *Orphans, pickpockets, degenerates, etc:* Time, Nov. 21, 1927. *"Black secrecy":*
      Aug. 22, 1927. *"Thousand daggers":* Jan. 12, 1925. *"Logic, reason:"* Dec. 26,
      1927. *"Work-fervor of Mussolini":* June 12, 1926. *The king and queen: Ibid.*
77   *"Across the Chamber":* Jan. 12, 1925. *Silence of Stalin:* Apr. 30, 1928. *"Spiritual
      veneration":* July 12, 1926. *Trotsky leaving Moscow:* Jan. 30, 1928. *Castor oil:*
      Aug. 6, 1923.
78   *"Egotistical, ruthless":* Time, Nov. 12, 1928. *"Exact dynamic utterance":* Dec.
      27, 1926.
79   *"I, Briton Hadden":* George Frazier in *Boston Herald,* n.d. June, 1963 (TA).
80   *"Hold my stock": Ibid.*
80   *"I don't know":* Gottfried told author.
80   *Luce buys shares:* Elson, *op. cit.,* 124–25.

VIII

81   *Chrysler, Man of Year:* Time, Jan. 7, 1929. *Morgan on cover:* Feb. 25; *Taylor:*
      Apr. 22; *Sarnoff:* July 15; *Macaulay:* July 22.

81 *Walter Teagle on cover:* Dec. 9, 1929.

82 *"Banana peel":* Hodgins's speech, Time's twentieth anniversary (TA).

82 *Whitney as Horatius:* Time, Nov. 4, 1929.

82 *Lamont on cover:* Nov. 11, 1929; *Owen D. Young:* Jan. 6, 1930.

83 *"Normal social life":* NYP, Jan. 4, 1957.

83 *Luce hires MacLeish:* MacLeish told author.

83 *Luce on Pittsburgh:* Fortune, Dec., 1930.

84 *Macdonald complaint:* The Nation, May 8, 1937.

84 *Hall of Fame:* Vanity Fair, Aug. 1930.

84 *"S for Singer":* Margaret Bourke-White, *Portrait of Myself* (Simon & Schuster, NY 1963), 69.

84 *Luce meets Hoffman:* Hoffman told author.

85 *San Diego Union attack:* n.d., Feb. 1930 (TA).

86 *"Peach of an idea":* Script, Mar. 7, 1931 (TA).

86 *Billings diary:* Entry for Nov. 12, 1931.

87 *Rutland Herald complaint:* Date missing, 1934 issue (TA).

87 *"Flexing his muscles":* Bernays told author.

87 Quotations are from Post-Dispatch Aug. 19, 1929; Ottawa paper Sept. 3, 1929; Fairmont Sentinel, Feb. 24, 1932; Baltimore Afro-American, n.d., 1932, all TA.

88 Quotation from SR, Feb. 18, 1933; from Editor & Publisher, Nov. 4, 1933; from Variety, n.d. Oct. 1929, all TA.

88 Quotation from NYHT, Apr. 17, 1933.

88 *"The trouble with me":* Brooklyn Eagle, Oct. 6, 1929.

89 *Mrs. Hobson's observations:* She told author.

90 *"All Against Russia":* Time, Mar. 10, 1930. *"Prayers must be numerous":* Ibid.

90 *"Stalin & Friends":* Time, June 9, 1930. *"In return for an order":* Time, Feb. 10, 1930. *Boycott urged:* Time, June 9, 1930.

91 *Macdonald on Goldsborough:* Nation, May 22, 1937.

IX

93 *World trip:* The author listened to Severinghaus's account of the journey and also read his illuminating diary, cited here as SD.

93 *"We do muff news":* HRL letter, undated (TA).

94 Chiang was first on Time's cover Apr. 4, 1927; next, on becoming a Methodist, Oct. 26, 1931.

95 *Luce meets Soong:* HRL notes on China (TA). *Fortune on Soong:* June 1933 issue.

95 *"I didn't dance":* SD, entry May 30, 1932.

95 *"Filthy dining car":* SD, June 6.

96 *Mahan warned:* M. B. Young, *Rhetoric of Empire*, 222.

97 *Sacred Mountain ascent:* SD, June 17, 1932.

97 *"No interpreter":* HRL to Larsen, June 25, 1932 (TA).

97 *"Harry was like a ten-year-old":* SD, June 19.

98 *"You've never seen":* Letter to Larsen listed above.

99 *"At that late hour":* SD, July 2, 1932.

100 *"Atrocious body-odor":* HRL Aug. 1932 report (TA).

100 *"Harry won't double up"*: SD, July 5.

100 *"Platform crowded"*: SD, July 7.

101 *HRL reunion with Lila:* Mrs. Tyng told author.

102 *Olfactory Lesson:* Entire HRL report on Russia from TA.

X

104 *"Maloler the Roller"*: Dwight Macdonald, Nation, May 8, 1937.

104 *"Arms and the Men"*: In Fortune, Mar. 1934.

105 *Billy Sunday et al:* Richard Hofstadter, *Anti-Intellectualism in American Life* (Vintage, NY 1963), 116 and 268.

105 *"The characteristic"*: Ortega y Gasset, *Revolt of the Masses* (Norton, NY 1932), 18–19.

106 *"My God!"*: MacLeish told author.

106 *"The poor slob"*: Private source.

106 HRL Scranton speech delivered Apr. 19, 1934 (TA).

107 *"Taken the initiative"*: Time, Nov. 20, 1933.

107 *"Just as Pres. Roosevelt"*: Ibid.

107 *Time on Bullitt:* Nov. 27, 1933.

109 *Billings on Luce:* From his recorded recollections.

109 *At the Century of Progress:* Bernard Barnes told author.

110 *Miss Thrasher's recollections:* Narrated by her to author.

110 *HRL vs. father on liquor:* Sheldon Luce told author.

110 *Rev. Henry Luce on RD:* John Bainbridge, *Little Wonder* (Reynal & Hitchcock, NY 1946), 43.

111 *"The herd mind"*: Bainbridge, 11.

111 *Laski on Luce:* Laski's *The American Democracy* (London, 1949), 659–63.

112 *Luce observations on England:* Report dated July 16, 1934 (BP).

XI

114 MacLeish told author about the Commodore meeting.

115 *"Piano factory"*: Alden Hatch, *Ambassador Extraordinary* (Holt, NY 1956), 23.

115 *"Most conceited"*: Ibid., 39.

115 *"Affaire de coeur"*: Ibid., 44.

116 *"Her friends are familiar"*: Margaret Case Harriman, *Take Them Up Tenderly* (Knopf, NY 1944), 66.

116 *"Her status was vague"*: Edna Woolman Chase and Ilka Chase, *Always in Vogue* (Doubleday, NY 1954), 230–231.

116 *"Weekly staff luncheons"*: Fay Henle, *Au Clair de Luce* (Stephen Day, NY 1943), 44.

116 *"She would have her secretary"*: Harriman, op. cit., 66.

117 *"Darlingest"*: Postmarked Feb. 7, 1935.

117 *"A good many years"*: Postmarked Mar. 30, 1935.

118 *Longwell in Salzburg:* Mrs. Longwell to author Mar. 10, 1969.

118 *"I'd go weeks at a time"*: BR.

119   *The Richard Watts review:* NYHT, Nov. 22, 1935.

120   *"Harry, you have got to make up your mind":* Elson, *op. cit.,* 289–90.

XII

121   *"Time* is *a rewrite sheet":* HRL memo Oct. 17, 1933 (TA).

122   *"Miss Astor's diary":* Time, Aug. 17, 1936.

122   *"Strutting little venture":* T. S. Matthews, *Name and Address,* 216.

123   *Edmund Wilson on Time:* Princeton U. Library Chronicle, Feb. 1944.

123   The parody was in New Yorker, Nov. 28, 1936.

125   Conversation at Ross's is from the George Frazier ms., 186–89, and James Thurber, *The Years with Ross* (Little, Brown, Boston 1959), 219.

125   *Ross letter:* John Kobler, *Luce: His Time, Life and Fortune* (Doubleday, NY 1968), 74–77.

125   Morro Castle *story:* BR.

126   *"This motion":* Time, Nov. 25, 1935; *"Tall, fair Vittorio":* July 15, 1935; *"fashionably tallowed":* Jan. 6, 1936; *Red Cross shelter:* Jan. 27, 1936; *"squealing for protection":* Dec. 2, 1935; *"terrified":* Nov. 18, 1935; *"jabbered and shrieked":* Dec. 2, 1935; *"screaming savages":* July 20, 1936.

127   *Haile Selassie Man of Year:* Time, Jan. 6, 1936. *Mussolini's fifth cover story:* July 20, 1936.

128   *"We had a private dining room":* Billings diary, July 16, 1936.

128   *"Some orations":* Time, Mar. 16, 1936; *"The Treaty":* Apr. 13, 1936; *Blood Purge story:* July 9, 1934; *"Even to intelligent Germans":* Apr. 13, 1936.

129   *"Herr Hitler's technique":* Time, Mar. 16, 1936; *"the jam closet":* Apr. 22, 1935; *"The tone of the French press":* Apr. 13, 1936; *"toothy Anthony Eden":* Apr. 20, 1936.

129   *Time on Churchill:* Nov. 4, 1935; *"the salty admirals":* Dec. 30, 1935.

129   *Time cover story on Blum:* Mar. 9, 1936, issue.

130   *Dangerfield on MOT:* NR, Aug. 19, 1936; *NYHT on MOT:* Quoted in American Spectator, Mar. 1936.

131   *Cover story on Eleanor Roosevelt:* Nov. 20, 1933; *Time on Farley:* July 30, 1934.

131   *Time on Tugwell:* June 25, 1934; *on Gen. Johnson:* Jan. 1, 1934.

131   *Johnson again:* Time, Sep. 10, 1934.

132   *Landon cover story:* May 18, 1936.

134   *"A play about women":* Harriman, *op. cit.,* 69.

134   *"What, for God's sake":* Henle, *Au Clair de Luce,* 63.

135   Time, Jan. 4, 1937, reviewed *The Women.* Life, Jan. 25, featured it.

135   *"Unpopularity, distrust":* Harriman, 44; *"shrewd, cynical":* Henle, 200; *"two such sophisticated":* Hatch, 82.

136   "Beautiful façade": Harriman, 47.

XIII

137   *"Frog-faced,"* etc.: Time, July 20, 1936.

138   *"Glorious Government forces":* Time, Sep. 7, 1936; *on Caballero:* Nov. 16; *"emptied the jails":* Aug. 3; *"opened the arsenals":* Aug. 24.

138 *"Shoemakers," etc.:* Oct. 26; *"smiling Generalissimo":* Nov. 16; *MacLeish memo:* Jan. 16, 1937 (TA).

139 *Goldsborough reply:* Jan. 23, 1937 (TA).

139 *Luce memo:* Dec. 21, 1936 (TA).

140 *"Harry turned up his nose":* Hodgins told author; *"Why Harry kept this man":* MacLeish told author; *"And then there's you":* Aug. n.d. 1938 (TA).

141 *Luce memo:* Sep. 18, 1938 (TA).

142 *McLuhan appraisal:* View, Spring 1947.

143 *"Intelligent criticism":* Luce speech, Des Moines, Apr. 1933; *Williamstown speech:* Sep. 2, 1937; *White Sulphur Springs speech:* Apr. 30, 1937 (all TA).

144 *"Could edit a magazine":* Frazier ms., 152; *"Luce was in and out":* (BR).

145 *De Voto comment:* SR, Jan. 29, 1938.

145 *"Have no embarrassment":* Cleveland Plain Dealer, Nov. 11, 1937 (TA).

145 Of those mentioned in the "Luce vineyard," the author interviewed Kastner, Hodgins, Sheldon Luce, Mrs. Hobson, Hersey and Alexander.

150 *"Sausage meat":* Winthrop Sargeant, *In Spite of Myself* (Doubleday, NY 1970), 229.

151 *"Responsibilities of the writer":* Sargeant, 232.

152 *"Sparse-haired, pale":* Alexander King, *Mine Enemy Grows Older* (Simon & Schuster, NY 1958), 196.

152 *"Cheap little Jew":* Ibid., 254.

152 *"Everybody in his right mind":* King, *May This House Be Safe From Tigers* (Signet, NY 1960), 116–17.

XIV

153 *"Luce took me up":* Billings diary, May 11, 1938.

153 *". . . [W]e Americans":* Speech delivered Dec. 4, 1937 (TA).

154 *Kennedy cover story:* Time, July 22, 1935.

154 *Cassandra on Luce:* London Daily News, July 14, 1938 (TA).

154 *London Bystander on Luce:* June 1, 1938 (TA).

154 Luce's report of this trip, dated June 22, 1938 (BP), is quoted repeatedly in the narrative.

157 *"He sat on my picture table":* BR.

157 Kronenberger's review was in Oct. 10, 1938, issue.

157 Life's praise was in Oct. 17 issue.

158 *"Tended to shake my hand":* Louis Kronenberger, *No Whippings, No Gold Watches* (Atlantic-LB, Boston 1965–70), 121.

158 *"Really scathing attacks":* Time, Oct. 10, 1938.

158 *"Energetic Daladier":* Time, Oct. 17, 1938.

158 *Kronenberger on Goldy:* Kronenberger, *op. cit.*, 108.

158 *Ingersoll memo:* Oct. 28, 1938 (BP).

159 *Luce memo on Goldy:* Dec. 8, 1938 (BP).

159 *Retiring Weiss:* Weiss told author.

159 *"Why should I build?":* Hatch, *op. cit.*, 90.

159 *Million-dollar wager:* Der Spiegel, Dec. 20, 1961 (TA).

PAGE

160   "*I did not see*": Ingersoll profile, New Yorker, May 9, 1942.

161   "*It was in Harry's room*": Same as above.

161   "*Psychologically, Time*": High Time, Feb. 1939 (TA).

161   *New Republic on High Time:* NR, Feb. 15, 1939.

161   "*At 5:15*": Billings diary, n.d. Jan. 1939.

162   *Luce memo:* Jan. 30, 1939 (BP).

162   High Time second issue dated March (TA).

163   Long Luce memo on Time n.d. 1939 (TA).

164   *Matthews "empire building"*: Sargeant, *op. cit.*, 230.

164   "*I could no longer say*": Matthews, *op. cit.*, 240.

165   "*Young man!*": Matthews told author.

165   "*When Luce arrived*": Matthews, *op. cit.*, 243.

165   "*If I thought*": *Ibid.*, 274.

165   "*Even within our company*": Luce memo Sep. 18, 1938 (BP).

166   "*Speaking of Dictators*": Life, Apr. 18, 1938.

167   "*Comrade Earl*": Time, May 30, 1938.

167   *James Roosevelt story:* Time, Feb. 28, 1938.

167   "*Often at banquets*": Time, June 10, 1940.

167   "*I know I shouldn't*": John Brooks, *The Big Wheel* (Harper, NY 1949), 54.

XV

168   Billings diary entry, May 19, 1939.

168   Shaw postcard: Harriman, *op. cit.*, 56.

168   "*Dear Lila*": July 28, 1939.

169   *Alice Toklas comment:* Alice B. Toklas, *What Is Remembered* (Holt, NY 1963), 161.

170   "*Oh, God*": Elson, *op. cit.*, 408.

170   "*Luce went through*": Billings diary, Sep. 15, 1939.

170   "*I've met the man*": Marcia Davenport, *Too Strong for Fantasy* (Scribner, NY 1967), 259. Also, author's conversation with Mrs. Davenport.

171   "*Madame Pomaret*": Clare Boothe, *Europe in the Spring* (Knopf, NY 1940), 98–100.

172   *The Rex letter:* Apr. n.d. 1940, TA.

173   *Luce reply to Kennedy:* Recalled in Luce memo to Matthews, Aug. 23, 1952 (BP).

173   "*Grinning, cussing Joe*": Time, Sep. 18, 1939.

173   *Laski remark:* Recalled by Mrs. Laski, NYT Aug. 19, 1970.

173   "*A shocking thing*": Clare Boothe, *op. cit.*, 192.

173   "*Les Allemands!*" *etc.*: NYHT, May 16, 1940.

174   "*Your special correspondent*": May 10, 1940 (TA).

174   "*The remarks of Roosevelt*": May 12, 1940 (TA).

XVI

XVII

193 *Frillman ends party:* Paul Frillman and Graham Peck, *China* (Houghton Mifflin, Boston 1968), 156.

193 *Blow in kidney:* Hersey told author.

194 *"Harry urged me to run":* CBL told author.

194 *"Whatever Time prints":* Richard Pollak, "Time After Luce," Harper's, July 1969.

194 *"Nero needed only one":* NR, July 19, 1943.

194 *CBL and Bernays:* Edward L. Bernays, *Biography of an Idea* (S&S, NY 1965), 699; also, Bernays told author.

195 *"America's war":* Life, Feb. 16, 1942.

195 Freda Kirchwey in The Nation, Feb. 28, 1942.

196 *Luce meets Chambers:* Welles told author.

197 *Matthews and Barkham on Chambers:* From interviews with author.

197 Maxine Davis in Look, Jan. 25, 1944.

198 *Matches and cigarettes:* Matthews, *op. cit.,* 248.

198 *"Long delayed fury":* NR, July 19, 1943; Hatch, *op. cit.,* 154–5.

199 *Globaloney speech:* Haynes Johnson and Bernard Gwertzman, *Fulbright the Dissenter* (Doubleday, NY 1968), 63 ff.

199 *Eleanor Roosevelt comment:* Time, Feb. 22, 1943.

199 *Name-dropping:* Gretta Palmer in Look, Apr. 15, 1947.

200 *Hopkins remark:* Robert E. Sherwood, *Roosevelt and Hopkins* (Harper, NY 1948), 660.

201 *"This beautiful woman":* Life, Mar. 1, 1943.

202 *"Madame must have the best":* Private source.

XVIII

205 *Benét disapproval:* Charles A. Fenton, *Stephen Vincent Benét* (Yale, New Haven 1958), 362.

205 *Dr. Aaron on bran:* Time, Nov. 14, 1938; *Dr. Fantus on bran:* Time, Dec. 5, 1938.

205 *"What with Thanksgiving":* Nov. 30, 1938 (BP).

206 *"As you may recall":* Oct. 9, 1941 (BP).

206 *"The most important place":* July 10, 1941 (BP).

208 *Luce eats unawares:* Hersey told author.

209 *"Only if America":* Mar. 11, 1943 (BP).

209 *Luce southern trip:* Billings and Howland told author.

XIX

212 *"The central problem":* Time, Feb. 15, 1943.

212 *"The peace-loving nations":* Ibid.

212 *"If it can be believed":* Life, Dec. 20, 1943.

213 *"Most dangerous man":* Smethport Union, n.d. (TA). Luce sold his Blue Network holdings two years later.

215 *"Time does have policies":* Hodgins memo, Mar. 6, 1944 (BP).

Luce and His Empire

215   *Sumner Welles incident:* James McGregor Burns, *Roosevelt: The Soldier of Freedom* (Harcourt, NY 1970), 350; Dean Acheson, *Present at the Creation* (Norton, NY 1969), 46.

216   *"I never missed an opportunity":* Whittaker Chambers, *Witness* (Random, NY
1952), 477.

216   *"I began to see":* Ibid., 481; *"This was my first":* Ibid., 494; *"I cannot be
beaten":* Ibid., 479; *"The tacit ban":* Ibid., 497.

217   *"The World From Rome":* Life, Sep. 4, 1944.

218   *Murphy Fortune article:* June 1944 issue.

218   Protests from Pravda and others listed in Life Sep. 25; *Max Lerner:* PM, Sep. 6;
open letter: Daily Worker, Oct. 25.

218   *FDR asked watch on TLF:* Burns, *op. cit.,* 307.

219   *"After we left":* Bruce Gould and Beatrice Gould, *American Story* (Harper, NY
1968), 276.

219   *"Who is GI Jim?":* Hatch, *op. cit.,* 165.

220   *New Yorker's stomach:* Quoted in PM, Oct. 25, 1944.

220   *Busch and Luce:* Busch told author.

220   *Buell article:* Life, Oct. 30, 1944.

220   *FDR's debility:* Time, Oct. 30.

220   *Tom Dewey approval:* Time, Oct. 2, 23 and 30. *FDR denigration:* Time, Oct. 16
and 23.

221   *Miss Connors on CBL:* PM, Sep. 10, 1944.

221   *CBL on FDR:* Time, Nov. 20. *On Ickes:* Bridgeport Post, Aug. 10. *Winchell on
CBL:* NYDM, Oct. 27. *PM on CBL:* Oct. 25.

222   *Truman on CBL:* Alfred Steinberg, *The Man From Missouri* (Putnam, NY 1962),
224.

222   *Time on CBL:* Nov. 20, 1944.

222   *McLean party episode:* Steinberg, *op. cit.,* 231.

222   *"The attention-getter":* Life, Jan. 8, 1945.

XX

223   *Chambers supports Bullitt:* Time, Sep. 19, 1944. *Goebbels's line:* PM, Sep. 17.
Life's defiance: Sep. 25.

224   *Barkham on Chambers:* Barkham told author.

224   *Hersey cable:* Dec. 13, 1944. *Billings report:* n.d. late 1944. *Wertenbaker cable:*
Dec. 15. *Graebner's* was Dec. 12, *Osborne's* Dec. 21 and *Hersey's* Dec. 16 (all
BP).

225   *HRL's memo:* To Billings, Jan. 6, 1945 (BP).

226   *CBL rapport with Patton:* Hatch, *op. cit.,* 169.

226   *Six Timen resigned:* NYDN, Feb. 7, 1945.

227   *Rumors about the Soongs:* Barbara Tuchman, *Stilwell and the American Experience in China* (Macmillan, NY 1971), 148.

227   *Service's report:* Herbert Feis, *The China Tangle* (Princeton U. Press, 1953), 270.

227   *Time on Stilwell:* Nov. 13, 1944.

228   *Atkinson story:* NYT, Oct. 31, 1944. *Watts story:* NR, Dec. 3, 1945.

228 *"Harry saw Chiang"*: NYP, Jan. 6, 1957. White told author of these events. *White's Life account:* Dec. 18, 1944.

229 *Time's smörgåsbord:* A. J. Liebling, *The Press* (Ballantine, NY 1961), 166.

230 *"He gave it back to me"*: Matthews told author.

230 *"Is journalism necessary?"*: Matthews, *Name and Address*, 267.

XXI

233 *Stettinius talk:* HRL notes, Mar. 19, 1945 (BP).

233 *On hunting Communists:* Life, Mar. 26, 1945.

234 *Litvinov remarks:* NYT, Jan. 3, 1952.

234 *Luce-Alexander trip:* Alexander told author.

234 *Daily News comment:* June 4, 1945.

234 *"We should have"*: May 28, 1945. *"We are now fueling"*: May 27. *"In the tentative opinion"*: June 10 (all BP).

235 *Luce-Truman interview:* Robert Elson told author.

235 *Time on CBL:* July 30, 1945.

236 *Zaslavsky:* Daily Worker, Oct. 7. *Boris Izaakov:* NY Sun, June 15. *New Masses attack:* Sep. 11 (all TA).

236 *Matthews and Mrs. Moore:* Matthews told author.

236 *HRL and mother:* Private source.

236 *"One prominent Presbyterian"*: Private source.

238 *"Pigs flying past"*: Matthews, *Name and Address*, 246.

238 *Luce and Fuoss:* Fuoss told author.

239 *CBL and Lilienthal: The Journals of David Lilienthal* (Harper, NY 1964) II, 36–7.

239 *Luce notes on Germany:* n.d. 1946 (BP).

240 *"I had reservations"*: From Mrs. Bancroft (MB) to author Jan. 22, 1971, as are all her quotations given here.

241 *Luce and Von Hofmannsthal:* VH told author.

243 *Luce and Francis Brown:* Brown told author.

243 *"Proceed to Tsingtao"*: HRL to Bailey, Mar. 14, 1946.

243 *Bailey reply:* Apr. 16.

244 *HRL raises salaries:* To Larsen, July 2. *Cuts Washington staff:* To Grover, Aug. 24. *Bans Reds:* To Billings, Sep. 14 (all BP). *Luce and Jensen:* Jensen told the author.

245 *CBL letter:* NYHT, Nov. 24.

245 *Deep Freeze:* Bailey told author.

245 *Hiroshima:* New Yorker, Aug. 31, 1946.

246 *Luce addresses missionaries:* San Francisco Chronicle, Sep. 10, 1946.

246 Hsin Min Wan Pao dated Nov. 2 (TA).

247 *Stilwell warning:* Tuchman, *op. cit.*, 522.

248 *"It can be argued"*: John F. Melby, *The Mandate of Heaven* (U. of Toronto Press, 1968), 136.

248 *"Luce dominated"*: John Robinson Beal, *Marshall in China* (Doubleday, NY 1970), 264.

248 *Melby observations:* Melby, *op. cit.*, 161 and 208.

Luce and His Empire

249 *Dinner with Potter:* Alexander told author.

249 Hsin Min Wan Pao dated Nov. 3, 1946 (TA).

249 *Luce, MacArthur and Hirohito:* Elson told author.

XXII

251 *Life praises treaty:* Sep. 10, 1945, issue.

251 *Hailey report:* Foster Hailey, *Half of One World* (Macmillan, NY 1950), 52–53 and 67–68.

251 *Missionary disillusionment with Chiang:* Wilber C. Harr (ed.) *Frontiers of the World Christian Mission* (Harper, NY 1962), 5–6.

252 *Stuart's reflections:* John Leighton Stuart, *50 Years in China* (Random, NY 1954), 242.

252 *"Soong and entourage":* Melby, *op. cit.,* 188.

252 *Robert Allen broadcast:* WOR, Dec. 21, 1947.

253 *Life's attack:* Jan. 6, 1947.

253 *Luce and Forrestal:* Arnold A. Rogow, *James Forrestal* (Macmillan, NY 1963), 132, 152. *Fortune's article:* Dec. 1948. *Time smells plot:* Jan. 24, 1949.

254 *Time on Burnham:* Mar. 24, 1947.

254 *Elson sees Ross:* Elson letter to Billings, Apr. 9, 1947 (BP).

254 *Luce on Aranha:* HRL May 1947 report (BP).

254 *Luce Scranton speech:* Scranton Tribune, June 25, 1947.

255 *Luce-Potter wedding:* NY Sun, June 27, 1947. Also, Billings told author.

255 *Miller descriptions:* Merle Miller, *That Winter* (Wm. Sloane Associates, NY 1948), 15–16, 58, 67.

256 *Miller criticism:* Unidentified clipping (TA).

257 *Beka Doherty protest:* Frazier ms., 237–8.

258 *Fact magazine roundup:* Fact, Jan.–Feb. 1964.

258 *Lorimer complaint:* Frazier ms.

258 *Hough's editorial:* Reprinted in American Press, Dec. 1946. *De Voto attack:* Harper's, May 1949. *Daily Trojan attack:* Trojan, Apr. 7, 1948 (all TA).

260 *"Dreams of 1946":* Life, Nov. 25, 1946. *Galantiere letter:* NYHT, Jan. 3, 1947.

260 *Death of a Salesman:* Private source.

261 *"Noel Cowardish thing":* MB to author, Sep. 18, 1971.

261 *A Free and Responsible Press* (U. of Chicago, 1947). Among the thirteen members of the Commission (none newspapermen) were Zechariah Chafee, Archibald MacLeish, Reinhold Niebuhr and William E. Hocking.

262 *Czech peasant woman:* Time, Mar. 22, 1948.

262 *Luce protest:* Chicago Sun, Mar. 27, 1947. *Hutchins reply:* PM, Mar. 27, 1947.

262 Time's anniversary issue was dated Mar. 8, 1948.

XXIII

265 *Melby on Bullitt:* Melby, *op. cit.,* 227.

265 Bullitt's article was in Life, Oct. 13, 1947.

266 *Time on Marshall:* Mar. 10, 1947.

266 Eric Sevareid: CBS Mar. 12, 1948 (Radio Reports, Inc.). Luce-Vandenberg rumor: Robert Allen on WOR, Apr. 4, 1948.

267 Misleading apologia: Fortune, Feb. 1948.

267 "You can't win": Time, Mar. 1, 1948.

268 The Great Ones, by Ingersoll (Harcourt, NY 1948). Both NYT and NYHT reviewed it Feb. 16, 1948.

268 Rumored Luce scheme: NYDN, June 9, 1948 (TA).

269 Duff cover story: Time, June 21, 1948.

269 CBL at convention: NYJA, NY Sun and Post, all June 22 (TA).

269 Raymond Walsh: On WMCA, June 28 (TA).

269 MB's raillery: MB to HRL, Dec. 10, 1947.

270 Pegler on Luce: NYJA, Aug. 29, 1948.

271 Time on Truman: From Time issues Oct. 4 to Nov. 1, 1948.

271 Time on Dewey: From same issues.

272 "Mr. Dewey is supported": Raymond Walsh, WMCA, Nov. 2, 1948.

272 "The little old voter": Time, Nov. 8, 1948.

272 Wertenbaker letter to MB dated Nov. 6, 1948.

273 HRL to MB, n.d. Dec. 1948 (MBP).

274 MB to HRL on "ideas" is dated Dec. 9, 1950.

274 MB on HRL's blue soul: Feb. 25, 1952. On saving his soul: Dec. 10, 1947.

275 MB disputes Time: Jan. 15, 1951. On "master race": same. On capitalism: same. On "ardor & crusades": Aug. 27, 1956. On "American way of life": Jan. 15, 1951.

276 Wertenbaker cheers her: To MB, Nov. 6, 1948.

276 "As I am in a position to testify": John K. Jessup (ed.), The Ideas of Henry Luce (Atheneum, NY 1969), 204, 206.

277 Luce Milwaukee speech: Milwaukee Journal, Nov. 17, 1948.

277 Eric Sevareid: On CBS, Nov. 10, 1948.

280 "We have two hours": Grover told author. Panettone incident: Rospigliosi told author.

280 Wertenbaker telegram dated May 2, 1949.

280 "Monsieur Auriol sat me down": Mentioned in later (1953) HRL report from Indochina (BP).

281 Daily Express item, May 19; Standard, May 17.

281 Chinese checkers: Graebner to author, July 22, 1969.

282 Connally's query: Denis W. Brogan, Worlds in Conflict (Harper, NY 1967), 18.

282 Gen. Barr's report: Acheson, op. cit., 305.

283 MB on Chiang: Letter to HRL, Mar. 18, 1953.

XXIV

284 "Nonsense": Chambers, op. cit., 531. Following Luce-Chambers scene is ibid., 616–17.

286 Cooke view: Alistair Cooke, A Generation on Trial (Knopf, NY 1950), 9.

286 Winchell wisecracks in his column, ranging from Sep. 1948 to Mar. 1950.

288 Time on Hiss verdict, Feb. 6, 1950.

288 Goldy's suicide: NYT, NYDN, Feb. 15, 1950.

289   *MB on Chambers:* To HRL [Feb. 23, 1952].

289   *Luce Harrisburg speech:* TA and Harrisburg Patriot, Feb. 19, 1950.

290   *HRL to MB:* Feb. 22, 1950 (MBP).

290   Howland told author about the Columbia trip.

291   Christian Century, May 24, 1950, contained the criticism of Luce (TA).

291   Wertenbaker letter undated [May 1950].

292   *Luce in Munich:* MB to author, Feb. 8 and 18, 1971.

293   *CBL on war footing:* Denver Post, Aug. 14, 1950 (TA).

293   *Luce Mid-East tour:* Quotes are from Nov. 13 letter to Billings, Nov. 14 memo, Nov. 14 note to Billings, undated Luce report on Iranian tour, and report on Lebanon dated Nov. 29, 1950 (all BP).

296   *Luce and Tisserand:* Rospigliosi told author.

296   *MB letter to Jung,* Jan. 5, 1948.

297   *"Mr. Luce had a genius":* Winston-Salem Journal, Mar. 2, 1967 (TA). *"During this period":* Jack Anderson and R. W. May, *McCarthy* (Beacon, Boston 1952), 277.

298   *"The danger of Communism":* Life, Apr. 10, 1950.

299   *Dr. Schlag on HRL:* July 27, 1951 (MBP).

300   *NY Post on Life:* Mar. 20, 1950 (TA).

300   *Morano on CBL:* NYHT, May 25, 51 (TA).

301   *"Cumulative debasement":* Life, Sep. 27, 1951. *Time's McCarthy cover story:* Oct. 22, 1951.

303   *Rusk speech:* NYT, May 19, 1951.

304   *Matthews on Luce:* op. cit., 245. *HRL memo to Matthews:* Aug. 23, 1952 (BP).

307   *Luce on McCarthy:* San Antonio Light, Oct. 8, 1952 (TA).

307   Luce speech at Trinity University, Oct. 7, 1952; at Lafayette College, June 6, 1952; in New York, Apr. 23, 1951; in Philadelphia, June 1952; in Cincinnati, Nov. 15, 1951; at College of Idaho, Oct. 6, 1951; in Dallas, Apr. 19, 1951—all TA.

308   *Kingdon demurrer:* NYP, June 8, 1951.

308   Luce speech in Buffalo, June 26, 1951; editorial comment in Buffalo Evening News same date (TA).

309   *Life quotes: On Acheson,* quoted in NR, Sep. 28, 1953; *"The prospect is war":* Life, Dec. 11, 1950; *"War NOW":* Dec. 18, 1950; *"The enemy of the free world":* Feb. 27, 1950; *War with both Russia and China:* Jan. 8, 1951; *"Our terms":* Mar. 24, 1952 (italics added).

309   *"The War We May Fight":* Life, May 28, 1951.

310   *"Someday, a president":* July 10, 1950.

310   *Life on Indochina:* Aug. 28, 1950.

XXV

311   *Dr. Frank on ideology:* N. D. Houghton (ed.), *Struggle Against History* (Simon & Schuster, NY 1968), 87.

311   *Time on MacArthur:* July 10, 1950. *"Humility to believe in God":* Life, Apr. 23, 1951.

312 *"Seldom has . . .":* Time, Apr. 23, 1951. *Luce to Hughes:* Newsweek, Mar. 13, 1967.

313 *"In that concept":* Richard H. Rovere and Arthur M. Schlesinger, Jr., *The MacArthur Controversy* (Farrar, NY 1965), 221, 225.

313 *MB to HRL:* Apr. 19, 1951; *HRL to MB:* Apr. 29; *HRL next letter:* May 30.

314 *"WAS LATTIMORE?":* Life, May 1, 1950; *"carload of spies":* Time, Apr. 17, 1950. *"As far back as 1944":* Time, Aug. 15, 1949.

314 *"It was Acheson":* Life, July 24, 1950.

315 *Bagdikian:* NR, Feb. 23, 1959.

315 *Time on Acheson:* Jan. 8, 1951. *On Dulles:* Aug. 13, 1951.

317 *"There is a moral order":* Time, Aug. 13, 1951. *"There is a moral or natural law":* Life, May 19, 1952.

317 *Miller on Dulles:* Wm. Lee Miller, *Piety Along the Potomac* (Houghton Mifflin, Boston 1964), 170.

318 *The Reporter on Time and Life:* Aug. 15, 1950.

318 *"Save Southeast Asia":* Life, June 5, 1950.

319 *Time on Templer:* Dec. 15, 1952.

XXVI

320 *Morgenthau observation:* Hans J. Morgenthau, *A New Foreign Policy for the United States* (Praeger, NY 1969), 26.

320 *Life editorial:* June 5, 1950.

321 *HRL to MB:* Jan. 22 [1952] (MBP).

321 *Luce in Manchester:* Manchester Daily Dispatch, Feb. 1, 1952. London Observer story was in Feb. 10 issue (both TA).

321 *"I am in the middle":* Luce cable Jan. n.d. 1952 (BP). *Time on Eden:* Feb. 11, 1952.

322 *"Death of king":* Cable Feb. 8 (BP).

322 *HRL dinner with MB:* MB to author, Jan. 8, 1971.

322 *"One of Ike's great strengths":* MB to HRL, Feb. 18, 1952.

323 *"Dinner with Spaniards":* From tour itinerary (TA).

323 *CBL speech:* NYHT, July 2, 1952.

323 *HRL tiff with Roper:* Roper told author.

324 First Stevenson cover story was in *Time*, Jan. 28, 1952.

324 *Matthews-Welles prayer:* Welles told author.

325 *Matthews-Fuerbringer argument:* Alexander told author.

325 *"There was no holding Time":* Matthews, *op. cit.,* 271.

325 Kronenberger observation in his book, already cited, 135–6.

326 *HRL-MB shouting match:* MB letter to friend, May 13, 1952.

326 *Time on Ike:* From issues June 16 to Nov. 3.

326 Second Stevenson cover story: Time, Oct. 27, *Running comments:* From issues Sep. 29 to Nov. 3.

327 *Time on Nixon:* Aug. 25, 1952. *On Truman:* Oct. 20.

327 *Nixon on Stevenson:* Time, Oct. 20.

328 *Time defends Nixon:* Sep. 29 issue. *Drew Pearson disagrees:* Drew Pearson and

Jack Anderson, *The Case Against Congress* (Simon & Schuster, NY 1968), 427–8.

329 *Life applauds Nixon:* Oct. 6. *Replies to reader:* Oct. 27.
329 *MB letter to HRL:* Oct. 20.
329 *Life "savageries":* Oct. 27.
330 *HRL cable to MB:* Nov. 2, 1952.
330 *HRL speech:* Nov. 14, 1952 (BP).
332 *Time attacks NYT objectivity:* Oct. 30, 1950.
333 *HRL proposes Dewey:* Hughes told author.
335 *"Give us the tools":* Chiang quoted in Time, Feb. 9, 1953.
336 *"After Chiang has landed":* HRL to Billings, Dec. 22, 1952 (BP).
336 *"I wonder if":* MB to HRL, Mar. 18, 1953. Luce's article was in Life, Feb. 23, 1953.
337 HRL on Bao Dai and how to win the war appeared in his "Report on Indochina" (BP).
338 *"After all these encounters":* HRL memo, Dec. 22, 1952 (BP).
338 London Mirror quoted in NYT, Nov. 11, 1952. Concerning the Rome post, the belief is general that Eisenhower first offered it to Luce himself.

XXVII

339 *"Dulles's policies":* Life, quoted in Miller, *Piety on the Potomac*, 161.
339 *Dulles encircled:* Time, Feb. 9, 1953; Louis J. Halle, *The Cold War As History* (Chatto, London 1967), 233–4.
341 J. Edgar Hoover and Richard Nixon quoted in Miller, *Piety*, 45.
341 *Spellman on Reds:* Robert I. Gannon, *The Cardinal Spellman Story* (Doubleday, NY 1962), 202.
341 *"Religion, for many individuals":* Richard Hofstadter, *Anti-Intellectualism in American Life* (Vintage, NY 1963), 118.
341 *Mickey Spillane:* Quoted in Eric F. Goldman, *The Crucial Decade* (Knopf, NY 1956), 211.
342 *"The horse having run":* HRL to Alexander, Jan. 7, 1953 (BP). *Luce to Griffith:* Mar. 21, 1953 (BP).
342 *Conniff column:* NYJA, Feb. 20, 1953 (TA).
344 Finch and Miss Quimby told author of the Luce installation.
344 *Rumors about the Luces:* Later mentioned in Newsweek, Jan. 24, 1955.
345 *"Luce lunched with Churchill":* Cable, May 22, 1953 (BP).
346 *De Gasperi on cover:* Time, May 25, 1953.
346 *Barzini comment:* Harper's magazine, July 1955.
346 *"Grave consequences":* The Reporter, Feb. 23, 1956.
347 *"What can be done?":* Barzini article noted above.
347 *HRL on Nixon:* Memo to Alexander, June 26, 1953 (BP).
348 *"Year of the Snake":* Life, Aug. 3, 1953.
349 *L'Aurore on the Luces:* July 30, 1953 (BP).
349 *Luce-Duncan talk:* Duncan, *Yankee Nomad* (Holt, NY 1966), 376–7.
351 *"Why did you keep me":* To Roy Larsen, Aug. 19, 1953 (BP).

371 *"I have never been a man"*: NYT, Aug. 23, 1964.

371 *Gissen anecdote:* Gissen told author.

371 *Mrs. Roosevelt in Rome:* The Reporter, Feb. 23, 1956.

371 *Buchwald story:* NYHT, Nov. 6, 1956.

372 *Time on "hand-wringing":* Apr. 12, 1954; *on Oppenheimer:* June 14, 1954; *on "dental officer":* Mar. 1, 1954; *on Yalta:* Mar. 28, 1955.

372 *Dulles article:* Life, Jan. 16, 1956.

373 *London papers on Dulles:* Quoted in NYT, Jan. 12, 1956.

373 *HRL defends Dulles:* NYHT, Jan. 22, 1956.

374 *CBL to Gretel:* Baldrige, *op. cit.*, 297.

374 The Von Hofmannsthals described the party to author. Spectator, May 25, 1956 (TA), burlesqued Luce.

375 *Randolph Churchill on CBL:* Spectator, Oct. 26, 1956 (TA).

375 *"Arsenic for the Ambassador":* Time, July 23, 1956. It appears that Time was confused between arsenic, arsenate of lead and the lead poisoning possible from paint. Le Ore's reply was in the Aug. issue.

376 *Time lauds Dulles:* July 30, 1956.

377 *MB on Eisenhower:* Letter to HRL Feb. 19, 1956. *MB on confronting God:* same letter.

378 *Kefauver perspiration:* Time, Sep. 17, 1956; *Tediousness and banality:* Oct. 1; *manure-pitching cover story:* Sep. 17.

378 *Allen as clown:* Time, Jan. 28, 1946; *as hero:* Dec. 14, 1954.

378 *Nixon in Manila:* Time, July 16, 1956. *UAW rejoinder:* Ammunition, Dec. 1956.

379 *MB on Nixon:* In letters to HRL, Sep. 28 and Aug. n.d., 1956.

379 *Bagdikian judgment:* NR, Feb. 23, 1959. *"This is hokum":* Ammunition, Dec. 1956.

XXIX

381 *"Time today":* NYP, Dec. 29, 1956.

383 *"Do you imply?":* Quoted in PM, Sep. 3, 1944.

383 *"I am a Protestant":* Newsweek, Mar. 13, 1967.

384 *Bagdikian appraisal:* NR, Feb. 23, 1959.

385 Mrs. Hobson and Mrs. Bancroft told author independently of Luce's belief in the ending of poverty.

386 *Crosby on Guinness and Time:* NYHT, Jan. 25, 1958.

387 *MB on integrity:* Letter to HRL, May n.d., 1954.

388 *Kimball observation:* NYP, Dec. 26, 1956. *"I see my assignments":* NYP, Dec. 24, 1956. (From Post's ten-part series.)

389 *Dr. Blake's denunciation:* Private source.

XXX

390 *Life Sputnik issue:* Nov. 18, 1957. *Nation retort:* Nov. 23. Territorial Enterprise editorial, date missing (TA).

392 *Mrs. Hobson visit to Phoenix:* narrated by her to author.

393   *Goren on Luce's bridge:* Quoted by Herbert Mayes in SR, Mar. 18, 1967.

394   *Luce at Yale:* NYDN, Apr. 17, 1958.

395   *"Betrayal beyond belief":* Time, Jan. 5, 1959.

395   *Wright Organization:* Steele, *op. cit.*, 126. *"Money is the most important":* The Reporter, Apr. 29, 1952.

395   *MB on Daddy:* Letter to HRL, Apr. 22, 1958; *on McCarthyism:* to HRL, May 14, 1958.

396   HRL to first wife, Aug. 28 (1958).

397   *"Abolish Bolivia":* Time quoted in NYT, Mar. 3, 1959; *O'Rourke comments:* NYT, Mar. 4; *Andrade request:* NYT, Mar. 3.

398   *Truman wisecrack:* NYDN, Mar. 5; *Senatorial discussion:* Time, May 11, 1959.

398   *CBL statement:* NYHT, Apr. 29, 1959. *Sen. Young's verse:* NYHT, Apr. 30.

399   Mrs. Hobson's memo was dated Aug. 15, 1959.

399   Jacques Barzun, *The House of Intellect* (Harper, NY 1959), 41–43.

400   *Denis Brogan suggestion:* Brogan, *op. cit.*, 30.

400   *Eisenhower comment:* NYT, Aug. 26, 1959.

400   *Harriman article:* Life, Sep. 28, 1959. Time quotations are from Sep. 21 and 28 issues; Life's editorial "welcome," Sep. 21; Osborne piece, Oct. 5.

402   *Murray on Luce at golf:* Hughes told author.

403   *Cholly Knickerbocker:* NYJA, Sep. 27, 1959. *CBL repartee:* Leonard Lyons, NYP, May 5, 1961. *Suzy remark:* NYDM, Oct. 15, 1959; *Nancy Randolph:* NYDN, Oct. 21, 1959.

404   *Lady Jean on rumors:* NYWT, Oct. 22, 1959. *Elsa Maxwell:* NYJA Dec. 19, 1959 (all TA).

404   *Luce on Glarner:* Francis Brennan told author.

405   *Kronenberger view:* Kronenberger, *op. cit.*, 145–6.

406   Niebuhr quoted in NYP, Jan. 4, 1957.

406   Noel Busch told author of the dinner.

406   *Fuerbringer edits Luce:* NYP, Jan. 4, 1957.

407   Alexander described the world tour to author.

407   HRL talk to staff, June 9, 1960 (BP).

407   *Luce on Nasser:* Narrated in talk noted above.

408   *Luce-Nixon-Johnson chat:* NYHT, July 27, 1960.

408   *Luce addresses committee:* NYT, June 29, 1960. *Nation retort:* July 9, 1960 issue.

409   Luce's remarks to Benton and Mrs. Hobson related by them to author.

XXXI

410   *Kennedy, Sr., visits Luces:* John K. Jessup, *op. cit.*, 367–8.

410   *Time on Nixon:* Jan. 18, 1954; *on Mrs. Nixon:* Feb. 29, 1960.

411   *Luce denial of Nixon support:* NYT, Aug. 6, 1960. *Life clarifies his stand:* Life, Aug. 15, 1960.

413   Life declared for Nixon domestically Oct. 17 and in foreign outlook Oct. 24.

413   *Kennedy queries Benton:* Sidney Hyman, *The Lives of William Benton* (U. of Chicago 1969), 539.

413   *Kennedy asks Bowles to go easy:* Chester Bowles, *Promises to Keep* (Harper, NY 1971), 398.

414 *Kennedy resents Fortune article:* Theodore C. Sorensen, *The Kennedy Legacy* (Harper, NY 1965), 316 and 316n.

415 *Luce declares war:* May 15, 1961 (TA).

416 *The Goulds on the Luces:* Goulds, *op. cit.,* 303. Both Benton and Hoffman described the cruise to author.

416 *Nancy Randolph gossip:* NYDN, Dec. 18, 1961.

416 Luce's Eisenhower interview appeared in Life, Sep. 8, 1961.

416 *Kennedy's change on China:* Bowles, *op. cit.,* 391. *"This was my intention":* Bowles, 398n.

417 *JFK to Stevenson on China:* Arthur M. Schlesinger Jr., *A Thousand Days* (Houghton Mifflin, Boston 1965), 483.

417 *Commager view:* SR, July 10, 1965. *Cousins complaint:* SR, May 3, 1958.

418 *Luce and the unthinkable:* Dr. Read told author. *Luce talk on US and new order:* Jan. 28, 1961 (TA).

418 *Luce and Kennedy on Monroe Doctrine:* Jessup, *op. cit.,* 370; *Time on Doctrine:* Sep. 21, 1962.

418 *Reston on Luce:* NYT, May 19, 1961.

418 *Luce Missouri speech:* Mar. 14, 1962 (TA).

419 *Life twits Schwarz:* Sep. 1, 1961.

419 *Mosk on Schwarz:* Nation, June 20, 1962.

420 *Jackson speech: Ibid.*

420 Murphy claim in San Fernando Valley Sun, Nov. 5, 1961. *The Reporter on Life's courage:* Nov. 9.

421 *McGill, Cronkite and Luce:* L.A. Times, Oct. 31, 1961.

421 *John Crosby demurs:* NYHT, Oct. 30, 1961.

422 *Galbraith speculation:* John K. Galbraith, *Ambassador's Journal* (Houghton Mifflin, Boston 1969), 35–36.

422 Miss Mariano, Mrs. Wardell and Mrs. Edwards told the author their impressions.

423 *"Divine slaughter":* Herbert Wallace Schneider, *The Puritan Mind* (Holt, NY 1930), 40.

424 *"Luce's opus":* In student paper The Justice, Feb. 5 [1962?] (TA).

425 *"I like Luce":* Schlesinger, *op. cit.,* 63.

425 Donald Burke told author of talks with Luce.

426 Wilder to author July 25 and Aug. 1, 1968.

427 *"The other day at the zoo":* MB to HRL, June 17, 1951.

428 *Luce prefers best-sellers:* MB to author, Feb. 18, 1971. *Luce on cultivation:* MB to author, Oct. 2, 1971. *Dylan Thomas poem: Ibid.*

XXXII

430 *Niebuhr definition:* SR, Nov. 6, 1965.

430 *JFK on Time:* Sorensen, *op. cit.,* 316–17. *HRL on Fuerbringer:* Richard Pollak, "Time After Luce," Harper's, July 1969.

431 *JFK Man of Year:* Time, Jan. 5, 1962. *CBL article:* Life, Oct. 5, 1962. *Praise for JFK over Cuban ultimatum:* Time, Life, both Nov. 2.

431 *Life warns Khrushchev:* Nov. 9, 1962.

432 *Luce addresses staff:* Mar. 4, 1963 (TA).

433 *CBL and Elsa Maxwell:* NYJA, May 7, 1963. *HRL introduces CBL:* NYP, May 7. *President's telegram:* C.S. Monitor, May 8.

433 *Johnson, Rusk and Tillich speeches:* Time, May 17, 1963.

435 *Herblock remark:* "Books," Mar. 1964 (TA).

435 *Time on Hughes book:* Mar. 22, 1963. Hughes related circumstances to author.

437 *Longstreet on Luce:* Hollywood Canyon Crier, Apr. 13, 1967 (TA).

437 *"Lord Luce":* Thomas Griffith, *The Waist-High Culture* (Harper, NY 1959), 84.

438 *"Tough miracle man":* Life, May 13, 1952.

438 *CBL National Review article:* Quoted in unidentified newsclip dated Oct. 29, 1963 (TA). *Winchell on Mme. Nhu:* NYDM, Nov. 26, 1963.

439 *CBL Utah speech:* Stephen C. Shadegg, *Clare Boothe Luce* (Simon & Schuster, NY 1971), 291.

440 *Halberstam on Time:* Halberstam, *The Making of a Quagmire* (Random, NY 1965), 269.

440 *Liebling comment:* Liebling, *op. cit.,* 166. *Halberstam on Mohr: op. cit.,* 269. *NY changes Mohr story: Ibid.,* 270—Time, Aug. 9, 1963.

441 *Time blasts correspondents:* Sep. 20, 1963.

441 *LBJ conversation with Luces:* Henry Luce III told author.

441 *Cassandra eruption:* In Newsday (Garden City), Dec. 24, 1962.

442 *Luce "retirement":* NYT, Apr. 17, 1964; also "The Luce-Donovan Dinner" (TA).

443 *"Candidate B":* Joseph Epstein, "Henry Luce and his Time," Commentary, Nov. 1967.

XXXIII

444 Complaints by Zuroweste (S.F. Monitor, Jan. 17, 1964); Sylvester (letter in Life, June 5, 1964); about Boise (S.F. Examiner, Oct. 17, 1966); Cardinal Cushing (Boston Globe, Aug. 30, 1964 and America, Sep. 5, 1964); The Nation (Aug. 15, 1959); Columbia Journalism Review, Summer 1962; Liebling (quoted by John Leo in the National Catholic Reporter Mar. 16, 1966); Arapahoe Herald, Jan. 12, 1965 (TA).

445 *HRL on WABC:* "Issues and Answers," Jan. 24, 1965.

446 *HRL at Clurmans':* Mrs. Clurman told author.

446 *HRL "mum" about preference:* Henry Luce III told author.

447 *Life and Time on Tonkin:* Both Aug. 14, 1964.

448 *McNamara on PT's:* Joseph C. Goulden, *Truth Is the First Casualty* (Rand McNally, NY 1969), 41. *Stankevitz statement: Ibid.,* 158.

448 Life, Sep. 11, 1964, declared for Johnson.

449 *CBL on "unfairness":* NYT, July 8, 1964.

449 *"When France withdrew":* Life, Jan. 31, 1964. *Time on Red split:* Apr. 24, 1964.

450 *Luce Dallas speech:* Apr. 30, 1964 (TA). *CBL speech in Brooklyn:* NYT, June 26, 1964.

451 *HRL Danish decoration:* Washington Star, Mar. 8, 1963 (TA).

452 Luce interviews in China News, Oct. 6, China Post, Oct. 7, and Free China Weekly, Oct. 11, 1964 (TA).

452 *Luce Tokyo speech:* L.A. Times, Oct. 15, 1964.

453 *Luce-Greene argument:* S.F. Examiner, Dec. 13, Oakland Tribune, Dec. 14 and
       S.F. Dispatcher, n.d. 1964, all TA.
453 *Kopkind narrative:* NY Review, Sep. 12, 1968. *Luce policy memo:* Sep. 18, 1938
       (TA).
455 *Mrs. Chandler cover story:* Time, Dec. 18, 1964.

XXXIV

456 *Morgenthau on policy:* Morgenthau, *op. cit.,* 27.
456 *Luce and Cutty Sark:* Dallas Times Herald, Apr. 7, 1967.
456 *LBJ on top of crisis:* Life, May 14, 1965.
457 *Misleading reporting:* Time, May 7, 1965 ff.
457 *On U.S. nuclear power:* Time, Aug. 23, 1963.
457 *Luce on escalation:* WABC, "Issues and Answers," Jan. 24, 1965.
457 *Life approves bombing:* Feb. 19, 1965. *Time on Westmoreland:* Feb. 19, 1965.
458 *Life vs. MacLeish and Hersey:* June 25, 1965.
459 *Cover story on Bundy:* Time, June 25, 1964. *"Kill Luce" incident:* NYT, Nov. 29,
       1965.
459 *Luce Washington speech:* Jan. 26, 1965 (TA). *Memphis speech:* May 3, 1965
       (TA). *San Francisco speech:* Dec. 3, 1965 (TA).
460 *US should not back away from China:* Time, July 30, 1965.
460 *"Turning Point in Vietnam":* Time, Oct. 22, 1965.
460 *Time's four pronouncements:* All in Jan. 7, 1966, issue.
461 *"Mr. Luce's traps":* Tulsa Tribune, Mar. 1, 1967.
462 *Hoving anecdote:* Chicago Daily News, Sep. 15, 1966.
462 *Shadegg observation:* Shadegg, *op. cit.,* 276.
463 *Thanat praised:* Arizona Rebublic, May 13 and 15, 1965. *Fortune extols Thanat:*
       Oct. 1965.
463 *LSD experiments:* Kobler, *op. cit.,* 102; NYP, Mar. 2, 1968. *Dr. Leary:* On
       WMCA, Barry Gray show, Apr. 15, 1966.
464 *"If you read a column by Reston":* Yale Daily News, Apr. 20, 1965.
464 *Kobler profile:* Satevepost, Jan. 16, 1965.
464 *"Meaning was built into life":* Ottumwa Courier, May 31, 1966.
466 Time on the economy, opinion polls, the anxious LBJ, the chivalric bombing
       pause, the "peace offensive" and on Nixon: Jan. 14 and Feb. 4, 1966.
467 *China the "real enemy":* Time, Feb. 26, 1965.
467 *Life on moral elevation:* Oct. 29, 1965. *Murphy series:* Fortune, Oct. 1965 ff.
467 *Westy Man of Year:* Time, Jan. 7, 1966; *Rusk on cover:* Feb. 4; *Ky on cover:*
       Feb. 18, 1966.
468 *The three Time Essays:* July 30 and Aug. 6, 1965, and Jan. 14, 1966.
468 *Time shaft at Lippmann:* Jan. 7, 1966; *encomium for McNamara:* Feb. 26, 1965.
470 *Donovan editorial:* Life, Feb. 25, 1966. Donovan's reassessment five years later
       was in Time, June 14, 1971.
471 *Fulbright on T-L:* WCBS-TV, Mar. 13, 1966.
471 *Time on Cameron series:* Reported in NR, June 4, 1966.
471 *Salisbury in Hanoi:* Time, Jan. 6, 1967; Life, Jan. 20.

PAGE

472　*Rusk on Salisbury:* Gay Talese, *The Kingdom and the Power* (World, NY 1969), 447.

472　*"Man your trifocals":* National Catholic Reporter, Mar. 16, 1966.

XXXV

473　Der Spiegel, Dec. 27, 1961 (TA).

473　*"Open Mind" program:* Dr. Goldman told author.

474　*Life approves Johnson message:* Jan. 20, 1967.

474　*HRL calls Tito "hero":* Description of tour in Time Archives. *National Review upset:* Dec. 2, 1966 issue. *Time's announcement:* Nov. 11, 1966. NYT, Oct. 21, listed Time's Ad Manager.

475　Pierson Sun article in Feb. 25, 1966 issue (TA).

476　*Hersey book: Letter to the Alumni* (Knopf, NY 1970).

476　*Talk of LSD:* Hersey told author.

476　*Luce citation:* New Haven Register, June 13, 1966.

477　FDR Letter dated Nov. 20, 1940 (FDR Library).

477　Mrs. Clurman told author of the visit.

479　*Hutchins statement:* Western Advertising, Nov. 4, 1968.

479　Luce speech at Santa Barbara, Feb. 1, 1967 (TA).

479　*Luce and Buckley:* Buckley column, Arizona Republic, Mar. 12, 1967.

480　Roper told author of this meeting with Luce.

481　*"I showed it to Harry":* CBL told author.

Author's Note and Acknowledgments

This book, published so soon after Henry R. Luce's death, reflects access only to a fraction of the evidence that will accumulate in another decade or two. It emphasizes his journalism—that part of his lifework most open to observation even if its final propagandist results can still only be estimated. His astonishing career marks the transition from the Twenties, when few questioned the vigor and fearlessness of the free American press, to a stormy new era when it is under fire and its survival seems by no means certain. How did this come about? A study of the Lucepress through the violent stresses of several wars may at least suggest some of the reasons.

I am grateful for the generous help given by Luce's family: his first wife, Mrs. Lila Tyng; his second wife, Clare Boothe Luce; his two sisters and brothers-in-law, Mr. and Mrs. Leslie R. Severinghaus and Mr. and Mrs. Maurice T. Moore; his brother, Sheldon R. Luce and his oldest son, Henry Luce III. The great organization he founded, Time Inc., permitted me to read and quote some of the company records, to consult its enormous file of newsclippings and to borrow pictures. Lillian Owens, the company archivist, was continually imposed upon and gave the most skillful assistance. As I worked on this book, Robert T. Elson of Time was writing his two-volume company-sponsored history of Time Inc. of which only the excellent first volume has appeared at this writing. Although the two projects were not without conflict, he gave me friendly help, as did his staff, composed of Margaret Quimby, Elsa Wardell and Marie McCrum.

Whatever Luce's faults, he inspired loyalty. By the time I was in the middle of my work, benefiting from the help of all these kind people, I was unhappily aware that they were likely to disagree unanimously with my appraisal. I can only fall back on the hope that they may remember instances in which people have disagreed strongly with appraisals made of them in Time, Life or Fortune.

John Shaw Billings, the first TLF editorial director, now retired, talked with me for hours about Luce and lent me his tape-recorded recollections containing passages from his diary, as well as his collection of papers relating to his years at Time Inc. Allen Grover, now retired as a vice-president of the company and Luce's longtime "chief of staff," gave me his invaluable recollections and his counsel. I was fortunate to hear the accounts of three successive managing editors of Time, Manfred Gottfried, T. S. Matthews and Roy Alexander. Three classmates of Luce's prep-school and college years, Culbreth Sudler, John M. Hincks and Pierrepont I. Prentice, helped bring to life the days at Hotchkiss and Yale. Other important Luce colleagues who recalled the early years of Time, Fortune and Life were Archibald MacLeish, Noel Busch, Joseph

Kastner, Mrs. Daniel Longwell, Myron Weiss, Ralph Ingersoll and the late Eric Hodgins. A few people close to Luce, and some recently or still employed by Time Inc., preferred not to be named and are listed in the notes under the term "private source."

My friend Henry Wexler, M.D., the New Haven psychiatrist with whom I have discussed earlier biographical subjects, has "lent me his wisdom" once more. George Frazier, the Boston columnist and former Timan who years ago wrote an absorbing account of Luce and Time Inc. which he never saw through to the printer, let me read it and borrow from it. Tom Mahoney and George Scullin, both former Fortune writers, gave advice and help, as did Professor Irving Dilliard of Princeton and John Kobler, author of an earlier book about Luce.

Mary Bancroft's long friendship with Luce was of unusual dimensions because of their many discussions of journalism, politics and philosophy in which he "let himself go" more than was his custom, and because of her keen insights into his character. I am grateful for the privilege of reading a large part of her correspondence with Luce, and for her permission to publish some of her letters.

I am most grateful to Dr. Robert H. Ferrell of Indiana University for his skilled criticism of the text.

My thanks also to the following for kind help given in a variety of ways: Wesley L. Bailey, Mrs. Edgar Baker, John Barkham, Bernard Barnes, Luigi Barzini Jr., James Bell, William Benton, Edward L. Bernays, Francis Brennan, Mrs. Van Wyck Brooks, Dr. Francis Brown, Gilbert Burck, Donald Burke, Margaret Case, Mrs. Richard Clurman, Charles Colt, Patricia Divver Dagg, Marcia Davenport, Emeline Nollen Edwards, Dr. John King Fairbank, E. C. Kip Finch, Lael Wertenbaker Fletcher, Robert M. Fuoss, B. A. Garside, Max Gissen, Dr. Eric F. Goldman, Mrs. Laird Goldsborough, Walter Graebner, Thomas Griffith, Walter Guzzardi, Edward V. Hale, John Hersey, Mr. and Mrs. George Hiltebeitel, Laura Z. Hobson, Paul Hoffman, Mr. and Mrs. Raimund von Hofmannsthal, William S. Howland, Emmet John Hughes, Eliot Janeway, Oliver Jensen, John K. Jessup, Duchessa Elena Lante della Rovere, Roy E. Larsen, James A. Linen, Gloria Mariano, Merle Miller, Charles J. V. Murphy, Reinhold Niebuhr, Duncan Norton-Taylor, Dr. James O'Neill, Content Peckham, Dr. David H. C. Read, William A. Reuben, Elmo Roper, William Rospigliosi, Cornelius Ryan, Dorothy Seiler, Dr. Louis M. Starr, Celia Sugarman, Ralph Thompson, Joseph J. Thorndike Jr., Corinne Thrasher, Patricia Tucker, Susan Vadnay, Max Ways, Mr. and Mrs. Samuel Welles, Theodore H. White, Thornton Wilder, and the New York Yale Club library.

My wife and seasoned collaborator, Dorothy G. Swanberg, once more has read the manuscript and made wise suggestions. And this book marks the eighth on which Burroughs Mitchell of Scribners has worked with me—a length of pleasant association almost matched by that with my literary agent, Patricia S. Myrer of McIntosh & Otis, Inc.

W.A.S.

INDEX

Aaron, Dr. Harold H., 205
Abbott, Dr. Lyman, 33
Acheson, Dean, 286, 287–88, 293, 294;
   under steady Lucepress fire, 300; 301,
   306, 308, 313, 314; hatcheted by Time,
   315–16; 329, 335, 350, 358, 364, 396,
   432, 476
Adenauer, Konrad, 348, 356–57, 368
Adler, Brig. Gen. Julius Ochs, 238, 241,
   342, 386
Agee, James, 151, 244
Aguirre Cerda, Pedro, 190
Albee, Edward, 446
Aldrich, Winthrop, 338, 370
Alexander, Field Marshal Sir Harold,
   193, 226
Alexander, Roy, joins Time, admires
   Luce, 149–50; 193, 209, 226, 234–35,
   246, 248–49, 278, 324; named man-
   aging editor, 325; 333, 342, 347; cir-
   cles world with Luce, 406–408; 462
Alger, Horatio, 171
Allen, George E., 378
Allen, Robert S., 252–53
Alsop, Stewart, 392
American Century, The (Luce policy
   statement), 180–83, 184, 195, 211,
   224, 240, 249, 306, 393, 438, 473, 479
Amery, Julian, 374
Andrews, Roy Chapman, 94
Angell, James Rowland, 54
Anne-Marie, Princess of Denmark, 451
Anschluss, 153, 155
Aranha, Oswaldo, 254, 307
Arizona Republic (newspaper), 461
Architectural Forum, 133n, 147

Armstrong, Louis, 87
Arnall, Gov. Ellis and wife, 210
Arnold, Gen. Henry H., 202
Artzybasheff, 188, 335
Astor, Mary, 122, 143
Astor, Lady Nancy, 169, 173, 239
Atkinson, Brooks, 228
Attlee, Clement, 239, 321, 345, 358
Auchincloss, Douglas, 183
Auchincloss, Hugh, 45
Auer, Bernhard, 434
Auriol, Vincent, 280–81
Austin, Dr. Albert E., 115, 193–94
Azana, Manuel, 137, 138, 264

Babbitt, George F. (character in Lewis
   novel), 61, 64, 67, 72, 75, 81
Badger, Mary Jane, 322, 427
Bagdikian, Ben, 315, 379–80, 384, 386,
   399
Bailey, Wesley L., 9, 10; finds Luce "a
   wee bit tight," 11; 12–14, 194, 199,
   201, 213, 243; in "deep freeze," re-
   signs, 245
Bainbridge, John, 111
Baker, Ernest Hamlin, 188
Baldrige, Letitia, 361–62
Ball, George, 470
Baltimore News—Luce and Hadden on,
   49–51
Bancroft, Mary: meets Luce in Zurich,
   239–42; 246, 260–61, 269–70, 272;
   faults Luce's journalism, 273–76; 279,
   280–82, 288–91; HRL meets her in
   Munich, 292; 296–97, 298, 299; sees
   him in Paris, 321–22; 326, 329, 330,

515

Index

Index

Index

Index

123, 176–77, 205; its poll shows faith in Russia, 211

Fox, Dr. Emmet, 105

Franco, Francisco, glorified in Time, 137–41; 148, 160, 263

Frank, Dr. Jerome D., 311

Franklin, Jay, 176

Fraser, Mary, 61, 159

Frawley, Patrick, 419

Frazier, George, 122

Frederika, Queen of Greece, 370, 451

Freedom of the Press, Commission on, 214, 261–62, 306

French, Winsor, 62, 63

Freud, Sigmund, 87

Frillman, Paul, 193

Fuerbringer, Otto, 150, 325, 406–407, 412, 415, 417, 430; on Vietnam, 439–41; 449, 455, 465

Fulbright, Sen. J. W., 312–13, 449, 450, 468, 471

Fuoss, Robert M., 238

Gafencu, Gabriel, 169

Galantiere, Lewis, 259–60

Galbraith, John K., 421–22, 426

Gamble, James, 64

Gannett, Lewis, 268

Gardner, John G., 191

Garner, John Nance, 167

Garside, B. A., 183, 188

Gavin, Gen. James, 468

Geneva conference, 366–67, 394, 438

George V, 129

George VI, 140, 322

Gibbon, Edward, 26

Gibbons, Floyd, 49

Gibbs, Eric, 281, 349

Gibbs, Wolcott, 123–25

Gifford, Walter, 68

Gissen, Max, 371

Glarner, Fritz, 404

Gluck, Alma, 82

Goebbels, Joseph, 223, 236

Goldman, Eric F., 473–74

Goldsborough, Laird S., 62, 67, 76, 78, 91, 94–97; interviews Hitler and Mussolini, 108; 110, 121, 125–27, 128; lauds Franco, 137–41; 158–59, 164, 165, 195–96, 224, 232, 257, 288, 387

Goldwater, Sen. Barry, 420, 446–49, 451, 452, 480

Gooding, Judson, 481–82

Goren, Herbert, 393, 415

Gottfried, Manfred, joins Time, 55; 60, 62, 80, 126, 140; named managing editor, 164; 193, 206

Gould, Beatrice Blackmar, 219, 415–16

Gould, Bruce, 415–16

Goulden, Joseph C., 448n

Graebner, Walter, 208, 223–25, 238, 281

Graham, Billy, impresses Luce, 290–91; 341, 425

Greene, Felix, 453

Griffith, Thomas, 342, 388, 412, 437

Gromyko, Andrei, 215, 219, 236, 415, 431

Grover, Allen, 35, 134, 140, 159, 206, 223, 236; tours Europe with Luce, 279–81; 287, 422, 428

Grover, Mrs. Allen, 159, 428

Gruening, Sen. Ernest, 468

Gruenther, Gen. Alfred, 370

Gruin, Frederick, 306

Guinness, Alec, 386

Gunther, John, 188

Guzzardi, Walter, Jr., 336–37, 368–69

Gwirtzman, Milton S., 386, 399

Hadden, Briton, 32, 33, 34; rivalry with Luce at Yale, 35–43; 45, 49, 50; joins Luce to found Time, 51–56; 59, 62; journalistic innovations, 63–65; estrangement from Luce, 66; 74–75; illness and death, 79–80; 81, 85, 89, 127, 159, 191, 208, 231, 295, 415, 442, 463

Hadden, Crowell, 80

Hagerty, James A., 407, 436

Haile Selassie, Emperor, 126–27, 264

Hailey, Foster, 251

Hale, E. V., 35

Halberstam, David, 440, 465–66

Hamilton Wright Organization, 395, 456

Hamm, Margherita, 21

Hammer, Mike, 341–42, 449

Hammond, Judge Henry, 209

Hanes, John Wesley, 54, 68

Harding, Warren G., 44

Harkness, Edward S., 55

Harkness, William Hale, 55, 68

Harkness, Mrs. William L., 55

Harriman, Averell, 11, 353–54, 400–401

Harriman, Margaret C., 135, 136

Harvard Advocate, 55

519

Index

Harvard University, 55, 62, 86, 149, 184, 355, 386
Haskell, Frederick, 49
Hatch, Alden, 135
Hearst press, 48, 221, 235, 299, 314, 354
Hearst, William Randolph, 119, 154, 207, 305, 382, 425
Hearst, William R., Jr., 312, 422
Heath, Donald, 337, 338, 349
Hecht, Ben, Luce works under him, 48–49
Heffelfinger, Peavey, 37, 49
Hemingway, Ernest, 67
Henderson, Sir Nevile, 155
Henle, Fay, 135
Henty, H. G., 26
Hepburn, Audrey, 361
Hersey, John R., 148–49, 184, 193; seen as Luce "heir," 207; 208, 223–25, 226, 230, 237, 243; his *Hiroshima* outrages Luce, 245–46; 387, 440, 475–76
Herter, Christian, 397
Hibben, John Grier, 54
Hicks, Wilson, 207
Hillman, Sidney, 221
Hilton, Conrad, 455, 456
Hincks, John M., 35, 39, 40; with Luce in England, 44–45; 49, 59, 66
Hindenburg, Paul von, 86
Hirohito, Emperor, 143, 405
Hiroshima, 1, 237, 245
Hiroshima, by John R. Hersey, 245–46
Hiss, Alger; and Chambers, 284–89; 290, 299, 300, 303, 304, 307, 314, 318, 364, 396
Hitler, Adolf, 86, 108, 113, 127; coddled by Time, 128–29; 143, 148, 155–57; crisis over his Time cover, 160–61; 166, 168, 173, 176, 180, 195, 206, 212, 217, 221, 241, 297, 330, 396
Hobbs, Virginia Lee, 213
Hobson, Laura Z., 54, 89; works for Luce, 148; 385, 392–93; urges reform, 399–400; 409, 411, 424
Hobson, Thayer, 89, 116, 148
Ho Chi Minh, 310, 337, 348, 468
Hodgins, Eric, 82, 121, 140, 146, 147, 150, 206, 208, 223, 232
Hoffman, Paul G., 84, 184, 202, 265, 322, 416, 446, 478
Hofmannsthal, Raimund von, 241–42, 321, 374, 376

Hofmannsthal, Mrs. Raimund von, 321, 374
Hofstadter, Richard, 341
Holmes, Justice Oliver Wendell, 307–308, 331, 357
Hoover, Dorothy, 147–48
Hoover, Herbert, 23, 68, 70, 86, 104; Luce supports, 106; 124, 168, 199, 219
Hoover, J. Edgar, 253, 328, 341, 354, 396
Hopkins, Harry, 200
Hotchkiss School, 29, 31–34, 55, 65, 80, 147, 148, 415
Hotz, Lila Ross, meets Luce in Rome, 46; 47, 48, 49, 50, 55, 58; marries Luce, 59, *see* Luce, Mrs. Henry Robinson
Hough, Henry Beetle, 258–59
Howard, Roy, 154
Howland, William, 209–210, 290–91, 361
Ho Ying-chin, Gen., 6, 185
Hughes, Emmet John, 312, 327, 333–34, 360, 402, 405, 406; Luce ends friendship with, 435–36; 437
Hull, Cordell, 177, 187, 219
Hume, Edward H., 17
Humphrey, Sen. Hubert, 398
Hurley, Brig. Gen. Patrick Jay, 8
Hu Shih, Dr., 96, 426
Hussein, King, 406
Hutchins, Robert M., 214, 262, 273, 354, 355, 409, 478

Ickes, Harold L., 131, 221
Illinois, University of, 205
Ingalls, David S., 42, 55, 324
Ingalls, Mrs. David S., 55
Ingersoll, Ralph McA., 104, 120, 121, 123–25, 140, 145; attacks Goldy, 158–59; leaves Time Inc., 160–64; 207, 258; writes *The Great Ones,* 268
Ingersoll, Robert G., 308
Iococca, Lee, 455, 456
Iran, Luce visits, 293–95

Jackson, C. D., 110, 207, 327; Hollywood apology, 420–21; 461
Jackson, Justice Robert H., 239
Jacoby, Annalee, 5, 238, 243, 246
Jacoby, Melville, 5
James, Arthur Curtiss, 85
James, Sidney, 150, 350, 406, 408

Index

Index

Mme. Chiang, 201; 212, 215; "cold war" piece by Bullitt, 217–19; 233, 260; pro-Chiang piece by Bullitt, 265–66; new drive against Russia, 309–10; Indochina story by Duncan, 348–50; Chambers article on "freedom," 355–56; Dulles on brinkmanship, 372–73; article on Sputniks, 390–91; belittles Birchers and apologizes, 419–21; for LBJ in 1964, 448

Lilienthal, David, 171, 238–39

Lin Yutang, Dr., 189

Lindbergh, Anne, 187

Lindbergh, Charles, 187

Lincoln, Abraham, 6, 357, 401

Linen family, 38

Linen, James A., 446

Lippmann, Walter, 48, 52, 116, 262, 424, 457, 468

Literary Digest, 50, 53, 54, 55, 57, 65, 69; skids as Time prospers, 85; 86, 88; absorbed by Time, 153; 174

Litvinov, Maxim, 107, 233–34

Lloyd-Smith, Parker, 83

Lodge, Henry Cabot, Jr., 413, 446

Lollobrigida, Gina, 361

Longstreet, Stephen, 437

Longwell, Daniel, 118, 120, 159, 207, 256

Lorimer, George Horace, 258

Luce, Claire (actress), 343

Luce, Clare Boothe, 1, 9, 40, 133; her *The Women*, 134–36; 148, 151; to Europe with Luce, 153–57; 158, 159–60, 164–65, 168–69, 170; visits Europe, meets war, 171–74; campaigns for Willkie, 178–79; visits China, 183–87; Life correspondent in Asia, 191–93; elected to Congress, 194–95; "globaloney" debut, 197–99; death of daughter, 213; reelected in 1944 despite FDR opposition, 219–22; assails Soviet, 235–36; 238–39, 245, 259, 269, 270, 289, 290, 292–93, 300–301; backs Ike, 323–24; named ambassador, 338; on job in Italy, 342–50; 351, 361; Sulzberger on, 362–63; poisoned by paint?, 374-76; in Phoenix, 392–93; rejects Brazil appointment, 397–99; on Cuba, 431; on Vietnam, 437–39; backs Goldwater, 446–49; her San Francisco speech and death of Luce, 481–83

Luce, Elisabeth, 24, 30, 32, 34, 47, 68; *see* Moore, Mrs. Maurice T.

Luce, Emmavail, 22, 26, 28, 30, 32, 47, 68; *see* Severinghaus, Mrs. Leslie R.

Luce, Henry III, 62, 73, 101, 112, 133, 159, 198, 206, 234, 249; marriage, 254–55; 324, 393, 446, 451, 484

Luce, Henry Robinson, his 1945 visit to China, meetings with Chiang, T. V. Soong, Mao and Chou, his impressions and patriotic ardor, 1–14; birth and childhood, 15–30; first visit to America, 25–26; at Chefoo School, 27–28; alone to Europe, 29–30; at Hotchkiss School, 31–34; at Yale—rivalry with Hadden, 35–43; army interlude, 39–40; attacks Communists, 41–42; Europe and Oxford, 44–45; meets Lila in Rome, 46; works for Chicago Daily News, then Baltimore News, 48–51; with Hadden, starts Time, 51–56; marries, 59; honored by Yale, 66; anti-Communism and interest in Fascism, 70–73; possible ambition for Presidency, 74–75; his militant Presbyterianism, 79.

He controls company on Hadden's death and lauds big business, 80–84; restlessness, dynamism, 89; anti-Communism in Time and Fortune, 89–92; circles globe in 1932 with Severinghaus, 93–101; his reports on China and Russia, 101–103; belief in Ortega, 105; visits England, 112–13; his romance with Clare, divorce and remarriage, 114–120; big success and big salaries—New Yorker parody, 121–25; hatred for FDR and support of Landon, 128–33; reviews his wife's play, *The Women*, 134–36; his memo and speeches on "interpreting" news, 142–43; work on Life—his intensity, sarcasm, encouragement, 144–150; appraises Nazis in 1938, 153–57; crisis with Ingersoll and with Time Communists, 160–64; visits Poland and Rumania, 168–69; he muses on power, visits Europe again and meets war head-on, 172–75.

He backs Willkie in 1940, 176–79; his "American Century" policy essay, 180–83; visits Chiang in 1941, 183–87; and Whittaker Chambers, 195–96;

522

Index

publicizes Mme. Chiang, 200–203; as Boss, 204–208; begins his own Cold War, 211–12; his vast propaganda holdings and his use of Bullitt, 213–18; supports Dewey and Clare in 1944, 219–22; backs Chambers in Time revolt, 223–25; supports Chiang in Stilwell dispute, 226–29; visits Pacific in 1945, 234–35; meets Mary Bancroft in Zurich, 238–43; visits China in 1946, sees Chiang and Hirohito, 246–49; seeks more U.S. aid for Chiang, 252–53; rejects Press Commission report, 261–62; China called "Harry's mania," 265; yearns to be Secretary of State under Vandenberg but backs Dewey in 1948, 268–73; he parries Mrs. Bancroft's efforts to improve his journalism, 273–76; wines and dines Churchill, 278–79; in Hiss case, 284–87; finds Senate beyond him, is heavily despondent, 289–90; meets Billy Graham, 290–91; meets Mrs. Bancroft in Munich, 292; tours mid-East, 293–96; Luce and McCarthy, 297–306; his elevator prayers, 303–304; series of speeches on U.S. role as "liberator," 307–308; for MacArthur against Truman, 312–13.

His Presbyterian solidarity with Dulles, 316–18; checks out England and Eisenhower, 320–22; lectures staff on journalistic "value judgment," 330–33; circles globe after Eisenhower election, 1952, 334–38; promoter of Againstness, 341; helps ambassador wife in Rome, 344–50; pioneer of China Lobby, 351; attitudes on McCarthyism, 352–56; praises Adenauer and Dulles, 356–59; another Roman interlude, 361–65; similarities to Dulles, 367–68; praises Nasser, 374; imaginary confrontation with God, 377; his propagandist skill, 381–85; has heart attack, 392–93; gossip about Luce and Lady Jean Campbell, 403–404; circles globe in 1960, 407–408; "elects" JFK President, 410–14; pledges Time Inc. to defeat Communism, 414–15; interviews Eisenhower, 416; advocates U.S. international interference where necessary, 418.

Luce defends "anti-Communist schools," 421; seen as "square," 424; in India, 425–26; feelings on culture, God and death, 428–29; at Time's 40th birthday, 432–34; ends Hughes friendship, 435–36; gives up on Goldwater but attacks doves, 446–50; visits Athens and Taiwan, 451–52; assailed publicly in Berkeley, 452–53; favors escalation, 457; his life in Arizona, 461–63; tries LSD, 463; calls Tito a hero, 474–75; addresses Yalemen, 475–76; his last Christmas, 477–78; Santa Barbara speech, 479; busy last weeks and death in Phoenix, 481–85.

Luce, Mrs. Henry Robinson, 62, 73; vows to "kidnap" Luce, 74; selects Fortune title, 82; 89; meets Luce in Vienna, 101; 111–12; divorces Luce, 117–19; 133, 147, 168; Luce sends her gift, 396; he writes her, 480

Luce, Rev. Henry Winters, education and missionary work, 15–30; 34; 53, 96, 97, 98; against liquor ads in son's magazines, 110; 118–19, 142, 165, 177, 189

Luce, Mrs. Henry Winters, marries and sails for China, 17; 24, 27, 30, 34, 96, 101, 118–19, 236–37; worries about son's soul, 260; 276–77

Luce, Peter Paul, 69, 101, 133, 159, 198, 199, 255, 324

Luce, Sheldon, 28, 30, 47, 98; joins Time Inc., 147; 207n

Lucepress (Time, Life and Fortune), begins Cold War, 211–219; intensifies it, 252–54; lauds Dewey, rakes Truman, 271–72; its line on McCarthy, 297–306; lauds MacArthur, attacks Acheson and Lattimore, 311–16; for Ike and Nixon, 326–29; voice of the China Lobby, 352–53; Lucepress propaganda, 381–85; churlish to Khrushchev, 400–402; in 1960 election, 410–14; on Cuba crisis, 431; on Vietnam, 438–41; backs a Democrat—LBJ, 447–49; slanted coverage on war, 457–61, 464–72

MacArthur, Gen. Douglas A., 186, 198; sees Luce, 249; 264, 266; his recall, 311–13; 347, 466

Index

Index

Index

Index

Service, John S., 227, 314, 329

Sevareid, Eric, 266, 277

Severinghaus, Leslie R., 68; circles globe with Luce, 93–101; 119, 255

Severinghaus, Mrs. Leslie R., 68, 98, 119, 255

Shadegg, Stephen, 462

Sharp, Adm. Ulysses S. Grant, 447

Shaw, George Bernard, 168, 169

Sheen, Rev. Fulton J., 1, 238, 245, 253, 341, 363–64

Shepley, James, 365, 372–73, 408

Sherwood, Robert E., 116

Sidey, Hugh, 430

Simon, Norton, 455

Simon & Schuster, 206, 354

Simpson, Wallis Warfield, 122; see Windsor, Duchess of

Skull and Bones, 36; Luce tapped, 41; 49, 51, 54, 55, 75, 83, 89, 141, 148, 306, 323, 324, 459

Smith, Gov. Alfred Emanuel, 68

Smith, Howard K., 445

Solomon, Max, 42

Soong, Charlie, 7, 94

Soong, Ei-ling, see Kung, Mme. H. H.

Soong family, 5–7, 94, 264, 282

Soong, Mei-ling, see Chiang Kai-shek, Mme.

Soong, T. V., 9; visited by Luce in 1932, 95; 184, 185, 200, 202, 227, 247, 351, 432

Sorensen, Theodore, 430

Spaak, Paul-Henri, 279

Spellman, Cardinal Francis, 1, 253, 280, 312, 341, 354, 432, 438

Spillane, Mickey, 341–42

Sports Illustrated, 362, 391–92, 406, 409, 422

Stalin, Joseph, 8, 9; target of Time, 76–78; 90, 92, 107, 143, 166, 199, 200, 211, 212, 229, 230, 233, 235, 251, 266, 269, 274, 396

Stankevitz, James, 448

Steel, Johannes, 158

Stein, Gertrude, 169

Steinhardt, Laurence, 189

Stettinius, Edward R., 233

Stevenson, Adlai E., 324, 325; belittled by Lucepress, 326–29; 373, 378, 406, 413, 417, 428, 433, 449

Stewart, James, 420

Stillman, Charles L., 323

Stilwell, Gen. Joseph W., 2, 193; dispute over his recall, 227–28; 229, 246, 247, 299, 323

Stimson, Col. Henry L., 97, 187

Stone, Edward Durell, 133

Stone, Melville, 53, 69

Stover at Yale, by Owen Johnson, 29, 36–37, 41

Stratemeyer, Gen. George E., 3, 4, 6, 10, 12, 14, 311

Streicher, Julius, 155

Stuart, Dr. John Leighton, 10, 47; shipmate of Luce, 93–94; 96, 247, 248, 251–52

Sudler, Culbreth, 32, 34, 35, 38, 40, 48; with Luce and Hadden on Time, 53–54; 59, 415

Sulzberger, Arthur Hays, 342, 386

Sulzberger, Cyrus, 362–63, 370

Sun Yat-sen, 94, 95

Swift, Otis, 183

Swope, Gerard, 287

Swope, Herbert B., 49, 54

Sylvester, Arthur, 444

Symington, Stuart, 246

Syracuse University, 464

Taft, Horace, 322

Taft, Sen. Robert A., 176, 294, 300, 301, 323, 326

Taft, Seth, 191

Taft, William Howard, 21

Taiwan, invaded by Chiang, 282–83; 303, 335, 364

Taylor, Gen. Maxwell D., 414

Teagle, Walter, 81

Teller, Edward, 463

Templer, Sir Gerald, 319, 336

Tengchow, Luce birthplace, 15, 17, 22, 98, 124

Thanat Khoman, 463

Thomas, Dylan, 429

Thomas, Norman, 104, 182, 433

Thompson, Dorothy, 178–79, 182, 241

Thompson, Edward K., 207, 349–50, 355, 362

Thompson, Malvina, 219

Thornburg, Max, 293–95

Thorndike, Joseph J., Jr., 149, 189, 207

Thorpe, Dr. Franklyn, 122

Index

BOOKS BY W. A. SWANBERG

THE RECTOR AND THE ROGUE

PULITZER

DREISER

CITIZEN HEARST

JIM FISK:
The Career of an Improbable Rascal

FIRST BLOOD:
The Story of Fort Sumter

SICKLES THE INCREDIBLE

LUCE
and His Empire